PAUL MARTIN LESTER
CALIFORNIA STATE UNIVERSITY, FULLERTON

VISUAL COMMUNICATION

IMAGES WITH MESSAGES

FIFTH EDITION

WADSWORTH
CENGAGE Learning

Australia • Brazil • Japan • Korea • Mexico • Singapore • Spain • United Kingdom • United States

WADSWORTH
CENGAGE Learning™

**Visual Communication:
Images With Messages, Fifth Edition**
Paul Martin Lester

Senior Publisher: Lyn Uhl

Publisher/Executive Editor: Michael Rosenberg

Development Editor: Megan Garvey

Assistant Editor: Jillian D'Urso

Editorial Assistant: Erin Pass

Media Editor: Jessica Badiner

Marketing Manager: Bryant Chrzan

Marketing Coordinator: Erin Mitchell

Marketing Communications Manager: Christine Dobberpuhl

Content Project Manager: Aimee Chevrette Bear

Art Director: Linda Helcher

Print Buyer: Justin Palmeiro

Permissions Manager Text: Margaret Chamberlain-Gaston

Photo Manager: John Hill

Production Service: MPS Limited, A MacMillan Company

Compositor: MPS Limited, A MacMillan Company

For product information and technology assistance, contact us at
Cengage Learning Customer & Sales Support, 1-800-354-9706

For permission to use material from this text or product,
submit all requests online at **www.cengage.com/permissions.**
Further permissions questions can be emailed to
permissionrequest@cengage.com

Library of Congress Control Number: 2009936693

ISBN-13: 978-1-4390-8282-9

ISBN-10: 1-4390-8282-0

Wadsworth
20 Channel Center Street
Boston, MA 02210
USA

Cengage Learning is a leading provider of customized learning solutions with office locations around the globe, including Singapore, the United Kingdom, Australia, Mexico, Brazil, and Japan. Locate your local office at: **international.cengage.com/region**

Cengage Learning products are represented in Canada by Nelson Education, Ltd.

For your course and learning solutions, visit **www.cengage.com**

Purchase any of our products at your local college store or at our preferred online store **www.CengageBrain.com.**

Printed in the United States of America
1 2 3 4 5 6 7 14 13 12 11 10

for xtine

Contents

Preface

As a child you want all the presents you can get. If you are particularly persuasive, even a half-birthday (six months from the date of your actual birth day) is celebrated. After you reach a certain age in life, though, probably from 30 years old, the halves are long forgotten while the ones through fours and sixes through nines tend to receive fewer accolades in favor of zeros and fives. And so it is for book editions.

Because of a feeling of frustration over not finding a textbook for a visual communication class first taught 15 years ago, this fifth edition is in your hands. Between its covers comes a greatly improved and visually expanded textbook that should be used for visual communication classes of course, but also can work well for mass communication and society lecture classes. That's because visual communication *is* the history of mass communication. Every student in a mass communications program should know of the field's importance in telling stories with words and pictures that educate and persuade.

Where did the idea come from that words communicate better than pictures? Since they were first invented to communicate complex thoughts, words and pictures have been locked in a struggle for dominance, with words throughout history being the clear-cut leader.

With the widespread use of Johannes Gutenberg's commercial printing press, words became more important than pictures to convey complex thought. Images were relegated to an occasional medical diagram, a "pretty" border decoration, or a sensational eye-catching picture. Reading and writing became curriculum requirements, but visual literacy wasn't considered a necessary component of an individual's education.

However, with the inventions of motion pictures, television, and the computer with the ubiquitous spread of the web, these media

All our knowledge has its origins in our perceptions.

*Leonardo da Vinci,
1452–1519*
SCIENTIST, ARTIST, AND AUTHOR

have dramatically changed the role of visual messages in communication. Nowhere on Earth can a person avoid being confronted with some sort of visual message.

And so, because of the persistent and thoughtful comments from paid reviewers, academic friends who use the book in their classes, and students who as they use e-mail and text messaging in greater numbers become less shy about voicing their strong opinions, this fifth edition of *Visual Communication: Images with Messages* is a major overhaul. The chapter on light and the other on the eye, retinas, and the brain have been consolidated into the visual cues chapter; a section on political posters has been added in the visual persuasion chapter; details about such cultural groups as Arab, Asian, bisexual, gay, lesbian, transgender persons, and Latinos are included in the stereotypes chapter; a chapter on visual analysis has been added; all of the media chapters have been subjected to tighter editing, updated information, and new opening quotations; the illustrations have been increased by about 100, with 70 percent of them **new to this edition**; and weblinks incorporated within each chapter's discussion can be accessed from the book's website.

However, even with all these changes, the purposes of this edition are still the same. This work is an appreciation that visual messages that are *remembered* have the greatest power to inform, educate, and persuade, and it is an exploration into why some images are remembered but most are forgotten. Hopefully at the end of the last chapter, your conclusion will be that:

The most powerful, meaningful, and culturally important messages are those that combine words and pictures equally and respectfully.

The first step toward understanding visual communication is to be educated about the many ways that information is produced and consumed in a modern, media-rich society.

Typographic, graphic, informational, cartoon, still, moving, televised, computer, and web images are analyzed within a framework of personal, historical, technical, ethical, cultural, and critical perspectives in order to complete this first step.

For hundreds of years technology has kept writers and visual artists separate and unequal. Before Johannes Gutenberg's invention, less than 30 percent of Europeans could read. Seventy years after his printing press became commonplace, 80 percent of the population could read. Seventy years after the introduction of the daguerreotype, almost everyone had a Kodak camera and could see pictures in their local newspapers. And yet, educators never developed a visual grammar for photographs in the same way that a verbal grammar was developed for words after Gutenberg.

■ WE LIVE IN A VISUALLY INTENSIVE SOCIETY

Think of all the ways visual messages are displayed—billboards, cell phones, computer monitors, digital cameras, magazines, movie screens, newspapers, packaging, personal digital assistants, photo albums, refrigerator doors, storefronts, T-shirts, tattooed skin, television sets, and wall space. Bombarded daily with a steady, unrelenting stream of visual stimulation from all manner of media, we need to understand pictures. We see mediated images more than we read words. Some experts warn that if the trend continues, civilization will regress to illiteracy and lawlessness. But more optimistic researchers predict that technological advances will merge words and pictures in new ways to create innovative educational possibilities.

In this new convergent era, a person cannot afford to know only how to write, to know only how to make an image, or to know only how to make print or web designs. Today, you should be interested in all the ways words and pictures are used—advertising, entertainment, graphic design, journalism, motion pictures, photojournalism, public relations, television, or the web. The artificial walls between the various media imposed by tradition and outdated technology are crumbling.

This book can help you breach those walls and enter the brave new (visual) world on the other side.

■ FEATURES OF THE BOOK

This fifth edition of *Visual Communication: Images with Messages* is divided into an introduction, two main sections, and a conclusion.

- **Chapter One: Visual Communication** introduces you to the joy of discovery when you really look at pictures and of the philosophy of the author Aldous Huxley, who inspired this book.
- **Section One** comprises five chapters.
  - o **Chapter Two: Visual Cues** explains the four visual cues of color, form, depth, and movement and how they can be employed to grab a viewer's attention.
  - o **Chapter Three: Visual Theories** details the sensory theories of gestalt and constructivism and the perceptual theories of semiotics and cognition to show how designs and meaning can be improved through a knowledge of these significant theories.
  - o **Chapter Four: Visual Persuasion** teaches how visual messages are employed to convince others to buy a product, adopt a service, or advocate a point of view.
  - o **Chapter Five: Visual Stereotypes** gives a history of "images that injure" as portrayed in all the media, with special emphasis on six cultural groups.

  - o **Chapter Six: Visual Analysis** takes one, ordinary photograph used for a public relations purpose to make the point that through a 13-step analysis, any single image is more interesting and memorable if looked at closely.
- **Section Two** contains the nine media chapters that concentrate on the ways we see visual messages. Each chapter in Section Two is introduced with a detailed analysis of a significant example from the medium being discussed, followed by a general discussion of the medium from personal, historical, technical, ethical, cultural, and critical perspectives. Each chapter ends with a "Trends to Watch" section and a list of glossary terms.
  - o **Chapter Seven: Typography** is a discussion of Johannes Gutenberg's printing press improvements that revolutionized mass communication, a section on the history of writing dating from cave paintings to modern uses, the varying moods and styles of the six typeface families, the use of typography as artwork, Twitter messages, and digital book publishing.
  - o **Chapter Eight: Graphic Design** features the work of Saul Bass and his influences on logo designs, motion picture advertisements, and opening title credits, sections on how technology added to a graphic designer's palette, how design considerations are often driven by audience needs, the work of Shepard Fairey within an ethical discussion about appropriation, and how several free-form and grid artistic movements inspired graphic designers and illustrators with an appreciation of aesthetically pleasing word and picture displays.
  - o **Chapter Nine: Informational Graphics** features the colorful weather map from the national newspaper, *USA Today*, with a discussion about the

history of weather graphics for print and screen media, sections that detail the two types of infographics—statistical and nonstatistical, the importance of not misrepresenting the visual nature of column charts within an ethical perspective, and the increased use of infographics seen in music videos and art photography.

o **Chapter Ten: Cartoons** is a detailed discussion of one of the most enduring and longest lasting television series, "The Simpsons," from the mind of Matt Groening, the history of cartoons from caricatures scribbled on walls to three-dimensional (3-D) animated motion pictures, a technical discussion that includes the three types of animation production—cel, stop-motion, and computer-generated—and a section on the rise of the graphic novel for telling entertaining and important stories.

o **Chapter Eleven: Photography** features the social significance of Dorothea Lange's portrait titled "Migrant Mother" with emphasis on the ethical challenges in the making and distribution of the famous image, a history section that charts the medium's progress from the Greek philosopher Aristotle to digital materials, an ethical section that explores the important issues of using violent images, right to privacy of subjects, and picture manipulations, and a discussion on the significance of the stilled moment.

o **Chapter Twelve: Motion Pictures** discusses what is considered the greatest movie of all time, *Citizen Kane*, and why it is so admired, a history that took its initial technology from photography and greatly improved upon it, how the industry competed with television through the additions of sound, color, large screens, 3-D projections, and plush seats, and a critical look at the use of stereotypes, the lack of women directors, and the move to web-only productions.

o **Chapter Thirteen: Television** starts with the famous phrase "The tribe has spoken," well-known to fans of Mark Burnett's "Survivor" series, and then moves to a discussion on the genre of reality programs, followed by a historical discussion that starts with the first successful electronic television demonstration and leads to television/web collaborations, a section on the inauguration of high-definition, and ends with innovations in programs and viewing technologies.

o **Chapter Fourteen: Computers** begins with the work of James Cameron in promoting computer-generated images (CGI) in his critically acclaimed and wildly popular motion pictures, a look at the history of CGI in the movies, a history that begins with a calculator used by ancient Greek astronomers and ends with the successes from the Apple Computer Company, a section on popular, yet violent games, analyses of the IBM and Apple logos, and the implications of human/computer interactions.

o **Chapter Fifteen: The Web** has an opening discussion that features the lives and work of Sergey Brin and Larry Page, the two graduate students who invented the most popular web search engine in the world, Google, a section on the need for classifying and searching for information, a history of how the internet led to the web, and a section on the importance of the so-called Web 2.0 as it seems to be replacing all other media.

• **Chapter Sixteen: The More You Know, The More You See** emphasizes the point that creating designs that use both verbal and visual messages is the best methodology for maximum communicative effectiveness.

- **This edition also contains**:
  o An informal writing style that explains detailed information in a thorough, yet easily understandable way,
  o More than 400 illustrations, 70 percent of them new to this edition, which give life to the text's historical references and contemporary trends,
  o Expanded captions for each illustration, which act as elaborate footnotes that not only identify the image and those responsible for it, but often describes the picture in terms explained in the text,
  o Almost 300 weblinks within the text that you can click from the book's website while you read,
  o An expanded glossary that contains meaningful definitions of almost 300 words and phrases that are introduced in the text—150 more than in the previous edition, and
  o A website that includes assignments and discussion topics for each chapter, weblinks, a detailed bibliography, exam questions, syllabus suggestions, and other features http://communication. wadsworth.com/lester5.

In short, there's a reason this is the fifth edition of *Visual Communication: Images with Messages*. It stays current.

Every chapter has been updated and improved with, the most relevant and current images obtained from an international pool of photographers for inclusion within these pages. Furthermore, digital videos found primarily through YouTube give you added, moving insights to the verbal descriptions in each chapter, and these videos are only a simple click away when you access the book's website.

Finally, with its text, examples, and graphic design, this book exemplifies the best that words and pictures can provide when they combine to tell a compelling and vital story. Wherever you live on this planet and whatever language you choose to use, this book contains a narrative that links each one of us. Visual communication teaches that when messages are respectful, patient, and two-way, they are universal.

■ ACKNOWLEDGMENTS

To all who helped directly to make this edition better and to the rest of you who helped directly to make me better, I offer my heartfelt gratitude and sincere sympathy.

Paul Martin Lester
Fullerton, California

Visual Communication

A photograph published in the *New York Daily News* in 1963 of construction workers on a building site is almost forgettable except for one redeeming quality—you won't have a clue what's going on in the picture. I could come up with several guesses: Heads bowed for a moment of silence for a fallen comrade, waiting in line for their lunch, they all have to use the restroom. I would be wrong (Figure 1.1).

Another image of an abstract collection of frantic lines and a few shapes that fill the frame on all sides with black, heavy marks is equally perplexing. I might think a seriously disturbed child made the drawing. I would be wrong (Figure 1.2).

Consider the painting "A Bar at the Folies Bergère" completed in 1882 by the French master Édouard Manet. The work is a portrait of a young woman tending bar; a mirror behind her reflects her back, well-dressed patrons, and a male customer. With a vacant, slightly sad look, she stares into your eyes. This painting helped change the history of art as we know it. But I'm thinking, what's so monumental about this picture? It's simply shows a woman behind a bar. I would be wrong (Figure 1.3).

Or take the delightfully engaging Academy Award–winning short animation from British filmmaker Nick Park, *Creature Comforts* (1989). I might immediately conclude that the film, a brilliant example of the Claymation style of cartooning that Park spent years making, is concerned with animals that live in a zoo—some like it and others don't. I would be wrong (Weblink 1.1).

Finally, a news photograph from one of the most important and far-reaching stories from the first year of the 21st century—the September 11, 2001 airline attacks on American soil, property, and persons.

The hardest thing to see is what is in front of your eyes.

Johann Wolfgang Von Goethe, 1749–1832
POET, PLAYWRIGHT, PHILOSOPHER

Courtesy of Hal Mathewson and the *New York Daily News*

Figure 1.1
Originally published in the
New York Daily News *in*
1963, these workers are obvi-
ously straining for some mys-
terious reason.

Figure 1.2
Although seemingly a mish-
mash of confusing lines, blobs,
and letterforms, once you
know what the child is
trying to communicate by
this drawing, it all makes
perfect sense.

Kristen Brochmann of *The New York Times*
made the dramatic moment-of-impact
photograph of the second plane hitting the
South Tower of the World Trade Center

for the cover of a *Newsweek* magazine's
"EXTRA EDITION" (Weblink 1.2). Under
a banner headline "AMERICA UNDER
ATTACK" and framed by white and black
borders, the *Newsweek* name is shown in
white letters over a black background. The
copy reads, "9:03 A.M. TUESDAY, SEPT. 11,
2001 Hijacked United Airlines Flight 175
explodes into the World Trade Center."
I might think that this combination of
words and the dramatic photograph is the
highest form of photojournalism and is an
example for the ages of how an art director
for a magazine should display important
historical images. I would be wrong.

It's hard to imagine how the world has
changed since the tragedy of those attacks.
One telling effect of those changes has
been in visual messages in the media. Since
9/11 there have been the U.S. invasion of
Afghanistan later in 2001; the winter Olympic games, which were held in Salt Lake
City, Utah, in 2002; the in-flight destruction
of the Space Shuttle Columbia; the invasion of Iraq; the fall of Baghdad; President
Bush's "Mission Accomplished" speech on

Courtesy of Allison Lester

an aircraft carrier; the capture of Saddam Hussein in 2003; Janet Jackson's Super Bowl "wardrobe malfunction;" the torture of prisoners by U.S. forces in the Abu Ghraib prison captured on soldiers' digital cameras; the evacuation and siege of Fallujah, Iraq; the Indian Ocean tsunami that killed almost 300,000 people in 2004; the acquittal of Michael Jackson of sexual child abuse; the devastation of Hurricane Katrina in 2005; several small, rural churches burned by arsonists; Google's purchase of YouTube in 2006; 32 people killed by a Virginia Tech student in 2007; Cyclone Nargis, which struck Myanmar and killed more than 100,000 people; the global economic meltdown; shoes thrown at Bush while speaking in Iraq in 2008; and the start of the presidency of Barack Obama in 2009 (Figure 1.4).

These and other stories were mostly told with such powerful images that they were added to our collective memory. We remember them because of our emotional attachments and because they have been replayed many times on countless news reports. Through repetitive viewing combined with strong mental and emotional associations, over time the images have become permanent in our minds. When you see new images, you make new impressions and comparisons with these previously stored mental pictures. The content of the new and old images constantly bounces back and forth in our minds so that we learn from them. Otherwise, we forget them, as we do most words and pictures that stream across us as we journey through our lives.

Visual communication relies both on eyes that function and on a brain that interprets all the sensory information received. An active, curious mind remembers and uses visual messages in thoughtful and innovative ways. Knowing about the world and the images that it conveys

will help you analyze pictures. And if you can examine pictures critically, you have a good chance of producing high-quality images that others will remember.

All messages, whether verbal or visual, have literal and symbolic components. Many famous and often reproduced images throughout this book have visual messages that are so strong that millions of people who have seen them have memorized them. No doubt, you have seen some of them too. And when you see them again, you will learn something more because you will make new connections in your brain. These images are memorable because they have strong and compelling literal and symbolic messages. You understand what you are looking at (the literal component of a message) and you perceive a deeper, perhaps emotional connection with the message's content (the symbolic component). Consequently, images reproduced in this textbook have helped shape Western culture and how most of us feel about ourselves. Although separate and individual in

Figure 1.3

*"Un Bar aux Folies Bergère,"
oil on canvas, 1882, by
Édouard Manet. Manet
signed his name on the label
of the bottle at the left next
to a Bass ale, identified by its
red, triangular logo. Perhaps
there was a tour group from
England visiting that evening.
The painting was criticized
at the time for, among other
details, not accurately positioning the bottles reflected in
the mirror.
See color insert following page
178.*

Figure 1.4

The official portrait of President Barack Hussein Obama is filled with symbolism. He stands before the American and Great Seal flags, has a strong, direct, and confident eye-level expression with a slight smile, and wears a blue shirt and tie, possibly symbolizing his affiliation with the Democratic Party, and also wears a flag pin on his sports coat's lapel.

See color insert following page 178.

Official White House Photo

HIP / Art Resource, NY

Figure 1.5

Blind in one eye and nearly blind in the other, Aldous Huxley was forced to wear glasses with thick lenses, as shown in this 1934 portrait.

ity without the aid of glasses. However, his main purpose in the book was to convey the idea that seeing clearly is mostly the result of thinking clearly. Huxley summed up his method for achieving clear vision with the formula: "Sensing plus selecting plus perceiving equals seeing."

■ Sensing

The first stage of clear vision is to sense. To sense simply means letting enough light enter your eyes so that you can see objects immediately around you. Sensing also depends on how well the many parts of the eye work. Obviously, a darkened room and/or damaged or improperly functioning eyes will hamper sensing. If there is enough light where you are and your eyes are working properly, you will sense light. However, when you are sensing, only your brain is engaged with the outside world—your mind hasn't registered what it is you are sensing. Think of sensing as a camera without a memory card; that is, there is no mental processing of the image during this phase of visual perception.

■ Selecting

Huxley's next stage is to select a particular element from a visual array. To select is to focus and look at a specific part of a scene within the enormous frame of possibilities that sensing offers. That concentration is the result of the combination of the light-gathering and -focusing properties of the eye with the higher-level functions of the mind. In other words, selecting is a conscious, intellectual act. When you select, you engage more fully the objects in the scene than when you merely look when sensing. Selecting starts the process of classification of objects as harmful, helpful, known, unfamiliar, meaningful, or confusing. To select is to isolate an object within the area where the sharpest

their intent, content, and medium, all are linked by the inescapable elements common to all visual messages: They are objects that get their life from light. That life comes not only from the light of day but also from the light of revelation, the light of understanding, and the light of education.

Aldous Huxley, author of the novel *Brave New World* and 46 other books of philosophical and futuristic vision, detailed his efforts to teach himself how to see more clearly in his 1942 work *The Art of Seeing* (Figure 1.5). From the age of 16, Huxley suffered from a degenerative eye condition known as *keratitis punctata*, an inflammation of the cornea. One eye was merely capable of light perception and the other could only view an eye chart's largest letter from ten feet away. Today, the condition is rare and attributed most likely to bacterial or a viral infection. It can now be treated easily with medications.

In *Seeing*, Huxley described the physical exercises he used to overcome his disabil-

vision takes place in the eye. By selecting individual objects within a scene, you are doing what the eye's physiology is made to do—focus your mental activities on a single area that is isolated from all others.

■ *Perceiving*

The last stage in Huxley's visual path is the most important—to perceive. That is, you must try to make sense of what you select. If your mind has any chance of storing visual information for long-term retrieval and to increase your knowledge base, you must actively consider the meaning of what you see. To process an image mentally on a higher level of cognition than simply sensing and selecting means that you must concentrate on the subjects within a field of view with the intent of finding meaning and not simply as an act of observation. This process demands much sharper mental activity. Previous experience with specific visual messages is a key in seeing clearly.

Sensing without selecting will often lead to mistakes in perceiving.

Imagine that you are in a car stopped at a traffic light. There's another car stopped in the lane next to you. Although you are staring straight ahead, you notice out of the corner of your eye that there is furious hand motion going on between the two persons in the car next to you. You naturally conclude that the two are having a violent fistfight. Almost afraid to look, you turn your head slightly and look through the open windows·and smile at your "aha" moment. The light changes and your attention again is directed to the traffic on the road. The two were simply having an energetic conversation using sign language while waiting for the green light.

The adage "seeing is believing" was first expressed in 1639, and it meant "only physi-

cal or concrete evidence is convincing." But the eyes and the mind alike can be easily fooled. Optical illusions are perhaps the best examples. With illusions, even when you know the truth of them, you often cannot force your brain to make the correction. Consequently, they are powerful attention-getters used by advertisers and artists.

Two major classes of optical illusions are physiological and cognitive. Physiological illusions rely on the physical way our eyes are constructed and are called grid or simultaneous contrast. Black dots appear and disappear in the intersection of a grid of black boxes made from white lines in a grid illusion that relies on the stimulation and relaxation of photosensitive cells in the eyes' retinas. Volkswagen employed the grid for its Golf automobile in 2002 with the copy, "Now you see it. Now you don't," and Clearasil, an acne medication, used the grid illusion next year in an advertisement with the tag line, "As soon as a black spot appears, use Clearasil" (Figure 1.6). For the contrast illusion,

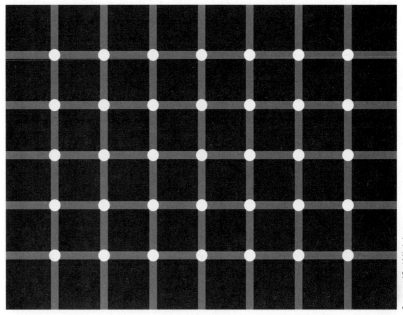

Courtesy of Paul Martin Lester

Figure 1.6

As you move your eyes from side to side, try to count the black dots that suddenly appear and vanish throughout the pattern. The optical illusion is not caused by graphic elements within the picture itself. The faint and fleeting black dots replace the white ones only within your mind. The illusion is a result of the photosensitive rods in your retinas being excited and then resting. Because of its attention-getting property, companies have used this illusion in print advertisements.

Figure 1.7

As a way of identifying edible plants, our minds evolved to be able to see the colors of berries and other fruits whether in sunlight or shade. This phenomenon is called color constancy and was detailed by the American inventor of the Polaroid camera, Edwin Land, in his retinex (a word formed by the combination of retina and cortex) theory in 1971. In this simultaneous contrast illusion, the thinner horizontal gradient is exactly the same tone of gray from left to right. You can prove this is so if you cover the background. Our minds change the color of the foreground bar depending on the colors behind it in order to compensate for changes in illumination.

Figure 1.8

Perhaps as a subliminal message symbolizing movement, the designer of the FedEx logo incorporated an arrow between the "E" and the "x" that is impossible not to see once the illusion is revealed.

the brain's tendency for colors to remain the same despite varying lighting conditions makes a horizontal gray line appear to have different tones depending on its background. The American inventor of the Polaroid instant camera, Edwin Land, used the word "retinex" in 1971 to describe the phenomenon that he thought was a combination of the retina and the visual cortex in the back of the brain (Figure 1.7).

One of the first scientists to write significantly about cognitive illusions was the German scientist Herman von Helmholtz, who later distinguished himself in the field of color perception. He believed that this type of illusion happened because of "unconscious interferences" that our minds make while looking at the objects. The three major types of cognitive illusions are ambiguous, distorting, and paradox. In 1915 the Danish gestalt psychologist Edgar Rubin, also known for creating a form of military camouflage, experimented with figure and ground patterns by drawing an object that could be interpreted as either a face or vase. The brain cannot see both images at once—you must make a conscious decision whether to see a face or a vase in the drawing. The package delivery company FedEx uses a variation of this illusion in its logo. The arrow that is seen only through conscious effort by the viewer leads outwardly to the right and symbol-

izes forward movement and progress (Figure 1.8). Famous distorting illusions are the Müller-Lyer and café wall illusions. With its horizontal lines the same length but with varying inward and outward arrows at their ends, they appear to be different measurements. The café wall illusion is named after an actual café wall in Bristol, England, which contained alternating black and white tiles so that the perfectly straight horizontal lines appear uneven (Figure 1.9). Paradox illusions create impossible objects in the minds of viewers. One famous example is the Penrose triangle made popular by Roger Penrose, an English mathematician in the 1950s, and employed by Dutch lithographic artist M.C. Escher particularly for his 1961 piece "Waterfall." The gestalt theory is often cited as a way to explain these illusions. The brain tries to make sense of confusing objects by organizing them the most efficient way that it can (Figure 1.10).

Although you can certainly select a particular visual element with little mental processing when it is a new or a surprising occurrence, analyzing a visual message helps ensure that you will find meaning for the picture. If you understand the image, it is likely to become a part of your long-term memory. As the American philosopher, writer, and pencil maker Henry David Thoreau once said, "The question is not what you look at, but what you see."

Consider for a moment all the visual messages that are a part of your life—a cracked bat given to you by a professional baseball player when you were six years old; your fingers on the handlebars during your first bicycle ride; the smile from your favorite teacher during your high school graduation; red blood dripping from a cut on your leg; the sight of a small stream during a quiet walk in the country; a passionate look from a lover. These pictures

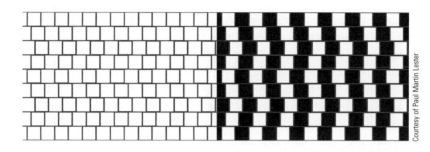

Figure 1.9
First seen on the tiles of an actual café in Bristol, England, by a student of the British psychologist Richard Gregory in 1973, the illusion makes the parallel horizontal lines appear to be angled.

are all a part of your repertoire of memories. Images weave themselves into your memory system, sometimes lying dormant for years. You remember and communicate these mental images because they are highly meaningful visual messages.

But think of all the personal visual messages you have experienced but may have forgotten—the billboard advertisements on the outfield wall during the baseball game; where you ended up on your first bicycle ride; the faces of your fellow graduates sitting next to you as you waited for your diploma; the face of the doctor who treated your cut leg; all the colors of the plants as you walked along the trail; the pictures on the wall of your lover's bedroom. Actually, the proportion of remembered to forgotten images is quite small. At the end of the classic science fiction movie *Blade Runner* (1982), the character played by Rutger Hauer recounts memories from his life to Harrison Ford. Hauer sums up the fragility of memory best when he confesses, "All those moments will be lost in time like tears in rain."

Why are select memories easily recalled, but a vast array of ambiguous memories lost?

To answer that question you must know how the brain works. The brain processes three types of visual messages: mental—those that you experience from inside your mind such as thoughts, dreams, and fantasies; direct—those that you see without media intervention; and

mediated—those that you see through some type of print (paper) or screen (movie, television, or web) medium. What you experience and what you remember are products of a mind that actively thinks, with images and words, the mental, direct, and/or mediated visual messages you imagine or experience in your life.

One reason dreams are so often forgotten is that the mental images are not translated into words. You will not remember much through visual messages alone. Memory happens when you think about pictures using words *and* images. If you immediately tell a friend or write down a dream, you have a better chance of remembering it. That's why a textbook about visual communication takes so many words.

■ *Back to the Images from the Beginning*

If you knew something about construction sites and the building techniques that were employed during the 1960s, you might have instantly known what the serious-looking men were doing. But there are other clues as well. Their sad, downturned faces clearly indicate they are not happy. In fact, they are all struggling. What are they struggling with? Look at their shoulders and their arms. Something is causing their limbs to be pulled down by the extreme weight they all hold. But a lunch plate couldn't possibly be heavy

Figure 1.10
Although the Swedish artist Oscar Reutersvärd first created the impossible triangle in 1934, the British mathematician and physicist Sir Roger Penrose popularized the illusion in the 1950s by calling it "impossibility in its purest form." The Dutch woodcut and lithographic artist Maurits Cornelis Escher often employed the illusion in his work.

enough to cause such discomfort. If you have photographic experience, there are clues in the picture that only a photographer might notice. For one, a flash bulb was used to take the picture. The shadow of the face of the third man from the right can be seen on the back of the man next to him. The flash's light is at an extreme angle—way off to the left of the frame. Another photographic clue is on the head of the man second from the right. See the discoloration of his hair and ear? Two other clues of note: There is a white, vertical line between the third and fourth men from the right, and the man on the upper level in the middle—can you imagine what he is doing? If you are still stumped, the words that accompanied the picture will explain it all. The caption read, "JOB IS REALLY A PANE. Workmen seem to be faking it for benefit of foreman as they strain under weight of invisible load at 42d St., near Third Ave. They're holding handles of suction cups gripped to huge section of plate glass which was installed in store." The glass appears transparent because the flash is off to the side. The light illuminates the scene but doesn't reflect back into the lens (try to make a portrait of yourself by using a flash with your camera and pointing it straight at a mirror). The slight discoloration on the man's head is a reflection from another light source (probably the sun) on the glass, the vertical line is from the glass pane itself, and the man in the middle is guiding the piece into place.

The child's drawing was made by the author's daughter Allison when she was four years old. She was given a white sheet of typing paper, a thick black marker, and an assignment to draw the story of one of her favorite songs. The picture contains elements that are meant to be letters and others meant to be images.

But since she hadn't yet learned how to write or the icons for simple pictures, the letters and forms seem to merge and are confusing. You might guess the song if you can imagine what the two major dark areas in the frame—top-center and bottom-center—might be and what all the squiggly lines might mean. The popular song is mostly known as "The Itsy Bitsy Spider." The words are thought to have been first published in a 1910 book, *Camp and Camino in Lower California*, by Arthur Walbridge North. In an account of his travels through the California peninsula and Mexico, North described writing down the words of two pioneer girls he met along the way:

> **Oh, the blooming, bloody spider went up the water spout,**
> **The blooming, bloody rain came down and washed the spider out,**
> **The blooming, bloody sun came out and dried up all the rain,**
> **And the blooming, bloody spider came up the spout again.**

The song can be thought of as an optimistic message of hope despite impossible odds. Admittedly, Allison learned a slightly different version, but you get the point. Still, her drawing looks strange. Luckily, she interpreted the elements for us: The little symbol at the top-left corner means that this work is a song, the blob of black near the center is the sun, the blob toward the bottom is the spider and its web, the marks that look like letters contains the message, "Don't get too near a spider or he might bite you," the seemingly random marks throughout the page designate rain, and the letters in a row at the bottom-right that start with what looks like an "A" is her attempt to write her name. If this assignment were given to you, chances are you would divide the story of the song into separate sections and tell it in narrative form as if seen in a comic book. But Allison, because she didn't know any better, relayed the entire song all in one go. Five years later she repeated the assignment. Sure enough, she had learned the images for a spider, its web, and the sun, with the parts of the song divided by clear borders. She also greatly improved upon her signature (Figure 1.11).

Seven years before the invention of photography was made public, the painter Édouard Manet was born in Paris. By the time he was an adult, artists throughout his country and the world were scared that their profession's days were numbered. Why would anyone pay for a sitting or even buy a painting when the camera recorded exact replicas of people, things, and places at a fraction of the cost? Summing up the artists' frustration was the phrase, "From today, painting is dead!" But of course, painting did not die after photography became popular. In fact, it can be said that painting and its practitioners were reborn and flourished *because* of photography. And one of the chief reasons cited by art critics and others for this renaissance was the painting of a bored barmaid by Manet.

Take a look at the painting again (Figure 1.3). It seems straightforward enough, right? A young woman stands behind a marble counter with bottles of alcohol for sale while she, a gentleman customer, and the expansive and raucous Folies Bergère are reflected in the mirror behind her. Look closely. In the mirror's reflection behind her, can you see all the chandeliers and other electric lights, the smoke in the air, the men in the crowd wearing top hats, the woman catching a view with her opera glasses, the woman with long, yellow gloves

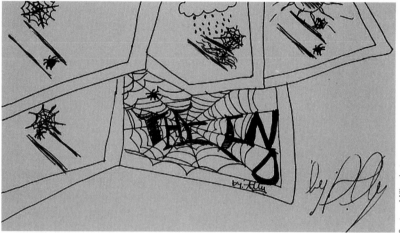

distracted by something beside her, and the green stockings of the trapeze artist? Now study the young woman. Notice her golden bracelet, the flowers in her bodice, the jewel-encrusted necklace, her earrings, her bright yellow bangs, and her gaze. She's looking right at you as you stand before her and she awaits your order. Still think all is ordinary in the painting? Wait a minute. The reflection of you and the barmaid should be directly behind her, and yet the reflected image is off to one side showing the backside of the woman and a face that isn't yours (of course), but that of a tall man with a mustache, top hat, and cane.

Manet changed the art of painting by showing through this example that the art world could move away from strict realism. In this work he portrayed a concept that is about as abstract as it gets—two moments in time. In one view he showed the life of a sad, young, bright-blonde barmaid as she thinks about being trapped in a job that she will have until her hair turns gray and her body becomes plump as a much older woman. Her future is depicted in the mirror's view. Manet helped accomplish the transition from

Figure 1.11

The same child who at four years old made the drawing of the "The Itsy Bitsy Spider" song in Figure 1.2 repeats the exercise at age nine. But since she learned to read English and became familiar with comic books, the narrative takes place within a storyboard composed of five panels separated by thick borders that are meant to be read left-to-right and top-to-bottom. With less background noise than before, the panels include easily identifiable images of the spider, rain cloud, sun, and cobweb. To solidify the link to motion pictures, the last panel shows a screen filled with the spider resting on its web and an elaborate "The End."

realism to a new art form that came to be known as Impressionism. Manet's "Folies Bergère" was his last great work of art and is a key in the transition between the literal and the symbolic as expressed on canvas.

Four-time Academy Award–winning animator Nick Park was born in a small town in northwestern England. As a young boy he was interested in drawing cartoons and making short, experimental movies. After college he worked for a time at a small animation studio, Aardman Animations. His first professional work was for the musician Peter Gabriel's music video for "Sledgehammer," a number one hit in several countries in 1986. Three and a half minutes into the video, you can see headless, dancing chickens brought to life by Park (Weblink 1.3). He became known early on as a master of the stop-motion animation technique using Plasticine, a pliable clay product that brings three-dimensional depth to animated characters. In 1989 he and his fellow staffers completed the five-minute film *Creature Comforts* that won him and his company its first Academy Award.

All forms of animation require a great deal of patience, but manipulating clay figures frame by frame (24 frames usually make up one second of film) requires particular dedication. For *Comfort*, Park worked on and off for about four years. In the motion picture a human reporter (early on you see a hand holding a microphone) conducts a series of interviews with various animals living in the London Zoo at Regent's Park—the oldest in the world, established in 1828 and opened to the public in 1847. The animals have varying opinions about their quality of life. Those that like their life in the zoo include a male polar bear with his two sons, an aardvark, a glasses-wearing koala, and a

chicken who makes a point that animals in the circus have to perform. However, a young hippopotamus, a tortoise, a lemur mother with too many children in her tight quarters, a female gorilla who counts the days by making marks on the wall, and a disgruntled jaguar who complains about the lack of space and fresh meat (a microphone attached to a long pole is used for his segment) complain about their environment. The literal message is readily apparent—if animals could talk, you would find out that some like living in a zoo and some don't. Four years' work and an Academy Award to make that obvious point? No.

Andrew, the younger polar bear, gives the point of Park's film away with his first line, "Oh well, the zoos are very important to animals. They're a bit like homes—like nursing homes for poor animals and people like old people." Most of the dialogue came from interviews Park and his assistants made with persons who lived in housing projects and retirement homes. The short animation is not about zoos at all. It's a commentary on institutional living arrangements—rest homes, prisons, school dorms, military housing, and a parent's or guardian's home. The conclusion that can be made by the movie is that a person living under such regulated conditions should have their individual needs respected. That's why the film won an Academy Award.

Newsweek's "Extra Edition" was similar to other magazine covers immediately after 9/11. *People, US News & World Report, Time,* and others featured a single photograph that dramatically showed the inconceivable confluence of fire and smoke after an airplane going full speed smashed into a skyscraper. With such a picture, few words were needed to help clarify the unexplainable. Look closely in the background of the *Newsweek* cover (Weblink 1.4). There is a hint of how beautiful September 11, 2001, was in New York City as a cloudless blue sky can be seen. In contrast to that tranquility are the words that are set in uppercase sans serif or clunky square serif typefaces that scream out at the reader as much as the angry orange and yellow fireball surrounded by smoke and a cascading shower of building debris. And yet, you would think that the distracting barcode, a pattern meant to be read by a laser scanner that gives pricing information and other details, could have been placed on the back cover's advertisement just this once.

But it wasn't the barcode that upset media critics and historians. This important photograph was altered to exploit the visual cue of depth for purely commercial reasons.

The background sky behind the stricken tower was removed with a software program so the building could be placed in front of the *Newsweek* name. The three-dimensional effect is popular with editors for their covers because it can catch a customer's eyes browsing near a bookstore's crowded magazine rack. However, to manipulate a photograph, particularly one with such historical and long-term value for a purely commercial reason, is the height of unethical behavior.

The greatest aid to clear seeing isn't eyes that function with or without glasses or a telescope that brings into sharp focus the craters of the moon. The process of sensing, selecting, and perceiving takes a curious, questioning, and knowledgeable mind. The goal of a visual communicator isn't simply to have an image published or broadcast.

The goal should be to produce powerful pictures so that the viewer will remember their content.

Images have little use if the viewer's mind doesn't use them.

As future image consumers and producers, you will want to see images that you remember and make images that others learn from.

The goal of this book is to give you a method for analyzing visual messages regardless of the medium of presentation. Without systematically analyzing an image, you may sense it and not notice the individual elements within the frame. You might not consider its content as it relates to a story. Without considering the image, you will not gain any understanding or personal insights. The picture will simply be another in a long line of forgotten images.

In *The Art of Seeing* Huxley wrote a phrase that sums up visual communication:

The more you know, the more you see.

A former baseball player watches and sees a game much more attentively than someone who is at her first game. The newcomer probably will miss signals from a manager, scoreboard details, the curve of the ball's flight as it speeds from pitcher to batter, and many other details observed by the former player. But the process is more than simply knowing and seeing.

The interim steps between knowing and seeing can be thought of as the visual communication circle dance: The more you know, the more your eyes and brain will sense. The more you sense, the more your mind will select. The more you select, the more you will understand what you are seeing. The more you perceive, the more you remember, as the images become a part of your long-term memory. The more you remember, the more you learn because you compare new images with those stored in your mind. The more you learn,

Figure 1.12

As the circle shape implies, Aldous Huxley's method for clear seeing spins as the more you sense, the more you will come to know.

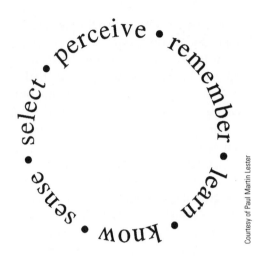

Courtesy of Paul Martin Lester

Analyzing visual messages makes you take a long, careful look at the pictures you see—a highly satisfying intellectual act. Those images become a part of your general knowledge of the world. You discover how images are linked in ways that you never thought of before. You also become a more interesting, curious person. Such is the goal of visual literacy—to sense, to select, yes, but more importantly, to perceive.

the more you know. The more you know, the more you will sense. For clear seeing and knowing, this circle should repeat itself on and on (Figure 1.12).

■ *KEY TERMS*

- Abstract
- Flash
- Impressionism
- Literal
- Long-term memory

- Memory card
- News photograph
- Realism
- Symbolic
- Western culture

 To locate active URLs for the weblinks mentioned in this chapter, please go to the companion site at http://communication.wadsworth.com/lester5 and select the proper chapter.

Section

1

The five chapters in this section—visual cues, theories, persuasion, stereotypes, and analysis—all make the point that it is the mind—not the eyes—that understands visual messages. Toward that end, we are programmed to notice the four visual cues and how they are employed in print and screen media to attract our attention so that we may learn from pictures. Visual communication theories further refine our understanding of why some pictures are remembered but most are forgotten. And because these visual messages can stimulate both intellectual and emotional responses, they are powerful tools that persuade people to buy a particular product or think a specific way. A creator of images also has an ethical responsibility to ensure that a picture is a fair, accurate, and complete representation of someone from another culture. Finally, if you don't engage intellectually with a visual message, there is little chance of understanding its meaning and purpose. Consequently, a 13-step methodology for studying any image—still or moving—is included that should change an emotional, short-term, and subjective opinion about a picture into a rational, long-term, and objective response.

Visual Cues

Chapter 2

It sounds like a horrible idea.

Put the head of a slightly anesthetized cat into a vice so that it's forced to watch a simple slide show while you poke the back of its brain with a microelectrode. But that scene was not a horror movie plot that would give nightmares to a member of PETA (People for the Ethical Treatment of Animals); two scientists won a Nobel Prize for that experiment in 1981 (Weblink 2.1).

The work of Canadian David Hubel and Swede Torsten Wiesel of the Johns Hopkins University in Baltimore provided clues to how the brain sees images provided by our eyes. The two jabbed a microelectrode into a brain cell in the visual cortex at the back of the brain of an anesthetized cat and connected it to both an amplifier and an oscilloscope. The amplifier converted electrical energy to a "put-put" sound, while the oscilloscope turned signals to a

blip on a screen so they could measure the response (Figure 2.1).

With the cat's eyes open and focused toward a screen, the scientists flashed simple straight and slanted light patterns. With their setup, Hubel and Wiesel could see and hear immediately the effect of any nerve cell stimulation by the patterns of light. After they flashed the light on the screen several times and adjusted their equipment, the scientists recorded what they had thought was possible: the stimulated activity of a single brain cell responsible for vision.

The visual cortex is composed of several thin layers of nerve tissue. By this tedious and perhaps ethically disturbing method of placing microelectrodes in various cells within each layer of a cat's brain, Hubel and Wiesel found that some cells responded to a spot of light while others noted the edges of objects, certain angles of lines, specific movements, specific colors, or the space between

A mind that works primarily with meanings must have organs that supply it primarily with forms.

Suzanne Langer, 1895–1985
PHILOSOPHER AND EDUCATOR

Figure 2.1

David Hubel and Torsten Wiesel shared a Nobel Prize for attaching a tiny electrode to a cat's visual cortex and identifying the types of brain cells responsible for sight. The simplicity of this line drawing masks the fear the animal must have felt at being restrained for this experiment.

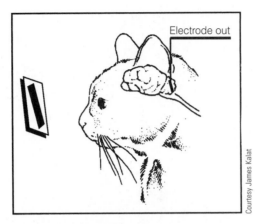

Electrode out

Courtesy James Kalat

Courtesy Autodesk, Inc.

Figure 2.2

The use of lighting in this computer-generated image helps create a sense of depth in this view of a chapel. The lighting effect also communicates religious meaning.

visual cues are the major concerns of any visual communicator when designing an image to be remembered by a viewer because they are noticed before a person even realizes what they are. The four visual cues, therefore, are what the brain sees, not the mind. Consequently, the four cues can be used to attract attention to a presentation, whether in print or on a screen.

■ COLOR

Throughout human history, people have been fascinated by light. Civilizations prayed and celebrated at each new sunrise and invented gods that ruled the sun. Religious leaders equate light with life, and most religions begin with its creation (Figure 2.2). When the light from fire was discovered, probably by accident through a lightning strike, most were awed by its power. Literary references and colloquial expressions about light and vision abound because of the importance placed on seeing. When we want to learn the truth, we say, "Shed light on the subject." After a revelation of some truth, we have "seen the light." If we are concerned that we are not getting the full story, we complain, "Don't keep me in the dark." New Orleans photographer Clarence John Laughlin once wrote, "One of my basic feelings is that the mind, and the heart alike . . . must be dedicated to the glory, the magic, and the mystery of light." Performers such as Daft Punk (Weblink 2.2), the French DJ artist Étienne de Crécy (Weblink 2.3), Radiohead (Weblink 2.4), and Trans-Siberian Orchestra (Weblink 2.5), among others, know the power of light to attract attention so they produce expensive light shows to accompany their concert performances (Figure 2.3). Light can intrigue, educate, and entertain, but nowhere is light so exquisitely expressed as through color.

lines rather than the lines themselves. In short, each brain cell in the cortex reacts almost in a one-to-one relationship with the type of visual stimulation it receives. From all this information, the brain constructs a map of the outside world, which is projected upside-down on our retinas.

More importantly for visual communicators, it was eventually discovered by other researchers that the brain, through its vast array of specialized cells, most quickly and easily responds to four major attributes of all viewed objects: color, form, depth, and movement. These four

Various philosophers, scientists, and physicians throughout recorded history have attempted to explain the nature of color. Aristotle reasoned correctly that light and color were different names for the same visual phenomenon. Much later, Leonardo da Vinci proposed that there were six primary colors—white, black, red, yellow, green, and blue. He came to that conclusion simply by reasoning that the six colors were wholly independent and unique. Da Vinci showed that by mixing these six colors in the form of paints in varying degrees, all the other colors capable of being seen by a normal human eye could be created. His interest in and theories on the mixing of colors came directly from his experience as one of the great masters of painting. Although all the colors desired by painters can be made by mixing those six color *pigments* together in varying degrees, this property of paints doesn't explain how *light* is mixed.

Thomas Young, a British physician and scientist, was the first to link color and the human eye. In 1801 he suggested that nerve fibers in the retina respond to the colors red, green, and violet. Twenty years later, the great German physiologist and physicist Hermann von Helmholtz was born. In 1851 he invented the ophthalmoscope, which enabled doctors to see inside a person's eye. In 1867 he published his greatest work, a handbook on optics, in which he refined Young's ideas on how humans see color. Their combined work became known as the Young-Helmholtz theory, or the tri-chromatic theory, and explained how the eye physically sees color. Their theory became a fact in 1959 after their idea was experimentally proven. Sir John Herschel, the scientist who invented the word "photography," praised Young as a "truly original genius." The immortal physicist Albert Einstein had kind words for von Helmholtz as well

Amra Pasic © 2009, used under license, Shutterstock.com

Figure 2.3

A typical stage lighting configuration can be seen for the English rock band Oasis in concert. Spotlights directed from the front illuminate the musicians while backlights help separate them from the background.

when he remarked, "I admire ever more the original, free thinker Helmholtz."

Every color we see can be made with three basic, primary colors—red, green, and blue. When these colors are mixed, it is called additive color. Equal amounts of these colored lights will add together to produce white light. The additive mixing of colors is the basis for color we see from our eyes and in photography, television and computer monitors, and stage lighting.

Some students get confused because they are taught that the primary colors are magenta, yellow, and cyan. But those colors are the primaries used for paint pigments and printing presses—not light. When paints are mixed together, the colors in the paint absorb every color except the wavelength that we see reflected back. This method of color mixing is called subtractive color because as they are mixed they become darker. Subtractive color is used in offset printing, in which four colors are used to create color photographs and illustrations on paper—magenta, yellow, cyan, and for added definition, black (Figure 2.4).

Figure 2.4

This simple graph illustrates the primary (red, green, and blue) and secondary (magenta, yellow, and cyan) colors. The graph also communicates the result when the colors are mixed—blue and red make magenta, whereas magenta and yellow make red, and so on.
See color insert following page 178.

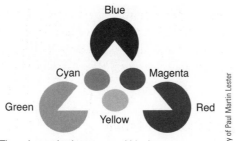

The primary (red, green, and blue) and secondary (magenta, yellow, and cyan) colors

Courtesy of Paul Martin Lester

Figure 2.5

Because red light has a longer wavelength than the other colors, it is used for warning lights and signs. Since blue light has a shorter wavelength, more data can be placed on a compact disc of the same size.

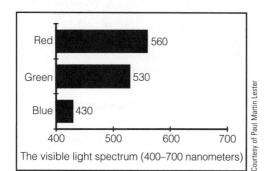

The visible light spectrum (400–700 nanometers)

Courtesy of Paul Martin Lester

Figure 2.6

Unlike the psychological response to blue light as cold and distant, the temperature of the blue-colored firelight near the gas jets is much hotter than the yellow-colored light that streams to the top of this artificial fireplace.
See color insert following page 178.

Courtesy of Paul Martin Lester

Three different methods can be used to describe color: objective, comparative, and subjective. The objective method for describing colors depends on known standards of measurement; the comparative and subjective methods rely on the evaluation of the person who sees the color.

■ *Objective Method*

The objective, or scientific, method for describing colors rests on the assumption that the perception of color is a result of various light wavelengths stimulating the cones along the back of the eyes' retinas. A color can be accurately measured by the location of its wavelength on the electromagnetic spectrum. The length of an energy wave is measured in parts per millimeter. The wavelength of the visible light spectrum is 300 nanometers wide. That's about one one-hundredth of an inch. The entire electromagnetic spectrum sensitive to the photoreceptors in the eyes is only from 400 to 700 nanometers on the visible light portion of the electromagnetic spectrum. Blue shows up on the visible spectrum at about 430 nanometers, green has a wavelength that starts at about 530 nanometers, and red has a wavelength beginning at 560 nanometers (Figure 2.5).

The objective method can also be used to measure a color's unique temperature that distinguishes it from every other color. The color red, for example, is about 1,000°K, and a deep blue color is a much hotter 60,000°K. Sunlight at noon, depending on the time of year, is between 4,900° and 5,800°K. The next time you look at logs burning in a fireplace, note the various colors produced. Yellow and red colors are cooler on the temperature scale than green or blue colors (Figure 2.6).

Because of its long wavelength and quick recognition by the eye, red is used for signal lights, stop signs, and other warning or attention-getting purposes. There are two reasons that the eye notices red more easily—one has to do with the length of the color's wavelength, and the other with the physiology of the eye. Since red has a longer wavelength, it is noticed from farther away and stays inside a person's eyes longer than any of the other visible colors. Plus, the slightly yellow-colored cornea protects the eye from harmful ultraviolet rays and also absorbs the shorter wavelength colors of blue and green, letting the longer wavelengths of red pass through to the retina easier.

■ Comparative Method

The second technique for describing colors is less accurate than the objective method. As with a dictionary definition, the color red might be compared to the color of blood, green with healthy plants, and blue with the sky on a clear, sunny day. But one person's conception of the color red isn't always the same as someone else's. Blood red is dark, but the red of poinsettia plant leaves and traffic lights are slightly different. For the comparative method to be of use, the color that another color is compared with must be accepted universally as a standard. A problem arises when the word for a color is not understood. For example, The Phrontistery, "A Thinking Place" website (Weblink 2.6) lists 168 color definitions you might not know—aeneous (shiny bronze) to zinnober (chrome green). Likewise, paints used for canvases, house walls, and automobiles are sometimes hard to compare if you are unfamiliar with their names. Automobile paint from the Dulux company used for Volkswagen cars from 1954 to 1982 could come in 28 shades of blue—andorra, bahai, bahama, baltic, belgrave, commercial, diamond, flipper, gemini, gulf, horizon, lavender, miami, mountain, neptune, ocean, pacific, pastel, pigeon, regatta, sea, seeblau, slate, space,

strato, summer, tasman, and zenith. Don't forget plain old blue. It should be clear that the comparative method could only be used to give a rough estimate of what a color might look like.

■ Subjective Method

This third technique for describing color is the most symbolic. A person's mental state or association with an object strongly affects the emotional response to a color. In their drawings, children tend to prefer abstract colors to shapes and lines. Girls generally use more intense colors than boys do in their early pictures. Educational psychologists consider such use of color to indicate enjoyment of social interactions and possession of higher reasoning abilities. Painters have known for years that the warm colors—reds and yellows—appear closer than the cooler colors—blues and greens. The terms *warm* and *cool* are psychological distinctions and are not related to the actual temperature of the color. (Recall that blue is one of the hottest colors.) Lighter colors tend to be viewed as soft and cheerful, and darker colors have a harsh or moody emotional quality about them. A room painted a light color will appear larger than the same room painted a dark color. Colors or hues that are tinted (made lighter) tend to recede, whereas shaded (made darker) colors advance toward the viewer, making the room look smaller (Figure 2.7). Because people associate colors with objects and events, this visual attribute is highly subjective and emotional.

We tend to associate a memorable experience, whether pleasant or bad, with the colors of the objects that constitute the event. Blood red might remind someone of an accident. Green might recall a pleasant

Figure 2.7

"Sea Chest," by Garth Chouteau. In this computer-generated image, the red fish appears to be in the foreground while the dark blue background gives a three-dimensional (3-D) illusion. See color insert following page 178.

Figure 2.8

"The Arnolfini Portrait," oil on oak panel, 1434 by Jan van Eyck. The Dutch artist Jan van Eyck's painting is a seemingly simple portrait of a man with his wife, and yet it is considered to be one of the most complex in Western art. The image is quite likely a memorial. It shows Giovanni di Nicolao Arnolfini and his first wife Costanza Trenta who had died the year before. With its use of natural, realistic lighting, a perspective probably achieved from the use of a camera obscura visual aid to create an illusion of depth, and numerous objects displayed throughout the work that have symbolic meanings, the work is a favorite of art history students. Although it is often mistakenly thought that the woman is pregnant, it was fashionable at the time for dresses to make their wearers appear to be with child. In the 15th century, the color green symbolized hope—in this case, hope that the couple would have a child by the green dress she wears. But as signified by the one lit candle in the chandelier on his side and the burned out candle on hers, their hope was dashed. See color insert following page 178.

Courtesy Autodesk, Inc

National Gallery, London / Art Resource, NY

walk on a grassy field. Yellow might be the color of a balloon bought at a circus. Imagine any color of your choosing. Do you relate it to a specific object? Most people never associate color with a formless blob, but with a definite object. For that reason, memory of an object affects the perception of its color.

Throughout recorded history, colors have been associated with magical spells, medical cures, and personality revelations. A general love for color is considered to be a sign of an enthusiastic person. An indifference to color is a trait of an introspective personality. In ancient Egypt, women so loved color that they used green powder topped with the glitter obtained by crushing beetles for eye shadow, black paint as lipstick, red rouge for their cheeks, blue paint to outline the veins of their breasts, gold paint to coat their nipples, and a reddish brown dye called henna to stain their fingers and feet. But Egyptian women did not use color merely to brighten their complexions; color was used to signify power relationships within the culture. Unfortunately, many of the paints and powders used as makeup contained toxic metals that slowly killed their wearers.

Green symbolizes fertility, youth, nature, jealousy, hope, and the Irish. In 1434 the painter Jan Van Eyck painted a portrait, "The Arnolfini Portrait," in which a woman wears a green dress and simulates pregnancy with her pose (Figure 2.8). The puppet Kermit the Frog was a logical choice as the spokesfrog for Ford's line of hybrid cars. Green is a favorite color of those who are outgoing and have large appetites. Emerald green connotes versatility and ingenuity, whereas a grayish green signifies deceitful behavior. Green stones worn around the neck were thought to promote fertility. Green also is believed to have a calming effect. Many backstage waiting rooms in theaters are called "greenrooms" because of the color of their painted walls.

Baby boys are dressed in blue because the color is associated with the color of the sky—where it was thought the gods lived. The color supposedly gives boys power and protects them from evil spirits. Some adults wear blue for the same reason—to ward off the evil eye. Parents once draped blue and violet stones around children's necks because they associated the colors with virtue and faith.

In ancient Egypt, red fingernails signified a woman's belief that she was a member of the highest social class. Red-colored objects supposedly relieved many medical ailments. In Ireland and Russia, red flannel clothing was believed to be a remedy for scarlet fever. Red woolen blankets were applied to a sprained ankle in Scotland, to a sore throat in Ireland, and to prevent fever in Macedonia. To prevent smallpox, the physician to Edward II demanded that the king's entire room be painted red. To prevent the scars caused by the disease, red light was used in Denmark. Red stones were often used to treat any disease. Some people still believe that an injury such as a black eye should be covered immediately with a red, raw steak. The Japanese thought that the color red overcame nightmares. The Chinese tied a red ribbon to a child's hair to promote long life. Parents dress baby girls in pink because a European legend claimed that girls were born inside little pink flowers. Many people believe that a room that is painted pink will calm children, whether girls or boys.

Jaundice has long been considered a condition that can be cured through exposure to sunlight. For many years, however, people mistakenly thought that the sun's yellow color was the curative agent. Consequently, to combat jaundice in Germany, patients ate yellow turnips and wore gold coins and saffron clothing. Russian physicians had their wealthy patients wear necklaces made of gold beads. In England, victims of the disease were forced to eat yellow spiders rolled in butter.

The color purple often is associated with dignity, wisdom, or sadness. Egyptians wore purple necklaces to thwart adversity. Many artistic people say that they prefer purple to other colors. It is often used to signify gay pride, as is a display of rainbow colors. In 1999, the Reverend Jerry Falwell made news when he accused the children's character Tinky Winky on the BBC's "Teletubbies" television show of being gay (Weblink 2.7).

Jeff Jacobson / Redux

"He is purple—the gay pride color, and his antenna is shaped like a triangle—the gay pride symbol," Falwell wrote. A BBC spokesperson said, "As far as we are concerned Tinky Winky is simply a sweet, technological baby with a magic bag." The symbolic qualities of purple make it a favorite attention-getter in photography, paintings, and print and screen media.

The photographer Jeff Jacobson often uses color to convey a dramatic effect or an important detail that might be missed if the image were in black and white. Born in Des Moines, Iowa, he graduated from Georgetown University Law Center in Washington, D.C., and traveled the South as an American Civil Liberties Union (ACLU) lawyer. He became interested in photography after taking pictures of people in jails and rural areas. Every image in his 1991 book, *My Fellow Americans . . .* is a rare collection of art and craft. In his pictures you see the red-tipped fingernails and the pinkish guts of the snake that Miss Rattlesnake Charmer holds, the tongue of a German Shepherd licking its chin as it eyes a baby on a wooden floor (Figure 2.9), the vibrant colors at sunset of

Figure 2.9

As a black and white photograph, the macabre humor of a German Shepherd licking his lips at the sight of a baby on the floor would most likely be lost to a viewer. Color enriches the meaning of the picture after you notice the dog's pink tongue.
See color insert following page 178.

Figure 2.10

"Soir Bleu," oil on canvas, 1914 by Edward Hopper. In this Parisian scene, painted when the American Edward Hopper was 32 years old, a sex worker with heavy makeup surveys possible prospects while her pimp sits alone, his eyes focused on another view. During this blue evening lit by oriental lanterns, she considers the strange trio of a bearded Vincent van Gogh look-alike in a beret, a military officer, and a "classically attired" clown in white, while an upper-class couple enjoys a late-night drink. Hopper's use of color is an "early attempt to create, rather than merely record, a sophisticated, anti-sentimental allegory of adult city life" that he duplicated later in "Nighthawks" (1942).

See color insert following page 178.

a boy being held by his grandfather, and the gaudy colors of a dancer performing for two men at a convention.

Another artist, the New York–born Edward Hopper, became a leader in the realist style of oil painting. A tall, shy, introspective person, Hopper often captured lonely people who were unable or unwilling to communicate with each other. His use of lighting and colors often gave an eerie, otherworldly spookiness to his works such as "Early Sunday Morning," "Chop Suey," "New York Movie," "Hotel Room," and his masterpiece, "Nighthawks" (Figure 2.10).

Graphic designers in print and screen media know the power of color to attract attention. Logo and poster designers are careful about their use of color. They must consider not only the possible symbolic meanings of color, but also how color should be used to make a logo memorable and prominent in a crowded media market. Two colors that are distinct but not too similar should be used (Figure 2.11). A website that uses too many colors that are too bright runs the risk of looking amateurish. Care should also be taken in choosing colored copy and backgrounds so that persons with low vision or color deficiencies can read the words. Since green and red colors are sometimes hard to see, a designer should avoid highlighting text in

those colors. Many times newspapers that must compete with other publications on a newsstand's rack for a reader's eyes often display red banners and photographs with the color prominently displayed.

The use of color on the front page of a newspaper can be controversial. In 1984, the worst mass murder in the history of America up to that time occurred when a gunman opened fire and killed 22 and wounded 19 at a McDonald's restaurant outside San Diego. The front page of *The Tribune* showed a ghastly pair of color photographs. In one, blood streams down the leg of a young victim sitting on an ambulance, and the other has a yellow "Golden Arches" logo and arrow pointing to rescue workers trying to save the life of a boy on the ground. Readers wrote letters and made phone calls to the editor of the San Diego newspaper complaining about the gruesome nature of the images. If the pictures had been printed in black and white, it is doubtful readers would have complained (Figure 2.12).

Animated cartoons are often the most colorful forms of entertainment, with their characters attracting the eyes of young and old. Brightly colored characters sitting on toy store shelves that look exactly like their animated equivalents also attract young eyes and elicit pleading requests to a parent or guardian. Animators should be aware of how their creations are marketed. Four-time Academy Award–winning British animator Nick Park, who produced such cartoon shorts as *Creature Comforts* (1989), which showed animals in a zoo talking about their experiences, as well as *The Wrong Trousers* (1993) and *A Close Shave* (1995) with the enduring characters Wallace and Gromit, knows that his Claymation technique provides a lifelike, three-dimensional (3-D) depth to his work and also brings out the color of his characters. Park sells cuddly and color-ful toys, backpacks, watches, and DVDs on his animation studio's website (Weblink 2.8). An animation artist with an opposite style, both in its execution and content, is Canadian John Kricfalusi (pronounced "Kris-fa-lose-ee"). His best-known cartoon is the adult-oriented "Ren and Stimpy," drawn in a traditional cel-animation style. It is often criticized for being too violent, too scatological, and for using language too strong for children. In "Sven Hoek," Ren threatens to torture and murder Stimpy and his cousin for vandalizing vari-ous rare collections while he was at work. As a result, Kricfalusi's creations are rare collectors' items, but are not so easily mar-ketable to children as Park's characters.

Color in the hands of an inspired movie director should be observed closely. British director Sir Ridley Scott's science fiction classic *Blade Runner* (1982) was one of many standout directorial achievements in his career, alongside *Alien* (1979), *Thelma & Louise* (1991), and *Gladiator* (2000), which won a Best Picture Academy Award. Two scenes from *Blade Runner* show why it earned two Oscar nominations for best art direction and visual effects. The scenes are similar in content—they both show a character taking a type of lie detector test that determines whether or not the subject is a robot, called a "replicant" in the film. In the first scene, the two characters don't like each other much. In fact, at the end of the scene, one of them is murdered. To show the animosity they feel for each other, the set is filled with a cold, blue, unemotional light. The other scene shows two charac-ters meeting for the first time. They will later fall in love. The scenery for this one is bathed in a warm, golden color indicat-ing their love interest. Likewise, in Disney's first three-dimensional animated cartoon *Up* (2009), co-directed by Pete Docter and

Courtesy of Crystal Adams

Bob Peterson, a flashback scene that tells the back story of the main character's life with his wife uses different color palettes to depict the passing of time—beginning with sepia tones reminiscent of photographs printed in the 1930s and then moving to bright blues and greens as their love and lives progress. As with a soundtrack for a movie or the choice of typography for

Courtesy of the San Diego Union-Tribune

Figure 2.11
Graphic designer Crystal Adams works for Simple Human, a company that makes products for use in the home. In her poster announc-ing a design competition, overlapping silhouettes of common household objects are set large and in the center of the poster, with a subtle gradated color scheme over a black background, for maxi-mum viewer effect.
See color insert following page 178.

Figure 2.12
The San Ysidro, California, a mass murder at a McDon-ald's restaurant on July 18, 1984, resulted in 22 deaths with 19 injured. Part of the horror of these front-page images comes from the added information supplied by color. Blood can be seen on the girl's leg, whereas the brightly colored and usually benign McDonald's "golden arches" and entrance sign points to an emergency worker strug-gling to the save the life of a young victim.
See color insert following page 178.

words, color can convey subtle, emotional meanings.

Color is a highly subjective and powerful means of communicating ideas. James Maxwell, the Scotsman who gave the electromagnetic spectrum its name and invented color photography in 1861, once wrote that the "science of color must be regarded essentially as a mental science." Despite the artist Francis Bacon's common-sense statement that "All colors will agree in the dark," no two individuals see a color in exactly the same way.

■ FORM

The brain responds to another common attribute of images, which is the recognition of three types of forms: dots, lines, and shapes.

■ *Dots*

The dot is the simplest form that can be written with a stylus. A dot anywhere within a framed space demands immediate attention. In the center, it becomes the hub of visual interest. If off to one side, it creates tension since the layout appears out of balance. Two dots within a framed space also create tension, since the viewer is forced to divide attention between the two forms. When three or more dots appear in an image, the viewer naturally tries to connect them with an imaginary line. It may be a straight or curved line, or it may take the basic shape of a square, triangle, or circle.

Hundreds of small dots grouped together can form complex pictures (Figure 2.13). In 1934 Walker Evans photographed the window of a photography studio, which was composed of hundreds of small, neatly aligned driver's license pictures. Each portrait acted as a dot of visual interest for passersby. Georges Seurat in the 19th century used a technique called pointillism in which he peppered his paintings with small colored dots that combined in the viewer's mind to form an image. His most famous

Figure 2.13

"Bottle House, Rhyolite, Nevada," 2002, by Gerry Davey. The thousands of beer, whiskey, soda, and medicine bottles that create a pattern of circles—besides being a relatively inexpensive alternative to lumber—provide a visually pleasing aesthetic and has been an eye-catching photographic subject since this house was built in 1906.

Erich Lessing / Art Resource, NY

Figure 2.14

"Un Dimanche après-midi à l'Île de la Grande Jatte," 1884–1886, by Georges-Pierre Seurat. *The 19th century French pointillist constructed his paintings by using a series of dots and only twelve separate colors, never mixing one color with another. This tedious, mathematically based painting technique found few advocates because the style lacked spontaneity. Nevertheless, this Sunday Parisian scene, his most famous work, can be appreciated on a technical level when the thousands of tiny dots are clearly discerned from a close-up view while its sunny optimism is communicated by its inherent vibrancy viewed from a few yards back.*

work, "Un dimanche aprè-midi à l'Île de la Grande Jatte" (1884–1886), is an invigorating concert of colored dots. If a security guard at the Art Institute of Chicago lets you get a few inches from the canvas, you can appreciate the technique involved, but you won't be able to discern the work's meaning. But if you view this work from 20 feet away, you see a scene of pleasant relaxation on a sunny day (Figure 2.14). Seattle-based photographer Chris Jordan (Weblink 2.9) produced a variation of Seurat's painting in which the surprising "points" that compose the image are revealed upon a close-up view. In "Cans Seurat," instead of dots of paint, Jordan used photographs of 106,000 tiny soda cans—"the number used in the U.S. every thirty seconds" (Figures 2.15–2.17).

■ *Lines*

When dots of the same size are drawn so closely together that there is no space between them, the result is a line. According to anthropologist Evelyn Hatcher, straight lines convey a message of stiffness and rigidity, and they can be horizontal, vertical, or diagonal. Horizontal lines, especially when low in the frame, remind viewers of a horizon with plenty of room to grow. If the horizontal line is high in the frame, the viewer feels confined, as the layout seems heavy. Vertical lines bring the eye of the viewer to a halt in a layout. The eye attempts to travel around the space created by the line. Diagonal lines have a strong, stimulating effect in a field of view. The most restful diagonal line is one that extends from one corner to its diagonal opposite. It is a perfect compromise between horizontal and vertical forces. Any other diagonal line strongly moves the eye of the viewer in the line's direction. Several diagonal lines within a composition create a nervous dynamic energy. Curved lines convey a mood of playfulness, suppleness, and movement. Curves have a gracefulness about them that softens the content of their active message (Figure 2.18). If lines are thick and dark, the message is strong and confident. If lines are thin and light with a clear separation between them, the mood is delicate, perhaps a bit timid.

Grouped lines form blank spaces that the eyes naturally want to inspect. When drawn as part of an object, they combine to simulate the sensation of touch. The lines that form the surface of an object

Figures 2.15 – 2.17

"Cans Seurat," 2007, by Chris Jordan. Viewed from far away, this photograph seems like a faithful reproduction of Seurat's famous painting. However, as you get closer to the work, the "dots" are revealed for what they are—soda pop cans. According to Jordan, the photograph contains "106,000 aluminum cans, the number consumed in the United States every 30 seconds." For Seurat, taking a faraway view of the work reveals the subject of his paintings. Jordan's photographs require the opposite focus—you need to put your eyes right up to them to understand the point.

Courtesy of Chris Jordan

Courtesy of Chris Jordan

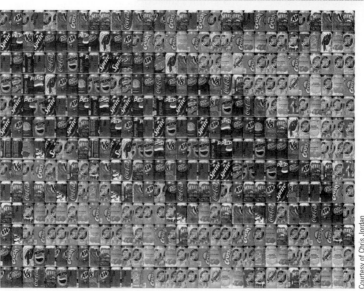

Courtesy of Chris Jordan

may be part of an illustration or part of the natural lighting where the object is located. A rough surface has several small curved lines that make up its bumpy exterior. A smooth surface has few lines that mark its coating. Texture stimulates the visual sense by the image itself and the tactile sense through memory. For example, previous experience with the sharp points of the needles of a cactus transfers to a picture of the plant.

Lines can be controversial when a graphic artist or photographer uses a Photoshop tool to stretch the legs of models to make them appear thinner and perhaps more attractive. Lines can also be powerful tools in conveying complex messages.

Commercials for AT&T's wireless network service cleverly repeat its logo, which comprises rising vertical lines. In "Sweet Pea," with music by Amos Lee, the logo can be seen as palm trees, buildings, newspapers, bread sticks, and playground equipment. Likewise, a public service announcement (PSA) for the Peace Corps starts with a hand's life line and continues the theme of a horizontal journey in its "Life is Calling" commercial narrated by Matthew McConaughey (Weblink 2.10). Finally, the simple, elegant lines that portray a human figure struggling to push a large boulder up a hill is a powerful animated presentation that advertises a GMC Yukon hybrid but also is a positive metaphor for living (Weblink 2.11).

■ *Shapes*

The third type of form, shapes, is the combination of dots and lines into patterns that occur throughout nature and in graphic design. Shapes are figures that sit on the plane of a visual field without depth and define the outside edges of objects. They can be as simple as a beach ball and as complex as the side of

Courtesy of Paul Martin Lester

a person's face. A shape that is quickly recognized is clearly separated from the background of the image. The three basic shapes are parallelograms, circles, and triangles. From these three shapes, variations that make all known or imagined forms can be created. The name of a form created by a combination of shapes is polygon. As with all visual attributes, cultural meaning is assigned to each shape. In 1987 American animator Bill Plympton was nominated for an Academy Award for his short cartoon, *Your Face*. In its short time frame, Plympton shows how a creative and talented mind can make variations on the shapes that combine to form a human face. Later, the same concept was used in a commercial for Taco Bell (Weblink 2.12).

Parallelograms

The parallelogram is a four-sided figure with opposite sides that are parallel and equal in length. The two major types of parallelograms are squares and rectangles. "Be there or be square" is often a challenge given by those organizing a party. In Western culture, a *square* is

Figure 2.18

Conceived by Danish architect Jørn Utzon and completed in 1973, the spherical rooflines and sail-like vaults of the Sydney Opera House constitute one of the most famous curved shapes in the world.

defined as an unsophisticated or dull person. Similarly, a square shape, with its formally balanced, symmetrical orientation, is the most dull and conventional shape. But strength also comes from its plain appearance. A square is considered sturdy and straightforward. In language, the equivalents are a *square deal* or a *square shooter*. The implication from the phrases is that the business transaction or person so described may not be flamboyant but that you can trust that the person or transaction is fair. Rectangles are the slightly more sophisticated cousins of squares. Of all the geometric figures, rectangles are the most common and are the favored shape of the frame for mediated images. High-definition television (HDTV) changed the shape of television screens from squares to the wide-screen rectangular form used in movie theaters. Composition in motion picture and still photography formats often takes advantage of the horizontal sides that a rectangle naturally creates. In a rectangular frame, the chief object of focus does not have to be in the center for the work to appear balanced. A clever commercial for the Volkswagen New Beetle aired in 2003. It compared the modern, oval shape of the car with everyday square objects—a clock, house, piece of toast, sponge, and so on, which made the point that you didn't want to drive just another box (Weblink 2.13).

Circles

The first shapes primitive humans probably took notice of were the bright, circular forms in the sky (the sun and the moon), the round shape of another person's head, and the two circular eyes staring at them. As Leonardo da Vinci once wrote, "The sense which is nearest to the organ of perception functions most quickly, and this is the eye, the chief, the leader of all other senses" (Figure 2.19).

Circles have always been important attention getters. No wonder advertisers of video games, picture agencies, and motion pictures use the human eye in ad campaigns. Photojournalists also know how telling a person's eyes are in understanding a subject's personality. If the subject stares straight into a camera's lens, the message might be one of bewilderment, defiance, innocence, happiness, or concentration. A specific genre of photography, the police mug shot, in which the person arrested must look into the lens, often reveals a hidden side of a celebrity caught doing something wrong, whether it's Mel Gibson in a nice shirt and a glowing smile in 2006 or Nick Nolte in 2002 with disheveled hair and a much too colorful Hawaiian shirt (Figures 2.20–2.21). Eyes that look away from a camera might signify embarrassment, disgust, longing, worry, a wish for privacy, or a disregard for being photographed (Figure 2.22). *Los Angeles Times* photographer Luis Sinco's riveting picture of Marine Lance Corporal James Blake Miller's "thousand-mile stare" after an assault on Falluja, Iraq, in 2004 captures the physical and mental exhaustion of war (Weblink 2.14). Finally, a person might close their eyes or hide them behind hands, sunglasses, or a veil.

Figure 2.19

Window to the soul: The eye not only absorbs light but also reflects it, while its round shape catches the eye of a viewer.

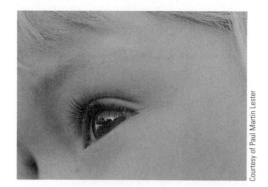

Courtesy of Paul Martin Lester

Such gestures could mean that the person wants to block out the world, to hide the extent of grief from others, to look fashionable, or to obey culturally bound religious restrictions against showing their eyes in public. Secret Service members and many security guards like to wear sunglasses so you can't see what their eyes are watching (Figure 2.23). The Dublin-born singer Sinéad O'Connor gained tremendous popularity early in her career with a 1990 music video directed by John Maybury, a British filmmaker known for his films *The Jacket* (2005) and *The Edge of Love* (2008). "Nothing Compares 2 U," written and originally performed by Prince with his 1980s band The Family, showed arresting, close-up images of O'Connor singing with her eyes mainly looking into the camera's lens. The intimate filmmaking technique allowed a viewer to feel her pain after losing a love (Weblink 2.15).

Circles are also associated with the endless rhythmic patterns of time, symbolizing eternity without clear beginnings or endings. A popular country song titled "Will the Circle Be Unbroken?" asks if a group of friends and family members will always maintain their closeness—even after death.

Triangles

These are the most dynamic and active of shapes. As energetic objects, they convey direction, but they can burden a design with the tension they can create. The two types of triangles—equilateral and isosceles—have vastly different symbolic meanings. All three sides of an equilateral triangle are the same length. Its shape conveys a serene mood because of symmetrical balance. Think of the silent stone pyramids of Egypt. They calmly watch the passing of each millennium and tourist with a camera. Seen from a distance, they are an abrupt change in the naturally sloping sand dune–filled horizon. Seen up close, their power obviously comes from their stable bases. The triangle juggles its two parts—the base and the apex—to

Figures 2.20 and 2.21
In their booking photographs by patrol and sheriff officials for being under the influence, actors Mel Gibson (top) and Nick Nolte are contrasts in demeanor, hair styles, and shirt choices. But they do have one thing in common—they look straight into the camera's lens, a requirement of such pictures. Gibson's eyes reveal playfulness and vulnerability, whereas Nolte's show defiance and anger.

Figure 2.22
"Woman Behind Glass Door, New York City," 2000, by Gerry Davey. Perhaps out of respect or low self-esteem, the woman inside the glass door bows her head so as not to look at the other entering the building.

Courtesy of Gerry Davey

Figure 2.23

"Worker, Las Vegas," 1999, by Gerry Davey. Although looking right at the camera's lens, this construction worker reveals little about his personality since a pair of sunglasses covers his eyes. Rather than an attempt to look cool, the man probably wears them to avoid harmful ultraviolet rays of the sun while working long hours in the intense heat of Las Vegas.

Figure 2.24

The Temple of Kukulcan, known as "The Castle" at Chichén Itzá, Mexico, is a Mayan structure built about 800 CE. At 30 meters high, the terraced pyramid with a temple on top is a masterwork that demonstrates precise architectural and construction skills. As with the pyramids in Egypt, its shape causes passersby to notice its silent, solemn dignity.

create a dynamic energy. From its base comes stability, but from its peak comes tension (Figure 2.24). In contrast, the isosceles triangle draws its power not from its base but from its sharp point. Think of the Washington Monument in Washington, D.C. When the point is vertical and used in architecture, the shape is called a

steeple and symbolizes a religious person's hoped-for destination. But pointed in any direction, isosceles triangles challenge the eye to follow. When using the isosceles shape, a visual communicator must be sure to give the viewer something to see at the end of its point (Figure 2.25).

■ DEPTH

If humans had only one eye and confined their visual messages to drawings on the walls of caves, there would be no need for more complex illustrations that could be made from dots, lines, and shapes. But because we have two eyes set slightly apart, we naturally see in three dimensions—width, length, and depth—rather than only the first two. In 1838, Sir Charles Wheatstone presented a paper to the Royal Society of London detailing his views on binocular vision. He concluded that our two eyes give different views and create the illusion of depth.

City Image/Alamy

The images are projected onto each two-dimensional (2-D) retinal screen at the back of each eye and travel to the brain, which interprets the difference between the images as depth. In 2009 researchers at the University of Texas at Austin discovered that areas of the brain behind the left and right ears, originally thought to be responsible only for 2-D motion (up, down, left, and right) also are used to detect 3-D objects or images coming toward a person.

Wheatstone used his studies in depth perception to discover the stereoscopic process. Based on his findings, the 3-D photographic illusion printed on stereocards was introduced to the public. Each card had two slightly different photographs mounted side by side on a cardboard backing. When each eye viewed them simultaneously through a viewer called a stereoscope, the brain merged the images into one, 3-D image. The difference between looking at an ordinary photograph and an image through a stereoscope is striking. Stereoscopically enhanced views were enormously popular as educational and entertainment sources from about 1860 until 1890. Before the invention of the halftone method for printing pictures in publications, stereocards viewed through stereoscopes were the main source of pictorial news for wealthy patrons (Figure 2.26).

The three-dimensional effect has been popular with the public and valued for medical purposes. A modern variation of the stereoscope is the View-Master from the Fisher-Price toy company. Circular cards displayed dozens of 3-D images, mostly of tourist sites. As a vintage toy, the View-Master and its cards are now collectors' items. The 3-D photographic process known as holography, introduced in 1947, was initially developed as an aid

Scott Bauer, U.S. Department of Agriculture

in viewing microscopic images, but later became popular as a medium for artists and as anti-counterfeiting procedures for printed money and credit cards. In the 1960s, a printing technique called the xography process produced a 3-D effect by interlacing two, slightly apart views

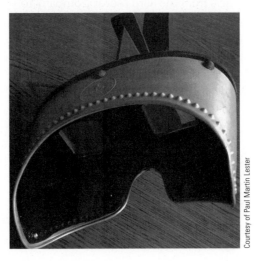

Courtesy of Paul Martin Lester

Figure 2.25

A gift from the people of Japan, cherry trees in full blossom ring the Tidal Basin in Washington, D.C., and frame the Washington Monument in the background. The powerful and striking shape of the monument against the clear sky is in contrast to the stable and constant pyramid shapes found in Mexico and Egypt.

Figure 2.26

After British scientist Charles Wheatstone published a paper in 1838 detailing the principle that creates a 3-D view from our two eyes slightly apart, Sir William Brewster invented an inexpensive viewer for seeing the 3-D effect. With Queen Victoria's interest in stereocards during the Great Exhibition in 1851 at the Crystal Palace in London, the public took notice of the effect. The American physician Oliver Wendell Holmes spread the fad further with his handheld viewer shown here. Home users subscribed to a stereocard company and received sets of images in the mail. Before photographs could be published in newspapers, stereocards were the main source for visual news.

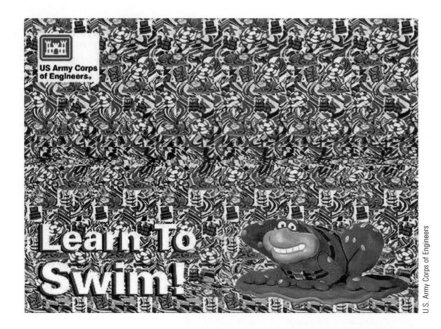

U.S. Army Corps of Engineers

Figure 2.27

*Autostereograms produced
by such companies as Magic
Eye Inc. are images that
create the illusion of a 3-D
picture floating on a graphic
background. If you focus your
attention at an imaginary
point behind the picture, you
may see a figure swimming
above the frog. Such images
were popular in the 1990s for
fun and in advertising, but
interest has waned since then.*

on parallel strips. These were popular as postcards. In 1977 the first human was tested using a magnetic resonance imaging (MRI) device to obtain a three-dimensional view of inside the body that was of much better quality than a simple X-ray or computer tomography (CT or CAT) scan could provide. In the 1990s Magic Eye Inc. started a fad using random dot stereogram images that gave most viewers a 3-D effect from color patterns. Advertisers from the Ford Motor Company to the U.S. Army Corps of Engineers have commissioned stereograms using Magic Eye's computer process (Figure 2.27). In 2006, the progressive metal band Tool released its fourth album "10,000 Days," which featured a stereoscopic viewer and several images as part of the compact disc packaging.

Since perception is such a complicated combination of eye and brain properties, researchers have identified eight possible factors, used singly or in combination, that give viewers a sense of depth: space, size, color, lighting, textural gradients, interpo-

sition, time, and perspective. All of these factors, when combined with our two eyes, help us to notice when one object is near and another farther away.

■ EIGHT DEPTH FACTORS

■ *Space*

This factor depends on the frame in which an image is located. With a natural scene, the illusion of space depends on how close you are to a subject. Standing in an open field gives the feeling of a large amount of space and enhances the feeling of depth. If an object is close to the eyes, depth perception is limited. Likewise, the placement of content elements is important for an image. Often, beginning photographers are told to add interest to their pictures by including a tree limb or some other object in the foreground of the frame (Figure 2.28).

■ *Size*

If a viewer is aware of an object's actual size, it can help in the illusion of depth perception. An airliner seen from a distance is a small size on the viewer's retina. If someone had no idea what the flying object was, she might conclude that it was quite small. But because we are familiar with the actual size of the aircraft, we know that it is far away and not as small as an insect (Figure 2.29). Size, consequently, is closely related to our ability to determine an object's distance. Distance is related to space and helps in our perception of depth. Size also is related to scale and mental attention. Without knowing an object's size, we have to view it next to an object of known size. Archaeologists take pictures of artifacts found at historical sites with a ruler in the frame

Figure 2.28
"Abandoned Restaurant Window, Pecos, Texas," 2005, by Gerry Davey. A cloudy day without direct sunlight makes it hard to determine which forms are in the foreground and which ones are in the back. Are the dark shapes on the right side the eyes of a space alien looking at you?

Courtesy of Gerry Davey

so that viewers will know how large the recovered object is. Tourists often are disappointed when they travel to Mount Rushmore in South Dakota because, with no frame of reference, the presidential faces carved in the rock do not convey a sense of their enormous size. Educational psychologist Jean Piaget found that if much attention is given to an object, its size will be overestimated. A small, refined figure often attracts attention within a visual frame because the viewer must concentrate on it. Scale and attention are related to depth perception because there is no illusion of depth if objects are all viewed as the same size.

■ Color

As indicated at the start of this chapter, an object's color can communicate depth. Warm-colored objects appear closer than cool-colored objects. High-contrast pictures with great differences between light and dark tones seem closer than objects colored with more neutral tones (see Figure 2.7).

■ Lighting

Differences in light intensities can communicate depth. A television studio technician will position a light above and behind a news announcer. Called a "hair light," the brightness level is slightly higher than the lights in front in order to separate the person from the background. The prevalence of shadows also indicates an object's

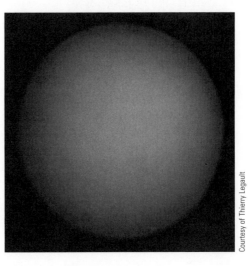

Courtesy of Thierry Legault

Figure 2.29
Captured via telescope, the space shuttle Atlantis is seen in flight in front of the sun in 2009. Knowing the relative size of objects helps determine the foreground from the background. The extreme telephoto effect also makes it appear that the spacecraft is quite close to the star.

Figure 2.30

In this computer-generated image, note how the lights in the background and the shadows in the foreground help create the illusion of depth.

Courtesy Autodesk, Inc.

volume and gives the viewer another depth cue. The light's brightness and position create shadows that the viewer notices (Figure 2.30).

■ *Textural Gradients*

The ripple effect seen in a still pond suddenly disturbed by a rock or the ridges

Courtesy of Paul Martin Lester

Figure 2.31

Our eyes can sense the illusion of depth in the photograph of this Southern California beach because the shadows within the footprints in the sand in the foreground are large compared with those farther back in the picture.

from the wind on a sand dune are called textural gradients. With water, the ridges appear closer together as they move away from a viewer's point of view. With sand, shadows in the foreground are larger than the shadows in the craters that are farther away. The difference in their size contributes to the illusion that the scene fades into the background (Figure 2.31).

■ *Interposition*

Graphic designers for *Sports Illustrated* magazine regularly use interposition for their covers with a picture of a player in front of a headline or the publication's name. The 3-D effect often shows a player seemingly leaping off the page. Such a graphic technique is employed so that the cover catches the eye of a potential customer within a crowded bookstore (Figure 2.32).

■ *Time*

As a depth factor, time refers to a viewer's attention to a particular element within an image. When something interests us, we tend to stare at it for a longer amount of time than other parts of a visual array. Examples might be someone you know or something you are attracted to because of past associations. To an outsider, the element may technically be considered in the background. In a magazine advertisement, for example, words, a model's face or clothing, or an unusual object in the background that triggers a memory might propel that element to the foreground for you (Figure 2.33).

■ *Perspective*

Probably the most complex depth factor is perspective. That's because it is equal parts brain function and learned behavior. A person's cultural heritage has more bearing on the interpretation of perspective attributes than any other one. The concept of perception as used in Western art is relatively new compared with the entire history of art. In Europe during the Renaissance, visual communicators usu-

Courtesy of Paul Martin Lester

Figure 2.32
Two schoolgirls in New Orleans ride a streetcar and demonstrate interposition with each having one leg and one arm before the other while they sit before the window and a view of the city that they pass in the background.

ally were artists and scientists. Probably the most famous during this era was Leonardo da Vinci. His paintings reflect an early attention to duplicating on a 2-D surface the illusion of depth as viewed in the real world. One of Leonardo's most famous works, *The Last Supper*, uses perspective to express the social importance of the Christ figure (Figure 2.34).

Courtesy of Paul Martin Lester

Figure 2.33
The Taos, New Mexico, Pueblo is an archeological site where Native Americans lived almost 1,000 years ago. Presently, about 150 persons still live there. Depending on your personal interest, you may spend more time looking at the adobe structure, the store "OPEN" sign, the window frame, the sleeping dog, the handwritten sign with the "F" letters drawn as two "7s," the elaborate smiley face, the parched ground, the play of light and shadow in the background, or some other detail. Consequently, whichever element you spend more time looking at becomes the foreground.

Figure 2.34

On a wall of a dining room in the convent of the Santa Maria delle Grazie ("Our Lady of Grace") church located in Milan, Italy, is a wall painting by Leonardo da Vinci called "The Last Supper." The masterpiece is a classic example of the use of linear perspective to emphasize the main subject. All of the diagonal lines in the painting converge on the face of the Christ figure at the vanishing point.

Figure 2.35

This 1525 woodcut by Albrecht Dürer demonstrates a drawing table called a Leonardo box (named after Leonardo da Vinci, but probably invented by Filippo Brunelleschi or Leone Battista Alberti). The perspective tool uses a frame to achieve an accurate linear perspective of an object.

His "Leonardo box" aided painters in duplicating depth by tracing a scene on a sheet of paper (later on glass) with the artist's eye remaining in the same position. Using this method, the artist could be sure that the drawn lines accurately mimicked an actual scene (Figure 2.35). But the "box" most commonly used by artists of the day to draw accurate landscapes was the *camera obscura*, or "dark chamber." A small hole in a box projects an upside-down view of the outside scene if lighting conditions are favorable. Artists inside a large camera obscura traced the outside view on a thin sheet of paper to replicate depth cues. Much later, light-sensitive material replaced paper and became the basis for modern photography. The medium, more than any other invention, spurred artists to render scenes in their proper perspective.

In her book *Visual Metaphors: A Methodological Study in Visual Communication,* Evelyn Hatcher identifies three major forms of perspective: illusionary, geometrical, and conceptual.

Illusionary Perspective

An illusionary perspective can be achieved through size, color, lighting, interposition, and linear perspective. When you stand on a railroad track and look down the ties, the steel rails seem to converge into a single area, or vanishing point, in the distance. This trait of parallel lines when seen at a distance is called linear perspective and provides the illusion of 3-D depth in a painting, photograph, film, or other flat surface (Figure 2.36).

Some artists played with the illusion of depth by having their subjects appear to be escaping from their frames. Called *trompe l'oeil*, or "tricks of the eye," artists such as Titian, Pere Borrell del Caso, Edward Collyer, and George Henry Hall used techniques that gave the illusion of 3-D depth. Contemporary British artist Julian Beever creates pavement chalk drawings that delightfully trick and intrigue the eyes (Weblink 2.16), and the Italian artist known as Blu further advances the artform with his large, 3-D animated drawings. In his piece named "Muto," Blu makes a drawing, a camera records the frame, he erases it, makes a new drawing, and repeats the process. When edited, the result is a captivating animated film of the 3-D public artwork (Weblink 2.17).

Those who make 3-D motion pictures and television shows are currently enjoying a renaissance of the genre. Instead of the poor quality sci-fi and horror 3-D pictures of the 1950s seen with red-and-blue cellophane pasted on cheap cardboard frames, audience members now are able to watch good quality motion pictures such as *Avatar* (2009), *Coraline* (2009), *Fly Me to the Moon* (2008), and *Monsters vs. Aliens* (2009) with comfortable glasses in theaters equipped to show digitally projected movies.

Phil "Captain 3-D" McNally, special effects wizard for *How to Train Your Dragon*, (2010), *Shrek Forever After* (2010), and *Monsters*, explains that 3-D movies are shot using two cameras—one records for the right eye and the other for the left. Adjusting the distance between the side-by-side cameras alters the extent of the illusion. McNally also knows how vision works. "3-D happens

Courtesy of Paul Martin Lester

Figure 2.36
Delta Airlines flight attendant Katherine Lee, dubbed "Deltalina" by her fans who think she resembles the actress Angelina Jolie, is placed within the center of the frame of the pre-flight safety video to maximize passenger interest and the linear perspective effect.

in your brain," he says. "It doesn't happen on the screen; it doesn't happen in your eyes; it doesn't happen in the camera. It only happens when your brain gets the two images."

Advertisers also produce commercials using 3-D technology. In 2006 a Norwegian animation studio named BUG created the first 3-D commercial for the Mitsubishi car company. In 2009, about 150 million glasses were handed out to viewers so that commercials for *Monsters vs. Aliens* and SoBe's Lifewater drink could be seen during the Super Bowl. Home watchers are also able to enjoy the effect with 3-D TV, which is particularly popular for sports and action movies. An episode of the NBC show "Chuck" was shown in 3-D.

Still photographers use illusionary perspective to create a sense of depth and to draw attention to the subject. Arnold Newman, known for environmental portraits showing people in their own surroundings, often exploited the vanishing point illusion to draw interest to his subject. One of his most famous pictures is of German Alfried Krupp, who was convicted as a war criminal after World War II for using slave labor in his factories. Being Jewish, Newman made an unflattering portrait of Krupp using low, side lighting that made him look evil and placed him

Figure 2.37

A denomination of Hinduism more than 20,000 years old, Shaktism acknowledges a Divine Mother named Shakti or Devi. In this painting by the Indian artist and musician Shri S. Rajam, the deity sits upon lesser gods and holds the traditional symbols in her hands—a sugarcane stalk, a bow, and a flower arrow. Contrary to Western traditions, this geometrical perspective uses the size and placement of Shakti in the frame to signify supremacy over the other gods.

Figure 2.38

After the Glorious Revolution of 1688, the Dutch Protestant Prince William III of Orange overthrew the Catholic King James II of England to become King of England, Scotland, and Ireland. Two years later, William's Protestant troops conquered the Catholic army in Ireland at the Battle of the Boyne. What followed was almost three hundred years of discrimination and attempted genocide of the Catholics in Northern Ireland. Despite recent progress in relations between the two religious groups, districts in Belfast are still segregated. With a simply drawn wall mural showing William of Orange on a white steed large in the frame, his dominance over the land is celebrated on an abandoned building within a Protestant neighborhood.

Dinodia/The Image Works

in the center of his factory to exploit the illusionary perspective (Weblink 2.18).

Geometrical Perspective

This type of perspective is common among traditional Japanese and Mayan

Courtesy of Paul Martin Lester

artwork. An Indian painting of Shaktism's Divine Mother shows, to Western eyes, the god in the background (Figure 2.37). But because the deity is higher and larger in the frame, it is in the foreground. So-called "naïve" wall murals as seen in Belfast, Northern Ireland, in the 1980s often showed the main subject of a painting higher and larger in the frame than all other elements (Figure 2.38). Young children without artistic training also often exhibit this type of perspective in their drawings.

Conceptual Perspective

This element of perspective is a compositional trait that relies on a more symbolic definition of depth perception. It can be divided into two types: multiview and social. With the multiview perspective, a viewer can see many different sides of an object at the same time. The picture is like an X-ray, or transparent view of the object. Near objects overlap far objects only by the outside edges or lines that make up their shapes. Pablo Picasso often used this type of perspective in which the subject's various moods and angles are seen all at the same time. Photographer Clarence John Laughlin in "The Masks Grow to Us" (1947) employed a double exposure technique in which the hard, cold stare of a mannequin's face starts to cover the soft features of a live model. His point was to say that if a person is not truthful, she might become permanently phony (Weblink 2.19).

In social perspective, the most important person in a group picture is often larger in size, centrally located, or separated from other, less important people (Figure 2.39). A viewer often assumes power relationships because of social perspective. A group picture of a large family often has older adults in the center with the children surrounding them on the edges. The owners and partners of a law firm may pose in the center for an advertising photograph. President Obama, when meeting with his Cabinet, sits in the center so that photographs from the meeting make it clear that he is in charge. In advertising images, a man nearer and larger in the frame with his hand resting or with an arm wrapped around a woman's shoulder often signifies his dominance over the woman. Over the past three decades, the feminist movement has made advertisers and others more sensitive to nonverbal, negative stereotypes such as these. Erving Goffman's content analysis *Gender Advertisements* is a classic collection of visual sexism in advertising.

One of the reasons the motion picture *Citizen Kane* (1941), directed by Orson Welles, is considered the greatest movie ever made is because of its technical innovations. One advance that particularly impressed director Roger Corman was the use of depth. Ordinarily, action within a film takes place along the so-called *x*-axis, an imaginary line along the horizontal

Courtesy of Apple Computers, Inc.

Figure 2.39
The low camera angle and position of the models emphasize that the man in front is the boss—an example of social perspective. Not surprisingly, he is the one holding the personal digital assistant.

plane, and the *y*-axis, a line that represents the vertical plane. But when the illusion of depth is introduced to an image, the *z*-axis, a line that moves into the frame, is introduced. With special lenses, lighting, and films, Gregg Toland, the cinematographer for *Kane*, created deep-focus photography—characters were in focus far into a scene, adding more information and the illusion of depth to the picture.

■ MOVEMENT

Color, form, and depth join movement to constitute the principal qualities of images that make the cells in the visual cortex respond quickly to a stimulus. Recognizing movement is one of the most important traits in the survival of an animal. Knowing whether an object or other animal is moving closer or farther away helps the animal avoid potentially harmful encounters. There are four types of movement: real, apparent, graphic, and implied.

■ *Real Movement*

This type of movement is motion not connected with an image presented in the media. It is actual movement as seen by a viewer of some other person, animal, or object. Because real movement does not involve mediated images, we don't emphasize it in this book.

■ Apparent Movement

The most common example of this type of movement is motion picture films. Moving images are a series of still images put together sequentially for film, videotape, or digital media and moved through a viewing device at a fast speed. Each single picture is shown only for a fraction of a second. Movement is perceived in the brain because of a phenomenon called *persistence of vision*. In 1824 Peter Mark Roget, who later became famous for his popular *Thesaurus*, proposed that this phenomenon, also called *diligence of foresight*, resulted from the time required for an image to fade from the cells of the retina. Scientists now know that persistence of vision is a result of the time needed for the brain to receive and recognize the picture. It takes about one-tenth of a second for an image to enter the eyes and register on the brain. Consequently, at 24 frames a second, a character or object in a film appears to move because of a blurring between individual frames as they pass through a projection device at that speed.

In printed still photography, two or more images placed together are called a series or sequence. A viewer's mind puts together the photographs into a mini, printed movie. In his picture book of dogs throughout the world, Elliott Erwitt in *Son of Bitch* shows a politician talking to citizens on a sidewalk while a dog seems interested. But in the second picture, it turns its back on the group of

humans and in the third urinates on a pole. The effect of the three-photo series is an amusing commentary on politics (Weblink 2.20). In 2005, Associated Press photographer Charles Dharapak photographed a series of President Bush having trouble opening a door while in China. The unflattering four-picture series was shown on the front pages of many newspapers including *The New York Times* (Weblink 2.21).

■ Graphic Movement

Graphic movement can be the motion of the eyes as they scan a field of view or the way a graphic designer positions elements so that the eyes move throughout a layout. Visual communicators often position the graphic elements in a design to take advantage of the eyes' movement around a picture and layout. A viewer's eyes will move through and notice elements in an image based on previous experiences and current interests and seeing certain parts of the picture and ignoring others. Nevertheless, a visual communicator can direct a viewer's eyes in a preconceived direction. The eye will usually follow a line, a slow curve, or a horizontal shape before it follows other graphic elements. Of course, colors, sizes of individual pieces, and placement of elements against a frame's white or background colored space also are crucial (Figure 2.40).

■ Implied Movement

Implied movement is motion that a viewer perceives in a still, single image without any movement of an object, image, or eye. Some graphic designs purposely stimulate the eyes with implied motion in order to attract attention. Optical or "op" art has been used in advertisements and in posters

Figure 2.40
At this newsstand in Los Angeles, magazine covers are prime examples of graphic movement.

to achieve frenetic, pulsating results. Visual vibration is the term used for these images. Through high-contrast line placement or the use of complementary colors, moiré (wavy) patterns seem to move as if powered by an unseen light source (Figure 2.41).

Implied movement also has roots in the beginnings of human communication. In 1994, while exploring a cave on his family's land in southern France, Jean-Marie Chauvet discovered the oldest known cave etchings and paintings. *Le Grotte Chauvet*

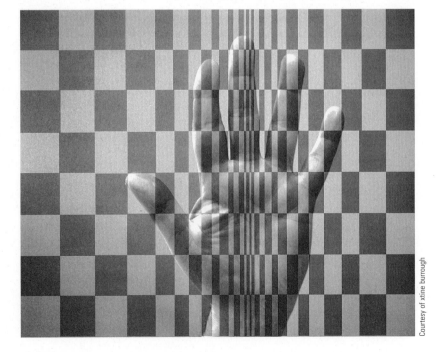

Figure 2.41
"A Hand for Riley," 2009, by xtine burrough. The British artist Bridget Riley is one of the most influential painters of the Op Art movement. After earning her degree from the Royal College of Art in London, she worked as a teacher and illustrator for the J. Walter Thompson advertising agency. In the 1960s she developed her distinctive style of black and white geometrical forms that created an internal, vibrant, visual energy and helped launch the Op Art movement. This piece is based on Riley's "Movement in Squares," 1961.

contains 416 cave paintings of extraordinary detail and cultural significance dating from approximately 30,000 years ago. One of the drawings shows a bison running but with additional legs. With so many other animals accurately displayed, archeologists puzzled why this one was not anatomically correct. Speculation about the artist's intent ended after someone brought in a flaming torch to see the drawing as the cave dwellers themselves would have seen it. With the aid of a fire's light, it could easily be seen that the extra legs gave the viewer the illusion that the bison was actually galloping across the cave. Perhaps this example of implied movement is evidence that early humans longed for motion pictures (Figure 2.42). Unfortunately (or fortunately) for these cave dwellers, buttered popcorn and flavored carbonated sugar water were invented much later.

New York City–born director Martin Scorsese won Academy Awards for Best Director and Best Picture for *The Departed*

(2006). In 1990 he made a critically acclaimed mobster movie, *Goodfellas*. The action leading up to a drug bust scene is a clinic in camera and actor movements synchronized to make an audience member feel the tension and paranoia that the characters have when taking drugs and performing other illegal acts. The scene starts with the character played by Ray Liotta snorting a line of cocaine and ends with him being busted in the driveway of his house. In between, the camera zooms in and out, pans left, right, up, and down, and moves in and out. The shots are quickly edited for maximum tension. The musical selections also enhance the frenetic tension. The actors are constantly moving, talking, and looking for surveillance helicopters. It is not only a brilliant example of the visual cue of movement, it is also a powerful anti-drug message.

David Hubel, Torsten Wiesel, and other scientists who built on their work through experiments with rats, monkeys, and people with brain injuries, demonstrated that the

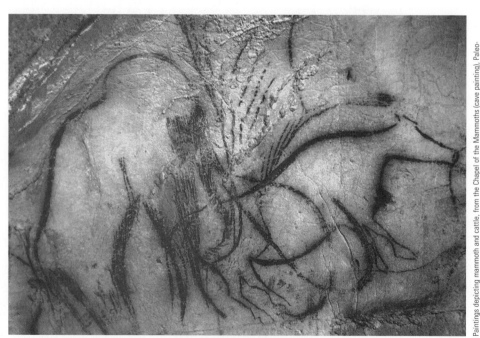

Figure 2.42
Estimated to have been painted about 25,000 years ago, the animals depicted in the "Chapel of the Mammoths" can be found within the cave known as Pech-Merle, located about 70 miles north of Toulouse in southern France. It is thought that the wispy, flowing lines of the mammoth and cattle depictions create an illusion of the animals running when viewed by the light of a flickering fire.

Paintings depicting mammoth and cattle, from the Chapel of the Mammoths (cave painting). Paleolithic / Grotte de Pech Merle, Lot, France / Index / The Bridgeman Art Library

cells in the visual cortex respond primarily to color, form, depth, and movement. But even without the knowledge of research, for many millennia visual communicators have used these four visual cues in their work, whether it has appeared on cave walls or on computer screens. An important lesson for image producers who want to make memorable messages is to understand that brain cells are complex "difference detectors." They are stimulated more by the relative differences between visual elements than by the intensity of each one. Consequently, a gaudy, colorful presentation may lose much of its impact if all its graphic elements have the same intensity. Differences between the visual cues detected by brain cells are only part of the reason that some messages are noticed and others are ignored. The content of a visual message, which we discuss next, also plays a vital role.

■ KEY TERMS

- Advertising campaign
- Banner
- Binocular vision
- Composition
- Computer tomography (CT or CAT scan)
- Cornea
- Cortex (Visual)
- Double exposure
- Electromagnetic spectrum
- Feminist movement
- Genre
- Gesture
- Halftone
- Layout
- Logo
- Magnetic Resonance Imaging (MRI)
- Microelectrode
- Moiré pattern
- Mug shot
- Pan
- Photoshop
- Public Service Announcement (PSA)
- Random dot stereogram
- Renaissance
- Retinas
- Shot
- Visual array
- Wavelength
- Zoom

 To locate active URLs for the weblinks mentioned in this chapter, please go to the companion site at http://communication.wadsworth.com/lester5 and select the proper chapter.

Chapter

3

Visual Theories

Students and practitioners of visual communication are often intimidated by the word "theory." But remember: Theories are simply best guesses made from a series of carefully considered observations.

A theory is not cut in stone; it is not a fact. As such, a theory should be questioned and rigorously defended without passion and with an open-minded attitude from both sides so that the exchange leads to its improvement or rejection. Over the centuries, psychologists, philosophers, and professionals have proposed many theories trying to explain how we see and how we learn from images.

The four theories we discuss in this chapter were selected for their direct connection to mass communications. They can be divided into two fundamental groups: sensory and perceptual. Those who advocate the sensory theories (gestalt and constructivism) maintain that

direct or mediated images are composed of light objects that attract or repel us. They are more concerned with what the brain sees—the visual cues of color, form, depth, and movement—but not how the mind considers them. The perceptual theories (semiotics and cognitive) are concerned mainly with the meaning that humans associate with the images they see.

The two sets of theories can be summed by the difference between what something looks like and what it actually is. To understand any of these approaches to visual communication, you must first know the difference between visual sensation and visual perception.

A sensation is a stimulus from the outside world that activates nerve cells within your sense organs. Wood burning in a fireplace activates the cells in your ears because you can hear the logs cracking and hissing, in your nose because you can smell the rich aroma of the wood, in your hands and face because you can feel the warmth of the fire, in your mouth if you pop a hot toasted marshmallow into it, and in your eyes as you watch the hypnotizing glow of the yellow flames. Sensations are lower-order, physical responses to stimuli and alone convey no meaning. Nerve cells in your ears, nose, hands, mouth, and eyes do not have the capacity to make intelligent thoughts. They are simply conveyors of information to the brain. Our minds make sense of all the sensory input. Conclusions based on those data are almost instantaneous. Our minds interpret the noises, smells, temperatures, tastes, and sights as a fire. Visual perception concentrates on the conclusions that are made from information gathered by our eyes.

■ SENSORY THEORIES OF VISUAL COMMUNICATION

Researchers and theorists who concentrate on sensory theories of visual communication are mainly concerned with how the brain can notice and miss the visual cues of color, form, depth, and movement. A useful motion picture that helps you imagine what it's like to be a brain cell is the documentary *Koyaanisqatsi* (1982) directed by Godfrey Reggio (Weblink 3.1). With the thousands of slow- and fast-motion images and quick and frenetic cuts between scenes of everything from crowded freeways to women who work on a snack cake assembly line, there are too many images to process and remember. Scenes in the film become a blur composed not of content but of the four visual cues. The film shows what being a brain cell in your visual

cortex at the back of your brain is like—the cell notes the stimulation and passes it on to your mind without considering it. As a general rule, sensory theories are not concerned with the literal meaning of what is possible to be seen. They help us understand how we can be attracted and distracted from visual messages.

■ Gestalt

The gestalt theory of visual perception emerged from a simple observation. German psychologist Max Wertheimer received his inspiration during a train trip in the summer of 1910. As he looked out the windows as the train moved through the sunny German countryside, he suddenly realized that he could see the outside scene even though the opaque wall of the train and the window frame partially blocked his view.

He left the train in Frankfurt, went to a toy store, and bought a popular children's toy of the day—a stroboscope, similar to what we call a flipbook today. The flipbook is a simple form of cartoon animation. On the first page of the book, a drawing—say, of a cartoon character in a running position—is displayed on the right-hand side of the page. On each subsequent page, the drawing of the figure is slightly different depending on the actions intended by the artist. To see the effect of the moving character, a viewer uses a thumb to flip the pages rapidly. A modern example of this animation technique can be seen in a music video from the Dutch pop group Kraak & Smaak for their 2007 hit, "Squeeze Me" (Weblink 3.2).

Wertheimer's observations during the train trip and using the flipbook led to more research at the University of Frankfurt. Wertheimer concluded that the eye merely takes in all the visual stimuli, whereas the

individual sensory elements. The word *gestalt* comes from the German noun that means form or shape. Gestalt psychologists further refined the initial work by Wertheimer to conclude that visual perception is a result of organizing sensory elements or forms into various groups. Discrete elements within a scene are combined and understood by the brain through a series of four fundamental principles of grouping that are often called laws: similarity, proximity, continuation, and common fate.

Similarity

This gestalt law states that objects that look similar will be automatically grouped together by the brain (Figure 3.1). Simple experiments with the basic shapes of filled-in circles and square forms made that clear to gestalt researchers. Whether for print or screen media, words are easily separated from images. However, when a page is composed of nothing but similarly sized words or pictures, the viewing of it can be tedious. Visual interest comes from *dis*similarity, not similarity (Figure 3.2).

Proximity

The brain more closely associates objects close to each other than it does two objects that are farther apart. Likewise, two friends standing near each other will be viewed as being more closely related than a third person standing 20 yards from the couple (Figure 3.3). Proximity is also a factor with the visual cue of depth. The illusion is enhanced if an object is perceived as being close to the viewer while another seems farther away. If two objects appear to be on the same horizontal plane or are the same size, their proximity is equal and the sensation of depth is reduced.

Courtesy of Paul Martin Lester

Figure 3.1

Six tourists who rest on a bench at Versailles outside Paris come from a similar cultural group and are linked together in our minds through their similarity. Because the woman to the right reads a book and is from a different generation, she looks as if she does not belong, or is dissimilar.

brain arranges the sensations into a coherent image. Without a brain that links individual sensory elements, the phenomenon of movement would not take place. His ideas led to the famous statement:

The whole is different from the sum of its parts.

In other words, perception is a result of a combination of sensations and not of

The Norwegian National Library

Figure 3.2

This Norwegian newspaper from 1905 was typical of print displays at that time. The six columns of vertical type graphically link the page as a single unit. However, the brief headlines and small display advertisements in the second column stand out and add a bit of visual interest because of their dissimilarity.

Figure 3.3

Three boys dressed in similar Mardi Gras costumes pose for a picture while they wait to be photographed with the queen of a ball in New Orleans. One of the reasons the brain links the boys as a single unit is because of their proximity. Regardless, look at their expressions closely— they have quite different personalities.

Continuation

The brain does not prefer sudden or unusual changes in the movement of a line. In other words, the brain seeks as much as possible a smooth continuation of a perceived movement. The line can be a drawing, or it can be several objects placed together along an imaginary line. Objects viewed as belonging to a continuous line will be mentally separated from other objects that are not a part of that line. Continuation also refers to objects that are partially blocked by a foreground object with a viewer's mind continuing the line in order to achieve a kind of graphic closure (Figure 3.4).

Common Fate

Finally, another principle of gestalt psychology is common fate. A viewer mentally groups five arrows or five raised hands pointing to the sky because they all point in the same direction. An arrow or a hand pointed in the opposite direction will create tension, because the viewer will not see it as part of the upwardly directed whole. Again, a visual communicator can use this principle to direct a viewer's eyes toward or away from a graphic element in a picture or design (Figure 3.5). The

placement of a warning label in a cigarette ad is made through research by tobacco industry graphic designers to be the least viewed part of a page.

Danish gestalt psychologist Edgar Rubin developed the principle of camouflage when he made patterns with little or no separation between the foreground and the background. Understanding and manipulating this trait of visual perception led directly to military applications of merging the colors of uniforms and

Figure 3.4

A billboard for a Target department store in Adelaide, Australia, demonstrates continuation as you continue the circles that make up the store's logo in your mind. This image also demonstrates that non-American advertisers can get away with more than their U.S. counterparts.

Figure 3.5

Besides their similar shapes, the two cola bottles are linked graphically by their upward movement, and yet, the two brands are set apart by their opposing directions, or differences in their fates.

Figure 3.6

The Danish psychologist Edgar Rubin used the gestalt principles to draw conclusions about how the mind tells the difference between a foreground and a background (also known as figure and ground). Noting how we see differences led to the idea of creating similarities and camouflage clothing for military uses. PFC Joel Graham applies camouflage paint as his unit prepares to board a ship that will take him to the verdant countryside of Puerto Rico for a military exercise. See color insert following page 178.

equipment with those of surrounding backgrounds in order to hide them (Figure 3.6). This principle also influenced the work of artists M. C. Escher and Paul Klee, both of whom were influenced by the writings and findings of several gestalt psychologists.

Visual communicators learned at least two important lessons from the gestalt theory—studying individual elements of a picture helps you to better understand its whole meaning, and the theory helps you create more noticeable print and screen media designs.

When analyzing a visual message, tiny details within a frame should be studied first to discover how they create a different and often surprising whole. For example, a photographic craze in the 1990s used a computer to mesh the exposures and compositions of hundreds of similarly themed single images into a gestalt whole. As a student at the Massachusetts Institute of Technology, Robert Silvers invented a photographic technique called "photomosaic" that can arrange hundreds of single photographs by their exposures into one picture. Through his company Runaway Technologies, he creates examples such as a picture of the Earth comprising single images from the ground, Leonardo da Vinci's "Mona Lisa" that is a composite of paintings from the artist's notebooks and the Renaissance period, and a close-up portrait of Nazi Holocaust victim Anne Frank as a combination of pictures from that era (Figures 3.7 and 3.8). Silvers has also produced images for use in advertisements for Audi, Coca Cola, MasterCard, and other corporations (Weblink 3.3).

In addition, gestalt helps to focus on a tiny, cropped version of a photograph so that additional insights can be learned when attention is turned to the entire image. Diane Arbus was an inspired portrait photographer who helped invent a genre of photography known as the "snapshot aesthetic." Many times she took pictures of unusual-looking persons—circus performers, nudists, identical twins, a giant, and so on—and

Courtesy of Robert Silvers

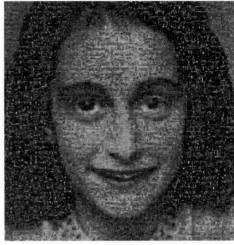

Figures 3.7 and 3.8

The photographic work of Robert Silvers is a demonstration of the gestalt phrase, "The whole is different from the sum of its parts." Looking closely at the individual images that compose the whole picture reveals clues to the subject of this portrait. Holocaust identification photographs, German officials, and prison camp views are placed within the work depending on their exposures. Once the whole image is revealed, it is obvious the portrait is of a smiling and vibrant Annelies "Anne" Frank, who hid with her family from the Germans within a house in Amsterdam until they were discovered in 1944. Seven months later she died of typhus at the Bergen-Belsen concentration camp at the age of 15. In 1952 the English translation of her The Diary of a Young Girl *was published to international critical acclaim.*

photographed them in such a way as to make the portrait look like an ordinary picture you would find in a family's photo album. If you look at just the face of Arbus's portrait titled "A Woman with her Baby Monkey, N.J., 1971," you won't see any signs of the animal that sits on her lap dressed like a baby. What you might notice with the close-up view, however, is the broken slat in the blinds and reflective wood paneling behind her, the cut and style of her hair, and her plain clothes that all indicate economic status. Studying her face, you will see her slight, closed-mouth smile is belied by the sadness evident in her eyes. Finally, the turn of her head and the distracting shadow in the background caused by a flash light are indications of the snapshot aesthetic style. After that concentrated and focused view, seeing the entire photograph confirms and also expands the initial observations. Poignancy is added to the photograph

when it is also considered that the portrait was made the year Arbus killed herself (Weblink 3.4).

Gestalt research radically changed the design philosophy of graphic artists. The strength of gestalt is its attention to the individual forms that make up a picture's content. Any analysis of an image should start by concentrating on those forms that naturally appear in any picture. Recall that color, form, depth, and movement all are basic characteristics of an image that the brain notices. Gestalt teaches a visual communicator to combine those basic elements into a meaningful whole. The approach also teaches the graphic artist to focus attention on certain elements by playing against the gestalt principles. For example, a company's logo (or trademark) will be noticed in an advertisement if it has a dissimilar shape, size, or location in relation to the other elements in the layout.

Gestalt also helped alter the front-page layouts of newspapers. Before the theory was advanced, newspapers were a mind-numbing collection of gray words on a page separated by six to eight long, vertical columns that ran the length of the page. The main story's small headline, followed by smaller subheads, and then even smaller body copy, started at the top-left of the page and continued on without breaks or pictures. These designs, intended for highly literate readers, were dull and unattractive. In gestalt terms, the page was an example of similarity, the columns showed equal proximity, continuation was imposed as the reader's eyes finished the bottom of one column to advance to the top of the next, and all the columns were meant to be read in the same direction, indicating a common fate (Figure 3.9). Today, a newspaper's front page is a varied, sometimes desperately cacophonous collection of different sized headlines, columns, and pictures.

In gestalt terms, the page is now dissimilar, because separate stories are easily differentiated, proximity is noted when two photographs for the same story are printed closely together, continuation is indicated by both a vertical and a horizontal flow of the eyes depending on the layout, and the relative importance of each story is shown by its position and size on the page (Figure 3.10). Modern newspaper design is a lesson in the application of the gestalt theory. Most experts agree, however, that gestalt design won't be enough to save the delivery of news on paper.

The work of gestalt theorists clearly shows that the brain is a powerful organ that classifies visual material in discrete groups. What we see when looking at a picture is modified by what we are directed to see or miss by photographers, filmmakers, and graphic designers.

Figure 3.9 (left)

This first edition of the Daily Globe *(St. Paul, Minnesota), published on January 1, 1880, illustrates how the four gestalt laws of similarity, proximity, continuation, and common fate do not necessarily create a graphic design that holds much visual interest for a reader.*

Figure 3.10 (right)

Modern newspaper design creates visual interest by displaying contrasts in headline, picture, and story styles, sizes, and locations, as shown in this fictitious newspaper created for a university project titled "News Design" in 2004.

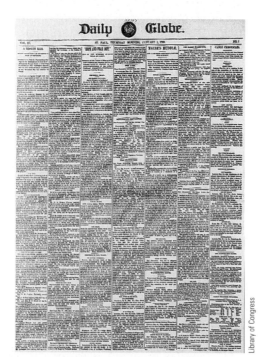

■ *Constructivism*

The gestalt approach has been criticized for describing perceptions rather than giving explanations of how these perceptions actually give meaning to an image. Consequently, several gestalt psychologists attempted to develop theories that helped explain the importance of the viewer's own mental state during active viewing. In 1970, Julian Hochberg, a professor of psychology at Columbia University, found that the eyes of his experimental subjects were constantly in motion as they scanned an image. These quick fixations all combined within the viewer's short-term memory to help build a mental picture of a scene. For Hochberg, a viewer constructs a scene with short-lived eye fixations that the mind combines into a whole picture. If memorable, the scene will be added to a person's long-term memory. The gestalt approach described a viewer as being too passive. In contrast, constructivism emphasizes the viewer's eye movements in an active state of perception.

Hochberg had his subjects use eye-tracking machines in his visual perception experiments. These devices can chart the way a viewer looks at an image. Since the area of sharpest focus that we see is about the size of the letter "e" printed on this page, the eye constantly moves in order to maintain focus. Eye-tracking machines simply made obvious the eyes' frenetic journey across a direct or mediated image (Figure 3.11).

Two graphic designers and researchers helped make Hochberg's theory practical for visual communicators by showing how viewers notice elements on a page or screen.

In 1990, Dr. Mario García of the Poynter Institute (Weblink 3.5) and García Media (Weblink 3.6) and Dr. Pegie Stark

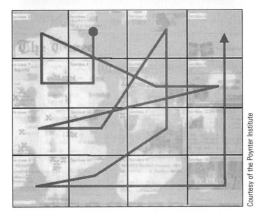

Courtesy of the Poynter Institute

Figures 3.11 and 3.12
In order to conduct research on graphic design attributes for print and online publications, subjects were asked to wear headsets that recorded eye movements and time spent viewing various elements. A typical eye path shows the starting point with a dot and the sweeping right, left, up, and down movements as the subject was attracted by graphic elements presented on a computer monitor.

Adam of Poynter used an eye-track testing machine to record on videotape the eye movements of participants as they read different versions of a newspaper. Participants wore special glasses that "contained two small cameras—one that recorded eye movement and another that recorded where the reader looked." The time spent on each element of a page could also be recorded. The researchers found that readers noticed the largest picture on a page first and a headline before a story. Captions under photographs were the third most viewed element on a page. Clearly, the results indicated how important graphic designs are in capturing a reader's attention.

Subsequent eye-track studies looked at the reading habits of online readers. One study found that web users noticed text on a screen first, unlike their print counterparts who noticed images first. For

García it was clear that reviewing online material "is more like reading a book, where one concentrates on the text and prefers photos to appear separately."

In 2007 a more elaborate study tried to find differences in readers as they navigated the various elements that make up print and online pages. Studying more than 350 elements that could be found on pages—headlines, stories, pictures, briefs, advertisements, podcasts, blogs, teasers, and so on—the study was an exhaustive use of the eye-track procedure. The research discovered several differences between online and print readers. Online users read more of a story than readers in broadsheet and tabloid formats; online users scanned through various stories whereas print readers tended to start at the beginning and read to the end. More attention by readers of all graphic formats was given if stories also contained informational graphics, sidebars, and lists. Bigger headlines and photographs got a lot of attention in print, but online readers noted navigational elements and links. Photojournalistic images of real people were preferred over studio set-up shots. Both groups liked color over black and white (Figure 3.12).

Ironically, the news organizations that participated in the study in order to find out how to keep the readers they have and attract new ones included the *Star Tribune* of Minneapolis and the *Philadelphia Daily News*, whose parent companies filed for bankruptcy in 2009, and the *Rocky Mountain News*, which quit publishing altogether the same year.

Although limited by their emphasis on "what the brain sees" and not what the objects seen mean, sensory theories can be thought to be limited in their application for visual communicators. Nevertheless, the gestalt and constructivism theories both have important uses for print and/or screen media graphic designers. No work is useful if readers, viewers, and users do not notice it.

■ PERCEPTUAL THEORIES OF VISUAL COMMUNICATION

The semiotics and cognitive theories of visual perception can be considered to be content driven. Although recognizing that vision cannot happen without light illuminating, structuring, and sometimes creating perceptions, these two theories stress that humans are unique in the animal kingdom because we assign complex meaning to the objects we see.

■ *Semiotics*

The flag that is raised high above a baseball stadium and is watched reverently during the singing of the national anthem by those in the stands and on the field is a sign. The right hand placed over the approximate location of the heart during the singing of the anthem is a sign. The words printed in a program about the players on the field are signs. The close-up photograph of a player holding a bat awaiting a pitch are signs. The refs' black outfits and the managers' hand signals are signs. The illuminated numbers on the scoreboard are signs. Even cleat marks in the dirt are signs. The "high-five" slap with a friend after a team's home run is a sign. The simple silhouette illustration of a woman on a restroom door is a sign. The green traffic light as you make your way home from the game is a sign (Figure 3.13).

A sign is simply anything that stands for something else. After reading the preceding list of signs you might well

Courtesy of Paul Martin Lester

Figure 3.13
Fans of the Los Angeles Angels of Anaheim wear a fake Mohawk and standard baseball caps along with a jersey to support their team. See color insert following page 178.

ask: What is *not* a sign? That's a good question, because almost any action, object, or image will mean something to someone somewhere. Any word or physical presentation, from a yelled comment to an orange jacket, is a sign if it has meaning beyond the object itself. Consequently, the meaning behind any sign must be learned. In other words, for something to be a communicated sign, the viewer must understand its meaning. But if you don't understand the meaning behind the orange color of a jacket, it isn't a sign for you. It's just a jacket.

Semiotics (called *semiology* in Europe) is the study or science of signs. The field is the culmination of Aldous Huxley's mantra: The more you know, the more you see. Images will be much more interesting and memorable if signs that are understood by many are used in a picture. The study of semiotics is vital because signs permeate every message, whether verbal or visual. The academic study of semiotics attempts to identify and explain the signs used by every society in the world.

Although semiotics has gained popularity relatively recently, it is an old concept.

In 397 CE, Augustine of Hippo, a Roman philosopher, linguist, and bishop of the Roman Catholic Church, first proposed the study of signs. He recognized that nature is filled with universally understood entities that afforded communication on many nonverbal levels. For Augustine, signs were the link between nature and humans—between the outer and inner worlds. More importantly, signs from nature also linked individuals to form cultural meaning that could be transferred to future generations. The word semiotics comes from the language of his country: *Semeion* is the Greek word for sign.

Contemporary semiotics emerged through the work of two theorists just before World War I. Swiss linguist Ferdinand de Saussure developed a general theory of signs while a professor at the University of Geneva (Figure 3.14). We know about his work in semiotics because of the notes written by his students during his lectures, which were later published. A lesson: Listen closely to your instructors and take good notes. At about the same time, American philosopher Charles Sanders Peirce (pronounced

Figure 3.14 (left)

Ferdinand de Saussure was a Swiss linguist who was monumental in establishing the symbolic interpretation of signs through his course in general linguistics taught at the University of Geneva. After his death in 1913, two former students published his lectures from their notes; this led to the founding of the field of semiotics, the study of signs.

Figure 3.15 (right)

Charles Sanders Peirce was an American philosopher and scientist considered to be the founder of the field of semiotics, but he led a troubled life. Appointed to teach logic courses at Johns Hopkins University, he was dismissed after it was learned he lived with a woman while he was separated but still married to his first wife. After the scandal, he could no longer find employment in academia. In 1887 he lost his family inheritance after purchasing 2,000 acres of farmland in Pennsylvania that never returned the investment. Wanted by the authorities for assault and failure to pay his debts, he was saved from prison by sympathetic friends and family members. To support himself until he died in 1910, he wrote articles for journals and gave lectures. Nevertheless, from his articles, lectures, and correspondence, the field of semiotics was established.

Library of Congress, Prints and Photographs Division, LC-US262-99929

National Oceanic and Atmospheric Administration, Office of NOAA Corps Operations

"purse") published his own ideas about the effect of signs on society (Figure 3.15). De Saussure and Peirce inspired others to concentrate in this field of study. The Americans Arthur Asa Berger, Charles Morris, and Thomas Sebeok, the Italian Umberto Eco, the French Roland Barthes, and many others have contributed greatly to the study of semiotics. Eco's novels *The Name of the Rose, Foucault's Pendulum,* and *The Island of the Day Before* are fascinating and amusing explorations of symbolic meaning.

De Saussure and Peirce weren't particularly interested in the visual aspects of signs. They were traditional linguists who studied the way words were used to communicate meaning through narrative structures. However, over the years semiotics has evolved into a theory of perception that involves the use of images in unexpected ways. For example, Sebeok, a professor emeritus at Indiana University who died in 2002, identified some of the topics that semiotics researchers have studied. Besides the obvious subject of visual signs and symbols used in

graphic designs, they include the semiotics of the theater, where performance elements are analyzed; the semiotics of puppetry, in which the colors, costumes, gestures, and staging of the characters are studied; the semiotics of television shows and commercials; the semiotics of tourism; the semiotics of the signs used in Boy Scout uniforms and rituals; the semiotics of notational systems used in dance, music, logic, mathematics, and chemistry; and urban semiotics, in which the growth and physical attributes of cities are seen as social symbols. The field has become so popular that journals, international conferences, and academic departments at universities are devoted to semiotics.

Peirce's contribution to semiotics was in the formulation of three different types of signs: iconic, indexical, and symbolic. All signs must be learned, but the speed of comprehension of each type of sign varies. Thinking about iconic, indexical, and symbolic signs is a way to really look and study a visual message in a much more thorough and critical manner. Once this process is done, you soon realize that even the simplest image has complex cultural meaning. However, it is important to realize that the three categories of signs are not mutually exclusive. The written and visual examples given in this section are meant to focus your attention on one particular type of sign.

A napkin from Hof's Hut, a popular chain of southern California restaurants, portrays the three types of signs through pictures and words and will be used as an example for this section (Figure 3.16).

Iconic Signs

Icon, from the Greek word *eikenai*, means "to be like" or "to seem." Iconic signs are the easiest to interpret because they most closely resemble the thing they are meant to represent. Examples of icons are the accurate cave paintings of animals by prehistoric humans; the simple drawings above restroom doors that communicate the gender allowed inside; the trash can, printer, and home images on the desktops of many computers; street signs that indicate dangerous road conditions; and—the most common of all—photographs and motion pictures that are meant to be representations of what they depict.

Almost any documentary photographer's images would be good examples of iconic signs. The portraits of German August Sander work well. Looking at his many images you cannot doubt that at some time the persons pictured resembled their portraits (Weblink 3.7).

Figure 3.16
The Hof's Hut restaurant napkin is a study of many different types of semiotic signs—iconic, the illustration of a pot pie; indexical, the "heat" lines emanating from the crust; and symbolic, the words and colors. See color insert following page 178.

Courtesy of Paul Martin Lester

For the restaurant's napkin, the tilted, brown illustration of a chicken pot pie in the top-left corner is an iconic sign—the drawing is meant to represent a pie similar to one you can order at the restaurant.

Indexical Signs

Indexical signs have a logical, common sense connection to the thing or idea they represent rather than a direct resemblance to the object. Consequently, their interpretation takes a little longer than that of icons. We learn indexical signs through everyday life experiences. Peirce used a sundial as an illustration of an indexical sign. The sun's shadow implied the movement of time. Other indexical signs can be a footprint on the beach or on the surface of the moon, smoke spewing out of a high smokestack or automobile exhaust pipe, or the high temperature reading of a sick patient. Footprints stand for the person who impressed them.

Figure 3.17

This 19th century drawing presents good examples of indexical signs. There are two possible sources for the smoke—a steam engine on the horse-drawn fire engine and a fire inside the house. But is there a blaze on the fire engine or is the man at the window simply smoking a (rather large) cigar? Experience helps us decipher indexical signs. But as with all images, there are other signs to analyze. The photographic quality of the image makes it an iconic sign, and the buildings, clothing, and horses are symbolic signs of an earlier age.

Figure 3.18

In Belfast, Northern Ireland, the Ulster Defense Association (UDA) is an ultraconservative paramilitary organization. The sans serif typeface urges the Irish hunger strikers in 1981 to starve themselves in the prison wing known as "H-Block." The cross for the "I" in "DIE" is an ironic religious symbol when it is associated with this violent message.

Figure 3.19

Clasped hands symbolize prayer or contemplation in many cultures. The unusually tight cropping of the top of the image emphasizes the importance of the gesture by a doctor who treats young patients who have been paralyzed from gunshots.

Uncensored Situations, 1966, The Dick Sutphen Studio, Inc.

Courtesy of Paul Martin Lester

Courtesy of Paul Martin Lester

Smoke represents the pollution generated by the furnace or engine. Fever indicates that the patient has an infection (Figure

3.17). A famous portrait of trumpeter Louis Armstrong taken in 1965 by John Loengard of *Life* magazine is a tightly cropped image that shows lines on two fingers and his lips, which are indexical signs of his age. The portrait captures him rubbing petroleum jelly to his lips to soften them before a concert (Weblink 3.8).

Back to the napkin, we have learned through our experiences that the six lines trailing from the pot pie are meant to represent heat. Someone's food is fresh and right out of the oven. However, to someone else, those lines might indicate that the pie is falling, a common visual device used in printed cartoons. More bizarre, a creative person might think that the lines mean that the pie is a marionette, a type of puppet controlled by strings, or even stranger, a pie full of rats, with the brown lines representing the tails showing through the crust. All of these interpretations come from the indexical sign on the napkin of lines exuding from the pie.

Symbolic Signs

The third type of sign is the most abstract. Symbols have no logical or representational connection between them and the things they represent. Symbols, more than the other types of signs, *have* to be taught (Figure 3.18). For that reason, social and cultural considerations influence them greatly. Words, numbers, colors, gestures, flags, costumes, most company logos, music, and religious images all are considered symbols (Figure 3.19). Because symbols often have deep roots in the culture of a particular group, with their meanings being passed from one generation to the next, symbolic signs mean more than iconic or indexical signs (Figure 3.20). The burning of a country's national flag as a protest gesture is a powerful symbol of defiance and anger. It isn't simply an act to create heat through the burning of a piece of fabric.

The meaning one gets from a symbol is highly personalized and often distinct. In the novel *The Da Vinci Code* by Dan Brown, a main character attempts to explain this fact of human nature: "Telling someone what a symbol 'meant' was like telling them how a song should make them feel—it was different for all people. A white Ku Klux Klan headpiece conjured images of hatred and racism in the United States, and yet the same costume carried a meaning of religious faith in Spain."

Symbols often evoke strong emotional responses among viewers. After cleaning fluid reacted to the surface of windows of the Seminole Finance Corp. building in Clearwater, Florida, in 1996, many claimed to see a 60-foot apparition of the Virgin Mary (Figure 3.21). Consequently, a shrine was established that included a large, wooden crucifix, an area where persons could light candles, and white, plastic chairs where you could sit and meditate. With the thousands that came to see the window's image, the building was abandoned by its owners and later sold to the Shepherds of Christ Ministries, which sold bibles and other religious works in its bookstore. But such a popular icon can be a tempting target. In 2004 a high school student admitted that he broke out the window and destroyed the giant "head" with a powerful slingshot (the author is not certain whether the perpetrator's name was David).

In 2007 Iranian officials, out of pride or to stir up the international community, introduced a 50,000-rial bank note (equivalent to about five U.S. dollars) with a graphic path of electrons

surrounding a proton—the symbol of atomic energy (Figure 3.22). The bank note corresponded with the controversial news speculating whether Iranian scientists were working on atomic experiments

Courtesy of Paul Martin Lester

AP Photo

Figure 3.20

A black cloth over the head of a person symbolizes death in many cultures. In reality, this man is simply avoiding the sun or the photographer on the boardwalk of Atlantic City.

Figure 3.21

The power of symbolic signs to emotionally connect persons with them is evident in this picture. After a cleaning solvent accidentally stained the outside glass of a building in Clearwater, Florida, in 1996, for many the result resembled the head of the religious figure, the Virgin Mary. Thousands came to the site seeking inspiration and comfort. Eventually, the window was broken.

Figure 3.22

The 50,000 Iranian rial sparked controversy in 2007 after the model of atomic energy, a reference to the country's nuclear power initiative, was printed on the bank note. The bill also features a map of the region and a quote from the prophet Mohammed that translates to "Even if science is at the Pleiades [a cluster of about 500 stars about 400 light years from Earth], some men from the land of Persia would attain it."

to provide nuclear energy for its citizens or armaments that might threaten the world's safety.

The printed words on the napkin are all examples of symbolic signs. Notice the typeface choice for "Hof's Hut." You will learn a bit later how a designer's typographic choices can provide additional meaning to a presentation. The typeface family used for the name of the restaurant is called blackletter. It originated from the first commercial printing press by the German Johannes Gutenberg in 1455. Consequently, over the years the typeface's symbolic meaning includes concepts such as German, religious, traditional, and long established. Although not a German restaurant, the Hofman family who owns the chain wanted to honor their German roots. Under the name is the word "RESTAURANTS" presented with a much different typeface, a sans serif. It has a clean and modern symbolic meaning enhanced by the extra space or kerning between the letters. Hof's Hut, then, has been around for a long time, their kitchen is tidy and

sanitary, and their restaurant is a pleasant place, despite what may be interpreted by its pot pie picture.

An example of all three types of signs used in portraits of the same person over several centuries can be seen in the portraits of Christopher Columbus. Since no portraits of him were made during his lifetime, a study of his pictures is an example of cultural relativism. After his death and when his exploits became known, the portraits were iconic—the public simply needed to know what the explorer looked like. Hundreds of years after his explorations, Italian American commercial interests used Columbus as a symbol for their own purposes. They wanted to use his name and history to promote the Columbian Exhibition in Chicago in 1892 and to try to change the name of America to Columbia. Consequently, his portraits were indexical—he was seen being guided by the light or voice of God. At the 500th anniversary, however, when opinions of Columbus and his voyages were severely critical, the portraits were symbolic—they showed his face as a collection of jigsaw puzzle pieces or as a sailing ship that had a death mask on its bow (Figures 3.23 and 3.24 and Weblink 3.9).

New Orleans photographer and poet Clarence John Laughlin made pictures of objects that for him had complex symbolic meanings. One image is of a statue by the side of a grave he named "Figure from the Underworld, 1951." His typically lucid and elaborate caption directs the viewer to notice all three types of signs. Iconic: "A horrible little stucco figure, probably turned out by the thousands in a mold, and found in a Louisiana country garden." Indexical: "The fierce suns and heavy rains of Louisiana

Figure 3.23

"Portrait of a Man, Said to be Christopher Columbus," 1519, by Sebastiano del Piombo (Sebastiano Luciani). This portrait is highly regarded and has been used in many descriptions and articles about the Admiral, but it is not Columbus. Born around 1485, Piombo would have been 21 years old when Columbus died, but there was no indication he knew the Admiral. Moreover, Piombo took up painting later in his life, having devoted his early years to music. As a portrait, it is a bit unusual because the subject wears a hat with a curled border. A deep-edged and ornate sleeveless coat or mantle hangs from his shoulders. His fingers are long and delicate. His face is round, his eyes blue, and a dimple is barely visible in his chin. Most striking about this painting is the legend that runs along the top. The inscription that identifies the sitter as Columbus was included much later to increase the value of the painting.

© The Metropolitan Museum of Art/Art Resource, NY

have eaten it as though by acid." Symbolic: "Leaving it as though with its brain exposed, and with a sweet smile turned sickly and defeated. It rises as if from some nether plane—the dark and ragged American world of the 1930s." His image becomes a powerful metaphor that makes a comment about our present economic times (Weblink 3.10).

Besides iconic, indexical, and symbolic signs, Roland Barthes described another way to think of individual elements within an image. He developed the concept of a *chain of associations* that make up a picture's narrative. To understand this concept, we must first discuss how we communicate through words.

In verbal language, the narrative or story we are telling/reading/hearing is linear. One word follows the next in a specific rule-based order known as its syntax, or grammar. These rules of syntax have been established and agreed upon over centuries for a language and its people. Pictures, on the other hand, are presentational. All the elements of an image, whether still or moving, are presented all at once with a viewer free to look at them in any order. Signs within an image are presented in various ways for a variety of media, many times depending on the style of the image maker. But since most of us think of images through thoughts composed of words within our minds, we usually link individual elements within a picture into a narrative whole. For Barthes, each element is a link that forms a chain of associations, or meaning. The common term for Barthes's chain of associations is codes. A code is an amalgamation of hundreds of ideas and/or elements into one, convenient concept. The next time you are stopped at a street corner and see a stop sign, think of all the underlying statutes and laws that regulate

Bildarchiv Presussischer Kulturbesitz / Art Resource, NY

Figure 3.24
"Columbus Discovering Land," oil on canvas, 1866, by Karl von Piloty. A German painter of considerable skill and reputation, Piloty was known for his historical works. He later was appointed keeper of the Munich Academy, was ennobled by the King of Bavaria, and was a respected educator. This painting is a good example of indexical signs. While a crewman sleeps, the bearded Admiral is seen on deck late at night, bags under his eyes from worry, and checking his progress on a map when a heavenly light rivets his attention as he nears land.

the sign itself—its color, location, shape, size, height, and so on—and its meaning—to stop, of course, but also where, for how long, and in which order if other cars are present (Figure 3.25). Asa Berger elaborated on Barthes and suggested four types of codes: metonymic, analogical, displaced, and condensed.

Metonymic Code

A collection of signs that cause the viewer to make assumptions about what is seen is a metonymic code. In that way, this type of code is closely associated with indexical signs. You assume something about what you see. Most advertisers, whether working in commercial, nonprofit, or political venues, want the viewer to make assumptions about a particular product or service. A viewer of a studio setup portrait of a smiling family—father, mother, daughter, and dog—playfully wrapped in bed linens used in an advertisement shown in a magazine makes a number of assumptions about the

Figure 3.25

As one of the few traffic signs that originated in the United States, the first stop sign was erected in Michigan, the home of the American automobile industry, in 1915 and showed the word "STOP" in black letters against a yellow octagon background. A common stop sign stands for a complicated set of legal specifications and codes. In 1954 the design was changed to a standard 30 inches across each side of its octagonal area with a three-quarter-inch white border. The white uppercase san serif letters forming the word "STOP" are ten inches high. The height of a sign from the base must be at least five feet. The color red was chosen because the same color is used for traffic lights. The sign is also retroreflective, as it reflects headlights back with a minimum of scattering. But the traffic sign also stands for a complex set of legal codes—for example, if you arrive first at an intersection you can proceed first, but if two or more drivers arrive at the junction at the same time, the one on the left must yield to the one on the right.

Courtesy of Paul Martin Lester

picture—that this is a real family, that they are actually happy, and that their choice of cotton comforters has brought them to this blissful state. Furthermore, it is hoped that when you see this pleasant quartet of good-looking models, you will think that if you had the same product on your bed you would be just as satisfied with your life (Figure 3.26).

Analogical Code

This type of code is a group of signs that cause the viewer to make mental comparisons. Examples, often called figures of speech, might compare an old tree to a human face, a live mouse to a computer device, and lined yellow paper to a lemon peel. A large piece of equipment, such as a blast furnace in a steel mill, might have

shapes and patterns that when seen at a particular angle and under specific lighting conditions resembles the face of a robot. It is unlikely that the architect of the factory positioned parts of the furnace to resemble the eyes, nose, and mouth of a face, but it is likely that an observant photographer would take a picture in such a way to show those features because it adds interest to the picture (Figure 3.27). During the 2009 U.S. Open tennis tournament, American Express introduced a commercial for its charge card that showed everyday objects, singularly and in combination, that resembled human faces when sad or happy. Produced by WPP's Ogilvy & Mather advertising agency, it puts the analogical code to creative commercial use (Weblink 3.11).

Displaced Code

Whenever there is a transfer of meaning from one set of signs to another, a displaced code is used. In the classic movie *Dr. Strangelove or: How I Learned to Stop Worrying and Love the Bomb* (1964) directed by Stanley Kubrick, rifles, missiles, airplanes, and other phallic shapes were photographed purposely to communicate the idea of sexual tension among certain military characters. The film's climax shows the character Major T. J. "King" Kong played by Slim Pickens gleefully riding the bomb to his and the world's doom (Figure 3.28).

Images of penises are not acceptable pictures for most members of society and so are displaced by their phallic equivalents. Liquor, lipstick, and cigarette advertisers also commonly use phallic imagery in the form of their products' shapes in the hope that potential customers will link the use of their products with possible sexual conquest. Ads from

Scarlett Johansson

Courtesy of the Advertising Archives

Figure 3.26

Actress Scarlett Johansson, with lively, flowing hair, direct eye contact, and a smile, is a picture of metonymic assumptions–buy a bottle of Moet champagne and you can party the same as her.

Skyy vodka, Tom Ford eyewear, and Sisley clothing regularly employ such symbolism. To attract attention and to link sex with their products, "shock ads" from these companies have used the shape of a tie, the placement of a bottle, a man's middle finger in the mouth of a woman, and a female model holding a snake and attempting to lick its head.

Condensed Code

In many respects, this type of code is the most interesting. Condensed codes are several signs that combine to form a new, composite message. Televised music videos and the advertisements inspired by them have unique and often unexpected meanings. The signs of musicians, dancers, music, quick-editing techniques, graphics, colors, and so on all form a complex message. Within the culture a message is intended for, a condensed code has relevant meaning. For those outside that culture being represented, the images can be confusing, random, and without purpose. But the way individuals combine signs and form their own meaningful messages often cannot be controlled by the creators of the signs. The photographic work of American

Jerry Uelsmann combines elements from several images to make intriguing composite pictures. In his 1980 photograph "Untitled," a cloud-filled sky contained within a box is suspended above the edge of an ocean with crashing waves. Without much help from the title, any meaning from this set of elements must come from the viewer (Weblink 3.12).

Semiotics teaches the importance of symbolism in the act of visual perception and communication. A viewer who knows the meaning behind the signs used in a complex picture will gain insights from it, making the image more memorable. The motion pictures of American director David Lynch (*Blue Velvet*, 1986; *Lost Highway*, 1997; *Mulholland Drive*, 2001) are often examples of complex semiotic

NASA Jet Propulsion Laboratory (NASA–JPL)

Figure 3.27

In the summer of 1976, the Viking Orbiter 1 took photographs of the Cydonia region of Mars in the planet's northern hemisphere to find possible landing sites for its sister spaceship, the Viking Lander 2. One of the images revealed what a NASA public relations person described as a "huge rock formation . . . which resembles a human head . . . formed by shadows giving the illusion of eyes, nose and mouth." The so-called "Face on Mars" became an instant popular culture phenomenon, with some using it as evidence of life on the planet. In 2001 the Mars Global Surveyor took another picture of the rock cropping. There was no face, but the analogical code lives on.

Figure 3.28

*Stanley Kubrick's
Dr. Strangelove or: How
I Learned to Stop Worrying
and Love the Bomb (1964) is
a classic study of the displaced
code. The nuclear warhead
prop that actor Slim Pickens
rides at the end of the movie is
the ultimate phallic symbol.*

Figure 3.29

*"The Doubting of St. Thomas,"
1601–1602, by Caravaggio. The
Italian painter Michelangelo
Merisi da Caravaggio popularized a technique called selective
illumination that became a
signature of the Baroque school
of art that he initiated. His use
of spot lighting and dark shadows added dramatic interest
to his works. He also preferred
to use ordinary people he met
on the streets as models in
his paintings to give them a
realistic quality, unlike the ideal-
ized religious works of the day.
"The Doubting of St. Thomas,"
hanging in the former summer
palace of Frederick the Great,
captures the moment told in
the Bible when St. Thomas
investigates the wounds of Jesus
and no longer doubts that he
has returned to life after his
crucifixion. A live actor reproduction of the painting can be
seen in REM's 1991 music video
"Losing My Religion," in which
it might be assumed that the
lead singer, John Michael Stipe,
doubts his fame.*

The Everett Collection

signs. The opening scene from *Twin Peaks: Fire Walk with Me* (1992) has a strange woman wearing a red dress and holding a blue rose who communicates through gestures important information to the characters played by Chris Isaak and Kiefer Sutherland.

Bildarchiv Preussischer Kulturbesitz/Art Resource, NY

The 1991 music video from the rock group REM for their song "Losing My Reli-gion" is a rich and potentially confusing collection of signs (Weblink 3.13). Its over-all meaning is aided by knowing the his-tory of the band and the biography of its members, the lyrics of the song, the fact that the director, Tarsem Singh, is from India, the "Myth of Icarus," the history of fascism, and the paintings of Italian Michelangelo Merisi da Caravaggio, par-ticularly his 1601–1602 oil, "The Doubting of Saint Thomas" (Figure 3.29).

The problem in using complex signs as a part of an image is that they may be misunderstood, ignored, or interpreted the wrong way. Nevertheless, the chal-lenge for visual communicators, expressed in the study of semiotics, is that signs can enhance the visual experience and edu-cate, entertain, and persuade a viewer.

■ *Cognitive Theory*

According to the cognitive theory, what is going on in a viewer's mind is just as important as the images that can be seen.

Figure 3.30

President Lincoln's funeral procession in New York City, with 11,000 members of the military and about 75,000 civilians marching along, was as elaborate in real life as it is shown here in this lithograph based on a photograph attributed to Matthew Brady and published in Harper's Weekly on May 13, 1865. If you are a history buff interested in Lincoln, or have been to funeral recently, this image may be of interest to you because it might trigger memories.

Mental activities focus attention on a visual element, but they can also distract a viewer. The cultural anthropologist Carolyn Bloomer identified several mental activities that affect visual perception: memory, projection, expectation, selectivity, habituation, salience, dissonance, culture, and words.

Memory

Arguably the most important mental activity involved in accurate visual perception, memory is our link with all the images we have ever seen. A historic photograph of President Lincoln's funeral in Washington, D.C., in 1865 or a crowd shot from the 1969 Woodstock, New York, music concert, might be of interest to you as they trigger memories and associations because of a funeral you have attended, a visit to America's capitol, something you read about the 16th president, someone you know who was at the historic concert, or a music festival you attended. Someone else might have no associations with either picture and quickly turn the page (Figure 3.30).

Projection

Creative individuals see recognizable forms in Cheerios floating in a bowl of milk in the morning or in rock patterns while sitting near a pool in Palm Springs, California. Others make sense out of clouds or trees, or find comfort in the messages learned from tarot cards, astrological forecasts, and the I-Ching. One reason the common inkblot test developed in 1921 by the Swiss Freudian psychologist Hermann Rorschach is used is that individuals often reveal personality traits by deriving meaning from the oddly formed shapes (Figure 3.31). A person's mental state of mind is thus "projected"

Figure 3.31

Hermann Rorschach was a Swiss psychoanalyst who while in high school made inkblot pictures to amuse his friends. Later in college he wondered why different persons see different things with the random ink drops. In 1921 he published a book, Psychodiagnostic, that introduced his test in which ten inkblots are shown to a subject with the responses compared with established norms. He might have been able to further refine his test, but he died the next year. In the inkblot shown here, whether you see an animal with wings sitting on a cliff, a powerful leader pointing to two subservient persons, or some other interpretation is an example of the cognitive element of projection.

onto an inanimate object or generalized statement. Someone may spend hours marveling at the humanlike face formed by the curves and shadows in a tree trunk while another will walk past. The difference between the two may be in the mental processes that affect what they see.

Expectation

Having preconceived expectations about how a scene should appear often leads to false or missed visual perceptions. Italian artist Guido Daniele (Weblink 3.14) paints images of zebras, elephants, eagles, and snakes on hands. The intriguing visual result is that a viewer often forgets that the animal paintings use a human hand as the substrate for the work. A clever magazine advertisement and commercial for Johnnie Walker's Blue Label whisky is at first an artistic collection of wavy lines—until a full-length image of a man standing before a woman sitting in a chair holding a bottle suddenly is noticed under the catch phrase, "For those who know what to look for" (Weblink 3.15). Researchers Robert Becklen and Daniel Cervone devised an experiment in 1983 in which subjects were asked to count the number of times a three-person team wearing black T-shirts passed a basketball. Not expecting to see a young woman holding an umbrella walking casually through the room, most who viewed the video didn't see her (Weblink 3.16).

Selectivity

Aldous Huxley discussed this cognitive element when he wrote of combining selecting with sensing and perceiving. Most of what people see within a complicated visual experience is not part of conscious processing. For example,

rarely do people think about their own breathing unless made aware of it. Most of visual perception is an unconscious, automatic act by which large numbers of images enter and leave the mind without being processed. We usually focus only on significant details within a scene. If you are trying to locate a friend sitting in the packed bleachers during a baseball game, all the other unknown faces in the crowd will have little significance. When you see your friend, your mind suddenly locks on that person as if with the help of a spotlight in a darkened room. Concentrating on people observing a funeral procession in a documentary photograph taken during the violent era of 1981 in Belfast, Northern Ireland, you might miss the covered face of an Irish Republican Army (IRA) soldier (Figure 3.32).

Habituation

To protect itself from overstimulation and unnecessary images that might fatigue and confuse, the mind tends to ignore visual stimuli that are a part of a person's everyday, habitual activities. When you walk or drive to school or work the same way every day, your brain will ignore the sights along your route. People like to travel to new areas because the images experienced in an unfamiliar place often are striking and interesting. One way to prevent your mind from thinking habitually is to search for new ways to think about familiar objects or events in your daily life so that you save money on a flight to Amsterdam. Practicing creative thought readies your mind to think actively about new images when you see them. Walker Evans, one of the most famous photographers in the medium's history, produced a series of pictures of everyday tools—a pair of pliers, a wrench,

Courtesy of Paul Martin Lester

Figure 3.32

Expectation is a mental condition that can lead to heightened observation if a scene matches your mental imaginings or to poor visual perception if your preconceived idea of what you will see is not matched by reality. A casual viewer would most likely over-look the masked Irish Republican Army (IRA) soldier at the lower right of the frame during a funeral for a hunger striker in Belfast, Northern Ireland, in 1981.

and so on—using high-quality studio lighting and camera techniques to celebrate their often overlooked designs. Accompanying his 1955 portfolio in *Fortune* magazine titled "Beauties of the Common Tool," Walker wrote, "Almost all the basic small tools stand, aesthetically speaking, for elegance, candor, and purity" (Figure 3.33). Likewise, another master of photography, Edward Weston, photographed ordinary objects such as a seashell, a bell pepper, and a toilet seat for the same reason (Weblink 3.17). Looking at their images, you can't help but find the sublime in their banality.

Salience

A stimulus will be noticed more if it has meaning for an individual. If you recently met someone you like whose favorite food is from India, whenever you smell curry, hear other people talking about the country, or watch *Slumdog Millionaire* (2008), you will be reminded of that person. If you are hungry you will notice the smells of cooking food emanating from an open window. A trained biologist will see more in a slide under a micro-

scope than the average person will; both individuals see all there is to see under the microscope, but what the biologist sees is consciously processed in the mind (Figure 3.34).

Dissonance

For many, trying to read while a television or stereo is loudly playing in the same room is difficult because the mind tends to concentrate on only one activity at a time. A book is set aside the moment a television program or the lyrics of a song become interesting. Television programs that combine written and spoken words,

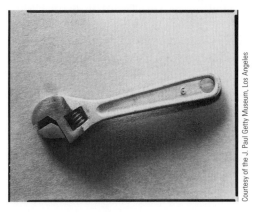

Courtesy of the J. Paul Getty Museum, Los Angeles

Figure 3.33

"Open-End Crescent Wrench, German Manufacture, 56 cents," gelatin silver print, 1955, by Walker Evans. Former Farm Security Administration (FSA) photographer Walker Evans made a series of pictures of everyday objects under studio lighting that demonstrate the cognitive element of habituation. Without being able to study Evan's photograph, you might miss the crescent wrench's metal texture, the contrast of curved versus straight lines, the shadows that define its thickness, the parrot-like "beak" of its clasping edges, the number 6 on its handle, the round hole to hang it from a hook, and the slight smudge on the sheet of paper.

Figure 3.34

The cognitive element of salience refers directly to Aldous Huxley's famous phrase, "The more you know, the more you see." If you are a geneticist, you will more likely find meaning from this electron microscope view of a strand of deoxyribonucleic acid (DNA) than someone who has never seen it. As a general rule, the more salience you bring to any visual message the more interesting it will be to you.

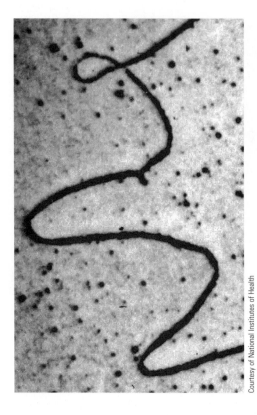

Courtesy of National Institutes of Health

multiple images, and music run the risk of creating visual messages that the viewer cannot understand because of all the competing formats. A classic example of dissonance came from the cable network CNN when it introduced in August 2001 its new version of the 1982 staple "Headline News." Television critics across the country voiced their negative opinion about the format because of all the competing bits of information—an anchorperson talking on camera or as a voice-over, still and/or moving images, graphics with headlines, stock details, weather reports, news "crawls" that updated news events, and advertising logos. Because of the negative feedback, CNN toned down most of its visual display, but kept the crawl along the bottom of the screen.

Dissonance can also happen if a room is too warm or too cold, if there is a

personal matter that you cannot stop thinking about, or if there are too many road sign advertisements competing for your attention on a highway. Too many distractions and you will find it difficult to concentrate on a single visual message (Figure 3.35).

Culture

As a manifestation of the way people act, talk, dress, eat, drink, behave socially, and practice their religious beliefs, cultural influences have a tremendous impact on visual perception. Religious icons, state and country flags, T-shirt designs, and hairstyles all have individual and cultural meanings. If you are aware of the signs that are a part of a particular culture you also will comprehend some of the underlying reasons behind their use. Culture isn't simply the concept of a country's borders or the idea of high-class or upper-class "culture." It spans ethnicity, economic situations, places of work, gender, age, sexual orientation, physical disability, geographic location, and many other aspects of a person's life. Franz Boas, a leader in the field of anthropology, in his book *Anthropology and Modern Life* explained that culture is "the community of emotional life that rises from our everyday habits." Boas thought that culture was more important than race. Culture determines the importance of the signs that affect the people who live with and among us (Figure 3.36).

Words

Although we see with our eyes, most of us think with words. Consequently, words, like memory and culture, profoundly affect our understanding and subsequent long-term recall of an image. One of the strongest forms of communication is when

Figure 3.35

"Little Chapel," Las Vegas, 1999, by Gerry Davey. Sandwiched between the Yucca Motel with its "UEEN" beds and the Oasis Motel with its adult movies, fantasy rooms, and Jacuzzis, you might miss the fact that if you get married in the Little Chapel of the Flowers you can get your wedding webcast FREE. Dissonance is a result of so many elements within a visual array that important details may be missed.

words and images are combined in equally respectful ways. That is why magazines and newspapers regularly have captions for each photograph printed, and news anchors and broadcast journalists use voice-overs to explain what is being shown. One of the best examples of the importance of words and knowing the language of those around you comes from a 1997 episode of NBC's "Saturday Night Live." The late, great comedian Chris Farley is lost in translation when he mistakenly becomes a contestant on a Japanese game show that turns ugly. Strangely, the skit was plagiarized in 2008 for the Russian show, "Проводы Старого года с Максимом Галкиным" or "With the Old Year with Maxim Galkin" (Weblink 3.18).

Semiotics and cognitive approaches to visual communication state that the

Figure 3.36

One of the most important determinants of what you notice and what you miss visually is your cultural identity. For this group of persons waiting for an Easter parade in the French Quarter of New Orleans, what each person notices may be a factor of race, age, gender, weight, and alcohol intake.

human mind is an infinitely complex living organism that science may never fully understand. But meaningful connections between what people see and how they use those images arise when mental processing is viewed as a human rather than an automatic, mechanical process.

The sensory theories of gestalt and constructivism and the perceptual theories of semiotics and cognitive teach visual communicators to look closely at their world, create designs that attract attention, be mindful of the varied messages that come from images, and understand the possible mental enhancers and distractions to anything that might be attempted graphically.

■ KEY TERMS

- Blogs
- Briefs
- Broadsheet
- Closure
- Cultural relativism
- Fascism
- Ku Klux Klan
- Podcasts
- Rituals
- Short-term memory
- Shrine
- Sidebars
- Social symbols
- Substrate
- Syntax
- Tabloid
- Teasers
- Visual perception

 To locate active URLs for the weblinks mentioned in this chapter, please go to the companion site at http://communication.wadsworth.com/lester5 and select the proper chapter.

Visual Persuasion

A newborn baby lies alone with an umbilical cord still attached; a black horse mates with a docile white; a young, attractive priest kisses a young, attractive nun romantically on the lips; a car engulfed in flames; sensitive portraits of death row inmates—the connection between these and other striking images is that they were all used as advertisements to sell clothing. They also generated an enormous amount of controversy in newspapers, magazines, and television news reports throughout the world (Figure 4.1).

There is a trite saying sometimes uttered by those slightly burned by the media's too glaring light, "Any publicity is good publicity." For even though most of the news articles and televised reports about the Benetton clothing company's advertising campaigns were negative, business boomed. The Italian magnate and politician Luciano Benetton, 74, sells about 100 million sweaters, shirts, and pants through some 5,500

outlets in 120 countries. Total sales in 2008 were more than $2.5 billion. But the strategy of using shocking images to generate editorial condemnation backfired when the company went too far portraying death row inmates almost as fashion models. Sears' executives decided to cancel a contract to sell Benetton sweaters on its shelves. After the controversy, Benetton apologized and promptly terminated the employment of Oliviero Toscani, who had been the creative director for the company and responsible for its campaigns for almost two decades.

■ SHOCK ADVERTISING

Because of photography's ability to arouse viewer interest and occasional condemnation, controversial and unusual pictures are sometimes used to shock potential customers to get attention. Although a sometimes risky marketing strategy,

The most important persuasive tool you have is integrity.

Hilary Hinton "Zig" Ziglar, b. 1926
MOTIVATIONAL SPEAKER, AUTHOR

Figure 4.1

Two models employed by Benetton wear the clothing of a priest and nun who kiss for the camera in this studio image. The picture upset many Catholics because it seemed to mock their religious beliefs.

Figure 4.2

"We Know What You Want, New York City," 2000, by Gerry Davey. If the larger-than-life size of the billboard doesn't attract attention, the advertiser hopes the topless model will. And yet, the potentially shocking picture seems to attract only the attention of a photographer.

company officials recognize the impact of shock that images can have on viewers. They get free publicity because the controversial ad campaigns generate stories in the news media as well as sales.

Brooke Shields probably began the manifestation of "soft porn" advertisements when she posed at age 14 in tight-fitting Calvin Klein jeans in 1980 and cooed, "Nothing comes between me and my Calvins." Klein has consistently used shock advertising as a way of generating enormous controversy and publicity. But sometimes he goes too far. A $6 million campaign was withdrawn in 1996 in response to a public outcry when teenage boys and girls were photographed in sexually provocative poses by Stephen Meisel, who took pictures of Madonna for her 1992 book *Sex.* Nevertheless, the Calvin Klein brand name generated news reports that acted like free advertising for the company.

Some art directors know that shock advertising can temporarily make a company a media standout and give a fresh, edgier look to a traditional company (Figure 4.2). Former *Playboy* magazine model Jenny McCarthy sat on a toilet, her panties below her knees, for the shoe company Candies. Media critic Collin Brooke noted that the ad's "taboo nature brought it attention." The 2009 spokesperson for Candies was Britney Spears, who has had her own personal dramas played out in the media. After Christian Dior introduced its "Addict" cosmetic line with perfume-crazed, open-mouthed, scantily clad, and sweaty models in 2002, the campaign was called "outrageous and irresponsible" by a member of Congress. But the 2005 "Addict

2" campaign featuring emaciated models was barely noticed by media critics. Sisley, a clothing brand owned by Benetton, showed young women with dark rings around their eyes "snorting" the white straps of a slinky dress from straws for its "Fashion Junkie" campaign, misspelled by its Chinese advertising company as "Fashioin." Humorous commercials can also get a company's product noticed. The Swedish vodka company Absolut, known for its advertising campaign in which it commissions artists to produce posters that incorporate the shape of the bottle in clever ways, asked comedian Zack Galifianakis (*Comedians of Comedy*, 2005, and *The Hangover*, 2009) to produce a series of web-only commercials that were as bizarre as they were funny and became a popular YouTube download (Weblink 4.1).

Linking sexual activity with products is a long-established tactic for advertisers. Ice cubes in a glass next to a bottle of Gilbey's gin spelled the word "SEX" and caused a brief uproar. Likewise, if you stacked two Pepsi cans produced in 1990 you could see the word "SEX," although a spokesperson said it was just a coincidence. An ad for Club Med, a singles resort company, can be seen on two levels—15 men and women enjoy various activities on a sunny tropical beach or 15 men and women enjoying themselves in various sexual poses on a sunny tropical beach. Executives of the preppy clothier Abercrombie & Fitch (A&F) discovered that sometimes controversy sparked by an advertising campaign does not sell more clothes. Nudity and sexual themes, some involving group sex, were depicted in the company's 2003 *Christmas Field Guide.* Many parents became enraged and boycotted the store. A media firestorm ensued, and A&F quietly withdrew the catalog. Meanwhile, Paris Hilton exploited her sex-crazed celebrity reputation in a 2005 commercial for the Carl's Jr. hamburger

chain (Weblink 4.2), which was hilariously parodied in an Accolo job-recruiting ad (Weblink 4.3). In 2008, a commercial that was leaked to the web, not produced or approved by JCPenney executives, was titled "Speed Dressing." It showed two teenagers removing their clothes and then dressing quickly in anticipation of doing the same in the girl's basement while her mother watched TV upstairs (Weblink 4.4). Saatchi & Saatchi, JCPenney's advertising agency, apologized for the spot.

Shockingly violent or sexual images used in ads are the culmination of corporate cynicism in which almost any sensational still or moving image is justified if it gets the attention of potential customers. But not all shock advertising is used for commercial reasons. Barnardo's, a London-based charity that aids more than 50,000 children and their families in more than 300 projects across Great Britain, is known for its striking and controversial campaigns. In 2000, an ad showed a baby about to inject heroin (Figure 4.3).

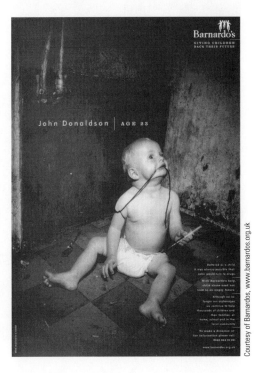

Figure 4.3

"John Donaldson Age 23." With harsh lighting and tilted frame amid a stark and dingy backdrop, the baby shocks a viewer and potential donor to the charity by its striking reality. Even though the child was a model, the campaign was called off because many were offended.

Another campaign featured five death and suicide scenes. One poster showed the legs of a fictional victim lying on the bloody floor of a grimy parking garage (Figure 4.4). The copy read: "From the age of three, Jane was neglected and a large part of her died. Her hope and self-esteem died. Her future died. 19 years later, after being lured into prostitution, she was beaten so badly by her pimp she died for real. What a waste." Despite the fact that donations grew by 5 percent and surveys showed public awareness of the charity had doubled, criticism of the graphic content of the ads caused Barnardo's executives to withdraw the campaign.

Other activist individuals and groups use shock images to get noticed. To protest invasive surgery as a cure for breast cancer, photographer Joanne Matuschka, who had a mastectomy, posed in 1993 for a cover story in the *New York Times Magazine* and created a series of posters showing her naked body from the waist up. People for the Ethical Treatment of Animals (PETA) often creates controversial advertising in order to gain the media's attention. The Anti-Defamation League and Germany's highest court denounced a campaign in 2003 produced by PETA that included photos of 60-square-foot panels of animals in cages next to photos

Figure 4.4

"Jane Kent. Died: Age 3 years." Like so much trash, the body of Jane Kent is cruelly discarded and photographed in a straight-on official way much like a police photographer's style. The eerie blue-green glow from a halogen light, the graffiti-inspired "MEAN" on a back window, and the text with a line through it add to a viewer's discomfort. The copy at the bottom reads, "NEXT time you read a story like Jane's in this newspaper (and you will) you'll say, 'this must never happen again.'" See color insert following page 178.

of Jewish concentration camp victims behind barbed wire, with the slogan "Holocaust on your plate." The German court called the campaign "an offense against human dignity." A PSA (public service announcement) commercial called "Sex and the Kitty," which was intended to promote animal birth control, was considered too racy for network television (Weblink 4.5). In 2009 PETA was again in the news for a PSA intended to promote vegetarianism, after NBC prohibited the spot from being shown during the Super Bowl telecast because it was considered too sexually suggestive (Weblink 4.6).

United Colors of Benetton 1991 spring/summer advertising campaign, OlivieroToscani

UNITED COLORS OF BENETTON.

■ BENETTON REMAINS SHOCK ADVERTISING'S LEADER

Benetton's target audience has always been young 18- to 24-year-olds, who are perhaps more socially conscious clothing buyers than other age groups. Beginning in 1989, Benetton used photographs in catalogs, store posters, and billboards to promote the company's idea of multicultural harmony. In all the advertising pictures, the only copy on the page was the Benetton logo. Later, a telephone number was added so that those interested could order a subscription to Benetton's monthly magazine *Colors*. Images of an African woman breast-feeding an Anglo baby, an African child resting on several Anglo teddy bears, a close-up of African and Anglo hands cuffed together, and an African and an Anglo child sitting side by side on matching toilets symbolically emphasized racial harmony and equivalence (Figure 4.5).

In 1991, the Benetton campaign switched to more overtly political images. One ad showed a picture of several rows of crosses in a cemetery. The ad was

banned in Italy, France, Great Britain, and Germany. Arab countries refused to print a picture of African, Anglo, and Asian children sticking their tongues out at the camera. Members of the Catholic Church were outraged that a picture of a priest and nun kissing was used in an advertisement. During this era, though, no picture received as much attention as that of a child photographed fresh from the womb of her mother. This image was printed on billboards, but was banned in Italy and Great Britain.

Never one to rest on previous publicity-seeking achievements, creative director Oliviero Toscani embarked on other Benetton campaigns that used previously published news photographs. The long list of disturbing images without context or explanation included a woman sobbing over the bloody body of a Mafia victim that was published only in Italy, a mercenary soldier holding the thigh bone of a human, the image of Albanian refugees escaping on an Italian ship, a red-eyed duck coated with oil after a recent spill, a Zulu woman with

Figure 4.5

Benetton has long maintained that its advertising campaigns attract attention and promote racial harmony. However, many have criticized their choice of images. Dr. Bette Kauffman, a professor at the University of Louisiana at Monroe, writes, "The black woman's face is completely confined, contained, imprisoned by the white man's hands and forceful kiss. Indeed, for his hand to cover her forehead like that, he has to have her entire head trapped in his left arm. This would be a problematic image if the woman were white! The goofy 'smile' on her face does nothing to combat the impression that she has no say in this matter."

albinism who appeared embarrassed next to two brown-skinned women who appear to shun her, an Indian couple wading through flood waters, South American children working as laborers, a man sprawled on the ground while being forced to submit to a radio interview by men on top of him, and the picture that has been called "the most shocking photo used in an ad," David Kirby surrounded by family members shortly before his death due to HIV/AIDS (Figure 4.6).

Ohio University student Therese Frare had been photographing in the Pater Noster House in Columbus, a hospice care home where Kirby received treatment. Kirby allowed her to take pictures of him that were to accompany a story for a school project. Their relationship eventually led to the moving, deathbed image that caused little reaction as an editorial picture in *Life*. Benetton executives saw the picture after it won the World Press Photo Budapest Award and came in second place in the association's general news category. Kirby's parents, Bill and Kay, gave permission to Benetton to

use the image in its ad campaign because they thought it would raise HIV/AIDS awareness around the world. Benetton executives donated $50,000 to the Pater Noster House to furnish and renovate the facilities.

David Kirby was from Stafford, Ohio, a small town of only 94 residents. Lured by the prospect of a better life, he traveled west after high school and eventually ended up in California in the 1980s. He soon lost touch with his family. But after contracting HIV/AIDS, Kirby telephoned his parents and asked if he could return home. He wanted to die with family members around him. Although there is no known cure, medications can extend the length and quality of life of those with the disease today. Kirby's parents immediately welcomed him back. His return to the town, however, caused panic among many residents who were uneducated about the disease. The emergency workers who took him to the hospital later burned everything in the ambulance that Kirby had touched. Schoolchildren screamed in horror about an "AIDS monster" living

Figure 4.6

David Kirby, 32, is on his deathbed surrounded by grieving family members. Therese Frare's photograph is an unforgettable emotional moment. But the green logo of Benetton makes it clear that the image is intended not only to make people care but to remind viewers to buy clothing.
See color insert following page 178.

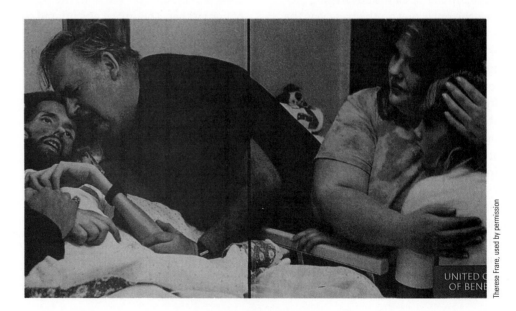

near them. But Kirby didn't shrink from the cruel characterizations. He often went door to door to educate neighbors about himself and HIV/AIDS. As an activist, he did much to calm the fears of Stafford's residents.

When the disease progressed to its conclusion, the 32-year-old Kirby was at the hospice with his family. Frare took the picture of Kirby surrounded by his father, sister Susan, and niece Sarah openly weeping over the loss of their loved one. His mother was in the next room crying.

The picture is a riveting moment in which a family faced with unspeakable tragedy is united by their grief. Barb Cordle, who was the volunteer director at the Pater Noster House and who helped care for Kirby, said that "the picture in the ad has done more to soften people's hearts on the AIDS issue than any other I have ever seen. You can't look at that picture and hate a person with AIDS. You just can't." But others, particularly HIV/AIDS activists, looked at the picture and felt horror, anger, and outrage over the image being used in an advertisement. They cite the use of the picture as another example of a large corporation exploiting a personal tragedy to sell a product. They wondered why a phone number for HIV/AIDS information could not be included in the ad if an 800 number was printed so that customers could obtain the company's new catalog. Critics asked whether using such an emotionally powerful image for commercial purposes without written copy in the advertisement to explain the meaning of the picture is ever morally acceptable.

The picture generated much discussion about shock advertising on television talk shows and in newspaper and magazine articles. The controversy over the image swirled around its use in the advertise-

ment. Such a narrow discussion ignored the fact that Frare's image was a sensitive example of the best photojournalism could offer. Nevertheless, because of all the media attention, more than one billion people around the world probably saw the Kirby family scene. But interest in the controversy didn't necessarily mean that more people became educated about HIV/AIDS around the world.

Peter Fressola, Benetton's director of communications and the person responsible for the company's publicity, asserted that the reason for the ad campaign was to make people think, to get them to talk about serious issues, and to promote worldwide multiculturalism. Toscani also wanted to expand the way advertisements were used. He believed that ads could be used to inform and spark commentary about serious issues. "Advertising can be used to say something that is real about things that exist," said Toscani. Both Fressola and Toscani admitted that they also wanted to create advertising that broke traditional banal presentations in order to focus more attention on the company. Without doubt, the campaign was a tremendous success. Estimated worldwide sales jumped 10 percent, or by more than $100 million, from 1991 to 1992 during the controversy.

■ END OF AN ERA FOR BENETTON?

But it was a $20 million advertising campaign launched in an issue of *Talk* magazine in January 2000 that caused Benetton to rethink the philosophy behind shock advertising. *Talk* contained a 96-page booklet entitled "We, on Death Row."

With the bright green Benetton logo interspersed on several pages, photographer Toscani posed 26 death row inmates from across the United States like models. None wore Benetton clothing. They simply answered questions about their favorite foods, activities, their mothers, and fear of execution. Benetton expressed hope that the campaign, which included billboards and pages in other national magazines, would draw attention to the issue of executions in America (Weblink 4.7). With its death penalty, the United States is a member of an exclusive group of countries that includes Afghanistan, China, Iran, Iraq, and North Korea. Regardless, many were outraged by the advertising supplement, particularly the families of those killed by the inmates.

Benetton was accused of glamorizing the murderers while ignoring their crimes. One outraged couple decided to fight back. Donata and Emery Nelson saw the image of Victor Dewayne Taylor on a billboard. Taylor kidnapped, sodomized, and murdered their teenage son along with

his friend. The Nelsons started a petition and began picketing branches of the Sears department store that had recently begun selling Benetton clothing. Donata Nelson explained, "I know they have strange ads for Benetton, but how low can they go? They've sunk about as low as the men on death row." Sears executives canceled the multimillion-dollar deal with Benetton and quit selling its clothing in about 800 outlets. In addition, the attorney general of Missouri, Jay Nixon, filed a lawsuit against the company, alleging that Benetton misrepresented its intent when gaining access to four murderers within a Missouri prison.

Faced with an enormous blitz of unfavorable publicity and a trial, the case was settled when Benetton paid $50,000 to a fund for victims of crimes in Missouri. Benetton also sent letters to the families of victims of the Missouri inmates in which the company expressed its regret for any pain the campaign may have caused them. Nevertheless, defending the campaign, Benetton said, "We wanted to attack the policy of the death penalty. We knew that a debate could emerge from our advertising but nevertheless we wanted to test and see what type of debate would emerge. A debate, as with our previous AIDS pictures, emerged." After 18 years of a controversial yet creative partnership, art director Toscani and Benetton parted ways.

Perhaps to rehabilitate the company's image, Benetton worked with the United Nations (the UN), which has no advertising budget, to bring social issues through media campaigns to the attention of consumers. In 2001, Benetton produced images for the "International Year of Volunteers," and in 2003 a $15 million campaign called "Food for Life" showed portraits of people from around

Figure 4.7

An HIV/AIDS reference in this studio photograph for Benetton using a male model provoked protests from various Jewish groups upset over the use of a tattoo that resembled a Holocaust victim's markings.

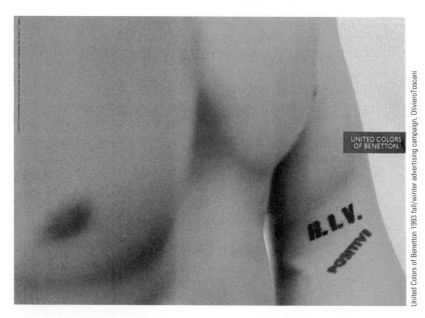

UNITED COLORS OF BENETTON.

United Colors of Benetton 1993 fall/winter advertising campaign, Oliviero Toscani

the world who received food from the U.N. (Figure 4.7). Since that time, the company has managed to stay out of the glare of media controversy.

However, since 2005, Toscani has been in the news. His photographs of men "participating in homosexual behavior" were used in a campaign for Ra-Re, an Italian clothing brand. The next year he ran unsuccessfully for a seat in the Italian parliament, perhaps inspired by Luciano Benetton, who was an Italian senator. In 2007 he introduced a new campaign called "No-l-ita," meant to be associated with the Vladimir Nabokov novel *Lolita* about a young seductress. The campaign featured French model Isabelle Caro, who has suffered from anorexia nervosa since she was 13 years old. At one point her five-foot, five-inch frame weighed only 55 pounds (Weblink 4.8). An Italian media watchdog group said it "breached its code of conduct" and banned billboards of her nude, emaciated body. However, Italian health minister Livia Turco said the billboards promoted "responsibility towards the problem of anorexia."

■ THE FINE LINE BETWEEN PERSUASION AND PROPAGANDA

Regardless of how you assign motives to actions, the Benetton campaigns that use editorial pictures in advertisements to generate enormous publicity highlight an important feature of mass communication: The fields of advertising, public relations, and journalism always have been closely related. The blurring between corporate and editorial interests is one of the most pressing concerns of media critics today.

Persuasion uses factual information and emotional appeals to change a person's mind and to promote a desired behavior. In contrast, propaganda uses one-sided and often nonfactual information or opinions that appear to be facts, along with emotional appeals, to change a person's mind and promote a desired behavior. Most information, whether factual or not, is communicated through the mass media. More and more, that information relies on the emotional appeal inherent in visual presentations.

In 1922 the journalist and media critic American Walter Lippmann published *Public Opinion*. It stressed the need for images to change a person's attitude. "Pictures have always been the surest way of conveying an idea," wrote Lippmann, "and next in order, words that call up pictures in memory." Recognizable symbols used in visual presentations will become long-lasting memories with the power to change attitudes if viewers have a chance to actively think about the content of the image and relate it to their own situation. All human communication—whether advertising layouts, lectures from parents and professors, closing arguments by lawyers in a trial, or campaign speeches—uses persuasion and sometimes propaganda in an attempt to mold or change a listener or viewer's attitude. Communications educator James Carey says that "communication is fundamentally and essentially a matter of persuasion, attitude change, behavior modification, and socialization through the transmission of information" (Figure 4.8).

■ *The Role of Persuasion*

In the 4th century BCE, Aristotle was the first to write about the art of persuasion. He defined it as communication designed to influence listeners' choices. According

Figure 4.8

As with the Benetton image of David Kirby, the advertising photograph for the Kenar clothing company is meant to alert the public about HIV/AIDS. But what is the connection between supermodel Linda Evangelista, seven older women wearing black dresses, an empty wooden chair, and the HIV/AIDS issue? The striking image attracts attention, but says nothing about the medical emergency to most people walking along Times Square in New York City.

Courtesy of Paul Martin Lester

to Aristotle, persuasion has three components: ethos, logos, and pathos. Ethos refers to a source's credibility. A professor for a well-known university will usually be more believable speaking about the state of the economy than someone nick-named "Joe the Plumber." Logos refers to the logical arguments used to persuade an individual. Whatever is being communicated should fit your personal view of how the world works. If the information seems far-fetched, you may reject the argument from the onset. Pathos refers to emotional appeals used in the persuasive argument. Testimonials from those with direct knowledge of a situation are often the most effective statements. Images of animals and children suffering, if used sparingly, also can be persuasive. Aristotle thought that if a speaker is believable or imbued with authority, uses factual arguments in a reasoned presentation, and gains an audience's attention through emotional means, persuasion is possible. The Canadian singer Sarah McLachlan participated in an effective PSA video to help prevent animal cruelty, which

featured sad-eyed cats and dogs looking right in the camera with her song "Angel" playing in the background (Weblink 4.9). Since the ad began airing in 2006, the American Society for the Prevention of Cruelty to Animals has received more than $30 million in donations.

Persuasion is a socially accepted way of attempting to change individuals' attitudes. In a pluralistic, democratic society, the government most commonly attempts to persuade the public through the news media. When the president introduces a new budget, the government mobilizes its huge public relations bureaucracy to "sell" the plan to the U.S. Congress and the American people. The president and the administration use the print, broadcast, and web media to communicate their ideas. Such a system naturally leads to tension between the government and the media, especially if independent journalists disagree with the government's message and report their findings.

Charlie Fisher of MoveOn.org created a PSA commercial, "Child's Play," that

CBS executives declined to show during the Super Bowl game in 2004. Because of the controversy, CNN aired the spot as part of a news segment. The short film is an excellent example of Aristotle's pathos because children are portrayed working dead-end, boring jobs in order to pay off the country's trillion-dollar deficit (Weblink 4.10).

■ *The Role of Propaganda*

The word propaganda started out as a neutral term, without negative connotations. It simply meant a way to spread or *propagate* an idea to a large population. In the 17th century, the Roman Catholic Church set up the *Congregation for Propagating the Faith* as an effort to bring more members into the church. But subsequently, its use by governments intent on conveying their version of the truth to citizens and enemies alike has given the term a pejorative connotation that can't be ignored. Whereas persuasion is the art of convincing someone that your position is correct through factual information, propaganda is thought of as the duping of an unsuspecting public through misleading or false information. The word has long been associated with the thought-control techniques used by totalitarian regimes, but critics have expanded the definition to include many of the persuasion techniques utilized by all governments and large corporations to persuade an unsuspecting public. Sociologist Harold Lasswell said that "both advertising and publicity fall within the field of propaganda." Media critic John Merrill enlarged the definition to include journalism, saying that "three-fourths of all media content . . . contains propaganda for some cause, idea, institution, party or person." In the end, the best definition of propaganda may be the use of spoken, written, pictorial, or musical representations to influence thought and action through debatable techniques.

Figure 4.9

"Together We Win," c. 1917, by James Montgomery Flagg. This World War I propaganda poster shows men of the Army, Navy, and industry in lockstep, with clenched fists and eager smiles, ready to wage war in Europe. More than 116,000 American members of the military were killed in the war, and more than 200,000 wounded. Although a serious artist, illustrator, and cartoonist, the American James Flagg is best known for his poster work.

Library of Congress, Prints and Photographs Division, LC-USZC4-1660

Figure 4.10

"I Want You for U.S. Army," c. 1917, by James Montgomery Flagg. Considered to be Flagg's most famous poster because it introduced Uncle Sam, a symbol of America to the public, it was an appropriation of an earlier work by the British illustrator Alfred Leete.

Library of Congress, Washington, D.C. [LC-USZC4-3859]

Figure 4.11

"Britons Join Your Country's Army!" 1914, by Alfred Leete. Since the striking face of Field Marshal Horatio Herbert Kitchener was so recognizable to British citizens of the day, his name did not need to be included on the recruitment poster. As with the Flagg version, the steely and direct eye contact and pointing finger is effective as it personalizes the message. The number of British military killed in World War I was more than one million, with over two million wounded. On a diplomatic mission to Russia in 1916, the armored cruiser was struck by a mine and sank. Only 12 crewmen of the 655 on board survived. The field marshal's body was never found.

© Daniel Deme / epa / Corbis

Beginning in earnest from the beginning of the 20th century, visual propaganda could be found in colorful and visually eye-catching political posters. Above the banner "TOGETHER WE WIN," a World War I sailor and soldier are arm-in-arm with a brawny steel worker carrying a sledgehammer (Figure 4.9). It was painted by American illustrator James Montgomery Flagg, who is better known for his recruitment poster of a stern Uncle Sam pointing his finger at a viewer (Figure 4.10). Flagg's "Sam" composition was based on a poster created three years earlier by illustrator Alfred Leete depicting the British military leader Lord Kitchener pointing his finger at a potential recruit (Figure 4.11). During World War II, a poster of a strong and confident woman under the words "We Can Do It!"—which was created by J. Howard Miller and modeled on a photograph of Geraldine Doyle—symbolized female factory workers who helped the war effort (Figure 4.12). After the popular American artist Norman Rockwell painted a similar

woman, she became known as "Rosie the Riveter."

In 1933 the Third Reich of Nazi Germany established the Ministry of Propaganda with Joseph Goebbels as its head. Probably most known for its classic propaganda movie *Triumph of the Will* by filmmaker Leni Riefenstahl, dramatizing Adolph Hitler during the 1934 Nazi Party Congress in Nuremberg, the Ministry was also responsible for poster production. Typical was one that showed a photograph of Hitler in a heroic stance in front of an army of swastika flag carriers, guided by light from the heavens, with, ironically, the dove of peace and the words, "Long live Germany!" (Figure 4.13). Another, labeled "LIBERATORS," is a complicated collection of visual symbols. A Ku Klux Klan hooded robotic giant meant to be the United States is in the act of destroying a city. With two muscular arms, one holding an LP record and the other a money bag, and two additional arms with one holding a machine gun and the other a grenade, the poster alludes to America's presumed racism, Jewish sympathies, and obsession with beauty, consumerism, and entertainment (Figure 4.14).

The Vietnam War sparked a different genre of the art form, the anti-war poster. An anonymous British artist created "Vietnam Skeleton," a clever variation of Flagg's Uncle Sam with the poster torn open to reveal a menacing skeleton (Figure 4.15). On the opposite end of the anti-war continuum is the simple graphic of a flower that includes the text "War is not healthy for children and other living things." Created by printmaker Lorraine Schneider, it became a powerful icon for the anti-war movement (Weblink 4.11). In 2005, Schneider's daughter Carol gave a necklace with the design to anti–Iraq War protestor Cindy Sheehan.

■ VISUAL PERSUASION IN ADVERTISING

Media critic and educator Everette Dennis defines advertising as "any form of non-personal presentation and promotion of ideas, goods, and services by an identified sponsor." The advertising industry in the United States employs more than 400,000 people and generates more than $650 billion in annual billings worldwide. According to Dennis, advertising benefits society because it funds most of the media, provides consumer information in the form of public service announcements, and stimulates the economy (Figure 4.16).

It is estimated that the average television viewer spends three years of her total life watching commercials. As such, visual messages are vital in those communications. Effective advertisers, therefore, make use of the semiotic code of metonymy. Through words, images, and situations, they want the potential customer to make assumptions about the ads they see related to their own behavior. A Johnnie Walker Black Label scotch ad that shows the opened gate of a long lawn headed to the front door of a three-story mansion is meant to convey the assumption that if you buy the alcohol you will be living like those inside the house. Likewise, other alcohol manufacturers, particularly Skyy vodka out of San Francisco, pose models in sexually suggestive scenarios to link consumption with sex.

Out of necessity, advertisers are also becoming more creative about where their ads are placed. With digital video recorders (DVRs) such as those made by TiVo, viewers can control what they

National Archives

watch and skip traditional commercials. As more and more consumers use the device, advertisers have to find clever ways to plug their products. For the show "How I Met Your Mother," CBS put life-sized pictures of two main characters on elevator doors. The network also stenciled ads for "CBS Mondays," "The Amazing Race," and "CSI" on eggshells. The rum brand Captain Morgan produced a small poster to stick to the door of a men's room in a bar that read, "Got a little CAPTAIN in you?" In 2009, the fast-food chicken chain KFC paid $3,000 to fill 350 potholes on the streets of Louisville, Kentucky, and was allowed to stamp each smooth surface with a chalk stencil that read, "Re-freshed by KFC."

Motion picture and television cross promotions are popular as well. Print ads for milk featured the Incredible Hulk. Hugh Jackman's Wolverine character in *X-Men: The Last Stand* (2006) was placed on a Diet Dr. Pepper can. Angelina Jolie's face hovered over a Jeep like the one she drove

Figure 4.12
"We Can Do It!" 1942, by J. Howard Miller. Since the reasons for Americans to enter World War II were clearer than those for WWI—after all, the country had been attacked at Pearl Harbor, Hawaii—recruiting posters were not as vital to the war effort as works that bolstered morale and home front efforts. J. Howard Miller, an American graphic artist employed by the Westing-house Company, created one of the most enduring images from the era. Based on a picture taken by a United Press International (UPI) photographer of Geraldine Doyle working in a factory, it was little seen during the war, as it was only shown for two weeks at Westinghouse. However, the image is widely used today as a symbol of feminism. See color insert following page 178.

Figure 4.13

"Es lebe Deutschland!" (Long live Germany). Adolf Hitler, the leader of Germany's Nazi Party, resolutely carries the party's flag and stands ahead of and above his soldiers. The title of the poster is printed in a blackletter, German-style typeface. The tilted horizon indicates the struggle will be hard, but the bird and the streaks of sunlight bursting through the clouds that frame Hitler's head are indexical signs that at least he believed that God sanctified his mission of world dominance. The swastika symbol dates back to the Neolithic prehistoric period from about 5,000 BCE in the Middle East and Europe. Over the centuries it has been used by Indian cultures as a symbol for Hinduism and Buddhism. Today, its use is outlawed in Germany, except for religious purposes. See color insert following page 178.

Bildarchiv Preussischer Kulturbesitz / Art Resource, NY

in *Lara Croft: Tomb Raider* (2001). The characters of NBC's "The Office" met at a Chili's restaurant. Tom Hanks worked for FedEx in *Cast Away* (2000), with the movie acting like a long commercial for the shipping company. During the 2003 Super Bowl telecast, FedEx did one better and used a Hanks stand-in actor to recreate a plot line from the film for a commercial.

Having a celebrity spokesperson will almost always assure viewer interest, but if the message is not accurate the ploy can backfire (Figure 4.17). Australian actress Kerry Armstrong (*Reservations*, 2008, and *Mind the Gap*, 2005) and Coca-Cola were criticized for a 2009 magazine advertisement which claimed that it was a myth that the sugar water soda "makes you fat, rots your teeth, and is packed with caffeine." The Australian Competition and Consumer Commission, which oversees accuracy in advertisements, forced the cola company to print retractions in all of the major newspapers.

Product placement (showing a product) and product integration (having the product part of a show's plot) in motion

pictures and television programs have long been effective staples of advertising for a good reason. In 2005, television producers alone earned almost $1 billion from advertising placements. *Wings* (1927), the first movie given the Best Picture Academy Award, contained an ad for Hershey's chocolate. The consummate spy James Bond often drove fast cars provided by Aston-Martin and BMW. Sales of Reese's Pieces candies increased by 65 percent after moviegoers watched the alien in *E.T.: The Extra-Terrestrial* (1982) follow the candy trail. Seagram's, the parent company for Mumm's champagne, paid $50,000 for Cher to drink that brand in the movie *Moonstruck* (1987). Interestingly, the 1950s-era drama *Revolutionary Road* (2008), in which many of the actors smoked heavily in the movie, contained an ending credit message that explained tobacco companies gave no money. Reality TV shows, however, are the real masters of the strategy called "advertainment." The *Wall Street Journal* reported that "The Biggest Loser" and "American Idol" each had more than 3,000 brand name placements on their shows.

To help television executives and advertisers work more closely together, digital imaging technology can be used to place products into old television shows. Princeton Video Image Inc., the company that created the imaginary scrimmage and first down lines for televised football games, now produces "virtual product placements" for marketers. Besides being able to place ads only the television audience can see behind goal posts, home plates, soccer fields, and on NASCAR racetracks, the technology can be used to put products in scenes. Imagine a rerun of "Grey's Anatomy" in which the characters gather at "Joe's Bar" to be seen drinking Miller beer. Media critic Jeff Smith explains, "Product placement is one of the ways to reach a captive audience. If you work your product into a TV show or a film, it's impossible for the viewer to zap it out."

Technology can also bridge the analog and digital worlds. Based on a process first developed by the Japanese company Denso-Wave in 1994, Quick Response (QR) graphic tags can be put on billboards, print ads, and websites and then photographed by a user with a cell phone that has an application that can process the image. Product information, a discount coupon, website, or an e-mail or telephone number can be displayed on a user's cell phone. For example, the company 2D Sense (2Dsense.com) offers a free application for Apple's iPhone that allows users to read these graphic tags and create their own (Figure 4.18). These two-

Galerie Bilderwelt/Getty Images

Courtesy of Paul Martin Lester

Library of Congress Prints and Photographs Division, LC-USZC2-665

dimensional codes are a common sight in Japan. In 2007 the British band Pet Shop Boys included a QR tag with their single "Integral." When it is processed through a cell phone, users are sent to their website.

Figure 4.14
"Liberators," 1944. In this symbolic-laden World War II German propaganda poster, American culture is feared as much as its might if Germany loses the war. Prone citizens near a town's traditional water fountain await the onslaught of American music, superficial beauty, racism, Jewish interests, and violence. The little figure in the foreground with the large ears holds a sign that sarcastically reads in Dutch, "The USA will save European culture from extinction."
See color insert following page 178.

Figure 4.15 (right)
"I Want You for U.S. Army" (after James Montgomery Flagg), offset lithograph, United Kingdom, c. 1972. During the Vietnam War, an anonymous British illustrator composed an anti-war poster in which the Uncle Sam in James Flagg's World War I recruiting poster is supplanted by a symbol of death—a menacing skeleton.

Figure 4.16 (left)
More than 50 years after the Japanese seaport town of Hiroshima was devastated by an atomic bomb, the city is a vibrant commercial municipality with large billboards hawking products just as in most other downtown districts.
See color insert following page 178.

Figure 4.17

Although denied by R. J. Reynolds Tobacco Company officials, the cartoon character Joe Camel, or "Old Joe," was criticized for enticing young people to smoke by making the habit look fun and sophisticated. In 1997, under pressure from the U.S. Congress and anti-tobacco groups, Reynolds voluntarily ended its Joe Camel campaign in America. After the U.S. Congress enacted strict anti-tobacco legislation in 2009, Senator Richard Durbin of Illinois remarked, "Joe Camel has been sentenced and put away forever."

Figure 4.18

Two friends pose for a photograph. On the T-shirt of the man on the right is a Quick Response (QR) tag created from the application 2D Sense. If you take a picture of it using the program, a web browser will show his webpage. Initiated by Japanese inventors, QR tags are becoming more common in magazine and billboard advertisements.

Clever website marketers use a variety of methods to get their advertising message noticed. Since the 19th century, pop-up books for children with intricately folded designs that spring into a 3-D shape when a page is opened have been popular. Inspired by the technique for attracting attention, Waldo Hunt used the graphic gimmick in magazine ads from the 1960s. In the 2000s the method received a high-tech update. Studies show that most people ignore banner ads on websites or set web browsers to block such ads, so-called webitisers (advertisers on websites) are creating more obtrusive "in-your-face ads." David Hallerman, an industry analyst, explained, "the inherent nature of advertising is to annoy people enough so that they pay attention. Advertising rarely doesn't irritate." In addition to the usual "pop up" windows that appear over the intended information and "pop under" windows that are placed under a website's window so you see them after you think you have closed down your browser, three new types of ads were introduced in 2009: The "fixed panel," in which the ad moves up or down the

page as a user scrolls, the "XXL box" that allows users to see video commercials, and "pushdown" ads that open to show a larger ad. These types of windows are sometimes effective in attracting customers because it is difficult to ignore the message.

Other types of ads are difficult to ignore. A billboard displayed on an entire side of a multi-story building. These so-called "supergraphics" produced by SkyTag and other companies can be as much as 20 stories high. However, city governments and anti-billboard activists are working together to try to prevent these visual eyesores (Figure 4.19). In 2009 the clothing retailer XOXO employed two models in skimpy dresses to sit in a window display in its New York City store and engage in everyday lounging activities to the amusement of (mostly) men on the sidewalk.

Ads on a different scale can attract attention as well. A clever way to get a reader's attention was seen within a small, one-column space in *The New Yorker* magazine. The overhead view showed the results of a Mini Cooper that had just run into an ad for the canoe/kayak hybrid Poke Boat below it. No one was injured in the collision. Likewise, an ad for Quaker instant oatmeal showed a bike ramp with the logo printed on it in the lower-left corner of a newspaper page, and a boy shown from the shoulders down on a bicycle at the top-right of the same page. Without text of any kind, the boy on the bike is suspended in white space. It is an arresting image with a satisfying "aha" moment when you put the two sections together and read the tagline, "Give your kids a boost." Other techniques blur the line between editorial and advertising. Stick-on ads and foldout flaps can be found on *ESPN The Magazine* covers and the *Los Angeles Times* front page, whereas *Esquire* magazine used mix-and-match covers with famous faces on its cover for an ad. Voicing concern for this practice was Sid Holt, chief executive of the American Society of Magazine Editors, "Everyone has to be able to tell the difference between advertising and editorial, and if you can't tell there's a difference, there's a problem."

Another ploy by marketing directors that blurs the line between reality and fiction for motion pictures is to create a website that strongly implies a movie's fictional content is real. Producers of *The Blair Witch Project* (1999) generated enormous interest in their movie before its release date by providing information on its website that made many moviegoers believe that the film was a recreation of actual events. Likewise, for the forgettable film *Godsend* (2004), a science fiction/supernatural story about a distraught couple who agrees to have their dead son cloned, its website looked so real and sincere that many didn't make the connection with the motion picture and believed there really was an American institution where human cloning took place. When parents who had lost a child called a number provided on the site, they were told of the hoax. Negative publicity about the film probably generated more viewer interest because of the controversy. Exploiting ancient Mayan mythology and end of the world fears, executives at Sony Pictures encouraged phony science websites and misinformation in order to promote *2012* (2009), a motion picture that fictionalizes the destruction of Earth. Cleverly advertising a movie using web resources that cause concern about a public panic is not an acceptable use of the medium.

Courtesy of Paul Martin Lester

Figure 4.19

Workers on a platform lift change an advertisement on a building in Hollywood from Disney's G-Force (2009) to the musical Mary Poppins. These huge, multi-story ads are controversial; some say they are urban eyesores and distractions for drivers.

■ VISUAL PERSUASION IN PUBLIC RELATIONS

Opinion makers, whether in government or business, long ago learned that what is reported in a news story sometimes isn't as important as how it is presented. Public relations specialists try to influence news reporters in the hope that favorable coverage will result. Public relations people also attempt to influence public opinion positively about a particular product, company, or issue. The public relations industry helps gain the public's support for issues and services identified as important by corporate executives. As part of that process, public relations employees contact journalists to help them identify important stories by giving them tips. Media ethicist John Merrill asserts that 50 percent of all the stories presented in the media—whether print or broadcast—probably are generated initially by a public relations person.

Politicians and their publicity handlers have readily embraced what has been called a photographic opportunity, shortened to "photo op." The photo op is a stage-managed, highly manipulated still or moving image. A successful photo op appears to look real but is actually a contrived fiction in which the source, his or her handlers, and sometimes the photographers themselves orchestrate the timing, location, subject, props (telephone, pen and paper, podium, and so on), lighting, foreground and background elements (banners, signs, supporters, and so on), and sometimes even the selection and placement of the photographers covering the "event." Although traditionally the photo op is thought of as a way to get positive publicity for a politician, the photographic genre can include all types of so-called media or pseudo-events that might include owners celebrating their store openings to portraits of corporate leaders in their offices. As the writer and political commentator George F. Will wrote, "A photo opportunity, properly understood, is someone doing something solely for the purpose of being seen to do it. The hope is that those who see the resulting pictures will not see the elements of calculation (not to say cunning) that are behind the artifice."

One of the most infamous photo ops devised by the Bush administration probably sounded like a good idea at the time, but it backfired. Less than two months after the invasion of Iraq by American and coalition forces in March 2003, President Bush gave a rousing speech aboard the aircraft carrier *USS Abraham Lincoln* under a large banner that read "Mission Accomplished." In the speech, he announced the end of all major combat operations in the Iraq War. But after the war dragged on for years, and thousands of American soldiers and Iraqis were killed and wounded, the stunt was criticized (Figure 4.20). Later, after Hurricane Katrina slammed into the Gulf Coast and flooded New Orleans in August 2005, Bush was pictured flying over the stricken land from the comfort of Air Force One (Figure 4.21). The photo op made him look detached and clueless, and helped send his approval rating to the low level he maintained until the end of his presidency.

In 2009 the Obama Administration was embarrassed by negative publicity over

Figure 4.20

With a banner that read "Mission Accomplished" and Navy personnel carefully arranged on the deck of the USS Abraham Lincoln, *President Bush participates in what came to be one of his most embarrassing photo ops of his presidency.*

Paul Morse / White House Photo

Figure 4.21

In a photo op arranged by Senior Advisor Karl Rove, President Bush looks out the window from Air Force One at the damage to New Orleans and the Gulf Coast two days after Hurricane Katrina struck land in 2005. For many, the picture symbolized the ineffectual response from government officials following the catastrophe.

Figure 4.22

In the first photo op controversy of the Obama Administration, a low-flying Air Force aircraft (it is only called "Air Force One" when the President is aboard) was photographed in 2009 over the Statute of Liberty, but not before frightening residents of Manhattan who thought another 9/11-type terrorist attack was taking place. The White House official responsible for the photo op later resigned from his position. See color insert following page 178.

an ill-advised photo op. Air Force One, but without the president on board, flew over Manhattan accompanied by two military jets with the objective of capturing a photo. It caused many residents and onlookers in New York City, site of the September 11th terrorist attack on the World Trade Center, to panic (Figure 4.22). President Obama, who had no knowledge of the flight ahead of time, was reportedly infuriated by the photo shoot that cost American taxpayers $328,835. The director of the White House Military Office who was responsible resigned from his position.

The public relations profession is criticized because it sometimes hides its commercial intent from unsuspecting readers and viewers. It can rarely be determined whether a persuasive public relations person originally suggested a news story to a reporter. More often than not, because of time constraints, budget cutbacks, and the history of commercialism of the mass media, a public relations person's information in printed and video news releases are published or aired with little criticism or cross-checking of facts. Moreover, social media websites such as Facebook, Digg, Twitter, and popular blogs are being used by savvy public relations personnel to get the word out to influential networkers to announce a birthday party, an innovative technology, a political campaign, or a website.

Fortunately, the public relations industry is filled with many bright, articulate, and caring individuals who work hard to overcome the historical stereotypes of the publicity hounds who spend their time glad-handing at cocktail parties and hacks who churn out press releases dictated by management. Concern about negative perceptions of the industry led to the 1948 formation of the Public Relations Society of America (PRSA), with student chapters around the world (Weblink 4.12). The society established a code of ethics, accredits public relations professionals and academic programs, promotes scholarly research in the field, and showcases successful public relations activities. Consequently, the public relations profession gets better publicity.

■ VISUAL PERSUASION IN JOURNALISM

Large, bold headlines with big, dramatic pictures, and short, easy-to-read stories are tactics used by newspaper graphic designers to attract new readers and hold onto the ones they have. Such displays are not new. When Tom Howard snuck a camera into the death chamber in 1928 and photographed Ruth Snyder, the first woman executed in the United States since 1899, the *New York Daily*

Figure 4.23

After Ruth Snyder was convicted of arranging for the murder of her husband, she became the second woman executed by the electric chair at Sing Sing prison in New York. The picture is blurry because Tom Howard, a Chicago Tribune *photographer brought in by the* Daily News *so state officials wouldn't know him, made at least two exposures with a hidden camera strapped to his leg. The newspaper's illustrator also retouched it. Nevertheless, the front page, with its dramatic headline and large photograph, is an iconic symbol of journalistic sensationalism. As an attention-getting combination of word and picture, it also acts as an advertisement for the publication.*

New York Daily News

News devoted about one fifth of the front page to the word, "DEAD!" and the rest of the page for the chilling photograph (Figure 4.23). Equally dramatic were the word and picture choices by the *New York Journal American* after the German airship, the *Hindenburg*, exploded in 1937. These displays are not only sensational and catch a customer's eye, they also act as advertisements for the publication. The message is: We present the news in exciting visual ways better than our competition. Television news stations engage in the same practice when they lead a newscast with dramatic live digital video and then later use that footage in commercials that promote the stations themselves. With subscriptions and advertising dollars dwindling, newspaper executives, journalists, and readers are seriously concerned with whether the news will cease to be printed on paper in the near future. What is clear is that simply altering the typography and making photographs larger will not be sufficient to save the news(paper) industry.

Many media critics and journalists look to the web for examples of the future of newspapers and serious, investigative stories. Almost every traditional newspaper in the world, from a large, metropolitan daily to a small, weekly publication, has a website that either copies a version of its print edition or creates exclusive content for its online editions. Journalists take pictures, shoot digital video, and record digital audio to include with copy and links to additional information. This type of display is designed for those who have lost, or never had, the news*paper* reading habit and are comfortable with gaining information from a computer monitor.

■ BACK TO DAVID KIRBY

Look at the Benetton advertisement of David Kirby on his deathbed surrounded by family members one more time (Figure 4.24). The original caption in *Life* magazine read, "THE END. After a three-year struggle against AIDS and its social stigma, David Kirby could fight no longer. As his father, sister and niece stood by in anguish, the 32-year-old founder and leader of the Stafford, Ohio, AIDS foundation felt his life slipping away. David whispered, 'I'm ready,' took a labored breath, then succumbed."

The caption for the Benetton ad read, "United Colors of Benetton."

The words in the journalistic context of *Life* magazine are meant to stir the reader's emotions, to educate the reader about a family's courage and love for each other, and perhaps to persuade the reader to do something tangible about the HIV/AIDS crisis. The words in the advertising context for Benetton are meant to sell sweaters.

Before assigning nothing but positive motives to the editors of *Life* magazine, take a look at what else is on the page with the Kirby family. Therese Frare's black-and-white image is on a double-page spread inside a black border framed by a thin, white rule. In 2003 the image was included in *Life* magazine's collection, *100 Photos that Changed the World*, along with Joseph Nicéphore Niépce's first photo and Dorothea Lange's "The Migrant Mother" (Weblink 4.13).

The cutline is at the lower left of the picture. The text is printed in white and set inside a black box. But stuck between the two pages—attached between the image of Kirby and his father on the left page and his sister and niece on the right—is a cheery insert printed with colorful holiday graphics. It is a promotion to get the reader to subscribe to the magazine. "Give the gift that shows you care . . ." the copy reads, "all year long. Give LIFE." When you turn the little card over it reads next to the crying face of David Kirby's father, "With LIFE

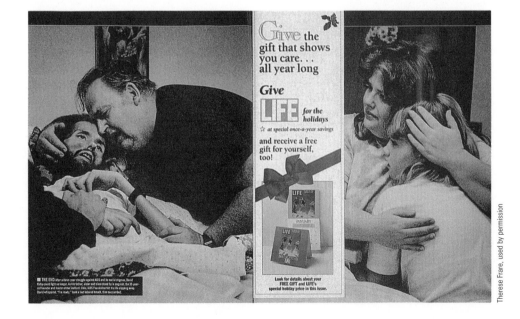

Therese Frare, used by permission

Figure 4.24

David Kirby's private family tragedy was published originally in a November 1990 issue of Life *magazine. The black and white tones give a documentary look to the photograph but contrast starkly with the brightly colored holiday advertisement insert. See color insert following page 178.*

your holiday shopping's a snap." Except, of course, if you are dead. Although explained away by a *Life* executive as a coincidence, the placement of the card that must be turned by a reader in order to see the entire Kirby photograph is a perfect location to get maximum attention for its own ad.

Advertising and journalism once again merge in a shockingly ironic and insensitive way.

■ KEY TERMS

- Advertising campaign
- Anorexia nervosa
- Blogs
- Caption
- Copy
- Death penalty
- Editorial picture
- HIV/AIDS

- Hospice
- Joe the Plumber
- *Life* magazine
- LP record
- News photograph
- Pater Noster House
- PSA
- World Press Photo

 To locate active URLs for the weblinks mentioned in this chapter, please go to the companion site at http://communication.wadsworth.com/lester5 and select the proper chapter.

Visual Stereotypes

Chapter 5

For many, Labor Day marks the end of the summer season. It is a U.S. holiday that recognizes the transition between lazy days full of relaxation and the start of a new season of productivity for students and workers alike. As that last picnic, last stroll along a trail, or last dive into a pool begins to fade into a pleasant memory, about 750 million viewers worldwide settle into comfortable chairs, turn on their television sets, and watch some or all of the 23-hour Jerry Lewis Muscular Dystrophy Association (MDA) telethon, the annual fund-raising program that has become a staple of the medium. The only other televised program that gets more viewers is the NFL's Super Bowl.

Jerry Lewis, 83, has been the national chairman of the MDA since 1952 and the emcee for the telecast since 1966. With his professional charm and slicked-back black hair, he introduces each perfor-mance, from comedians to singers, with the same level of enthusiasm, despite the many hours he has worked on the show.

Many Las Vegas performers are inter-spersed with filmed spots about muscular dystrophy (MD) research and people afflicted with the disease. Between danc-ers, singers, magicians, and comedians in the old theater tradition known as vaudeville, we see scientists in white lab coats mixing chemicals in test tubes, doc-tors talking passionately into the camera of the need for more money to further their research, and children in wheelchairs being pushed to their next physical ther-apy session. On stage, parents and other family members of these children talk with tears in their eyes about the shock of learning of their child's illness.

Filmed segments or cutaways to a local station's activities usually end with emotional monologues from Lewis. The

The whole idea of a stereotype is to simplify.

Chinua Achebe, b. 1930
NIGERIAN POET, NOVELIST, EDUCATOR

"poster child" for the year arrives in a wheelchair to the front of the small stage and recites a brief message. Lewis then delivers an emotional appeal for money. At the end of his performance, a spokesperson for a large corporation walks on stage, introduces a slickly produced video about the company's role in the fight against MD, and delivers a check in true photo op fashion. Lewis hoots with joy and announces that the check has a number "followed by lots of zeros." The lights flash, the audience applauds, and the camera zooms in to reveal the dancing numbers on the electronic tote board high above the stage as it registers a new total.

Muscular dystrophy is a name for several inherited diseases that affect the muscles attached to the skeleton. The most serious form of MD is called Duchenne, named for the French neurologist Guillaume Duchenne, who first described the condition in 1868. Duchenne MD affects only boys. The first sign of the

disease appears at about age four, when a child begins to have trouble walking. By age ten, the child must use a wheelchair. As the disease progresses, all the muscles eventually are affected, always causing a premature death. Without doubt, Duchenne MD is tragic, affecting one in 3,500 male births. Although the gene responsible for causing the disease has been identified, as yet there is no cure. In 2007 Dutch researchers announced that an experimental drug seemed to slow the disease's progress. However, the therapy costs as much as $250,000 per treatment and would need to be repeated several times during a lifetime.

The more than 40 other kinds of neuromuscular diseases do not receive as much emotional publicity because they are much less severe than Duchenne MD. These less life-threatening afflictions can affect both males and females. Despite numbness in the face and extremities, patients aided by physical therapy can lead long, productive lives, some with and some without the use of wheelchairs. Nevertheless, the public's stereotypical perception, promoted by the telethon, is that those with any type of muscular disease can't walk and always die prematurely (Figure 5.1).

To its credit, MDA gives money to further research and to sponsor worldwide scientific conferences. The organization also provides some funds for equipment, services, and summer camps for children. But the Muscular Dystrophy Association has been criticized for its high administrative costs. MDA has more than 1,300 paid staff employees, and its CEO earns about $350,000 a year. Charity Navigator, an independent organization that evaluates charities, gives MDA two out of four stars, the lowest rating compared with similar charities. Only 15 cents of every dollar donated goes to help those who need it.

Figure 5.1

It was rare for President Franklin Roosevelt to be photographed using a wheelchair because it was thought he would look weak, especially during wartime. Nevertheless, he probably didn't object to this picture because he thought it would never be released to the public. Taken in 1941 at Top Cottage, his private residence in Hyde Park, New York, he has his dog Fala on his lap while he entertains a friend's granddaughter.

FDR Library

The Jerry Lewis/MDA telethon almost always starts with an ironic twist. As a fundraiser that exists to help many who do not have full muscle function or who have other mobility challenges, the program usually begins with the most energetic activity that one can possibly do with two healthy legs–dance. Over the years the opening has been a production of men and women tapping, kicking, clogging, and stomping. For example, one year the opening featured STOMP!, a troupe of frenetic stomping dancers who smash garbage can lids and other objects on floors and other surfaces (Weblink 5.1). Imagine that you are watching the performance while sitting in a wheelchair, and you might start to understand why the telethon is criticized every year for insensitivity toward those whom it supposedly supports.

It is the "pity approach" to fund-raising that most irks those who use wheelchairs to navigate through their daily lives. In 1990, an essay Lewis wrote for *Parade* magazine caused controversy when he characterized persons with MD as "half a person." Although he later apologized for his remarks after a public outcry, Jerry Lewis made clear the connection between making money and exploiting pity. In 1994, former telethon poster children calling themselves "Jerry's Orphans" started to publicly object to the pity campaign by calling it a "pity-thon." Lewis also showed his contempt for those who criticize this Aristotle-based pathos tactic during an interview on the show "CBS Sunday Morning." In 2000 Lewis told correspondent Martha Teichner, "I'm telling about a child in trouble. If it's pity, we'll get some money. I'm giving you facts. Pity. You don't want to be pitied for being a cripple in a wheelchair? Stay in your house." Harriet Johnson, a lawyer from South Carolina with a neuromuscular disease, said that

Lewis's remark was an example of "shocking bigotry."

He has also sparked outrage by remarks on other subjects. In 2000, as he was receiving an award from the U.S. Comedy Arts Festival (now known as the Comedy Festival), he admitted that he didn't like female comics because each one is "a producing machine that brings babies in the world" and by implication shouldn't be telling jokes and performing skits. In 2007, during a telethon he jokingly described the son of a camera operator using an anti-gay slur. After news reports criticized him, he apologized. Nevertheless, in 2009 he received the Jean Hersholt Humanitarian Award, the honor given by the Academy of Motion Picture Arts and Sciences (AMPAS) at the Academy Award ceremonies for "outstanding contributions to humanitarian causes." The Oscar was presented to him by actor/comedian Eddie Murphy, who had reprised Lewis's role as the Nutty Professor. Lewis humbly and graciously accepted the award without causing controversy. In 2010 Lewis plans to direct a musical version of the 1963 comedy *The Nutty Professor* on Broadway.

For those who use wheelchairs, the telethon is an annual reminder of how mainstream media communicate stereotypical attitudes, even for a good cause. Those in wheelchairs aren't seen as active, independent, and normal. They are viewed as helpless and fragile individuals to be pitied—and who can exist only if a viewer picks up the telephone and pledges a donation.

■ REINFORCING STEREOTYPES WITH IMAGES

Whether an individual is identified because of gender, age, cultural heritage,

Courtesy of Paul Martin Lester

Figure 5.2

The girl posing for a photographer in a Southern California neighborhood reflects her age and social group. But she goes against the stereotype of a pretty girl in a pink dress by holding a toy (let's hope) submachine gun.

economic status, sexual orientation, or physical disability, the visual message generally communicated about that person often is misleading and false (Figure 5.2). Because pictures affect a viewer emotionally more than words alone do, pictorial stereotypes often become misinformed perceptions that have the weight of established facts. These pictures can remain in a person's mind throughout a lifetime.

When pictorial stereotypes are repeated enough times, they become part of a society's culture. Culture is a culmination of learned, mutually accepted rules that define communication for a group of people during a particular time period. People form attitudes about others, both within and outside their own culture, through direct experiences, interactions with family members and friends, educational institutions, and the media. Culture tells us what we should do to get along within a particular society as well as what our actions mean to others. Communication is easier when people share the same cultural meanings (e.g., speak

the same language or use the same visual symbolism).

Through everyday experiences, a person acquires a certain set of beliefs and attitudes about other people, places, objects, and issues. Perhaps as a youth you were punished by a high school principal and thus dislike all persons in positions of authority. Maybe you have heard that Mexico City has high pollution levels so you never want to visit there. Perhaps your father doesn't like to eat broccoli and so neither do you. Maybe someone you admire opposes capital punishment, influencing you to adopt that same attitude. What you believe, what you think is true, forms your attitudes. Attitudes are general and long-lasting positive or negative feelings. If information is limited or its source isn't trusted, a belief can become an enduring attitude that can lead to stereotypical generalizations. The goal of education is to teach an individual how to seek factual information and base beliefs and attitudes on reasoned conclusions.

To be successful, communication (from the Latin word for *commonness*) requires mutual understanding of the symbols used. By definition, different cultures attribute different meanings to similar actions. Consequently, members of one culture often are easy to identify and have trouble communicating with members of another culture. In a multicultural society, members of other cultures often are stigmatized because of their inability to use the symbols of the dominant culture. Dominant cultures are not designated by having the most members, but by having the most economic and political influence over an entire society. Dominant cultures can also have as members individuals who cross ethnic, racial, gender, and other lines.

Throughout the world, an estimated 17,000 distinct cultural groups almost never receive media attention within their societies. In Latin America, for example, 600 separate tribes live in lowland regions alone. In the United States, some 20 million people belong to so-called "fringe" religious groups, and 75 million classify themselves as belonging to more than 120 separate ethnic cultures. But the faces that most often appear in still photographs and moving images are Anglo. In 1790 the U.S. Census identified the country's four most numerous ethnic groups—German, Irish, English, and African. Those same four groups also headed the 2000 census. The dominant cultural groups—those with the most power and influence in the social structure, including the media—are the ones that control which images get seen. It is always to the advantage of the dominant groups to stereotype other groups in order to secure their dominance.

One of the chief functions of the brain is to categorize visual information into basic units that can be easily and quickly analyzed. Unfortunately, this trait of the brain also leads to instant categorization of people. Noticing a person's gender, age, ethnic background, and the like is perfectly natural. But having preconceived attitudes that may or may not be true about that person are learned and often misguided.

Stereotypical media coverage manifests itself as a sin of admission or omission. Media coverage of individuals who belong to a specific cultural group usually presents them as special cases to be pitied for their terrible living situations, admired for bettering themselves, or, most often, reviled for their violent criminal actions. The stories of hardworking, decent members of various cultural groups often are ignored. Accounts of their lives simply are not considered to be "news." Part of the problem with the media's portrayals of diverse groups is that few practicing journalists are from those groups. At least 86 percent of the daily newspapers in the United States do not have any diverse staff members and 78 percent have no diverse group members in management positions. Sensitivity to the stereotyping of ethnic and other groups isn't a high priority when newsrooms all exhibit the same skin color. In addition, schools of communication have few if any culturally diverse professors or students. A test for your own school or workplace is easily conducted— find the racial/ethnic percentages for your geographical area. The ratios would ideally be the same at school or work.

For example, the percentage of African Americans living in Orange County, California, is 2 percent. The percentage of African Americans who attend California State University, Fullerton, is about 3 percent, an acceptable number. Therefore, the percentage of African Americans playing on the basketball team should be between 2 and 3 percent. During the 2008–2009 season, African Americans comprised 71 percent of the team.

Obviously, such a large discrepancy indicates a racial issue that should be addressed.

■ SPECIFIC EXAMPLES OF STEREOTYPING

Every form of prejudice is based on the assumption that members of one group are better than members of another because of false opinions about physical, intellectual, and social characteristics. Throughout history, the dominant groups in societies have discriminated against various ethnic and other groups. Some groups have managed to overcome discrimination and become a part of the dominant societal force. Most others have not been so successful.

Almost any group you can think of has been the target of prejudice and discrimination at some time—children, older people, religious and political conservatives and liberals, people who are homeless, those who have disabilities, students, professionals, unemployed people, the poor and the rich, foreigners, city and country dwellers, people with Southern accents, people with Brooklyn accents—and on and on until every person can find his or her own category. Men must always be strong, have well-developed pecs, and be interested in women, hunting, and—as Full Throttle's "Get Your Man Out" commercial would want you to believe—energy drinks. Religious fundamentalists are fanatics. News photographers and paparazzi are "animals." Anglos are racists. Blind persons cannot live successfully alone, as reflected in a scene with Gene Hackman and Peter Boyle in Mel Brooks's *Young Frankenstein* (1974). Likewise, African Americans represent about 13 percent of the American population and yet more than 48 percent of prisoners within jails and prisons are African-American. Intellectually disabled individuals are easy fodder for jokes in motion pictures. The First Lady of California, Maria Shriver, denounced a character named Simple Jack played by Ben Stiller in the movie *Tropic Thunder* (2008). In the movie, "retard" is repeated several times and refers to the character. With an estimated eight million intellectually disabled Americans, Shriver says that the word is "equal to the impact of the 'N-word' on an African American."

African Americans; Arabs; Asians; Latinos; women; bisexual, gay, lesbian, and trans-gender persons; and Native Americans are groups that have long been discriminated against. Pictorial stereotypes presented in the media of all these cultural groups shape the public's perception of them.

■ *African American Stereotypes*

African American history is directly tied to past U.S. government-sanctioned enslavement. Consequently, African Americans have faced tremendous difficulty in overcoming stereotypes, despite legal, economic, and social reforms. Racism is the belief that one race is better than another because of the genes in a person's chromosomes. When European explorers came into contact with Africans in the 16th century, many concluded that Africans must not have European mental processing abilities because African societies lacked the technological advances common in Europe. Later, evolutionary theory became a scientific justification for racism, with western Europeans thought to be on a higher evolutionary plane than other races. Those with economic interests in the slave trade used all these rationalizations. Thinking of Africans simply as animals on the same level as apes often was used as an excuse for severe treatment during capture, transport to the New World, enslavement, and forced labor (Figure 5.3).

Unlike other ethnic groups that immigrated voluntarily and retained their own cultures, African Americans were not allowed to re-create their own African cultures in the slave colonies. The master–slave mentality also made assimilation extremely difficult even after the Thirteenth Amendment outlawed slavery following the Civil War. Few in the North had ever had any contact with African Americans. Until 1860, there were more

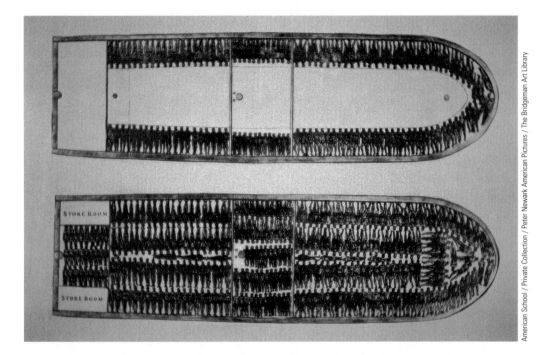

American School / Private Collection / Peter Newark American Pictures / The Bridgeman Art Library

Figure 5.3

This diagram of a typical slave ship that crossed the Atlantic Ocean to America in the 18th and 19th centuries can only hint at the horrific travel conditions of the kidnapped Africans. It has been estimated that up to 30 percent of the victims from each voyage died, their bodies left to decay next to the living.

Figure 5.4

"Colored Entrance, New Orleans, Louisiana," 1997 by Gerry Davey. Evidence of racial discrimination against African Americans lasted on the wall of this French Quarter structure as late as 1997. It has since been painted over.

than 500,000 free African Americans living in the South. They had been born of free mothers, had paid for their own freedom, or had been set free by their owners. In the South these freed slaves had occupations as diverse as architects and hotel clerks. But in the North, discrimination in jobs, housing, and education was much more common and institutionalized, making the assimilation of African Americans into the dominant culture particularly difficult. Nevertheless, separate and unequal treatment, demonstrated though different water fountains, theater entrances, restaurants, schools, and businesses, existed in both the North and South (Figure 5.4).

Prejudice and discrimination continue to this day. In a study of 700,000 cases in which officers of the Los Angeles Police Department stopped pedestrians or drivers in 2003 and 2004, conducted by the Southern California branch of the American Civil Liberties Union (ACLU), it

was found that African Americans were 127 percent more likely to be stopped than Anglos. The study brought criticisms of racial profiling to the department.

Recent studies of African American pictorial coverage in print and broadcast media have noted the pictorial legacy of

Courtesy of Gerry Davey

discrimination based on stereotyping. Although more African Americans are seen in the media, the most common pictures of them still relate to crime, sports, and entertainment. Having African American entertainment and sports heroes is important for children, but the message being sent is that they can "make it" in society only if they excel in those fields (Figure 5.5). As of 2009, there were only three African American men who were head coaches among the 119 major college football teams.

African Americans shown in movies, music videos, and on television often present a stereotypical pattern that concentrates on sexual and violent acts while motion pictures with good intentions—*The Color Purple* (1985), *Boyz n the Hood* (1991), and *Precious: Based on the Novel Push by Sapphire* (2009)—were criticized for their realistic telling of tough stories. *Precious* with a storyline about a young ghetto-living overweight girl divided audiences into those who though the movie was uplifting and other who were concerned about perpetuating negative stereotypes.

A recent trend in African American stereotypes is created by male actors wearing wigs, makeup, and heavy body suits to portray overweight, insensitive, and crass women. Martin Lawrence in *Big Momma's House* (2000) and *Big Momma's House 2* (2006), Tyler Perry in *Madea's Family Reunion* (2006) and *Madea Goes to Jail* (2009), and Eddie Murphy in *Norbit* (2007) all perpetuate the loud, large woman stereotype through their distorted, oversimplified images (Weblink 5.2). They reinforce prejudicial thinking that continues social discrimination.

Other negative examples are unfortunately easy to find. After Hurricane Katrina slammed into the Gulf Coast in 2005, the captions for two news pictures taken in New Orleans made the images controversial. The photographs showed survivors performing the same action— wading in chest-high polluted water while carrying food and drinks from a store. The African American man in one picture was categorized as "looting" the store, whereas the Anglo couple had left the store after "finding" their items. Besides showing how racial profiling can creep into a caption, these examples also show that images in themselves are ethically neutral—it is often the words that accompany visual messages that cause misrepresentations and misunderstandings (Weblink 5.3).

Visual symbols are often the most controversial. In 2007 four nooses were found hung on the campus of California State University, Fullerton, before a rally promoting tolerance. During the 2008 presidential campaign, then-candidate Barack Obama commented on a cover of *Golfweek* magazine with a noose on its cover "to illustrate the controversy over a Golf Channel anchor's use of the word 'lynch' in a comment about Tiger Woods." Said Obama, "We have to have a culture

Figure 5.5

During the 2000 Sydney Olympic Games, the gold medal 4x400 relay team of (from left) Jearl Miles-Clark, Monique Hennagan, LaTasha Colander-Richardson, and Marion Jones pose for pictures. Since that happy time, Jones pled guilty to lying to federal agents about using steroids. She served six months in prison in 2008. She also was stripped of all medals, including those she and her team won in Australia.

Courtesy of Mike Powell / Allsport / Getty images

that understands that there's nothing funny about a noose."

President Barack Obama's election to the presidency has triggered unfortunate racial stereotypes. Soon after he signed an economic stimulus bill into law, a tragic news story was reported in 2009 of a woman severely mauled by a pet chimpanzee. The animal was shot and killed. Sean Delonas of the *New York Post* drew a cartoon depicting a police officer killing a chimpanzee and the other saying "They'll have to find someone else to write the next stimulus bill." Critics immediately decried the cartoon as racist and inflammatory. One said, "To compare the nation's first African American commander in chief to a dead chimpanzee is nothing short of racist drivel." Since the 19th century, motion pictures and cartoons have portrayed African Americans as apes. Social psychologists Phillip Goff and Jennifer Everhardt call this attitude "a kind of racial programming, a legacy even something as progressive as Obama's election cannot obliterate." The editor of the *Post* defended the work by calling it a parody and claiming that it simply mocked "Washington's efforts to revive the economy." Nevertheless, the newspaper printed an unusual apology, not for the cartoon itself, but to those whom the cartoon might have offended. The same year, the mayor of the Southern California city of Los Alamitos resigned his position after a storm of protest over an e-mail he sent that included a picture of the White House in which the lawn was covered with large, green watermelons. He claimed to not know that watermelons shown in that context were a symbol of racial insensitivity. He does now.

■ *Arab Stereotypes*

Unlike many other groups, Arab culture is not only a social construct that comprises

Arab-speaking peoples, but is distinct from others by differences in shared histories, religion, music, culinary specialties, and artworks. As such, those who identify themselves as Arab can have light or dark hair and skin and identify themselves as a Muslim, Christian, or any other religion. In the United States, most Arabs are Christians who immigrated from Lebanon and Syria. Nevertheless, in news and entertainment media, the prevalent stereotypes of Arabs as convenience store counter workers, unintelligible taxicab drivers, and cold-blooded religious fanatics are commonly featured (Figure 5.6). Well before the events of 9/11, stereotypical generalizations, discrimination, and assaults against Arabs had occurred. The list of media examples is long and injurious.

The folk tales of Aladdin and his lamp and Ali Baba and his 40 thieves are ancient stories that were included in a collection called *One Thousand and One Nights*. Unfortunately, these stories, as well as the equally popular Sinbad the Sailor, are examples of powerful popular culture positive icons that were turned into stereotypes by Hollywood and others

Figure 5.6

Unfortunately, the stereotype of an Arab as a terrorist comes from images such as this one of Iraqi policemen on patrol in the city of Hit, located on the Euphrates River within the Al Anbar province.

Figure 5.7

From an illustration by Albert Robida in an 1895 edition of Ali Baba and the Forty Thieves, *Hollywood directors later exploited the violent nature of Arab swordsmen. The son of a French carpenter, Robida escaped his humble beginnings by becoming a renowned caricaturist, illustrator, and the editor of his own magazine,* La Caricature. *He became most known for his fanciful inventions, including the téléphonoscope, a large flat-screen television "that delivered the latest news 24 hours a day, the latest plays, courses, and teleconferences," which he conceived in the 1870s.*

(Figure 5.7). From such motion pictures as *Alladin and the Wonderful Lamp* (1900) came *The Thief of Bagdad* (1924), starring Douglas Fairbanks, and its parody *Grief in Baghdad* (1925), with the principal actors strangely played by chimpanzees. Cartoons such as *Gypped in Egypt* (1930), *Popeye the Sailor Meets Sinbad the Sailor* (1936), *Popeye and Ali Baba's Forty Thieves* (1937), and *Porky Pig in Ali Baba Bound* (1940) added to the notion that Arabs were dumb-headed and money-crazy. More recently, Disney's *Aladdin* (1992) sparked controversy. Marvin Wingfield and Bushra Karaman wrote, "The film's light-skinned lead characters, Aladdin and Jasmine, have Anglicized features and Anglo-American accents. This is in contrast to the other characters who are dark-skinned, swarthy and villainous—cruel palace guards or greedy merchants with Arabic accents and grotesque facial features."

Without a doubt, the depiction of Arabs as maniacal terrorists is hard to shake. Jack Shaheen, a Lebanese American

writer, laments, "There is never an Arab hero for kids to cheer." In such pre-9/11 films as *Raiders of the Lost Ark* (1981), *Back to the Future* (1985), *True Lies* (1994), and *The Siege* (1998), Shaheen's assertion is supported. The director of the Islamic Council of New England said, "*The Siege* hideously distorts the religion of Islam." Many protested the linking of Islam and violence. After the 9/11 attacks, motion pictures and television programs such as *Team America: World Police* (2004), *American Dreamz* (2006), *You Don't Mess with the Zohan* (2008), *Iron Man* (2008), and most episodes of the television series "24" were criticized for their portrayal of Arabs as terrorists. In *Iron Man*, Egyptian-born actor Sayed Badreya played an arms dealer who kidnaps the character played by Robert Downey, Jr. In a *Los Angeles Times* feature, Badreya explained that "when he first arrived in Hollywood in 1986 'I couldn't work. I was too handsome,' he laughs. 'So I put on some weight and grew a beard, and suddenly I was working every day and playing the angry Arab.'"

After the Oklahoma City bombing in 1995 that killed 168 people, numerous assaults were made against Arab Americans, because news agencies repeated a false rumor that Arab terrorists were involved. In fact, it was homegrown Anglo terrorist Timothy McVeigh who was responsible for the bombing. Six years later, not much had changed. Less than a month after 9/11, the U.S. Justice Department issued a report that the agency had "received numerous reports of violence, threats of violence, and discrimination against Arab-Americans and other Americans of Middle Eastern and South Asian descents. Any threats of violence or discrimination against Arab or Muslim Americans or Americans of South Asian descents are not just wrong and un-American, but also are unlawful and will be treated as such."

Violent behavior against those who appear Arab is not limited to real-world assaults. Dr. Tom Denson, a communications researcher at the University of New South Wales, conducted a study with students regarding their stereotypes of Arabs. In a first-person shooter video game, "innocent figures in the game were more likely to be shot at if they were wearing turbans or hijabs." Denson called this response the "turban effect" and noticed it in both male and female players. He concluded, "People learn about negative stereotypes from their parents, their peers, their education and the media. Muslims tend to be portrayed negatively in the media so the findings make sense, even in an otherwise tolerant Western society like Australia." He also warned that such negative behavior might be more prevalent in the United States and Great Britain. A Gallup poll of Muslim Americans taken in 2008 showed that although they have achieved high levels of education and employment, they report "feelings of unease" with increased stereotypical media coverage and perceived suspicion of Islam since the terrorist attacks of 9/11. On the plus side, although Barack Obama is not Muslim, the fact that his middle name is Hussein and he was elected president of the United States heartened many Arab and Muslim Americans that there might be a spirit of tolerance evolving within the country.

■ Asian Stereotypes

Asian American students often tell personal anecdotes in which they have been stereotyped as being good at math, bad drivers, golf obsessed, and wealthy. In the final "Newhart" episode in 1982, for example, Japanese investors bought the entire town and turned it into a golf course. A "South Park" episode titled "The China Problem" featured the main characters uncovering a plot to take over the world hatched at a P.F. Chang's restaurant. More serious and embedded stereotypes are discussed by academics Farah Mahdzan and Norlinda Ziegler in their analysis of Asian American stereotypes in the media. They identify the "exaggerated depictions of exotic, sex-hungry Asian women to the gangster-involved, sexually abusive characteristics of Asian men" in mainstream motion pictures. The evil and diabolical crime genius Fu Manchu, first featured in the books by English author Sax Rohmer in the 1910s, was often a character in motion pictures (Figure 5.8). *The Mysterious Dr. Fu Manchu* (1929) starred the Swedish actor Warner Oland who later was better known for his portrayal of detective Charlie Chan.

Library of Congress Prints and Photographs Division LC-DIG-jpd-02216

Figure 5.8

Many of the early stereotypes of evil and diabolical Asian villains seen in Hollywood films come from actual portraits of warriors, a noble and honored profession. This 1760 hanging silk scroll shows a portrait of Wu Fu, Brigadier General of the Gansu Region of north central China.

Fu Manchu inspired a host of "Yellow Peril" characters in various media in which Asian criminals were out to dominate the world. In movies, Ming the Merciless was an evil influence in the *Flash Gordon* serials of the 1930s, and James Bond's first nemesis was Dr. No, who was played by Canadian actor Joseph Wiseman. On TV, Doctor Zin was shown in the 1960s "Jonny Quest," and Wo Fat, played by Khigh Dhieg, was in "Hawaii Five-O." In print cartoons, Marvel comic books featured antiheroes such as Mandarin and the Yellow Claw, and DC Comics' Wonder Woman battled the giant Egg Fu, who closely resembles Jabba the Hutt from *Star Wars: Episode VI—Return of the Jedi* (1983).

The opposite of the male gangster is the "Dragon Lady" stereotype exemplified in Lucy Liu's character O-Ren Ishii in Quentin Tarantino's *Kill Bill: Vol. 1* (2003). In *The Joy Luck Club* (1993), Asian men were portrayed as being cheap, egodriven, and bad sexual partners. In *The Year of the Dragon* (1985), the "China Doll," a "sexually active, exotic, overly feminine and eager to please" female stereotype was shown. In television, Asian actors have been hard to find since Anglo actor David Carradine appeared in the series "Kung Fu" in the 1970s.

In 2009, after the first Asian American was named the president of the Ivy League school Dartmouth College, hate e-mails circulated among students. Jim Yong Kim, a South Korean–born health expert in HIV/AIDS with the World Health Organization, grew up in Iowa. In high school he was the class valedictorian and quarterback for the football team. In 2006 he was named one of *Time* magazine's 100 most influential people for his work in helping the world's poor. But a daily e-mail update sent to about 1,000 students run by a group not associated with the college called him a

"Chinaman" and warned of the "Asianification" of the campus. The writer of the e-mail reportedly "is full of regret" and "did not mean to offend anyone."

The term Asian Americans comprises many groups from diverse lands, including the most prevalent Chinese, Japanese, and Koreans, as well as Vietnamese, Pacific Islanders, Hmong, Samoans, Bengalis, Sri Lankans, Pakistanis, Indians, Thai, and so on. With such diversity, the individual cultures should never be lumped together.

■ Latino Stereotypes

As with Asians, the Latino culture is wonderfully diverse with members from Cuba, Puerto Rico, Mexico, Central and South America, and Spain. And yet, even though about 13 percent of the American population is Latino, a recent study sponsored by the National Association of Hispanic Journalists reported that less than 1 percent of the stories on network newscasts feature Latinos. Out of that small percentage, the overwhelming topics covered are crime, terrorism, poverty, welfare, and illegal immigration. Subsequently, the Hispanic American Culture website noted a study in which high school students were asked to come up with words to describe Latinos: "Taco. Cactus. Poverty. Welfare. Sombrero. Mules. Lots of children. Chicken. Farmers. Tequila. Migrant workers. Illegal aliens. Chips-n-dip. Pollution. Ponchos. Limited variety of food. Markets. Gangs. Cameros. Field workers." Most if not all of these negative generalizations stem from media portrayals.

Motion pictures and live-action commercials have created controversy. *Viva Max* (1969), about the retaking of the Alamo by a gang of inept soldiers, and *¡Three Amigos!* (1986) played up the Mexican bandit stereotype and sparked protests. A Chihuahua as a spokesperson for Taco

Bell offended many in the Latino community because fast food is not considered "home cooking" by most Latinos. The little dog was pulled in 2000. To its credit, Disney's *Beverly Hills Chihuahua* (2008) has voices of Latino stars Edward James Olmos, George Lopez, and Andy Garcia, but the plot of the film "shows an ignorance of Mexican culture that could offend Latinos." For example, a statue that is shown as a history lesson of the Mexican Aztec culture is actually Machu Picchu, an Inca structure in Peru (Figure 5.9). The Warner Bros. character Speedy Gonzalez was noted as "the fastest mouse in Mexico." In his second appearance in 1955, he stole cheese from security guard Sylvester the Cat for his fellow drunken mouse friends and his lazy and slow-witted cousin Slowpoke Rodriguez (Weblink 5.4). After the Cartoon Network obtained the Speedy collection, the episodes were taken off the air in 1999 "for perpetuating stereotypes about Mexicans."

From 1967 to 1971, a cartoon character created by the famous Warner Bros. animator Tex Avery and voiced by Mel Blanc, who also played Bugs Bunny, Elmer Fudd, and Speedy Gonzales, offended many for its stereotype of Latinos. The Frito Bandito, a creation of the Foote, Cone & Belding advertising agency for Fritos corn chips, was a short bandit with a gold tooth and a long, thin mustache, sporting two pistols with crossed ammunition belts and a huge, yellow sombrero who tried to steal your corn chips. The commercials ran from 1967 until pressure from protest groups caused the end of the character in 1971 (Weblink 5.5).

Kristy Acevedo offered a critique of the animated film *Happy Feet* (2006) that was produced by the Australian animation house Animal Logic for Warner Bros. (Weblink 5.6). In the film, the character Mumble is banished by the Emperor penguins and forced to live in a penguin ghetto where the males speak with "heavy Mexican accents, including Ramon, played by the Anglo Robin Williams." Writes Acevedo, "The messages embedded in the film are undeniable. The tall Emperor penguins, white, sometimes stodgy, are definitely the haves, and the Latino misfit penguins are the have-nots. Why should cartoon penguins ever be sorted into ethnic communities in a children's film? Are we trying to teach children that 'birds of a feather flock together'? We are teaching children segregation, not the integration Martin Luther King, Jr. dreamed about."

■ Female Stereotypes

Males in almost every culture in the world and throughout the history of social

Figure 5.9

In contrast to where the producers of Disney's Beverly Hills Chihuahua (2008) thought Machu Picchu is located, this photograph shows the actual mountain with evidence of a vast pre-Columbian Inca civilization located in the Urubamba Valley of southern Peru.

Amy Harris / iStockphoto.com

interaction have thought that they are the dominant and more important gender. Such patterns of thought have led to prejudice and pervasive discrimination against women (Figure 5.10). At birth, girls are treated more gently than boys. Traditionally, girls were taught to stay home and attend to household duties. Boys were encouraged to be adventurous and active. Women were expected to find happiness in marriage and motherhood. Men were expected to find fulfillment in their careers. Women were valued for their appeal as sexual objects. Men were valued for their intelligence, strength, and energy.

Cultural norms are learned behaviors and are based on several interrelated factors.

A study of 156 separate societies worldwide revealed that cultures that had high incidences of rape competed for limited natural resources, tended to engage in wars, tolerated high levels of violent crime, and supported the male (macho) image of toughness.

During the Industrial Revolution in the 19th century, many poor women were allowed to work in factories for the first time because of labor shortages. Despite this advance in social thinking, women were still not allowed to vote, own property, testify in court, make a legal contract, spend their wages without getting permission from their husbands, or even retain guardianship over their children. *Abolitionist* activism on behalf of freedom for slaves in the South led many also to consider freedom for women in the North. Eventually, Wyoming became the first state to give women the right to vote. In 1920, the Nineteenth Amendment, which gave women national voting rights, was ratified. Although voting reform was an important step, efforts to reform other discriminatory practices were unsuccessful. The late Texan columnist Molly Ivins noted that women's rights were especially slow in coming to Texas, for example. "Until June 26, 1918," she writes, "the Texas Constitution mandated that all Texans had the right to vote except 'idiots, imbeciles, aliens, the insane and women.'" Women weren't allowed to serve on juries in Texas until 1954.

During World War II women again were needed in the factories, this time to produce armaments, to replace the men serving in the armed forces. When the war ended, these "Rosie the Riveters" succumbed to tremendous social pressure to take care of their returning men, have babies, and let the male "breadwinners" have the jobs they needed in order to support their families. The result was the "baby boom," named for the large number of children born during the late 1940s and the 1950s.

Figure 5.10

Many women throughout the world are forced by cultural restrictions—including religious and/or social customs—to cover their faces while in public, as this 19th century woodcut demonstrates.

Uncensored Situations, 1966, The Dick Sutphen Studio, Inc.

In spite of this social progress for women in the 1960s and beyond, media stereotypes of women in news, entertainment, and advertising contexts constantly remind viewers of society's male-dominated view. To some, the political world hasn't changed that much. Cokie Roberts, reporter and political commentator for National Public Radio (NPR) and author of *We Are Our Mothers' Daughters*, criticized the characterizations of and questions to Senator Hillary Clinton and Governor Sarah Palin during the 2008 presidential campaign. In an interview with NPR host Scott Simon, Roberts said, "I think that the words used about them, words like 'shrill' were not words you would hear applied to a man. You certainly have never, ever, ever, ever, ever had a male politician asked who's going to be taking care of the children when he runs for office including the current president of the United States who has small children when he started on the campaign trail. It is still just so much a double standard when it comes to politicians."

On television, women often are portrayed as sex objects designed only for a man's pleasure, as wives whose chief duty is to serve their husbands, and as mothers who often must rear children without a husband's help. In the 1950s, women were portrayed as being less intelligent than men, being dependent on men for support, and thus being inferior. Obviously, such stereotypes do not portray men and women equally (Figure 5.11). Early television situation comedies such as "I Love Lucy," "The Adventures of Ozzie and Harriet," "Father Knows Best," "The Donna Reed Show," and "Leave It to Beaver" reinforced the view that the women should stay home and take care of the house and children (Weblink 5.7). Set in the 1960s, the 2010 hit series "Mad Men"

offers the same stereotypical messages about women.

Nowhere is the unequal status of men and women as obvious as in advertising. Images in magazine ads and in television commercials show women as sexual objects to attract the attention of potential customers to the product. Hair care, clothing, and makeup advertisements regularly give women the impression that they are inferior if they do not measure up to the impossible beauty standards demonstrated by high-priced models. Research on television commercials has revealed that men are used as voice-overs when an authority figure is desired, women are portrayed mainly in a family setting in which men are benefited, women often are noticeably younger than their male counterparts, and fewer girls and women are used in advertisements than boys and men. Although never the only cause for gender discrimination, print, television, movie, and web images that show bikini-clad models holding phallic-shaped beer bottles reinforce the idea that women are mentally inferior to

Figure 5.11
This billboard in Southern California for Mervyn's department stores and Levi's jeans presents at least two stereotypes: that old men are content to fritter away the day in a pool hall and that young women like to pose seductively. Look closely: Is she posing for a blind African American man? Carefully composed advertising images are rich in semiotic meanings.

men and good only for sexual pleasure (Figures 5.12 and 5.13). Major female actresses such as Nicole Kidman and Sarah Jessica Parker as well as female cast members for the television shows "Gossip Girl" and "The Hills" have posed while wearing only their underwear for such magazines as *Vanity Fair* and *Rolling Stone*. Such objectification of women, although seemingly innocent, can lead to degradation, intimidation, stalking, assault, rape, and murder.

■ Bisexual, Gay, Lesbian, and Transgender Stereotypes

If someone were to advocate that people with disabilities, or Native Americans, African Americans, or women should be forced to suffer the physical and emotional scars of discrimination, most people would roundly condemn that person as a crackpot. That's because prejudice and

discrimination generally are opposed on legal and moral grounds. However, the approximately 25 million gay and lesbian members of our society belong to one of the few groups that can be discriminated against legally.

Ironically, gays and lesbians are the most diverse of any cultural group. In fact, data from the 2000 U.S. Census showed that same-sex couples head nearly 600,000 homes in the United States, which puts on average at least one gay or lesbian couple in nearly every county in America. Bisexual, homosexual, and transgender persons cannot be isolated by race, gender, economic situation, social position, region of the country, religious belief, political orientation, or any other physical attribute. Many are extremely hesitant to admit their sexuality, fearing an employment, housing, and/or social backlash.

When the HIV/AIDS crisis became known in the early 1980s, homosexuals

Figure 5.12

In this advertisement for Cointreau liqueur, the shape and position of the models' fingers and the bottle itself are meant to link drinking the alcoholic beverage to sexual conquest.

Figure 5.13

Although at first glance the man appears to be holding the woman's breasts in the Seagram's billboard, she is actually touching herself. Media critic Irving Goffman has written that such a gesture by women connotes subservience to men. The metonymic code of dress style, jewelry, and background details communicates an upscale environment. Ironically, the JVC advertisement (on the right) displays the words that Seagram executives hope male buyers of their gin (on the left) will believe: "Hold everything."

Courtesy of Neil Chapman

Courtesy of Neil Chapman

were cast as either victims or villains, with little concern about an objective presentation. Independent and well-financed videos produced and distributed by conservative religious organizations that operated their own cable networks played on the fear of HIV/AIDS. Such programs included "The Gay Agenda" and "Gay Rights/Special Rights." For example, in "Gay Rights," an HIV/AIDS patient talked of having 50 sexual partners in one night—hardly representative of homosexuals as a group. Pro–gay rights commercials—one featuring a gay soldier who was killed in Vietnam with the message "End Discrimination"—are seldom seen, as the major networks refuse to air most political advertisements.

Discrimination continues. In 2003 during the MTV Music Video Awards show, singers Madonna and Britney Spears kissed on the lips. Although the calculated act created a brief media stir, there was little harm to their careers. Yet after openly gay "American Idol" runner-up Adam Lambert kissed a male musician during his 2009 performance on the American Music Awards, appearances were canceled on several television programs. Earlier that year, after a Microsoft Xbox Live game user identified herself as a lesbian in her profile, she was subjected to offensive comments from other gamers. Instead of an investigation by Microsoft officials, her account was canceled. After news of this story was made public, the company apologized.

Many saw as progress several television programs with bisexual, gay, lesbian, and transgender characters since the first lesbian kiss on NBC's "L.A. Law" in the early 1990s. NBC's "Will and Grace," ABC's "Grey's Anatomy," Bravo's "Queer Eye for the Straight Guy" and "Boy Meets Boy," and Showtime's "Queer as Folk" and "The

L Word" all had homosexual characters and plotlines. "The L Word," which aired its last episode in 2009 after six seasons, was praised for showing lesbian professional women with everyday life challenges. The actress Daniela Sea was praised for her sensitive portrayal of a female-to-male transsexual (Weblink 5.8). Viacom's MTV Networks offers programming aimed at bisexual, gay, lesbian, and transgender viewers on its Logo channel. Two groundbreaking movies released in 2005, *Brokeback Mountain* and *Transamerica*, introduced mainstream audiences to story lines that included two tough bisexual ranch hands in love with each other and a male-to-female transsexual who learns of a son she never knew she had.

The Internet Movie Database (Weblink 5.9) lists 315 motion pictures in which a bisexual character is part of the plot. Movies include *Spartacus* (1960), *Cabaret* (1972), and *Mulholland Drive* (2001). The database lists 597 movies with a gay male character, including *Little Miss Sunshine* (2006) and *Milk* (2008), which won a Best Actor Academy Award for Sean Penn, who played the assassinated politician and gay rights activist Harvey Milk. A lesbian character can be watched in 1,213 movies including *Sin City* (2005) and *V for Vendetta* (2005). Finally, 72 films feature a transsexual character, as in *Boys Don't Cry* (1999) and *Hedwig and the Angry Inch* (2001). Gay and lesbian activists, although pleased with the number of shows on television and in motion pictures, are nevertheless still concerned with stereotypical portrayals. After Mary Glasspool was elected a suffragan, or an assistant bishop of the Episcopal Church in 2009, the openly lesbian priest lamented that headlines did not state a "Well Qualified Priest Elected Bishop" but instead had "Lesbian Priest." Said Glasspool, "It segregates out one of the many, many aspects of my personality."

In 2004 the Massachusetts Supreme Judicial Court gave full marriage rights to same-sex couples, a right beyond the civil union arrangements granted in a few other states. Four years later the Supreme Court of California overturned the ban on same-sex marriages. However, in the same election that was a victory for Barack Obama, California's Proposition 8 was passed and negated that ruling. But in 2009 the Iowa Supreme Court overturned a ban on same-sex marriages, writing, "We are firmly convinced the exclusion of gay and lesbian people from the institution of civil marriage does not substantially further any important governmental objective." Gay rights advocates were jubilant, while those against the ruling took an example from California and "began lobbying lawmakers for a constitutional amendment to ban same-sex

marriage." Perhaps the most far-reaching development was when the Vermont legislature overrode the governor's veto, allowing same-sex couples to marry. The state became the first to allow marriages "through legislative action instead of a court ruling." In 2009, Democrat Annise Parker was elected mayor of Houston, the first openly lesbian head of a major US city while John Perez, a gay lawmaker from Los Angeles was named the speaker of the California Assembly.

Overcoming ingrained stereotypes takes many years for a culture to achieve. The process could be sped up if the images of culturally diverse groups, including bisexuals, gays, lesbians, and transgender individuals, showed them as ordinary people who have ordinary needs, fears, and hopes and lead ordinary lives (Figure 5.14).

■ *Native American Stereotypes*

Portrayed as bloodthirsty savages, alcoholic indigents, romantic princesses, and silent but wise sidekicks, Native Americans have long been a staple of paperback, movie, and television stereotypes. But the practice of stereotyping Native Americans probably goes as far back as the 17th century. In *Publick Occurrences Both Domestick and Foreign*, the first English-language newspaper in America, there were two stories concerning Native Americans: One praised "their industry and communal spirit in staving off starvation" and the other accused them of "kidnapping white children, presumably to ravage or eat them." It seems the dominant culture has always wanted to portray Native Americans both ways—as noble savages and as feared adversaries—in order to pigeonhole their culture and justify the treatment of Native peoples throughout American history (Figure 5.15).

Figure 5.14

Two women publicly proclaim their love for each other by gestures and signs during an International Women's Conference in Houston, Texas. Images of bisexual, gay, lesbian, and transgender individuals can depict sweet, personal, and universal moments, just as with everyone else.

Courtesy of Laurie Williams

There is always debate, it seems, whether Hollywood and other portrayals honor or marginalize Native peoples. "Cowboys versus Indians," despite Americans encroaching on Native lands, was a staple of early Hollywood films. D. W. Griffith, infamous for his flawed classic *Birth of a Nation* (1915), made the first picture that had the classic scene of a wagon train being terrorized in *The Last Drop of Water* (1911) (Weblink 5.10). He also directed *Fighting Blood* (1911) and *The Battle of Elderbrush Gulch* (1913). Cecil B. DeMille's first movie was named *The Squaw Man* (1913). The word "squaw" is a derogatory word for a Native woman. Other angry Native movies followed, including the box office hit *The Covered Wagon* (1923), *Northwest Passage* (1940) starring Spencer Tracy, and *Red River* (1948) with John Wayne. After 1950 the cowboy/Indian genre lost popularity among movie producers, as audiences became more interested in gunslinger westerns.

University of Alaska professor Dan Rearden cited *Eskimo* (1933), *On Deadly Ground* (1994), and Disney's *Snow Dogs* (2002) offensive. In *Dogs*, the character played by Cuba Gooding, Jr., tells of a nightmare in which he was an Eskimo. "Children are watching this in a Disney film," Rearden said. "The message is, if you're Eskimo, that's a nightmare. What's at stake with kids watching movies like this?"

In 1995 Disney released an animated movie about a Powhatan woman named Pocahontas. In defending the romantic princess stereotype in the movie, Roy Disney wrote that the film is "responsible, accurate, and respectful." However, Chief Roy Crazy Horse said, "It is unfortunate that with this sad story, which Euro-Americans should find embarrassing, Disney makes 'entertainment' and perpetuates a dishonest and self-serving myth at the expense of

Medicine Man—A Story of Indians on the War Path
"BLONDY" RYAN TALKS BASEBALL

Courtesy of the Advertising Archives

Figure 5.15
First published in 1919, The Open Road for Boys was a typical magazine for boys that promoted camping, hiking, and shooting things with air rifles. In this 1934 cover story, a "Medicine Man," one of the most sacred leaders responsible for the tribe's spiritual and physical health, is distorted in this common, violent stereotype.

the Powhatan Nation" (Figure 5.16). Native American stereotypes have been seen in such popular television shows as "My Favorite Martian," "Star Trek," and "Quantum Leap." In one episode of the popular 1990s television sitcom "Seinfeld," Jerry is considered a racist by his friends when he buys a cigar store Indian for his Native American girlfriend (Figure 5.17).

No debates, however, are as heated as those outside huge professional sports arenas and small-town grass fields. Groups such as the National Indian Education Association, the National Congress of American Indians, the American Civil Liberties Union, the U.S. Commission on Civil Rights, and others have condemned the use of Native American symbols as sports mascots. Nevertheless, the use of Native mascots is still popular. Almost 2,000 school athletic programs around the United States still have Native mascots.

Figure 5.16

"Baptism of Pocahontas," 1840, by John Gadsby Chapman. Commissioned by the U.S. Congress, the painting shows an event believed to have taken place around 1613. Matoaka, nicknamed Pocahontas (a Powhatan word referring to her outgoing personality), the daughter of Wahunsuna-cawh, chief of the Powhatan nation, is baptized with the name Rebecca in Jamestown, Virginia. Her future husband, the British John Rolfe, stands behind her. Her brother Nante-quaus turns his back on the proceedings while fellow tribes-men also express their misgiv-ings. The painting was used in a propaganda campaign to convince the American public that Native Americans should be Christianized.

Courtesy of Susan Isakson / Alamy

Figure 5.17

Wearing a skirt depicting an American flag, this wooden sculpture outside a cigar store shows a Native American scout with one hand shading his eyes and the other holding a package of cigars. Since Native Americans introduced tobacco to European explorers and settlers, the use of "cigar store Indians" became an advertise-ment symbol. Today, however, use of these statues is limited, since many compare the figure with African American racist lawn ornaments and other stereotypical representations that are seen as demeaning.

Courtesy of Paul Martin Lester

Alumni of schools and universities and fans of professional teams throughout the United States use the same defense: "Indian people should be proud that there are people who want to represent them and follow in their footsteps and conduct themselves with dignity and honor." But names like the Washington Redskins, which is a racial slur on par with "nigger" or "kike"; cartoon images like the toothy grin of Chief Wahoo, the Cleveland Indians' mascot; the "tomahawk chop" employed by fans of the Atlanta Braves; and the "Sacred Ground" at the Kansas City Chiefs' end zone do not honor Native peoples and are denounced by experts who offer a variety of reasons for ending such depic-tions (Figure 5.18). About the Redskins' NFL mascot, Suzan Shown Harjo, execu-tive director of the Morning Star Institute, a non-profit advocacy group for Native American rights, said that Redskins "is the most derogatory thing Native Peoples can be called in the English language."

Another argument against the use of mascots is because of "collateral use." Fans from opposing teams often use racial slurs and obscene cartoon depictions based on a Native mascot (Figure 5.19). Lucy Ganje, Professor of Communications with the University of North Dakota, writes, "Native children have the right to grow up believing they're more than mascots for products and sports teams. They have the right to attend a football game without standing next to someone yelling, 'Scalp the Indians!'"

■ WHERE DO WE GO FROM HERE?

Reverend Martin Luther King, Jr., wrote those words as the title of his last book and also used them as the title of a speech he gave to the Tenth Anniversary Convention of the Southern Christian Leadership Conference in Atlanta on August 16, 1967, eight months before he was assassinated. In the speech he said:

> When our days become dreary with low hovering clouds of despair, and when our nights become darker than a thousand midnights, let us remember that there is a creative force in this universe, working to pull down the gigantic mountains of evil, a power that is able to make a way out of no way and transform dark yesterdays into bright tomorrows. Let us realize the arc of the moral universe is long but it bends toward justice.

During the historic 2009 inauguration of President Obama, the first African American elected president of the United States, Reverend Joseph Lowery, who founded the Southern Christian Leadership Conference with King, gave the benediction. Later, Lowery delivered a sermon to contemporary civil rights lead-

ers including Eric Holder, the nation's first African American attorney general, on the anniversary of "Bloody Sunday," when civil rights marchers were beaten in Selma, Alabama, in 1965. Lowery related how during the inauguration he tried to see the site where King made his famous "I Have a Dream" speech in 1963:

> "But I couldn't make out the Lincoln Memorial," Lowery said. "These old eyes have grown dim. But the eyes of my heart saw the Lincoln Memorial and the ears of my soul heard a 34-year-old preacher standing on the steps, issuing a summons to a nation to climb out of the pits of racism to a higher ground of character and competence. And there I was, never dreaming that I would even see a black president. And here I was not only seeing, but participating. And I was glad to be there to say that today, January 20, is the nation's response to that summons issued by that 34-year-old preacher in 1963."

In his book *A Theory of Justice*, John Rawls writes of the "veil of ignorance." He asserts that members of all cultural

Figure 5.18
Named in 1933, the Redskins, the team mascot for the Washington, D.C., NFL football team is defended by team boosters as it "refers to the red paint used on the skin of Indian warriors." Bill Plaschke, sports columnist for the Los Angeles Times *writes "How does a team from the nation's capital, supported by a fan base of some of the nation's greatest thinkers, maintain a nickname that is the Native American equivalent to the N-word?"*

Figure 5.19
The University of North Dakota has the "Fighting Sioux" as its mascot, despite protests from students, faculty, and others. An example of "collateral use" is this T-shirt worn by fans of North Dakota State University, a football rival.

groups must retreat to an "original position" in which cultural rules and social differences disappear. When all barriers between individuals are lifted, everyone is freed to experience what it is like to be in the "other person's shoes." At that point, Rawls believes, everyone in a society will have equal status and access to the goods and services produced by that society. The need is to build solid bridges between people that are not based on superficial, stereotypical, and visible symbols.

The only place where people regularly and over a long time see members from other cultural groups is in the pages of newspapers and magazines, on television, in the movies, and on computer screens. But when most of those media images are misleading, viewers aren't challenged to examine the basis of their prejudices and do something about them. To change people's minds about diversity may require far-reaching changes in the entire society.

As a hopeful sign, many of the images we see in the media are positive. In 2009 Disney introduced its first African American animated starring role in *The Princess and the Frog* that featured an interracial romance (the Prince is Anglo). Photographer Bruce Davidson produced a coffee table book, *East 100th Street*, which documented the everyday lives of persons living in Harlem, New York City, and returned almost 30 years later to update his work. The increasing popularity of *lucha libre* ("free wrestling") in the United States fills many assimilated Mexicans with pride for their heritage. As one fan noted, "This is part of the culture. It's the fiesta of the people." Latino culture was further enhanced in 2009 after Puerto Rican American Sonia Sotomayor was inducted as the first Latina to become a member of the Supreme Court of the United States.

Actors from diverse backgrounds can be seen on popular television shows—Sandra Oh in "Gray's Anatomy," Margaret Cho in "Drop Dead Diva," Dennis Haysbert who plays the president on "24" and a special ops leader on "The Unit," D. L. Hughley on CNN's "D.L. Hughley Breaks the News," Tracy Morgan in "30 Rock," Masi Oka in "Heroes," and many contestants on reality game shows.

Other examples of positive portrayals can be found. With women comprising 11 percent of U.S. soldiers in Iraq and Afghanistan as of 2009, several photographers have shown in pictures their hard work and unique challenges; *Murderball* (2005) is a documentary film about paraplegics who play the grueling game of full-contact rugby on basketball courts (Weblink 5.11); the Fox series "Glee" featured Kevin McHale playing a high school student who uses a wheelchair; above the slogan, "Not all blind people sell pencils," a public service advertisement from the American Foundation for the Blind shows portraits of a successful professor, wrestling coach, district attorney, and sports announcer (Figure 5.20); whether for credit cards, jewelry, or automobiles, advertisers are using more and more actors from diverse cultures; shot in black & white filmstock, portraits of many of the Latinos encountered along the journey of Ernesto "Che" Guevara and Alberto Granado portrayed at the end of *Diarios de Motocicleta* (2004) were respectful of the individuals and their culture; Arab American director Cherien Dabis's *Amreeka* (2009) tells the sensitive and real-life story of a divorced Palestinian woman who immigrates to the United States with her son after the invasion of Iraq in 2003.

Many times over-the-top parodies teach important lessons about sexism. A popular faux commercial on "Saturday Night Live" showed a boy and girls playing two different versions of chess in "Chess for Girls." The boy became frustrated after the girls were provided with pieces that resembled toys and dolls, with some that smelled of strawberries, and a Queen piece holding a sleeping baby. Another example of an artist showing stereotypes in order to make a point *against* stereotypes is the music video "Stupid Girls" by Alecia Moore (aka P!nk; Weblink 5.12). A girl is offered two ways of life—conforming to traditional standards of behavior and beauty that leads to breast enhancement and bulimia or being socially aware, intelligent, articulate, and playing the male-dominated sport of football.

Another example of anti-stereotypical behavior is a 1997 Volkswagen commercial in which two young men, one Anglo and the other African American, ride in a car, pick up a smelly chair, and get rid of it set to the tune of "Da Da Da" by the German band Trio (Weblink 5.13). The commercial was praised for showing an everyday lifestyle activity in which the races of the two men didn't matter. In 1995, the Nike sports clothing company launched its "If You Let Me Play" advertising campaign, in which mostly pre-teen girls spoke directly into the camera. They told of the benefits of playing sports, which included statements such as "I will suffer less depression," "I will be more likely to leave a man who beats me," and "I'll be less likely to get pregnant before I want to." Although criticized for the adult themes the girls addressed, the statistics and social issues addressed in the ad were factual and important (Weblink 5.14).

In 2005 the National Collegiate Athletic Association (NCAA) announced that it would ban from postseason play any team that used a Native American mascot. Consequently, sensitivity to the mascot issue seems to be gaining ground. Because of pressure from the NCAA, alumni, and other concerned citizens, educational institutions around the United States

Dennis Shulman, Ph.D. Psychoanalyst and Professor Fordham University

Vivian Yacu, Staff System Designer Port Authority of New York/New Jersey

Erik Weihenmayer, English Teacher and Wrestling Coach Phoenix Country Day School (AZ)

Don Wardlow, Sportscaster New Britain Red Sox

Lou Calesso, Computer Systems Analyst AT&T Bell Labs

Celeste Lopes, Asst. District Attorney Brooklyn, NY

N O T   A L L   B L I N D   P E O P L E   S E L L   P E N C I L S .

have changed from their Native mascots in recent years. The Redmen of St. John's University in New York became the Red Storm; Southern Nazarene University in Oklahoma were once the Redskins and are now the Crimson Storm; Ohio's Miami

Figure 5.20

This American Foundation for the Blind advertisement counters the stereotype of those who cannot see as helpless and dependent on others.

University changed their mascot from the Redskins to the RedHawks; and Marquette University changed from the Warriors to the Golden Eagles. In addition, Native groups praised *Little Big Man* (1970), *A Man Called Horse* (1970), *Dances with Wolves* (1990), and *Smoke Signals* (1998) for their honest portrayals (Figure 5.21).

Considered a groundbreaking advertising promotion in combating stereotypical thinking was the "Real Beauty" campaign by the personal product manufacturer Dove, which was founded in 1955 with a popular line of soaps and skin creams. In 2004 ordinary-looking women posed for British fashion photographer John Rankin Waddell and American photographer Annie Leibovitz. The images were used in billboard and magazine advertisements created by Ogilvy & Mather, Canada. Dove also started the "Self-Esteem Fund" to promote various projects related to posi-

tive self-awareness and anti-mainstream advertising messages directed at women. Several short videos associated with the campaign received international praise. *Dove Mothers and Daughters* (Weblink 5.15) was shown during Super Bowl XL in 2005. *Evolution* (2006; Weblink 5.16) and *Onslaught* (2007; Weblink 5.17) won awards at the prestigious Cannes Lions Advertising Festival. In *Evolution*, a "pretty, but ordinary girl," the model Stephanie Betts, is transformed into a billboard beauty through lighting, makeup, hair products, and Photoshop. But before too many accolades are given to the Dove campaigns, it should be noted that the British and Dutch company Unilever that owns Dove also promotes its Axe line of men's fragrances with commercials that are considered stereotypical and misogynistic.

Unequal power, ownership, privilege, and respect are at the core of communication problems between cultural groups. And when the media regularly celebrate cultural diversity with words and images instead of concentrating on conflict and stereotypes, the goal of ending prejudice, racism, and discrimination will come a little closer to being reached.

Figure 5.21

A page from the Nordisk Familijebok, *a Swedish encyclopedia from 1904, shows Native and South Americans from 33 tribes, from the Aleuts in Alaska to the Fuegians from the southern tip of Tierra del Fuego. Studying closely the diversity of their headdresses, hairstyles, facial attributes, expressions, and clothing, it is difficult to imagine anyone lumping them together as one cultural group.*

Courtesy of the Bibliographisches Institut, Leipzig

■ KEY TERMS

- Assimilation
- Aztec culture
- Discrimination
- Gallup poll
- Hijab
- HIV/AIDS
- Inca culture
- Islam

- Muslims
- Poster child
- Prejudice
- Proposition 8
- Racial profiling
- Terrorists
- Vaudeville

To locate active URLs for the weblinks mentioned in this chapter, please go to the companion site at http://communication.wadsworth.com/lester5 and select the proper chapter.

Chapter 6

Visual Analysis

British critic and artist John Ruskin, who died in 1900, was best known for initiating the Arts and Crafts aesthetic movement that celebrated handiwork. The Bolshevik revolutionary Leon Trotsky called him "one of those rare men who think with their heart." Ruskin once wrote, "The greatest thing a human soul ever does in this world is to see something. . . . To see clearly is poetry, prophecy, and religion, all in one" (Figure 6.1). As you have learned by now, the first step in seeing clearly is to think clearly. Analysis is a way the mind not only engages with the outside world, but also internalizes its lessons and learns from them.

Critics throughout the history of literature have used many methods to analyze works created by others. For example, David Lodge, in his book *Small World: An Academic Romance* (1984), lists 14 different analytical perspectives: allegorical, archetypal, biographical, Christian, ethical, existentialist, Freudian, historical, Jungian, Marxist, mythical, phenomenological, rhetorical, and structural. Although most analyses don't require so many approaches, you must be able to use some sort of critical method to analyze pictures to fully appreciate visual communication.

Image analysis teaches two important lessons about the creation of memorable pictures: A producer of messages should have an understanding of the diversity of cultures within an intended audience, and she should also be aware of the symbols used in images so that they are understood by members of those cultures.

Although visual analysis is vital in understanding a picture's place within a cultural context, the concept of visual analysis is fairly new given the long history of visual message production—over

Analysis reveals the person making the analysis—not really the piece itself.

David Lodge, b. 1935
NOVELIST AND PLAYWRIGHT

Figure 6.1

"John Ruskin," watercolor on paper, 1879, by Sir Hubert von Herkomer. Ruskin said of his portrait that it is "a beautiful drawing of me, the first that has ever given what may be gleaned out of the clods of my face." Von Herkomer was a British painter, filmmaker, and composer. After a long career as a painter of portraits and landscapes, he established his own Herkomer School for art education. In 1896, Queen Victoria knighted him.

Courtesy of the National Portrait Gallery, London

30,000 years. But from the dawn of modern typography—Johannes Gutenberg's commercial printing press, first developed in the 1440s—the visual media were rarely employed for any purpose other than as margin drawings or as sensational, attention-getting pictures to attract the non-reading public to performances. At best, images might be used as maps or medical diagrams. Consequently, those who produced pictures were often regarded as lesser than their written word counterparts. For example, newspaper photographers in the first half of the 20th century were often considered to be "reporters with their brains knocked out." However, later in the century, critics and educators such as Rudolf Arnheim, John Berger, Roland Barthes, Susan Sontag, and others took image production and visual communicators seriously. Consequently, visual literacy gradually developed into a serious study.

John Berger is a British critic, artist, and novelist born in 1926. For visual communicators he is best known for his landmark book on visual culture, *Ways of Seeing* (1972), which was developed into a television series for the BBC. For Berger, an image must be analyzed within its presentational context. A quick-click photograph viewed on an iPhone, a somber and respectful gallery exhibit with viewers enjoying cheese and drinks, a series of travel images on Facebook or Flickr, murals sprayed on subway trains, any photograph published in this book, a newspaper front page or magazine cover picture, a movie in a theater or shown on television or a computer monitor, a large advertisement on a billboard—all create unique contexts of meaning and, thus, of analysis (Figure 6.2). But as varied as

Figure 6.2

Facebook is one of the most popular websites for storing pictures and sharing them with friends. Here, an album contains 10 images of a user's trip to Australia in 2008. With a mouse click on a small, thumbnail photo, you can see a larger version with any caption details the user cared to include.

Courtesy of Paul Martin Lester

the contexts are for viewing images, so too should be the varied ways in which images are analyzed.

Historian and educator David Perlmutter identifies eight ways to help understand an image: production (how was the image physically produced and how are elements combined within a frame), content identification (what are the major elements and what is the story being told), functional (what is the context for the image and how was it put to use), expressional (what emotions are conveyed by the content and how are those feelings translated across cultures), figurative (how are the symbols and metaphors employed and what are any culturally sensitive elements), rhetorical/moral (what are the philosophical justifications for making and showing the work and what are any responsibilities the producer has to the subject and viewers), societal or period (how does the image reflect the culture and mores of the time it was produced and what does it communicate to future generations), and comparative (how is the image similar to previously created works and how does it fit within the body of work of the image creator). Not surprisingly, Perlmutter admits that such an analysis "involves a great deal of effort."

Analytical approaches, although time-consuming, are valuable because they help you notice the smallest details that make up an image, which often leads to greater, universal truths. Meaning/perceiving should be the goal of any type of visual analysis—whether for personal, professional, or cultural reasons. The process also requires that you become familiar with the biography of an artist, the details of her culture and her life, that led to the picture's creation. Analysis should come after a detailed viewing of the work itself and the impact, if any, the work had on the artist, other artists, the subjects, the viewers, the genre, the culture, and society. As such, an analysis of *any* image, whether still or moving, seen in print or screen media, should not be taken lightly.

As you will note in the subsequent chapters, six perspectives for analysis—personal, historical, technical, ethical, cultural, and critical—will help explain a wide variety of presentation media, from the use of typography in graphic designs to the way websites present almost unlimited links. But before using any of these six analytical perspectives, there are a few preliminary steps you should take in order to prepare yourself for a thorough analysis. These 13 steps include making a detailed inventory list of all you see in a picture; noting the unique compositional elements within a frame; discussing how the visual cues of color, form, depth, and movement work singly and in combination to add interest and meaning; looking at the image in terms of the gestalt laws of similarity, proximity, continuation, and common fate; identifying any iconic, indexical, and symbolic signs; thinking of how the four semiotic codes of metonymy, analogy, displaced, and condensed contribute to its understanding; isolating any cognitive elements that may be a part of the image; considering the purpose the work might have; and whether the image can be thought of as aesthetically pleasing.

A picture taken by *National Geographic* photographer Clifton Adams of Secretary of Commerce Herbert Hoover and Secretary of War Dwight Davis standing among children in a relief camp at Natchez, Mississippi, during the flooding of the Mississippi River in 1927 is used as an example of visual analysis. For a more in-depth analysis of this image, see *On Floods and Photo Ops: How Herbert Hoover and George W.*

Bush Exploited Catastrophes by Paul Martin Lester and published by the University Press of Mississippi. Before you read the author's analysis, study the image yourself and get your own interpretation. Your response may be quite different. Also, even though a photograph is used for this demonstration, the procedure described here should be used with any form of visual message (Figure 6.3).

camera. The other man looks down. Nine children no older than ten years old are standing with the men. Most of the children are barefooted (Figure 6.4). One boy wears a hat. All stand on worn-down grass. Behind them are two teepee-style tents tied with stakes to the ground. A woman sits in the tent at the left. She wears a hat. Her left hand covers her mouth. Behind the tents is a forest.

■ Inventory

Make a list of all you see—animal, vegetable, and mineral—in the picture. If it helps, imagine a grid with horizontal and vertical lines superimposed upon the picture so that you actively consider every possible part of the picture.

Two adults are seen standing. They are formally dressed. Both wear hats. The man at the left is in a dark suit and looks at the

■ Composition

Actively notice the picture's elements. How do the individual parts contribute or distract from the picture as a whole? How do the gestalt laws of similarity, proximity, continuation, and common fate contribute to compositional elements?

The camera angle is straight on in the horizontal view. The photographer is probably standing at eye level with the adults.

Figure 6.3

The original caption for the picture as it appeared in the April 1927 issue of National Geographic *read: "'YES, WE HAD BREAKFAST, BUT WE HAVE NOTHING TO PLAY WITH' It was not easy to explain to children why pets and toys had to be abandoned when families fled before the rising floods. At Natchez, Mississippi, Secretaries Hoover and Davis visited the youngsters in camp. One bashful boy, dodging the camera, hid behind the friendly coattails of Mr. Hoover."*

Herbert Hoover Presidential Library and Museum, Clifton Adams, Photographer

Figure 6.4

A close-up look at the feet of the children reveals the approximate time of day by the shadows on the ground, the presumed temperature since most wear short pants, and the fact that most are not wearing shoes.

The group of men and children are in the center and front of the frame. There is extra space on all four sides of the frame. The woman in the background is not a part of the group and is a bit distracting (Figure 6.5). Similarity: Although wearing different colored jackets, the two men are easily grouped separately from the others in the picture by their age, similar height, and position in the frame. Proximity: The children are an identifiable group since they are all standing so close to each other. Continuation: The point of the tent at the left can be imagined as its triangle shape continues beyond the top. Common fate: Since only one child actually looks up at an adult while the other man looks down at the children, this gestalt law is invoked with the man at the left looking directly into the camera's lens. In other words, the viewer of this image is the designation of the subjects' gaze.

■ *Visual Cues*

Study the visual cues of color, form, depth, and movement within the image. Note how they interact and conflict. How are colors used? Look for the source and direction of light in the picture. Does light come from a natural or artificial source? How are shapes and lines utilized within the frame of the image? If there are persons in the image, take notice of their eyes to see whether they are looking at or away from the camera or are hidden from view. How is the illusion of depth achieved? Are your eyes actively moving around the frame?

Color: The photograph is black and white with a wide variety of light, gray, and dark tones. The dense and dark shadows on the ground from the persons standing indicate a bright day, sometime during the early afternoon. Form: A boy wears a hat that is pyramidal in shape, similar in form to the tent in the background. In fact, a reverse pyramidal "V" shape is formed by

Figure 6.5

A close-up of the mystery woman sitting on a footlocker at a tent's opening shows that she looks away from the camera's lens with her hand attempting to cover her face. She wears a distinctive, tight-fitting, bell-shaped cloche hat (cloche is French for "bell"), made popular by "flappers" of the 1920s. This type of modern hat is strangely out-of-place in this rural, relief camp setting. She wears a skirt perhaps made of leather and a jacket. The out-of-place woman distracts from the politicians with the children and was cropped out from the National Geographic *printed version. Could she be a friend of the photographer?*

the negative space of the tent edges in the background that mimics a similar triangle from the man at the left down to the child in the front and up to the hat of the other man. The eyes of the children look up at the man to the left, who looks at the camera. The other adult looks down. Depth: The group in the front is separated from the background not only by their interposition but also because they are more in focus than the elements behind them. They are also more in the light than the objects behind them. Because the man at the left in the dark suit is slightly separated from the group and is looking toward the camera, he appears to be the central focus of the picture and the most important element. Movement: The moment captured is static, with everyone stopped for the photographer, but there is graphic dynamism with the "V" forms mentioned earlier and the direction of the eyes of the man at the right (Figure 6.6).

■ Semiotic Signs and Codes

What are any iconic, indexical, and symbolic signs that can be identified in the image? Do any of the metonymy, analogy, displaced, or condensed codes contribute to its understanding?

The photograph itself is an example of an iconic sign, since there is little doubt that the individuals pictured lived and are accurately portrayed. The fact that most of the children are without shoes is an indexical sign that perhaps the weather was warm. The dress of the two men is a symbolic sign of their superiority, power, and separation from the others, since they are not wearing clothes you would normally see in a camping environment.

■ Cognitive Elements

How do the cognitive concepts of memory, projection, expectation, selectivity, habituation, salience, dissonance, culture, and words contribute to the image's understanding?

Memory: As an historical photograph featuring a future president, Herbert Hoover, the image evokes other memorable scenes dating from 1929 and

Figure 6.6
Visual interest is directed toward the children in the photograph by the graphic "V" shape that is made from the outline of the two tents in the background. Furthermore, the tall, lean form of Secretary Davis looking down on the children also directs a viewer's eyes to them.

the Great Depression. Projection: The strangely shaped object that appears to hang from a tree at the top-right might be the carcass of a deer or other large animal after it has been field dressed (Figure 6.7). Selectivity: There are many elements of the photograph that might catch your eye, but the sweet, polite girl with the blonde curls looking up at Hoover with her hands calmly clasped at her waist stands out (Figure 6.8). Habituation: Perhaps this image is interesting to you because you live in a desert climate and are not accustomed to a forest scene. Salience: If you have broad experience camping you may notice the style of the tents, which are open at the bottom to allow more air to circulate. Dissonance: The mystery woman in the background may be a distraction from the main focus of the image. Culture: Although everyone in the image is Anglo, there is a clash of cultures between the woman in the back and the men, the men and the children, and city dwellers and country residents. Words: The caption in *National Geographic* (See Figure 6.3) indicates that it is probable that the mood of the children was not as cheerful as the caption writer might suggest.

■ *Purpose of the Work*

Where do you think the picture was made? What do you think is the image's purpose? Is it news, art, scientific, a personal snapshot, or some other type of image?

The photograph might have been taken in a large, open clearing surrounded by woods. With the man at the left looking at the camera and the stiff and formal collection of strangers, the image appears to be a publicity shot used by government officials to promote themselves in their effort to help children during a natural disaster (Figure 6.9).

Herbert Hoover Presidential Library and Museum, Clifton Adams, Photographer

Herbert Hoover Presidential Library and Museum, Clifton Adams, Photographer

Figure 6.7
A bizarre element in a photo op meant to spread positive publicity by government officials visiting children in a relief camp is revealed by this close-up of a shape against one of the trees in the background. Rob Draper of the Federal Highway Administration noted that "the thing hanging in the tree could be what remains of [a] deer carcass. Looks like a thoracic cavity minus the loin and rear legs." If true, what does that say about the relief efforts if those living in the camp are forced to eat wild game?

Figure 6.8
The sweet-faced girl who peers respectfully up at the future president shows a maturity beyond her years (she would be about 86 years old today). Out of the entire group of children and perhaps the adults as well, she stands out.

Herbert Hoover Presidential Library and Museum,
Clifton Adams, Photographer

Figure 6.9

Although often excruciatingly shy even with friends and labeled arrogant by his critics, Herbert Hoover was one of the first American politicians to know how to find a camera. He understood the power of publicity to paint a positive picture of himself. No wonder he is the only person in the photograph looking straight into the camera's lens with the best smile he could muster.

■ *Image Aesthetics*

Is there anything about the image that makes it particularly compelling to look at? Does it have formal and/or creative elements that make it particularly beautiful? Does the image make you want to see more of the artist's work?

Although there is a certain charm to an historic black-and-white documentary image, because of its utilitarian purpose—to make two politicians look helpful in the eyes of the public—any formal determination of the picture's aesthetic worth is tempered. The picture is perhaps one step from a family snapshot, but has little aesthetic value otherwise.

Now you are ready for an in-depth analysis. The rest of this chapter details the six perspectives for analyzing images:

Personal: An initial reaction to the work based on your subjective opinions.

Historical: A determination of the importance of the work based on the medium's time line.

Technical: The relationship between light, the recording medium used to produce the work, and the context in which the work is shown.

Ethical: The moral and ethical responsibilities that the producer, the subject, and the viewer of the work have and share.

Cultural: An analysis of the metaphors and symbols used in the work that convey meaning within a particular society at a particular time.

Critical: The issues that transcend a particular image and shape a reasoned personal reaction.

The goal of this analysis is to move from a subjective, quick, and emotional opinion, often expressed from a personal perspective, to an objective, long-term, and reasoned judgment reflected by the critical perspective.

■ *Personal Perspective*

Upon first viewing any image, everyone draws a quick conclusion about a picture based entirely on a personal response. When asked about a movie, words and phrases such as "good," "bad," "I like it," or "I don't like it" are the usual quick responses. These answers indicate that a person initially analyzes the picture on a superficial, cursory level. Personal perspectives are important because they reveal much about the person making the comments. But such opinions have limited use simply because they are so personal. These comments cannot be generalized beyond the individual, nor do they reveal much in the way of how others in the present or future should think of an image. A memorable image, perhaps one that is considered a masterpiece by critics and the public alike, always sparks strong personal reactions, either negative or positive, and also reveals much about the culture from which it was made. A viewer who rests a conclusion about an image on only a personal perspective denies the chance of perceiving the image in a more meaningful way.

Although the image was published in *National Geographic* magazine as part of its coverage of the devastation unleashed by the Mississippi River flood of 1927, the photograph at first glance is not worth a second look. By most professional standards, the picture of two American government officials posing with children in a relief camp would not even be published in a daily newspaper. The picture is obviously

a set-up and stage-managed photo op or media event so that politicians can show their concern and advance their own political self interests. Additionally, on technical and content criteria, it does not deserve much notice. Consequently, an initial reaction of the picture is rather negative.

Historical Perspective

Each medium of presentation—from typography to the web—has a unique history of circumstances that were set in motion and fostered by individuals interested in promoting the medium. For typography, the history of writing dates from the dawn of recorded history. For the web, the developments are relatively recent. Knowledge of a medium's history allows you to understand current trends in terms of their roots in techniques and philosophies of the past. Innovative and aesthetically pleasing visual messages come from an awareness of what has been produced before, and contemporary pictures will influence future image creation. Since images are artifacts that immediately are thought to preserve past events, an historical analysis is of utmost importance in understanding the present meaning of any image.

Ask yourself: When do you think the image was made? What major developments were happening in the area where the image was produced and throughout the world? Is there a specific artistic style that the image imitates?

The Mississippi River flood of 1927 started out as an ordinary rainstorm during August 1926. But the storm never let up. By September, all the river's tributaries were full. The storm persisted throughout the winter.

Rain and then snow accumulated until February. By April, the soaked land couldn't take any more water. Over a 19-hour period beginning on Good Friday, April 15, 1927, Greenville, Mississippi, received 10 inches of rain. Six days later a levee about 18 miles north of the city collapsed. The Mississippi River widened to 80 miles. The flood eventually covered 25,781 square miles in seven states, the approximate size of the state of South Carolina. The estimated number of persons killed was about 1,000. Total damages were about $230 million ($2.7 billion in today's value). More than 600,000 persons were made homeless, with about 540,000, or 90 percent of them, African Americans.

Although orphaned by the time he was nine years old and considered withdrawn and hard to get to know, by the age of 46 Herbert Clark Hoover was a multimillionaire and considered one of the most admired Americans in the world. He parlayed his knowledge of mining, learned from his degree in geology from Stanford University, into a means of becoming a wealthy man. During World War I he accepted governmental positions to aid Americans trapped in Europe and helped Belgian citizens survive the war. He also saved Russians from starvation. By the time of the Mississippi River flood he was Secretary of Commerce under President Calvin Coolidge and selected to head the massive relief effort. The positive publicity he garnered from journalists that followed him to every relief camp helped his candidacy for president, which he won in the election the next year. However, because of his handling of the economic crisis called the Great Depression, historians and others consider his term in office as one of the worst in American history.

At the time the picture was taken, mass circulation newspapers and magazines were popular, television was still in an experimental stage, and sound had just been introduced in motion pictures (Figure 6.10). The style of photography most common was typified by the image analyzed—a straight-on perspective with the main subjects in the center of the frame aware of the camera.

 Technical Perspective

You must know something about how each medium of presentation works. A thorough critique of any visual presentation requires knowledge of how the producer generated the images you see. Whether clay for stop-motion animated films, camera settings with still and moving pictures, or software controls for computer-generated images, knowing the ways they are produced gives you a clearer understanding of the meaning and purpose of a work. With an understanding of the techniques involved in producing an image, you are also in a better position to know when production values are high or low, when great or little care has been taken, or when much or little money was spent to make the images. Ask yourself: How was the image produced? What techniques were employed? Is the image of good quality?

The black-and-white photograph was made using a normal lens, a medium-sized aperture, without fill-in flash, and 10 to 20 feet away from Hoover and Davis. Adams probably used the "Top Handle" Speed Graphic model that was manufactured by Graflex of Rochester, New York, from 1912 to 1927. There is a moderate amount of depth-of-field, indicating a mid-range aperture opening of the lens. Although the woman in a tent and the trees behind can be clearly seen, they are not in clear focus. Since no one is moving, a fast shutter speed might have been used (Figure 6.11). The overall quality of the image suffers from being slightly overexposed. From the grassy area in the front to the sky in the background, white-colored areas in the picture are washed out, without detail, to the point that the clothes worn by the two children to the right seem to blend together.

 *Ethical Perspective*

Ethics is the study of how persons, other sentient beings (those that can feel pain), and systems (such as governmental agencies and the environment) behave (known as *descriptive ethics*) and how they *should* behave (known as *normative ethics*). You should try as much as possible to concentrate your analyses on normative, rather than descriptive, ethics. You want to come to a conclusion of what someone

Figure 6.10

Hoover recognized the promotional opportunities presented by the visual media, and on April 7, 1927, he became the first politician to be publicized through the new medium of television. This live picture from a funeral home in Washington, D.C., was shown to newspaper reporters and dignitaries gathered at the AT&T Bell Telephone Laboratories auditorium in New York City.

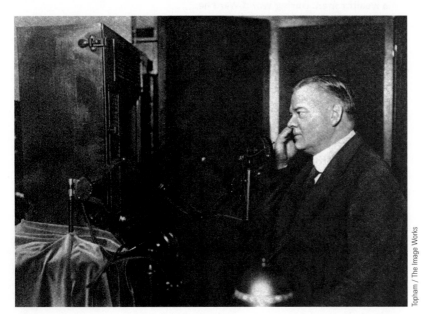

Topham / The Image Works

Figure 6.11
Normally fidgety children are stopped by the camera's relatively fast shutter speed.

Herbert Hoover Presidential Library and Museum, Clifton Adams, Photographer

should do rather than simply describe what someone did.

Anyone considered to be practicing ethical behavior should abide by all the role-related responsibilities that a job requires and should not during the execution of those duties cause unjustified harm. Every profession, from graphic design to website production, has a unique set of requirements or role-related responsibilities that combine to form the concept of a person's "job." For example, a visual journalist for a news organization develops sources, conceives stories, takes images, records audio, interviews sources, writes captions, voice-overs, and copy, edits the words and pictures, checks to make sure all facts are accurate, and arranges to display the work in print, on television, and/or the web.

Doing your job and not causing unjust harm has been called the "ethics mantra." As long as those professional obligations are met, the first part of the mantra is satisfied. But to be considered ethical, you must also make sure that any harm that may ensue must be justified. A nurse causes some discomfort that might be interpreted as harm with a needle stick, but the pain is justified in order to get

well. A professor assesses your exams and papers that may cause harm to your GPA, but it is justified to help you learn. Showing a video of a celebrity in an embarrassing situation on a local newscast may be harmful to that person's reputation, but as long as the airing is deemed acceptable for reasonable, objective persons, the harm can probably be justified. Any action that causes physical or mental harm without adequate justification is unethical.

Six principal ethical philosophies can and should be used to analyze a picture. Knowledge of philosophies is important because they help explain how actions can or cannot be justified. In chronological order, they are golden rule, hedonism, golden mean, categorical imperative, utilitarianism, and veil of ignorance. Although there are many more useful philosophies that could be discussed, these are the principal theories that have survived for more than 2,500 years of Western moral philosophy. Even if the names are new to you, their basic ideas should be familiar to all who have grown up in the United States or other European-influenced cultures. Aspects of these theories are used to justify our public policies, laws, and social conventions.

Golden Rule

The golden rule, or the ethic of reciprocity, teaches people to "love your neighbor as yourself." This theory has been attributed to ancient Greek philosophers such as Pittacus of Mytilene (died 568 BCE), considered one of the "Seven Sages of Greece," who wrote, "Do not to your neighbor what you would take ill from him;" Thales of Miletus (died 546 BCE), another Sage of Greece who said, "Avoid doing what you would blame others for doing;" and Epictetus (died 135 CE), a Stoic philosopher who wrote, "What thou avoidest suffering thyself seek not to impose on others." In fact, every major religion has some variable of the golden rule as a part of their scriptures and/or teachings. This philosophy holds that an individual should be as humane as possible and never harm others by insensitive actions.

A television producer who decides not to air close-up footage of family members mourning the loss of a loved one at a funeral, because seeing themselves on television might compound their grief and the image might make viewers feel bad, invokes the golden rule.

> **For the Hoover relief image, it is a positive "feel-good" moment despite the reality of what life must be like under such living conditions. As such, it probably made readers of *National Geographic* smile to see children taken care of by powerful and famous members of their government.**

Hedonism

From the Greek word for pleasure, hedonism is closely related to the philosophies of nihilism and narcissism. A student of Socrates, Aristippus (who died in Athens in 366 BCE) founded this ethical philosophy on the basis of pleasure. Aristippus believed that people should "act to maximize pleasure now and not worry about the future." However, Aristippus referred to pleasures of the mind—intellectual pleasures—not physical sensations. He believed that people should fill their time with intellectual pursuits and use restraint and good judgment in their personal relationships. His phrase sums up the hedonistic philosophy: "I possess; I am not possessed." Unfortunately, modern usage of the philosophy ignores his original intent.

The Renaissance playwright and poet Ben Johnson, a contemporary of William Shakespeare, once wrote one of the best summaries of the hedonistic philosophy, "Drink today, and drown all sorrow; You shall perhaps not do it tomorrow; Best, while you have it, use your breath; There is no drinking after death." Phrases such as "live for today" and "don't worry, be happy" currently express the hedonistic philosophy. If an opinion or action is based purely on a personal motivation—money, fame, relationships, and the like—the modern interpretation of hedonistic philosophy is at work.

When an image maker considers *only* the aesthetic pleasure, monetary gain, or possible awards a picture might bring, hedonism is the dominant philosophy. It is rare for a visual communicator or anyone else to admit to a purely hedonistic justification for an act that others might judge unethical.

A freelance professional photographer, known as a paparazzo after a character in the movie *Irma la Douce* (1963), who stands in wait for a celebrity to exit a concert, restaurant, or her home so that a picture can be made solely for the purpose of making money from it uses the hedonism philosophy. As such, this philosophy is probably the least admitted to by practitioners out of the six principal ethical philosophies.

The relief image demonstrates hedonism because the photographer wanted to feature the notable person in the picture, Herbert Hoover, and his work in aiding those affected by the flood in the most positive light possible. The commerce secretary is using hedonism too as he wanted to be seen with children to seem more compassionate.

Golden Mean

The Greek philosopher Aristotle was born near the city Thessaloniki in 384 BCE. As his parents were wealthy, he studied at the Athens-based Academy led by the renowned Greek philosopher Plato. After learning and teaching at the Academy for 20 years, he traveled throughout the region studying the biology and botany of his country. He was eventually hired as a tutor for Alexander the Great and two other kings of Greece, Ptolemy and Cassander. When he was about 50 years old he returned to Athens and began his own educational institution, the Lyceum, where he wrote an astounding number of books on diverse subjects that made breakthroughs in science, communications, politics, rhetoric, and ethics. He was the earliest known writer to describe the phenomenon of light noticed in a *camera obscura* that eventually led to a further understanding of how the eyes and the photographic medium work.

Although the golden mean was originally a neo-Confucian concept first espoused by Zisi, the only grandson of the Chinese philosopher Confucius, Aristotle elaborated on it for Western readers in his book *Nicomachean Ethics*. The golden mean philosophy refers to finding a middle ground or a compromise between two extreme points of view or actions. The middle way doesn't involve a precisely mathematical average but is an action that approximately fits that situation at that time. When using the golden mean philosophy, you must first think of the two most extreme examples. For a particularly violent or controversial news photograph or video, there are two extreme choices. The first is to take and then use the picture large and in color on a front page of a newspaper, the cover of a magazine, or in the lead for a news broadcast. The other extreme choice is not to use the image at all. A compromise or middle way might be to use the image in black and white, small, on an inside page, as a short, edited video, or on a website where users are warned before clicking a link to it. Generally speaking, most ethical dilemmas are solved with the golden mean approach.

The relief camp picture is a compromise between close-up images of the children in their harsh day-to-day living conditions, in their tents with their fellow family members, and not taking any pictures at all.

Categorical Imperative

Immanuel Kant was born in Königsberg, the capital of Prussia (now Kaliningrad, Russia) in 1724. The fourth of 11 children, at an early age he showed intellectual promise and escaped his crowded household to attend a special school. At the age of 16 he graduated from the University of Königsberg, where he stayed and taught until his death. Kant never married and never traveled farther than 100 miles from his home during his lifetime. Thirteen years before his death in 1804, he published *Critique of Pure Reason*. It is considered one of the most important works in philosophical history. Kant established the concept of the categorical imperative.

Categorical means unconditional, and *imperative* means that the concept should be employed without any question, extenuating circumstances, or exceptions. Right is right and must be done even under the most extreme conditions. Consistency is the key to the categorical imperative philosophy. Once a rule is established for a proposed action or idea, behavior and opinions must be consistently and always applied in accordance with it. But for Kant, the right action must have a positive effect and not promote unjustified harm or evil. Nevertheless, the categorical imperative is a difficult mandate to live up to.

If a visual reporter's rule is to document any situation and take pictures regardless of whether she thinks her newspaper will print them because she considers that action to be part of her job and to be performed without objections, then this decision becomes a categorical imperative. She takes photographs because it is her duty to do so, and it leads to a positive conclusion—the pictures document an activity for historical purposes if for no other reason.

As a *National Geographic* photographer, Clifton Adams had little choice but to take a picture of a posing Herbert Hoover and Dwight Davis with a group of children. Regardless, Adams no doubt felt it was part of his professional role-related responsibility to take the picture in order to publish it in the magazine. Therefore, his categorical imperative would be to perform the same act under any similar set of circumstances.

Utilitarianism

This philosophy is usually considered the combined work of British thinkers Jeremy Bentham and John Stuart Mill. The legal scholar and philosopher Jeremy Bentham developed his theory of utility, or the greatest happiness principle, from the work of Joseph Priestley, who is considered one of the most important philosophers and scientists of the 18th century. Bentham acknowledged Priestley as the architect of the idea that "the greatest happiness of the greatest number is the foundation of morals and legislation." John Stuart Mill was the son of the Scottish philosopher James Mill and was tutored for a time by Bentham. When he was three years old, he was taught to read Greek; by the time he was 10 he read Plato's works easily. With the aid of his wife Harriet Taylor, he developed the philosophy of utilitarianism expressed in his books *On Liberty* (1859) and *Utilitarianism* (1863). He gave credit to Taylor for her influence but, as was the custom of the time, did not give her co-authorship credit.

Mill expanded on Priestley and Bentham's idea of utilitarianism by separating different kinds of happiness. For Mill, intellectual happiness is more important than the physical kind. He also thought that there is a difference between happiness and contentment, which is culminated in his phrase, "It is better to be a human being dissatisfied than a pig satisfied; better to be Socrates dissatisfied than a fool satisfied." In utilitarianism, various consequences of an act are imagined, and the outcome that helps the most people is usually the best choice under the circumstances. However, Mill specified that each individual's moral and legal rights must be met before applying the utilitarian calculus. According to Mill, it is not acceptable to cause great harm to a few persons in order to bring about a little benefit to many. However, if everyone is being treated justly, then it is acceptable to do something that might provide a large benefit to the community as a whole.

Editors and news directors frequently use and misuse utilitarianism to justify the printing of disturbing accident scenes in their newspapers, magazines, on television, and on websites. Although the image may upset a few because of its gruesome content, it may persuade many others to drive more carefully. That action is acceptable under the utilitarianism philosophy because people do not have a moral right to be sheltered from sad news on occasion. For many, the educational function of the news media—from the typographical and graphic design displays that can be easily read to informational graphics that explain a complex concept—is most often expressed in the utilitarian philosophy.

Clifton Adams most likely thought that by producing the relief camp picture he would be educating *National Geographic* readers that although camp life could be rough, the children looked reasonably well fed and happy to be visited by Hoover and Davis.

Veil of Ignorance

Articulated by the American philosopher John Rawls in his book *A Theory of Justice* in 1971, the veil of ignorance philosophy considers all people equal as if each member were wearing a veil so that such attributes as age, gender, ethnicity, and so on could not be determined. No one class of people would be entitled to advantages over any other. Imagining oneself without knowing the positions that one brings to a situation results in an attitude of respect for all involved. The phrase "walk a mile in someone's shoes" is a popular adaptation of the veil of ignorance philosophy. It is considered one answer to prejudice and discrimination.

Rawls taught at Harvard University for almost 40 years. In 1999 he received the National Humanities Medal from President Bill Clinton, who said that he "helped a whole generation of learned Americans revive their faith in democracy itself."

A viewer of a print or screen display might invoke this philosophy in an e-mail of thanks to a visual communicator or journalist, if the viewer were made to think of her own loved ones after seeing a picture of subjects of a visual message.

A *National Geographic* magazine reader might think of a child she knows and imagine her living in a temporary camp after a terrible environmental catastrophe. Thinking of such a connection with "the other" and feeling empathy for those affected by the Mississippi River flood might result in contributions to the Red Cross and Salvation Army.

After a thorough study of the six ethical philosophies briefly described, an analysis of the Hoover picture might also include the following:

Herbert Hoover was the first American politician to understand that "public relations could change behavior." Consequently, he and the people who worked for him tried to promote him at every step of his career. He was the first politician to make extensive use of the radio and the first to be broadcast via the new television medium. He was the first to use motion pictures and sound in his presidential campaign films. Hoover orchestrated his appearances at flood-damaged sites and camps for maximum public exposure. But the picture demonstrates the exploitation of the good graces, best wishes, and innocent hopes of those most vulnerable—the children—who naively looked up to the powerful adults visiting them.

The other compelling aspect of the photograph is the fact that there are no African Americans. In 1927 the United States was deeply segregated, and the relief camps reflected that racist era. Nevertheless, since an estimated 90 percent of those affected by the flooding were African Americans, it seems fitting that Hoover and his entourage should have visited and been pictured with non–Anglo Americans.

Cultural Perspective

Here is your chance to further refine your analysis given the influences from the historical, technical, and ethical perspectives. Cultural analysis of a picture involves identifying the symbols and metaphors used in an image and determining their meaning for the society as a whole. Symbolism may be analyzed through the picture's use of heroes and villains, by the form of its narrative structure, by the style of the artwork, by the use of words that accompany the image, and by the attitudes about the subjects and the culture communicated by the visual artist. The cultural perspective is closely related to the semiotics approach.

Metaphors combine a viewer's experiences with the meaning of a visual message. Aristotle, in *Rhetoric*, wrote, "It is a great thing, indeed, to make proper use of poetic forms, . . . But the greatest thing by far is to be a master of metaphor." Real world experiences infuse an image under analysis with special meaning for the viewer so that underlying metaphors can be discovered. Educator Stuart Jay Kaplan defines metaphors as "combinations of two or more elements in which one element is understood or experienced in terms of the other." For Kaplan and others, "Metaphors serve as

interpretive frameworks for organizing information about the world and making sense of experiences." George Lakoff and Mark Johnson, in *Metaphors We Live By*, expand the point when they write, "No metaphor can ever be comprehended or even adequately represented independently of its experiential basis." The American anthropologist Evelyn Payne Hatcher, author of *Art and Culture: An Introduction to Anthropology of Art*, wrote that metaphors "are a matter of trying to understand and comment upon what is going on [within a picture] in terms of our previous experience." As such, metaphors that are commonly understood across time and cultures "rest on the common experiences of the human." For Hatcher, "Visual art is not merely a matter of aesthetics, but one of visually developed ideas, usually conceived in some metaphorical form."

Ask yourself: What is the story and the symbolism involved in the elements of the visual message? What do they say about current cultural values? What metaphors can be expressed through the work?

The symbolism of Anglo power and dominance as expressed through social perspective is clearly evident in the photograph. Hoover is in the front and slightly separated from the others. He is dressed in somber, almost funereal clothes that add seriousness to his demeanor. However, his light-colored fedora hat doesn't match the rest of his outfit, perhaps indicating a slight air of informality fitting for the campsite setting. The barefoot girl to his left looks up at him with her arms respectfully held in front. She has a bright, pleasant expression on her face. But Hoover, with his arms at his sides, has all his attention directed toward the camera. Hoover knows that the most important element

is to see his face clearly. Everyone else is secondary.

The hat and coat of Davis match his informal attire and the setting. The fact that the two men stand so far apart from each other indicates that the two are not close. In fact, Hoover considered Davis a political rival. After he was elected president, Hoover appointed Davis Governor General of the Philippines to keep him out of the political limelight.

The barefoot children seem at ease in the natural environment, whereas the overly dressed adults, symbols of technological progress and an urbane attitudes, stand awkwardly and look out of place. As seen by their clothing and poses, the city versus country conflict is a metaphor for modernism that divides those who are content and secure from those who have lost everything and must begin anew.

🔍 Critical Perspective

The final step in analyzing a picture is to apply a critical perspective. In this last step, you should attempt to transcend a particular image and draw general conclusions about the medium, the culture from which it is produced, and the viewer. A critical perspective allows the viewer to use the information learned about a medium, its practitioner, and the image produced to make more general comments about the society that accepts or rejects the images. As such, a critical perspective redefines a person's initial personal perspective in terms of universal conclusions about human nature.

Ask yourself: What do I think of this image now that I've spent so much time looking at and studying it? What lessons does it have for those who view the image?

As an artifact that illustrates the history of the public relations profession, the Hoover/Davis relief camp photograph has value for cultural historians who would note the absence of African American faces and for visual communicators who study the photo op genre. It also is useful for biographers of Herbert Hoover, who may use the image to illustrate an aspect of his personality and media savvy. Consequently, an initial negative opinion of the picture is changed to one of positive worth through the analytical process.

Whether it is a still or moving image, if you study it by first making an inventory list, then by noting its compositional elements including the gestalt laws, visual cues, semiotic signs and codes, cognitive elements, possible purposes, and aesthetic qualities, and then from personal, historical, technical, ethical, cultural, and critical perspectives, you become intellectually engaged with the picture. Using the six perspectives will encourage you to base conclusions about images on rational rather than emotional responses. You will find that all images have something to tell you because every picture created, no matter how banal or ordinary it may be at first glance, has some meaning to communicate. The producer of the image took the time to frame and make the picture for a reason. The message that the artist wants to communicate may be simply a literal summary, or the hope that the viewer will appreciate the image's aesthetic beauty, or an underlying political agenda. Just because you cannot initially see any purpose for an image is no reason to discard it. Many large lessons are lost because of a failure to study small, captured moments. An image, regardless of its medium of presentation, is forgotten if it isn't analyzed. A forgotten image simply becomes another in a long stream of meaningless pictures that seem to flood every aspect of communication. Meaningless pictures entertain a viewer only for a brief moment and do not have the capacity to educate. But an analyzed image can affect a viewer for a lifetime.

The nine chapters on typography, graphic design, informational graphics, cartoons, photography, motion pictures, television, computers, and the web are analyzed within the six-perspective analytical framework outlined in this chapter. Although analysis is time consuming at first, practice reduces the amount of time required. It is up to you, and only you, to find meaning and use for a picture. If you take the time to study images carefully, you will become a much more interesting and knowledgeable person. You will also be more likely to produce images that

have greater meaning for more people. These images are also remembered longer than unconsidered pictures.

Your ultimate goal with regard to any analysis of a picture is to understand your own reaction to the image. Through this analytical process, you review, refine, and renew your personal reaction to an image. Being critical is a highly satisfying intellectual exercise.

■ *KEY TERMS*

- Allegorical
- Archetypal
- Bolshevik
- Cropped
- Depth of field
- Existentialist
- Field dressing
- Freudian
- Jungian
- Marxism
- Mythical
- Phenomenological
- Rhetorical
- Shutter speed
- Structural

 To locate active URLs for the weblinks mentioned in this chapter, please go to the companion site at http://communication.wadsworth.com/lester5 and select the proper chapter.

Section

The previous chapters gave you vital background information and a procedure for analyzing visual messages. However, you are only halfway to fully being able to articulate why some images are remembered and most others are forgotten. The following nine chapters will complete your journey by detailing how pictures are used within the various media. With each chapter there is a quotation from an innovator of the field, an introductory section that details a famous example with an analysis, a concentrated breakdown of the chapter's topic in terms of the six personal, historical, technical, ethical, cultural, and critical perspectives, a section that discusses trends to look out for now and in the future for the medium, and a list of terms that you can find in the glossary. Plus, as with the subsequent chapters, be sure and study the still images printed alongside the copy and read closely the captions associated with each picture. Many times valuable information is conveyed about visual communication through the captions. Finally, if at all possible, you should have a computer open to the weblinks section of the book's website so you can refer to the examples mentioned within the text.

Typography

For $39 (US) dollars, you can download the typeface "textur" from the Linotype.com website. That's the typeface Johannes Gutenberg used to print his Bibles. He took about four years and spent more than he could afford to complete the process from typeface to the printed page, but in minutes you can copy and paste a King James version of the Bible found on the Electronic Text Center website provided by the University of Virginia Library (Weblink 7.1) into a word processing program and with the command "Select All," replace the typeface with the one Gutenberg used. Send the file to your laser printer and your version is complete.

Gutenberg chose to make copies of the Bible, printed in Latin and set in textur, not because he was a religious person, but because he was a smart businessman (Figure 7.1). He knew that once church officials heard of the product of his print-ing invention, which used the language they preferred in the style of handwritten copies, he would be rich.

Gutenberg labored in his workshop and eventually produced a marvel in technology with a commercial printing press that ushered in a revolution in mass communications. In four years he produced 140 Bibles on paper and 40 on vellum, or animal skin. The two-volume, mostly 42-line double-column book, with hand-painted borders and enlarged letters, measured 11 × 16 inches, weighed over 50 pounds, and was introduced in 1455, 100 years before William Shakespeare wrote his first sonnet.

But there were two flaws in Johannes's get-rich plan—he couldn't pay back the money he borrowed to support his lifestyle, experiments, and printing operation, and he never included a personal logo or printer's mark on a single printed page.

Typographical design should perform optically what the speaker creates through voice and gesture.

Lazar Lissitzky (El Lissitzky), 1880–1941
TYPOGRAPHER, PHOTOGRAPHER, AND ARCHITECT

Figure 7.1

Johannes Gutenberg's Bible doesn't start with the Old or New Testaments. The first page of his printing masterpiece comes from the Epistle of St. Jerome, an introduction written in the 5th century by the saint who translated the religious book into Latin, called the Vulgate. In his introduction he mainly defends his reasoning for using a Hebrew Bible as the base for his translation into Latin rather than a Greek version. Besides using the language of the Catholic Church of the day, Latin was a good choice because of the many ways it can be abbreviated. Nevertheless, a reader is helped through the rigid, two-column page by painted red markers for the start of each sentence. Plus, Gutenberg left space for artists to later add colored text and fanciful enlarged or drop cap letters. See color insert following page 178.

Mansell / Time & Life Pictures / Getty Images

From early childhood, Johannes must have been a precocious, problem child. For one thing, he didn't like his last name. He was born Johannes Gensfleisch, German for *goosebumps,* and is believed to be the third son of wealthy parents from Mainz, Germany. Maybe because he was teased as a child, he changed his name to the town of his mother's birth. His uncle was the master of the mint at Mainz, so he learned the skills of metal-working, engraving, mirror making, and decorating objects with precious stones—all crafts he would put to good use later in life.

Unfortunately for his family's economic status, around 1430 there was an uprising of the working class against the aristocracy. Gutenberg's upbringing and outgoing personality earned him a leadership role in the dispute, but he and his father were forced to leave Mainz because they feared for their lives. The two settled in Strasbourg, France, then a German city,

about 100 miles southwest of Mainz, leaving his mother behind to manage the family's home.

In Strasbourg Johannes developed a reputation for being quick tempered and a borrower of large sums of money. In 1437 he asked for a woman's hand in marriage. All was well and good until he changed his mind and called the wedding off. Her family promptly sued him for breach of contract. At his trial, he so berated one of her witnesses that the man later sued him for slander. The experience must have soured him on marriage, for he remained a bachelor his whole life (Figure 7.2).

But the funds required to support his printing experiments were enormous, and trying to secure enough money to continue his work caused most of the troubles in Gutenberg's life. When he needed additional funds to continue his printing experiments, he agreed to a five-year contract to teach two partners his secret method. After one of his associates died, his former partner's sons sued for the advance their father had given to Gutenberg. Court documents reveal that he won that case. An important part of the official court document, an inventory of his workshop, shows that it included a press, various examples of type, and a "mysterious instrument" that was probably a device for casting type molds in metal. For historians, this record is crucial in establishing the fact that Gutenberg was indeed a printer. Also interesting was the court's inventory of his personal property, which revealed that he had the equivalent of 2,000 bottles of wine.

He borrowed a large sum of money from the Church of St. Thomas in Strasbourg, which he failed to repay. The church elders sued him for the money, and Gutenberg fled back to Mainz in 1443, where he lived the rest of his life.

Seven years later Gutenberg borrowed money from a wealthy Mainz gold merchant, Johannes Fust. This transaction would cause his downfall, because he used his printing equipment as collateral for the loan. In 1455, with the work nearly completed on the Bibles that could easily pay off his debt, Fust grew impatient or greedy and brought suit against him. Fust won the case and was awarded the presses and all of the work in progress. Gutenberg was locked out of his own print shop. Fust traveled to several European capitals selling the books, but caught the plague and died. It has been assumed that the German legend of Faust, a man who sells his soul to the devil, which has been retold throughout history by such diverse authors as Christopher Marlowe, Oscar Wilde, and Randy Newman, was inspired by Fust's actions.

Gutenberg went bankrupt but was saved by a Mainz doctor who offered him financial support to open another print shop. Later, Archbishop Adolf of Mainz gave him the rank of nobleman with an annual pension that allowed him to live the last years of his life in relative comfort. He is believed to have died in 1468 and was buried somewhere in the cemetery of the Franciscan church in Mainz. No marker was erected to identify his grave (Figure 7.3).

Although the popular assumption is that Gutenberg invented printing, that isn't quite the case. His genius was in combining what was known at the time with some of his own ideas. He combined a type mold acceptable for printing, a suitable metal alloy, ink, paper and parchment, bookmaking, and a press. He wasn't even the first to use movable type as a substitute for writing by hand. Pi-Sheng, a Chinese alchemist, invented movable type with characters made from heat-

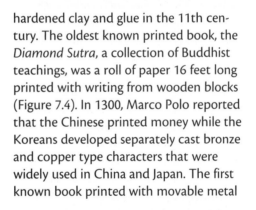

hardened clay and glue in the 11th century. The oldest known printed book, the *Diamond Sutra*, a collection of Buddhist teachings, was a roll of paper 16 feet long printed with writing from wooden blocks (Figure 7.4). In 1300, Marco Polo reported that the Chinese printed money while the Koreans developed separately cast bronze and copper type characters that were widely used in China and Japan. The first known book printed with movable metal

Figure 7.2

Johannes Gensfleisch zur Laden zum Gutenberg wears traditional garb and inspects a printed page from his commercial press.

Figure 7.3

This woodcut shows the city of Mainz, Germany, on the river Rhine, as it looked in 1493, roughly the time that Gutenberg inhabited the town.

Figure 7.4

Printed in the year 868 CE, *the* Diamond Sutra *is the world's earliest surviving printed book. It is one of the most sacred works of the Buddhist faith. The words of the document run along a column to the left, while an elaborate image featuring the Buddha large and high in the frame fills the rest of the page.*

The British Library / Imagestate RM / PhotoLibrary

type—almost 80 years before Gutenberg's book—was titled *Jikji*, another book of Buddhist teachings, produced in a Buddhist temple in Korea in 1377 (Figure 7.5). However, Gutenberg and everyone else in Europe probably were unaware of the extent of printing developments in Asia because of the limited communications of the day.

Gutenberg was well aware of the method of relief printing from wooden blocks used in the Netherlands, France, Italy, and his own country to produce popular holy images, playing cards, and advertising handbills. But wood wasn't acceptable for a mechanical printing process because it tended to warp easily. Gutenberg may have learned of experiments by Propius Walkfoghel of France, who was supposedly working on "alphabets of steel" in about 1444, but with no known result.

Gutenberg most likely used his metalworking skills and borrowed funds to eventually develop an alloy that was soft enough to cast as an individual letter and hard enough to withstand several thousand impressions on sheets of paper, and would not shrink when it cooled in a type mold. Through hundreds of experiments, Gutenberg developed a mixture of lead, tin, and antimony that satisfied his strict requirements.

Fortunately, printing inks and paper were common by that time and easier to adapt. The Egyptians and Chinese had used writing ink as early as 2600 BCE. By the 11th century, ink-making in China was a treasured art in which earth colors were mixed with soot and animal fat and used to produce colorful documents. European relief block printers made their own inks from secret formulas learned from painters of the day. Many of these inks were combinations of iron sulfate and gum arabic, a glue derived from the hardened sap of the acacia tree. The mixture unfortunately oxidized with exposure to light and

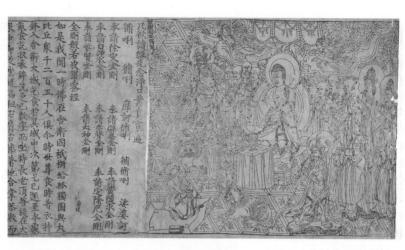

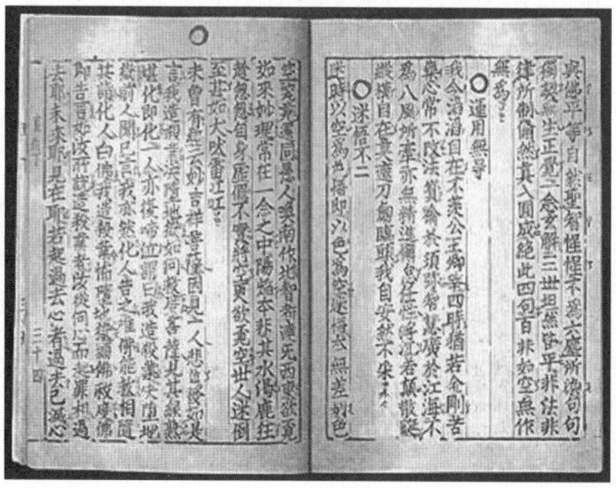

Figure 7.5

"The Monk Baegun's Anthology of the Great Priests' Teachings on Identification of the Buddha's Spirit by the Practice of Seon," known as the Jikji, *is the world's oldest book printed with metal type. It was produced in Korea about 80 years before Gutenberg's invention. Vertical grid lines on the pages are a result of the metal type process, an artifact that Gutenberg eliminated.*

Bibliotheque Nationale de France

turned the letters brown. Consequently, modern curators must display these works in dark exhibition rooms. Nevertheless, it was a popular ink medium from the 5th century until the end of the 18th century. Gutenberg probably used ink that was developed by the Dutch artist Jan Van Eyck 20 years earlier. His formula called for the boiling of linseed oil and soot, which produced a thick, tacky ball that could be smeared on metal type.

The Egyptians had long used papyrus, a crude paper made from reeds that grew along the banks of the Nile River, as a substrate for the writing. The eunuch Ts'ai Lun for the emperor's court in 105 CE probably invented paper in China. Paper as a medium for writing gradually made its way to the West. After Arab warriors defeated the army of the Chinese Tang Dynasty at the Battle of Talas in 751, prisoners were forced to make paper, which led to the first paper mill located in Samarkand, Russia. Consequently, mills were established throughout the Muslim world and eventually spread as far west as Spain. By Gutenberg's time, paper mills were well established in Germany, Spain, France, and Italy.

Although it was vastly more expensive, Gutenberg preferred the use of parchment as a printing substrate. Vellum is the name for the highest-quality material made from the skins of young or stillborn calves, goats, or sheep. The Old French word *velin* means "calf" and is the basis for the English word veal. Vellum is a long-lasting leather that can be printed on both sides. Because inks are better preserved on its surface, it was used for the most colorful illustrations. Another reason for Gutenberg's money woes, however, was that he had to maintain a herd of cattle to supply animal skins for his copies.

The modern concept of a book—individual pages bound together—was well known to Gutenberg. Every abbey library contained a collection of handwritten books produced by monk scribes who used a similar style of calligraphy. For example, the abbey library at Canterbury housed more than 2,000 books. The most common type of book was religious, such as Bibles, collections of psalms, and other religious works; most were written in Latin. Semiologist and author Umberto Eco's novel *The Name of the Rose* tells the story of the murder of scribes in an Italian monastery. In 1986 the work was made into a motion picture starring Sean Connery and Christian Slater. The novel and movie are accurate representations of the grim life of a scribe in the 14th century.

Printing also requires a press. The machine had to be sturdy enough to withstand the weight of the platen and the type itself. Presses at the time were used to produce wine, cheese, and bailing paper. With his interest in wine, not surprisingly, Gutenberg's printing press was a modification of wine presses in use at that time. His press was simply a large screw that lowered a weight onto a sheet of paper or parchment against a plate of inked type. This basic design remained the same until the invention of steam-powered presses about 350 years later.

After Gutenberg's invention became known, print shops opened in France and Italy and quickly spread throughout Europe. By 1500, there were 1,120 print shops in 260 towns in 17 European countries. More than 10 million copies of 40,000 different works had been printed by that year. As books became plentiful and inexpensive, literacy and educational opportunities quickly grew. Societies moved from oral presentations to reading as the primary method of teaching. As people became better educated, democratic ideas spread. Secularism challenged traditional ideas about religious attitudes. Business opportunities and cities expanded as printing sped the recording of transactions. More than any other single invention, the printing press signaled an end to the Dark Ages that followed the collapse of the Roman Empire and the beginning of the Renaissance.

The Gutenberg Bible not only showed the world the potential of the print medium, it also signaled the start of typography—the reproduction of words through a mechanical process. Typography, as exemplified in Gutenberg's work, put printed words on an equal artistic footing with hand-lettered words.

A few years after Gutenberg's achievement, typographic artists—specialists in the creation and use of various typographical styles—combined the craft of sculpture with the art of graphic design to produce lettering that was both practical and beautiful.

Typography, of course, has its roots in writing. The story of writing is the gradual acceptance of the idea, over thousands of years, that words and images are separate and different. But writing and reading without knowledge of design reinforced the notion that words are more important than pictures in formulating messages. Typography reminds us that words are graphic elements with pictorial and emotional qualities as important as any illustration.

Johannes Gutenberg will always be credited for inventing the first commercially viable printing press. But he was a person with all-too-human frailties. Despite the events in his life, or because of them, he accomplished what he set out to do. Perhaps in the end he dedicated so many years of his life to printing a Bible as an act of contrition for his relationships with other people. We will never actually know his motives because, ironically, the inventor of commercialized printing left no printed record of his own life.

■ ANALYSIS OF THE GUTENBERG BIBLE

Gutenberg's work should be praised for at least three technical achievements: its typeface, its design, and its longevity (Figure 7.6). Gutenberg magnificently mimicked the textur typographical style of the abbey scribes. The design is a pleasing combination of text and graphic elements arranged to connote power, prestige, and artistic beauty—a perfect fit for the content of the work. Finally, the book's longevity—48 are known to exist today—is another credit to his craft. Few books in human history have lasted as long. Nevertheless, the Bibles that remain are considered almost priceless. In 2009,

Figure 7.6

The three-volume Gutenberg Bible on display within the respectful and elaborate display case in the east corridor of the Library of Congress in Washington, D.C., is only one of three surviving perfect vellum copies in the world. The distortion of the lines of type comes from the glass that protects the volumes.

a single page on display at a Southern California university is said to be worth as much as $100,000.

Production of the Gutenberg Bible marked the start of the printing profession, but it also is a commentary on ethical business practices. Both Fust and Gutenberg were tarred by their business dealings with each other. Fust should have been more patient and allowed Gutenberg to finish his work instead of locking him out of his own print shop and trying to take credit for printing the book. Gutenberg should have been more careful about handling other people's money in the operation of his printing business.

The commercial printing press demonstrated how much people of the day yearned for reading matter beyond the simple printed playing cards or religious tracts available to them. When more people learned to read, writers supplied them with words. For example, humanist writers supported by the Pope believed that turning to the Greek and Roman philosophers for answers could solve all ethical dilemmas. The humanist movement became the dominant philosophy during the Renaissance, but was later denounced by the Catholic Church when philosophers questioned the content of the Bible.

Since the introduction of the Gutenberg Bible and the printing press, the Bible is considered to be the best-selling book in the history of publishing. Contemporary efforts have tried to package the work in a more modern, young-adult-friendly version. For example, *Revolve 2009* is the New Testament packaged in a magazine format marketed to teen girls with additional stories such as "Beyond Beauty," "Faith Quest," and "What Is He Thinking?" *Bible Illuminated: The Book* also presents

Courtesy of tthe Illuminated World

Figure 7.7

In 2008 the latest addition to the vast number of Bibles printed since Gutenberg's day, Bible Illuminated: The Book, was published by a group of Swedish advertising executives. Described as a work that is the "intersection of religion and pop culture," it includes the text of the New Testament while featuring striking, thought-provoking photographs, as evidenced by its cover image, with pictures of celebrities and a world in crisis.
See color insert following page 178.

the New Testament, but with a fashion magazine's graphic style that has "a mixed bag of richly colored pop culture–driven photographs." From Swedish advertising executives, its cover displays a close-up of a woman's eye with heavy makeup in a provocative stare (Figure 7.7).

■ TYPOGRAPHY AND THE SIX PERSPECTIVES

Because words are so important in communicative messages, the way those words are presented form a vital link between what the words mean and how the words are seen. The study of typography is vital for students of communication, because poor typographical use in print and screen media is often an indication of amateurish presentations. In addition, not being aware of the many typographical choices available to a designer is like watching a motion picture only because of its plot—much is missed.

Personal Perspective

Typographical designer Jonathan Hoefler once remarked, "Typography is to writing as soundtracks are to movies." If the music for a motion picture is too loud or too soft, too intense or too calm, or in an inappropriate style, an audience member is distracted from the plot. Typographical choices can guide a viewer toward understanding the literal message of the words and toward perceiving symbolic meaning. But the wrong choices can make words hard to read and distract from their message. *How* words are presented, then, are just as important as *what* those words are.

A graphic designer has many variations of type at her disposal. In addition to the obvious choice of the particular typeface style, a single word or a block of copy varies in its size, placement, color of the letters, the background, column width, length, and justification style. If a designer is working in a screened media either for television, motion pictures, or online, other variables can include pacing, the length of time letters are shown on a screen, and direction, the placement of where the words enter and exit a frame. Unless the letters are the main thrust of a presentation, it is a safe bet that most typographic choices made for print and screen media go unnoticed by an untrained viewer.

Artists, however, seldom want their work to have a neutral reaction. They want their choices seen and responded to by a viewer. The typographical artist Tauba Auerbach (Weblink 7.2) uses letterforms in her pieces that often demonstrate how the same word can have different messages depending on the typographic choices employed (Figure 7.8). The Seoul, Korea, artist duo of Marc Voge and Young-Hae Chang of Young-Hae Chang Heavy Industries (Weblink 7.3) work primarily with online animated typographical forms set to music that make statements about social customs and practices. In their piece called "The End," they demonstrate through mostly large, uppercase sans serif letters that breaking up is hard to do in English, Korean, and Galician, a language spoken by about 3 million persons mainly residing in northwestern Spain. Voge and Chang vary the music and pacing depending on the letterforms inherent within each language. Again, the literal message remains the same, but the effect on viewers is quite different. New York artist Yael Kanarek, perhaps more well known for the integrated media piece "World of Awe" first conceived in 1994 (Weblink 7.4), also works with word sculptures made from rubber cutouts. In "Lemon," the word is displayed in 32 languages in a collage of rubber characters glued together to form a kind of crocheted piece in order to investigate the "territorial properties of language."

Figure 7.8

"Blah, blah, blah," 2006, by Tauba Auerbach. The New York–based typographic artist Tauba Auerbach shows in this work how the same word can have different symbolic and emotional meanings depending on the choice of typeface.

Courtesy of Tauba Auerbach and Deitch Projects

In a similar technique, "Untitled (Lace)" weaves together a phrase from "World of Awe," "Yours forever, your sunset/sunrise forever yours, your forever yours" written in English, Hebrew, and Arabic. The piece conveys simplicity within its chaos through its webbed structure (Figure 7.9).

Historical Perspective

Although the art of typography officially began with the first edition of Gutenberg's Bible, typography is linked directly to the history of writing. And even though anatomically modern humans have been on the Earth for about 180,000 years, the practice of placing symbolic messages on a medium of presentation is probably 40,000 years old. Since then it has transitioned from drawing and writing to mechanical and then digital production.

■ Drawing

As evidence of higher intelligence over other animals, early humans began to preserve images of animals by drawing or carving petroglyphs on the walls of caves, on mountains, on desert plateaus,

and on the bones of slaughtered animals (Figure 7.10). Paintings and petroglyphs were a realization by early humans that they could make their thoughts permanent by preserving them. Later, drawings of human figures and symbols for the sun and moon abounded, but overwhelmingly the main subjects were the animals that were hunted in the part of the world where the drawings were found. The drawings represent two kinds of visual messages: pictographs and ideographs. Pictographs are pictures that stand for objects, plants, or animals. Ideographs are images that represent abstract ideas. Modern humans can easily understand ancient pictographs, but the ideographs created by early humans remain a mystery (Figure 7.11).

In the Lascaux and Chauvet caves in southern France, for example, early artists mixed charcoal or colors from the soil with animal fat or their own saliva. They spread these paints with their fingers, spit them from their mouth, or used crude reed brushes to produce paintings of animals with remarkable clarity and artistry. These drawings represent the first known attempts to create a written language.

Courtesy of Yael Kanarek, Bitforms Gallery, New York City, and John Berens

Figure 7.9

"Untitled (Lace)," 2008, straight pins and rubber words in English, Arabic, and Hebrew, by Yael Kanarek. In the typographical artwork, the hypnotic flow of words in rubber merge in organic patterns in which the foreground is as interesting as the negative spaces between the forms and the background shadows.

Figure 7.10

You may find it hard to believe that the words you are presently reading evolved from cave paintings on walls in prehistoric times. Over the millennia the wall space on caves of the Lascaux region of southern France gradually became limited.

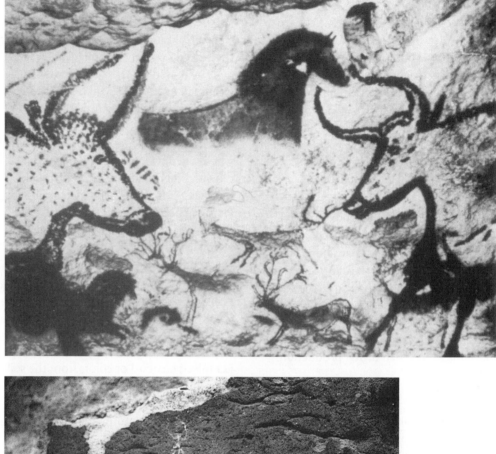

Courtesy of the French Tourist Office

Figure 7.11

"Petroglyph, Rural New Mexico," 2002, by Gerry Davey. Human, animal, and symbolic forms scratched in rocks have been found throughout the world.

Courtesy of Gerry Davey

Sadly, because of all the attention, many cave drawings are in danger of being taken over by a creeping fungus, caused by rising temperatures from high-powered lights and poor circulation as well as human contact.

■ *Writing*

The Sumerians

Like the animals they hunted, for thousands of years early humans were wanderers who constantly searched for food, shelter, and water in small tribes of individuals with similar interests. But around 12,000 BCE in what is now Iraq, thousands of these nomads started to congregate in the lush valleys that formed an arc from Lower Egypt to the Persian Gulf, known as the Fertile Crescent (Figure 7.12). Between the Tigris and Euphrates rivers, the Sumerians lived in Mesopotamia, or the "Land Between the Rivers," for more than 10,000 years. They planted crops, domesticated animals, initiated the Bronze Age when they mixed copper with tin for stronger tools and weapons, invented the wheel, created a complex system of religious and social discipline, buried their dead in organized services, and invented the first system of writing (Figure 7.13).

At the temple in Uruk in about 3500 BCE, scribes wrote on clay tablets for the first time in history. This monumental step in human development took the form of crude pictographic text arranged in columns from right to left. The pictures described the agricultural lives of the people and reported the number of cattle, sacks of grain, and barrels of beer that people possessed (Figure 7.14). Specially educated scribes used a sharp-edged stylus to make impressions in damp clay

tablets that they later dried in the sun or in kilns. In about 2800 BCE, the scribes started to turn the pictures over on their sides to ease in their production. Three hundred years later, the scribes replaced their pointed sticks with triangular-tipped styluses that they pushed into, rather than dragged through, the clay (Figure 7.15). Unfortunately, many historical and irreplaceable ancient pieces remain missing after the looting of the museum in Uruk following the U.S. invasion of Iraq in 2003.

Figure 7.12

The Fertile Crescent is the name for the arc-like region of the Middle East where humans about 14,000 years ago quit being nomads and started to settle in large numbers. The Crescent included Ancient Egypt, the Levant, or the eastern Mediterranean, and the "Land Between the Rivers," Mesopotamia.

Figures 7.13 and 7.14

"A cast of a stone tablet from the Uruk period," 3300–3100 BCE (left). Without a translation, the meaning of early writing forms is largely lost in time. However, because it was used so often and was so popular, the symbol for beer (an upright jug with a pointed base) can be found in the piece on the right.

Figure 7.15

Compared with the previous examples, this writing sample from a later period of the Uruk region is much more organized and symbolic. The scribe used a pointed stick to make the marks in the clay.

B. Speckart / © 2009, used under license of Shutterstock.com

This innovation, along with more abstract representations of objects and ideas, meant that those with less artistic skill than earlier pictographic scribes could produce Sumerian writing. Nevertheless, this writing style called *cuneiform* (Latin for "wedge-shaped") required strict schooling from childhood on, because there were hundreds of characters to learn (Figure 7.16). One of the oldest written stories is the *Epic of Gilgamesh*. In 12 tablets using cuneiform, believed to be written in 2100 BCE, it told of a devastating flood. The cuneiform story became known because of a later Akkadian-language version of the story. Akkadian was a Semitic language, later replaced by Aramaic (Figure 7.17).

The Egyptians

Stretching more than 4,000 miles, the Nile is the longest river in the world. Sometime

Figure 7.16

Eventually, highly stylized cuneiform writing, which employed a slanted wooden stylus pressed into soft clay, became the norm for the Sumerian scribes.

Courtesy of Paul Martin Lester

in 3100 BCE, Sumerian ideas about writing reached the Egyptians. Hieroglyphs remained the chief written language of the Egyptians until the Romans conquered the area in 390 CE. The name is derived from the Greek words *hieros* for "holy" and *gluphein* for "engrave." This "writing of the gods" reveals that the Egyptians were much more sensitive to the pictorial qualities of writing than the Sumerians. Egyptian hieroglyphics not only told the story of their culture, but also did so in a poetic, beautifully visual way (Figure 7.18).

From an initial symbol set of 700, hieroglyphs eventually expanded to more than 5,000 characters. By 1500 BCE, hieroglyphic writing divided into two forms: hieratic and demotic scripts. The hieratic form is the most familiar style of writing and was used for official business, religious documents, and the pyramids. The demotic script was more popular for everyday types of writing because it was less illustrative. Its characters were also more abstract and symbolic.

For hundreds of years, the meaning of Egyptian hieroglyphs remained a mystery for researchers. But in 1799, during Napoleon's expedition to Egypt, the Rosetta Stone was found near the port city of Rashid. Written in 196 BCE, the stone contained the same information in hieroglyphic, demotic, and ancient Greek versions. The message carved into the stone came from the king of Egypt, Ptolemy V Epiphanes, who proclaimed that the priesthood was exempt from various taxes and set forth an order to erect statues in his likeness in their temples. In 1808 the French scholar Jean-François Champollion was able to translate most of the Rosetta Stone with the help of others, including Thomas Young, who also helped developed the tri-chromatic theory. The stone

is now on exhibit in the British Museum in London (Figure 7.19). By 1822, Champollion could translate any hieroglyphic text. Just before his death at age 42, he published a dictionary to enable Egyptologists to learn about the ancient culture.

The Chinese

In 1800 BCE, Tsang Chieh, after noticing tracks left behind by a bird, supposedly invented calligraphy. Chinese calligraphy

Figure 7.17

The Epic of Gilgamesh is the oldest surviving literary work in the history of civilization. Written in Sumerian and Akkadian, the vertical line denotes the two versions of the cuneiform classic, believed to have been written between 2150 and 2000 BCE. It tells the story of the mythological King Gilgamesh in 12 tablets. Shown here is the 11th or "Deluge" tablet that tells of a great flood, which many believe is the basis for the story of Noah in the Bible.

Figure 7.18

A detailed view of aesthetically beautiful Egyptian hieroglyphics immediately shows how much more labor intensive the writing style was than cuneiform writing because of its larger and detailed symbol set.

Figure 7.19

Created in the year 196 BCE, the Rosetta Stone's horizontal lines divide the telling of the same edict in three different languages—ancient hieroglyphics, a more modern style called demotic, and classical Greek. Discovered in 1799 by a French Army engineer in preparation of Napoleon Bonaparte's attempt to seize Egypt, the sight of the historical treasure, which measured 45 inches high, 28.5 inches wide, and 11 inches thick, stunned the army officers. Nevertheless, after Napoleon gave up his quest to capture the country, British troops seized the stone and brought it to London in 1802, where it resides today. The British medical doctor Thomas Young, who, with Hermann von Helmholtz, developed the tri-chromatic theory of color perception, was the first to translate the demotic text, while the French scholar Jean-François Champollion expanded on the translations and created a dictionary for future researchers. Although the message of the stone is somewhat banal—it gives the temple priests a tax break—the reason modern anthropologists know so much about ancient Egyptian culture is because the Rosetta Stone could be used to translate the hieroglyphic writings found on papyrus and on the pyramids.

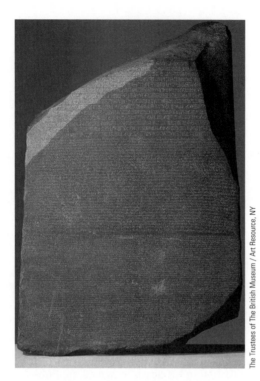

is one of the most complicated forms of communication known. It was never reduced to abstract symbols, as were many of the other systems; it remained a written language comprising more than 44,000 individual symbols for centuries.

By royal decree in 210 BCE, the Chinese writing system was simplified to about 1,000 basic characters that are still in use today. Such a writing system made the use of the language in mechanical presses difficult. Devising metal typefaces, as Gutenberg had done, for every Chinese character was simply too costly and time consuming. Chinese printers would spend all their time finding and sorting symbols. Consequently, the Chinese developed a pictorial calligraphic style that is praised as an art form throughout the world.

The Phoenicians

Between Egypt to the west and Sumer to the southeast, the great society of mer-

chants known as Phoenicia prospered along the Mediterranean Sea in the area now known as Lebanon, Syria, and Israel. By about 2000 BCE, the Phoenicians possessed some of the fastest sailing ships known and traded goods throughout the region. They learned the Egyptian and Sumerian writing systems in order to trade with them successfully, but cultural pride led them to develop their own.

The Phoenician culture is forever linked to one of the greatest advances in the history of communication: the alphabet (Figure 7.20). Derived from the first two letters of the Greek alphabet, *alpha* and *beta*, an alphabet is a collection of symbols in a specified order that represents the sounds of spoken language.

The genius of an alphabet was that it reduced to a handful the number of characters needed to write a language. The Egyptians used about 5,000 symbols, the Phoenicians only 22. Found in the limestone of a sarcophagus in the Phoenician city-state of Byblos, the 22 abstract symbols represent the final phase in the transition from pictorial to purely symbolic characters. The English language alphabet uses 26 letterforms that represent the sounds made while speaking. However, a close inspection of a dictionary reveals that in reality, 26 letter symbols are not enough. Over 40 characters are needed for a more complete pronunciation of all the words (Figure 7.21).

The Greeks

Because the Greeks obtained their papyrus from the Phoenician capital of Byblos, they gave their papyrus writing paper the same name. The English word *bible* is from the Greek phrase that means "a papyrus book." The Greeks also learned the Phoenician alphabet sometime between 1000 and 700 BCE. The Phoenicians had little use for vowel sounds, but the Greeks did. They changed five consonants to the vowels *a, e, i, o,* and *u* and added two other vowel sounds for a total of 24 characters. The Greeks introduced uppercase and lowercase letters; capitals were reserved for writing on stone, whereas lowercase letters were used on papyrus (Figure 7.22).

The Romans

Roman society was one of the largest and most influential in the history of Western civilization. Growing from a sleepy little village in 750 BCE on the Tiber River in what now is central Italy in a region known as Latium, the "Latins" built and ruled an empire in about 700 years that stretched from England to the north to Egypt to the south, and from Spain to the west to Mesopotamia to the east. As they did with all the peoples they conquered, when they overwhelmed the Greeks, the Romans absorbed much of their culture, including its alphabet. The Romans made

Courtesy of the Advertising Archives

Figure 7.20

Although the idea of an alphabet, a highly symbolic symbol set of letters consisting of the sounds one makes when speaking, was discovered earlier in the region, the Phoenicians are credited with spreading the concept throughout the known world. Consequently, the word phonetic *is a tribute to the Phoenicians, as the alphabet became the basis of almost all modern languages.*

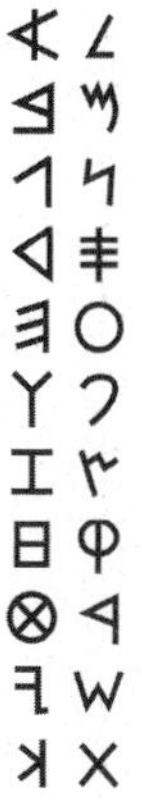

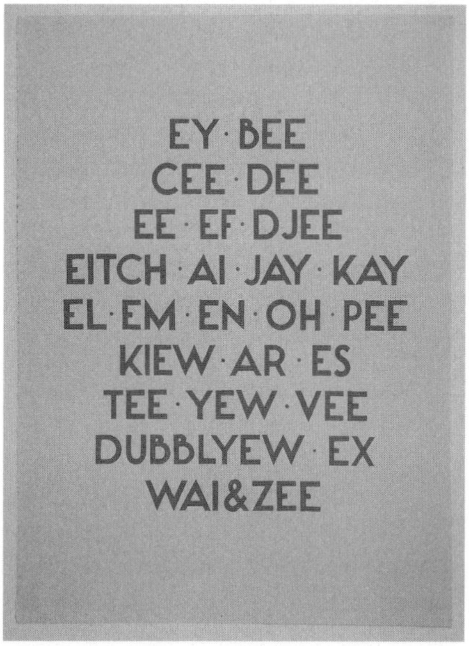

Courtesy of Paul Martin Lester

EY · BEE
CEE · DEE
EE · EF · DJEE
EITCH · AI · JAY · KAY
EL · EM · EN · OH · PEE
KIEW · AR · ES
TEE · YEW · VEE
DUBBLYEW · EX
WAI & ZEE

Courtesy of Tauba Auerbach and Deitch Projects

Figure 7.21

*"How to Spell the Alphabet," 2005, by Tauba Auerbach. The artist provides her own take on the English 26-letter phonetic alphabet.
See color insert following page 178.*

many adjustments to the Greek writing system. Late in the 10th century CE, the Latin letter W, a variation of the common letter V, was added. Finally, in the 14th century, some 400 years after Latin had died as a spoken language, the 26th letter, J, was added to complete the alphabet.

As the Greeks had done, the Romans used uppercase letters (usually painted

Figure 7.22 (left)

As the Greeks were more attuned to nature, their writing examples usually contained a more flowing, natural, wave-like aesthetic feel to them. Sensitivity to their environment is shown with the Greek headline for a flyer printed in France in 1896 promoting the first Olympic games in the modern era.

Figure 7.23

For writing on stone, Romans used all uppercase letters, as seen in this example housed in the Louvre Museum in Paris.

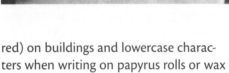

Courtesy of Paul Martin Lester

red) on buildings and lowercase characters when writing on papyrus rolls or wax tablets (Figure 7.23).

Other civilizations around the world had their own histories and writing styles. In 2006 a stone block about 1,000 years old contained drawings believed to be a writing system developed by the pre-

Columbian Olmec civilization in Mexico. It is the oldest such find on the continent. Zapotec and Maya cultures developed writing styles 500 years later. However, for all these writing examples, no translation has been found (Figure 7.24).

■ *Hot Type Production*

One of the great early printers after Gutenberg was the Venetian Aldus Manutius. His Aldine Press published high-quality works by Greek and Roman philosophers and illustrated works of fiction. In 1498 he finished a five-volume set of Aristotle's works. He also published *The Dream of Poliphilus*, a curious tale about a young man searching for his lover. The book is noted for its sexually explicit illustrations. Aldus also was known for promoting italic type. Unlike today, when the slanted script is reserved for titles of books or movies, Aldus used italic to save money—it allowed pages to be filled with more characters, thus using less paper (Figure 7.25).

Evidence of Gutenberg's legacy is found throughout the world. In 1704, the *Boston*

Figure 7.24

Beside the impressive pyramid structure, the pre-Columbian site known as Chichen Itza, built by the Mayan empire on the Yucatán Peninsula in Mexico, contains several buildings and recreational facilities where the walls have carved figures of humans and symbols that probably formed a written language. No translation has ever been discovered.

Felix Stensson / F1 Online / PhotoLibrary

News-Letter became the first single-sheet American newspaper (Figure 7.26). When the French Revolution erupted in 1789, a call for the freedom of the press was answered with the establishment of more than 300 newspapers in France the next year.

The principal invention of the Industrial Revolution (1760–1840) was James Watt's steam engine, invented in 1769. Johannes Gutenberg's quaint converted wine press became a historical relic in 1814 when the German Frederich Koenig used the steam engine to power a printing press in London that could print 1,110 sheets a day. Police had to guard the press from printers who feared the loss of their jobs and were angry about this technological development. Known as "Luddites," named after a popular fiction character named Ned Ludd, this social movement started with workers upset by automated clothing looms three years before Koenig's press. In 1828, a four-cylinder press that could handle 4,000 sheets a day for *The Times* of London was invented. Later improvements increased that output

to 8,000 sheets per hour. The American Richard Hoe made an important advance when he introduced the rotary press in 1847 (Figure 7.27). With the invention of lithography and the halftone photo-engraving screen, color illustrations and photographs could be printed during the same press run as the type. By the late 1880s, most high-circulation publications used a web perfecting press with coated papers that allowed high-quality, fast-paced printing on both sides of a long roll of paper. The advent of stereotype plates further sped up the printing process, as several duplicate pages could be printed on different presses at the same time.

High-speed presses wouldn't have been of much an advantage if printers still sorted and set the many typeface styles by hand, as in Gutenberg's day. A skilled person could set 1,500 letters per hour

Courtesy of Vis-Com, Inc.

Figure 7.25 (left)

This woodcut portrays a typical print shop during the first century after the invention of the commercial printing press. Typesetters in the background set the printing plates with metal type molds. Meanwhile, the man in the front right inks a plate of type with two ball-like pads. After he lowers the platen, the other man removes the printed work from the press.

Figure 7.26 (right)

The Boston News-Letter, in 1704, was the first American newspaper with a regular circulation. With its two columns of aligned type introduced by an enlarged letter, it is similar in style to Gutenberg's Bible.

Courtesy of M. Thomas Inge

Figure 7.27

The Hoe press was used primarily to publish Sunday newspapers that used color. The symmetrical composition of this woodcut helps organize the complicated structure of the steam-driven press.

by hand. But in 1886 the Linotype automated typesetting machine was invented, which could set 9,000 letters an hour. It cast a whole line of type in lead from letters typed on a keyboard. When an entire story had been set, the type could be fitted onto a form for printing with other stories. After printing, the lead was simply melted and used again—the origination of the term *hot type*.

The next year, the Monotype machine was introduced, which could set individual letters. Corrections were much easier than with the Linotype machine because a mistake did not require that a whole line be reset. In 1928, Walter Morey introduced the Teletypesetter, which used perforated tape similar to that used for years for printing stock market prices. When attached to a Linotype machine, the Teletypesetter automatically produced the copy in lead slugs. These noisy and huge machines were still common in newspapers until the 1960s, when they were replaced by cold type technology.

Many visual communicators prefer the handcrafted look of printed pieces using metal letters and a press in the style of Gutenberg-era technology. Especially suited

for invitations, small press books, zines, and other works, hot type printing has a tactile aesthetic—when you run your finger over hot press printed letters you can feel the raised ink on the paper. This sensation is not experienced with letters printed with the aid of a computer (Figure 7.28).

■ Cold Type Production

Inspired by the relatively new invention of photography, phototypesetting, or *cold type*, was a method for creating typeface letters without the need for metal. The transition from metal hot type methods to photographic and later digital cold type procedures produced a radical change in typeface design. Fonts, all of the variations of a typeface including bold, italic, and so on, could be made cheaply, quickly, and with nearly the same quality as with metal (some mistakenly refer to a typeface as a "font"). More important, designers could create and manipulate type placement easily once the physical limitations of metal type were eliminated.

With computers, cold type production has moved away from the photographic-based technologies of phototypesetting, photocomposition, and photo-optic or filmsetting to digital typesetting in which an operator uses a computer to generate letters. In 1984, Apple introduced its Macintosh computer with on-screen controls for the production of words and graphics on the same system. The next year the inexpensive LaserWriter printer from Apple was launched, and the desktop computer revolution officially started.

Technical Perspective

In order to analyze the use of typefaces in print or screen communications, you must be aware of the various choices available to a typographer. A designer who uses words must make choices about various typeface styles in relation to overall size, color, fonts, text block size, justification, space, and animation.

■ Typeface Families

Typography is a big business. It is estimated that computer companies, typesetters, printers, publishers, advertising agencies, and writers spend more than $300 million a year to purchase typefaces. Johannes Gutenberg had an easy time selecting the typeface style for his Bible because there was only one—textur. Since Gutenberg's day, at least 40,000 different typeface styles have been created, with more than 176,000 attribute variations. With so many choices, a method was devised to group all of the typefaces into categories or families. The resulting six basic typeface families became blackletter, roman, script, miscellaneous, square serif, and sans serif. Think of each typeface family as separate colors or musical styles, each with their own mood and purpose (Figure 7.29).

Blackletter

Sometimes called gothic, old style, old English, renaissance, or medieval, the blackletter typeface family is highly ornate and decorative. Individual strokes that make up the letters are thick and have sharp diagonal lines. Many of the strokes in capital letters are connected with thinner supporting lines. The ends of the letters usually have small stylized strokes that were early predecessors of the serif. Because it happened to be the style that scribes in monasteries used for their handwritten works, Gutenberg fashioned his metal type characters accordingly.

Courtesy of xtine burrough

Figure 7.28
"Paradise Obscura," 2007, handmade, letter press–printed bags for City Lights Bookstore, San Francisco, by xtine burrough. On the 50th anniversary of the publication of Jack Kerouac's On the Road, *50 bookstore shoppers received a bag for their purchases printed with a phrase from the novel. Artifacts from the printing process—vertical lines and uneven inking—add to the artistic pleasure of the lettering.*
See color insert following page 178.

Consequently, the family is associated with traditional, conservative, religious, or German content. A newspaper's name was often set in this typeface family to communicate to readers that the publication had traditional values and was long established (Figure 7.30). The cartoonist Jules Feiffer, for example, used the typeface to illustrate the voice of God. For the motion picture *Inkheart* (2008), makeup artist Jenny Shicore was asked to simulate blackletter tattooed text on some of the characters' faces.

Roman

The roman typeface family is the most commonly used of them all. Body copy in books, magazines, and newspapers use roman because it is familiar to readers and exceedingly legible. The gently curved serifs create lines that are easy to read (Figure 7.31). Development of the style of roman used today took approximately 300 years from the time it was introduced

Figure 7.29

"Periodic Table of Typefaces Popular, Influential, & Notorious," by Camdon Wilde. Arranged as a periodic table for chemical elements, Wilde sorted and arranged 100 typefaces based on lists generated by typographical experts. The sans serif typeface family seems to be the winner with more than 30 examples on the table.

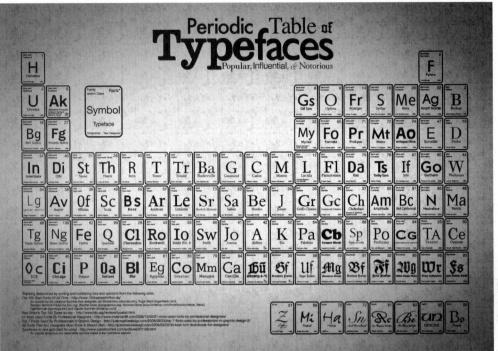

in 1465. During that period, three forms were introduced: *old style*, created by two Venetian printers, Nicolaus Jenson and Aldus Manutius, and the French Claude Garamond, who shaved the metal of the blackletter characters so that the strokes were not quite as thick or ornate; *transitional*, for which William Caslon and John Baskerville of England in the 18th century made the letters more vertical

and allowed a bit more contrast between the thin and thick strokes with less ornate serifs; and *modern*, from the Italian Giambattista Bodoni, who produced more than 100 different alphabet collections. As a result, roman lost its early link to blackletter and became a distinctive family, with letter strokes changed from thick lines with little contrast to thinner strokes with a noticeable difference in width.

Figure 7.30

Like this 1902 issue of The Washington Times, *the blackletter typeface family is still used for the modern version, but over time the period at the end of the name was removed.*

Script

Cursive writing is defined as letters that are linked. In 1557, Robert Granjon of France introduced the first typeface designed to mimic the handwriting of ordinary people. Ironically, the script typeface family is now used almost exclusively for documents and publications that want to promote a high-quality, high-class appearance (Figure 7.32). Wedding invitations and licenses, for example, commonly are printed in script because the fine letters, perhaps more than any other family's style, give the piece an air of handmade attention to detail (Figure 7.33).

Miscellaneous

Sometimes referred to as novelty or display type, the members of the miscellaneous typeface family, as the name suggests, cannot easily be sorted into the other families. Miscellaneous type first began appearing for advertising purposes during the Industrial Revolution. As more people made more money because of the efficiency of new machines, they needed more products and services. Printing came to be thought of as not simply a means of disseminating information and news through books, magazines, and newspapers, but also as a way to attract potential customers through advertising. The miscellaneous family's unique feature is that its style purposely draws attention to itself (Figure 7.34). For example,

Courtesy of Paul Martin Lester

creative typographers designed typefaces with letters formed by collections of flowers or contorted human figures.

The Industrial Revolution also spurred the final two typeface families discussed.

Square Serif

In 1815, probably inspired by the architecture and other sights reported after Napoleon's conquest of Egypt, Vincent Figgins designed a typeface similar to the modern roman but with right angle curves jutting from the letter strokes. Sometimes called 3-D, slab, or Egyptian, the square serif typeface family is intended, as is

Figure 7.31

The urgency of the upper-case warning on the window of a parking lot booth in downtown Dallas, Texas, is diminished by the choice of a roman typeface family for the sign. A more stern sans serif family typeface would have been a better choice. However, if you have to worry about rattlesnakes in your place of employment, perhaps your typeface choice should not be your first concern.

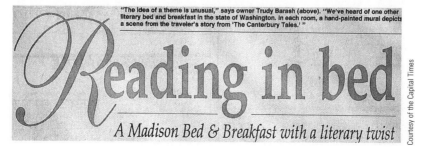

Courtesy of the Capital Times

Figure 7.32

The script typeface family "R" reinforced by an italic roman subhead lends an air of sophistication to a story on a bed and breakfast inn.

Figure 7.33 (left)

"V," 2005, by Tauba Auerbach. The flowing, swirling lines capture the dynamic and elegant energy of the script typeface family and the letter "V."

Figure 7.34 (right)

Although this typeface generated by a computer program has roots in the sans serif family, it is considered an example of a miscellaneous typeface because its metallic appearance matches its verbal message.

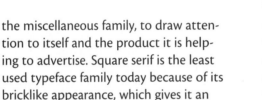

used commonly on storefronts in pioneer towns in the Western movies made in Hollywood. It is also a favorite choice, for some reason, of college graphic designers for university initials on caps and sweatshirts (Figure 7.35).

Sans Serif

In 1832, William Caslon IV introduced the first member of this family. It was immediately controversial. The French word *sans* means "without." Caslon simply took existing letters and trimmed off all their serifs. The result was a typestyle that Caslon named "block type." Typographical critics of the day immediately voiced their

the miscellaneous family, to draw attention to itself and the product it is helping to advertise. Square serif is the least used typeface family today because of its bricklike appearance, which gives it an unpleasant rigid look. Curiously, in American culture this typeface family is associated with the Wild West because it was

Figure 7.35

"Restaurant Bar, Austin, Nevada," 2003, by Gerry Davey. The seldom used typeface family of square serif is nevertheless popular for signs that evoke a spirit of the old American West. The connection probably comes from Hollywood westerns that used the family for its storefront sets.

objections to the type family as being too simple and without style.

Despite the early criticism, sans serif typefaces have enjoyed several periods of popularity. Printers in the 1880s liked the new style, because many felt that the streamlined, clean-looking letter strokes fit the new machine age. Plus, they saved money. Typefaces with serifs often snapped off because of fast-moving presses. Printing had to be stopped to replace letters, and flawed pages were discarded. With sans serif types, printers didn't have to stop the presses to replace broken letters. But the sans serif fad eventually faded. During the 1920s there was a rebirth in interest. Architectural and graphic design styles of de stijl, bauhaus, and art deco revived the type family, as artists thought the simple lines matched the illustrations they created. In the 1970s, newspaper publishers asked designers to modernize their front pages. Many turned to the sans serif family for headlines and photo captions to offset the roman type of the body copy for their print and online editions (Figure 7.36).

Screen media presentations have demonstrated the importance of the sans serif style, as it is easy to read. Consequently, sans serif typefaces are used most often in motion picture titles and credits, in captions for television news programs, and for menu and text announcements on a computer screen. Without serifs, the type style connotes a no-nonsense, practical approach to lettering in which a viewer isn't distracted by the addition of serifs. For that reason, stop, warning, and exit signs most often are printed in the sans serif style (Figure 7.37).

Austrian graphic designer Stefan Sagmeister stunned the art world with his 1996 poster for Lou Reed's "Set the Twilight Reeling," with inked text on the musician's face (Figure 7.38). Three years later he upped the ante for an AIGA (American Institute of Graphic Arts)

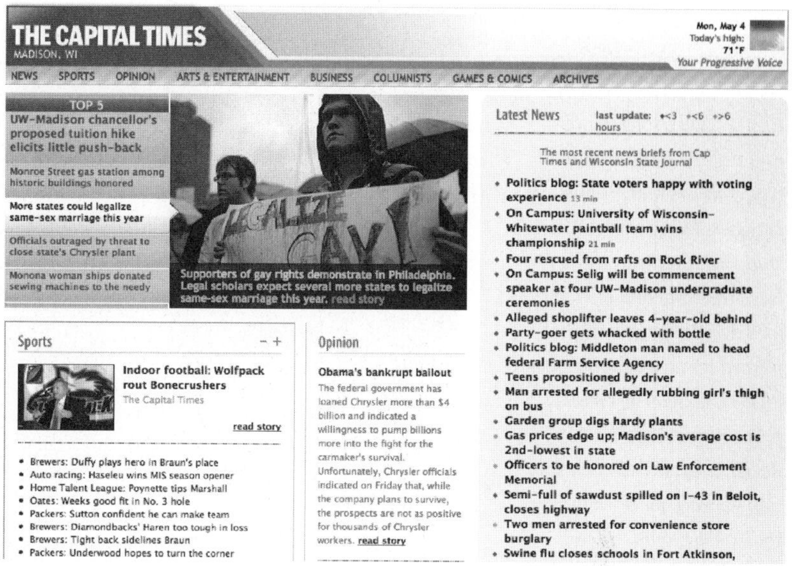

THE CAPITAL TIMES
MADISON, WI

Mon, May 4
Today's high:
71°F
Your Progressive Voice

NEWS SPORTS OPINION ARTS & ENTERTAINMENT BUSINESS COLUMNISTS GAMES & COMICS ARCHIVES

TOP 5
- UW-Madison chancellor's proposed tuition hike elicits little push-back
- Monroe Street gas station among historic buildings honored
- More states could legalize same-sex marriage this year
- Officials outraged by threat to close state's Chrysler plant
- Monona woman ships donated sewing machines to the needy

Supporters of gay rights demonstrate in Philadelphia. Legal scholars expect several more states to legalize same-sex marriage this year. read story

Sports — +

Indoor football: Wolfpack rout Bonecrushers
The Capital Times
read story

- Brewers: Duffy plays hero in Braun's place
- Auto racing: Haseleu wins MIS season opener
- Home Talent League: Poynette tips Marshall
- Oates: Weeks good fit in No. 3 hole
- Packers: Sutton confident he can make team
- Brewers: Diamondbacks' Haren too tough in loss
- Brewers: Tight back sidelines Braun
- Packers: Underwood hopes to turn the corner

Opinion

Obama's bankrupt bailout
The federal government has loaned Chrysler more than $4 billion and indicated a willingness to pump billions more into the fight for the carmaker's survival. Unfortunately, Chrysler officials indicated on Friday that, while the company plans to survive, the prospects are not as positive for thousands of Chrysler workers. read story

Latest News last update: <3 <6 >6 hours

The most recent news briefs from Cap Times and Wisconsin State Journal

- Politics blog: State voters happy with voting experience 13 min
- On Campus: University of Wisconsin-Whitewater paintball team wins championship 21 min
- Four rescued from rafts on Rock River
- On Campus: Selig will be commencement speaker at four UW-Madison undergraduate ceremonies
- Alleged shoplifter leaves 4-year-old behind
- Party-goer gets whacked with bottle
- Politics blog: Middleton man named to head federal Farm Service Agency
- Teens propositioned by driver
- Man arrested for allegedly rubbing girl's thigh on bus
- Garden group digs hardy plants
- Gas prices edge up; Madison's average cost is 2nd-lowest in state
- Officers to be honored on Law Enforcement Memorial
- Semi-full of sawdust spilled on I-43 in Beloit, closes highway
- Two men arrested for convenience store burglary
- Swine flu closes schools in Fort Atkinson,

Courtesy of the Capital Times

Figure 7.36

In order to connote a modern appearance, the nameplate for this online version of a newspaper is taken from the sans serif typeface family. Further proof of a forward-thinking approach to typographical design is the use of illustrations, text, and white space on the layout. Newspaper front pages usually are tightly packed word and picture displays with little room for anything else.

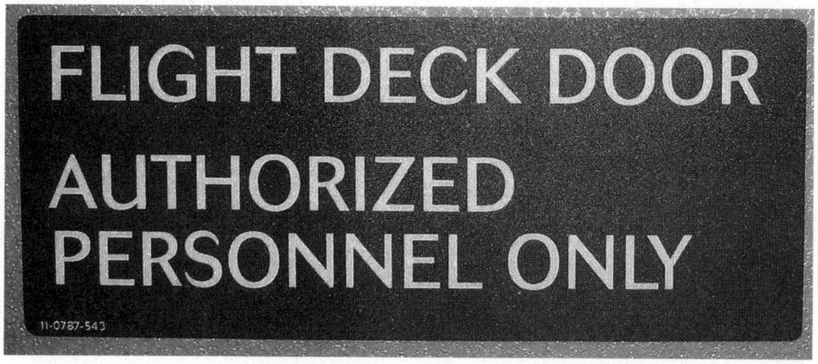

Courtesy of Paul Martin Lester

Figure 7.37

The sans serif typeface family is used to communicate a serious message. Since 9/11, this warning sign has appeared on the cabin door of some airlines. By the way, flight attendants get really nervous when you take a picture like this one. Best to leave it to a professional.

Figure 7.38

"Lou Reed Poster," 1996, by Stefan Sagmeister. Born in Austria, Stefan Sagmeister is one of the most respected typographers and graphic designers in the world. After studying at Pratt Institute in New York City and working for advertising agencies, he formed his own design studio in 1993. In 2005 he received a Grammy Award for Best Boxed or Special Limited Edition Package for art directing the Talking Heads album, Once in a Lifetime. Examples of his work can be found in galleries throughout the world. In this striking poster for Lou Reed's Set the Twilight Reeling, *hand-drawn sans serif song titles were used because, as Sagmeister explains, "The lyrics are extremely personal. We tried to show this by writing those lyrics directly over his face."*

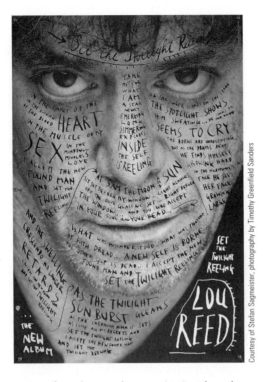

Courtesy of Stefan Sagmeister, photography by Timothy Greenfield Sanders

poster for a lecture he gave in Cranbrook, Michigan. An assistant scratched the title, location, subject, day, and time of his lecture with a sharp blade on Sagmeister's naked torso (Figure 7.39).

The MTV Music Video of the Year award for 1992 was presented to director Mark Fenske for his video of the Van Halen song "Right Now." The visual interpretation of the song uses mostly sans serif, with some miscellaneous typefaces for sentences such as "Right now science is building a better tomato" and "Right now your parents miss you." In 2004, for the band's reunion tour, scenes were added with updated messages such as "Right now a 13-year-old is illegally downloading this song" and "Right now nothing is more expensive than regret" over two portraits of former President George W. Bush (Weblink 7.5).

One of the most enduring and universally used sans serif typefaces is Helvetica, created in 1957 by the Swiss designer

Max Miedinger. In 2007 Gary Hustwit released a documentary of the same name that featured interviews with many of the most famous designers in the world (Weblink 7.6).

■ *Typeface Attributes*

Whether for print or screen presentations, a graphic designer must make choices about seven major type attributes: size, color, font, column, justification, space, and animation.

Size

Type is measured in points. A single point is 0.0138 inch. For printed text blocks, the best type sizes are between 9 and 12 points. Display type is considered to be anything larger than 14 points. Banner newspaper headlines for some significant event are 72 points or larger (Figure 7.40). Screen presentations require a type size twice that of printed body copy.

Color

Actually two colors are implied—the color of the type and the color of the background, sometimes called, regardless of the actual color, "white space." Research on type consistently shows that the most legible combination of colors for long blocks of copy is black type against a white background. For eye-catching headlines, designers occasionally use white type against a black background (called reverse type), colored type against a white background, or white type against a colored background. Motion picture title artists often make movie credits white and the title of the movie, the most significant part of the copy block, another color. Television graphic artists often place white text on top of a colored box, banner, or a shadow to identify the person speaking.

Font

Typically, a font refers to all of the letters and symbols that are possible with an individual typeface. For many graphic designers, font also means the attributes of plain text, boldface, *italic*, <u>underline</u>, and any other attention-grabbing graphic devices available (Figure 7.41). Most designers, whether for print or screen mediums, use such fonts conservatively.

Column

Two factors are involved with a column's size: line width and column length. For the best reading width, lines should contain no more than 12 words. While two columns in print or online are more readable than one wide column, books are set in one column, magazines usually in two to four, and newspapers can have up to eight columns on a page (Figure 7.42).

Justification

Text may be presented with margins that are aligned left and/or right, or centered. Left justified text is the most common style, with the right side of the text not justified (also called ragged right). Right justified, called ragged left, and centered types are seldom used for long passages because a viewer has trouble determining where the next line starts. Completely justified type, as used by Gutenberg, has a rigid, conservative, but organized appearance.

Space

Kerning is the term used to describe the space between individual letters. A modern, informal appearance can be achieved if the kerning is made an obvious design factor. When kerning is too little, too much, or uneven, the copy may be difficult to read. Leading (pronounced "ledding") describes the space between

horizontal lines of type. The space between two columns of type is called the alley, and the space between the pages of a book or magazine is called the gutter (Figure 7.43).

Animation

Besides all the other considerations mentioned above, a visual artist who works

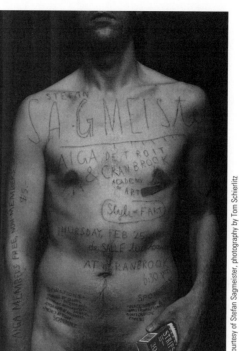

Courtesy of Stefan Sagmeister; photography by Tom Schierlitz

Figure 7.39

"Sagmeister AIGA Detroit Poster," 1999, by Stefan Sagmeister. For a poster announcing the details of a lecture, Sagmeister had an intern scratch the details on his body in a sans serif typeface. Says Sagmeister, "We tried to visualize the pain that seems to accompany most of our design projects." Then he added, "Yes, it did hurt real bad."
See color insert following page 178.

Figure 7.40

The streamlined and bold headline across the entire width of the page, with illustrations and text in separate modules, gives a modern look to this early 20th century newspaper.

Modified after Howard Finberg and Bruce Itule, Visual Editing, Wadsworth Publishing Company, 1990

Figure 7.41

A drop shadow box behind the capital "Q" gives a three-dimensional illusion to the layout, helping to attract attention to the display.

Courtesy of the Capital Times

Figure 7.42 (left)

The New York Times *was created in response to the sensational illustrations and stories in many publications of the day. As indicated by the conservative nature of the layout, this publication was meant for those who wanted to read long, in-depth stories.*

Figure 7.43 (right)

In this 1920s era advertisement for Instant Postum, a caffeine-free coffee substitute, the night sky, full moon, and sleepy owl on a branch, and the leading between the lines of type help reinforce the calming effect of the beverage.

with typography in motion for screen media must also consider such variables as position, the location of the entrance and exit points for the text, timing—at what point words appear or disappear, pacing—how fast or how slowly words appear and disappear, and other visual effects such as fades, dissolves, wipes, and so on. With screen media, the choices for

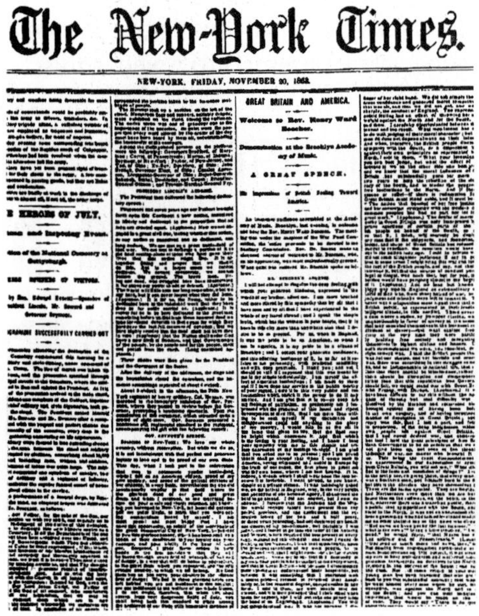

a graphic designed with regard to typography become much more complex and potentially rewarding. The online media artist xtine burrough creates visual poems with animated text set in a roman typeface over edited video. In *Nighght*, a tribute to Aram Saroyan's 1965 dada poem "lighght," the soft quality of the roman typeface matches the revolving and weaving letterforms of her poem (Weblink 7.7).

Ethical Perspective

Typographical designers usually invent and use typefaces that combine the philosophies of utilitarianism with the golden rule. In other words, a design is useful, the words can be easily read, and it adds beauty to our lives with an aesthetically pleasant design. But if typefaces are made to draw attention to them or to satisfy a designer's personal needs, hedonism may be at work. Graphic artist Milton Glaser, responsible for the design of *New York* magazine and the "I [HEART] NY" logo,

The New-York Times.

NEW-YORK, FRIDAY, NOVEMBER 20, 1863.

Courtesy of Vis-Com, Inc.

Sleep nights
Keep awake days
drink
INSTANT POSTUM
Instead of Coffee

Courtesy of The Advertising Archives

among others, warns, "There's a tremendous amount of garbage being produced under the heading of new and innovative typographical forms." Despite the criticism of typefaces being designed solely for the amusement of a particular graphic artist, the prevalent use of typographical computer programs produce ways of thinking about the use of type never before imagined. Glaser could be referring to graphic designer David Carson, for many years the innovative art director for *Ray Gun* magazine. He has been called the founder of grunge typography because of his non-traditional displays of text on a page that includes lines of type that overlap, columns of varying lengths on the same page, and an interview with the musician Brian Ferry he considered so boring that he set the text in the symbol set known as Zapf Dingbats.

Jonathan Hoefler, who created typefaces for *Sports Illustrated* and other magazines, likes "unusual fonts that challenge typographical assumptions. After all, design is about breaking the rules. Rule-breakers become rulers." The world is certainly large enough to support both dynamic, cacophonous displays and quiet, traditional typographical presentations.

Cultural Perspective

Because typography gives the artist's style to a text, it is linked, as is any art form, to a particular culture at a particular time. The history of typography may be divided into five major eras: pre-Gutenberg, Gutenberg, industrial, artistic, and digital.

Pre-Gutenberg (before 1455)

During this era, words and images were linked as equal partners in communication. Scribes, with their power to shape what future readers of their texts thought of their civilizations, had enormous power and were pampered by their leaders. For example, the 950 fragments known as the Dead Sea Scrolls, originally discovered in 1947 in 11 caves along the shore of the Dead Sea east of Jerusalem, can be dated between 150 BCE and 70 CE. They were handwritten biblical documents on vellum and papyrus. Later, beautifully aesthetic illustrated manuscripts combined words and images in the tradition of the Egyptians. Ireland's *Book of Kells*, containing four Gospels of the New Testament, printed about 800 CE, as well as lushly illustrated works from Persian and European crafters, elevated the concept of aesthetic beauty when applied to printed materials in the form of scrolls, maps, manuscripts, and books.

Gutenberg (1456–1760)

This era is marked by its influence of the printed word in typographically heavy designs with practitioners that often thought of images as afterthoughts. The rise in literacy and the need for books of all types produced a tremendous explosion in the number of publishing houses. Unfortunately, pictures were reserved for illustrative decorations around text blocks or for medical and other scientific textbooks and not appreciated for their own unique communicative value.

Industrial (1761–1890)

This period is known as the "dark ages" of typographical design. Machine mentality ruled style. Efficiency in design and the ability to attract attention to advertisements, rather than the appearance of a typeface, were praised. The increase in all kinds of printed advertising called for typefaces that customers noticed. Elaborately shaped typefaces, often used in combination with several others and sprinkled around the images of products in an advertisement, gave the appearance of a "typographical car wreck." The style was popular in an era of fast-paced efficiency.

Artistic (1891–1983)

Artists such as the French master Henri de Toulouse-Lautrec elevated typography into a respected art form through their painted posters for theatrical openings and other purposes. The art nouveau decorative style, inspired from Asian calligraphy and designs on screens and vases, revolutionized the combination of words and images on a page. Later, several modern art styles of the 20th century (dada, de stijl, bauhaus, art deco, pop art, punk, new wave, and hip-hop) were linked with specific cultures and expressed messages related to political content, architecture, and product design. These art movements

used typography as an integral part of their graphic design.

Digital (1984–present)

The introduction of relatively inexpensive Macintosh computers with on-screen user controls by Apple in 1984, combined with high-quality laser printers with networking capabilities, allowed graphic artists to more easily match their original design concepts with tools that were relatively inexpensive and easily mastered, for a global audience. Consequently, designers have learned to create typefaces for print and screen media, whether for a small circulation flyer or for a web presentation that receives several million user hits a day.

Critical Perspective

The field of typography reminds us that what is considered acceptable or good is when the text choices match the expectations of an intended audience. An early print advertisement for a biscuit is an excellent example (Figure 7.44). With its sober presentation in black and white and justified copy that relates how the biscuit can help with a person's digestion, it is obviously not meant as a chewing gum for a younger audience. If this product were intended for children, the advertisement would show words in various colors, typefaces, and off-centered in a dynamic, three-dimensional, page-jumping, and exciting layout, similar to a typical cigarette ad. Likewise, the serious business of investment banking, especially given the present severe economic downturn, demands a serious justified column with increased leading for added legibility. Not surprisingly, a website for an upcoming concert with the Cincinnati Symphony Orchestra will employ much different typographical

Figure 7.44

Many of the typographical choices in this old advertisement for Huntley & Palmers' oval digestive biscuits, otherwise known as cookies—lack of color, mostly set in a roman typeface, and a single justified column of copy—indicate that the product was not marketed to children.

When day begins——

Huntley & Palmers Oval Digestive Biscuits will make the first meal of the day a better meal.

Their lightness, their purity, and their high nutritive value should commend their use with any meal.

As a temporary 'stay,' especially with a glass of milk or wine, they are excellence itself.

HUNTLEY & PALMERS
OVAL DIGESTIVE
BISCUITS

Made, like all Huntley and Palmers manufactures, with an unfailing regard for purity. Always ask for H & P's Oval Digestive

Courtesy of The Advertising Archives

choices than one for the indie rock band Wilco (Weblinks 7.8 and 7.9).

Early scribes lost much of their political power when alphabets were invented and anyone could easily learn to write. But when artists developed calligraphic and illustrative skills, they turned words into works of art. Today's scribes are the graphic designers who can use a computer to make sure that the words match the style of the illustrations, the content of the piece, and the intended audience.

■ TRENDS TO WATCH FOR TYPOGRAPHY

Every medium of presentation—from typography to the web—is dominated by computer technology. Fewer artists prefer the analog crafts of handset type printing and chemical-based photographic darkrooms. Most work today is all digital. With individuals linked with others around the world, computer technology has sparked a rebirth in writing and reading, just as Gutenberg's printing press did 50 years after its invention.

For example, an estimated 20,000 homemade magazines are produced in the United States alone every year in garages, dens, and bedrooms with pens, typewriters, copy machines, and computers. With names like *Official Facilities Meeting Guide, Tight Fit, Return Whence You Came*, and *Fever*, creators of these specialty publications called *zines* (pronounced "zeens") comment on fringe culture, creative products, political and social issues, and alternative lifestyles with a freestyle, hand-drawn typographical and visual exuberance (Figure 7.45). The modern roots of these publications date back to science-fiction comic books of the 1930s and Hollywood fan magazines

Courtesy of Paul Martin Lester

of the 1950s. Sold in bookstores, record shops, and through mail orders, zines typically have low circulations, are under 20 pages, and have irregular issue dates. They nevertheless often make important contributions to the global environmental and anti-consumerism movements expressed in the DIY (Do-It-Yourself) ethic. With the advent of web logs, shortened to "blogs," and online magazines, the web version of the printed zine makes it possible for anyone with a wireless computer connection to have her views, both in words and images, showcased for a world of users to comment. Creative typographical choices are a vital part of the success of a zine or blog. Once on the margin of popular culture, zines are now in the mainstream with such web-based publications as *Slate* and *Salon* and blogs such as *The Huffington Post* and *Bag News Notes* (Weblink 7.10).

One of the most accomplished new artists working with the typographical medium for online presentations is Evan

Figure 7.45

As shown by the covers of these zines, homemade publications offer a variety of typographical and graphic design layout choices for producer and viewer.

Roth, aka fi5e. Created with partner Max Asare, such works as "Typographic Illustration," "Graffiti Taxonomy," and "Typoactive" expand and challenge established rules regarding traditional typographic displays. In "Illustration" (Weblink 7.11), users are allowed to select a typeface, which is then used for images on a screen. If Garamond is selected, an image of Bob Dylan is formed with the typeface as his song "Don't Think Twice It's Alright" plays. For Century Gothic, a map of California is created as Jose Feliciano sings "California Dreamin'." "Graffiti Taxonomy" as Roth notes, "presents isolated letters from various graffiti tags, reproduced in similar scales and at close proximity. The intent of these studies is to show the diversity of styles as expressed in a single character." For "Typoactive" (Weblink 7.12), you can type in your own text that pulsates on the screen in a hyperactive, dynamic dance of letters that you can capture with a screen saver and save to your computer to print (Figure 7.46).

Book publishing and reading have been dramatically changed by recent technological advances. What has been called the "ATM of books," OnDemandBooks' Espresso Book Machine is in use at bookstores, libraries, and museums around the world. Per a user's demand, it can print an entire paperback book with a cover in a matter of minutes. Someday this technology may be available for customers at convenience stores and coffee shops.

With print-on-demand self-publishing companies such as authorHOUSE, iUniverse, Lulu.com, and Scribd.com, an author can skip many of the traditional steps in the editorial process and make a book available to readers as an electronic and/or printed version. These author-commissioned works must still be approved by the publishers and checked for accuracy to avoid libel lawsuits. With Lulu, authors can publish works such as paperbacks, hard covers, photography books, and calendars. An ISBN assignment, professional cover design, and marketing services increase the cost. When completed, an author can charge as much as she wants for the work, and it can be ordered through bookstores and online companies such as Amazon.com, BarnesandNoble.com, and Borders.com. With Scribd, authors set their own price for the books, and readers can purchase the entire work or any portion of it, just as is common with music on iTunes. Perhaps this model may be employed by the newspaper industry some day. Another innovation comes from the Massachusetts Institute of Technology (MIT). Through its OpenCourseWare, textbooks from more than 1,800 courses in 33 disciplines can be accessed by a student and read on a computer screen or printed if desired.

With portable readers such as Amazon's Kindle 2, Sony's Reader, and cell phones such as Apple's iPhone, downloaded books, newspapers, magazines, and websites can be listened to or read off the screen via wireless connections (Figure 7.47). Herman Melville's *Moby Dick*, for example costs 80 cents from

Figure 7.46

"images with messages," 2009. Using Evan Roth's online "Typoactive" program, any combination of letters can be turned into a modern form of the kidnapper's ransom note.

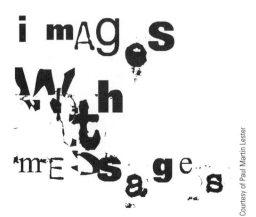

Courtesy of Paul Martin Lester

Amazon.com's Kindle book site. Transferred to an iPhone, it takes as many as 9,461 screens to get through the classic. A user of the Sony Reader can download more than 500,000 free books in the public domain that have been digitized by Google. In 2009, the Washington Post Co. and New York Times Co. announced a partnership with Amazon to provide content for the Kindle DX. In addition, Gabriel Stricker, the director of Google's book search communications, calls his company's internet-based book access method a "digital book ecosystem." Instead of users downloading books to their computers or portable devices, reading materials will be available from the web, avoiding those pesky copyright laws.

Another text-based system is the online service Twitter.com, which began its service in 2006 and is now the third most popular social network behind Facebook and MySpace. Through "mobile texting, instant message, or the web," short text updates of no more than 140 characters called "tweets" in a clean, sans serif typeface can be sent to your "followers" while you can follow friends and celebrities. In 2009, Twitter messages mobilized more than 10,000 protestors for a rally against the Communist leadership in Moldova and helped organize opposition to the presidential election in Iran.

In 2009 author Stephen King took a stand for the printed book after selling 1,500 signed copies of his novel *Under the Dome* from the publisher's website for $200 each. As more and more computer users become comfortable reading text on a screen, will there be a need for paper and ink, manufactured from two precious natural resources? Kevin Kelly, writing in *The New York Times Magazine*,

Figure 7.47

The title page of Robinson Crusoe *by Daniel Defoe, as seen using an iPhone application, is a simple text-based reading experience. Many think that in the future, books, magazines, and newspapers will be delivered and read through digital rather than analog means.*

Courtesy of Paul Martin Lester

believes the switch from analog to digital is good for the book medium. He thinks that as Google, the Library of Congress, the Chinese, and countless other entities and individuals gradually complete the process of turning all analog print books into digitalized versions, they will become more valuable as an intellectual resource. Readers will learn of unknown and once isolated works, discover connections between them, and share them with others. Regardless, the proper use of typography is just as vital in the analog as the digital realms.

■ KEY TERMS

- AIGA
- Alloy
- Analog
- Banner
- Blogs
- Bronze Age
- Calligraphy
- Dark Ages
- DIY
- Engraving
- Filmsetting
- Handbills
- Hit
- Ideograph

- Lithography
- Maya
- Olmec
- Petroglyphs
- Photocomposition
- Photo-optic printing
- Phototypesetting
- Pictographs
- Platen
- Ptolemy V
- Renaissance
- Roman Empire
- Sarcophagus
- Scribe
- Secularism
- Serif
- Slander
- Small press books
- Stereotype plate
- Stylus
- Substrate
- Type mold
- Uruk, Iraq
- Vellum
- Web perfecting press
- Zapf dingbats
- Zapotec

To locate active URLs for the weblinks mentioned in this chapter, please go to the companion site at http://communication.wadsworth.com/lester5 and select the proper chapter.

Chapter 8

Graphic Design

Although you may not know it, your life is unavoidably connected to a Bronx-born graphic designer by the name of Saul Bass.

You see his pictures in your kitchen, on your television screen, on charities' stationery letterheads, on grocery store shelves, in magazines and newspapers, in gas stations, in movie theaters, atop corporate buildings, and on airplanes. Bass has designed packages for everyday food products and corporate trademarks for Fortune 500 companies. He has designed gasoline stations for major oil companies. He has made an Oscar-winning film and has produced the titles and ending credits for numerous well-known motion pictures. Unlike many other designers, Saul Bass was equally at home with print and screen media presentations (Figure 8.1).

Born in 1920 to immigrant parents in New York, Bass earned an early reputation for spending all his free time drawing whatever he saw and reading whatever he could find. He trained at the Art Students' League and Brooklyn College. At the age of 18, he worked as an apprentice in the art department of the New York office of Warner Brothers Studio. His job was to help create movie posters (or "one sheets") used to promote motion picture releases. Movie posters in the late 1930s and 1940s tried to show as much of the content of a movie as possible, considering the limited space. Large, miscellaneous typeface family lettering usually identified the movie's title. Close-up colorful paintings of the film's stars captured during an emotional moment usually were surrounded by smaller drawings of other scenes from the movie. These posters were important marketing pieces before the advent of television; they were used in newspaper advertisements and adorned the front of movie theaters to attract

Design is the method of putting form and content together.

Paul Rand, 1914–1996
LOGO DESIGNER AND EDUCATOR

Figure 8.1

Saul Bass was the first designer to create a visual style that was used in an advertisement in conjuction with an opening title sequence for a movie—the poster for The Man with the Golden Arm.

Figure 8.2

György Kepes was a Hungarian-born artist, educator, and theorist. While living in Berlin in 1930 he became involved in the bauhaus movement through his friend Laszlo Moholy-Nagy. In 1937 Moholy-Nagy and he moved to Chicago to teach at the New Bauhaus school. Kepes headed the study of light and color that he later used for his published works in which he explained his ideas on design theory. In 1943 he took a teaching position at Brooklyn College. One of his students was Saul Bass. After World War II, Kepes taught at the Massachusetts Institute of Technology (MIT) until he retired in 1974.

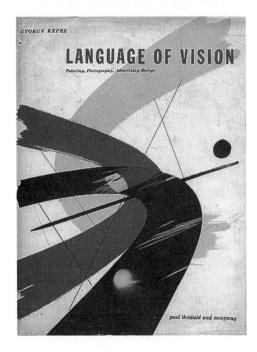

ticket buyers. Almost always they were graphically extravagant and appealed to emotions.

While Bass attended Brooklyn College, he was fortunate to have as an instructor one of the leaders of the bauhaus graphic art movement, György Kepes. One of the books that Bass read on his daily commute to work changed his life. It was *Language of Vision: Painting, Photography, Advertising-Design* by Kepes (Figure 8.2). The bauhaus art movement advocated focusing on essentials. For movie posters, the philosophy implied that instead of throwing in every possible significant scene in a movie, as in many previous and modern-day previews or trailers, a poster should feature a single idea or theme expressed in the film that would catch the imagination of potential customers. Bass decided to follow the bauhaus design philosophy for movie posters and title sequences and in all the other graphic work he produced.

In 1949 Bass moved to Los Angeles. He soon landed a job working for Howard Hughes and his movie studio, RKO. But Bass became frustrated when he realized that Hughes controlled every aspect of his company and allowed few ideas other than his own to be used. By 1955 he quit and formed his own design studio. His first employee, Elaine Makatura, later became his wife.

For the next 30 years, the team of Bass and Makatura, with their employees for their firm Bass/Yager & Associates, produced company logos, product packaging, and title sequences for many major motion pictures. His work inspired generations of graphic designers in print and for the screen.

■ BASS'S CONTRIBUTIONS TO GRAPHIC DESIGN

With such a stunningly diverse portfolio of work in all manner of media, Saul Bass is an able follower of Johannes Gutenberg and his commercial printing press.

■ Film Work

Bass's early interest in motion pictures translated into print advertisements and opening title credits—he worked on several movies as a storyboard artist and director. He was responsible for one of the most memorable visual messages in the history of motion pictures—the "shower murder scene" with Janet Leigh and Anthony Perkins in the movie *Psycho* (1960). As a storyboard artist, Bass produced a kind of comic book version of the film that showed the characters within each scene of the movie. Although the famous director Alfred Hitchcock directed the actual shooting of the scene, Bass's 48 drawings included such features as the torn shower curtain and the famous transition from the drain to a close-up of Leigh's eye.

Bass also produced short movies about the creative process. He won a Grand Award at the Venice Film Festival for *Searching Eye* (1964), a Gold Hugo award at the Chicago Film Festival for *From Here to There* (1964), and Oscar nominations for his films *The Solar Film* (1980) and *Notes on the Popular Arts* (1977). In 1968 he won an Academy Award in the short subjects category for his film about human creativity, *Why Man Creates*. In 1974 he directed his one and only major Hollywood movie for Paramount, *Phase IV*. The ecologically themed disaster film, a science fiction thriller about ants who team up to try to destroy human civilization, was a box office bomb. Perhaps as a private joke or not, ironically, the movie did not have an opening title sequence.

■ Packaging and Logos

Bass designed the visual elements seen on such diverse products as Wesson oils, Lawry's seasonings, Northern towels, and Ohio Blue Tip matches. In 1970, he redesigned the logo for the Quaker Oats Company to give it a more modern look (Figure 8.3). In an ultimate design package, he and his firm designed the entire visual system, including architecture, for the BP America and Exxon worldwide networks of service stations. Before being acquired by Philip Morris, General Foods had Bass redesign its logo. The leaf pictograph within a thick, black, open-ended line symbolizes wholesomeness, growth, strength, and dynamism (Figure 8.4). He has also designed logos for United Way, the YWCA, the Girl Scouts, Continental Airlines, United Airlines, Warner Communications, and Minolta (Figure 8.5). When U.S. District Judge Harold Green ordered AT&T to break up into regional telephone companies in 1983, he

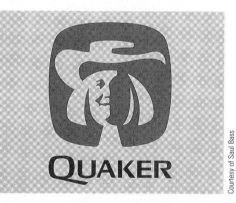

Courtesy of Saul Bass

Figure 8.3

The Quaker graphic reminds the consumer of the company's historic link to its oats breakfast cereal product, but also conveys a modern, forward-looking message.

Courtesy of Saul Bass

Figure 8.4

The round shape of the General Foods logo conveys wholesomeness and natural goodness.

also demanded that the parent company change its "bell in a circle" logo (designed by Bass in 1969). Bass came up with a blue globe encircled by white lines varying in width that connotes a worldwide network that cares about its customers (Figure 8.6).

■ *Advertisements, Posters, and Title Credits*

The first movie poster Bass designed was for the Kirk Douglas film *Champion* in 1949. It was a startling, full-page demonstration of reductionism. Centered within a black page was a tiny image of Douglas and actress Marilyn Maxwell. Interestingly, the text above the embracing couple was a compromise to previous sensational displays. The copy read, "Fighting or loving he was the…CHAMPION." But the total visual effect was anything but traditional. The small amount of text and the tiny picture of the stars surrounded by black supported the theme that the Douglas character was anything but a champion. The design shocked advertisers because it was a visually dramatic departure from previous movie posters. His advertisement cemented Bass's idea of the importance of bauhaus design and that a poster should reduce a subject's elements to one dominant idea.

In 1954, Bass met famed film director Otto Preminger and designed a poster for his movie *Carmen Jones* (Weblink 8.1). Preminger liked it so much that he used it as part of the title sequence for the movie. Until that time, the titles for motion pictures rarely set the mood of a picture. Exceptions were epic dramas that showed a well-manicured hand turning the pages of a book that contained the title and credits.

At first, Bass was nervous about designing for the motion picture medium. He once admitted that "I…found myself confronted with a flickering, moving, elusive series of images that somehow had to add up to communication." But the success of his work, as noted by historian Estelle Jussim, demonstrates "the ingenuity of a brilliant graphic designer conquering the difficulties of a new medium."

In 1955, Bass inspired the creative design of future movie titles with the opening sequence for the film *The Man with the Golden Arm* (Weblink 8.2). Bass admits that he used the title sequence "to create a little atmosphere." The mood that Bass established in the animated sequence perfectly matched the storyline for the movie. In the film, Frank Sinatra plays a drug-addicted poker dealer.

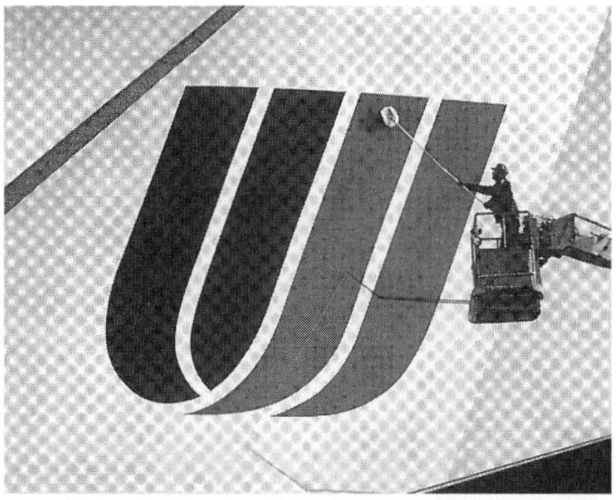

Figure 8.5
The United Airlines logo uses long, curved lines that simulate flight.

Figure 8.6
The AT&T logo, with its pulsating horizontal lines within a circular shape, connotes the worldwide communication network of the telephone company.

Courtesy of Saul Bass

Courtesy of Saul Bass

Backed by Elmer Bernstein's staccato jazz score, white bars with text moved across the screen in a tense, abstract dance, eventually forming a jagged pictographic arm that became the symbol of heroin addiction (Figure 8.7). In 1959, Bass again used jazz music, this time by Duke Ellington, to introduce another Preminger movie, *Anatomy of a Murder* (Weblink 8.3).

Besides creating the title sequences, Bass also designed the advertising posters for the movies, using minimal pictographs that symbolically presented the essence of the plot. Theater owners were uncomfortable with the posters because they wanted traditional works with large, close-up images of the stars. But when Preminger threatened to pull the movie from theaters that didn't use the posters, the owners capitulated. The public had no objections to the new poster presentations and title sequences.

In 1960, Bass created the emotionally charged title sequence for the film *Exodus*, with raised arms holding a rifle in triumph. In a 1962 movie, *Walk on the Wild Side*, the opening sequence showed a catfight that was a metaphor for the street life of New Orleans portrayed in the motion picture. He also made the titles for the movies *The Seven Year Itch* (in which the "t" in "itch" scratches itself, 1955), *Around the World in 80 Days* (1956), *The Big Country* (1958), *Vertigo* (1958), *North by Northwest* (1959), *Psycho* (1960), *Ocean's Eleven* (1960), *It's a Mad, Mad, Mad, Mad World* (1963), *Bunny Lake Is Missing* (1965), *Grand Prix* (1966), *That's Entertainment: Part 2* (1976), *Broadcast News* (1987), *War of the Roses* (in which the titles are supposedly in front of a red, satin sheet, which turns out to be Danny DeVito's handkerchief, 1989), Martin Scorsese's *Goodfellas* (1991), *Cape Fear* (1992), *The Age of Innocence*

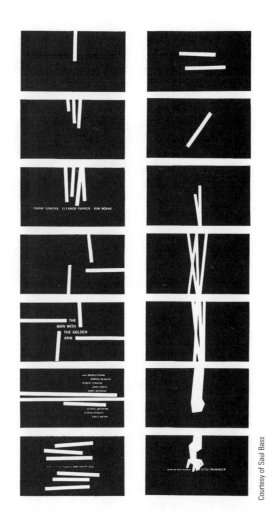

Courtesy of Saul Bass

Figure 8.7

The opening sequence for The Man with the Golden Arm *conveys the desperation and confinement of drug addiction. As Bass explains, "The intent of this opening was to create a mood . . . spare, gaunt, with a driving intensity. The staccato movement of white bars against a black background creates a strident geometry that finally forms 'The Arm,' the symbol of the distorted, disjointed life of a drug addict."*

(1993), and his last, *Casino* (1995). Scorsese said of Bass that he "fashioned title sequences into an art, creating in some cases, like *Vertigo*, a mini-film within a film. His graphic compositions in movement function as a prologue to the movie—setting the tone, providing the mood and foreshadowing the action." For Bass, title sequences are the first chance to set a mood for the motion picture. Consequently, a film director should never lose that opportunity. "Titles can be sufficiently provocative and entertaining to induce the audience to sit down and look," he explained, "because something is really happening on screen." Bass inspired

Figure 8.8

Lynda Kahn and her twin sister Ellen have designed opening title credits since 1987. In 2006 the team won an Emmy for the main title design and graphics package for "The Ellen DeGeneres Show." In this partial storyboard of the opening of the critically acclaimed yet canceled Fox television network's "Arrested Development," the quirky characters and plot lines are communicated through asymmetrical image placement, tilted text lines, colors, and arrows. See color insert following page 178.

several generations of title designers for movies—Susan Bradley (*Monsters, Inc.*, 2001), Josh Comen (*Napoleon Dynamite*, 2004), and Kyle Cooper (*Se7en*, 1995) and television—Ellen and Lynda Kahn of TwinArt ("Arrested Development" and "The Ellen DeGeneres Show") and Digital Kitchen ("Six Feet Under" and "True Blood") (Figure 8.8).

■ ANALYSIS OF *CASINO*

A year before his death, Saul Bass's last and greatest opening title sequence, for Martin Scorsese's *Casino*, was released. His work should have been considered for an Academy Award, if there were such a category. The title sequence demonstrated that graphic design elements could match the content of the piece, contribute to the emotional power of the movie, and add to an audience member's anticipation of seeing the film. Words, pictures, and music, in other words, are employed to complement rather than conflict with each other.

The movie tells the story of the rise and fall of two Las Vegas mobsters. The title sequence opens with actor Robert De Niro as Sam "Ace" Rothstein as he walks out of a casino and gets into his two-door 1978 Cadillac Eldorado. As soon as he starts the engine, an explosion propels him into a fireball that fills the screen. As he falls through the fire in slow motion, the title credits are seen in a white, sans serif typeface in the center of the frame. With Johann Bach's "St. Matthew Passion" playing, the background scene morphs from fire to the neon lights of Las Vegas, an obvious metaphor of the gambling mecca as a fiery hell. Instead of being randomly located in order to create tension in a dada design tradition, word and picture elements are purposely presented in the frame in a tightly controlled manner. Bass extended the life of the bauhaus design movement by incorporating its philosophy of reductionism into a popular visual art form. He also elevated the opening title credits for motion pictures into a highly respected art form (Weblink 8.4).

■ GRAPHIC DESIGN AND THE SIX PERSPECTIVES

Graphic design is the art and craft of bringing organized structure to a group of diverse elements, both verbal and visual. Although graphic design is usually thought of as an art form for print, because of the spread of design applications to all the media, its meaning has expanded to include the use of words, pictures, and sounds in motion pictures, on television, and through computers.

Personal Perspective

Saul Bass once said, "Design is thinking made visual." The next time you look at a print page or view a screen presentation, take the time to note the various graphic elements within your field of view. Most people are unaware of the many decisions a graphic designer makes in order to communicate the literal message of the design and also to convey the emotional quality or mood of the piece. Selecting and placing all the word and image elements of a presentation is the task of the graphic designer.

Historical Perspective

Designer William Addison Dwiggins first used the term *graphic design* in 1922. During his career he created more than 300 book designs for the Alfred A. Knopf publishing company. Although the term may be relatively new, the practice is as old as recorded history. As with the history of typography, the history of graphic design may be divided into five eras: pre-Gutenberg, Gutenberg, industrial, artistic, and digital.

Pre-Gutenberg (before 1455)

The Egyptians were the first culture to produce illustrated manuscripts and wall decorations that combined their writing system with illustrations. *The Books of the Dead* (2300–1200 BCE) are excellent examples of illustrated scrolls that were commonly used for both exalted and less well known members of Egyptian society who could pay for the service (Figure 8.9).

Another important pre-Gutenberg development was the combination of nature and art by the Greeks. The founder of the Academy in Athens and one of the most important figures in Western philosophical thought, Plato, and the writer, architect, and engineer Marcus Vitruvius Pollio expressed a "dynamic symmetry" composed of natural shapes found in the world: the square, the triangle, and the circle. In architecture, typography, and graphic design, naturally occurring objects inspired Greek designers who were particularly drawn to the similar shapes found

Figure 8.9

The cover of Stanislav Grof's Books of the Dead: Manuals for Living and Dying *gives a hint of the combination of words and images employed by Egyptian scribes in telling the stories of their rulers' afterlives. The book also describes similar renderings within Tibetan, Mayan, Aztec, and European cultures.*

Figure 8.10

Natural forms inspired many of the letter and graphic design concepts invented by the Greeks. Note how the shell of a nautilus can be divided into eye-pleasing divisions or "golden sections."

Courtesy of Ole Skaug

Figure 8.11

The Greeks created classic architecture inspired from natural forms (such as the shell from a nautilus). The lines imposed on the sections of the Parthenon show how Greek architects used the concept of the "golden ratio" for their buildings.

hand. Consequently, more care could be given to typography, illustrations, and graphic design. A publisher or art director for a book had assistants design pleasing typefaces; arrange the text in functional and aesthetically pleasing ways; draw elaborate cover, border, and whole-page illustrations; and put all these elements together in a unified format. In Germany, enlarged letters, colored borders, and wide alleys and margins were the common stylistic elements in books (Figure 8.12). In Italy and France, roman typefaces were commonly used to improve readability. Pages were illustrated with floral decorations or drawings related to the story.

in the shell of a nautilus, some pinecones, pineapple scales, daisies, and sunflowers (Figures 8.10 and 8.11).

Gutenberg (1456–1760)

With the invention of the commercial printing press, less time was needed for the actual production of lettering by

Industrial (1761–1890)

Steam-powered printing presses, mechanical typesetting machines, and a great need for advertising materials promoted the idea that graphic design's sole purpose was to attract the attention of potential customers through advertising. An important invention—lithography—expanded the range of graphic design by making easier the use of images with words. Before that invention, pictures could be included with their verbal counterparts in print material only through hand-drawn illustrations or crudely fabricated drawings in wood or metal.

Aloys Senefelder of Munich in 1800 patented the lithographic process, which is a printing method based on the principle that oil and water don't mix (Figure 8.13). The word lithography means "writing on stone" (from the Greek *lithos*, for "stone," and *grapho*, "to write"). In 1837, Godefroy Engelmann of France invented color lithography. Magazines soon began to exploit this new technology, combining words and images in a single press run. In 1857, one of the first illustrated magazines, *Harper's Weekly*,

Jill Britton / Camosun College

employed the first "visual artist," Thomas Nast. He was famous for his sketches of Civil War battles that were published on the cover of the magazine (Figure 8.14). Nast later became one of the most noted American cartoonists in history.

In 1868, Richard Hoe made improvements to his steam-powered press so that color lithographs could be easily and economically reproduced in great numbers. From 1860 to 1900, lithography was used to place images on paper and tin containers for art reproductions, political posters, all kinds of novelty items used as souvenirs, and for greeting and business cards. Printed, colored cards became enormously popular gifts when the American printing firm of Currier & Ives distributed them in the middle of the 19th century. Nathaniel Currier and James Ives published more than 4,000 color drawings that pictured everyday and historic American events. These early postcards are valued collectors' items today. But until the invention of the halftone

Figure 8.12

This 1552 publication, Jüdische Chronic *or* Jewish Chronicle, *shows a scribe standing at his podium adding handwritten text to a paper book.*

Mary Evans Picture Library / Alamy

Figure 8.13

Invented by the German Aloys Senefelder in 1796, lithography became the main way in which text and artwork was printed on paper. The technique relies on the principle that water and oil don't mix. A lithographer makes a drawing with a greasy crayon on a smooth section of limestone. The stone is then coated with water. Because it is porous, the limestone soaks up the water. Oil-based ink is rolled on the stone, which attaches itself to the greasy drawing. After paper is pressed on the stone, the image is transferred.

Figure 8.14

Before the use of the halftone printing process for photographs was introduced, engraving artists for newspapers and magazines often made images more dramatic through "artist license." The horror of the dead soldiers and horses after a Civil War battle, in an image originally seen in Harper's Weekly, *is intensified because the image is a composite of a photograph taken by Timothy H. O'Sullivan and eyewitness accounts.*

Courtesy of Paul Martin Lester

engraving process, printing high-quality photographs along with text on a press was still impossible (Figure 8.15).

American Stephen Horgan introduced the first crudely reproduced photograph using a printing press. On March 4, 1880, "A Scene in Shantytown," photographed by

Henry J. Newton, was printed in the New York *Daily Graphic* (Figure 8.16). The next year, the first color photographs were reproduced in a Paris magazine, *L'Illustration*, but the process was much too complicated and costly for widespread use. Frederic Ives of Philadelphia introduced a halftone screen

Figure 8.15

After the assassination of President Lincoln by John Wilkes Booth in 1865, Currier & Ives, the largest printer of postcards in the United States at that time, commissioned an artist to make an engraving of the murder based on eyewitness reports and photographs of the participants. Despite the gruesome nature of the image, the cards were enormously popular.

Library of Congress, Prints and Photographs Division, LC-USZ62-2073

composed of horizontal and vertical lines printed on a sheet of film in 1885. When a photoengraved plate was used with such a screen, the result was a much higher quality image than Horgan was able to reproduce. Two other Philadelphians, Max and Louis Levy, introduced a halftone plate in 1893 that reproduced even higher quality printed images. Advances in photoengraving and halftone techniques allowed the regular use of photographs in print media by World War I; these techniques are still used in the present day.

Artistic (1891–1983)

The artistic period merged graphic design art styles with various technological advances, including the halftone photographic screen process, color lithography, motion pictures, television, and computers. This important period in the history of graphic design will be discussed in depth in the Cultural Perspective section.

Digital (1984–present)

A machine that changed the face and practice of graphic design, whether for print or screen media—the computer—marks the digital era. The combination of small, inexpensive, easy-to-use computers and high-quality laser printers and networking innovations led to a proliferation in the use and presentation of words and images. For example, because of the computer, methods for working with and presenting photographs have radically changed. Halftone screens can now be simulated with computer programs that sidestep the entire photoengraving process. Furthermore, with the global distribution possible with the web, still and moving pictures can be taken with digital cameras or cell phones and uploaded to a server so that a worldwide audience can see the images minutes after they are taken.

Television news graphic artists have learned to organize complicated visual messages. They make bold presentations

Steven Henry Horgan / George Eastman House

Figure 8.16

Henry Newton of the Daily Graphic *took this photograph of a "shantytown" village near the newspaper's office, the first photograph printed in a newspaper. Although Stephen Horgan is credited with inventing an early form of halftone printing, this photograph was reproduced through a lithographic process and then transferred to an engraving plate for the printing press.*

that combine the on-screen elements of announcer or reporter, moving video shot at a story scene, icons or logos, and textual information, all within the small television format. Web presentations for commercial, educational, and entertainment programs have introduced sound and user interactivity as design elements that graphic designers must incorporate into their work.

 ## Technical Perspective

Attempting to identify "good" graphic design is always dangerous because, like beauty, it is often a highly subjective determination. What is considered good design changes over time and varies among cultures. Styles, as do fads, can capture immediate interest but become outdated just as quickly. But humans are rational and need to quantify all types of things, including what constitutes good graphic design. One method for determining good design is to be aware of the visual cues that the brain most readily responds to and the sensory and perceptual theories. Without question, some designs are noticed more than others are, some designs are remembered longer than others are, and some arrangements of words and images soothe while others cause nervous tension.

Out of that mix of sensory and perceptual elements, most graphic design experts have come up with four suggestions that lead to the concept of good design: contrast, balance, rhythm, and unity. Because good graphic design can follow or challenge them, they are called suggestions, not rules or principles. The discussion of the four suggestions that follows is in accordance with mainstream graphic design thought. A designer should always have a clear reason for using each one in a presentation. It's rare that a design is more important than the literal message it is supposed to communicate.

Contrast

The design suggestion of contrast refers to differences in color, size, symbolism, time, and sound in print or screen designs. A lot of contrast among elements signifies a busy and youthful design. Little contrast usually indicates a no-nonsense and conservative approach. For screen media, little time between the showings of images indicates highly dynamic displays. A good design will usually use colors that complement each other slightly, rather than contrast with each other greatly. For example, a colored rule used to separate a headline from body copy should be close in hue to the dominant color in a photograph that accompanies the story. A design with colors that contrast with each other (e.g., yellow and blue) will create tension in the viewer. Of course, if that kind of an emotional reaction is desired, such a design strategy is warranted.

The size of the graphic elements should vary but be proportional to the overall frame of the design. Proportion, or scale, refers to the spatial relationship between design elements and the size of the page or frame. Sometimes a small element within a large frame has more visual impact than a large element that fills the frame (Figure 8.17). Designer and educator Mario García asserts that every design should have a "center of visual impact." A design should have one element that is emphasized, most often by its dominant size, more than the others. That is the element the viewer notices first. For the most part, viewers prefer a design that presents the most important element in an obvious way because it minimizes the

Figure 1.3

Figure 1.4

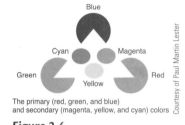

Blue

Cyan   Magenta

Green   Red

Yellow

The primary (red, green, and blue)
and secondary (magenta, yellow, and cyan) colors

Figure 2.4

Figure 2.6

Figure 2.7

Figure 2.8

Figure 2.9

Figure 2.10

Figure 2.11

Figure 2.12

Figure 3.6

Figure 3.13

Figure 3.16

Figure 4.4

Figure 4.6

Figure 4.12

Figure 4.13

Figure 4.14

Figure 4.16

Figure 4.22

Figure 4.24

Figure 7.1

THE BOOK
NEW TESTAMENT

Figure 7.7

EY · BEE
CEE · DEE
EE · EF · DJEE
EITCH · AI · JAY · KAY
EL · EM · EN · OH · PEE
KIEW · AR · ES
TEE · YEW · VEE
DUBBLYEW · EX
WAI & ZEE

Figure 7.21

I SAT THERE
with these two
MADMEN

Figure 7.28

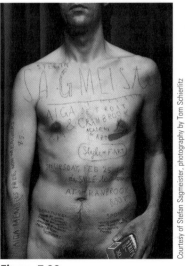

Figure 7.39

arrested
DEVELOPMENT

Figure 8.8

Figure 8.22

Figure 8.26

Figure 8.29

Figure 8.31

Figure 8.35

frustration that occurs when they must hunt for the significant elements.

Space is related to size because the scale of the elements determines how much space is available. Spaces among the various elements keep the eye from becoming fatigued. The front pages of most daily newspapers have little white space because they are filled with stories and pictures. Space is sacrificed in order to fit as many important news stories as possible on a page. Inside each section the stories tend to be more feature oriented and thus allow the designer more freedom in using layouts with space separate from typographical space (kerning and leading). As a general rule, space should be present around the edges of a frame and not trapped in the center. A design with a lot of space is considered modern or classy, whereas a crowded design with little space is viewed as traditional and serious (Figure 8.18).

Designers of screen presentations also have to deal with decisions related to contrasting lengths of time and sounds. An element shown on the screen for a long time gains emphasis over one that flashes on the screen and quickly disappears. Transitions between various segments may be long slow fades or quick editing cuts. A long, fading transition from one scene to another has a romantic, restful connotation; quick cuts signify action and energy.

When designers work with screen presentations, sound becomes an important consideration. Sound refers to all the audio aspects involved with a presentation—music, narration, dialogue, and sound effects. Sometimes television commercials are slightly louder than the program in order to gain the attention of potential customers. The late Robert Altman, director of *M*A*S*H* (1970), *The Player* (1992), *A Prairie Home Companion*

Don't let the low price scare you off.

Figure 8.17

The Volkswagen Beetle and the VW logo in this advertisement from the 1960s get noticed because of their small sizes.

(2006), and many other movies was known for his use of sound to make smooth transitions between scenes. Graphic designers who use computers have a wide variety of sound options for their educational and entertainment programs. Digital music and sound effects add drama, realism, and explanations to web presentations.

Balance

This design suggestion refers to the placement of elements within a design's frame. A design is considered balanced if it equalizes the weight between the x (horizontal) and y (vertical) axes. A single design element set in a square, rectangle, or circle midway along both axes results in a perfectly symmetric design. The frame, like the human face, may be divided into two similar parts. A balanced design is most appropriate for formal and classy presentations in which a traditional or conservative approach is desired. Like the square from which

Figure 8.18

Although both layouts use well-executed photographs, the design on the left is much more unified. If there is too much space between graphic elements, as in the layout on the right, the images seem to be floating on the page rather than linked into a coherent whole. Plus, the eyes become trapped in the white space between the pictures.

it comes, a symmetrical design is stable, but a bit dull. William Dwiggins once remarked, "Symmetry is static, that is to say, quiet; that is to say, inconspicuous." Stefan Lorant, picture editor for *Lilliput* and *Picture Post* magazines in the 1930s, used a symmetrical grid to showcase what he called "the third effect." Two photographs printed the same size and side by side created a new meaning in the mind of the reader that each photograph

alone could not achieve. Because Lorant had escaped Nazi Germany, he expressed his criticism of the appeasement policy of the British government just before World War II when he ran a picture of Prime Minister Neville Chamberlain next to that of a braying llama. A contemporary version of the third effect can be found in Lawrence Weschler's beautifully illustrated book, *Everything that Rises*, in which he compares the similarities of

such works as photographs of Civil War Army engineers lounging at a campsite in 1861 to firefighters resting in a break room after 9/11.

Asymmetric designs are less formal and create dynamic tension within the frame by a visual tilt toward one element over another. This design approach is used to add interest to a dull collection of visual elements or to attract attention, particularly with younger viewers.

Rhythm

The way design elements are combined to control movement of the viewer's eye from one element to another is called rhythm (Figure 8.19). Sequencing and simplicity help determine a viewer's path through a piece. Sequencing is the positioning of individual elements so that a viewer naturally views one and then another element in the order desired by the designer. Placing material on separate pages naturally sequences newspapers and magazines. Because motion pictures are a collection of moving, single frames, they are automatically sequenced as well. But within a single page or frame, elements can be positioned to lead the viewer through the design. A large, banner

Figure 8.19

Until the 1960s, newspaper front pages usually comprised eight highly vertical columns of text with small photographs, as in this 1925 issue of The World. *Readers were expected to start at the top left and read down each column of text. The lead story at the top right includes a sensational photograph of Floyd Collins supposedly taken the day of his death. In 1925, he became trapped while exploring Sand Cave a few miles from the famous Mammoth Cave in rural Kentucky. For 17 days, rescue workers attempted to free Collins. During the time, 50 reporters on the scene turned Collins into a national martyr, and more than 20,000 people from 16 states jammed into the area after reading the newspaper articles. In the movie* Ace in the Hole, *Billy Wilder critically presented the sideshow atmosphere surrounding the hole in the ground. Competition was intense among journalists on the scene to get interviews and pictures no other newspaper had. William Eckenberg, a photographer for* The New York Times, *learned that a farmer had a picture of Collins taken ten days earlier while inside another cave. Eckenberg found the picture, made a copy, and sent it to New York. Many papers used it across the country, including this one. Despite the rescue efforts, Collins died within the cave.*

Courtesy of Vis-Com, Inc.

Figure 8.20

The large headline, sensational artist's drawing of the sinking ocean liner, and the portraits of the rich and famous within variously shaped borders that are scattered haphazardly like pictures in a family photo album, all contribute to a chaotic rhythm that adds dramatic interest to one of the most important stories of the century.

Library of Congress

headline attracts the reader's attention, and the placement of a photograph and the story close to the headline provides a sequence for the three elements. A sequence also can be initiated within an image. The direction of a person's eyes or hands in a picture will cause the viewer's gaze to move toward that part of the frame. A designer should be sure that it makes sense for a viewer to look in that direction.

Simplicity is part of the rhythm of a design. A simple design—one that contains few elements—will attract little viewer eye movement. But a complex design with several units will create tension as the viewer's eye dances from one element to another. The front page of *The New York Herald* announcing the sinking of the luxury ocean liner *Titanic* is a classic example of a clash of design elements—a large three-row headline, the photo album display of portraits of the rich and famous passengers, and an artist's re-creation

of what the ship might have looked like going down. The frenetic display matches the event (Figure 8.20). Contrast the front page with the quiet, respectful, and dignified collection of words and images displayed on most university websites. A careful alignment of elements is the key to a simple design (Figure 8.21).

Unity

This design suggestion is composed of related content as well as stylistic consistency. Elements within a design should all be similar in content, with words and pictorial elements fitting the same mood. For example, a bright color used as a background for a somber subject may not be appropriate. Stylistic consistency refers to a design concept in which multiple pages or frames of a piece appear to be unified. Graphic designers take great care in organizing typographical and pictorial elements so the pages form a unified look (Figure 8.22). *The New Yorker*, *Wired*, *USA Today*, and *The New York Times* all express different styles. For example, the table of contents page is radically different for *The New Yorker* as compared with that of *Wired* magazine. Traditional black type on a white background typifies *The New Yorker's* conservative graphic style (even though the editorial content of the publication is considered liberal), while many colors and images fill the *Wired* display.

Contrast, balance, rhythm, and unity are guidelines for designers to either follow or challenge. When used traditionally, they are design considerations that can result in clear, noticeable, pleasing, and useful visual messages. But when the rules are bent or broken, exciting results can happen. Remember that good design is audience dependent—what works in one context may be confusing or silly in another.

Figure 8.21

In this 1960s-era advertisement for Olympic Airlines, the official airplane company for the Greek government, the bad weather and scowl of the bundled-up man is eased by the pleasing and careful alignment of text blocks. The layout is in contrast to the frenetic rhythm of the Titanic front page.

Ethical Perspective

A graphic designer must balance three conflicting approaches—utilitarianism, hedonism, and the golden mean. The philosophy of utilitarianism stresses the educational benefits of a publication. In the context of graphic design, it means that a design should be readable, legible, and useful. Concentrating on the hedonism philosophy may lead to designs that attract attention only for the purpose of satisfying commercial interests, shocking viewers, or expressing a personal state-ment. As Saul Bass said, "Sometimes we design for our peers and not to solve communications problems." Between those two extremes is the golden rule approach, which advocates design decisions based on a "middle way" between the two extreme display styles. To achieve Aristotle's golden mean philosophy, then, the designer must reach a difficult compromise by juggling the purpose of the piece, the need for it to be noticed, the idea that it should be pleasing to look at, and the desire to create a unique style. But because innovation seldom comes from designers who follow

Figure 8.22

From typographical choices of the magazine names and headlines to the choice of illustrations—one photojournalistic the other a humorous cartoon—you know you are seeing two separate publications because their styles are so different. Saul Steinberg's "View of the World" cover was his most famous work out of the almost 90 covers he made for The New Yorker *magazine.*
See color insert following page 178.

the "golden mean," being sensitive to conflicting ethical philosophies is one of the reasons that the field of graphic design is challenging and rewarding.

Graphic designers and all other visual communicators also must be sensitive to other ethical considerations: stereotypes, certain product promotions, appropriation, and the reasons for editorial decisions.

Because the combination of text, graphic elements, and images forms a powerful communications link, a print or screen media message can easily persuade a viewer by its content. A graphic designer's choices can reinforce stereotypes in the media that can leave lasting impressions.

Many products that are sold legally to consumers are harmful if used regularly and over a long period of time. Cigarettes, alcohol, and other drugs certainly fall in that category. The production and use of some products harms the environment. Every graphic designer must decide whether to work for a company that sells such

products to consumers. There is a growing trend among graphic designers to pay attention to this issue when selecting clients. For example, Saul Bass and his associates made a conscious effort not to work for companies that make harmful products.

The concept of fair representation involves giving credit for a design when credit is due. Most graphic designers are not geniuses suddenly inspired to produce a completely new style of design. Many ideas are appropriations of previously created compositions, but with an artist's unique style added to create a new piece. South Carolinian graphic designer and so-called "street artist" Shepard Fairey borrows from popular culture images and phrases for his reconstituted art. His meme "Obey" campaign came from slogans on billboards from John Carpenter's *They Live* (1988), and his graphic version of "The Medium is the Message" is a famous phrase attributed to the Canadian media critic Marshall McLuhan. In 2008, Fairey received additional notoriety after he made a poster that featured a head-and-shoulders portrait of Barack Obama over the word "HOPE" from a photograph taken by Associated Press photographer Manny Garcia in 2004. Garcia believes he should have been compensated for the work, whereas Fairey argues that the appropriation is a form of "fair use." Despite the controversy, the U.S. National Portrait Gallery acquired the poster in 2009 for its permanent collection and in a competition organized by the London Design Museum, Fairey's poster with "PROGRESS" under the image won the Design of the Year award (Weblink 8.5). However, Fairey confused the issue in 2009 when he admitted that his poster came from a full-frame portrait of Obama rather than one of him and the actor/activist George Clooney with Obama much smaller in the frame, both taken by Garcia. A graphic designer who reproduces wholesale someone else's work without credit or compensation is acting unethically and courting legal problems. Designers should be inspired by other work, but not copy it exactly.

Graphic designers sometimes need to make difficult image selection and placement choices when a news event has more than one storyline. Elián González, the young boy rescued off the coast of Florida in 1999 and later involved in a highly public custody battle between U.S. and Cuban relatives, is a good example. After several months of highly public but unsuccessful negotiations, in the early morning of April 22, 2000, a SWAT team of federal agents came into the house where Elián was staying. A Pulitzer Prize–winning photograph by Alan Diaz shows a SWAT team member with a submachine gun about to take the screaming child (Weblink 8.6). He was shortly returned to his father in Cuba (Figure 8.23). Editors had a difficult choice—emphasize the taking of Elián in a

AP Photo / Photo courtesy of Juan Miguel Gonzalez

large photograph, as on the cover of *Newsweek* magazine; feature his reunion with his father, as on the *Time* cover; or try to balance the two storylines with images about the same size side by side, as on the *Washington Post* front page. Whichever choice is made, an editor should make a decision after a reasoned discussion with fellow journalists and not for sensational, economic, or political considerations.

Cultural Perspective

Most of the trends in graphic design initially began as styles for political and advertising posters that were nailed to walls in cities with large numbers of pedestrians. After a time, other designers and mainstream media outlets adopted the technique. Nine of the art movements discussed here have had the most influence on graphic design. They may be divided into two main groups: free form and grid. Leading proponents of both groups have expressed not only aesthetic foundations for their art but political intent as well. These and other art movements used words and pictures in equally respectful ways and saved design from the "car wreck" styles of the Industrial Era.

The free-form artistic styles of art nouveau, dada, art deco, pop art, punk, new wave, and hip-hop are noted for their free-flowing placement of text and other graphic

Figure 8.23
One of the choices for editors wanting to tell the Elián González story was this happy snapshot of Elián reunited with his father, which was taken by a U.S. government official at Andrews Air Force base a few hours after the boy was taken from the home of his Florida relatives on April 22, 2000.

elements within a design's frame. In many of their graphic messages, designers communicated angry rebellion and frustration over political and social structures that allowed world wars and injustice to flourish. They hoped that calling attention to obvious hypocrisies of society would prompt people to act to change such conditions. Other designers, however, created works that were meant to be commercially successful.

The grid artistic approach, exemplified by the de stijl and bauhaus styles, was less obvious in its political message. The grid styles attempted to give objective, unemotional organization to graphic design. Designers developed a geometric approach based on horizontal and vertical lines and the basic forms of squares, rectangles, and circles, and usually combined the use of the colors red, yellow, and blue with black, gray, and white. They carefully placed each design element within a frame to ensure unity in the gestalt tradition—individual elements are not as important as the whole design.

Free-form and grid approaches are not limited to print design. It is important to consider how these two approaches also apply to television and film messages. For example, the technique seen in the opening title sequences of such television series as HBO's "True Blood" and Showtime's "The L Word," in which the camera constantly moves through a set or location as if it were a character itself (sometimes referred to as the "single-camera" technique), is an example of the free-form approach for moving images. Conversely, almost any situation comedy with characters in a tightly controlled and choreographed theater set (e.g., NBC's "The Office" and CBS's "How I Met Your Mother") in which a director uses one to four cameras and quickly cuts between actors in a scene (sometimes called the "multicamera" style) is an example of the grid approach.

■ *Free-Form Approaches*

Art Nouveau

Modern graphic design was saved from the crass commercialism of the Industrial Era designs with the introduction of the art nouveau (or "new art") style around 1890. Art nouveau was the first commercial art style intended to make products and their advertisements more beautiful. Art nouveau was highly influenced by traditional Asian vases, paintings, and screens, particularly from Japan and Korea (Figure 8.24). Borders were marked by stylized, plant-like vines, and typography mimicked the

Figure 8.24

"Waves at Matsushima," 17th century, by Tawaraya Sotatsu. Matsushima, a group of 260 islands on the eastern side of Japan, is ranked as one of the three best views in the country. With its flowing lines and shapes expressing the beauty and power of the crashing waves, the work is a classic example of the Japanese style of art that inspired the Western art nouveau movement.

flowing curves of the graphic elements. At first, critics severely criticized art nouveau, using such phrases as "linear hysteria," "strange decorative disease," and "stylistic free-for-all" to describe the art style. Eventually, however, the movement gained credibility after Henri Marie Raymond de Toulouse-Lautrec-Monfa gained popularity for his posters for various performances (Figure 8.25). A child of two first cousins, Toulouse-Lautrec suffered from a number of health problems. As a teenager he broke his right and then his left leg, which failed to heal properly. As a consequence, he grew to be only five feet tall, was unable to walk easily, but threw himself into creating artwork. He died at the age of 36 in 1901 as a result of alcoholism and syphilis. In 2005 one of his early paintings was sold for $22.4 million.

Although much more popular in Europe, the movement was best demonstrated in the United States on the covers of *Harper's Monthly*. Artists such as Maxfield Parrish and Will Bradley produced graphic designs for advertisements in the mid-1890s that were so praised for their beauty that they soon became collectors' items. Besides cover and poster work, Parrish was also known for his dreamy landscapes filled with golden nymph-like characters (Figure 8.26). Bradley started as an errand boy and apprentice to a printer in Chicago and went on to become art director for *The Chap-Book*, where he worked with other art nouveau artists such as Toulouse-Lautrec and Aubrey Beardsley, the controversial British illustrator known for his erotic drawings (Figure 8.27). Bradley also created his own striking covers for the literary journal *The Chap-Book* (Figure 8.28) He later became art director for *Collier's* magazine, and in the 1920s he supervised all the graphic production for William

Randolph Hearst's newspapers, magazines, and motion pictures. The movement inspired other designers to link artistry with functionalism for the first time

Figure 8.25

"Divan Japonais," 1893, by Henri Marie Raymond de Toulouse-Lautrec-Monfa. With their flowing graphic elements and matching typography, the posters of Henri Toulouse-Lautrec are excellent examples of the art nouveau movement that propelled graphic design out of the "dark ages" of advertisements inspired by the Industrial Revolution.

Figure 8.26

"From The Story of Snow White," 1912, by Maxfield Parrish. The son of an engraver and painter, Maxfield Parrish was encouraged to create art at an early age. After earning a degree in fine arts from the Pennsylvania Academy, he found work illustrating books and magazine covers and producing illustrations for various advertisements. Parrish eventually developed a unique style of artistic expression using luminous colors in thick layers that produced a three-dimensional quality with dramatic use of lighting for his often-fantastical subject matter. See color insert following page 178.

Figure 8.27

"The Peacock Skirt for Oscar Wilde's play Salomé," 1892, by Aubrey Beardsley. Born to middle-class parents in Brighton, England, Aubrey Beardsley had to quit school at the age of 16 to work as a clerk for an insurance company. Encouraged by the British painter Edward Burne-Jones, Beardsley attended art classes and became an illustrator. The gracefully flowing lines and high contrast drawing style of his pen and ink artwork helped define and promote the art nouveau movement. His illustrations for magazines and plays were often controversial for their exaggerated erotic features. His career was cut short due to his early death at the age of 25 from tuberculosis.

Victoria & Albert Museum, London / Art Resource, NY

since Gutenberg's time. It was a revolutionary art movement because it rejected the Victorian traditions of commercial excesses and a machine mentality.

Figure 8.28

"Cover for The Chap-Book," 1895, by Will Bradley. Nicknamed the "Dean of American Designers," Will Bradley has also been unflatteringly called the "American Aubrey Beardsley" for his similar flowing style that helped define the U.S. art nouveau movement. Born in Boston, he became a printer at an early age and eventually an illustrator most famous for his poster work after he moved to Chicago. At one point it was said he was the highest paid graphic designer in the early 20th century. In this Thanksgiving cover, his distinct style is evident as twin women beckon the reader with trays of food.

Library of Congress, Prints and Photographs Division, LC-USZ62-944

Dada

In 1916 Europe was preoccupied with the horrors of World War I. Dada emerged as a critical examination of the social structures that allowed such an event to occur. It expressed artists' rage with political leaders by the use of absurd, asymmetric designs. Writings and graphics were intended to confuse, educate, and gain attention. One of the founders of the movement, Romanian-born poet Tristan Tzara, said simply, "Dada means nothing." The name supposedly came out of a meeting of poets, painters, and graphic designers at the Cabaret Voltaire in Zurich, Switzerland, in 1916. The German refugee and poet Hugo Ball sponsored the social gathering. Opening a French dictionary at random, one of the members quickly pointed to the word for a child's hobbyhorse: *dada*. Its practitioners viewed harmony and symmetry as stifling. For the dada artists, graphic design elements reflected the way modern life actually was lived—quickly paced and tense. It was hoped that by using such designs they could communicate criticism of the many hypocrisies they perceived during and after the "War to End All Wars." Politicians and wealthy individuals were particular targets of dada publications.

Dada graphic designs consisted of typography of different sizes and styles randomly distributed on a page (Figure 8.29). At first glance, such designs are extremely difficult to read. However, Marshall McLuhan argued that dada showed a way to escape the confines of the Western tradition of reading from left to right in tightly controlled rows as the only way to present verbal messages. He preferred the "words in liberty" demonstrated by dada artists. Dada later went on to inspire artists such as "Walt Whitman, Allen Ginsberg, yippies, hippies, and punks."

Painters, graphic designers, filmmakers, and cartoonists experimented with nontraditional image-making. Painters Jean Arp, Max Ernst, and Marcel Duchamp, famous for his "Nude Descending a Staircase, No. 2," (1912) and "Bicycle Wheel" (1913), stretched the boundaries of acceptable fine art. Graphic designers introduced montage or composite techniques in which they cut out and arranged pieces of pictures on a page.

In film, this innovation was best demonstrated by Sergei Eisenstein's classic 1925 film *Battleship Potemkin*, in which more than one image was presented on the screen. In 1970, an engineer for General Dynamics, Sidney Laverents, made a humorous film called *Multiple SIDosis* with a 16-millimeter film camera and a two-track, reel-to-reel tape recorder, which featured multiple images of him playing various instruments on the screen at the same time. The short film was selected for the prestigious National Film Registry collection (Weblink 8.7). Finally, American George Herriman's comic strip "Krazy Kat," which ran in William Randolph Hearst's newspapers from 1913 to 1944, featured the tribulations of Krazy Kat, who was in love with a mouse named Ignatz, who in turn couldn't stand him and threw bricks at his head. Herriman's dada influence is credited with inspiring the rule-breaking, adult-themed line of cartoonists that includes Friz Freleng of Looney Tunes and Matt Groening of "The Simpsons," as opposed to the "family values" cartoons from the Walt Disney Studios.

Art Deco

Called "the last of the total styles," art deco united buildings, objects, fashions, and typographical and graphic designs by its stylish and distinctive look. Art deco (called *art moderne* in Europe) takes its

Courtesy of the Centre Georges Pompidou

name from a 1925 exhibition in Paris titled "Exposition Internationale des Arts Décoratifs et Industriels Modernes," which covered both banks of the Seine River.

The distinctive art deco style was noted for its streamlined shapes and curved sans serif typographical lettering that presented a modern graphic look. Advertisers at first didn't like the style because the conservative nature of U.S. design at the time favored function over form. Critics viewed art deco as anti-utilitarian. Nevertheless, *Harper's Bazaar* signed one of the most famous art deco artists, Erté, to a ten-year contract to make erotically styled drawings for its covers (Figure 8.30). Today his posters are valuable collectors' items. As the public embraced the style, advertisers started using art deco designs. Use of the style spread to department stores, corporate headquarters, and even automated vending machines. The Chrysler Building in New York City is a classic example of art deco architecture, as are the multicolored hotels and apartment buildings on Miami Beach (Figure 8.31).

Figure 8.29

"Und" ("And"), 1919, by Kurt Schwitters. Born in Hanover, Germany, Kurt Schwitters was fearless in experimenting with all kinds of artistic expressions that included the styles of dada, constructivism, and surrealism and the media of painting, graphic design, typography, sculpture, and music. Although never officially a member of the dada art group, he nevertheless incorporated its free spirit to his work. For nine years starting in 1923 he published the influential art journal Merz. One issue was edited and typeset by El Lissitzky. Barely escaping the Nazis, Schwitters fled to Norway and then England, where he remained until his death in 1948. This mishmash of text, overlapping torn and pasted poster parts, and colors by Schwitters is a classic dada art expression of the time. It is no wonder that the American collage artist Robert Rauschenberg counts Schwitters as one of his influences.
See color insert following page 178.

Figure 8.30

The French art deco master Erté poses with a model and examples of his graphic design work. Romain de Tirtoff was born in St. Petersburg, Russia, to a wealthy and influential family in 1892. Despite urging from his father, who wanted him to become a naval officer like himself, Erté moved to Paris to become a graphic designer when he was 18 years old. To avoid embarrassing his family, he took up the pseudonym of Erté, the pronunciation of his initials, R.T. In 1915 he worked regularly for Harper's Bazaar magazine as an illustrator. He also created costumes and set designs for the famous Parisian dance hall Folies Bergère (the site of the famous Manet painting) and several Hollywood movies.

Courtesy of Paul Martin Lester

Figure 8.31

With its sleek lines, curved shapes, and sans serif name, the Marlin Hotel in Miami Beach is an example of the art deco graphic design movement as an architectural expression. In 1979 Miami Beach's art deco district was placed on the National Register of Historic Places. See color insert following page 178.

Bruno Perrousse / age fotostock / PhotoLibrary

Pop Art

The pop art movement combined the organic vines of art nouveau designs and the rebellious philosophy of dada. Pop art gets its name from a group of London artists and designers who met in the mid-1950s. *Pop*, short for "popular," was the label given to objects—from sensational movie posters to the tail fins of Detroit automobiles—that were viewed as unworthy of serious artistic attention and yet were a part of a society's popular culture.

The style was connected with alternative lifestyles and rebellion against authority demonstrated by the "beatnik" culture. The poem "Howl" by Allen Ginsberg, the novel *On the Road* by Jack Kerouac, the peace sign designed by Gerald Holtom in 1956 as a nuclear disarmament symbol, and the photographs published in Swiss photographer Robert

Frank's *The Americans* (1956) were verbal and visual examples of artists questioning traditional cultural values. In 2009 an expanded edition of Frank's portrait of America was published with an accompanying exhibit at the National Gallery of Art in Washington, D.C.

In the 1960s, pop art combined grass-roots political movements concerned with civil rights and anti–Vietnam War opinions with the "hippie" culture, centered on the corner of Haight and Ashbury streets in San Francisco. Posters that advertised rock concerts and political rallies displayed psychedelic art that tried to represent the visual sensations people experienced after taking a hallucinogenic drug. Intensely contrasting colors in vinelike forms with hand-drawn lettering in the same style were visually arresting but hard to read for a viewer who was not part of the culture. Consequently, the designs were a symbolized code that relayed factual information but also served to link those within the culture. Artist Peter Max brought pop art into the mainstream with his colorful posters, as did New York artist Andy Warhol, who used innovative printing techniques depicting common American icons (e.g., Campbell's soup cans and Marilyn Monroe) to create strikingly visual works of art. By the early 1970s, pop art had reached its peak, but not before influencing fast food restaurants, comic books, and supermarket product packaging. San Francisco Bay area artist Jason Munn, a graphic designer who works in the pop art style, was inspired by the movie posters of Saul Bass. Using images of everyday objects such as paint buckets, bicycle wheels, and 45-rpm records, Munn has created concert posters for the bands Why?, Built to Spill, the Decemberists, and the musician Beck (Figure 8.32).

Punk

In the late 1970s, a new form of graphic design, initially called neo-dada and then punk, emerged. Creators of punk placed typographical and other visual elements on pages in angry, rebellious, and random ways in the style of "ransom note" cutouts. In that way, punk was greatly influenced by the earlier dada movement. Underground comic books and zines as well as music and fashion styles were the first outlets for this art form (Figure 8.33). Punk artists were critical of the lavish spending habits of the wealthy, as were their dada predecessors.

New Wave

Punk, as with other art movements, quickly became absorbed into mainstream culture. Cartoonist Gary Panter decried the transition into respectability when he said, "Punk was an honest expression, while new wave is a packaging term." New wave, founded by the Swiss Wolfgang Weingart and American April Greiman, was highly influenced by the ease of typographical and visual manipulations made

Figure 8.32

"Record Release for Why?," 2008, by Jason Munn. Jason Munn's clever use of the gestalt law of continuation creates a dynamic visual pun for the indie band Why? His use of vinyl record parts is also a trademark of pop culture artists—showing viewers new ways to think of ordinary objects. Munn, originally from Wisconsin, lives outside San Francisco. He started his The Small Stakes studio in 2003, which produces book covers, album packaging, T-shirt designs, screen-printed posters, and illustrations. His work has appeared in Print, Communication Arts, *and* Creative Review. *His posters are also part of the permanent collection at the San Francisco Museum of Modern Art.*

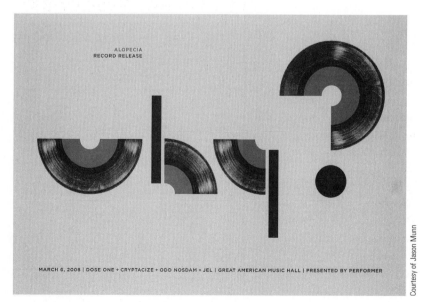

Figure 8.33

"Upcoming Genocide, El Monte, California," 2005, by Kevin McCarty. With roots in the rule-breaking and angry artists of the dada movement, punk can be an anti-establishment expression through music, artwork, and fashion. And yet, photographer and educator Kevin McCarty captures the dual personalities of a young punk advocate with his shaved head, heavily gelled, bird-like hair style, and leather jacket that is in contrast with his soft facial features, curious expression, and a framed studio portrait in the background of the treasurer of an Elks Lodge, the site of a punk music show.

Courtesy of Kevin McCarty

possible by computer technology. It was connected with a youthful culture that viewed all new technology as exciting. The colorful cutout titles that Tiber Kalman and Alexander Isley made for the movie *Something Wild* (1986) were examples of new wave that have been critically praised (Weblink 8.8). The design was also influenced by the music and the fashions of such bands as Depeche Mode, Devo, and the Pet Shop Boys.

Hip-hop

Started as a fashion, graphic design, graffiti art, and dance accompaniment to rap music in the 1970s, hip-hop eventually gained mainstream attention (Figure 8.34). The quick editing of visual messages to the beat of pulsating rhythms is combined with pictographic images on walls, clothing, and within the pages of such magazines as *Blaze* and *Vibe* until they quit publication, *Blaze* in 2000 and *Vibe* in 2009. Musically,

Figure 8.34

As with other graphic design and art movements, hip-hop is evidenced in music, fashion, typography, and spontaneous forms of expression. On a wall in the college town of Eugene, Oregon, a hip-hop artist communicates the exuberance of the art form with multi-colored, spray-painted bold, sans serif-based miscellaneous typeface family letters.

BCS/Alamy

hip-hop diversified to include various forms of rap (alternative, gangsta, jazz, and Southern). The high mark of hip-hop was 2004, when OutKast's album *Speakerboxxx/The Love Below* won Album of the Year at the Grammy Awards, and the movie *You Got Served* about a dance contest was a surprise hip-hop hit. Since then, however, albums by hip-hop artists have declined in sales.

■ *Grid Approaches*

The idea of a grid came from graphic designers who wanted to create organized and efficient presentations—whether for print or for architecture.

De Stijl

In the summer of 1917 several Dutch painters, including Theo van Doesburg and Piet Mondrian, perceived the use of a grid as a way to search for universal harmony in the wake of World War I. Unlike dada artists, de stijl designers believed that an unemotional use of lines, common shapes, and the colors of red, yellow, and blue would usher in a new utopian spirit of cooperation among the people of the world. De stijl, translated as *the style*, introduced contemporary graphic designers to the grid format through a journal of the same name. Today, editors commonly use a variation of the grid format for newspaper front pages to express a modern approach.

Like Mondrian, Doesburg composed abstract paintings of thick black horizontal and vertical lines that divided his canvases into basic shapes, which he filled in with colors (Figure 8.35). His artwork inspired graphic designers to use the same system with text and images.

Architect and designer Le Corbusier made an important contribution to the use of the grid in architecture with his 1948 book *Modulor* and the design system of

the same name. Le Corbusier was a pseudonym, taken from the name of a maternal relative, of Swiss-born Charles-Édouard Jeanneret. By the 1960s modular design, named after Le Corbusier's book, became the dominant force in modernizing the front pages of newspapers around the world. In modular design, text and images for each story are placed within rectangular shapes called *modules*. A newspaper redesigned modularly has more of a horizontal than vertical orientation and is meant to remind readers and potential customers that its stories and pictures are as easy to read as those found on television.

In his 1981 book *Contemporary Newspaper Design* and workshops at newspapers around the world, Mario García spread the modular design approach. When the national newspaper *USA Today* was introduced in September 1982, its design was heavily influenced by the philosophies of García and other modular advocates (Figure 8.36).

Bauhaus

In 1919, architect Walter Gropius headed a design workshop and think tank in Weimar, Germany, called the *Das Staatliches Bauhaus*. Bauhaus comes from the German words *bauen*, "to build," and

Figure 8.35

"Contra-Composition XVI," 1925, oil on canvas, by Theo van Doesburg. Born Christian Emil Marie Küpper, he took the surname of his stepfather after he started to paint professionally. After seeing Piet Mondrian's work, van Doesburg contacted him and the two helped found the de stijl movement. As with many duos in the history of visual communications, Mondrian was the shy creator of original work and van Doesburg, although a respected painter, was more outgoing and did much to promote de stijl. This work by Doesburg, perhaps a visual pun as the primary colors for light are not red, blue, and yellow, is an example of his style that caused a falling out in 1924 among the two artists. Doesburg preferred diagonals while Mondrian thought straight lines best represented the art movement. Although the two reconciled in 1929, van Doesburg died in Switzerland of a heart attack two years later.
See color insert following page 178.

Figure 8.36

As a demonstration of modular design that was influenced by the grids of de stijl artists, this mock newspaper contains four discrete rectangular modules, two with and two without a photograph. The visual effect is a more horizontal and modern-looking layout than early 20th century newspaper front pages.

Figure 8.37

From 1925 until 1932, the bauhaus school, founded by Walter Gropius, was located in Dessau, Germany, shown here. During part of that time, the famed German architect Ludwig Mies van der Rohe, also known for his catchphrases "Less is more" and "God is in the details," was its director. Although typography and graphic design were taught at the school, bauhaus is recognized more as an architectural movement. As the photograph shows, the soothing symmetrical grid of windowpanes, railings, and chairs define bauhaus.

The Daily News (Not)

This Is The Top Story Of The Day

Another Important Story Is Here

This Space is reserved for a daily column

The Third Top Story Goes Here

Courtesy of Paul Martin Lester

haus, "house." Bauhaus was originally intended as an architectural school; the grid-like look of skyscrapers with their individual cubicles for similarly dressed office workers comes from bauhaus architectural design (Figure 8.37). The design style quickly embraced the de stijl concept of creating harmony in the world by unifying art and technology. Bauhaus is characterized by its emphasis on useful, simple, and clearly defined forms. Abstract painter Paul Klee, designer and photographer Laszlo Moholy-Nagy, and his assistant, designer Gyorgy Kepes, who is the author of ten books including *The Language of Vision* (1944) and *Sign, Image, Symbol* (1966), which inspired the work of Saul Bass, were important bauhaus designers and educators.

Critical Perspective

What is considered "good" graphic design almost always depends on the audience. As with different generations that often do not appreciate the musical tastes of younger or older generations, design

Keith van-Loen/Alamy

sensibilities are shaped by the values expressed from other cultures. Milton Glaser is concerned about the prevalence of poorly designed websites. He observes, "There's a whole mess of very ugly things on the web. And to some extent that's because technicians are doing the design." Web design has been greatly improved by designers who appreciate the constraints of grid construction in the organized alignment of words, pictures, links, and navigational elements on a page.

Graphic design education is a key in using computer technology to produce work that is functional and aesthetically pleasing. But because the dominant, product-oriented culture in the United States relies on television and other screen media for educational and entertainment purposes, marketers, not artists or their fans, make many of the decisions that determine whether a graphic design style remains popular. As more and more persons are educated about good design, computer technology, which allows everyone to produce works that are sensitive to graphic design issues, may take style decisions out of the hands of the commercial interests. If not, graphic design may revert to the consumerism popular during the Industrial Era.

■ TRENDS TO WATCH FOR GRAPHIC DESIGN

Computer programs make it possible for every individual to create a graphic design for any purpose. Whether the style is free form, grid, or a totally new kind of graphic innovation, a person's selection and placement of pictorial elements within a frame will express that individual's personality. With the computer, television, and telephone merging into the same machine through cell phones and digital television (DTV) sets, sophisticated home design studios are linked to other workshops throughout the world producing programs and applications for these innovative communicative devices.

Virtual reality presentations, either dedicated systems with elaborate helmet and body-suit gear or simulated online communities found in such games as World of Warcraft and the social networking site of Second Life, will further revolutionize interpersonal communications by creating "cyberspace" worlds in which the designer actually becomes a visual element within the frame.

■ KEY TERMS

- Banner
- Consumerism
- Cut
- Cyberspace
- Family values
- Functionalism
- Halftone
- Lithography
- Meme
- Montage
- Morphing
- Photoengraved plate
- Reductionism
- Rule
- Situation comedy
- Storyboard
- Victorian Era
- Virtual reality

 To locate active URLs for the weblinks mentioned in this chapter, please go to the companion site at http://communication.wadsworth.com/lester5 and select the proper chapter.

Chapter

9

Informational Graphics

There is no such thing as information overload, only bad design.

Edward Tufte, b. 1942
DESIGNER, WRITER, PUBLISHER, AND EDUCATOR

Whether a national tragedy on the scale of 9/11, coverage of the wars in Afghanistan and Iraq, the historic election of Barack Obama to the presidency, or an airplane crash in western New York, words written and spoken and images still and moving can't tell the whole story to a waiting, curious world. With such complicated news stories, a third tool used by visual journalists is necessary—informational graphics.

Informational graphics (also called infographics, information design, and news graphics) are visual displays that can be anything from a pleasing arrangement of facts and figures in a table to a complex, animated interactive diagram with accompanying text and audio that help explain a story's meaning. With headlines, copy, and photographs in print as well as video, audio, and interactive features online, informational graphics are included in media presentations in order to explain aspects of a story that words, traditional pictures, and video alone could not explain fully.

Typical of news organizations worldwide, soon after the airliners crashed into the twin towers of the World Trade Center in 2001, researchers and graphic artists for print and screen media as well as for the U.S. government were at work completing several informational graphics that showed the airliners' flight paths, the location of the planes' hits upon the towers, and the reason for the collapse of the buildings, among other details of the story (Figure 9.1).

USA Today, the country's national newspaper, also offered several infographic displays during the 2008 presidential election with links to interactive displays such as "Campaign Finance Tracker," which allowed users to see the

196

amount of funds that were donated to Senators McCain and Obama by state and by source; "Campaign Ad Tracker," where users could see the videos produced for each candidate; and "Presidential Poll Tracker," with polling data provided for each state at various points in time (Weblink 9.1).

Soon after an airplane crashed outside Buffalo, New York, killing all 49 passengers and one person on the ground in February of 2009, data from the websites FlightAware.com, which provides live tracking of airline flights, and Google Earth, which offers satellite pictures of locations throughout the world, showed the path of the ill-fated airline and an interactive map with mouse-over hot spots that gave more information. In addition, a fact box reported "commercial airline crashes with fatalities" from 1995 to 2006, and a diagram included side, overhead, and front views of the aircraft involved in the crash with basic information about its capacities.

It is no accident that the newspaper website offers such advanced communication techniques. *USA Today's* has been at the forefront of the use of informational graphic design and has inspired countless other media entities since it was introduced on Wednesday, September 15, 1982.

The Gannett newspaper chain, headed by Allen Neuharth until he retired in 1989, saw an unfilled niche in the newspaper market. After being an editor for the *Miami Herald* and working for the Knight newspaper chain, later named Knight-Ridder, Neuharth took over as head of the Gannett chain of publications. At the time the United States had no national, general interest daily publication. In 1979, Neuharth sent some of his key staff members to a covered-window bungalow (to

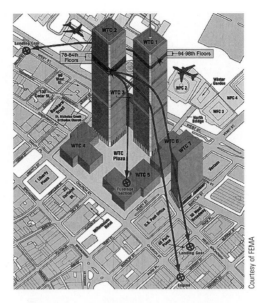

Courtesy of FEMA

Figure 9.1

A diagram and a locator map show where landing gear and other airplane parts fell after two jet airliners crashed into the World Trade Center towers on September 11, 2001. Such information could not be visually conveyed in any other way.

avoid spies) a few blocks from his Cocoa Beach, Florida, home to develop the national newspaper. One of the experts in the early days was graphics editor George Rorick who had been recruited specifically to create the stunningly aesthetic and technologically advanced national weather map.

From the start, the newspaper was created to attract the attention of the generations brought up on television. *USA Today* is a kind of printed version of the Cable News Network (CNN) channel. Its brief story treatment, combined with multicolored graphic illustrations, pays tribute to the printing industry's chief rival—television. Even the paper racks designed by Fred Gore resemble television sets. But it was the *look* of the newspaper that attracted the most attention. George Cotliar, managing editor of the *Los Angeles Times*, admitted that *USA Today's* "major contribution to journalism is, of course, its graphics. And it has helped bring a lot of newspapers into the twentieth century." The most striking graphic feature in the newspaper is the infographic on the back page of the first section (Figure 9.2).

Figure 9.2

Designed by Fred Gore, the paper racks for USA Today *were designed to look like the newspaper's chief competition—television sets, although it is rare to see a TV on a sidewalk that accepts quarters. Except for cooler temperatures in Colorado, the weather map indicates through its use of color that most of America experienced warm air on the day this photo was taken. See color insert following page 338.*

Figure 9.3

Although unable to afford the same type of colorful, full-page map as USA Today's, *many small newspapers run regional weather information and a U.S. data map supplied by the Associated Press.*

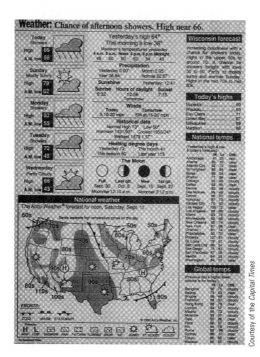

The large weather map has received universal acclaim since its introduction. Media critic Peter Boyle called the map "the most imitated feature in American journalism." In a 1987 poll of newspaper editors, more than half had increased their weather coverage since the introduction of *USA Today*, and 25 percent of them admitted that it was because of the popularity of the large, colorful weather map. Soon after its introduction, newspapers around America started printing their own version of the map—but in regional versions more suited for their readers (Figure 9.3). In addition, other publications began dropping their drab, black-and-white satellite photographs and introduced color graphic elements, color pictures, and a variety of infographic illustrations in order to attract more readers.

■ WEATHER MAPS

The *USA Today* weather infographic would not have been possible had it not been for many factors in weather map–making history. No other kind of map—printed or broadcast—enjoys such a favorable and persistent following or is so dependent on the telecommunications industry for the delivery of its data.

■ Newspaper Use

The first printed weather map did not show high and low temperatures or warm and cold fronts. Drawn by Edmond Halley in 1686, its symbols simply indicated wind directions over the oceans (Figure 9.4). Based on reported observations, his map was crudely drawn and showed the direction of trade winds and monsoons. As such, it was an early aid to mariners.

Halley is best known for the comet that bears his name. In 1682 he accurately predicted that the comet would return every 75–76 years. If you were born after 1986, you missed it, but take heart. You get another chance in 2061.

Introduction of the telegraph in 1848 allowed weather observations from around the country (and later the world) to be depicted on a map. It wasn't until April 1, 1875, that *The Times* of London printed the first daily weather map, which was composed by a pioneer of statistical presentations, Francis Galton, cousin of Charles Darwin. Because of the large landmass of the United States, getting

weather reports for the entire country was much more difficult than it was in Great Britain. However, the U.S. Weather Service, formed in 1870 as a branch of the U.S. Army Signal Office, supplied weather information to the *New York Herald* and the *New York Daily Graphic*. As a one-time experiment in 1876, the *Herald* published America's first weather map. Three years later, the *Daily Graphic* began regular publication of a weather map. Stephen Horgan, inventor of the halftone engraving screen, made the weather maps for the *Daily Graphic*.

It was 55 years later, however, before *The New York Times* signaled the beginning of the weather map's regular use when it published its first map in 1934. The next year, the Associated Press (AP) Wirephoto network began transmitting weather maps electronically via telephone lines to its member newspapers across the country. Publishers liked the maps from the AP because they could use them in local newspapers without alteration.

In 1960, NASA launched the first geosynchronous weather satellite, TIROS-1, which sent pictures of the United States back to Earth from 22,000 miles away in space. The National Weather Service provided the images to newspapers and

Figure 9.4

One of the first data maps, in which a map was combined with statistical information, was this 1686 infographic by Edmond Halley. Prevailing wind currents throughout the world are indicated by the direction of the tiny strokes.

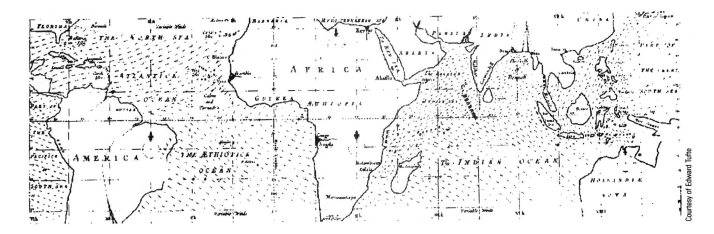

Courtesy of Edward Tufte

Figure 9.5

Web users can find detailed weather information supplied by the U.S. National Oceanic and Atmospheric Administration (NOAA). The colors alert residents of numerous warnings, including those for floods, fogs, and freezes. See color insert following page 338.

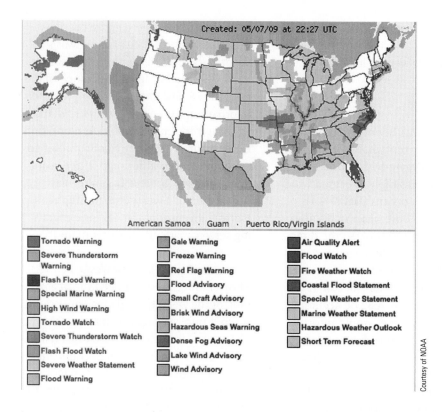

Courtesy of NOAA

television stations for use in their weather coverage (Figure 9.5).

■ Television Weather Segments

Before the 1970s, weather segments of local TV news programs were intended as lighthearted diversions from the other, more important news and sports segments. Sexy women with no apparent qualifications other than their appearance or people dressed up in clown suits and makeup read the weather reports in comical ways. CBS talk show host David Letterman began his television career explaining the weather for an Indianapolis station, and Fritz Coleman, the weather reporter for the NBC affiliate in Los Angeles, started as a stand-up comedian and disc jockey. Today the trend is toward more professionalism among weather personnel. Many now have degrees in meteorology

and receive the "seal of approval" from the American Meteorological Society after finishing a training session for television meteorologists.

The epitome of thorough weather presentations with an often folksy, informal delivery is Chicago-based WGN-TV's Tom Skilling III. Brother of Jeffrey, the jailed former CEO of the disgraced Enron Corporation, Tom is a member of both the American Meteorological Society and the National Weather Association. His weather segments during the hour-long newscast often last several minutes and are filled with numerous computer-generated maps that flood the chroma-keyed effects screen behind him with colorful numbers and isobar lines, but perhaps to distraction.

Another indication of the popularity of weather information is The Weather Channel, the first nationally broadcast

24-hour cable weather service, which was launched by John Coleman, the weather personality for ABC's "Good Morning America," the same year as *USA Today*. The channel and its reporters are particularly valuable during severe weather conditions such as hurricanes.

■ ANALYSIS OF THE INFOGRAPHICS IN *USA TODAY*

USA Today is a cheery, easily readable example on paper of what is offered on a portable computer screen. Many communications experts think that the future of newspapers is a move to web-only presentation, such as the non-print publications of the *Christian Science Monitor* and the *Seattle Post-Intelligencer*. If so, *USA Today* may be considered to be a transition between print and computer, between the analog and digital eras. The stories are written in a short, feature-oriented style that could easily fit on a few computer frames. The headlines are easily distinguished from the other elements on the page and are written in a light, casual style. The typography is a mixture of sans serif and roman typeface families, which creates variety on the page and is eminently readable. Photographs, infographics, and most lines are in color to maximize visual impact. Graphic elements are selected for their eye-catching impact. Consequently, a reader needs to expend only a little more effort than when watching thirty minutes' worth of national news on television (Weblink 9.2).

Although the newspaper has been criticized for its abbreviated writing style of easily consumed "fast food" stories, and has often been referred to the "McPaper," its more important contribution is in its use of colorful graphic elements that show how informational graphics can be a vital and accepted way to enhance stories.

Through the use of computer technology, an enormous number of infographics can be created and printed in each day's edition. For example, a content analysis of the editorial content for March 24, 2009, revealed that the 40-page edition contained 159 stories, 111 photographs, and 209 informational graphics—an average of 5.2 infographics per page. The editors of *USA Today* demonstrate their bias toward news graphics by publishing many more infographics than stories and photographs. In the same edition, there were 126 tables, 39 fact boxes, 15 icons, two illustrations, two diagrams, and one television guide, which together made up 88.5 percent of the total. Only 11.5 percent of the infographics were in the form of more sophisticated examples, including 18 charts, three data maps, one pie chart, and one pictograph.

The weather map infographic deservedly receives the most praise (Weblink 9.3). It is a tribute to the efficient, competent, and innovative use of computers, which allow such technological marvels to happen daily. The map itself takes up approximately one-third of the page. It is a bold rendering of the United States with separate areas that show Alaska, Hawaii, and Puerto Rico. Logically, cool colors on the map represent lower temperatures, and yellow and red indicate higher temperatures. Tables, fact boxes, precipitation and forecast maps, and a diagram constitute about half of the rest of the weather infographic on the page. An advertisement section, first added to the page in February 1986, runs along the bottom of the page to complete the layout.

Color is used on the page not only to show in an instant the high temperature in a major city but also to attract attention to the page and the newspaper because of its high quality. It is hoped that if business executives notice the newspaper at their hotels or between flights, they may decide to purchase advertising to run along the bottom of the weather page and elsewhere in the paper.

The market plan must be working. With many critics predicting the end of news delivered on paper, *USA Today* has the largest daily circulation of any newspaper in the United States, with about 2.25 million copies every weekday.

■ INFORMATIONAL GRAPHICS AND THE SIX PERSPECTIVES

Statistical designer, author, and former Princeton University professor Edward Tufte has been called the "da Vinci of data." He estimates that between 900 billion and two trillion informational graphics are printed annually worldwide in print and screen media. Television meteorologists stand before colorful animated weather maps. Presidential candidates use multiple-colored charts when making campaign infomercials. Business executives and educators put charts they created with an Excel spreadsheet within a PowerPoint page. Magazines, newspapers, corporate annual reports, and textbooks are filled with graphics. The informational graphic helps tell a story that is too tedious for words, yet too complex for photographs alone.

Personal Perspective

Besides creating a record of a society's major news and trends, the media also provide a place for corporations to advertise their goods and services. But one of the main utilitarian missions of the media is to educate. Reporters attempt to construct stories that answer the six journalistic questions of who, what, when, where, why, and how. The first four satisfy the basic requirements for most news stories, but *why* and *how* are part of the educational function of journalism and require more space or time. Research indicates that a reader or viewer learns and remembers better if the journalistic questions are answered with a combination of words, images, and infographics.

In this increasingly visual age, communicators find that images and graphics often help clarify factual accounts that in the past were the domain of word descriptions alone. As Tim Harrower reports in the sixth edition of his popular workbook *The Newspaper Designer's Handbook*, "When we want information, we say show me—don't tell me."

Infographics combine the aesthetic sensitivity of artistic values with the quantitative precision of numerical data in a format that is both understandable and dramatic. A company's growth and decline over several years can be communicated simply with a line chart that replaces several thousand words. It may be impossible for a photographer to capture the scene of a late-breaking news story in some remote part of the world, but a locator map can at least let a reader know where the event occurred. Infographics combine the intellectual satisfaction of words with the emotional power of visual messages.

Infographics can be powerful and even life altering. Three informational designs helped change the way persons saw themselves, their place in history, and the environment. We would not have a clear visualization of evolution without Charles Darwin's 1859 drawings of finches;

we would not have a mental representation of our genetic makeup without the diagram of DNA's double helix structure, formulated by Francis Crick and James Watson from X-ray images by Rosalind Franklin and incorporating additional research by Maurice Wilkins in 1953; we are better able to understand our contribution to global warming because of Charles Keeling's elegantly simple and alarming graph that shows the rise of carbon dioxide in the atmosphere since 1958 (Figures 9.6–9.8).

Informational graphics is concerned with using sometimes dry, statistical data for visual presentations that engage the viewer and help her to understand the information in a new way. One of the best practitioners in the field is Nigel Holmes, a British information designer who worked for *Time* magazine for 16 years and is the author of *Wordless Diagrams* (2005) and *On Information*

Design (2006) with Steven Heller, in addition to authoring four other books. Holmes wrote, "Information graphics should be GRAPHIC. A reader or new media user should SEE the subject and the data." Holmes once gave a seemingly simple exercise to conference attendees: Explain in a meaningful way the difference between a million, a billion, and a trillion. With the 2009 U.S. national debt estimated to be more than $10 trillion, understanding the meaning of these numbers is important. But simply adding zeros, or creating an inaccurate chart with three vertical columns at different heights, will not suffice. Holmes told his audience to convert the numbers to seconds. With 86,400 seconds in a day and 31,556,926 seconds in a year, one million seconds is about 12 days. One billion seconds is about 32 years. And one trillion seconds is about 32,000 years from now. As with Holmes' demonstration,

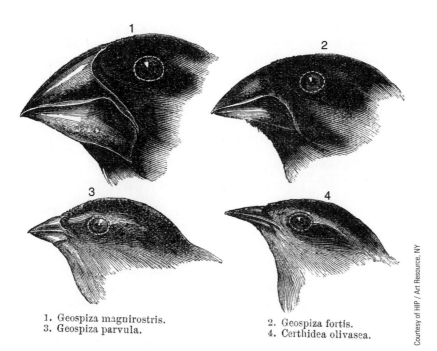

1. Geospiza magnirostris.
3. Geospiza parvula.

2. Geospiza fortis.
4. Certhidea olivasea.

Courtesy of HIP / Art Resource, NY

Figure 9.6

"Darwin's finches," 1845, by John Gould. During Charles Darwin's second voyage on the HMS Beagle *from 1831 to 1836, he collected what turned out to be about 14 separate species of finches while exploring the Galápagos Islands. Significant were the alterations in the birds' beaks—each one was slightly different, having adapted to the unique food sources they had on their home islands. With drawings by the English ornithologist John Gould, Darwin used this example as proof of his theory of evolution detailed in his 1859 book* The Origin of the Species.

Figure 9.7

Deoxyribonucleic acid (DNA) is a large molecule that contains the genetic instructions for the development and functioning of all living creatures. It exists as a pair of entwined molecules in the shape of a double helix. The diagram shows the two spiraling sugar phosphate backbones that support the four chemical base pairs (like steps on a ladder). A human has about three billion bases with more than 99 percent of them the same in all persons. Although the Swiss physician Friedrich Miescher first discovered DNA in 1869, the double helix structure wasn't identified until an article written by James Watson and Francis Crick was published in Nature *in 1953.*

Figure 9.8

From 1958 until his death in 2005, the Pennsylvania-born scientist Charles Keeling made recordings of carbon dioxide levels from the Mauna Loa Observatory atop the volcano of the same name on the Big Island of Hawai'i. He discovered a trend of rising atmospheric concentrations of carbon dioxide, with dips in the levels each year during the spring and early summer in the northern hemisphere, when plant growth increases and consumes the gas. The rise is correlated with an increase in fossil fuel emissions. In 1997 Keeling was given a special achievement award from Vice President Al Gore, who used his work in his 2006 Academy Award–winning documentary An Inconvenient Truth.

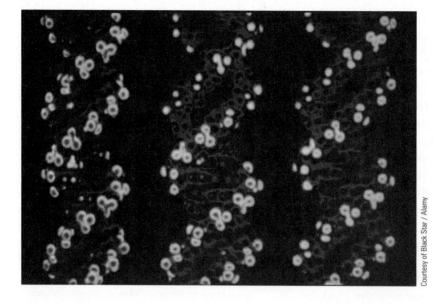

the best informational graphics cause the viewer to rethink the way she thinks of the world.

Historical Perspective

Some anthropologists have noticed that around the neck and head areas of animal cave paintings from 30,000 years ago

(about one trillion seconds in the past) are chips in the stone that appear to be made from spears. Such observations lend credence to the hypothesis that perhaps the paintings were early diagrams to help cave residents practice their aim.

The first clear-cut use of informational graphics by an advanced civilization took the form of maps. Carved in the Sumerian clay in about 3800 BCE, crude maps showed

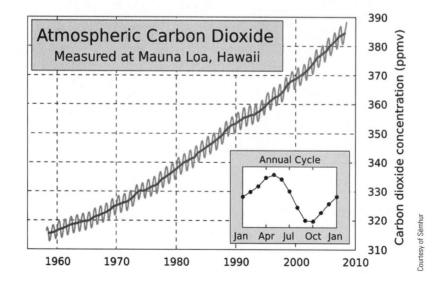

a vast agricultural estate in Mesopotamia. Two thousand years later, the Egyptians used simple maps to denote boundaries between properties.

After the Greeks invented the concepts of longitude and latitude for dividing the world into a grid of set coordinates in about the 6th century BCE, their maps became much more accurate. That innovation enabled mariners to explore farther regions of the world with the confidence that they could find their way home. Much later, in 1137 CE, a three-foot-square stone was the medium for a detailed map of the eastern coast of China. The map called the "Yü Ji Tu" ("Map of the Tracks of Yü the Great") was produced with a sophisticated grid system for a highly accurate representation (Figure 9.9).

With the spread of printing during the Renaissance, maps and detailed medical illustrations were regularly included with text. Sketch artists often used a camera obscura to render accurate diagrams of the human skeletal system. In his notebooks, Leonardo da Vinci often illustrated

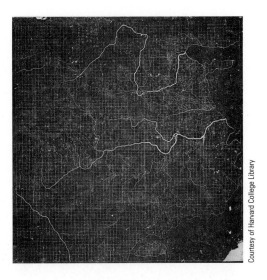

Courtesy of Harvard College Library

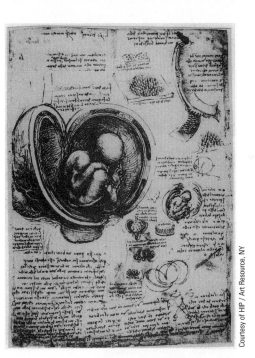

Courtesy of HIP / Art Resource, NY

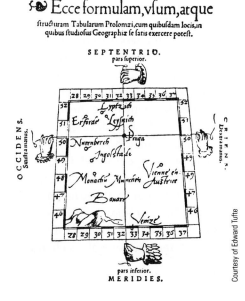

Courtesy of Edward Tufte

his innovative ideas with infographics. A diagram in one of his notebooks, estimated to be drawn in 1510, purportedly shows a fetus in the womb (Figure 9.10). A 1546 edition of Petrus Apianus's *Cosmographia* contained a map that showed many details of the European continent (Figure 9.11).

Figure 9.9

"Yü Ji Tu" ("Map of the Tracks of Yü the Great"), 1137. Unearthed in the Forest of Steles in Xi'an, capital of northwest China's Shaanxi Province, this early map carved in stone shows a portion of China's geography, emphasizing its river systems, with incredible accuracy using a grid. The map was rubbed on paper to produce a positive image about 650 years before the invention of lithography.

Figure 9.10

"Studies of Embryos," c. 1510, pen over red chalk on paper, by Leonardo da Vinci. Although da Vinci helped in dissections of human bodies with the anatomical expert Marcantonio della Torre, this drawing of a four-month-old fetus was based on that of a cow and not from direct experience.

Figure 9.11 (left)

Western map accuracy improved greatly when locations were superimposed on a grid representing latitude and longitude—an innovation from the Greeks but a technique perfected by the Chinese more than 400 years earlier. In his 1546 edition of Cosmographia, *the German mathematician, astronomer, and cartographer Petrus Apianus plotted the location of various European cities with the help of bodiless hands holding threads.*

Figure 9.12

"The Tree of Mans Life," 1659, engraved by John Goddard. With the sun labeled "Christ," the heavens shine down upon the leaves, branches, trunk, and roots of all humankind. Typical of science of the day was to mix religious views with natural observations to create infographic metaphors for the assumed steady and positive progress of human civilization.

THE TREE OF MANS LIFE

Courtesy of the British Museum

Figure 9.13

To honor John Venn, the inventor of the simple circular infographic named for him, the dining hall of Gonville and Caius College in Cambridge, England, displays a stained glass window designed by Maria McClafferty. With his father and grandfather both reverends for a sect of evangelical Christians who advocated prison reform and the end of slavery, John Venn naturally became a priest of the church in 1859. While teaching "moral sciences" at Gonville and Caius College where he had graduated, he wrote three books on logic and philosophy. His Symbolic Logic, published in 1881, contains examples of his famous diagram.

Besides location maps, so-called "concept maps" use a tree structure with roots, trunk, branches, and leaves as a popular metaphor for presentations of genealogical and known knowledge. One of the earliest examples was an engraving published in 1649 called "THE TREE OF

JOHN VENN
FELLOW 1857-1923
PRESIDENT 1903-23

Courtesy of Frederic Schutz

MANS LIFE," written by the English author Richard Dey and engraved by John Goddard (Figure 9.12). The point of this tree infographic is made clear by the piece's subtitle (with spelling not corrected): "Or an Emblem declareing the like, and unlike, or various condition of all men in their estate of Creation, birth, life, death, buriall, resurrection, and last Judgment, with pyous observations out of the Scriptures upon the severall branches." Much later, John Venn, an English mathematician added to the contribution of concept maps when he published his way of organizing data within simple oval sets he modestly called Venn diagrams in an 1880 article titled "On the Diagrammatic and Mechanical Representation of Propositions and Reasonings" (Figure 9.13).

■ *Informational Graphics Pioneers*

Informational graphics might forever have been limited to simple maps or diagrams if not for individuals who had the creative intelligence to understand that graphics could be more than simple drawings. The power of a graphic representation of empirical data lies in its explanation of complex processes by an immediate visual message. William Playfair, Dr. John Snow, and Charles Minard, in particular, had the insight to link numbers with traditional graphic forms to tell complex stories with eloquent simplicity.

Playfair, a Scottish political economist, is considered by many to be the founder of infographics. He was educated by his brother, a mathematician at the University of Edinburgh, and learned drafting while working for an engineering company. In his 1786 publication *The Commercial and Political Atlas*, he printed 44 charts that gave details about the British economic system. But one of his charts

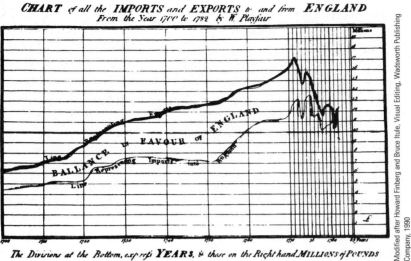

CHART of all the IMPORTS and EXPORTS to and from ENGLAND
From the Year 1700 to 1782 by W. Playfair

The Divisions at the Bottom, express YEARS, & those on the Right hand MILLIONS of POUNDS

Modified after Howard Finberg and Bruce Itule, Visual Editing, Wadsworth Publishing Company, 1990

Figure 9.14

The Scottish engineer William Playfair is an important figure in the history of informational graphics because he was one of the first to substitute time and money data for the latitude and longitude coordinates of Western maps. Charts, then, may be thought of as maps that plot economic positions against time rather than geographic locations.

was unlike any graphic previously seen (Figure 9.14).

To show one year's data for Scottish exports and imports, Playfair invented a graph that used black bars for exports and ribbed bars for imports. He showed dollar amounts at the top and listed individual countries down the right side. His innovation became the first bar chart, showing that infographics could convey complex messages powerfully and simply. Today, bar charts are one of the most common elements of infographics. Playfair is also credited with inventing the pie chart—a graphic representation of 100 percent of some quantity within separate pie wedges. His 1801 chart showed the extent of the Turkish Empire in Africa, Europe, and Asia (Figure 9.15).

Another innovative use of infographics was a result of mass deaths from disease. London in the 1850s, like many overly crowded and unsanitary cities of the day, was often ravaged by outbreaks of cholera, which could kill thousands of people. Dr. John Snow, a physician concerned about the cause of the dreaded disease, obtained the names and addresses of

about 500 of those who had died during an 1854 epidemic. When faced with all the street numbers written on several sheets of paper, Snow could make little sense of the data and could see no patterns. But when he plotted each death on a street map of a tiny section of central London, the visual representation of the data clearly showed the deaths clustered around the Broad Street water pump and

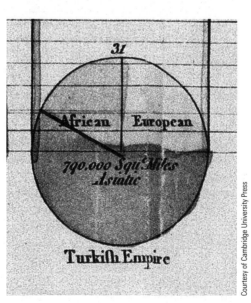

Courtesy of Cambridge University Press

Figure 9.15

Although noted for his advancements in informational graphics, William Playfair never seemed to be able to keep a job. In 1777 at the age of 18, he became an assistant to the renowned Scottish inventor, James Watt, whose improvements to the steam engine advanced the Industrial Revolution. Five years later he left to start his own silversmith shop, but it failed. In 1787 he moved to Paris where he helped bring down the Bastille during the French Revolution. Returning to London, he opened a bank that failed. To make ends meet he wrote books and political pamphlets. His 1801 book Statistical Breviary is credited with the publication of the first pie chart. The chart shows the relative influence of the Turkish Empire in Africa, Asia, and Europe. Asia wins.

Figure 9.16

British physician Dr. John Snow was one of the first to study the use of ether and chloroform for surgical operations. He also is responsible for the medical field known as epidemiology, or the science of population health and illness. A close-up of a London street map from 1854 shows the dots that Dr. John Snow marked to indicated a death from the latest outbreak of cholera. The "X" in the center is the location of the public water pump. His infographic clearly showed a problem with the pump, and it was dismantled. However, city officials refused to believe that fecal pollution of the water, as was later proved to be the case, caused cholera. A vegetarian and teetotaler who never married, Snow died of a stroke four years after his water pump finding.

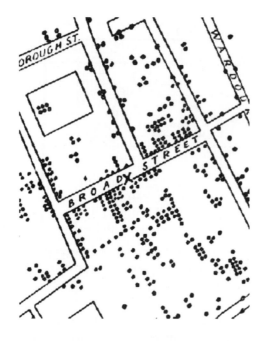

not any other source (Figure 9.16). Snow asked that the pump be dismantled by removing its handle. The plague ceased.

As with Snow, French engineer Charles Minard in 1869 combined statistical information and a map to tell a complicated story in a simple, direct way (Figure 9.17). Minard created an

infographic of Napoleon's disastrous march to Moscow and retreat during the War of 1812 that has been called "the best statistical graphic ever drawn." Historian E. J. Marey complimented the infographic as "seeming to defy the pen of the historian by its brutal eloquence." Minard told the incredible story of the loss of about 400,000 soldiers and support staff in one military campaign through an infographic that combined five different series of information. He showed the size and the location of the army and the direction of its movements on a two-dimensional surface, as well as the temperature on various dates. Minard proved that a complex story could be reduced to its simplest elements in a compelling visual format.

■ *Infographics for Storytelling*

Beginning in the 19th century, highly skilled visual artists fashioned maps and illustrations from eyewitness accounts and photographs for numerous publications. In the United States, two leaders in

Figure 9.17

Charles Minard eloquently portrays Napoleon's disastrous military advance on Moscow in 1812 in an informational graphic that has been called the best ever produced. The width, shading, and position of the horizontal lines indicate troop strength, direction, and position. This single visual message clearly shows why Napoleon started with 422,000 troops and ended with 10,000.

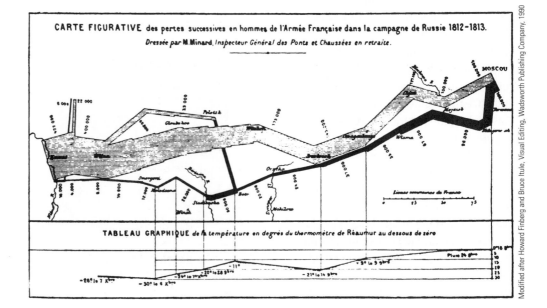

the use of illustrations were publications established in 1850—*Frank Leslie's Illustrated Newspaper* and *Harper's Weekly*. With the halftone engraving process for photographs not becoming standard practice for decades, the *Philadelphia Inquirer* and other newspapers used maps mostly to tell about important Civil War battles (Figure 9.18). These infographics had a side benefit for graphic design generally. Large, horizontal maps caused front-page designers to rethink the customary rigid, vertical column look of newspapers of the day. Because these horizontal, hand-drawn maps had to extend across more than a single column, designers of front pages let headlines and stories follow that same pattern.

Maps always have been the chief infographic in wartime. During the two world wars, hand-lettered maps and diagrams dominated the pages of newspapers and magazines as readers eagerly sought information about military actions around the world. With many unsure about the location of battles during the world wars and later the geography of Korea, Vietnam, Afghanistan, and Iraq, maps were the main type of infographic used during those conflicts (Figure 9.19).

With computer technology becoming affordable and easily manageable, newsrooms could produce custom-made illustrations. Television stations and graphics firms under contract made logos, titles, and other graphics for TV shows. As a result of the new emphasis on graphic design in television, newspaper editors saw a need to give their newspapers a more modern appearance. Graphics editors were hired to oversee both the photography and graphics departments.

In 2007 Adobe Systems, the company that helped launch desktop computing in 1985 with PostScript, a software

Modified after Howard Finberg and Bruce Itule, *Visual Editing*, Wadsworth Publishing Company, 1990

Figure 9.18

Before the halftone printing process, photographs could not be used to illustrate news stories. For Antietam, one of the bloodiest battles of the Civil War, only words and a map could be used to describe the horror of the fighting.

program for Apple LaserWriter printers, acquired the multimedia platform program Flash from its rival Macromedia. With programs such as InDesign, Photoshop, Dreamweaver, and many others, Flash helped make Adobe the most popular software company for visual communicators. Flash is the chief program used for infographic producers because it can combine audio, text, still and moving images, animation, and navigational elements to web pages. One of the best sources of some of the most recent examples of infographics using Flash and other programs is from Paul Nixon, a graphic designer for the University of Arizona. Besides featuring a favorite example he's found online, he maintains links to information designs from around the world (Weblink 9.4).

Technical Perspective

There are two main types of informational graphic: statistical and nonstatistical. Statistical infographics are visual displays that present empirical, quantitative data. Non-statistical infographics are visual displays that rely on a visually pleasing arrangement of verbal and visual qualitative information.

■ Statistical Infographics

The two main types of statistical infographic elements are charts (also called graphs) and data maps. Line, relational, pie, and pictograph are the primary examples of charts, but other variations include bubble, doughnut, radar, surface, and scatter plots. Data maps usually combine numeric data and locations within a simple locator map to form a powerful story-telling combination.

Charts

Much of the news contains numeric information. The president's budget, the value of the U.S. dollar compared with the values of currency in other countries, the increase or decrease in criminal activity, and election results are examples of stories that are primarily about numbers. Reading a story that simply listed in sentence form all the figures generated by such stories would be tedious and mind-numbing. Charts (graphs) were invented to display numerical information concisely and comprehensibly and to show trends visually.

A line chart contains a rule that connects points plotted on a grid that correspond to amounts along a horizontal, or *x*-axis and a vertical, or *y*-axis. Designers often use line charts to show variations in quantities over a period of time. They are most effective when the quantities change dramatically over time. A significant upsurge or decline in a company's sales or a politician's rise and fall, for example,

Figure 9.19

Maps have always helped readers understand conflicts in foreign locales. Many battlefield stories were illustrated with maps during the Korean War and the Vietnam War (bottom). Arrows and shading often are used to show troop movements and areas secured.

Courtesy of Vis-Com, Inc.

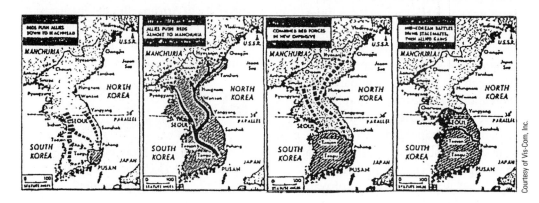

Courtesy of Vis-Com, Inc.

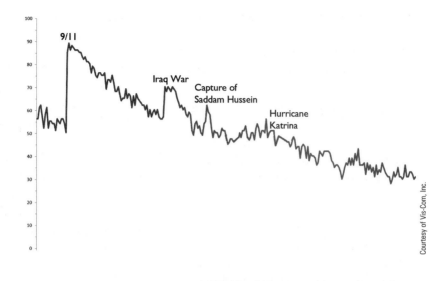

Courtesy of Vis-Com, Inc.

Figure 9.20

The job approval rating of President George W. Bush during his time in office, taken from surveys, is visually represented here as a line chart. Although there are positive spikes after 9/11, the start of the Iraq War, and the capture of Iraqi President Saddam Hussein, the downward trend to an historic low for a president started after Hurricane Katrina. Charts are effective because if the data were displayed as a table full of numbers, the visual effect of the information would be lost.

can be easily shown on a line chart (Figure 9.20). Occasionally, information designers will color the area below the line of the chart for a more dramatic effect. The graph then is called an area chart.

Although it depends on the type of data used, the *y*-axis for line charts should begin at zero. Intervals of time usually are displayed along the *x*-axis and should be consistent and evenly spaced to avoid visual misrepresentation of the data.

In contrast to line charts, which best show broadly based trends over time, relational charts show significant changes in two or more specific items during a particular time period. For example, two bars of different heights would best represent gold and silver prices for a particular year. When horizontal boxes present the amounts, the chart is called a bar chart. When vertical bars represent the amounts, the chart is called a column chart. Whether the graphic is a bar or column chart depends on a designer's preference.

Edward Tufte proposed a stripped-down and elegant type of chart he dubbed the "sparkline." Similar to a Kagi chart, first seen in the 1870s in Japan to show changes in the price of rice, a sparkline

Sparklines U.S. stock market activity (7 February 2006)			
Index	**Day**	**Value**	**Change**
Dow Jones		10765.45	−32.82 (−0.30%)
S&P 500		1256.92	−8.10 (−0.64%)
Nasdaq		2244.83	−13.97 (−0.62%)

Courtesy of Edward Tufte

reduces the noise of too much text and numbers accompanying a typical chart. It can reduce a complicated and busy series of numbers to an elegant, visual-only display (Figure 9.21).

A pie chart compares amounts individually and for the whole (Figure 9.22). The only way that pie charts can be used

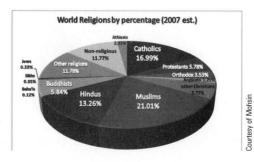

Courtesy of Mohsin

Figure 9.21

Infographic advocate Edward Tufte in his book Beautiful Evidence *(2006) argues for charts with fewer distractions from unnecessary grid lines, words, and numbers. Consequently, his sparkline charts, especially useful for long-range stock market data, present the information without getting in the way of it.*

Figure 9.22

This pie chart shows the percentages of the major world religions as of 2007 according to the World Factbook *of the Central Intelligence Agency (CIA). A pie chart can be useful as a way of splitting 100 percent of some entity; however, if the slices get too small, as they do in this example, a table is a better choice.*

to show complex trends is to use several pie charts, which isn't effective. Designers usually avoid pie charts because they often can get crowded with too much information to show. A pie chart should have no more than five slices and no slice should be smaller than one percent of the total. A pie chart with too many or with skinny, low percentage slices is difficult to read. Colors of individual slices should contrast, and each slice should be labeled clearly. Finally, all the wedges should be drawn accurately to correspond to the percentages they represent. Use of computer graphics software ensures pie-slice accuracy. Although pie charts are distinctive and immediately attract attention by their round shape, as Tufte points out, "a table should almost always be used over a dumb old pie chart."

A pictograph is a type of graph that uses illustrations that represent the items or concepts compared. For example, instead of showing the shrinking costs of computer hardware on a line or relational graph, the designer shows the cost differences by using smaller and smaller computer monitors. Pictographs are the most criticized of all graph forms because they often employ cute, contentless drawings to represent numerical information for the sole purpose of attracting the reader's attention. These visual representations often are misleading and wrong. Although pictographs are dismissed for insulting the intelligence of readers, they are widely used (Figure 9.23).

Data Maps

Maps that combine geographic information with numeric data can be the most eloquent type of infographic produced. Data maps can represent hundreds of figures in a visual format that an unsophisticated reader can instantly analyze. They combine the drawing techniques used in diagrams with quantitative data to help tell a complicated story in a simple presentation (Figure 9.24). The *USA Today* weather map with colored strips representing different temperatures is the type of data map most commonly used in the media. The maps produced by Dr. Snow and Charles Minard are classic examples of the use of numbers combined with simple geographic maps.

Investigative reporters have discovered the power of visually combining numeric data and geographic locator maps in telling their stories. For example, cancer death or crime statistics overlaid on a city's map enable readers to notice patterns that words alone could not emphasize as well (Figure 9.25).

■ Nonstatistical Infographics

Although not as numerically sophisticated as the statistical infographic elements,

Figure 9.23

A pictograph is a chart, but instead of lines or columns that stand for numbers, a picture is used. Hopefully, the image chosen will be conceptually linked to the subject of the chart. In this German illustration concerned with the percentage of feeds to give to pigs in order for them to gain the most weight, the three different figures at the bottom are in the form of pictographs of lead weights representing each column.

Courtesy of the German Federal Archive

nonstatistical infographic elements are a vital part of story-telling in this visual age. They comprise fact boxes, tables, nondata maps, diagrams, and miscellaneous formats.

Fact Boxes

Fact boxes contain a series of statements that summarize the key points of a story (Figure 9.26). These boxes catch the reader's attention in a graphic and entertaining way. They closely resemble the journalistic sidebar—a short article that elaborates on a specific topic mentioned in a longer story. Fact boxes rarely stand alone; they usually are part of a story. However, television and presentation graphic frames often use a variation of the fact box as subject headings for voice-overs by announcers. Fact boxes in print media are also used with photographs, icons, and other infographics in an attempt to attract new readers.

Tables

If you simply want to display numbers or words, a table puts them in an orderly format of rows and columns, with enough white space for readability. The most familiar types of tables in print media are stock market results for the day and baseball box scores after a game (Figure 9.27). Henry Chadwick, a British cricket enthusiast and transplanted American, is called the "Founder of Baseball" because of his promotion and innovations to the game and is credited with the creation of the box score. Writer Stanley Cohen wrote, "The box score is the catechism of baseball, ready to surrender its truth to the knowing eye." Some have suggested that a baseball's box score should be named the "baseball accounting table," or BAT. Although they are the least visually appealing of all graphics, tables are useful in presenting data in

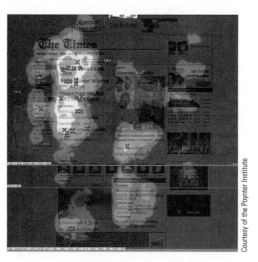

Courtesy of the Poynter Institute

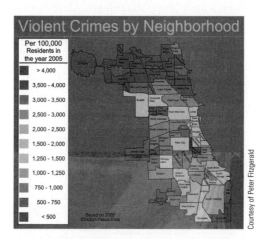

Courtesy of Peter Fitzgerald

Courtesy of the *Capital Times*

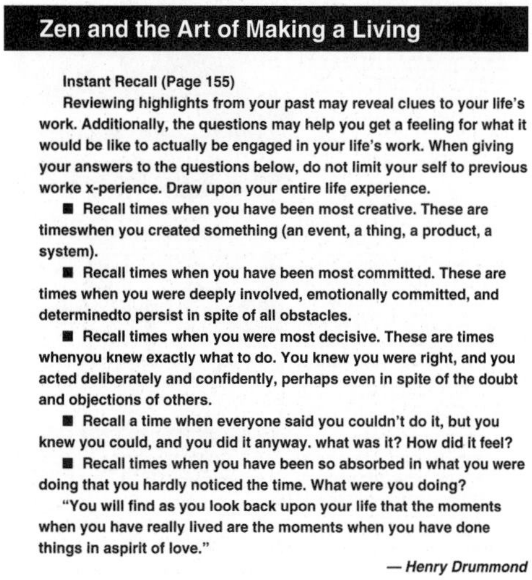

Zen and the Art of Making a Living

Instant Recall (Page 155)

Reviewing highlights from your past may reveal clues to your life's work. Additionally, the questions may help you get a feeling for what it would be like to actually be engaged in your life's work. When giving your answers to the questions below, do not limit your self to previous worke x-perience. Draw upon your entire life experience.

■ Recall times when you have been most creative. These are timeswhen you created something (an event, a thing, a product, a system).

■ Recall times when you have been most committed. These are times when you were deeply involved, emotionally committed, and determinedto persist in spite of all obstacles.

■ Recall times when you were most decisive. These are times whenyou knew exactly what to do. You knew you were right, and you acted deliberately and confidently, perhaps even in spite of the doubt and objections of others.

■ Recall a time when everyone said you couldn't do it, but you knew you could, and you did it anyway. what was it? How did it feel?

■ Recall times when you have been so absorbed in what you were doing that you hardly noticed the time. What were you doing?

"You will find as you look back upon your life that the moments when you have really lived are the moments when you have done things in aspirit of love."

— Henry Drummond

Figure 9.24

From the Poynter Institute's EyeTrack III study of 2003, a heat map reports where and for how long an experimental subject looked at a web version of a fictitious newspaper. The red color indicates the most interest in a page element; the blue color the least. The "X" marks are mouse clicks. From this example it can be seen that this subject was interested in the headline links, but didn't look that much at the pictures presented on the page. See color insert following page 338.

Figure 9.25

When maps are combined with complex data, they provide viewers with a more complete picture of an area. From a 2005 Chicago Police annual report, this data map shows the total incidences of violent crimes for Chicago neighborhoods. Depending on where you live, you may feel ease or discomfort at the visual display.

Figure 9.26

Fact boxes are studies in the visual organization of textual information. A reverse, sans serif typeface makes this headline stand out. The leading is tight, but square bullets instantly identify each fact presented. Finally, the name of the person quoted is set in italics and justified to the right. These visual elements attract readers to a quick synopsis of a longer story.

71st Regt. N.Y.S.S. Tenallytown, Md.	O	R	National B.B. Club August 7, 1862	O	R
P. Hudson	3	2	S.S. Walden	3	4
3B. Meshutt	3	2	C. Kenney	2	3
2B. Dallon	3	1	P. Hibbs, Geo.	3	4
C. Coomb	3	1	2B. Williams	4	2
R.F. Openshaw	1	3	3B. Gorman	2	3
1B. McCauley	3	2	1B. Hibbs, E.F.	6	1
L.F. Madden	5	0	R.F. Pope	3	3
C.F. Garner	4	0	L.F. Parker	2	4
S.S. Inslee	2	2	C.F. Campbell	2	4
		13			28

Scorer Geo. D. Walcott. Scorer, R.A. Cronin.
Umpire Geo. W. Moore,
Atlantic. Brooklyn.

Courtesy of National Baseball Hall of Fame and Museum

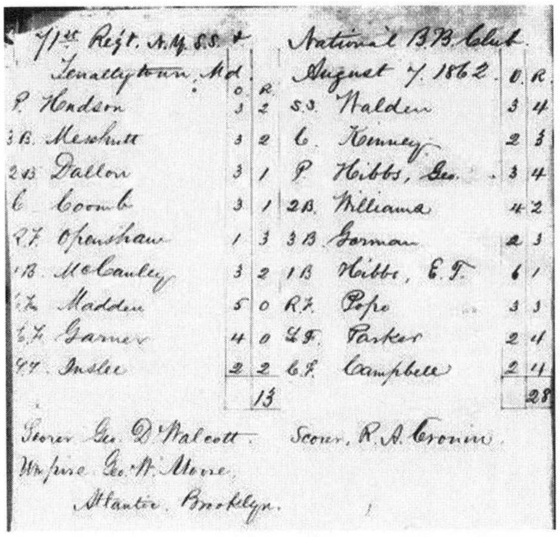

Figure 9.27
Henry Chadwick, a British sportswriter, historian, and statistician, is considered the "founder of baseball." He introduced the batting and earned run averages, promoted the new field of sports journalism, served on the rules committee to influence the way the sport was played, and invented one of the most popular features of the game—the box score. Adapted from a cricket scorecard, his handwritten summary shows the results of a game played in 1862 between the 71st Regiment of New York and the National Baseball Club in Tenallytown, Maryland. The neatly aligned columns give the positions, the players' last names, how many times they batted, and the number of runs each player batted in. Obviously, both teams could have used a pitcher with a better fastball.

a logical and ordered way. Headings run horizontally along the top and identify categories of information placed under them in vertical columns, enabling the reader to compare numbers or items easily.

Nondata Maps

Research supports the widely held belief that Americans generally lack geographic knowledge. One of the reasons that so many maps are published during times of war is that the public needs to be educated about foreign locations. But simple maps also may be used to answer an important journalistic question—they show immediately where a news story has taken place. One of the first maps published in a newspaper was in *The Times* of London on April 7, 1806, as part of a story about a murder (Figure 9.28). The simple floor plan of a house printed on the front page revealed, in almost Clue-like fashion, that Richard Patch shot Isaac Blight in the back parlor. It was used for the same reason similar maps are used today—words are too tedious and photographs are impossible to obtain. Maps enable understanding at a glance.

There are two types of nondata maps: locator and explanatory. Locator maps show a geographic location or a road system in a simplified design that lets the reader or viewer know where something of importance has occurred (Figure 9.29). In large cities, television news programs

The Times.
NUMBER 6704
LONDON, MONDAY, APRIL 7, 1806.
PRICE SIXPENCE.
Mr. BLIGHT's HOUSE.
Ground Plan of Mr. Blight's House.

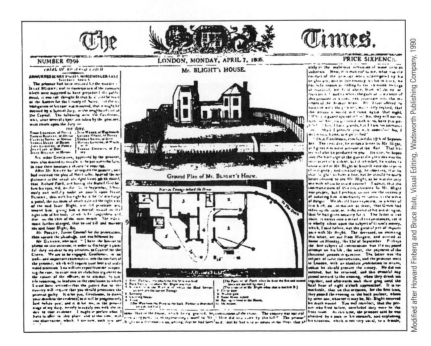

Modified after Howard Finberg and Bruce Itule, Visual Editing, Wadsworth Publishing Company, 1990

Figure 9.28
One of the first infographics ever printed in a newspaper was the floor plan of a house in which a murder had been committed. The Times of London in 1806 satisfied curious readers with its illustrations.

Figure 9.29

For a news story in 1999 concerned with the conflict between NATO allied forces and Yugoslavia over Kosovo, three locator maps with different scales remind users of msnbc.com where the region is located. In addition, users are encouraged to click on an icon on the map at the left to find more information.

include a traffic report about which highways are heavily congested and identify each one with a circle on a map. If a major news story happens anywhere in the world, a locator map might be the only visual information available until pictures can be taken at the scene. Explanatory maps not only reveal where a news story has occurred but also tell how a series of events has taken place. Usually designated with numbers, events leading to the arrest of a serial murderer, for example, are plotted on a locator map. Readers not only learn where a news story has taken place but also discover the background and time frame of events leading up to it.

Diagrams

Some of the most dramatic and artistically rendered infographics involve the use of diagrams. Diagrams can reveal the details of how processes and machines work with line drawings and color

(Figure 9.30). Because diagrams are complex, designers often prepare them in advance. A team of graphics researchers and artists works with the graphics editor to find verbal and visual resource materials that will ensure accuracy. During the first O. J. Simpson trial in 1995, Failure Analysis, Inc., created a realistic animated diagram based on evidence collected after the murders of Nicole Simpson and Ron Goldman for the software distribution and technical information company CNet. Although the jury never saw the video, it was shown on national television on the tabloid journalism show "Hard Copy." Companies such as Z-Axis Corporation in Denver and Decisionquest in Torrance, California, produce courtroom graphics in still and animated platforms. In 2009 Next Media, a Hong Kong company produced a controversial animation for the *Apple Daily* newspaper of Taiwan that presented two possible scenarios for the golfer Tiger

Figure 9.30

The British graphic designer Nigel Holmes is one of the most respected informational graphics practitioners in the world. After earning a degree from the Royal College of Art in 1966, he worked for Time *magazine for 16 years creating infographics. He then resigned to form his own company and work on books concerned with the field. Since 1984 he has written or co-written eight books concerned with news graphics and/or graphic design. His latest work,* The Enlightened Bracketologist: The Final Four of Everything *(2007), shows his skill as a typographical and graphic designer. This diagram explaining the digestion process is a good example of Holmes's bright and easily understandable style.*
See color insert following page 338.

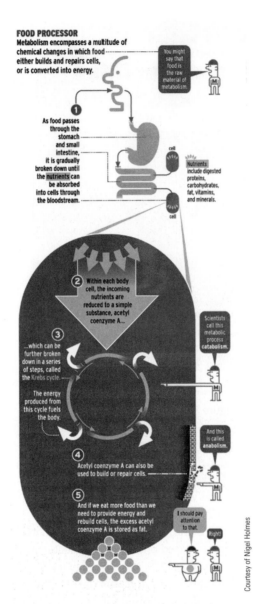

Courtesy of Nigel Holmes

Woods' car crash outside his home. Some suggested that such techniques may be the future for journalism (Weblink 9.5).

Miscellaneous Formats

Infographic artists also are asked to produce a variety of designs that don't fit any of the preceding categories. Again, because of the widespread use of desktop computers, print and screen media regularly present these types of graphics to catch the viewer's attention and help explain a story. Miscellaneous formats include courtroom sketches, television schedules, calendars, icons and logos, flowcharts, time lines, and illustrations.

Courtroom Sketches Sensational courtroom trials generate communitywide and sometimes nationwide interest. Most readers and viewers want to know what the participants in a trial look like and how they acted. Many courts do not allow still or moving pictures of the proceedings. A sketch artist is a highly specialized individual who is usually hired on a freelance basis by a media organization to produce courtroom drawings during a trial. A good artist reveals not only what the participants look like, but also how they feel about being called to testify (Weblink 9.6). To protect the identity of those involved, some judges do not allow sketch artists to reveal identifying facial features. The media must respect the privacy of the people involved when the court orders them to do so or they may be held in contempt of court. In Great Britain, courtroom sketch artists are not allowed to make drawings during a trial; they must make their illustrations later from memory. New York City–based illustrator Janet Hamlin was asked by the U.S. Pentagon to make sketches during hearings of Guantanamo Bay detainees. When one of the prisoners, alleged 9/11 mastermind Khalid Sheikh Mohammed, complained that his nose was too large in her drawing, she made an extra effort to correct the image so he would be happy with his picture.

Television Schedules A common infographic element is the television schedule. The wide-scale use of cable and satellite broadcasting since the 1980s has made the task of designing the TV program table much more complicated than when there were only three major networks. A large community may have several competing cable companies that offer different services and as many as 50 separate channels. Color coding and alignment aid in the readability of these complex tables.

Calendars Business meetings and other kinds of events often are shown in a calendar format because it is a graphic design that everyone understands. An artist or draftsperson will draw the background template or shell for the calendar and reuse it each month. New information is written in the days of the calendar.

Icons and Logos In the past 30 years, executives have realized the importance of visual symbols that identify their companies and products. Such symbols, or logos, are important visible links to consumers. Graphic designers such as Saul Bass and Paul Rand have created eye-catching icons and logos for some of the most important businesses in the world (Figures 9.31 and 9.32). Print and screen media infographic artists have extended those ideas to simple line drawings that attract attention to a story, briefly summarize its content, and help anchor a reader or viewer to the page or frame.

Flowcharts Depending on the type of story, an infographic artist may also be called upon to produce a flowchart that shows a corporation's organizational structure, a series of mechanical or chemical processes, or steps in a decision-making process (Figure 9.33). Most flowcharts use a specialized symbol system that must be explained to the novice reader in order for the labels and the connections between them to have meaning. An innovative variation of the classic flowchart

Modified after Nigel Holmes, Designing Pictorial Symbols, Watson-Guptill Publications, 1985

Figure 9.31

Icons and logos communicate vital messages visually, as demonstrated by these examples. A well-designed logo not only presents a clear message but also can provide a memory link to the company, service, or function. While working for Time *magazine, Nigel Holmes created pictographs for use with sports stores. The simple, easy-to-understand icons rely on our ability to combine the white background with the black foreground pictures.*

Courtesy of Paul Martin Lester

Figure 9.32

One of the most recognizable traffic icons is the familiar disabled parking icon, shown here before a spot overlooking Hoover Dam.

is a computer program developed by Jonathan Feinberg, a researcher for IBM and a former drummer with the indie band *They Might Be Giants*. His program, Wordle (Weblink 9.7), creates a word or tag cloud of the most numerous words in a block of text or website (Figure 9.34).

Figure 9.33

Flowcharts can be complex, book-length tools for solving a complicated technical problem, or simple demonstrations to help you figure out what to do if the light in your desk lamp is not working. Meant to be read from the top to the bottom, this flowchart still does not answer the question of how many persons are needed to change a lightbulb.

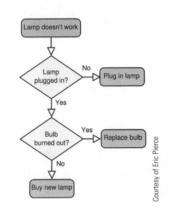

Courtesy of Eric Pierce

Time Lines Some stories that detail events over a long period of time benefit from a more graphic representation than a chronological fact box. A time line shows significant events along a horizontal or vertical line where important dates are indicated (Figure 9.35). The most effective use of time lines involves a combination of two or more such lines, making relationships between them visually obvious.

Illustrations The least factual form of graphic, the good ones instantly attract readers' attention and make them want to read the accompanying story. Illustrations

usually exhibit traditional artistic techniques. Illustrators favor pen, ink, brushes, and paints over computers because they more easily can create pieces that have a unique style. However, recent developments in hardware and software make determination of whether an illustration has been created with traditional or innovative tools irrelevant (Weblink 9.8).

Infographics evolved from simple maps and line charts to complex combinations of visual and textual elements. Many newspapers and magazines seldom use just one type of infographic to tell a story anymore. For a complex story, diagrams and icons might be combined with fact boxes, line and pie charts, and tables. Television producers still hesitate to use many infographics because viewers need time to absorb a complex array of information. Web presentations, however, allow viewers the option of repeating frames for better understanding.

Ethical Perspective

Through accident, ignorance, or intent, visual representations of empirical data

Figure 9.34

Another type of flowchart is the word or cloud tag. Here, all of the words appearing in this chapter are combined into a word cloud using the Wordle online program. Since the most common words used are presented larger, note the size of the word "MAPS." It is true that one of the most prevalent forms of infographics is a map.

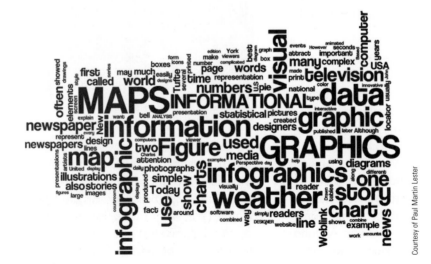

Courtesy of Paul Martin Lester

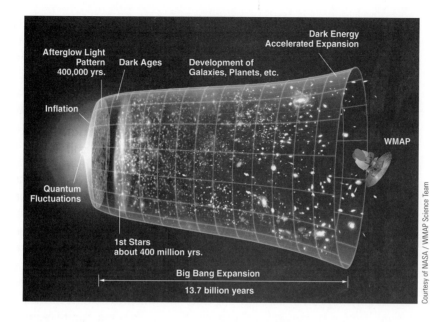

Courtesy of NASA / WMAP Science Team

Figure 9.35

This deceptively simple time line represents 13.7 billion years measured from the so-called "Big Bang" to the present day. Launched in 2001, the Wilkinson Microwave Anisotropy Probe (WMAP) measures and maps the cosmic microwave background radiation, "the oldest light in the universe." The left side of the infographic depicts the earliest time period that can be measured after a period called "inflation" produced a burst of energy and created the universe. The gradually rising vertical height of the timeline indicates that the size of the universe is expanding.

can easily mislead unsuspecting and trusting readers and viewers. Critics of the field cite two main reasons why errors and visual distortions occur frequently—few infographic producers have much experience with statistical information, and many designers believe that if the sole purpose of infographics is to grab the reader's attention, presentation errors and decorative flourishes can be overlooked.

It is the rare staff member in print or screen media who has taken a statistics class. Moreover, infographics production usually isn't offered as a separate university course. Consequently, few individuals are knowledgeable enough about words, numbers, pictures, and computer operations to know when an infographic is inaccurate or misleading.

Edward Tufte advocates more education for infographic producers (Figure 9.36). He has been a consultant for the visual display of empirical data for such corporations as CBS, NBC, *Newsweek*, the *New York Times*, the Census Bureau, and

IBM. His self-published books *The Visual Display of Quantitative Information*, *Envisioning Information*, *Visual Explanations*, and *Beautiful Evidence* were instant classics because of the combination of useful information and pleasing graphic design presentations. He travels around the world giving workshops in how best to link graphic design and statistical information.

For Tufte, a high-quality infographic should have an important message to communicate, convey information in a

Courtesy of Robert Del Tredici

Figure 9.36

Edward Tufte gives a lecture while he holds one of his published books on informational graphics.

clear, precise, and efficient manner, never insult the intelligence of readers or viewers, and always tell the truth. Tufte argues for a conservative approach in which the presentation is never more important than the story. "Ideally," he admits, "the design should disappear in favor of the information."

Tufte calls infographics loaded with gratuitous decorations or window dressing "chartjunk." Such graphic devices serve merely to entertain rather than to educate readers, he maintains. Tufte is particularly critical of the Microsoft Office popular presentation software PowerPoint. In his second edition of *The Cognitive Style of PowerPoint: Pitching Out Corrupts Within*, he rails against ready-made templates that "usually weaken verbal and spatial reasoning, and almost always corrupt statistical analysis." Anyone who has ever sat through a PowerPoint presentation with a presenter reading every word of multiple bullet points embellished with much too cute clip art graphic images, overly dressed graphic elements, and dizzy transitions knows Tufte is correct.

Charts should accurately reflect the numbers they portray. For example, dollar amounts over many years should be adjusted for inflation and monetary values of different currencies should be translated into one currency value. Because images generally have a greater emotional impact than words, the potential to mislead with visual messages is higher. Inappropriate symbols used to illustrate an infographic can be confusing. A serious subject, for example, demands serious visual representation and not cartoon characters. Such graphic devices may attract attention, but the risk is that the audience will be offended.

Inaccurate charts can be produced inadvertently when the y-axis is not based on the number zero. If the numbers of a graph are not based on zero, lines in a chart will be a roller coaster ride of dramatic up and down swings, making the presentation visually misleading. But because of space limitations, using a zero base for certain graphs (e.g., of stock market data) might take up too much space. Often a designer will insert a line break near the bottom of a chart to indicate that numbers have been removed. However, the lines in the chart still should be produced on a scale that begins at zero, and not at some higher number above the break. In the former, the line will be a visually accurate representation of the data. In the latter, the data are condensed and the line is a distortion. CNN sparked controversy in 2005 when the results of a poll concerned with Terry Schiavo, a Florida woman in a severe degenerative state, were not zero-based. The result was a visual representation that made Democrats appear much more in favor of a court's decision to have her feeding tube removed than Republicans or Independents. After criticism, CNN published a second chart that more accurately reflected the slightly higher results from Democrats, but similar responses as the other two groups. The second display was zero-based (Figures 9.37 and 9.38).

Although computers have greatly aided the production of infographics, the technology also makes easy the inclusion of decorative devices that distract the reader from the chart's message. Three-dimensional drop shadows, colored backgrounds, icons, and other illustrations may catch the reader's eye but not engage the brain. Tufte notes the trend in television and computer presentations in which the numbers get lost in animated, colorful

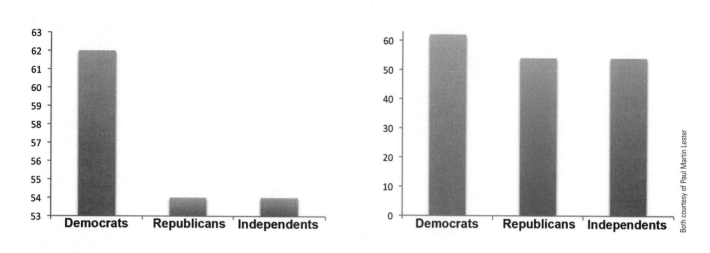

Both courtesy of Paul Martin Lester

effects. Weather maps for television and newspapers sometimes are so crowded with cute illustrations that their informational content is lost. Designers should avoid the temptation to base designs solely on aesthetic or entertainment criteria, a hedonistic approach. They miss an opportunity to educate a reader or viewer whenever they rely on decorative tricks. At best, such gimmicks distract from the message, and at worst they give wrong information. Tufte said it best: "Consumers of graphics are often more intelligent about the information at hand than those who fabricate the data decoration. And, no matter what, the operating moral premise of information design should be that our readers are alert and caring; they may be busy, eager to get on with it, but they are not stupid. Disrespect for the audience will leak through, damaging communication."

Cultural Perspective

The key to understanding infographics from a cultural perspective is to know a visual symbol or sign's context and its possible interpretations. Austrian statistician Otto Neurath wrote in 1925, "Words

divide, pictures unite." In 1936 Neurath introduced a set of pictographic characters he called Isotype (International System of Typographic Picture Education) that he hoped would become a universal visual language and help unify the world. One of the illustrators who worked with Neurath was the German Gerd Arntz who drew more than 4,000 Isotype symbols (Weblink 9.9). Traffic and Olympic competition sign designers owe their careers in large part to the efforts of Neurath. People from different cultures may be united in their common understanding of the information conveyed by the pictures contained in informational graphics as they become more visually literate. Toward that end, designers need to be concerned that mass audiences can understand their work. Carefully choosing the symbolism for communicating a message is vital in infographic production (Figure 9.39).

Critical Perspective

Computer technology makes using words and numbers with pictures to produce sophisticated visual messages in the form of informational graphics easier than ever before. Computer hardware and software

Figures 9.37 and 9.38

In 2005, CNN was criticized after it presented the results from a telephone survey of adults concerning the Terry Schiavo case, a Florida woman who was in a severe degenerative state for about 15 years. She ultimately died after her feeding tube was removed following a court's order. The question asked of the survey participants was "Based on what you have heard or read about the case, do you agree with the court's decision to have the feeding tube removed?" On the left are the results by political party that was originally presented on the CNN website. However, after users complained about the misleading visual message conveyed by a graph that was not zero-based, CNN corrected the column chart to show a more accurate view (right).

Figure 9.39

Based on the work of Otto Neurath and others in creating Isotype universal images, few of the simple pictures have recognizable women's shapes. One exception is the one used for bathroom doors, tattooed on this woman's leg.

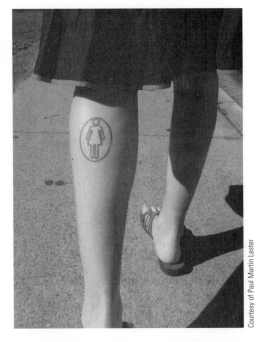

Courtesy of Paul Martin Lester

can make up for a lack of artistic talent. Unfortunately, much of the power of the computer is given to the creation of entertaining, decorative illustrations on subjects of little social importance. The computer can be used to make associations and inferences about seemingly incomprehensible data only if an operator has the skill to work comfortably with numbers.

The best infographic designs "draw the viewer into the wonder of the data" and represent the true merging of word and image. The convergence of verbal and graphic reasoning should be a prime concern of educators, students, professionals, and consumers. Mark Monmonier in his book *Maps with the News* makes the point that most individuals view infographics as "a means of analysis, not of communication." A simple locator map, argues Monmonier, is equivalent to third-grade prose. And yet, a graphic is praised as if it were a thing of wonder simply because it can be produced quickly. If

words and pictures are not united in form and function, the typical locator map suddenly becomes ridiculously rudimentary. Locator maps that show meaningful physical relationships, reveal an event's sequences, and explain complicated patterns within a specific area are intriguing and challenging. Infographics run the risk of becoming an entertainment medium when only entertainers use computers.

If there is any hope for newspapers to attract more readers, a news story presented with the traditional treatment of a story and a photograph, whether in print or online, will not suffice. Informational graphics will have to be included to engage viewers and fully explain the cause. An interactive locator map that shows the approximate site of the story, with an interactive time line and a diagram that explains how the story unfolded, are now mandatory parts of a journalism message.

■ TRENDS TO WATCH FOR INFORMATIONAL GRAPHICS

The FlowingData.com website created by UCLA student Nathan Yau is a popular source to discover the latest use of informational graphics from designers located around the world (Weblink 9.10). The site "explores how designers, statisticians, and computer scientists are using data to understand ourselves better—mainly through data visualization." The website was inspired by the work of data analysis expert John W. Tukey, who was a professor at Princeton University and a researcher for AT&T Bell Laboratories. While at Princeton, Tukey gave joint seminars on information design with a young professor, Edward Tufte. Besides his interest in visualizing statistical results, in 1958 he coined the word "software" to refer to computer programs. Tukey said, "The greatest value of a picture is when it forces us to notice what we never expected to see."

Out of the hundreds of infographic examples Yau makes known through his Twitter "tweets" and his website, he features what he considers to be the top six uses of data visualization for the year: Wordle.net, a decision tree using poll data from U.S. counties that shows how race, education, and income could influence whether Senator Hillary Clinton or Senator Barack Obama would win the Democratic Party nomination; a music video of Radiohead's "House of Cards" in which images were created with a rotating scanner for a 3-D eerie effect; an elegant flowing chart that uses motion picture box office receipts from 1986 to 2008; a New York Museum of Modern Art's commissioned work, "I Want You to Want Me," which converts data from online dating sites into free-floating balloons "hoping to find their match;" and his number-one visualization, "Britain From Above," a series shown on BBC television and available on its website, uses GPS data to trace such diverse activities as taxicab drivers, airline flights, telephone conversations, and ship traffic about England (Weblink 9.11). MSNBC political television host Rachel Maddow maintains a website that is "a collection of maps, infographics and primary documents to supplement the viewing of 'The Rachel Maddow Show.'" Charts, maps, and aircraft flight pattern art are featured on the informative site (Weblink 9.12).

Another example of showing information in unique, fascinating ways is the work of Seattle-based photographer Chris

Jordan, introduced in Chapter 2. Two collections on his website titled "Running the Numbers" present a series of manipulated photographs that when seen from a distance have unique communicative messages, but when viewed close-up become powerful informational graphics that convert raw data into surprising insights. For example, from about 20 feet, you see a pattern of colored dots with two swimming shark silhouettes. Move closer and it is revealed that the image "Shark Teeth, 2009" is composed of 270,000 images of fossilized shark teeth, "equal to the estimated number of sharks of all species killed around the world every day for their fins." Likewise, "Shipping Containers, 2007" becomes "38,000 shipping containers, the number of containers processed through American ports every twelve hours," "Plastic Bags, 2007" becomes "60,000 plastic bags, the number used in the US every five seconds," and "Constitution, 2008" transforms the Preamble to the U.S. Constitution into "83,000 Abu Ghraib prisoner photographs, equal to the number of people who have been arrested and held at the U.S. detention facilities with no trial or other due process of law, during the Bush Administration's war on terror."

An illustration of how informational graphics infiltrates popular culture is a music video from the Norwegian duo known as Röyksopp for their 2002 song "Remind Me" (Weblink 9.13). Produced by the French graphics studio H5, the video shows the day in the life of a young professional woman working in London using everyday products with animated diagrams, maps, and charts in a cartoon style known as cel-shading (Figure 9.40). H5 also produced music videos for such bands as Goldfrapp, Massive Attack, and Super Furry Animals as well as commercials for Audi, Volkswagen, and Cartier.

Figure 9.40

In 2002, the Norwegian duo of Torbjørn Brundtland and Svein Berge known as Röyksopp commissioned the French graphic studio H5 to make a music video for their song "Remind Me." This screen save shows a cutaway and top view of the brain of the young woman featured in the video. The work is a reminder that through advancements in technology and innovative thinking, informational graphics will continue to surprise, engage the mind, and be seen in unexpected places.

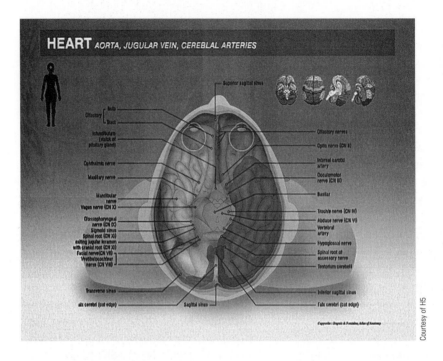

HEART *AORTA, JUGULAR VEIN, CEREBLAL ARTERIES*

Courtesy of H5

A television commercial for Areva, a French nuclear power supply company, used the same infographic style and was synchronized to the tune of the 1980 disco hit "Funkytown" by Lipps, Inc. (Weblink 9.14).

When all media—newspapers, magazines, books, movies, television, and computers—become combined through the web, viewers will not be satisfied with static, traditional displays. Users will want to be engaged, challenged, and awed. It is up to infographic designers now and in the future to reveal the rich and often hidden mysteries when everyday facts and events are combined in innovative and informative designs.

■ *KEY TERMS*

- Adjusted for inflation
- Analog
- Bullet points
- Cholera
- Chroma key
- Digital
- Engraving
- Freelance
- Geosynchronous orbit
- Halftone
- Hot spot
- Infomercials
- Isobar
- Logos
- Newspaper chain
- Noise
- Quantitative
- Renaissance
- Rule
- Sidebar
- Visual journalist
- Wirephoto

 To locate active URLs for the weblinks mentioned in this chapter, please go to the companion site at http://communication.wadsworth.com/lester5 and select the proper chapter.

Cartoons

Homer, Marge, Bart, Lisa, and Maggie need no introduction. You have known them for 20 years (Weblink 10.1).

Matt Groening (rhymes with "raining") created Homer, a beer-and-pork-chop-loving family man and inattentive safety inspector for a nuclear power plant, his stay-at-home wife, Marge, with her blue-colored, beehive hairdo, and their three children. Ten-year-old Bart (an anagram for Brat) is easily one of the most popular troublemakers on television; Lisa, the troubled, saxophone-playing, intellectual younger sister, is a favorite of all viewers who are sure that, when born, they were switched with another infant in the hospital; and Maggie, the quietly observant and untroubled baby of the family, constantly sucks on a pacifier. The Simpsons never age, they live by their own set of rules, and are not easily killed—perhaps they are vampires (Figure 10.1).

"The Simpsons" is a result of three powerful television forces—writer-producer James L. Brooks, writer Sam Simon, and Groening. Brooks is a savvy Hollywood veteran. He's the writer and producer of such highly respected motion pictures as *Terms of Endearment* (1983), *Broadcast News* (1987), *Big* (1988), and *As Good as It Gets* (1997). He was also the creator and multi-Emmy winner for such television hits as "The Mary Tyler Moore Show" (1970–1977), "Lou Grant" (1977–1982), and "Taxi" (1978–1979). In 1986 he formed his own production company, Gracie Films. Sam Simon was a writer for such shows as "Taxi," "Cheers," "It's Gary Shandling's Show," and "The George Carlin Show."

In 1987 Brooks and Simon were executive producers for the fledgling Fox television network's comedy series "The Tracey Ullman Show," starring the British comedienne. Groening was asked to produce

Comics as an arrangement of images in a sequence that tell a story are a very old form of graphic communication.

Will Eisner, 1917–2005
AUTHOR, ARTIST, AND EDUCATOR

Figure 10.1

Bart, Marge, and Homer Simpson dolls hang from a toy store at Universal Citywalk in Los Angeles. See color insert following page 338.

Courtesy of Paul Martin Lester

20-second animated cartoons that would air between the live action skits.

Matt Groening was born in Portland, Oregon, in 1954, the son of a retired filmmaker and cartoonist named Homer (Figure 10.2). His real-life family resembles his cartoon creation—his mother is named Margaret and wore her hair in a beehive, and his sisters are Lisa and Maggie. "When

Figure 10.2

Matt Groening, creator of "The Simpsons."

Courtesy of Phil McCarten / Reuters / Corbis

I was a kid," Groening says, "my friends and I used to put on puppet shows, make comic books, and I decided that's what I wanted to do." Groening did well in school, although he was frequently sent to the principal's office for muttering wisecracks in class. What a shock.

After briefly attending a local college, in 1977 he moved to Los Angeles to become a writer. One of his first jobs was a low-paying position for a photocopying shop. Groening's Southern California experiences, however, gave him a lode of rich material for his first cartoon, *Life in Hell*. The satirical comic features the characters Akbar and Jeff. When asked if the two characters are lovers or brothers, he answered, "Whatever offends you the most." *Life in Hell* was originally published in the Los Angeles new wave graphics innovator, *WET* magazine. In 1980, he sold his cartoon to the independent newspaper, the *Los Angeles Reader*. After a collection was published in a book in 1984, the cartoon's popularity soared. In 2002, it won the prestigious National Cartoonist Society's Reuben Award. Groening still draws one *Life in Hell* cartoon a week—it is syndicated to as many as 250 publications (Weblink 10.2).

Brooks, a fan of Akbar and Jeff, asked Groening to use those characters for Ullman's show. But Groening, either because the *Life in Hell* characters are limited in their situations or he didn't want to lose his marketing rights, came up with the Simpson family. Although the Ullman show was a critical success, it was not popular with viewers. However, Groening's Simpson shorts were a surprise hit. Brooks, Simon, and Groening then decided to produce a separate animated situation comedy (sitcom). When "The Simpsons" hit the air in 1989 as a separate series, it won an Emmy Award that first year.

To date, "The Simpsons" has won 24 Emmy Awards, 26 Annie Awards from the International Animated Film Association, and a Peabody Award for television excellence. In 2000 the characters were awarded a star on the Hollywood Walk of Fame next to the musician Kenny G (Figure 10.3). With more than 400 episodes and its 21st season starting in 2009, it is the longest running animated program, the longest running sitcom, and the longest running American prime-time entertainment show in television history, beating out the classic western series "Gunsmoke." As an indication of the scope of the cultural influence of the television show, during its 13th season in the fall of 2001, the *Oxford English Dictionary* added Homer's catchphrase "D'oh." It is defined as "expressing frustration at the realization that things have turned out badly or not as planned, or that one has just said or done something foolish." In 2007 the feature-length motion picture *The Simpsons Movie*, co-written by Groening and Brooks, was released. Its worldwide ticket sales grossed over half a billion dollars. The next year "The Simpsons Ride" opened at Universal Orlando theme park, an IMAX-style motion ride that is (big surprise) a parody of a theme park attraction (Figure 10.4). In 2009 Marge posed for the cover and an inside spread within the pages of *Playboy* magazine, the first time a cartoon character made such a revealing distinction while the U.S. Postal Service issued a first-class stamp that featured the Simpson family, the first ever given to television characters while the show still aired on prime time (Weblink 10.3). Said James Brooks, "We are emotionally moved by the Post Office Department's selecting us rather than making the lazy choice of someone who has benefited society."

Currently, Groening has backed off from much of the production work for the show and is now an executive pro-

Courtesy of Paul Martin Lester

Figure 10.3
"The Simpsons" star on Hollywood Boulevard.

ducer and creative consultant for the series. However, his work load picked up after his 1999 futuristic cartoon *Futurama*, which ran on Fox until 2003, was bought by Comedy Central and began airing new episodes in 2010. In the meantime, he can be seen at comic book conventions signing autographs. He also occasionally plays with a rock band composed of famous authors such as Mitch Albom, Stephen King, and Amy Tan. Groening plays the cowbell.

Figure 10.4
The Simpsons Ride at Universal Studios Hollywood. Bart seems out of character as he holds the rail of the roller coaster car.

Courtesy of Paul Mounce / Corbis Entertainment / Corbis

■ ANALYSIS OF "THE SIMPSONS"

Reaction to the barely functional cartoon family is as varied as the life experiences and attitudes of the viewers who watch it. If you are a fan of animated films, the cartoon may be appealing because it reminds you of your childhood. If you grew up in a similar home, you may laugh about like situations involving your family. If you enjoy watching the symbols of popular culture being gently nudged off their pedestals, you will appreciate the humor of the program. But if you think cartoon characters should be reserved for children and their concerns, you probably will be offended at the social satire and adult themes and jokes expressed during the half-hour. Its ultra-violent cartoon-within-the-cartoon, "The Itchy and Scratchy Show" that the Simpson children love, for example, is meant to be a commentary on those that criticize violence in children's animated shows.

"The Simpsons" has roots in every type of comic presentation, both single- and multiframed. When the drawings match the faces of media personalities frequently featured in story lines, the history of the caricature is evoked. The rich tradition of the editorial cartoon is featured in situations that comment on political issues. For example, Homer's careless attitude when it comes to working with highly toxic nuclear waste reflects Groening's view about the dangers of the nuclear power industry. Viewers can easily identify the influence of humorous cartoons that ridicule social hypocrisies in the comical situations, dialogue, and graphic style. Comic strips that make viewers laugh, think, and feel are popular among both children and adults. The yellow hair of Bart Simpson reminds us of one of the earliest wisecracking cartoon characters published, Richard Outcault's "Yellow Kid." Also part of the show's appeal are the celebrity guest appearances over the years voiced by such notables as Jerry Lewis, Johnny Carson, Michael Jackson, and former British Prime Minister Tony Blair.

"The Simpsons" is drawn in a decidedly elementary graphic style. As Groening says, "I've been drawing this way since fifth grade—people with big eyes and overbites." His *Life in Hell* cartoon also is marked by a minimalist style. "The Simpsons" is composed of such simply rendered images for three important reasons: time, money, and intent. Detailed, realistic drawings require an enormous additional output from animators and cost far more. Spending less time on the visual message allows the producers to concentrate more on the writing and acting.

Beginning with Season 14 in 2002, a switch in production was made from hand-drawn cel animation to digital ink and paint with animator drawings scanned and then colored with a computer. The February 15, 2009, episode marked the start of high-definition production of the series that anticipated the switch in American television sets to DTV (Digital Television). For this change, a new opening sequence replaced the one that had been featured for the past 20 years. However, the popular musical score remains by experienced Danny Elfman, composer of over 60 movie soundtracks including *BeetleJuice* (1988), *Good Will Hunting*, (1997), and *Terminator Salvation* (2009).

Groening's characters look ordinary (some might say unattractive) on purpose. The cartoon is deliberately in opposition to the 1950s and 1960s family-oriented situation comedies on television in which, in the words of radio personality Garrison Keillor, "all the women are strong, all the men are good looking, and all the children are above average." In both look and deed, "The Simpsons" celebrates all who are plain and average.

However, ethicists find fault with an aspect of the program that involves the way the shows are produced. For each episode, an American production company draws storyboards, new characters, and backgrounds. A South Korean animation company completes the frames necessary for each program. From start to finish the process takes about four months. The only reason for this long-distance arrangement is that Asian workers are paid much less than their U.S. counterparts. Even though the South Korean workers acquire specialized skills and money that they might not obtain in any other way, the cost of the exploitation is high. Those in a position to hire others have the moral responsibility of paying a fair and living wage.

As a blue-collar, middle-class family, the Simpsons follow in the comedic footsteps of "The Honeymooners," "Roseanne," and "The Office." Upper-middle-class, white-collar baby boomers and their children constitute the primary audience for the program because they enjoy laughing at these cartoon oafs. Although many real-life working-class families do not appreciate most of the cynical jokes that are directed at them, they still watch the show.

The show teaches that rich people are greedy, politicians are corrupt, police officials are stupid, teachers and parents are easily manipulated, and children are devious. At the same time, it contains symbols that transcend this one family—Homer's love for bowling, beer, and bacon, Marge's simpleminded support of her sexist husband and ungrateful children, Bart's smart-aleck retorts, Lisa's angst and alienation, and Maggie's . . . no, Maggie is okay. Yet despite their many personality disorders, the Simpson family members manage to support one another and stay together. Although flawed in many ways, the Simpsons all love each other, and

given the show's continued popularity, so too do the viewing public.

■ CARTOONS AND THE SIX PERSPECTIVES

Personal Perspective

For most of the history of cartoons, researchers have considered them unworthy of serious attention. Few academic programs or private art schools offer courses in the production or theory of cartoon art. Editorial cartoonists for financially strapped newspapers are often the first to be let go. Comic strips, comic books, and animated movies are considered by many to be junk for children and unworthy of serious attention. But with the rise in the use of visual messages in all media and the highly respected graphic novel genre, this pictorial art form has gained new converts, with serious studies written by scholars.

Historical Perspective

Since the elaborately animated characters in motion picture, television, and computer programs all started as crudely rendered line drawings, it is important to know how cartoons developed in order to fully analyze present efforts.

■ Single-Framed Cartoons

The historical roots of cartoons can be found in simple, unsigned visual messages that poked fun at others. Scrawled on walls by untrained artists (today we call such examples graffiti), these single-framed cartoons reveal an average person's opinion about someone in power that is missing from many mainstream historical documents. There are three types of single-framed cartoons: caricatures, editorial, and humorous.

Caricatures

As an artistic and communicative medium, the cartoon began as a caricature (Figure 10.5). The oldest known caricatures clearly intended to ridicule the individuals portrayed were found in Egypt. In about 1360 BCE, some unknown cartoonist painted an unflattering portrait of Akhenaten, the unpopular father of the boy King Tutankhamen. Artists satirized the actions of other unpopular Egyptian leaders by drawing animals performing similar activities. Throughout the world, visual ridicule was appreciated. In India, cartoonists made fun of their Hindu god Krishna. Greek terracotta vases and wall paintings often were decorated with profane parodies of overweight Olympian gods. Dating from at least 2,500 years ago, ancient Latino cultures used to keep the skulls of their vanquished as trophies. This ritual led to the *Dia de Los Muertos*, or Day of the Dead, a ritual that celebrates the dead and the promise of rebirth on All Soul's Day on Halloween. Paintings and sculptures feature skulls with exaggerated features similar to caricatures (Figure 10.6). Early Romans also ridiculed religious leaders. For example, the Christian Alexamenos is shown in a drawing standing at the crucifixion of Jesus, who has the head of a donkey. Almost every country in the world has a tradition of wearing elaborate, often brightly painted masks during festivals, theater performances, and other rituals (Figure 10.7).

Figure 10.5

At Universal Citywalk in Los Angeles a couple bravely poses for a caricature artist's portrait in front of examples that include the exaggerated features of such celebrities as Richard Pryor, Whoopi Goldberg, President Barack Obama, and Jay Leno.

The word *caricature* comes from the family name of Middle Ages artists. Annibale Carracci, his brother Agostino, and his cousin Ludovico—all from Bologna, Italy—painted caricatures around 1590. The Carraccis filled their naturalistic paintings with exaggerated yet recognizable human faces from their community to entertain their friends (Figure 10.8).

Today, a single-framed caricature is an important illustrative device created by such artists as David Levine, Dorothy Ahle, and Al Hirschfeld. Hirschfeld started his long career in 1926 drawing caricatures of Broadway theater stars. His distinctive graphic style often included a number next to his byline that indicated how many times he had worked in his daughter's name, Nina, within a drawing. In later years, his caricatures often appeared in the pages of *The New Yorker* magazine and *The New York Times*. Hirschfeld died at the age of 99 in 2003.

The art of the caricature eventually became fused with cartoon representations of public figures as a part of editorial cartoons. One of the most striking caricatures turned into an editorial statement was based on a news photograph by Associated Press photographer Charlie Tasnadi of President Lyndon Johnson incredibly revealing the scar from his recent gall bladder surgery. In his cartoon, David Levine changed the scar into a map of Vietnam, a commentary on the war as a scar on the Johnson presidency (Weblink 10.4).

Editorial Cartoons

The founder of the English editorial cartoon is considered to be William Hogarth. Fascinated with drawing since his early childhood, he became an apprentice to an engraver and later started his own print shop at the age of 23. Hogarth established

Courtesy of Paul Martin Lester

a solid reputation for creating illustrations for coats of arms, crests, bookplates, and advertisements. He created ads for companies that were printed on handbills, posters, and handheld fans. He also displayed ready-made artwork (called *clip art* today) from which patrons could select drawings to make their party announcements more visually appealing. After Hogarth became enthralled by a set of political cartoons smuggled from France, he started to create his own satirical drawings. In 1731, he published his most famous collection of drawings, *A Harlot's Progress*. Because he was appalled by the living conditions of the poor of his day, he intended his drawings to be moralistic lessons rather than entertainment (Figure 10.9).

After Hogarth, James Gillray was the leading cartoonist during the reign of King George III, whom he labeled "Farmer George." Gillray bitterly opposed the king's intervention in the affairs of the

Figure 10.6

One of the most popular El Dia de los Muertos ("Day of the Dead" or "All Souls Day") figures is that of the high society woman, "La Catrina." Popularized by Jose Guadalupe Posada, a Mexican engraver and illustrator, his lithographic calaveras or skulls often satirized the upper class with exaggerated, caricature figures. Here she is used to sell paletas, a fruit-based ice drink.

Courtesy of Musee di Quai Branly / Scala / Art Resource, NY

Figure 10.7

"Fang mask used for the Ngil ceremony," wood, Gabon, Africa, 19th century. Members of the religious and legal secret society known as Ngil wore masks during ceremonies meant to maintain social order and their power. Lawbreakers and those accused of sorcery feared for their lives by their rulings. When illuminated by firelight, the mask, with its long shape, double arched eyes, ape-like mouth, and pale color symbolizing the spirit of the dead, were dramatic and fearsome.

Figure 10.8

"Giovane Che Ride" ("Young Man Who Laughs"), 1583, *by Annibale Carracci. The Carracci family of painters would often make character studies of friends and strangers and incorporate them into their paintings. With the light in his eyes and mouth contorted from laughing, there is little wonder why the word caricature came from this family's name.*

Figure 10.9

"Plate 1 of Harlot's Progress," 1732, *by William Hogarth. This first engraving in the series shows the destitute and tentative Molly arriving in London and being greeted by a syphilitic brothel madam. Leering in the background is the likeness of Colonel Frances Charteris, an actual person nicknamed "The Rape-Master General," as he was convicted of raping a servant girl two years before the cartoon was drawn. He was pardoned, but died soon afterward. Hogarth became one of the most influential editorial cartoonists in history, particularly responsible for sequential narratives that led to comic books and motion picture storyboards. A prolific and popular artist who overcame his humble beginnings, seven years before his death he was named the "Serjeant Painter" to George II, King of England, essentially the monarch's personal artist.*

American colonies. He also was famous for his satirical portraits of Napoleon, whom Gillray and other cartoonists called "Little Boney." Sadly, at the top of his form Gillray went insane. In 1811 he tried to kill himself by jumping from a barred window, but his head became caught. Two years later, he died. But his strong graphic style combined with a powerful political message influenced many subsequent cartoonists (Figure 10.10).

The most famous American editorial cartoonist during this period was Thomas Nast. A native of Landau, Germany, Nast was brought by his mother to America when he was six years old. At the age of 15, he was employed as an illustrator for *Frank Leslie's Illustrated Weekly.* In 1862, *Harper's Weekly* hired him as a battlefield artist to cover the Civil War. His drawings improved morale enormously as they were circulated in Union towns, encampments, forts, and ships. General Grant praised Nast as having done "as much as any one man" to preserve the Union. President Lincoln called him "our best recruiting sergeant." Nast is responsible for the popular elephant symbol used by

Gillray, James (1757–1815) / © Courtesy of the Warden and Scholars of New College, Oxford / The Bridgeman Art Library

MERRY OLD SANTA CLAUS.

Library of Congress, Prints and Photographs Division, LC-USZ62-42027

Figure 10.10 (left)

The French Emperor Napoleon Bonaparte can't believe the news that his fleet was destroyed by the British Navy commanded by Rear-Admiral Horatio "Lord" Nelson in the Battle of the Nile in 1798. Soon afterward, Napoleon left Egypt, allowing the British to take the valuable Rosetta Stone to England. With his sharp pen, sharper wit, and fearless opinions, James Gillray is considered to be England's most influential political cartoonist in history.

Figure 10.11 (right)

Although Thomas Nast originally penned a portrait of Santa Claus in an 1863 issue of Harper's Weekly, *it proved to be so popular that in 1889 he made the drawing seen here that became the icon for the gift-giving character.*

the Republican Party and for the popular image of Santa Claus (Figure 10.11).

He is also known for his campaign to bring down the corrupt politician William "Boss" Tweed of Tammany Hall. Tweed and his Democratic cronies stole from the New York County treasury. Nast drew more than 50 editorial cartoons for *Harper's Weekly* criticizing Tweed. After Tweed fled the country because of a criminal investigation, a police official in Vigo, Spain, recognized him from Nast's cartoon. Tweed was returned to America, tried, and put in prison (Figure 10.12).

Figure 10.12

As "Emperor" Tweed looks on, the Tammany tiger, a symbol created by cartoonist Thomas Nast to graphically illustrate the corruption in New York, devours Liberty, a symbol of democracy and freedom in the United States.

"WHAT ARE YOU GOING TO DO ABOUT IT?"

North Wind / North Wind Picture Archives

At the start of the 20th century, newspaper publishers used cartoons for propaganda purposes, and editors of literary magazines used them as humorous diversions. William Randolph Hearst asked artists to draw cartoons of fake Spanish atrocities to whip up support for a war against Spain. During the world wars, blatant propaganda for the war effort replaced the earlier creativity of many cartoonists. Three of the top editorial artists in the United States—Bill Mauldin, Herbert Block, and Paul Conrad—rebelled against the propagandistic use of cartoons.

Sergeant Bill Mauldin drew cartoons for *Stars and Stripes* magazine while a soldier during World War II. His popular characters Willie and Joe boosted morale while letting the readers back home know what the average foot soldier thought. After the war, he worked for the *Chicago Sun-Times*. His most famous cartoon probably is the 1963 drawing of the Lincoln Memorial grieving the death of President Kennedy (Figure 10.13). Mauldin

also was known for his devastating attacks against the Ku Klux Klan and other segregationist groups.

Herb Block, professionally known as "Herblock," was the editorial cartoonist for the *Washington Post* and was at his best when taking on the politically powerful. He invented the word "McCarthyism" to describe the Wisconsin senator's communist witch hunt (Figure 10.14). His drawing of the shifty-eyed, unshaven Richard Nixon became an unshakable symbol of that political leader from early in his career. Before Nixon's 1968 presidential campaign, a public relations expert advised him to come up with a new image for himself. "I have to erase," he said, "the Herblock image." Block won three Pulitzer Prizes for his cartoons during his long career. He died in 2001.

Paul Conrad, the angry and insightful liberal voice of the *Los Angeles Times*, graduated from the University of Iowa and worked for the *Denver Post* before starting with the *Times* in 1964 (Figure 10.15).

Figure 10.13 (left)

After President Kennedy was assassinated in 1963, Bill Mauldin drew this famous cartoon of President Lincoln's statue hiding its face in sorrow. At such times words would serve only to diminish a highly emotional visual message.

Figure 10.14 (right)

This cartoon from Herbert Block illustrates the hysterical McCarthy era when many patriotic Americans were accused wrongly of being communists. Here, Herblock uses symbolism to make his point: The open-mouthed man with "HYSTERIA" written across his pants and a water bucket spilling its contents suggest a rush to douse the flame of Liberty.

"Fire!"

Cartoon by Paul Conrad. Copyright 1992. Tribune Media Services. Reprinted with permission.

ONE PICTURE IS WORTH ZERO

Figure 10.15

In a re-creation of the beating of Rodney King, retired Los Angeles Times *editorial cartoonist Paul Conrad demonstrates his anger at the acquittal in the state trial of the four police officers with a direct and powerful drawing style.*

Conservative publisher Otis Chandler constantly asked him to tone down his cartoons. In 1969, former mayor Sam Yorty sued the *Times* for $2 million for libel (and lost) because of one of Conrad's cartoons. Ronald Reagan, governor of California before becoming president, complained many times to Chandler that Conrad's cartoons were "ruining his breakfast." In an effort to divert criticism, Chandler moved the cartoon from the editorial to the opinion page, where comments from nonstaffers usually are printed. Conrad's stark visual style and direct messages are an outgrowth of his philosophy about cartoons. He once said, "I figure eight seconds is the absolute maximum time anyone should have" to understand a cartoon's meaning.

Editorial cartoons filled with emotionally symbolic visual messages can spark great controversy. In September 2005 after the Danish newspaper *Jyllands-Posten* printed 12 cartoons with most depicting the Islamic prophet Muhammad in satirical or silly ways, many in the Muslim world organized protests, with some that turned violent. There was also a boycott of all things Danish. In March 2008, Al-Qaeda head Osama Bin Laden reportedly threatened the European Union after one of the cartoons was reprinted in the newspaper (Weblink 10.5).

Humorous Cartoons

The 19th century saw the introduction of two humorous magazines—*Puck*, one of the most successful publications, which began in 1871, and *Judge*, formed in 1881 by disgruntled *Puck* employees (Figure 10.16). But Harold Ross, a high school dropout who learned journalism while copyediting as an employee of the U.S. government's *Stars and Stripes* magazine, started *The New Yorker* magazine in 1925 as a sophisticated alternative, and it outlasted both of them. Ross had a gift for hiring excellent personnel. One of his first hires was art director Rea Irvin. Irvin not only created the cartoon icon for the first cover—the aristocratic, top-hatted "Eustace Tilley"—but also established the style for typography and graphic design that continues to this day. Some of the most famous *New Yorker* cartoonists include Charles Addams, of "The Addams Family" fame, and Gahan Wilson. The magazine is credited with having almost single-handedly developed the art of the humorous cartoon to its highest intellectual potential. Ever in the forefront of trends, for its June 2009 cover, the magazine published a drawing by Jorge Colombo that was produced with an iPhone application, Brushes, which costs $4.99.

■ Multiframed Cartoons

All multiframed cartoons have similar historical roots. Egyptian scholars found a burial chamber mural from about 1300 BCE that showed two wrestlers fighting one another in several sequential frames (Figure 10.17). Many Greek vases were decorated with circular drawings of fighting warriors or gymnasts. Turning these vases gives an illusion of movement. Friezes on Greek temples also contained drawings that depicted sequential movement when viewed horizontally. Japanese continuity paintings, called *emakimonos*, appear to move when the viewer unrolls the long scroll. Completed in 1067, the Bayeux Tapestry is a huge embroidered cloth wall decoration over 200 feet long that depicts the Norman conquest of England with figures within separate frames or borders (Figure 10.18). In the 1500s, Chinese and Indonesian dancing silhouette toys were popular. The European version was the more crude "flipbook"—a series of small pictures drawn on separate sheets of heavy paper. When the viewer thumbed the pages, the images moved. Many of the drawings were adult-oriented and showed women dancing or undressing. Later, the drawings were modified for children's viewing.

Publications for children to teach reading and life's lessons also had a major

Figure 10.16

One of the most popular cartoonists for the humor magazine Puck *was the American Louis Dalrymple. He also worked for newspapers in Chicago, Philadelphia, and Baltimore. Sadly, in 1905 he was committed to a New York sanitarium after becoming "violently insane," a mental condition brought about by complications over a personal matter. He died that same year. A collaborator with Dalrymple for this and other covers, Samuel Ehrhart, was schooled in art in Munich, Germany, and worked for* Puck, Judge, *and* Harper's Weekly.

Figure 10.17

Found on a wall of the burial chamber of Baqet III, governor of the Oryx district in central Egypt, is a sequence of about 200 wrestlers in various poses. Estimated to be about 3,500 years old, the images are often cited as one of the earliest examples of multiframed cartoons.

influence on the medium. In 1744, John Newbery of London published children's illustrated stories as inexpensive pamphlets under the title *Little Pretty Pocket-Books* (Figure 10.19). Today, the most prestigious award given to children's book authors is called the Newbery Medal. One of the most frightening set of children's stories, meant to teach stern lessons of proper behavior, was Heinrich Hoffmann's *Der Struwwelpeter*, first printed in Germany in 1845 (Figure 10.20). Typical

Figure 10.18

More than 950 years old and measuring about a yard high and more than 75 yards long, the Bayeux Tapestry is one of the finest examples of visual narrative storytelling. Although misnamed a tapestry, it was not fabricated with a loom, this handmade embroidered work tells of the 1066 Norman victory at the Battle of Hastings. After the Norman Conquest, England became ruled by French-speaking royalty, which significantly changed the English language. In this fragment of a panel, Harold Godwinson, or Harold II, the last Anglo-Saxon King of England, is seen holding an arrow that has penetrated his eye, causing his death. It has been speculated that the embroidered arrow was not a part of the original work.

Figure 10.19

The title page of a 1744 edition of John Newbery's A Little Pretty Pocket-Book includes "A Little Song-Book" that is "A new attempt to teach children the use of the English alphabet, by way of diversion." The "diversion" is the addition of cartoon drawings.

Courtesy of © The British Library Board

Figure 10.20

Some of the most severe examples of teaching children how to behave properly were the stories by the German psychiatrist Heinrich Hoffmann in his Der Struwwelpeter ("Lazy Peter") series, first published in 1845. A publisher friend of his, who knew that he illustrated his own short stories to give as gifts to his children, persuaded him to produce a book. The collection, which included a child burning to death after playing with matches and another having his thumbs snipped off, was popular with the public and considered humorous, not cruel. Hoffmann had three children, but only two survived him.

of Hoffmann's work was "The Story of Little Suck-a-Thumb," in which an incorrigible thumbsucker is taught a lesson by the "Scissor-Man," who snips the boy's thumbs off (Weblink 10.6).

Courtesy of The Art Archive / John Meek /Picture Desk

Comic Strips

The German Wilhelm Busch has been called the founder of the modern comic strip because his cartoon, *Max and Moritz*, was the first published in a newspaper in 1865 (Figure 10.21).

During the last decade of the 19th century, William Randolph Hearst and Joseph Pulitzer were locked in a bitter circulation war in New York, and they believed that pictures were important to gaining readership.

The first color comic strip was Richard Outcault's *Hogan's Alley*, first published on May 5, 1895, in Joseph Pulitzer's *Sunday World*. It instantly was a smash hit. The cartoon provided social commentary in the disguise of a collection of orphaned, unkempt children living among the tenement houses in New York City. The central character was a towheaded, unnamed boy in a nightshirt who smoked cigars. A printer in Pulitzer's back shop made the boy yellow to help him stand out in the crowd of children (Figure 10.22).

Soon afterward the strip became known as *The Yellow Kid of Hogan's Alley*. In a battle between two giant egos, Hearst and Pulitzer publicly bid for Outcault's services. Hearst's *New York Journal* hired the famous cartoonist, but Outcault later returned to Pulitzer's paper at a higher salary. However, Hearst was determined and hired Outcault back. The unethical tactic of paying for a story or interview was thereafter labeled "yellow journalism" after the battle for the Yellow Kid.

The dada art movement inspired the *Krazy Kat* comic strip of George Herriman. Introduced in 1915, the cartoon described a surreal and often violent world of a mean-spirited mouse named Ignatz and an alley cat who loved him (Figure 10.23). Sadly, in an effort to keep from getting fired, the light-skinned Herriman hid the fact that he was African American by always wearing a hat to hide his hair. The strip inspired Fred "Tex" Avery, Friz Freleng, and Chuck Jones to produce "Bugs Bunny" and other popular characters in an equally wisecracking, absurd, and often violent style.

An important innovation in the continuing popularity of comic strips—the serial— appeared in the 1920s and 1930s. Harold Gray's *Little Orphan Annie* in 1924 championed the virtues of helping yourself without relying on government aid. Al Capp's *Li'l Abner* in 1934 criticized big business practices at first but gradually became conservative over the years. Such strips with not-so-subtle political messages were a link between the funnies and the editorial cartoon.

Adventure stories that continued from day to day were enormously popular comic strips. Many newspapers depended on them for their survival. In 1929, two important strip characters who also had lives as motion pictures were introduced.

Courtesy of M. Thomas Inge

Figure 10.21

Created by Wilhelm Busch, the childish imps Max and Moritz have found a way to steal chickens from a woman putting sauerkraut on her plate. Instead of horizontal movement of the action, as in most comic strips, this cartoon uses a vertical cutaway view of the house.

Richard Calkins and Phil Nowlan produced the 25th-century space traveler "Buck Rogers," and Harold Foster brought Edgar Rice Burroughs's "Tarzan" character to visual life. These adventure cartoons inspired all kinds of western, detective, and superhuman strips. Chester Gould's *Dick Tracy* (1931), Milton Caniff's *Terry and the Pirates* (1934), and later his *Steve Canyon* (1947) continued the adventure strip tradition.

But one of the most popular cartoon strips was *Peanuts* by Charles Schulz, originally published on October 2, 1950. His tale of a band of small children and a dog drawn in the minimalist artistic tradition became a symbol for America (Figure 10.24). At its peak the strip reached

Figure 10.22

Considered the first regularly published American news-paper cartoon, the Sunday, November 15, 1896, issue of Richard Outcault's The Yellow Kid of Hogan's Alley *as seen in William Randolph Hearst's* New York Journal *is a dense collection of words and images titled "Inauguration of the Football Season in McFadden's Row." The alley is a noisy, crowded place ruled by children, with their expressions reflecting the political cynicism of the day.*
See color insert following page 338.

Figure 10.23

"Krazy Kat as published in the New York Evening Journal," January 21, 1922, by George Herriman. Influenced by the dada art movement, George Herriman inspired cartoonists such as Chuck Jones and Tex Avery of Warner Bros. In this rare story line, Krazy Kat gets the better of Ignatz the mouse, if only accidentally.

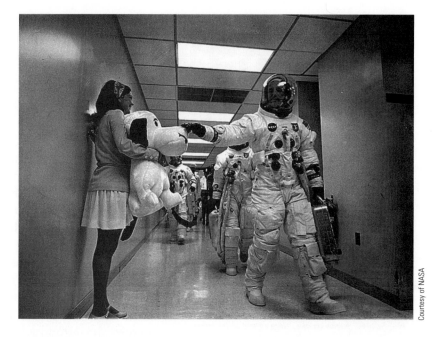

Figure 10.24
*One of the most beloved car-
toon characters in the world
is Charles Shultz's Snoopy. In
1969 the beagle, along with
Charlie Brown, were the unof-
ficial mascots for the Apollo
10 mission to the moon. Here,
Commander Thomas Stafford
pats the nose of the dog for
good luck on his way to the
launch complex.*

Courtesy of NASA

300 million readers in 75 countries and appeared in 2,600 newspapers in 21 languages. With books, television specials, and a Broadway musical, "You're a Good Man, Charlie Brown," the Peanuts gang was the most popular cartoon in the world. The Apollo 10 astronauts even carried a copy of the cartoon into space. Distributed by the United Features press syndicate, the strip helped make Schultz "the wealthiest contemporary cartoonist in the history of comics." Schultz had a complex personality, often moody and emotionally distant to his family. He died on February 13, 2000, but reprints of *Peanuts* continue in newspapers around the world.

Other cartoonists, inspired by such blatantly political strips as *Little Orphan Annie*, *Li'l Abner*, and *Pogo*, disguise social commentary as humorous comic strips—a tradition that has its roots in the *Yellow Kid*. Robert Crumb's irreverently humorous characters, Fritz the Cat, the Fabulously Furry Freak Brothers, and Mr. Natural poked fun at the hypocrisies he saw in the emerging hippie social

movement. These comic strips were published mostly in underground newspapers of the day. Garry Trudeau began *Doonesbury* in 1968 while a student at Yale. In 1970 he started publishing in only 28 newspapers. Today *Doonesbury* appears in nearly 1,400 papers. In 1975, Trudeau became the first comic strip artist to win a Pulitzer Prize for his cartoons about the Vietnam War, former president Richard Nixon, and the Watergate scandal.

Comic Books

In 1929, newspaper publishers started to promote their comic strip offerings through inexpensive giveaway inserts. Dell, a publisher known for its paperback books, was the first to offer color comic strips in a 16-page newspaper insert called *The Funnies*. Four years later Eastern Color published *Funnies on Parade*, an eight-page tabloid-sized collection. Maxwell Gaines, a salesperson for Eastern, convinced his bosses to fold the tabloid-sized publication to more resemble a book. The result contained 36 pages and was named

Figure 10.25

Originally, comic books were specially prepared publications produced by newspapers as an advertisement for their comic strips. Max Gaines printed 35,000 copies of Famous Funnies *in 1934. The comic book proved to be enormously successful.*

Famous Funnies: A Carnival of Comics, and it is considered the first comic book (Figure 10.25). Gaines went on to establish

Figure 10.26

William Gaines began Entertaining Comics, or simply EC, as a way to interest adults in reading science fiction and horror comic books. This 1950s era cover is a typical example of the genre with its mix of typeface styles, font sizes, and action-oriented illustrations.

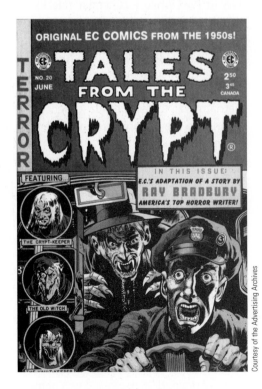

Educational Comics or EC Comics specializing in crime and science fiction stories.

Inspired by the success of a separate book of cartoons, action adventure stories soon followed. The first major superhero character, Superman, was the brainchild of two Ohio high school students, Jerry Siegel and Joe Schuster. Originally produced as a comic strip for newspapers, the original Superman was a criminally insane bald terrorist. After Siegel suggested he might work for the good rather than for evil, the benevolent hero was born in Action Comics #1 in 1938. In 2009 issue #1 sold in an internet auction for $317,200. There are only about 100 known copies in existence. Action Comics eventually became Detective Comics or DC Comics and introduced such characters as Batman, Wonder Woman, and the Flash. With DC's success, the other major publishing company for comic books at the time, Marvel Entertainment, introduced memorable characters from the minds of writer Stan Lee and artist Jack Kirby such as The Fantastic Four and the X-Men while Lee and artist Steve Ditko created The Amazing Spider-Man in 1962, one of the most successful superhero characters that has rivaled Superman's popularity. In 2009 the Walt Disney Co. paid $4 billion to Marvel to create motion pictures, television programs, and video games based on the more than 5,000 superheroes in the comic book company's catalog.

After Max Gaines died in a boating accident in 1947, his son, William, took over EC and introduced popular titles such as *Tales from the Crypt*, *Weird Fantasy*, *Weird Science*, and in 1952, the irreverent parody of popular culture, *Mad* magazine (Figure 10.26). With its laconic mascot Alfred E. Neuman and his famous phrase "What, Me Worry?," *Mad* inspired such diverse writers as Monty Python's

Terry Gilliam, movie critic Roger Ebert, and musician Patti Smith.

Comic books (sometimes called "floppies") also can express serious subjects in a nonthreatening way. Author Harvey Pekar's 1976 *American Splendor* (with many issues illustrated by Robert Crumb) was his effort to tell everyday stories with quirky observations, in contrast to the superhero comic books of the day. A motion picture was produced in 2003 based on Pekar's *Our Cancer Year* (written with his wife, Joyce Brabner).

In addition, the action adventure characters brought to the big screen by Sylvester Stallone (*Rocky* and *Rambo*) and Arnold Schwarzenegger (*The Terminator, The Last Action Hero*) are cartoon characters disguised as humans.

In Japan and other Asian countries, comic books are called *manga*. The art form started in pre-World War II Japan with traveling storytellers using cartoon images on poster boards called *kamishibai*. With the introduction of television, the practice ended but was replaced by its cartoon cousins, *manga* and *anime* for films. Popular with children and adults, *manga* works dominate entire bookstores (Figure 10.27). Although many depict violent and sexual themes, some are epic tales that usually pit a young protagonist who must face a formative foe with a visual aesthetic that resembles the free-flowing graphic style of art nouveau. A recent example is *Gimmick!*, a tragicomic manga series from a Japanese writer-artist team Youzaburou Kanari and Kuroko Yabuguchi that is a "powerful denunciation of the war in Iraq."

Graphic Novels

Art Spiegelman showed American readers that a graphic novel could be literature worthy of respect. His retelling of the Holocaust in an animal fable called *Maus* won

Courtesy of SAIYUKI © 2002 Kazuya Minekura / ISSAOSHA Inc.

Figure 10.27

The cover image from the graphic novel Saiyuki Vol. 2 by Kazuya Minekura is a classic example of Japanese manga with its free-flowing penmanship, youthful characters, and dynamic action.

a National Book Critics Award in 1987, the first time the award had ever gone to a cartoon. In 2004, his autobiographical *In the Shadow of No Towers* told the story of the attacks on 9/11. His work inspired others such as Chris Ware's *Jimmy Corrigan: The Smartest Kid on Earth* (2000), Matt Madden's *99 Ways to Tell a Story* (2005), and Brian Selznick's *The Invention of Hugo Cabret* (2007). *The Photographer* (2009) is a documentary graphic novel based on photographs by Didier Lefèvre and drawings by Emmanuel Guibert about a 1986 journey through Afghanistan accompanying Doctors Without Borders. In 2009 underground comic book artist Robert Crumb put his talents to work to produce a provocative and literal visual translation of all 50 chapters of the first book of the Bible in his *The Book of Genesis Illustrated by R. Crumb.* A note on the cover warns, "Adult supervision recommended for minors."

Many cartoon and comic book titles have been adapted for the screen. Frank Miller's stark style in such graphic novels as his *Sin City* series, *300*, and *Batman: The Dark Knight Returns* and in Daniel Clowes's cynical take on life as told in *Ghost World* and *Art School Confidential* were made into movies. Author Alan Moore and illustrator Dave Gibbons teamed to produce *Watchmen*, the only graphic novel honored by *Time* magazine as one of the top 100 English-language books ever written. The film of the same name, released in 2009 and directed by Zack Snyder, who also directed *300* (2006), re-created many of the iconic illustrations in the printed work.

The worldwide appeal of seeing cartoon characters in the movies is further evidenced by the Belgium character Tintin, seen in more than 20 books and translated into dozens of languages. The creation of cartoonist Georges Remi, known as Hergé, Tintin comes to life with the help of Steven Spielberg (*Jurassic Park* and *Schindler's List*) and New Zealand director Peter Jackson (*The Lord of the Rings* and *King Kong*) in *The Adventures of Tintin: The Secret of the Unicorn* (2011).

Animated Films

A week before Outcault's *Yellow Kid* was first published, the Lumière brothers in Paris showed their simple movies to a paying audience for the first time. The history of animated film, naturally, is tied to the history of the motion picture. And yet the early apparatuses for producing animation were mainly curiosities, today seen as children's toys, with many having really bad names.

The first evidence of a device that created the illusion of moving pictures reportedly comes from the Chinese inventor Ting Huan who in 180 CE hung paper with sequential drawings over a small fire. The heat caused vanes to spin, allowing the images to move. About 1,650 years later a Belgian physicist Joseph Plateau invented a device that used two discs to show animated drawings through slits, which he called the phenakistiscope, Greek for "to cheat through optics." Simultaneously and independently, the Austrian mathematician Simon von Stampfer came up with the same invention, but he named his viewing device the stroboscope. That name stuck.

The British mathematician William Horner in 1833 invented a spinning wheel with slits. When you looked through one of the apertures as the wheel spun, you saw a paper printed with sequential, moving drawings. He named it the daedalum or "The Wheel of the Devil." The name turned out to be a bad marketing decision, as it was not popular with the public. Nevertheless, American William Lincoln renamed Horner's mechanism the zoetrope or "Wheel of Life." It was a slightly better name and one that the esteemed director Francis Ford Coppola used for his studio, American Zoetrope. Another simple animation effect that is still popular today came from the British lithographer John Linnett, who was the first to patent a flip book in 1868. You made the images dance with your thumb.

Eight years later Professor Charles-Émile Reynaud of France managed to combine several drawings and a projection system he called a praxinoscope, basically a projected zoetrope effect. In 1882 he opened the first public theater for showing animated films, the *Théâtre Optique* (Figure 10.28). Reynaud showed thousands of cartoons, many drawn by his assistant Émile Cohl. Unfortunately, the public had become more interested in the live-action short films of the Lumière brothers, who

introduced their more popular movie theater in 1895. Frustrated, in 1910 Reynaud threw all his equipment in the Seine River, and at the end of World War I he died in a sanitarium.

In 1879 the photographer and adventurer Eadweard Muybridge initiated the switch from a child's toy to a viable form of adult entertainment. He introduced his awkwardly named zoopraxiscope that projected sequential stop-motion photographs on rotating discs that provided the illusion of movement (Figure 10.29). Muybridge's invention inspired the American inventor Thomas Edison and his assistant William Kennedy Dickson to develop the Kinetoscope in 1888, and the motion picture industry was born.

The founder of the American animated film industry is considered to be the cartoonist Winsor McCay. Born in Michigan in 1871, McCay worked in Chicago as an illustrator of circus posters and later for a Cincinnati newspaper. In 1903, he moved to New York to draw cartoons for the *New York Herald* and the *Evening Telegram*, owned by publisher James Gordon Bennett. In 1906, as part of his *Little Nemo in Slumberland* newspaper cartoon, McCay printed a series of drawings of a

trapeze artist inspired from a child's flip book. These sequential pictures inspired McCay to make animated movies. In 1914, McCay created *Gertie, the Trained Dinosaur*, a charming, crowd-pleasing animated brontosaurus that happily performed according to McCay's stage instructions (Weblink 10.7).

Although Walt Disney usually is credited with making the first feature-length animated movie, the honor actually goes to Berlin-born Lotte Reiniger. In 1926, *The Adventures of Prince Achmed*, about the tales of the Arabian nights, was first shown.

Figure 10.28

Charles-Émile Reynaud in 1882 showed hundreds of cartoon animations to paying audiences in his Théâtre Optique. Behind a screen and hidden from the audience, he would turn wheels that moved his images, creating the animation effect. A lamp illuminated the pictures while a mirror projected them on a screen. Reynaud's setup predated the Lumière brothers' public motion picture showings by 13 years.

Figure 10.29

"#29 Mule—Bucking and Kicking," 1896, by Eadweard Muybridge. In 1879 Eadweard Muybridge invented a movie projector he called the zoopraxiscope. The illusion of animation was created by sequential painted pictures and, later, hand-colored photographs that were transferred to glass discs and spun within a cabinet. A lamp illuminated the pictures through a lens with which the images were projected on a screen. Muybridge demonstrated his invention to audiences in America, England, and France, and in 1888 showed it to the American inventor Thomas Edison. And yet, as a still photographer, Muybridge never realized the enormous social and economic implications of what he had invented.

Reiniger made more than 60 films during her 62-year career. Her most famous animated works, introduced in 1955, include the cartoon classics *Hansel and Gretel*, *Jack and the Beanstalk*, and *Thumbelina* (Weblink 10.8).

Walt Disney grew up on a small farm in Missouri and went on to become the undisputed king of American animation. After his family moved to Chicago, Disney took night classes at the Art Institute and drew cartoons for his high school newspaper. After graduation and a brief stint as an ambulance driver in France for the Red Cross during World War I, he settled in Kansas City where he created advertisements for an art studio and met fellow artist Ubbe (Ub) Iwerks. After the two were laid off, Iwerks, Walt, and his brother Roy teamed up to create short cartoons called *Laugh-O-Grams* that they sold to local movie theaters. The three then moved to Hollywood in 1923 and obtained a contract to produce 15 movies under the series name *Alice in Cartoonland*, which combined a live-action girl with drawn characters. By 1927 the public had grown weary of live-action/animation combinations and preferred all-animation features such as those starring Felix the Cat. To counter the popularity of Felix, Disney with his team created the animated series *Oswald the Lucky Rabbit*, which was wildly popular. However, after a contract dispute with his New York distributor, Disney was forced to give up his rabbit character. He needed a new animal character and thought of a pet mouse he had during his Kansas City studio days. In 1928, Disney introduced *Steamboat Willie*, which had a fully synchronized sound track and, perhaps more important, the famous mouse, originally named Mortimer. Fortunately, the name was nixed by Disney's wife Lillian, and Mickey was chosen. Walt Disney provided the character's high-pitched voice, and Iwerks created the drawings (Weblink 10.9). Mickey Mouse became so popular that Nazi leader Adolf Hitler banned the cartoon from Germany. In 1929, the trio produced the first of their *Silly Symphonies—The Skeleton Dance*. The *Silly Symphonies* were an expert mix of motion and music, with skeletons dancing to tunes. The 1933 Disney short *The Three Little Pigs* is considered an animation landmark because each of the three central characters had a distinctive personality (Weblink 10.10).

The first color cartoon, *Flowers and Trees*, won the team an Oscar in 1933. *Snow White* (1937), *Pinocchio* (1939), *Fantasia* (1940), *Dumbo* (1941), and *Bambi* (1942) followed. Bambi is also significant because the Disney animators studied actual animals—deer, rabbits, and owls—to raise the level of realism without sacrificing the emotions and expressions expressed by the characters. By 1945, the Disney studio employed hundreds of artists and produced several cartoon classics. Disney introduced the concepts of preplanned storyboards to organize a film before a single cel, a cartoon's frame drawn on clear acetate, was drawn. He also organized the animation artists into several different departments in which workers would complete separate pieces of a long animated project independently. Iwerks invented the multiplane camera that separated cels from the background to allow realistic, real-time camera movements.

After World War II, Walt Disney concentrated on live-action nature films, the merchandising of his characters, television shows, and theme parks—Disneyland in Southern California and, later, Disney World and Epcot Center in central Florida.

Critics originally praised Disney for his animation innovations, but as the studio became more profitable, they criticized his movies for being too sentimental and pretentious. Because his films were aimed at a large, family-oriented audience, they were necessarily bland and free from controversy. Still, the crowning achievement for the studio, *Beauty and the Beast* (1991), was the first-ever animated motion picture nominated in the Best Picture category along with the other live-action features by the Academy Awards. *The Silence of the Lambs* won that year. In 2008 Disney Studios entered the huge Indian film market with *Roadside Romeo* in the style of the country's Bollywood tradition.

At the other extreme of the animation spectrum was a set of popular animators who were inspired by the absurd violence and cynicism of George Herriman's *Krazy Kat* cartoon—Fred "Tex" Avery, Friz Freleng, and Chuck Jones who, at Warner Bros. studio, created such classic *Looney Tunes* and *Merrie Melodies* characters as Bugs Bunny, Porky Pig, Daffy Duck, Elmer Fudd, Wile E. Coyote, and the Roadrunner (Weblink 10.11). The team made more than 800 films. When Warner closed its animation studio in 1963, Jones went to work for MGM. In 1965, he won an Oscar for his cartoon *The Dot and the Line*. In 1980 Warner reopened its animation division and is known for its television productions based on the Batman and Superman characters and motion pictures such as *Space Jam* (1996) and Brad Bird's critically acclaimed *The Iron Giant* (1999).

Other famous cartoon animators provided popular characters. Friz Freleng invented Tweety Pie, Sylvester, and the Pink Panther. Walter Lantz created Woody Woodpecker. Jay Ward produced the popular "Rocky and Bullwinkle" Saturday morning television show with stories that appealed to both children and adults. William Hanna and Joseph Barbera had Mr. Magoo, Huckleberry Hound, and Yogi Bear. The duo also proved that adults, as well as children, would like animated films. In 1960, the team produced the first prime-time television cartoon, "The Flintstones" (Weblink 10.12). With the success of that Stone Age family, the production company moved the familiar family situation comedy genre ahead a few centuries to create "The Jetsons" (Weblink 10.13). The success of the prehistoric cave dwellers and the futuristic family in the sky showed studio heads that animated films could attract adult audiences; this paved the way for Matt Groening's "The Simpsons."

Pixar Animation Studios started as a computer division of *Star Wars* (1977) director George Lucas's company, Lucasfilm. After Apple Computer co-founder Steven Jobs bought the division in 1986, it was renamed Pixar. One of the animators that worked for Lucasfilm was the talented John Lasseter. He won an Academy Award for the first all-computer-generated short feature *Tin Toy* (1988) (Figure 10.30). He also directed *Toy Story* (1995), the first feature-length animated cartoon produced solely with computer technology, as well as *A Bug's Life* (1998), *Toy Story 2* (1999), and *Cars* (2006), also all-computer productions. Pixar and Disney collaborated to produce *Monsters, Inc.* in 2001, which featured innovations in computer-generated technology. Another collaboration with Disney was *Finding Nemo* (2003), which won the 2004 Academy Award for best animated motion picture. In 2006 Disney acquired the Pixar Company, and John Lasseter became its CEO the next year. A friend of Lasseter's and an animator for Warner and Disney, Brad Bird, won Academy Awards for Best Animated Feature for *The Incredibles* (2004) and *Ratatouille* (2007).

Figure 10.30

Director John Lasseter of Pixar won an Academy Award for the first short subject film created entirely on computers, Tin Toy (1988). The use of perspective and lighting gives a realistic rendering to the enduring characters. In 2003 it was included in the National Film Registry of the Library of Congress for its "culturally, historically, and aesthetically significance."

See color insert following page 338.

Both courtesy of Pixar, Inc.

With its serious theme of environmental conservation, Pixar Animation Studio's *WALL-E* (2008) is considered a masterpiece in animation. Its mesmerizing soundtrack and long stretches emphasizing visual messages helped make the picture a milestone that won the 2009 Academy Award for Best Animated Film (Weblink 10.14). Pete Docter, who co-wrote and co-directed *Monsters, Inc.*, shared an Oscar for the script for *WALL–E* and co-directed *Up* (2009). Other highly anticipated movies from the studio were the hand-drawn cel musical *The Princess and the Frog* (2009) and the computer-rendered *Rapunzel* (2010).

Another major producer of animated films is DreamWorks SKG, which was started by Hollywood heavyweights David Greffen, Jeffrey Katzenberg, and Steven Spielberg in 1994. The company has produced three types of animated movies: hand-drawn cel, seen in *The Prince of Egypt* (1998); stop-motion, through a partnership with Aardman Animations headed by the British animator Nick Park, for *Chicken Run* (2000), and *Wallace & Gromit: The Curse of the Were-Rabbit* (2005); and computer-animated, such as *Antz* (1998), *Shrek* (2001), and *Madagascar: Escape 2 Africa* (2008). The 2009 3-D *Monsters vs. Aliens* was an unqualified smash hit for the film company. Many

critics thought that its success was a breakthrough for 3-D movies and compared it with *The Jazz Singer* (1927), which featured sound, and *Becky Sharp* (1935), which introduced audiences to color.

 Technical Perspective

Whether cartoons are intended for print or screen media presentations, the cartoonist uses specific devices to convey information to the viewer. The meaning of these graphic conventions often is not obvious because as symbolic codes, they must be learned (Figure 10.31). In order to analyze cartoons, you need to be aware of the various terms used to describe illustrative techniques. Once you know the name of an element, you will notice it more easily. One of the most respected sources to help you understand print cartoon production is Scott McCloud's *Understanding Comics: The Invisible Art* (1994).

There are at least eight separate technical considerations for cartoonists in print and screen media:

■ *Frame*

Top and bottom boxes or panels often contain narration and story explanations. Different sized frames increase visual interest (Figure 10.32).

■ *Setting*

The background illustrations might be highly stylized and simple as in a *Peanuts* cartoon or realistic and elaborate as in the *Spider-Man* comic strip. The degree to which elements of reality are removed from a cartoon is called *leveling*. Often the artist conveys the seriousness of the cartoon by a high or low degree of leveling (Figure 10.33).

■ *Characters*

As with the setting, the degree of realism with which the characters are drawn often indicates whether the strip is humorous or serious. *Assimilation* is the term used to describe the technique of exaggerating features, usually for a stereotypical effect. Homer Simpson's large belly and Marge's high beehive are examples. As with any pictorial representation of the human face, expressions connote emotional states that may help explain a character's motives (Figure 10.34).

■ *Motion Lines*

Mort Walker, creator of the popular strip *Beetle Bailey*, gave names to various movement lines: hites—horizontal movement, vites—vertical motions, dites—diagonal movement, agitrons—wavering or repetitive motions, briffits—little puffs of smoke or dirt, waftaroms—odors that float in the frame, and plewds—sweat beads that pop up on a character's forehead that indicate nervousness (Figure 10.35).

■ *Typography*

Unlike in any other art form, the reader of a comic strip, comic book, or graphic novel is asked to supply a dramatic reading of a character's dialogue by means of typographical variations. By recognizing

Courtesy of the Dick Sutphen Studio, Inc.

Figure 10.31

Editorial cartoons often are filled with symbols—some understandable, but many dependent for their meaning or a thorough knowledge of the time in which they were produced. Justice gives up her seat for an unknown corrupt politician in this woodcut.

Courtesy of Patricio Ruales Lopez

Figure 10.32

Although Colombian artist and illustrator Patricio Ruales López has been a professional for only a short time, she has developed comic books, book covers for a Spanish publisher, and illustrations for video games for companies based in Canada, Mexico, and the United States. In her "good vs. evil" futuristic action comic Cancro, *the use of differently sized frames—square, horizontal, and small verticals—heighten the dramatic action and compel the viewer to think of the page as a motion picture on paper.*

differences in letter size and thickness, the reader becomes an actor, emphasizing important words either in the mind or out loud (Figure 10.36).

Figure 10.33

Little Sammy Sneeze was the print and screen media animation artist Winsor McCay's first regular comic strip. Begun in 1904 in the pages of the New York Herald, *every week his main character, an innocent-looking boy, would be placed in a variety of settings and end with a sneeze that would usually create great havoc. In this series, McCay uses the simplest setting possible, a blank background to emphasize the innocence of the lone child who has no one else but himself to blame for destroying the cartoon's frame with his sneeze.*

HE JUST SIMPLY COULDN'T STOP IT   LITTLE SAMMY SNEEZE   HE NEVER KNEW WHEN IT WAS COMING

Courtesy of the Sunday Press

■ *Balloons*

The way dialogue of characters in comic strips is encircled is an example of a complicated semiotic structure. The reader must learn to interpret the symbolism of the various balloon types: unbroken line—normal, unemotional speech; perforated line—a whisper; a spiked outline—loud yelling; little bubbles instead of lines—thoughts by the character; icicles hanging from a balloon—conceited or aloof speech; tiny words within a large balloon—astonished or ashamed emotional speech; a zigzag line—sound from a telephone, TV set, or computer; the tail of a balloon outside the frame—similar to an off-camera voice (Figure 10.37).

■ *Action Sequences*

All the techniques utilized by motion picture directors are also used in cartoons. Artists use close-ups, perspective

Figure 10.34 (left)

The fear of the Frankenstein monster is enhanced with an illustrator's technique that emphasizes his facial and arm gestures in this Classics Illustrated production of the Mary Shelley horror story. The comic book series based on famous novels debuted in 1941 as Classic Comics, changed its name in 1947 to Classics Illustrated, and ceased publication in 1971.

Figure 10.35 (right)

Online editorial cartoonist Peter Welleman employs a variety of motion lines for a cartoon illustration for verbal abuse.

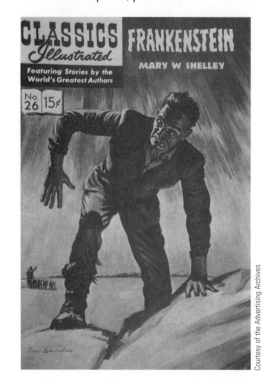

Courtesy of the Advertising Archives

Courtesy of Peter Welleman/CartoonStock

and framing variations, special lighting effects, montage techniques, and panning and quick-cut editing to help move the action from frame to frame. These film techniques once led cartoonist Will Eisner to say, "Comics are movies on paper." Of course, with all the absurd plot lines, killings, explosions, and digital special effects in today's action-adventure movies, we can also say that movies are comic books on film. Not surprisingly, film directors such as George Lucas (*American Graffiti*, 1973, and *Star Wars*, 1977) and Steven Spielberg (*E.T.: The Extra-Terrestrial*, 1982, and *Saving Private Ryan*, 1998) admit that early in their careers they learned about perspective, framing, and plot techniques by being avid adventure comic book readers.

■ Animation Techniques

Almost all the cartoons intended for the print medium are created with either traditional pencil, pen, and ink materials or through computer software. Animated films, however, are made using three major techniques: cel, stop-motion, and computer-generated imagery (CGI).

Cel Animation

Also called traditional and hand-drawn animation, this technique is divided into three types: full, limited, and rotoscoping.

Full animation This technique requires 24 frames per second for realistic movement—or for a 10-minute movie, more than 14,000 drawings. The process is enormously expensive and time consuming. Early Disney classics as well as the recent critically acclaimed *Les Triplettes de Belleville* (2003) used traditional cel animation. British animator James Baxter, who was responsible for Belle in the Disney classic *Beauty and the Beast* as well as supervising *The Lion King* (1994), *Shrek 2* (2004), and *Kung Fu Panda* (2008), prefers

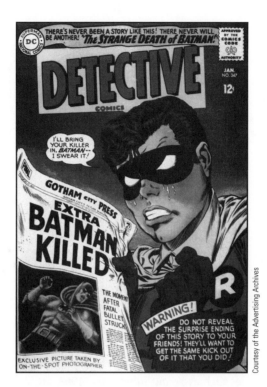

Courtesy of the Advertising Archives

Figure 10.36

For this cover illustration of Robin mourning the supposed death of his mentor and fellow crime fighter Batman as reported in the Gotham City Press, *typography is used by illustrators of this Detective Comics (DC) issue to emphasize the title of the story, the publisher, Robin's spoken dialogue within a bubble, the importance of the story in the newspaper, and the warning to readers not to reveal the surprise ending to others.*

hand-drawn techniques to the computer for action scenes. Using see-through paper and a pencil, he makes each drawing on a page so he can see how they line up. Baxter explains, "It's basically like making a flip book, page by page."

Uncensored Situations, 1966, The Dick Sutphen Studio, Inc.

Figure 10.37

In this 19th century woodcut, warriors are comically polite, as indicated by the dialogue within the balloons.

Another full animation technique, Japanese *anime*, has a distinctive style often noted for its hand-drawn cels with bright colors, supernatural characters, and out-of-this-planet landscapes. Popular in the United States only in the last ten years, *anime*—like its print counterpart, *manga*—is gaining support. One of the leaders of Japanese anime is director Hayao Miyazaki. His critically acclaimed films *Spirited Away* (2001), which won an Academy Award, and *Princess Mononoke* (1997) have reached general audiences around the world (Weblink 10.15). In 2009, *Ponyo* Miyazaki's adaptation of Hans Christian Andersen's *The Little Mermaid* received critical success.

Limited animation As the name implies, this technique of cel animation uses fewer frames per second for a more stylistic and jerky appearance and can be seen in movies such as *Yellow Submarine* (1968, art directed by the famous poster artist Heinz Edelmann who claimed to never have tried hallucinogenic drugs) and the television programs produced by the Hanna-Barbera production company (Weblink 10.16).

Rotoscoping This animation technique was invented by Max Fleischer in 1917. Fleisher's animation company produced such classic movie characters as Betty Boop, Popeye, and Superman. With this technique, live action movements were traced by hand frame by frame. The director Richard Linklater used the rotoscoping method with computers to produce the visually arresting films *Waking Life* (2001) and *A Scanner Darkly* (2006) (Weblink 10.17). The investment company Charles Schwab also employed rotoscoping for a series of commercials shown in 2009.

Stop-motion animation

This animation technique describes a wide variety of object manipulations that might include models, clay, and puppets.

Model animation Willis O'Brien used this technique in his 1925 classic about angry dinosaurs, *The Lost World*. Tooled steel formed the animals' skeletons, which were then covered with foam latex and painted. Animators moved these models slightly and photographed them frame by frame to produce the effect of the dinosaurs walking and fighting. The technique also was used in the popular movie *King Kong* in 1933. Ray Harryhausen was 13 years old when his aunt took him to see *King Kong* at Grauman's Theater in Hollywood. The movie so inspired him that he devoted the rest of his life to the animation field. In 1963 Harryhausen's animated work in *Jason and the Argonauts*, which includes a memorable scene in which the intrepid crew of the Argos fights sword-wielding skeletons, inspired future directors George Lucas, Steven Spielberg, and James Cameron (Weblink 10.18).

Clay animation Plasticine, the favorite brand for Claymation animators, is commonly used for animation because it gives characters depth. In 1953, Art Clokey introduced the popular clay characters Gumby and Pokey in the film *Gumbasia* (Weblink 10.19). Clay in the hands of master Nick Park becomes a powerful emotional element in which facial gestures reveal the inner feelings of the lifelike characters. His *Curse of the Were-Rabbit* (2005) won the Best Animated Feature Academy Award.

Puppet animation Similar to clay animations, this technique usually employs wood, rubber, or plastic puppet figures that interact with each other within constructed worlds. One of the masters is Henry Selick who worked for Disney where he learned stop-motion techniques. After he left to form his own company, his creativity revitalized the Doughboy for Pillsbury commercials. When an innovative film he made for MTV, *Slow Bob in the Lower Dimensions* (1990), got the attention of director Tim Burton, he was asked to direct *The Nightmare Before Christmas* (1993) (Weblink 10.20). His latest work is the ambitious *Coraline* (2009) with animator Travis Knight, son of Nike billionaire Phil Knight. The inherent depth of using puppets is further enhanced by a 3-D version in which moviegoers wear special glasses for an even more realistic view (Weblink 10.21). Another critically acclaimed animated motion picture that used puppets was director Wes Anderson's *Fantastic Mr. Fox* (2009) based on Roald Dahl's book of the same name. During the production, Anderson sent scene ideas through his iPhone from this Paris home to his animators based in London.

Computer-Generated Imagery (CGI)

Computer imaging has come a long way from its roots as simple lines on a screen for military purposes and quarter-hungry consoles at a local bar. CGI comes in 2-D, 3-D, and performance capture variations.

Two-dimensional With 2-D effects, animation can be accomplished with traditional animation techniques that are transferred to a computer screen, as in the television series "SpongeBob SquarePants" and by various software applications such as Flash and PowerPoint. Most animations seen on the web through the Adobe Flash software program employ 2-D methods. A popular web-based animation studio known for its political satires, JibJab, is the work of Evan and Gregg Spiridellis. Their "viral videos" spread around the world via links provided by fans to their friends (Weblink 10.22). In 2009 Walt Disney Animation Studios directors Ron Clements and John Musker (*The Little Mermaid*, 1989 and *Aladdin*, 1992) introduced their 2-D hit *The Princess and the Frog*, which

reminded critics and viewers of the richly textured traditional look of Disney classics from the 1950s (Weblink 10.23).

Another common special effect is to combine live action and 2-D animated characters in the same scene. This collaboration between humans and cartoons is as old as the stage work of Winsor McCay and his pet dinosaur Gertie. Walt Disney tried the technique in an animated series in which a young actress, Virginia Davis, interacted with an animated cat named Julius in the "Alice Comedies" of the 1920s. Later in 1946, *Song of the South* and the 1964 classic *Mary Poppins* featured dance numbers among actors and cartoon characters (Weblink 10.24). Walt Disney would often interact with some of his animated characters for television. More recent examples can be seen in *Who Framed Roger Rabbit* (1988) and *Looney Tunes: Back in Action* (2003) (Weblink 10.25).

Three-dimensional With 3-D animation, lifelike simulations of body movements are possible. The films *Toy Story*, *Shrek*, and *Monsters, Inc.* have a simulated realism about them that 2-D animation cannot supply. A kind of hybrid between 2-D and 3-D can be seen in the documentary movie *Waltz with Bashir* (2008). Written and directed by Israeli Ari Folman, it tells the story of his experience as a 1982 Lebanon War veteran. To simulate a 3-D look, the animators used Flash, traditional animation, and 3-D computer techniques. A related procedure, cel-shading, turns 3-D CGI images into a style that looks like hand-drawn cel animations. The technique is popular for video games, films, television shows, and commercials—examples include "The Simpsons Game," *Hey Arnold!: The Movie* (2002), "Family Guy," and Procter & Gamble's Mr. Clean commercial character (Weblink 10.26).

Performance capture Also called motion capture or mocap, this technology creates the most startling example of lifelike human characters and can be found in television commercials, digital computer games, and motion pictures. Sony Pictures Imageworks hired professional baseball players to re-create their body movements for its "MLB 2009: The Show" video game. Using 55 sensors attached to a spandex bodysuit, special cameras captured a player's every move for a realistic effect. *Final Fantasy: The Spirits Within* (2001) from directors Hironobu Sakaguchi and Moto Sakakibara was a quantum leap for technical achievement in mimicking the lifelike qualities of humans (Weblink 10.27). Other standouts include *The Polar Express* (2004), *Beowulf* (2007), and *Watchmen* (2009). The actor Andy Serkis was rendered as Gollum and Smeagol in *The Lord of the Rings* trilogy (2001–2003) and as the mighty ape in the remake of *King Kong* (2005). The technique has also been used for courtroom and journalistic creations discussed in Chapter 9. A popular variation of performance capture is demonstrated with the seamless morphing technique seen at the end of Michael Jackson's 1991 music video for "Black or White" discussed in Chapter 14. However, James Cameron in *Avatar* (2010) takes the technology to a higher level of perfection with many claiming it will revolutionize the making of motion pictures and lead to the maturing of 3-D movies on a level with sound, color, and widescreen presentations.

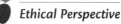

Ethical Perspective

Critics most often cite four main ethical issues as problems for cartoons: marketing cartoon characters to children, using too few multicultural characters, introducing political opinions in comic strips, and showing inappropriate sexual and violent themes.

■ Marketing

Product tie-ins are as old as comic strips. When the *Yellow Kid* was introduced in 1895, the popularity of the strip sparked one of the first mass-marketing campaigns in the United States. Illustrations reproduced on buttons, metal cracker boxes, and fans promoted the cartoon character and the newspaper. But the clear-cut winner of the marketing race and the model for other cartoonists and studios is Walt Disney. Disney gave up illustrating his motion pictures himself to organize and manage the lucrative product lines inspired by his company's characters. It seemed that every American child had to have a Mickey Mouse doll. With a popular movie, every animation studio makes an enormous profit on international ticket sales, video rentals, soundtrack albums, and product licensing agreements (from lunch boxes to dolls). At the same time, Saturday morning television programs and motion picture characters frequently appear in advertisements promoting everything from dolls to bicycles. Children are particularly vulnerable to such persuasive commercial techniques, but adults also are easily manipulated.

■ Stereotypes

As with other mass media images, Anglo males have almost exclusively dominated comic strip and cartoon visual messages. For example, of the 25 comic strips and five single-framed humorous cartoons on two pages featured in the *Los Angeles*

Times for February 19, 2009, there were a total of 53 human characters portrayed: 48 Anglo (90 percent), two Latino (4 percent), and three African American (6 percent). There were no other cultural groups shown in any of the strips. Male characters also beat out women with 35 characters, or 66 percent, to 18 characters, 34 percent. Such demographics, to say the least, do not match those of the Southern California region. It's a male, Anglo world after all.

In addition, African Americans had to endure extremely offensive racist stereotypes in Bugs Bunny cartoons in the 1940s from *Looney Tunes* and *Merrie Melodies*, distributed by Warner Bros. One particularly racist animated short showed a slow-talking, slow-walking, and slow-thinking African American boy resembling Elmer Fudd attempting to shoot Bugs Bunny with a shotgun. The title, *All This and Rabbit Stew*, was originally released in 1941 and directed by Tex Avery, although his name is not in the credits. After media mogul Ted Turner purchased the Warner Bros. collection, he vowed to never show the 11 most racist cartoons on television, although they can be found on DVD collections and other sources, including YouTube.com (Weblink 10.28).

■ Controversial Themes

Many readers object to serious messages disguised as children-oriented comic strips, often because they do not agree with the political messages. *Little Orphan Annie* frequently criticized President Roosevelt's New Deal politics, and *Pogo* often went after Senator Joseph McCarthy. In the 1960s, underground or alternative comic books were intended to shock traditional audiences and establish a counterculture readership. One cartoonist used to such criticism is Garry Trudeau. *Doonesbury* so regularly offends conservative readers with its liberal perspectives that it is often placed on the editorial or opinion page of a newspaper instead of in the comics section. As cartoons can be enjoyed by persons of all ages, a wide variety of political and thoughtful issues should be a part of the comics pages.

⊕ Cultural Perspective

Many times the Sunday comic pages are a child's first introduction to the magical world of reading. Upon seeing the brightly colored funnies, a child is interested immediately. But cartoon strip characters that are amusing to a child no longer provoke the same response in adults. Part of the reason that comic books are not considered a serious art form is that traditionally they have been intended for younger audiences. One of the most common causes of cultural division between people is difference in age. Consequently, the kinds of comic material you read help identify you as belonging to a particular cultural group. With adult-oriented graphic novels, the gap between young and old is narrowing.

Cartoons are an essential part of any country's culture. The types of cartoon subjects seen in a society reflect the values and beliefs common to the culture at that time.

As with many visual messages, cartoons can be studied in terms of society's myths (good vs. evil), their various genres (from westerns to soap operas), and their use of symbolism (both visual and verbal). Large numbers of readers enjoyed the *Yellow Kid* comic strip because the story about a group of lost children, seemingly abandoned by their parents, struck a sympathetic chord with readers, many of whom were immigrants living far away from their families. The threat of world domination by totalitarian regimes beginning in the 1930s inspired comic strips with conservative views or super-human characters who would fight for the values expressed by the "American way of life," whatever that phrase happened to mean at the moment. Visual symbols expressed in drawings also reflect the culture from which they are produced. Editorial cartoons, much more than any other type of comic, regularly feature symbolic images in the form of religious icons, military designations, and national emblems as a visual shorthand to make the point of the cartoons clear. Consequently, meaning resides in an understanding of these verbal and visual codes.

Critical Perspective

A cartoon, although packaged within a deceptively simple frame, is a complex exercise in semiotic analysis. No other art form, in print or screen media, combines words, pictures, and meaning in such an interwoven way. Like the effects created by motion picture and television images, cartoons form complex intellectual and emotional unions of text and images in a highly personal way. By reading a cartoon out loud, a reader becomes a character in the unfolding frame-by-frame drama. Cartoons have a powerful yet not fully understood effect on those who never outgrow their charm. In corporate advertising, government propaganda, and instructional aids, cartoon art is used because it is a powerful communication medium. To simply label

Figure 10.38

Cartoons can be used to attract a viewer's attention to a social problem. In a program called "Art Attacks AIDS," Mike McNeilly shows his work on the back of a bus stop bench.

comics as "children's art" and unworthy of serious attention is to deny the impact of all words and pictures that communicate a message. Such an attitude also discounts the enormous effect that cartoons have on all generations of readers and viewers.

Cartoons teach us not only how to combine words and pictures in symbolic ways, but also how to confront the significant issues that all societies face. It is unfortunate that cartoon messages are discounted by a narrow view of their importance (Figure 10.38).

■ TRENDS TO WATCH FOR CARTOONS

With the global economic downturn combined with a drop in subscriptions, newspaper publishers and their parent corporations have been pressured to reduce their staffs. Two of the first positions to go for many newspapers were the editorial and syndicated comic strip cartoonists. In place of editorial cartoons, newspapers may on occasion print work from artists who reside anywhere in the world on important issues. Nevertheless, this action is a shame as only a local cartoonist can make visual commentaries on local issues. With newspaper page counts being reduced to save money, some publications have made the strips smaller to fit more in the same space, cut long-time comic strips altogether, or run them only on their websites.

Graphic novels on specialized, serious subjects and distributed through major publishing houses, comics stores, and the web will become more common. One of the best recent examples is the work of Sid Jacobson and Ernie Colón

who produced an achievement in comic book art, *The 9/11 Report: A Graphic Adaptation*. They enhanced the reputation of the medium with their cartoon version of the governmental report requested by the President and Congress (Weblink 10.29). In 2008 the two produced a follow-up, *After 9/11: America's War on Terror*.

The Academy Awards separate category honoring the best achievements in mainstream animation sparks interest among indie producers of short- and long-form animations, and graphic novels produce compelling work. The Cartoon Network, popular among children during the day for its typical selections of classic and current cartoons, changes late at night into a visually stirring collection of animations called "Adult Swim." *Anime* and other styles present mature fare that can be found in such shows as "Bleach," "Fullmetal Alchemist," and "Shin Chan." However, because of competition from children's animated series offered by Nickelodeon and Disney, the network introduced live-action reality shows featuring children, which were not popular. Consequently, the network is struggling. Nevertheless, Fox television's adult-oriented "Animation Domination" on Sunday evenings usually features two hours of prime-time animated sitcom hits such as "The Simpsons," "Family Guy," "King of the Hill," and "American Dad."

The web has also increased the number of cartoons being produced, because comic strips, comic books, and animated films have all merged in the new medium. As the status of cartoons improve, they will also be used in informational graphics, not for their entertainment value, but to increase the knowledge of viewers about complex subjects.

■ *KEY TERMS*

- Anime
- Beehive hairdo
- Blue-collar
- Bollywood
- Cel
- Clip art
- Cut
- Digital television
- Doctors Without Borders
- Frieze
- Kinetoscope
- Live-action
- Manga
- Montage
- Morphing
- Panning
- Reuben Award
- Serial
- Short
- Situation comedy
- Storyboards
- Syndication
- Upper-middle class
- Viral videos
- Working class

 To locate active URLs for the weblinks mentioned in this chapter, please go to the companion site at http://communication.wadsworth.com/lester5 and select the proper chapter.

Chapter 11

Photography

Once you see the forlorn face of Florence Thompson, you will never forget her (Figure 11.1). With furrowed forehead, a faraway look, hand cupped to her chin in a gesture of uncertainty, two children shyly hiding their faces in the warmth of her shoulders, and an infant sleeping on her lap, the photograph is more than a simple portrait of a family. The image is reminiscent of the "Madonna and Child" religious icon known to millions because painters throughout the history of Christianity have captured it on canvas. But here in black and white is a real-life symbol for all parents struggling to survive and feed their families during the Great Depression and for all uncertain economic times. "Migrant Mother" is probably the world's most reproduced photograph in the history of photography because it makes people care about this mother on a deep, personal level.

But it was a picture that almost was not taken.

Dorothea Nutzhorn was born in Hoboken, New Jersey, in 1895. When she was 12 years old she took her mother's maiden name of Lange after her father left the family. As a child she suffered from polio that gave her a limp in her right leg for the rest of her life. Although she'd never held a camera, at 14 she wanted to be a photographer, because she said that her disability "gave her an almost telepathic connection with those who suffered." After studying at Columbia University under the photographer Clarence White, she moved in 1918 to San Francisco, where she enjoyed the Bay Area's bohemian lifestyle. She married the painter Maynard Dixon and had two sons. She supported her family through her studio photography business. By 1932, she had become an able portrait photographer

If your pictures aren't good enough, you aren't close enough.

Robert Capa (Endre Ernő Friedmann) 1913–1954
PHOTOJOURNALIST

259

Figure 11.1

"Migrant Mother," 1936, by Dorothea Lange. The disturbing and touching story line of a woman alone with her children during the height of America's Great Depression spurred many to help others. But is she posing or wishing the photographer would leave?

with a reputation for capturing the personalities of the rich San Francisco matrons of the day.

News reports of the terrible living conditions of rural Americans prompted Lange to want to document their lives. The country was undergoing the worst drought in its history; dust storms blew away the once-fertile topsoil. The stock market crashed in 1929 and farm prices plummeted, throwing millions out of work. People lived from day to day, and thousands of farmers from the Midwest

and Great Plains who had lost their land and livelihoods took off in mattress-topped automobiles for the golden West. Lange obtained a job with the State of California to document agricultural labor conditions. She was teamed with social economist Dr. Paul Schuster Taylor, whom she later married.

After completion of the project, the head of the Resettlement Administration (RA), Rexford Tugwell, reviewed her pictures in Washington and promptly hired her.

The RA, later renamed the Farm Security Administration (FSA), was an agency of the U.S. Department of Agriculture. President Franklin D. Roosevelt created it to help relocate farmers to more fertile farmland, obtain massive subsidies to offset the low prices farmers were getting for their crops, and convince the American public that controversial social programs needed to be passed by the conservative Congress. Thus, the FSA was more of a propaganda wing that the government used to get New Deal legislation through Congress than a direct aid to rural residents. Besides Lange, famous photographers who worked for the FSA were Walker Evans, Russell Lee, Gordon Parks, Arthur Rothstein, and Marion Post Wolcott (Figure 11.2).

The FSA photographers produced an exhaustive document of rural and urban life in America during the 1930s and 1940s that has never been equaled. Newspapers and magazines used their pictures because they were free. However, in 1943 the FSA was eliminated and its employees transferred to the Office of War Information, which was ended in 1945. Nevertheless, the images succeeded in helping pass New Deal legislation and also inspired other photographers to follow in their documentary footsteps. More than 250,000 of their images are stored in the collection at the Library of Congress, and a copy of each one can be purchased at a nominal price.

But *the* image in the collection—the most revered and reproduced—is Lange's "Migrant Mother."

Tired, hungry, and anxious to get home after a month-long project taking pictures in central California, Lange drove her car north along the cold and wet Camino Real Highway (101) in early March 1936. Along the way she noted a migrant workers' camp of about 2,500 people outside the small town of Nipomo. On the side of the road someone had placed a sign that simply proclaimed, "Pea-Pickers Camp." These sights were all too common, with poor people from all over the country forced to stop for lack of money and gasoline and earn a few dollars picking local crops.

For 30 minutes, Lange drove toward home and thought about the camp she

had passed. Finally, the image of the people she had briefly seen overpowered her desire to get home. She turned her car around and drove back to the camp. Lange retrieved her press camera, a portable version of the tripod-bound,

Figure 11.2

"Fleeing a Dust Storm," 1936, by Arthur Rothstein. Oklahoma farmer Arthur Coble and his two sons weather a storm. During the Great Depression, the Farm Security Administration of the U.S. government produced numerous classic documents such as this Dust Bowl picture by Arthur Rothstein.

Figure 11.3

Photojournalists call the first picture taken at a scene a "cover shot." If you are asked or are forced to leave, at least you have something. With the older girl avoiding the camera, the younger one smiling for the lens, and Florence Thompson looking back at a daughter hiding behind her, this image is almost a snapshot—not a particularly telling moment.

Figure 11.4

Perched atop her 1933 Ford Model C four-door wagon, Dorothea Lange poses with a Graflex 4 × 5 Series D camera. She was driving this car when she spotted Florence Thompson and her family at the side of the road and used this camera for her famous photograph.

Corbis

large-format camera, and immediately found Florence Thompson sitting in the barely adequate shelter of an open tent with her daughters (Figure 11.3). With the crop destroyed by a freeze, there was no work at the camp. An engine chain had broken on their Model T Ford, so they were stuck. Thompson's two sons, along with a man living with Thompson at the time, went to town to get the car fixed, leaving her to care for her daughters. She

Figure 11.5

The book jacket of An American Exodus: A Record of Human Erosion *by Dorothea Lange and Paul Taylor shows a typical sight along the roads during America's Great Depression—a truck filled with household goods. With Lange's pictures and Taylor's words, the two documented the migration of many from ruined Dust Bowl farms to migrant worker camps out West.*

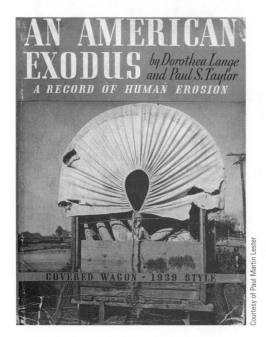

Courtesy of Paul Martin Lester

was pregnant with her sixth child. She would eventually have seven children.

In notes about the brief encounter, Lange later wrote, "Camped on the edge of a pea field where the crop had failed in a freeze. She said that she had been living on frozen vegetables from the surrounding fields and birds that the children had killed." Lange did not ask her name or anything about her past history. She stayed ten minutes and made six exposures (Figure 11.4).

When she returned home, Lange made several prints and gave them to an editor of the *San Francisco News*, where they were published under the headline, "FOOD RUSHED TO STARVING FARM COLONY." Two of Lange's photographs accompanied the story that detailed the situation of the migrants and the efforts of relief workers to bring food and cleanup crews to the camp. The famous close-up was not published. Because of the story and pictures, the camp residents received about 20,000 pounds of food from the government, but Thompson and her family had left before help arrived.

But back in Washington, the historical and social significance of the Thompson portrait were recognized immediately. The picture soon became an American classic with a life of its own. Newspapers across the country reproduced it. In 1941, the Museum of Modern Art in New York City exhibited it. When John Steinbeck saw the picture, it inspired him to write *The Grapes of Wrath*. Without question, the picture made Lange famous. And despite her later achievements as a staff photographer for *Life* magazine, her collaboration with Paul Taylor on their book *An American Exodus: A Record of Human Erosion*, and her documentation of Japanese American internees during World War II, she is forever linked to it (Figure 11.5). Frustrated over that fact, she once complained that she was not a "one-picture photographer." In 1965, Lange died at the age of 70 after a long and event-filled life made possible by her photographic skills and her sensitivity to the important moments in everyday life.

But Florence Thompson's life didn't change for the better after the picture was published.

Born to poverty in rural Oklahoma in 1903, her father died when she was a baby. When she was 18 she married Cleo Owens, a logger. Finding little work in their home state, they moved to California in 1922 to work in the sawmills. By 1929 the couple had five children. After Owens lost his job, they moved from field to field to pick peaches until he caught a fever and died at the age of 32. She moved with her children from town to town seeking help from her family, went back home to Oklahoma for a brief time, and returned to California to continue the farm-picking migrant life, traveling from camp to camp.

When she first saw it in print, she didn't like the image and tried to get it suppressed. When that effort failed, she tried to get Lange and/or the government to pay her for being in the picture. In 1979, 44 years after the picture was taken and 14 years after the death of Dorothea Lange, Thompson was finally identified as the woman in the famous photograph after she wrote a letter to the *Sacramento Bee* and was still bitter about the fact that the photograph made Dorothea Lange famous but didn't improve her life. In a newspaper article that followed, Thompson, living in a mobile home in Modesto, California, complained to a reporter, "That's my picture hanging all over the world, and I can't get a penny out of it." In 1983, Thompson suffered from colon cancer and couldn't pay her medical bills. Family members alerted the local newspaper and a national

story was published about her situation. Readers who saw the story and remembered the emotional image were moved to send money to her—more than $15,000 ($33,500 today)—before she died. Many of the letters that contained money noted how the writers' lives had been touched by Lange's close-up portrait of the "Migrant Mother."

In 1998, a print signed by Lange was sold for $244,500 ($328,000 today) at Sotheby's auction house in New York to an anonymous collector who promptly sold it to the J. Paul Getty Museum in Los Angeles for a higher undisclosed sum.

In a 2008 interview with a CNN reporter, Thompson's daughter Katherine (the girl on her mother's right shoulder in the famous photograph) said that the "photograph's fame made the family feel shame at their poverty." And yet, on Florence Thompson's gravestone at the Lakewood Memorial Park in Hughson, California, about 250 miles north of Nipomo, it reads, "Migrant Mother—A Legend of the Strength of American Motherhood." And in Nipomo, one of the major north–south streets that runs parallel with Highway 101 is named Thompson.

■ ANALYSIS OF "MIGRANT MOTHER"

Any great work of art always has many stories to tell. There is the story of the subjects within the frame, why and how it was created, and what happened after it was made public. But one of the most important stories any visual message tells is the one the viewer makes up. The way you interpret an image is the story of your life.

Even a casual glance at "Migrant Mother" reveals without question an

Figure 11.6

*"Madonna dell Granduca,"
c. 1505, oil on wood, by Raf-
faello Sanzio. Known simply
as Raphael, the High Renaissance Italian painter shared
the era with Leonardo da
Vinci and Michelangelo.
Typical of the times, he was
orphaned at an early age
but through an uncle found
apprenticeship work where he
learned his craft. Best known
for his religious works, many
of his paintings can be found
at the Vatican. He died on
his birthday at the age of 37
after having exuberant sex
with his mistress. Many have
compared Lange's "Migrant
Mother" with Raphael's
Madonna and Child because
of the downward, worried
gaze of the mother in the
painting.*

Courtesy of Erich Lessing / Art Resource, NY

emotionally charged, sad moment in a woman's life. Much of the picture's power comes from its obvious symbolic link to religious paintings. But where the Madonna icon is a positive affirmation of future possibilities for her child, the Thompson portrait is an anti-Madonna icon filled with uncertainty about the future for herself and her children (Figure 11.6).

With a normal perspective, medium-sized lens opening for limited focus, medium shutter speed to avoid camera blur, black and white film to avoid any distractions color might provide, and a 4-by-5-inch negative for maximum resolution, the picture demonstrates the highest quality possible using the gelatin dry plate photographic process in combination with a large format, portable press camera.

Legally, Dorothea Lange did all that was required. Her job as a visual reporter was to record Thompson's image on film and give prints to a newspaper for publication, not to help Thompson and her family

directly. But what is strictly legal and what is ethical do not always absolve a person's moral responsibility to help someone in a more direct way. Lange should have at least asked Thompson's name. The public learned her name only after newspaper accounts published her complaints about the image. Lange was one year younger than Thompson, and under different circumstances, they might have had much to say to each other. But Lange was anxious to get home and stayed for a short time. Realistically, however, given the differences in their cultures based on their economic situations alone, communication between them would have been difficult.

Another controversial aspect of the photograph was the way it was manipulated in two different ways. In a later version of the print, part of a hand and a thumb holding a tent flap was airbrushed from the image (Figure 11.7). But more significantly, the picture was a stage-managed setup by Lange. This fact should not be surprising given Lange's roots as a portrait photographer. Linda Gordon in the *Los Angeles Times* wrote, "Always a portraitist, she never sought to capture her subjects unaware, as a photojournalist might."

When one studies the images of Thompson and her family members in the order they were taken, the collaboration between Lange and the children is especially marked by an obvious degree of stage managing. The initial image shows 14-year-old Viola sitting glumly on a rocking chair inside the tent. Daughter Katherine smiles at the camera while Thompson holds baby Norma and looks behind her for Ruby who hides behind her back. The next picture is a formal and stiff portrait of the family group. Viola is now in front of the lean-to tent sitting awkwardly on the rocker.

Inside the tent Ruby, who wears a wool cap, has been coaxed to join the others for a picture (Figure 11.8). As an experienced image maker, Lange knew that a family portrait with an older girl would not be an emotionally powerful image, so for the next three pictures, Lange moved in close to concentrate on Thompson with her small children. In one, she nurses the baby (Figure 11.9). In another, Ruby rests her chin on her mother's shoulder *without her knit cap* (Figure 11.10). In the third Ruby leans her head more comfortably on the shoulder while grasping the tent pole. With its vertical view that includes the crude camp-life necessities of a kerosene lamp, a tin plate, a suitcase used as a table, a wedding ring, and a view of the barren ground beyond the tent, this image is a strong document of the Dust Bowl and further demonstrates Lange's photographic artistry (Figure 11.11). Finally, the famous portrait is a close-up of Lange looking into the distance with the two children told to turn

Courtesy of [LC-USF34- 009058-C] / Dorthea Lange / Library of Congress Prints and Photographs Division Washington, DC 20540

Figure 11.7
Compare the lower-right corner of this original version of "Migrant Mother" with the retouched photograph that starts this chapter and you will notice the distracting thumb that is probably her eldest daughter Viola's as she holds the tent flap out of the way. The retouched, darkened thumb is a picture manipulation that was common in the day.

away to avoid the distraction of their faces. Although such overt manipulations of a news photograph would be discouraged today and could get a photojournalist fired, the ethics of that time were different.

Courtesy of The Library of Congress

Figure 11.8
In this formal portrait of the family group, the older Viola strikes a model's pose as she sits awkwardly on the cane rocking chair as (from left) Ruby, coaxed from behind her mother and wearing a wool cap, Katherine, Florence, and baby Norma are inside the lean-to tent. Lange is now obviously stage-managing this situation, an ethical violation for documentary and news photographs by today's standards.

Figure 11.9 (top left)

Wisely, Dorothea Lange quit taking overall portraits and moved in closer to concentrate on Florence Thompson. Although much richer in content than the famous portrait, with the breast-feeding baby, kerosene lamp, and wedding ring, this photograph does not have the same emotional quality as "Migrant Mother." Notice that the edge of the canvas tent flap hangs parallel with the wooden pole.

Figure 11.10 (top right)

Dorothea Lange moves in a little closer. Five-year-old Ruby unnaturally rests her chin on her mother's shoulder, is not wearing her wool cap, and the tent flap has been pulled back, probably by Viola. All of this stage managing was no doubt suggested by Lange.

Lange and Thompson came from different worlds with no common bond except being at the same place at the same time. The camera became the basis for their relationship that lasted a little longer than the shutter was open. For Thompson the person, not Thompson the public icon, the image revealed a weary numbness in which she was probably too polite or helpless to refuse being photographed. But she was saying "no" in the photograph the only way she could. She looked off as if wishing this "city girl" would move on and leave her alone. The image forever stereotyped Florence Thompson as a homeless matriarch who could survive only with contributions from the public. Never mind that she had worked hard to feed and clothe her family as best she could, given the country's and her family's economic hard times. That is why she was probably upset that the picture was published. As such, "Migrant Mother" is a study not only of Great Depression photography but also a commentary on the ethics of manipulation and the right to privacy of those pictured.

■ PHOTOGRAPHY AND THE SIX PERSPECTIVES

Photography runs the gamut from simple, amateur snapshots to enormously expensive professional enterprises. Artists use images to express their inner emotions, commercial photographers to sell products and ideas, visual journalists to illustrate the lives of those in the news, and scientists to make an unseen world visible. With equipment that ranges from less than ten dollars to several thousand dollars, photographers take and preserve millions of images every year. The great Irish playwright and humorist Bernard Shaw, himself an amateur photographer, once said about the medium, "I would willingly exchange every single painting of Christ for one snapshot." Such a sentiment speaks directly to the power of photography. An image is considered truthful and believable—so much so that it is used as evidence in courts of law. Time will tell if the notion of "seeing is believing" remains for the medium in the digital era.

Personal Perspective

After learning how to use paint on fingers, a pencil, and a brush, many children are introduced to a simple point-and-shoot camera, often their first contact with the image-making process using a machine. Although their first attempts may be out of focus, blurred, off-center, or incorrectly exposed, they are nevertheless awed by the magic of capturing light and seeing it on a computer screen. Part of the joy of photography is that high-quality pictures can be taken with relative ease—the machine itself is easy to master.

Moments captured by amateur photographers are a combination of space and time that often are prized possessions preserved in ornate frames and leather-bound albums. Pictures give evidence of a trip once taken, a car long since sold, and a baby who is now a grown woman. We use photographs not simply to show others where we have been, what we possess, or whom we have loved, but to remind ourselves of those important events, things, and people in our lives

Courtesy of The Library of Congress

(Figure 11.12). Not surprisingly, most victims of catastrophic events caused by wind, water, or fire report that after the secured safety of their loved ones, what they most regret and wish could have been preserved from their destroyed houses were their precious photographs.

Figure 11.11

If "Migrant Mother" had never been created, this photograph would have been revered as a powerful portrait of migrant life, with probably as much attention given to it as its famous cousin. Florence looks just as forlorn as in "Migrant Mother" and little Ruby now seems more comfortable with one hand on her mother's shoulder as she grasps the pole with the other, but this image also contains more information with the addition of the simple metal plate and worn trunk used as a table and the outside, forbidding farm field beyond the tent's inadequate shelter.

Courtesy of Paul Martin Lester

Figure 11.12

Although inexpensive cameras with automatic exposure and focus capabilities do not produce professional quality images, they make photography a fun and popular hobby for millions of persons. A tourist (the author's mother) in New York City captures a memory from her hotel window.

Historical Perspective

The camera predates the photographic process by at least 1,000 years. Aristotle wrote about the phenomenon of light that produces an upside-down view of the outside world through a pinhole in one wall of a darkened chamber, called a *camera obscura*. From what is now Iraq, Abu Ali Hasan Ibn al-Hayitham, or simply al Hazen to his Western friends, was the first to use the principle to watch an eclipse of the sun inside a tent in the year 1000 to solidify his ideas about the speed of light and the fact that light travels in straight lines for his scientific work *Book of Optics* published in 1021 (Figure 11.13). Artists used the camera obscura as a tool to trace rough sketches of natural scenes on paper or canvas, to be filled in later with paint. In the 2003 motion picture *Girl with a Pearl Earring*, the artist Jan Vermeer shows the maid, Griet, how to see images with the device. The camera obscura device led to the idea of using photosensitive materials in place of a canvas (Figure 11.14).

Throughout the history of photography, nine main photographic processes have preserved the views captured through the camera obscura: the heliograph, the daguerreotype, calotype, wet-collodion, color emulsions, gelatin-bromide dry plate, holography, instant, and digital (Figure 11.15).

■ Heliography

Joseph Nicéphore Niépce has been called the founder of photography because he produced the first permanent photograph, which can still be viewed. Born to rich and well-educated parents in 1765 in the town of Chalon-Sur-Saône, France, about 350 kilometers southeast of Paris, he became interested in the many

Figure 11.13

Abu Ali al-Hasan ibn al-Haytham or al Hazen is the figure on an Iraqi ten-dinar bank note (worth about one U.S. penny) in 1982. Born in Basra in 965 CE, his scientific achievements include significant contributions to astronomy, medicine, and visual perception. He is considered the founder of modern optics.

Courtesy of SSPL / Getty Images

scientific and technological discoveries of the day. At the age of 51, Niépce began work that eventually led to the photographic process. In an attempt to improve upon the recently-invented lithographic process for making printing plates, he discovered that bitumen of Judea (a type of asphalt) hardened when exposed to the sun. After the soft, unexposed parts of the picture were washed away, the result was a positive image. Niépce placed his asphalt emulsion on a pewter plate within a crudely constructed camera obscura and produced the world's first photograph—the view outside his home—in 1826 (Figure 11.16). It was the first and only photograph that Niépce ever made. The image now is a part of the Gernsheim photography collection at the University of Texas. The faint picture is encased within a Plexiglas frame where xenon gas protects it from deterioration.

Niépce named his process heliography (Greek for "writing with the sun"). The process never attracted much public attention because the exposure time required was about eight hours, the image was extremely grainy in appearance, it appeared to be out of focus, and the public never learned of the procedure until many years after Niépce's death. Nevertheless, the process did attract the attention of Louis Daguerre, a theatrical artist

Courtesy of the Dick Sutphen Studio, Inc.

and amateur inventor who used Niépce's basic work to produce the first practical photographic process.

■ Daguerreotype

Louis Jacques Mandé Daguerre was born in 1789 in Cormeilles, France, just north of Paris. He became famous in that city for his dioramas, illusionary pictorial effects with painted backdrops and lighting changes. An optician who supplied lenses

Courtesy of ©NMPFT / SSPL / The Image Works

Figure 11.14 (left)

This replica of the tabletop camera obscura used by the inventor William Henry Fox Talbot was built for the Science Museum (London). Similar to a photographic camera, an artist would look through the viewfinder at the top, focus the image by sliding the lens in front back and forth, and make a drawing on thin tissue paper. Little wonder inventors thought of this device as a way of preserving images through chemical means.

Figure 11.15 (right)

As this 19th-century woodcut shows, before light meters were invented, photographers looked to the sky to gauge the intensity of the sun during an exposure.

Figure 11.16

"View from the Window at Le Gras," heliograph, c. 1826, by Joseph Nicéphore Niépce. For photography to become a successful medium for visual communication, inventors needed to use light-recording materials within a camera that (1) could produce a sharp image, (2) stop fast action, (3) could be easily reproduced, and (4) was simple to operate. With this heliograph, considered the first photographic image produced by the French inventor, none of those conditions were met.

Figure 11.17

The incredible sharpness of the daguerreotype process is evident in this image taken by an unknown photographer before 1851. The view shows retail stores and homes of Portsmouth Square in San Francisco. The area is now known as the "Heart of Chinatown."

Library of Congress, Prints and Photographs Division, LC-USZC4-7422

Figure 11.18

Born in Massachusetts in 1791, Samuel Finley Breese Morse was an accomplished painter most famous for his invention of the telegraph and his dot-dash code. In 1830 he traveled to Europe to study painting where in Paris he met Louis Daguerre, the co-inventor of the daguerreotype. Morse helped spark its development in America by establishing one of the first studios in New York and taught Matthew Brady, among others, the process. The one-of-a-kind special quality of the image is indicated by the elaborate frame and case.

Library of Congress Prints and Photographs Division LC-USZC4-12153

for Niépce's camera obscura told Daguerre about the heliographs. At the age of 64, in ill health and in serious financial difficulties, Niépce reluctantly signed a contract with Daguerre to share information about the heliographic process. In 1833, Joseph Niépce died before seeing the results from Daguerre's experiments, but his son Isidore maintained the partnership. Daguerre switched from pewter to a copper plate and used mercury vapor to speed the exposure time. These technical changes resulted in a one-of-a-kind, reversed image as if seen in a mirror, of extraordinary sharpness (Figures 11.17 and 11.18). Daguerre *modestly* named the first practical photographic process the daguerreotype (Greek for "Picture by Daguerre").

On January 7, 1839, the French astronomer Arago formally announced Daguerre's invention to the prestigious Academy of Science. Upon seeing the wondrous examples, the American physician and author Oliver Wendell Holmes Sr. dubbed the reversed daguerreotype image a "mirror with a memory," while John Ruskin wrote in a letter to his father in 1845, "Daguerreotypes taken by this vivid sunlight are glorious things. It is very nearly the same thing as carrying off a palace itself—every chip of stone and stain is there." The French government paid Louis Daguerre and Isidore Niépce an annual pension in return for making the process available to the public.

The precious, positive, one-of-a-kind portraits were an instant hit because common people could finally afford to have a picture made of themselves. Before, only the wealthy could afford to hire an artist to paint a picture, which is why museums are mostly filled with images of the rich. Daguerreotypes were often displayed within elegantly crafted miniature boxes made of papier-mâché, leather, or highly finished wood. Samuel F. B. Morse, inventor of the dot-dash code used in telegraphy, opened the first photographic studio in New York City and taught many entrepreneurs, including the famous photographer Mathew Brady, the process. With a faster chemical process, a larger lens that let in more light, and a smaller plate size, exposure times were reduced to 30 seconds.

The new process needed a name other than a derivative of Daguerre. England's Sir John Herschel coined the word *photography* for the new light-sensitive process, from the Greek words that mean "writing with light." However, the process, as stunning as it was, had two significant drawbacks—it produced a positive image that couldn't be reproduced, and depending on lighting conditions, exposures were too long for fast action.

■ Calotype

Coincidentally, a different photographic process was announced the same month as the daguerreotype. Sometimes referred to as the talbotype, the calotype (Greek for "beautiful picture") was invented by William Henry Fox Talbot. The process is the foundation for modern photography.

Talbot was born in Dorset, England, in 1800. After being educated at Trinity College in Cambridge, he devoted the next 50 years of his life to studying physics, chemistry, mathematics, astronomy, and archaeology. In 1833, while vacationing in Italy, he came to the conclusion that images from a camera obscura could be

preserved using light-sensitive paper. After several experiments upon his return home in August 1835, he produced a one-inch-square paper negative of a window of his house. He then produced a positive picture by placing another sheet of sensitized paper on top of the negative image and exposing it to the sun. The exposure time was about three minutes in bright sunlight. Talbot continued to produce many views of his estate, which were later collected in the first book illustrated with photographs, *The Pencil of Nature*, published from 1844 to 1846 (Figure 11.19). The work was published without binding to subscribers who were meant to collect all 24 plates and pay to have the pages bound. But due to a lack of interest from the public, only six plates were created (Figure 11.20). The calotype process never became widespread because of two reasons—its quality when compared with daguerreotypes, and Talbot's insistence on making the process available

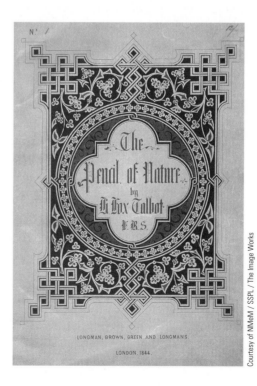

Figure 11.19
Cover of The Pencil of Nature, *1844, by William Henry Fox Talbot, the first book printed with photographs.*

Figure 11.20

*"Plate VI—The Open Door,"
1844, by William Henry Fox
Talbot. What Talbot wrote
about the picture is also a
call for being more observant
generally: "This is one of the
trifling efforts of [photogra-
phy's] infancy, which some
partial friends have been
kind enough to commend.
A painter's eye will often be
arrested where ordinary people see nothing remarkable.
A casual gleam of sunshine,
or a shadow thrown across
his path, a time withered oak,
or a moss covered stone may
awaken a train of thoughts
and feelings, and picturesque
imaginings." With Talbot's
calotype process, photography satisfied one other condition for its popularity—a
negative image that could
easily reproduce any number
of positive prints, but the
pictures weren't as sharp as
daguerreotypes.*

Courtesy of Stapleton Collection / Heritage /
The Image Works

only to those who paid for the formula.
Because a positive image had to print
through the paper fibers of the negative
view, Talbot's pictures never achieved the
sharp focus of daguerreotypes. Furthermore, unlike the daguerreotype process
that was released by the French government, Talbot charged interested parties
a large sum to learn the secret of the
calotype. Consequently, few took him
up on his offer. Nevertheless, the process
represents the first instance in which the
modern terms *negative* and *positive* were
used. Once a negative image was created,
any number of positive prints could be
made. This concept is the basis for modern
photography and encouraged economic
development of the medium until it was
replaced by digital photography.

■ *Wet-Collodion*

In March 1851, the year Louis Daguerre
died, Frederick Scott Archer published his
formula for all to read in a popular journal of the day, *The Chemist*. Archer was a
British sculptor and part-time calotype
photographer. He had grown weary of
the poor quality of prints obtained from
using paper negatives. He suggested glass
as a suitable medium for photographic
emulsion. The problem with glass, however, was in making the emulsion adhere
to its surface. However, the invention of

collodion in 1847 solved that problem.
A mixture of guncotton or nitrocellulose
dissolved in alcohol and ether, collodion
was used to protect wounds from infection. When poured on any surface, it
forms a tough film. Archer mixed collodion with light-sensitive silver nitrate.

His wet-collodion process produced
glass negatives of amazing detail and
subtlety of tone that could be used to
make hundreds of positive prints. The
exposure time was a remarkable 10 seconds. Although the process required that
the glass plate be exposed while moist
and developed immediately, serious portrait and documentary photographers
around the world used the wet-collodion
process for the next 30 years. Most of the
photographs taken during the American Civil War, for example, utilized the
wet-collodion process. However, with
the long exposure times, only before and
after battle scenes could be captured
(Figure 11.21). This era also saw the introduction of several processes that were
popular with the public such as inexpensive wet-collodion tintypes (images on
metal plates), ambrotypes (images on
paper), and albumen prints, a process that
used egg whites to bind the photographic
emulsion to paper, which was usually
used to print small calling cards that were
handed out between friends and business
associates called *carte de visites*.

■ *Color Emulsions*

Scottish physicist James Clerk Maxwell
is credited with producing the first color
slide. In a lecture to the Royal Institution in London in 1861, he admitted
that his work was influenced by Thomas
Young's discoveries about the eye's color
perception. Maxwell made three separate
pictures of a ribbon through red, green,

Figure 11.21

"Battle-field of Gettysburg—Dead Confederate sharp-shooter at foot of Little Round Top," 1863, by Timothy H. O'Sullivan. Since the famed photographer Mathew Brady was practically blind by the time of the American Civil War, he hired several photographers to take photographs for him. One of those was Timothy O'Sullivan, who made this silent study of a young sniper's body using Frederick Archer's wet-collodion process. Now, the photographic medium had two conditions met—sharp images that were reproducible.

and blue colored filters. When he projected the three separate images with the colored light from each filter at the same time and aligned the views, a color slide was the result (Figure 11.22).

But because of the impracticality of Maxwell's discovery, attention soon focused on color print materials. In 1903, Auguste and Louis Lumière, important figures in the history of motion pictures, started selling their *autochrome* photographic plates to the public. The Lumière brothers mixed red, green, and blue

colored potato starch grains randomly throughout a photographic emulsion. Although the film was quite expensive for the day, photographers immediately favored autochrome because of the quality of the images produced.

■ *Gelatin-Bromide Dry Plate*

Dr. Richard Maddox of London was an amateur scientist who helped change the face of photography and sparked motion pictures. A medical doctor and amateur

Figure 11.22

"Tartan Ribbon," 1861, by Thomas Sutton. The Scottish physicist James Clerk Maxwell had Thomas Sutton photograph a Scottish "tartan" ribbon three times, each time with a different color filter over the lens. Ironically for Maxwell, who identified the electromagnetic spectrum, the photographic emulsion used for the picture was not sensitive to the red wavelength. However, the red dye of the day used in the ribbon fluorescently created the "red" color for the film.
See color insert following page 338.

scientist and photographer, he was looking for a substitute for collodion as a photography emulsion. After experimenting with a number of sticky substances, he tried gelatin, an organic material obtained from the bones, skins, and hooves of animals. The result was a light-sensitive emulsion with silver bromide that could be manufactured, stored, and exposed much later by a photographer, unlike the wet-collodion process that had to be taken with the emulsion damp and developed immediately.

With his invention, photography was advanced to a point at which it could truly be a successful mass medium. It now had exposure times that could stop fast action, sharply focused images, and a negative that could produce any number of positive prints. Maddox's discovery led to the invention of motion picture film after

the American Thomas Edison saw stop-motion images of animals and persons as discussed in Chapter 12.

His photographic process also started the amateur photography craze after an innovation by an American inventor. George Eastman of Rochester, New York, invented cameras that used gelatin dry plate films in long rolls. In 1888, he introduced his $25 Kodak camera (in today's dollars, the camera would cost about $500). Kodak simply was an easily pronounced and remembered name that he invented (Figure 11.23). With the motto "You push the button—we do the rest," the camera came loaded with 100 exposures. After taking all the pictures, a customer mailed the camera back to Rochester where the round negatives were printed. The camera was reloaded with film and sent back. By 1900, Eastman was

Figure 11.23

Frank Church made one of the first snapshots in the history of photography. It shows George Eastman holding his invention—a Kodak camera—that made amateur photography possible. Now the photographic process was complete with sharp images, fast shutter speeds, easily reproducible images, and so simple a child can be a photographer.

Courtesy of Frank Church / George Eastman House

selling his enormously popular cameras for one dollar each ($20 today).

■ Holography

In 1947, Hungarian scientist Dennis Gabor developed holography to improve the sharpness of views obtained with an electron microscope. The unique aspect of holographic images is that they reproduce a three-dimensional view of an object photographed on one sheet of film. Russian researcher Yuri Denisyuk created a slightly different process that is used today to display logos on credit cards, unique jewelry and art presentations, novelty stickers for children, and for publications (Figure 11.24). One of the first mass-produced holographic displays was a picture of an eagle for the March 1984 cover of *National Geographic*, which featured stories on holography, China, Calgary, Canada, and the rhinoceros. In 2009 an opening bid for the issue was set at $2.99.

■ Instant

Edwin Land was a prolific American inventor with more than 500 patents to his name. In 1948, he introduced his most famous invention—the black-and-white Polaroid 50-second film camera. Instant photography was born. About 15 years later he announced a color version, calling it Polacolor. Once popular with married couples on their honeymoons and with artists and other professional photographers, the process has been replaced by digital cameras (Figure 11.25). However, artists such as William Wegman have used large-format, 20 × 24-inch cameras to produce fine-quality, one-of-a-kind Polaroid portraits. Another such artist is Stephanie Schneider, who manipulates the colors with heat and pressure to produce

Courtesy of Holography Collection, MIT Museum

Figure 11.24
A holographic image, such as this one from the Massachusetts Institute of Technology (MIT) Museum, when printed in a textbook will not reproduce the engaging three-dimensional effect when viewed on an acetate sheet from a single light source.

striking results. The Australian musician Sia Furler used about 2,500 Polaroid images in an animation style for the production of a video for her song, "Breathe Me," in 2004 (Weblink 11.1).

■ Digital

In 1981, Sony introduced its electronic still video camera, the Mavica (Magnetic Video Camera). Its two-inch disc could record only 50 color images, which were viewed on a television screen. As such, the camera was not technically a digital camera because it recorded an electronic video signal. Nevertheless, the camera started the era of digital photography, with all the major camera companies producing true digital models. After an exposure, photographers can use a program such as Photoshop and make exposure,

Figure 11.25
Polaroid photographs were once the process of choice for recording weddings and subsequent honeymoons such as these from a wedding and reception taken on a beach near San Francisco in 1989. These one-of-a-kind images should remind you of the early daguerreotype pictures—they are in sharp focus, but not easily copied.

Courtesy of Andi Stein

color balance, and cropping adjustments, just as in a traditional darkroom. The computer images can then be sent to anyone in the world via a cell phone or a wireless connection.

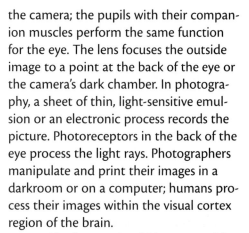

Technical Perspective

It shouldn't be surprising that a camera's parts and functions are similar to those of the eye. Knowledge of the physical workings of the eye directly helped in the camera's development. The essential elements of a camera are housed within a protective box; the eye is protected by an outgrowth of the skull. A visual artist often uses a drop of solution to clean the glass elements of the lens of dust and smudges; the eye has a built-in lens-cleaning system with its salty tears. The shutter regulates the amount of time a computer chip is exposed to light; the eyelids open and shut so that vision is possible. The aperture is an opening that lets light enter

the camera; the pupils with their companion muscles perform the same function for the eye. The lens focuses the outside image to a point at the back of the eye or the camera's dark chamber. In photography, a sheet of thin, light-sensitive emulsion or an electronic process records the picture. Photoreceptors in the back of the eye process the light rays. Photographers manipulate and print their images in a darkroom or on a computer; humans process their images within the visual cortex region of the brain.

Specifically, you should be aware of five main technical considerations when analyzing your own or someone else's image: lens type, lens opening, shutter speed, lighting, and image quality.

■ Lens Type

Lenses come in three variations: wide-angle, normal, and telephoto. As their names imply, a wide-angle lens gives a viewer an expansive, scene-setting view. The visual array photographed also has great depth of field—more is in focus. A normal lens mimics the angle of view as seen by the human eyes and is seldom used by professionals. A telephoto lens produces a close-up, narrow perspective of a scene with the foreground and background compressed. It also has a shallow depth of field with little in focus. If a photographer wants a viewer to see many details at once, a wide-angle lens is preferred over a telephoto (Figure 11.26).

■ Lens Opening

The opening of a lens is like the pupil in the eye—it regulates the amount of light that enters the camera. If you squint your eyelids, your pupils get smaller and more will be in focus. The same is true for a

Figure 11.26

"Firebomb Damaged Sale," 1981. Life and sales go on in Belfast, Northern Ireland, despite violent actions from terrorist organizations. A wide-angle lens is used not only to show as much information along the edges of the frame as possible but also to give a viewer the illusion of being in the scene.

Courtesy of Paul Martin Lester

lens. A small opening or aperture will produce an image with much a greater depth of field, whereas a large lens opening will have a shallow depth of field. Like the choice of the type of lens, a photographer can select elements of a scene she wants a viewer to notice by the choice of lens opening (Figures 11.27 and 11.28).

■ *Shutter Speed*

The amount of time a camera's shutter stays open—its shutter speed—can greatly affect a picture's content. A speed of 1/30th of a second or longer will usually cause blurring of anything that moves. A faster shutter speed will stop motion and is required to overcome shaking of the camera during exposure (referred to as *camera blur*). An important feature of many modern cameras is motion stabilizer technology that produces a sharp image during longer shutter speeds and/ or jarring conditions such as on a motorboat. An extremely fast shutter speed is necessary to photograph fast-moving subjects without blur. Sports photographers

typically use shutter speeds of 1/500th of a second and faster (Figure 11.29).

■ *Lighting*

Photography exists because of light. Knowledge of how lighting is used by photographers is essential in the analysis of an image. There are two kinds

Courtesy of Gerry Davey

Courtesy of Gerry Davey

Figures 11.27 and 11.28
"Vinton Cemetery #1, California," and "Vinton Cemetery #2, California," 2002, by Gerry Davey. With a small aperture setting on a camera's lens, objects close in the foreground as well as those in the distance are in focus. However, if a large aperture setting is chosen, a photographer can chose what to emphasize within a picture's frame by controlling focus.

Figure 11.29

An example of the stopping quality of a camera's shutter is provided by this picture of a young boy seeking relief from the 100-degree heat in Del Rio, Texas. Note how the mesquite tree in the background seems to cradle the boy in space.

of lighting: lighting that comes from available sources and lighting that the photographer brings to a location. Natural lighting, most often called available light, is illumination that already exists within a scene. Although its name implies light from the sun, it can also refer to incandescent bulbs, neon light tubes, or fire from a candle. Lighting equipment that a photographer brings to a photography shoot or that is contained within a studio is called artificial lighting. The most commonly used artificial light for location work is the electronic flash.

■ Image Quality

Learning how to evaluate the quality of an image in terms of its exposure and contrast is important. A picture that will reproduce well in a publication or for a web page must have a full range of tones supplied by proper exposure and contrast. As a general rule, a picture is considered properly exposed if it shows detail in the shadow areas and in the light areas. Contrast is defined as the difference between the black and white tones of the image. A low contrast image has little differences in light and dark areas; a high contrast picture has extreme differences (Figure 11.30). With color correcting software within a program such as Photoshop, a photographer can make most images, even those poorly exposed, acceptable for viewing. For web presentations a pixel-per-inch, or dots-per-inch (DPI), resolution of 72 with GIF, JPG, or PNG picture formats is fine. For printed work, however, a DPI of 300 or greater saved as a TIF file is preferred.

Ethical Perspective

Visual communicators must be aware of five major ethical concerns whenever images are used. Two of those concerns—visual persuasion and stereotypes—have been discussed. The three other main ethical issues are showing victims of violence, violating rights to privacy, and picture manipulations.

■ Victims of Violence

After the publication or broadcast of a controversial image that shows, for example, either dead or grieving victims of violence, people often make telephone calls and write letters attacking the photographer as being tasteless and adding to the anguish of those involved. And yet, violence and tragedy are staples of American journalism because readers have always been morbidly attracted to gruesome stories and photographs. It is as if viewers want to know that tragic circumstances exist but don't want to face the uncomfortable details (Figure 11.31).

During the war in Iraq that began in March 2003, about 500 journalists were "embedded" with military troops during the initial stage of the conflict. What resulted was an unprecedented access to fighting areas. Editors were faced with tough choices. Many of the images taken by photojournalists showed bloodied combatants and civilians—victims of the ravages of war. In a *New York Times* article, for example, a picture submitted to *Time* magazine was described as "the bloodied head of a dead Iraqi with an American soldier standing tall in the background." And yet, few images of corpses were ever shown to American print readers or television or web viewers. Arab and other news agencies around the world, however,

showed their viewers the full extent of the war with gruesome depictions and wondered why their Western media counterparts were sanitizing the violence. The difference may be one of editorial intent.

The executive director of "NBC Nightly News" explained, "You watch some Arab

Figure 11.30

With a selected exposure that creates a high contrast between the dark shadows and the sunlit wall, the diagonal lines and outline shape of the wild parrot are emphasized.

Figure 11.31

The front page of the Bakers-field Californian is a study in contrasts. Mickey Mouse and Edward Romero's grieving family share the front page. A reader firestorm of 500 letters to the editor, 400 telephone calls, 80 subscription cancellations, and one bomb threat resulted. Many readers probably were sparked to protest publication of the picture because of its insensitive display near the popular cartoon character.

coverage and you get a sense that there is a blood bath at the hand of the U.S. military. That is not my take on it." The difference may also be a judgment call based on the taste for such images by readers and viewers. The managing editor of *Time*, James Kelly, admitted, "You don't want to give the reader a sanitized war, but there has to be some judgment and taste."

Susan Sontag, author of *Regarding the Pain of Others*, took a skeptical view when she stated, "I am always suspicious when institutions talk about good taste. Taste belongs to individuals." Taste—the presumed appetite of viewers to stomach gruesome and/or controversial images—is a matter of etiquette, not ethics. The news media should report what a government does in its people's name. Sometimes that means grisly images must be a part of those reports. As Ted Koppel, then of ABC's "Nightline" said, "The fact that people get killed in a war is precisely what people need to be reminded of."

Although against the Geneva Conventions, prisoners are also tortured during

wartime—whether during a declared war or the so-called "War Against Terrorism" waged by the United States and other countries. But it is rare to see visual evidence of such abuse. The chilling images of the torture of Iraqi prisoners at Abu Ghraib in 2003 and 2004 with many that were hooded, naked, and forced to simulate sexual acts by military personnel was appalling and shameful to most everyone who saw them (Figure 11.32). In this age of high quality and relatively inexpensive digital cameras and camera phones, battlefield images taken by the soldiers themselves will no doubt reveal other horrors of war to which seasoned photojournalists will not have access. Perhaps not surprisingly, the Pentagon has banned digital cameras—including camera phones—from U.S. Army bases in Iraq. In 2009 President Obama reversed an earlier decision to release photographs "depicting alleged abuse of detainees by U.S. soldiers" for fear it might "further inflame anti-American opinion and to put our troops in greater danger." However, newspaper editorials and the American Civil Liberties Union make the point that the images are part of the historical record and should be made public. Regardless of the outcome that will be decided by the court system, the controversy shows how images more than words are highly emotional objects.

Gruesome images closer to home can have a longer impact on viewers. Reporter Charlie LeDuff of *The Detroit News* received a telephone call telling him that there was a body "encased in ice, except his legs, which are sticking out like popsicle sticks" within an elevator shaft of an abandoned warehouse. Wanting to make sure of the facts before he called police, he investigated and found the gruesome scene. The resulting story and published image shocked the citizens of Detroit and

Figure 11.32

Images of tortured victims taken with digital cameras and shared via CDs and e-mails by U.S. military personnel stationed at the Abu Ghraib prison in Iraq in 2003 and 2004 were eventually released to the public and shocked the world. Most of these gruesome pictures were not printed in newspapers, but can be easily found on the web.

Courtesy of Washington Post / Getty Images

the nation. LeDuff's report illustrated that hard economic times, with over 20,000 persons homeless, sometimes caused callous behavior that should be prevented whenever possible. A month after the gruesome find, the body was identified as a homeless man named Johnnie Redding. LeDuff described his sad life and burial in subsequent stories (Weblink 11.2).

Print and broadcast journalists have a duty to report the news as objectively, fairly, and accurately as possible. Editors and producers should be mindful that some images, because of their emotional content, have the potential to upset many people. However, decisions should be guided, never ruled, by readers and viewers. One solution attempted by some media organizations is to show controversial pictures on a website with a strong disclaimer. That way a user can decide whether or not she wants to click on the link and see the image.

■ *A Right to Privacy*

Florence Thompson looked away from Dorothea Lange's camera lens in the famous "Migrant Mother" photograph because that was the only way she thought she could protect her privacy. When subjects of news events and their families, through no fault of their own, are suddenly thrust into the harsh light of public scrutiny, they often complain bitterly, as Thompson did the rest of her life.

Many readers of newspaper and magazine special editions recoiled in horror at the images of people falling from the World Trade Center twin towers. Some of the complaints from viewers were made because it was thought family members might be able to recognize the person falling.

U.S. military officials banned photojournalists from taking pictures and videos of returning war dead at Dover Air Force Base in Delaware in 1991. It was said that the policy was made out of respect for the families' privacy. But when Russ Kick of "The Memory Hole" website was given 288 images of war dead from Afghanistan and Iraq after filing a Freedom of Information Act request, he posted the images on his website (Weblink 11.3). Many newspapers around the country published an image from the collection on their front pages (Figure 11.33). John Molino, a deputy undersecretary of defense, explained that the photographs, taken by military photographers for historical purposes, were censored because "we don't want the remains of our service members who have made the ultimate sacrifice to be the subject of any kind of attention that is unwarranted or undignified." However, a *Boston Globe* editor said, "I don't know how [the publishing of the images] can be disrespectful to the families. They are official photos of flag-draped coffins being treated with respect by military personnel." In 2009 during the Obama Administration, the Pentagon changed its policy and allowed families of the war dead to decide

Figure 11.33

Flag-draped coffins line the inside of a military transport plane as soldiers honor the dead by standing at attention and saluting. From World War II on, government officials have often censored photographs of those killed in combat from the public on the grounds that they violate the privacy of the soldiers and their families, but more often than not, such images honor those who have fallen rather than exploit them.

Courtesy of Russ Kick

whether to invite the media to their reunion with their loved ones in a casket. The return of the flag-draped coffin containing the body of 30-year-old Air Force Staff Sergeant Phillip Myers of Hopeville, Virginia, was the first fallen soldier covered by the media under the new policy.

The judicial system in America has recognized that private and public persons have different legal rights in terms of privacy. Privacy laws are much stricter in protecting private citizens not involved in a news story than they are for public celebrities who often invite media attention. As many as 60 paparazzi (if it's Britney Spears or Paris Hilton) regularly stake out the places where celebrities shop and go clubbing on a 24/7 basis. The general public often justifies such extreme behavior because of the intense interest in the celebrities. Tabloid magazines, television shows, and websites pay as much as $100,000 for an exclusive picture that shows a private moment of a troubled star. Although photographers need to be aware of the laws concerning privacy and trespass, ethical behavior should not be guided by what is strictly legal.

■ *Picture Manipulations*

Since the birth of photography, photographers have manipulated subjects and images to produce the result they desired. Hippolyte Bayard was the French inventor of a unique photographic process who did not receive the attention or pension of Louis Daguerre. In protest, he faked his own death in an 1839 photograph. It is the first example of a manipulated image in the history of photography (Figure 11.34). Roger Fenton, one of the most respected war photographers in history, moved cannonballs during the Crimean War in 1855 to make his "Valley of the Shadow of Death" image more harrowing. Coming from a painting tradition in which subjects and compositions were regularly manipulated, the Swiss Oscar Rejlander in 1857 produced a good versus evil tableau called "The Two Ways of Life" using at least 30 separate pictures within the composition (Figure 11.35). Before the invention of the halftone process, skillful engravers regularly altered the content of photographs. For example, artists regularly added and subtracted subjects portrayed in photographs for their printed engravings of the American Civil War. A curious artistic process common in newspaper photographs from the turn of the 20th century until as late as the 1970s was the heavy retouching of news images. Retouchers with paints, inks, airbrushes, and scissors "would remove backgrounds to make stark silhouettes or add additional elements, including cut-in vignettes or cutaway diagrams of events."

Critics get most upset when images intended for documentary and news purposes are altered for aesthetic reasons. The wake-up call for many was a 1982 cover story on Egypt in *National Geographic.* A pyramid in Giza was moved

Figure 11.34

"Self-Portrait as a Drowned Man," 1840, by Hippolyte Bayard. The French inventor Hippolyte Bayard created the first practical photographic process that predated the daguerreotype, had the first public exhibition of photographs, made the first self-portrait, and created the first manipulated picture in the history of medium. Frustrated by not receiving recognition from the French government that Daguerre and Niépce enjoyed, Bayard staged a photograph with a caption that read, "The corpse which you see here is that of M. Bayard. The Government which has been only too generous to Monsieur Daguerre, has said it can do nothing for Monsieur Bayard, and the poor wretch has drowned himself."

Figure 11.35

One of the first images to be manipulated by a photographer was Oscar Rejlander's "Two Ways of Life." He spliced 30 separate pictures together to form the composite. Gambling, drinking, sexual activity, and vanity are the themes to the young boy's right, and pious behavior, education, philanthropy, and hard work are presented on the other side.

by computer software to accommodate the vertical format (Weblink 11.4). Readers who had been to Egypt immediately contacted the magazine to question how the image could have been produced. As a result, the director of photography at the time was forced to resign, and all of the images *and* words within the magazine were subject to question. You may purchase this famous cover on eBay for a starting bid of $9.99.

The police mug shot of O.J. Simpson arrested for the murder of his wife and her friend in 1994 was used for the covers of *Time* and *Newsweek* magazines the same week (Weblink 11.5). The *Time* cover was criticized for illustrator Matt Mahurin's darkening of O.J.'s facial features, which some said was a slap at all African Americans, and yet *Newsweek* was never criticized for the manipulation of the words on the cover, "A Trail of Blood." Brian Walski of the *Los Angeles Times* was fired for a photo composite he created while a photojournalist covering the war in Iraq (Weblink 11.6). No doubt fatigue, tough conditions, and competition were factors responsible for him combining parts of

two images into a third. However, there is no good reason for such an ethical lapse. Credibility is a precious commodity that should be protected with as much fervor as can be mustered.

But there is little credibility with some types of photography. Wedding and portrait photographers remove unwanted warts and wrinkles from their subjects. Advertising art directors customarily combine parts of pictures, change colors, and create fantasy images to attract customers. Most persons are well aware of such practices and knowingly suspend disbelief when looking at portrait and advertising images. Still, examples such as a *Newsweek* cover photograph of Martha Stewart's smiling face just after she was let out of prison sitting on top someone else's body, a portrait of CBS News anchor Katie Couric with a digitally slimmed waist, and tennis player Andy Roddick with computer-enhanced arms on the cover of *Men's Fitness*, all help to degrade the photographic medium's credibility as a whole. Ironically, during the 2008 presidential campaign, many criticized a close-up portrait of Governor Sarah Palin on the cover of *Newsweek* because it *wasn't* touched-up.

 Cultural Perspective

The story of photography, as with any other medium, is never simply about the technical contributions made by scientists and inventors to improve the process. Technological advances allow photographers to communicate the cultural values of the time, but a photographer's style is formed by the culture in which the pictures are made. Studying the images produced within a certain time period is a study of the society from which they come. Throughout the history of photography, various photographic styles have reflected the people and the times.

■ *Photographer as Portraitist*

One of the earliest uses of the photographic medium was to capture the faces of people, both famous and ordinary.

Eventually, photography became a great equalizer. Because long exposure times and bright sunlight were required for early photography, Victorian portrait subjects appear to be grim, unsmiling people. In reality, they had to keep still in order to get the best picture possible.

In the 19th century, several photographers created a photographic style that reflected the culture of the times. Scottish calotype photographers David Octavius Hill and Robert Adamson made sensitive studies of ordinary people. Julia Margaret Cameron, one of the few women in visual communication history, made dynamic images of her famous friends: Alfred Tennyson, Sir John Herschel, Thomas Carlyle, Charles Darwin, Robert Browning, and Henry Longfellow (Figure 11.36). Gaspard Felix Tournachon, or Nadar, as he was known, matched his bold shooting style with the strong personalities of the day. Before he photographed the Civil War, Mathew Brady had portrait galleries in New York and Washington. Brady is credited for the daguerreotype image of President Lincoln that appears on the redesigned five-dollar bill that was first issued in 2008 (Figure 11.37).

The portrait tradition continued with August Sander's portraits of everyday German citizens before World War II, Diane Arbus's direct and sensitive portraits of extraordinary subjects, Irving Penn's series of everyday workers, Richard Avedon's large-format images of known and unknown Americans, and Philip-Lorca Di Corcia's "Heads," portraits of random pedestrians at Times Square, New York. A standout in this genre is Annie Leibovitz, who made the sensitive portrait of John Lennon and Yoko Ono taken for *Rolling Stone* early on the day of the Beatle's death, the naked and pregnant Demi Moore on the cover of *Vanity Fair*, and

Figure 11.36

"Sir John Herschel," 1867, by Julia Margaret Cameron. One of the most respected individuals in the history of photography is the British astronomer and scientist Sir John Herschel. He not only discovered a way to make photographic images so they wouldn't eventually fade if exposed to light, he also invented the cyanotype photographic process later called "blueprints" used by the English botanist Anna Atkins and in architecture, created the first picture on glass, and came up with the terms "snapshot," "negative," "positive," and most importantly, the word "photography," Greek for "writing with light." Julia Margaret Cameron, born in India, took up photography when she was 48 years old. She eventually made portraits of many of the most important figures in the worlds of literature and science at that time.

Courtesy of Stapleton Collection / Historical Picture Library / Corbis

Queen Elizabeth II during her state visit to Virginia (Weblink 11.7). Another is the relative newcomer Suzanne Opton, whose close-up portraits of American soldiers who have served in Iraq or Afghanistan have been shown in print, on websites, and on public billboards (Figure 11.38).

■ Photographer as Painter

Many painters feared that photography would soon replace their profession. To hedge their bets, some artists became photographers who mimicked the style of allegorical painters to tell a story with photographs in the tradition of paintings of the day. Two photographers who worked in this style during the 19th century were Oscar Rejlander and Henry Peach Robinson. Rejlander's "The Two Ways of Life" was discussed earlier. Robinson's most famous image, "Fading Away," is a combination print using five separate pictures to show a young woman on her deathbed. Other photographers thought that the new medium should have its own style distinct and apart from that of painting. A photographic school known as "straight photography," headed by Edward Weston and Ansel Adams, shunned manipulated work. Contemporary photographers Vicky Alexander, Richard Prince, and Mike and Doug Starn use "cut-and-paste" techniques to produce elaborate artistic renderings from their own or previously published pictures (Figure 11.39).

■ Photographer as Landscape Documentarian

Photographers have always enjoyed taking pictures of natural scenes. When the American Civil War ended, Timothy O'Sullivan and William Jackson traveled west to explore and photograph scenic

Courtesy of the Library of Congress, Prints and Photographs Division, LC-US26-2064

views with their awkward wet-collodion technology. In 1873, O'Sullivan made one of his most famous pictures at the ruins of "White House" at the Cañon de Chelle in Arizona (Figure 11.40). The power of photography to shape the opinion of others is demonstrated by these views of the land. The images became synonymous with what people thought of as natural and beautiful. Jackson, who lived to be 99 years old, made the first photographs of the Yellowstone area in 1871, which helped convince Congress to set aside the land as the country's first national park because the land was viewed, within the photographs, as naturally beautiful. Following in the footsteps of the early landscape photographers, Ansel Adams, Wynn Bullock, and Harry Callahan all have made photographs that record exquisitely nature's beauty and sharpen our sense of wonder of it. Contemporary New York photographer Paul Raphaelson captures hauntingly beautiful post-apocalyptic urban landscapes (Weblink 11.8).

Figure 11.37

"Abraham Lincoln," daguerreotype (reversed), 1864, by Mathew Brady. Born in upstate New York, Mathew Brady moved to New York City when he was 18 years old and learned the daguerreotype process from the American inventor of the telegraph, Samuel Morse, who had his own studio. Three years later Brady opened his own studio, and by the time of the American Civil War he was the most famous photographer of his day. Despite reservations from friends, Brady hired and outfitted more than 20 photographers, including Alexander Gardner and Timothy O'Sullivan, to document the battles of the Civil War; Brady took credit for their photographic work. He spent more than $100,000 of his own money (equivalent to about $2.4 million today) and never recouped his investment. Depressed over his financial situation and the death of his wife, he died penniless in the charity ward of a New York hospital after being struck by a streetcar in 1896.

Figure 11.38

"Birkholz—353 Days in Iraq, 205 Days in Afghanistan," 2007, by Suzanne Opton. For her "Soldier" series, Suzanne Opton photographed nine American soldiers who were between tours in Iraq and Afghanistan stationed at Fort Drum, New York. Of her series, Opton says, "We all experience strategic moments when we feel most alive. These are the moments we will always remember, be they transcendent or horrific. After all, what are we if not our collection of memories? In making these portraits of soldiers, I simply wanted to look in the face of someone who'd seen something unforgettable."

Figure 11.39

"Attracted to Light 1," toned silver prints on Thai mulberry paper, 4 × 7.3 yards, 1996–2002, by Doug and Mike Starn. The size of this composite piece might evoke the Japanese science fiction classic Mothra (1961), the first of the Godzilla monster genre of movies, metaphors for the use of weapons of mass destruction. At once aesthetically pleasing with subtle tones, textual intricacies, and a gestalt sensibility, it is also slightly menacing as you become hypnotized by the insect's incessant stare.

See color insert following page 338.

Courtesy of Suzanne Opton

■ *Photographer as Artist*

Many traditional artists have looked down on photography, thinking it a simple craft. Another problem artists had with photography was that any number of images could be made from a single negative. Therefore, acceptance of photography as a fine art on the same level as painting was slow in coming. One of the most important figures in elevating the medium to a fine art was the American Alfred Stieglitz (Figure 11.41).

Not only did he exploit photography's unique technological features, he also opened a gallery that exhibited painting and photography on an equal footing and published a critical journal about photography, *Camera Work*. Married to artist Georgia O'Keeffe, he was a strong proponent of modern art photography and inspired many photographers to build that tradition. Recent photographers who view photography as a way of expressing a deeply personal statement include Lucien Clerque, Yasumasa Morimura, and Sandy

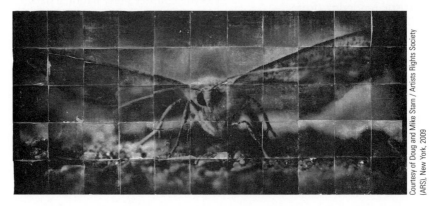

Courtesy of Doug and Mike Starn / Artists Rights Society (ARS), New York, 2009

EXPEDITION OF 1873.

1st Lieut. GEO. M. WHEELER,
Corps of Engineers Commanding.

LC-DIG-stereo-1s00363

Figure 11.40

Stereocard of "Ancient Ruins in the Cañon de Chelle, New Mexico," 1873, by Timothy O'Sullivan. Born in New York City, Timothy O'Sullivan was a teenager when he was hired by Mathew Brady to work in his studio. After fighting in the Civil War as a Union Army officer and honorably discharged, he joined Brady's team of photographers to document war participants and the aftermath of battles. One of his most powerful images is the eerily disturbing "The Harvest of Death," taken after the battle at Gettysburg, Pennsylvania, as seen in Figure 8.14. Perhaps disgusted by the death and destruction, after the war O'Sullivan joined several expeditions exploring the western United States and Panama. But after an expedition's boat capsized while exploring the Colorado River, he lost most of his 300 glass negatives. However, the image of the majestic Native American ruins precariously set within a canyon's wall survived. Nine years after he made the photograph, O'Sullivan died of tuberculosis at the age of 42.

Skoglund. In a reversal of the process, Marc Trujillo makes large paintings that feature a street corner with gas a station, workers in a fast food drive-in restaurant, and passersby in a shopping mall that look like color photographs (Figure 11.42).

■ *Photographer as Social Documentarian*

Because images have the capacity to spark interest and convey emotional messages, many photographers have used the medium to shed light on social problems in the hope of getting the public to act. In 1877, John Thompson teamed with writer Adolphe Smith for a book about London's poor, *Victorian London Street Life*. Newspaper reporter-turned-photographer Jacob Riis used photography to illustrate his writings and lectures on the slums in New York City (Figure 11.43). In 1890, he published his work in a book, *How the Other Half Lives*. In 1909, Lewis Wickes Hine managed to help enact child labor laws with his sensitive portraits of children working in dangerous, backbreaking occupations around the country (Figure 11.44).

Following in their tradition, French photographers Eugene Atget in the 1920s, a social documentarian with a view camera, and Henri Cartier-Bresson in the 1930s, with a small, handheld camera, showed views of ordinary people. Cartier-Bresson captured the "decisive moment"—a term he used to describe the instant when content and composition are at their most revealing.

The FSA photographers documented living conditions of homeless people for the U.S. government during the Great Depression. Photographers for *Life* magazine, most notably W. Eugene Smith, produced photographic stories that illustrated the lives of diverse individuals. Mary Ellen Mark, James Nachtwey, Eugene Richards, and Sebastião Salgado are photojournalists who continue in Smith's documentary style tradition. Greg Constantine is an independent photojournalist who travels the world documenting displaced persons, and his images are used by such groups as Doctors Without Borders and the United Nations Refugee Agency (Figure 11.45; Weblink 11.9).

Figure 11.41

"A Bit of Venice," 1894, by Alfred Stieglitz. One of the most important figures in the history of photography as a practitioner, editor, and advocate, Alfred Stieglitz elevated the medium into a respected fine art form. Born in New York to upper-middle-class parents, he studied mechanical engineering in Germany where he happened to enroll in a chemistry class taught by the photographer and inventor Hermann Vogel. Intrigued with the medium, Stieglitz entered and won several competitions. He later promoted photography through two publications, Camera Notes *and* Camera Work, *the Photo-Secession pictorial art movement, and his galleries "291" and "An American Place." Taken while on his honeymoon with his first wife, whom he left in 1923 to marry the American artist Georgia O'Keeffe, who was known for her erotic paintings of flowers, "A Bit of Venice" reveals the ethereal and transformative power of photographs over paintings after you realize that this corner of the canalled city actually existed in the real world.*

Courtesy of Allen Memorial Art Museum, Oberlin College

 *Critical Perspective*

Photography was invented at the height of the Industrial Revolution, during which millions of people around the world eventually had more money and free time to spend taking pictures. Photography, with its emphasis on realistic scenes, freed artists to be more expressive. Impressionism and surrealism, for example, flourished because painters no longer had to render natural scenes exactly on canvas.

Photography educated people about social problems within their own communities and among native peoples around the world. Visual messages inspired immigrants to learn to read words after pictures hooked them into buying a newspaper. But photography also was used to mislead and misinform. Government agencies in both totalitarian and democratic countries used photography to persuade citizens to adopt a desired point of view.

Photographs entertain and educate. They provide a historical record that relies on the idea that a camera does not lie. Throughout the history of photography, the picture enjoyed far greater credibility than the printed or spoken word. But computer operators who can alter the content of a digitized news picture as easily as an advertising image are undermining the picture's credibility.

■ TRENDS TO WATCH FOR PHOTOGRAPHY

Photography is undergoing exciting and challenging changes. This era in its history is not unlike the time when the wet-collodion process was replaced by the gelatin bromide dry plate. Of the nine major advances in the technological history of photography, only four have significantly changed the way people think about the medium. The daguerreotype introduced the world to the medium. The wet-collodion process proved that photography could be a high-quality and reproducible method of communicating visual messages to large numbers of people. The gelatin-bromide dry plate process made photography easy for both amateurs and professionals. Finally, digital photography, which combines the medium with the computer, promises unlimited possibilities for visual communicators. As more of us view photographs on monitors, paper prints are less important. Home computers contain collections of images that can be easily shared through wireless connections. Viewers can share their precious pictures with anyone anywhere in the world.

Courtesy of Marc Trujillo

Figure 11.42

"6800 Hayvenhurst Avenue," oil on canvas, 2008, by Marc Trujillo. Although photography is not used in his artistic process, Marc Trujillo's paintings of drive-thru restaurants, big box stores, and shopping malls display a photographic presence combined with an Edward Hopper unease.
See color insert following page 338.

Still cameras may be replaced by digital camcorders that enable the recording of still and moving images with the same quality. If a viewer wants to see a single frame from a recording, the equipment satisfies that option with simply the press of a key or utterance of a word or two. But the stilled moment will always be a vital component of mass communication messages because there is no way to escape its underlying power. As Carina Chocano, a critic for the *Los Angeles Times*, wrote, "Video may dominate the visible world, but still photography trumps it when it comes to administering electric jolts to the imagination."

Examples of the need for still images are easy to find in both the art and documentary worlds. For example, director Steven Soderbergh's trailer for his 2005 motion picture *Bubble* was a tribute to still photography, with spooky images taken within a doll factory (Weblink 11.10). David Crawford (Weblink 11.11) takes hundreds of still images of persons riding subways throughout the world and then creates stop-motion studies. When seen on a computer, the effect is a moving, still

image. A commercial for the Olympus PEN camera used a stop-motion animation technique with about 10,000 photographs that told the story of a man's life in an intriguing and compelling visual array (Weblink 11.12). Artists who use the stop-motion technique with still photographs present their work on YouTube.com. Noah Kalina took one picture of himself

Courtesy of Bettmann / CORBIS

Figure 11.43

"Bandit's Roost," New York City, 1888, by Richard Hoe Lawrence. Social reformer Jacob Riis was not a trained photographer, so he often hired them to accompany him on his nightly journeys through New York's seedy underworld. He used the pictures in his lectures and for his book, *How the Other Half Lives.* One of the most famous photographs that he took credit for, *"Bandit's Roost,"* was actually taken by Richard Hoe Lawrence. Taken in an alley off Mulberry Street, today located within New York's Chinatown district, a menacing and accommodating street gang poses for the photograph. The lines of laundry in the background were a favorite of Riis who wrote, "The true line to be drawn between pauperism and honest poverty is the clothesline. With it begins the effort to be clean that is the first and best evidence of a desire to be honest."

Figure 11.44

"Newsboys Selling on Brooklyn Bridge, 3 a.m.," 1908, by Lewis Wickes Hine. The American sociologist Lewis Hine encouraged his students at New York's Ethical Culture School to use photographs to document the immigrants arriving daily into the city. After he tried it himself, he devoted the rest of his life to documentary photography. Working for the National Child Labor Committee, he made thousands of pictures of children suffering under long hours in dangerous situations throughout the United States so that the images could be used as evidence to persuade members of Congress to enact child labor laws. He also documented the efforts of the Red Cross in America and in Europe, the construction of the Empire State Building, and served as the chief photographer with the government's Works Progress Administration (WPA), which concentrated on how work affects workers.

Figure 11.45

"Bihari woman," by Greg Constantine. During Pakistani rule, the Bihari were a prosperous and privileged community, but after a civil war in East Pakistan resulted in the birth of Bangladesh, they were fired from government jobs and lost ownership of their land. Since 1971 more than 300,000 live in 66 refugee camps where they are exploited, harassed, and unwanted.

Courtesy of the Library of Congress, Prints and Photographs Division, LC-DIG-nclc-03189

every day starting in 2000 and continues to add to the collection the first day of every month (Figure 11.46; Weblink 11.13), "madandcrazychild" took a photo of herself every day for 200 days (Weblink 11.14), and in a parody of the genre, "Phil" took a picture of himself every day for two days (Weblink 11.15).

One still image project didn't require a camera. A flash mob called "Improv Everywhere," comprising more than 200 individuals, dispersed randomly within the Main Concourse of Grand Central Station in New York City (Weblink 11.16). At the same moment they all stood perfectly still for five minutes. Commuters and tourists were obviously intrigued by the stunt and gave a round of applause when the frozen players started moving again.

For documentary presentations, Brian Storm (Weblink 11.17) maintains one of the premiere websites to see the work of still photographers within multimedia presentations that also include voice-overs, sound, music, and interactive navigation features. With a master's degree in photojournalism from the prestigious University of Missouri and experiences as the former director of multimedia for MSNBC.com and vice president of News, Multimedia & Assignment Services for the picture agency Corbis, Storm runs a multimedia production studio, MediaStorm, that presents stories created by journalists throughout the world. He also trains professionals and academics how to make

Courtesy of Greg Constantine

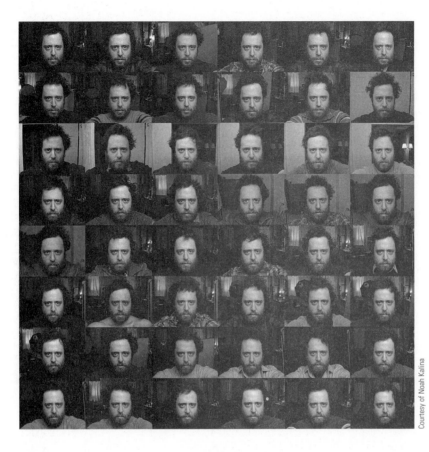

Courtesy of Noah Kalina

Figure 11.46

"Everyday," detail, 2009, by Noah Kalina. New York based Noah Kalina is primarily an advertising photographer with clients that include Motorola, Sony, and Neiman Marcus, but he possesses an artist's independent spirit. On January 11, 2000, he started to photograph his face every day, a project that continues. A video of the collection was a YouTube favorite and inspired many imitators.

their own multimedia programs. Its "Crisis Guide: Darfur" produced for the Council on Foreign Relations and "Kingsley's Crossing" by Olivier Jobard won Emmy Awards. Other stories tell of the lives of women raped in Rwanda in 1994, drug addicts in a New York City apartment, and the lives of Kurdish people in northern Iraq—stories you rarely can find on paper (Figure 11.47).

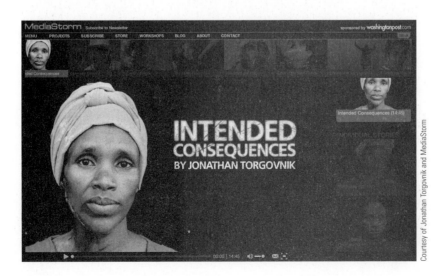

Courtesy of Jonathan Torgovnik and MediaStorm

Figure 11.47

"Intended Consequences by Jonathan Torgovnik," 2009. The MediaStorm interactive multimedia website is a showcase of the best photojournalism can offer with text, audio, and video presentations. "Intended Consequences" records the aftermath of the 1994 Rwanda war between the native tribes of Hutu and Tutsis that resulted in more than 800,000 persons killed. It is estimated that 20,000 children were born from rapes of women perpetrated by soldiers. There was also a rampant spread of HIV/AIDS. Women survivors tell their stories in words and pictures on the website.

Regardless of how still and moving images are combined and presented, the stilled moment will always be important. A moving image shocks, illuminates, and entertains, but it is fleeting, quickly replaced by another picture. A stilled image, one that freezes time forever in a powerfully arresting moment, will always have the capacity to rivet a viewer's attention so that long-term analysis is possible.

■ *KEY TERMS*

- Abu Ghraib
- Airbrush
- Allegorical
- American Civil Liberties Union
- Aperture
- Bitumen of Judea
- Collodion
- Contrast
- Crop
- Darkroom
- Depth of field
- Dioramas
- Doctors Without Borders
- Dust Bowl
- eBay
- Electromagnetic spectrum
- Emulsion
- Flash
- Flash mob
- Geneva Conventions
- Gelatin
- GIF
- Grain
- Impressionism
- Industrial Revolution
- JPG
- Large-format camera
- *Life* magazine
- Lithography
- Paparazzi
- Plate
- Polio
- Silver bromide
- Silver nitrate
- Surrealism
- TIF
- Visual cortex
- Visual journalists

To locate active URLs for the weblinks mentioned in this chapter, please go to the companion site at http://communication.wadsworth.com/lester5 and select the proper chapter.

Motion Pictures

Chapter 12

According to the Internet Movie Database (imdb.com), there have been 578,442 motion pictures made throughout the world from 1895 to 2010, or an average of about 5,000 movies a year.

Only one of those movies is consistently rated the best film ever—*Citizen Kane* (Figure 12.1).

The American Film Institute (AFI), founded in 1967, is a nonprofit organization that helps to preserve the future of filmmaking. In 2007 it polled 1,500 film artists, critics, and historians to determine the greatest movies of all time. The top ten, starting from tenth place, were *The Wizard of Oz* (1939), *Vertigo* (1958), *Schindler's List* (1993), *Lawrence of Arabia* (1962), *Gone with the Wind* (1939), *Singin' in the Rain* (1952), *Raging Bull* (1980), *Casablanca* (1942), *The Godfather* (1972), and *Citizen Kane* (1941).

The AFI website hints at the reason for the movie's exalted position: "[Orson] Welles broke all the rules and invented some new ones with his searing story of a newspaper publisher with an uncanny resemblance to William Randolph Hearst." Orson Welles was fortunate that his first Hollywood movie matched his brash, self-confident personality.

But he could not have made such a respected film alone; he had a lot of help. Herman Mankiewicz, a Hollywood writer for the previous 15 years for more than 50 movies such as *Gentlemen Prefer Blondes* (1928) and uncredited for *The Wizard of Oz* (1939), helped Welles write the screenplay. Joseph Cotten, Agnes Moorehead, and several other radio actors—many making their film debuts—were brought to Hollywood for the picture. Welles also assembled a technical team second to

The movies are the only business where you can go out front and applaud yourself.

Will Rogers (1879–1935)
COWBOY, ACTOR, HUMORIST

Figure 12.1

A "one sheet" for Citizen Kane *not designed by Saul Bass shows the lead characters and their opinions of Kane.*

none. Vernon Walker, a photographer for the spectacular movie *King Kong* (1933), coordinated the many special effects in the movie. The film editor, a young RKO staff employee named Robert Wise, would go on to direct *The Day the Earth Stood Still* (1951), *West Side Story* (1961), *The Sound of Music* (1965), and *Star Trek: The Motion Picture* (1979). Mercury Theater colleague Bernard Hermann, who won an Academy Award for his scoring of *All That Money Can Buy* (1941), composed and arranged the music for *Kane* and other productions such as *Psycho* (1960), "The Twilight Zone" (1959–1963), and *Taxi Driver* (1976). Famed cinematographer Gregg Toland, who had just won an Academy Award for his work in *Wuthering Heights* (1939), was in charge of photography.

Yet despite its best intentions, *Citizen Kane* was a financial disaster. Although

praised by critics, mass theater audiences of the day were accustomed to seeing lightweight action and comedic films— not a dark, moody psychological drama with an unhappy ending. Film critic André Bazin wrote that the motion picture was "decidedly above the mental age of the average American spectator." Although nominated for several Oscars, the film won only one award—for best screenplay.

Born on May 6, 1915, George Orson Welles was the second son of a troubled, yet creative, family in Kenosha, Wisconsin. His father, Richard, was a frustrated inventor who died early from alcoholism. His mother, Beatrice, was a strong supporter of women's rights, an excellent rifle shot, and a failed professional pianist.

From an early age Orson attracted media attention. In newspaper articles he was praised as a "boy genius"—at the age of two he could read fluently, at seven he could recite passages from Shakespeare's *King Lear*, and at ten he started producing backyard plays of his own. At 16 years old Welles made a walking tour of Ireland and ended up at the famous Gate Theater in Dublin. He convinced the Irish owners that he was a famous actor from the New York Guild Theater. Consequently, he became the first American actor ever to guest star with the Abbey Players of Dublin. After returning to New York and getting more acting experience, his booming voice landed him radio work (Figure 12.2). For the NBC broadcast "The March of Time," he supplied the voices for the dictators Mussolini and Hitler. He also played the popular mystery character Lamont Cranston on "The Shadow."

In 1938, CBS offered the theater group a contract to produce radio dramas, naming the program "Mercury Theater on the Air." The acting troupe regularly produced classic works such as *Treasure Island* and *Jane Eyre*. But Welles wanted to stage a

Library of Congress, Prints and Photographs Division, LC-US262-119765

Library of Congress Prints and Photographs Division LC-US262-49253

Figure 12.2 (left)
Orson Welles in 1937 when he was 22 years old, four years before the release of Citizen Kane.

Figure 12.3 (right)
The American newspaper magnate William Randolph Hearst in 1906 when he was 43 years old.

science fiction piece for Halloween and selected H. G. Wells's *War of the Worlds.* The night before the broadcast, however, he thought the script too dull and rewrote it in a documentary style similar to the "March of Time" news program of the day. The result was one of the most sensational broadcasts ever produced. Despite numerous reminders that the show was a fictionalized account of a novel, millions of radio listeners were convinced that Martians had invaded Earth. People fled in all directions to escape cities, limbs were broken in fights as people tried to get away, and priests were called to hear final confessions. One of the readers of the "War of the Worlds" controversy was RKO Pictures president George Schaefer. At the time the studio was close to bankruptcy. Schaefer thought Welles could offer a lifeline. With a promise of complete freedom over production and a three-picture deal worth $100,000 ($1.5 million today) each, Schaefer lured Welles to Hollywood to make movies.

After considering and rejecting several ideas, Welles decided to produce a

movie that he and screenwriter Herman Mankiewicz had conceived. Originally titled *American*, it was an obviously critical biography of newspaper publisher William Randolph Hearst (Figure 12.3). As a former newspaper reporter, Mankiewicz was familiar with the intricacies of Hearst's financial empire and his personal strengths and failings. As a visitor to Hearst's castle in central California, San Simeon, Mankiewicz had witnessed many of the excesses made possible by the publisher's enormous wealth (Figure 12.4). Hearst's passion for collecting art objects from around the world, staging elaborate picnics, and supporting his mistress, the actress Marion Davies, all were a part of Mankiewicz's screenplay. The script was written by Welles and Mankiewicz with editorial supervision by the actor John Houseman during the summer of 1939, and the idea might have come from a novel by Aldous Huxley, *After Many a Summer Dies The Swan*. Published that same year, Huxley's book told the story of an egomaniacal newspaper magnate who

Frank Vetere / Alamy

Figure 12.4

The Hearst castle, called San Simeon, now a California historical monument, overlooks the central California coastline and features 30 fireplaces and 38 bedrooms. It is so large there are five separate tours visitors can take. A view of the Roman-style indoor pool gives a hint of the castle's excessive opulence.

lived in an even larger castle than San Simeon and who had a mistress. Although Welles always denied the connection between Hearst and Kane, no one was convinced there wasn't one.

Shooting for *Citizen Kane* began on July 30, 1940, and was completed on October 23. Extremely tight security fanned rumors about its connection to Hearst. The film was scheduled to be released on Valentine's Day, 1941, but the opening was delayed after Louella Parsons, Hollywood correspondent for the Hearst newspapers, viewed an early screening. She relayed the message to Schaefer that Hearst would sue the studio if it released the film. Schaefer quickly invited the press for a sneak preview after which the movie received favorable reviews. But because of the threats from Hearst's organization, Schaefer had trouble finding theaters that would show the movie. For the public openings in New York, Chicago, and Los Angeles, RKO-owned theaters were hastily prepared. When Hearst felt that the published attacks on the film gave it

too much publicity, the negative stories ceased, but Hearst allowed no advertising about the movie to appear in any of his newspapers. In a last, desperate attempt to have the film shown, Schaefer sent the picture as a package deal with other RKO movies. Nevertheless, most theater owners did not show the movie (Weblink 12.1).

Despite receiving nine nominations including Best Picture, Best Director, and Best Actor for Welles and winning an Oscar for the screenplay, the film was booed at the Academy Awards ceremony. In 2003, Beatrice Welles, the youngest of the director's three daughters, tried to sell the golden statue at an auction sponsored by Christie's of New York. It was expected that someone would buy it for more than $300,000. However, the piece was withdrawn after the Academy of Motion Picture Arts and Sciences bought back the Oscar for $1, an arrangement it has with its awardees.

Welles was labeled a troublemaker, but he continued to direct and act in such highly revered motion pictures as *The Magnificent Ambersons* (1942), *Touch of Evil* (1958), and *Chimes at Midnight* (1965). The prestigious British Film Institute rated him the greatest film director of all time over Alfred Hitchcock, Jean-Luc Godard, and Jean Renoir. The Institute also rated *Citizen Kane* as the greatest movie of all time.

Late in his life, grossly overweight but still in possession of a Shakespearean voice and able to tell insider Hollywood stories, Welles made commercials for Eastern Airlines and Paul Masson wines and appeared regularly on the talk shows of Johnny Carson and Dick Cavett. Two hours after he taped an interview on Merv Griffin's show, Welles died of a heart attack at the age of 70 in his Los Angeles home in 1985 (Weblink 12.2). Unlike

Kane, no one heard his last word. Welles once said, "Hollywood is a golden suburb for golf addicts, gardeners, men of mediocrity, and satisfied stars. I belong to none of these categories."

■ ANALYSIS OF *CITIZEN KANE*

The opening of the movie is a metaphor for the entire picture. In a series of tracking shots that begin outside the castle gate of the once stately Xanadu estate showing a NO TRESPASSING sign, the camera moves us closer to a light from Kane's bedroom window, which always maintains the same position in various shots.

And just when the window is reached, the light suddenly goes off and Kane speaks his last word, the enigmatic "Rosebud" (Figure 12.5). The scene loudly shifts to a newsreel that serves as an obituary for the publishing tycoon. But toward the end of the footage, the documentary stops and the scene shifts to a smoky room filled with journalists who are given the task to discover, through interviews with his associates, why Kane uttered the word "Rosebud." The rest of the film is divided into four sections in which his banker reveals Kane's early life, his business associate tells about the newspaper empire and details of his first marriage, his former best friend analyzes his personality and the reason for his downfall, and his second wife, in an alcoholic haze, gives details about the frustrated and sad old man Kane had become. In the end, none of his associates could solve the mystery of "Rosebud." But the audience learns the secret. The scene of workmen burning some of the objects that had accumulated over the years in his castle shows the name "Rosebud" on a sled given to Kane as a boy (Figure 12.6). A symbol of

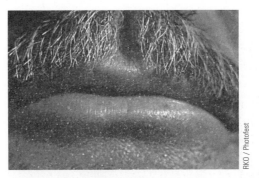

RKO / Photofest

Figure 12.5

One of the most famous dying words ever uttered by a real or fictional person, "Rosebud," is said at the start of the movie by the Orson Welles's character Charles Foster Kane. Close-up photography and enhanced audio effects emphasized this important scene in the movie.

The Everett Collection

Figure 12.6

In the end, the mystery of Kane's last word was relatively simple—the name of the sled young Charles possessed as a child. But the symbolism of the toy is quite complex. While clutching "Rosebud," eight-year-old Kane (Buddy Swan) is introduced to Thatcher (George Coulouris), his future guardian, while his parents (Harry Shannon and Agnes Moorehead) observe.

lost youth, missed opportunities, or an acknowledgment of Kane's love of objects over people—viewers are left to make sense of the movie's central riddle on their own.

As with Gutenberg's invention in which established components were combined into a commercial printing press, Welles didn't invent the film techniques used in the movie. He simply combined many different ideas into one work. Until *Kane*, movies of the day were dominated by snappy dialogue and unusual situations, but the visual messages weren't as important. Orson Welles combined the

Figure 12.7

*The "deep-focus" effect cre-
ated by cinematographer
Gregg Toland, as evident in
this scene from* Citizen Kane,
*allowed the viewer more
control in selecting which
part of a set to watch. Note
also that the top of the set is
covered—another innovation
of the motion picture.*

Figure 12.8

*Orson Welles during the
filming of* Citizen Kane.

most recent technical innovations for
producing visual messages with choreographed actions by actors to move the
plot along on several levels. Gregg Toland
took advantage of new lighting and film
stock to perfect a technique called "deep
focus." With higher-quality lights, faster
film, and wide-angle lenses, Toland could

have a depth of field that carried from
20 inches to several hundred feet (Figure
12.7). Consequently, Welles was able to
exploit this technical advantage in his
staging of the actors. Action could take
place simultaneously in the foreground
and in the background. Film critic André
has written that the technique gave viewers much more freedom in deciding which
part of the screen they wanted to watch.

Welles also requested that the sets
include muslin ceilings so that extreme
up-angle perspectives could be used.
Few directors ever thought to bother
with ceilings for their sets because most
shots were at eye level. Also, lighting and
microphones were hung from the top
of sets. Nevertheless, Welles presented a
much more realistic visual message with
the addition of ceilings. Lighting was high
in contrast and usually from behind. The
effect dramatically separated the actors
from their surroundings.

When asked if he knew that he was
making a masterpiece, Welles answered
simply, "I never doubted it for a single
instant." The trouble with creating a
perfect work of art your first time out is:
Where do you go from there? Unfortunately, Welles could not improve upon his
initial work because such an effort would
have been almost impossible for anyone.

David Denby, movie critic for *The New
Yorker* magazine, wrote about motion
pictures, "Almost every movie, of course,
is a fantasy, or a fable, or a fairy tale of one
kind or another. In a great movie, though,
narrative and technological magic combine to produce heightened intimations
of the real, and that ecstatic merging of
magic and reality is what imprints the
movie on our emotional memory." *Citizen Kane*, as a great movie, will always be
remembered (Figure 12.8).

Copyright, 1878, by MUYBRIDGE.   MORSE'S Gallery, 417 Montgomery St., San Francisco.

THE HORSE IN MOTION.

Illustrated by
MUYBRIDGE.   AUTOMATIC ELECTRO-PHOTOGRAPH.

"SALLIE GARDNER," owned by LELAND STANFORD; running at a 1.40 gait over the Palo Alto track, 19th June, 1878.

Figure 12.9

"The Horse in Motion," 1878, by Eadweard Muybridge. To publicize the successful technical feat of taking stop-motion images of Leland Stanford's horse "Sallie Gardner," Eadweard Muybridge arranged to have a postcard made for sale by Morse's Gallery of San Francisco. As his unusual name might suggest, Eadweard Muybridge, born Edward Muggeridge in England, was a unique character in the history of photography. He changed his last name to Muybridge when he started his photographic career in San Francisco and then changed his first name to match that of King Eadweard who was consecrated at Muybridge's hometown in 900 CE. In 1855 he arrived in San Francisco, but had to return to England after he suffered brain damage from a stagecoach accident. Returning in 1866, he became known for his landscapes of Yosemite and was asked to be a photographer for the U.S. Army's expeditions of the Western states. In 1872 Stanford contacted him to take pictures of his running horse. Two years later, he discovered that his wife had a lover, whom he then murdered. During the trial he pleaded insanity because of his earlier head injury. Nevertheless, the jury found the action "justifiable homicide" and acquitted him. Stanford had paid for his defense. The trial is the subject of the 1982 opera "The Photographer" by Philip Glass.

■ MOTION PICTURES AND THE SIX PERSPECTIVES

Personal Perspective

Motion pictures began as jerky films of everyday activities, capturing ordinary events to show the capabilities of this new medium. Soon, however, visionaries discovered that motion pictures could be much more than static camera shots. Early in the history of the movies, filmmakers exploited aesthetic, political, and economic advantages. The three primary functions probably explain why so many different terms—*motion picture, cinema, documentary, film, show, picture, movie,* and so on—have been used to describe the presentation of single-framed, sequential images that move through a machine so rapidly that they create the illusion of movement when projected on a screen.

Historical Perspective

The history of the motion picture can be summed up in one word—adaptation. Innovative inventors, directors, and studio executives worked to make sure that movies would become and remain a popular source of entertainment. Whenever movie sales dipped, the industry created better stories, turned up the publicity about the stars, and developed innovative technology to attract more viewers.

With the invention of Richard Maddox's gelatin-bromide dry plate process in 1871, fast action could finally be captured on film. One of the first to take advantage of this new medium was the English photographer Eadweard Muybridge. He was famous for helping the governor of California, Leland Stanford. He took stop-action pictures, clocked at 1/500th of a second, which proved a horse ran at some point with all four legs off the ground (Figure 12.9). He also invented an early movie projector, the zoopraxiscope in 1879. It used rotating glass discs to simulate movement with separate images. Muybridge sold collections of images on discs as well as prints of people and animals in various poses. However, there is no evidence that he realized the significance of combining his images with his projector.

Someone who did see the potential of these flickering images was the American inventor Thomas Alva Edison. In 1888 he bought 90 of Muybridge's motion studies. After numerous experiments, he and his assistant William Kennedy Laurie Dickson invented the first motion picture camera, the Kinetograph and the Kinetoscope, a peephole viewer. In 1891, Edison and Dickson made the first motion picture

to be preserved in the collection of the Library of Congress. The short film was a close-up of a slightly self-conscious Edison mechanic pretending to sneeze for the camera in *Fred Ott's Sneeze* (Figure 12.10). Within three years, Edison had established Kinetoscope arcades in which phonographs, another Edison invention, could be heard, and 30-second movies could be seen. Dickson made most of the

Figure 12.10

The first motion picture in the Library of Congress collection is the short Thomas Edison film Fred Ott's Sneeze *of 1891. Ott's sneeze should be viewed column-by-column starting from the top left. Edison believed if anyone wanted to watch a motion picture, it would be through a peephole viewer, and the subject would be fictionalized works.*

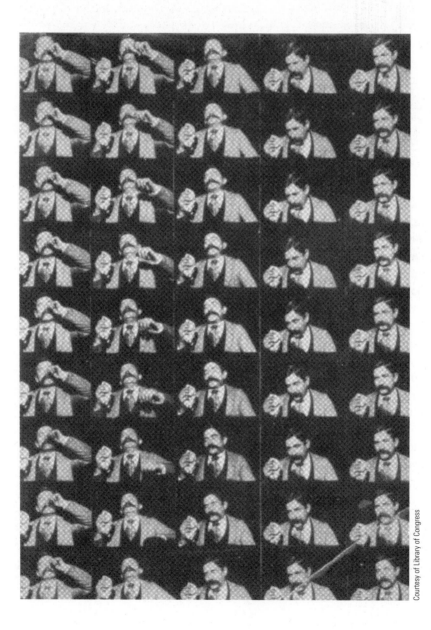

films, which were 50 feet long, with no editing or camera movements. Early movies simply showed dancers, clowns, and other entertainers performing in front of the camera. However, one of the first commercial productions for the public was called scandalous by social critics of the day. Directed by William Heise who worked with Dickson, *The Kiss* (1896) showed a reenactment of an amorous exchange between two characters in the play *The Widow Jones* (Weblink 12.3).

But Edison never thought much of the new medium. He was content to offer peephole films in his arcades where he featured what he thought would be more popular phonograph recordings. Consequently, he didn't bother to secure patent rights for his film equipment in Europe. An English scientific instruments maker, Robert Paul, bought a Kinetograph and made an important technical improvement—he replaced Edison's electrified mechanism with a more portable hand crank. In 1894, two French brothers, Auguste and Louis Lumière, purchased one of Paul's Kinetographs.

The brothers improved the device so that not only could they make films with it but could also use it to process and project the movies. They named their invention the *Cinématographe*, which soon was shortened to *cinema*.

The Lumières' first films were similar to those created by purchasers of video cameras—glorified home movies. Early in 1895, the two previewed their first effort, *Workers Leaving the Lumière Factory*, with a group of friends and family members (Figure 12.11; Weblink 12.4).

On December 28, 1895, the first public audience for motion pictures was treated to a series of short films in the basement of the Grand Café in Paris and the modern concept of motion pictures—movies seen with an audience—was born (Figure 12.12).

Edison's short films differed from the Lumière works in a fundamental way. Instead of a documentary approach, in which the camera filmed people and situations often without their being aware of its presence, Edison favored heavy-handed staged productions in the fiction genre that could be seen by only one viewer at a

Figure 12.11

Unlike Edison, Auguste and Louis Lumière thought motion pictures would be viewed in theaters with large audiences and that the type of films most would want to see would be documentaries. One of the first films by the Lumière brothers is the 1895 film Workers Leaving the Lumière Factory. *With its objective camera approach, the work has a contemporary documentary style.*

Figure 12.12

On a busy street in Paris, the plaque mounted on the wall at the top left commemorates the location of the Lumière brothers' motion picture theater, then called Le Salon Indien du Grand Café.

Figure 12.13

The grave of French director George Méliès, located in Pére Lachaise cemetery, Paris, is adorned with flowers laid by fans of the man who introduced the field of special effects to the motion picture industry.

But what they clamored for were fictionalized productions seen in a theater.

One of the first to realize the aesthetic potential of movies was George Méliès of France, considered the founder of special effects (Figure 12.13). The son of wealthy parents, Méliès started his career as a caricaturist, stage designer, magician, and actor. Méliès purchased a camera from Robert Paul and made his first movie, *A Game of Cards*, in 1896. By 1900 the public had grown bored with documentaries. Méliès filled the void with surreal films inspired by his experiences as a magician and stage performer. His most famous work is the 10-minute classic *A Trip to the Moon* made in 1902. Roughly based on the Jules Verne stories of *From the Earth to the Moon* and *Around the Moon*, the movie shows a group of professors who take a voyage in a rocket ship that lands in one of the "eyes" of the face on the moon (Weblink 12.5).

One of the early innovators in filmmaking who understood the public's desire to see action movies produced outside a studio was the American Edwin Stratton Porter.

In 1896, he had left the U.S. Navy and went to work for Edison as a mechanic, electrician, and film operator. He soon left Edison, bought his own camera, made films, rented a theater, and showed his movies under the name of Thomas Edison, Jr. He made his two most famous pictures in 1903—*The Life of an American Fireman* and *The Great Train Robbery*, in which much of the action was shot outside of a studio (Figure 12.14). He also invented the important concept of "cinematic time." Instead of simply leaving the camera on during an entire film, Porter edited scenes to create interest for the audience (Weblink 12.6).

time. As it turned out, both the Lumières and Edison had it wrong *and* right. What most of the public did *not* want to see were documentaries through a peephole.

Courtesy of Paul Martin Lester

Figure 12.14

The first action-adventure motion picture was the 1903 classic The Great Train Robbery *by Edwin Porter. Unlike the films produced by Thomas Edison, Porter filmed his movies outside of a stage set. Here, three train robbers make their escape while ducking gunfire.*

During the silent era, the rise and fall of David Wark Griffith is a metaphor for the entire early time period. Born in Kentucky to a Confederate Civil War hero, Griffith had been a reporter for a Louisville newspaper and had written and acted for the stage when he was signed up as an actor at five dollars a day ($120 today). With his stage experience, Griffith was offered a director's position with Biograph Studios in New York City and then moved to Hollywood. Griffith is best known for the infamous *Birth of a Nation* (1915). The movie is a demonstration of the maturity of Griffith's film work, but unfortunately is a mean-spirited and racist story. Originally titled *The Clansman* from Thomas Dixon, Jr.'s book *The Clansman: An Historical Romance of the Ku Klux Klan*, the movie tells of the history of the United States immediately after the Civil War. When a struggling community is attacked by a ravaging group of African Americans (Anglo actors played with heavy black makeup), the people are saved by white-hooded members of the Ku Klux Klan (KKK) who ride into town on horseback (Figure 12.15).

Compared to the other Biograph movies, *Birth* was an incredible gamble. Most films of the day cost no more than $100 (about $2,300 today) for the total production. *Birth* cost about $83,000 (about $1.8 million)—the most ever invested in a motion picture at that time (Weblink 12.7). To offset the cost of making the movie, the ticket price was an incredibly

Figure 12.15

In this scene from the 1915 movie Birth of a Nation, *the Ku Klux Klan (with toilet plunger head ornaments that today's Klan decline to wear) catches up with Gus, played by the Anglo actor Walter Long in blackface makeup. Thought responsible for the death of a young Anglo woman, Gus is tried, convicted, and executed by the Klan.*

high $2—that is the equivalent of $45 today. Obviously, the movie was intended for wealthy audience members. The three-hour movie premiered at Clune's Auditorium in Los Angeles (a grand movie palace that was demolished in 1985) to immediate controversy as Klansmen in full robes helped publicize the movie. The NAACP issued a pamphlet called "Fighting a Vicious Film" and began a boycott of the studio. Many leading politicians and civic leaders were unanimous in their condemnation because of the racist message of the movie. When it was shown in Boston, a race riot followed, but attendance at road show engagements was high. Nevertheless, after President Woodrow Wilson saw it in the White House, he said it was "like writing history with lightning. And my only regret is that it is all so terribly true." Although the KKK had disbanded in 1869, the film was responsible for the racist extremist group's revival.

Over the years, *Birth of a Nation* reportedly made $20 million (almost $300 million today). In 1919, Griffith, Charles Chaplin, Douglas Fairbanks, and Mary Pickford formed their own film company that they named United Artists (Figure 12.16). But in his later years, Griffith lost much of the creative energy associated

with his early films. In the 1930s, he tried to make movies with sound, but his lack of technical experience and his reputation among audio and studio executives who viewed him as a quaint, silent-movie dinosaur prevented him from doing so. For the last 17 years of his life he lived as a virtual hermit in Los Angeles. He died in 1948 on his way to a Hollywood hospital from a hotel where he had been living alone.

This early, silent film era is important because during that time the motion picture industry established itself as a powerful business force, started the careers of numerous directors, and began the concept of "stars," which were elevated to a higher status than mere actors. The triad of dealings, directors, and stars was crucial to filmmaking during that time, and the relationships between the three remain vital in today's world of moviemaking.

Because many European movie companies were forced to stop commercial production during World War I, Hollywood was able to dominate the business with its good climate, varied geography, inexpensive real estate, and war-free environment. By 1915, most American studios had established complexes in the Los Angeles suburb of Universal City. Many Europeans who migrated because of the war became successful in the film industry. The proliferation of studios indicated the rise in popularity of motion pictures generally, with the public asking for new movies to satisfy their film appetite. The numerous business deals among producers, distributors, and banking groups (e.g., J. P. Morgan and John D. Rockefeller) reflected the rising costs of movies.

Although making movies has always been a collaborative effort, the role of the director is the key to a production. A director turns the words of a screenwriter, the talent of the actors, and the

Figure 12.16

Standing behind a seated, camera-aware Charlie Chaplin are D. W. Griffith, Mary Pickford, and Douglas Fairbanks as they prepare to sign the contract establishing United Artists motion picture studio in 1919.

Library of Congress Prints and Photographs Division, LC-USZ62-137195

expertise of the technical crew into an art form with a unique visual style. Some of the most powerful studio executives had humble beginnings. Mack Sennett was an actor under Edison and later worked for Griffith. In 1912, he financed his own production company, the Keystone Film Company of Los Angeles. The studio became famous for its madcap chase scenes involving the Keystone Kops and romantic comedies featuring the sophisticated star Gloria Swanson. Keystone launched the careers of writer-turned-director Frank Capra and comedic actors Harold Lloyd and Charles Chaplin, the most famous silent film star. But when the silent film period ended, Sennett's comedies were no longer popular. Hal Roach was Sennett's biggest competitor. Roach wooed Lloyd away with more money. With his alter ego, whom he called the "Glass Character," Lloyd made more than 100 one-reel comedies that exhibited his acrobatic skills and a sophisticated sense of visual humor (Figure 12.17). Roach went on to direct Stan Laurel and Oliver Hardy in several comedy classics as well as the *Our Gang* comedy series, which was popular in theaters and on television.

One of the most famous silent film directors was Cecil B. DeMille, who often clashed with studio executives over his high budgets. His 1923 *The Ten Commandments* cost more than a million dollars ($12.8 million today) to produce. DeMille had been inspired to become a director after watching Porter's *The Great Train Robbery*. He initially worked for Samuel Goldwyn and moved his production facilities to a barn in Hollywood in 1914 to begin making feature films. DeMille was popular with the public because his movies always contained a hint of sensuality as opposed to Griffith's sentimentality.

Hal Roach / Pathe Exchange / The Kobal Collection / Kornman, Gene / Picture Desk

Figure 12.17

Suspended above Los Angeles during the filming of Safety Last! *in 1923 is Harold Lloyd, one of the most popular physical comedians of the silent era, lesser known than Charlie Chaplin and Buster Keaton. Lloyd made about 200 pictures, and is best known for his "Glass Character" who thrilled audiences with his elaborate chase scenes and self-performed stunts. Attesting to his popularity, his hand- and footprints, along with the outline of his eyeglass frames (in reality, sunglass frames) are preserved in the cement in front of Grauman's Chinese Theatre on Hollywood Boulevard. In 1994 the U.S. Postal Service issued a stamp that included a caricature of him by Al Hirschfeld.*

One of the most influential directors in the history of silent films was the Russian Sergei Eisenstein. Like Orson Welles, Eisenstein was known primarily for his innovative film technique in one motion picture. He studied architecture and engineering before being bitten by the theater bug. He gave up his engineering career when he landed a job with an experimental theater where he designed sets and directed plays. He became interested in filmmaking after watching Griffith's use of montage sequences in *Birth of a Nation* to tell the story of rich and poor characters. In 1925, he released his classic *The Battleship Potemkin*, which told the story of the 1905 sailors' rebellion in Odessa and the Tsar's brutal reprisal. The movie is probably best known for its famous "steps" scene in which montage and quick-editing techniques created dramatic tension (Figure 12.18). Eisenstein was inspired by the dada art movement, in which multiple images were shown on the screen at the same time for maximum visual effect.

GOSKINO / THE KOBAL COLLECTION / The Picture Desk

Figure 12.18

Adding to the horror of the famous steps scene in the 1925 classic by Russian director Sergei Eisenstein, The Battleship Potemkin, *is the abandoned baby carriage that is left on its own to perilously travel down the steps between dead and dying citizens.*

With film pieces as short as 1/16th of a second, the murder of Russian civilians by the Tsar's troops (an incident that probably was not as severe as shown) is one of the best examples of the art of editing in the history of film (Weblink 12.8). Eisenstein became a teacher of motion picture art and wrote several books about the power of film as a communication medium before his death in 1948.

Hollywood sensuality on and off the big screen caused many people to become concerned that movies could have a corrupting influence on the morals of the nation. Sparked by the sensual love scenes on the screen and the personal scandals of a handful of stars, a private censorship board was established to regulate the industry. In 1920 Mary Pickford divorced her husband and two weeks later married

Douglas Fairbanks. Fans were shocked, thinking Pickford's own personality was the same as her sweet, girl-next-door characters. The actor and director Roscoe "Fatty" Arbuckle was involved in a 1921 scandal when a young actress died during a party at his rented 12th-floor suite in the St. Francis Hotel in San Francisco, and Arbuckle was charged with rape and murder. Even though he was found not guilty, his reputation was ruined because of vicious attacks in the Hearst newspapers.

Mary Pickford's hasty post-divorce marriage and the Arbuckle affair led to the 1922 formation of the Motion Pictures Producers and Distributors of America by Will Hays, former Postmaster General during the Harding administration. A Presbyterian elder, Hays and his committee members offered informal advice to movie executives about studio scandals and movie content. More important, the office issued a seal of approval for work that they considered acceptable for mass audiences. Without that approval, a film was doomed to a low-budget status. This early form of censorship led to sanitized and banal works in the 1930s and 1940s that could win easy approval from the Hays office. From that idea came the Motion Picture Association of America's (MPAA) rating system, initiated in 1968. Kirby Dick directed a documentary about the MPAA's rating procedure in *This Film Is Not Yet Rated* (2006).

As a public relations ploy to help dignify the criticized film industry, the Academy of Motion Picture Arts and Sciences first presented its Academy Awards on May 16, 1929. The treasured eight-pound, gold-plated award originally was called "The Statuette," but when an Academy librarian remarked that the standing man looked like her uncle Oscar, the name stuck.

The 1930s and 1940s are considered by most motion picture historians to be Hollywood's great technical age. Technical innovations brought improvements in presentation, and the public flocked to films in record numbers. One of the innovations, sound, was an instant success.

■ Sound

Amplified sound that could be heard by large audiences was made possible by Lee De Forest's invention of the audio tube. Based on an earlier idea of Edison's, De Forest created a vacuum tube that eventually led to public address systems, radio, stereo equipment, and television. The American Telegraph & Telephone Company (AT&T) bought De Forest's technology and developed it in the company's

Western Electric Bell Laboratories subsidiary. General Electric's scientists also were working on sound development. Both Western Electric and General Electric announced their amplification systems at about the same time.

The advent of "talking pictures" was delayed because there were two different sound systems that competed for adoption by the studios. Another reason for the delay was that theater owners were not convinced of the necessity to fit their movie houses with expensive sound equipment.

Sound for movies required that synchronized dialogue, music, and sound effects be recorded during a movie's filming. Two sound systems—the Vitaphone (sound on disc) and the Phonofilm (sound on film)—became available to filmmakers at about the same time. The Vitaphone process was an adaptation of Edison's phonographic cylinder invention in which a recording disc was made when the film was shot. To produce sound during a movie, a theater exhibitor had to run the picture and the cylinder with two different machines. Occasionally problems arose (considered humorous by early audiences) when the two didn't match or a haphazard projector technician accidentally played the wrong disc. Phonofilm, the technology that eventually won the competition, was a sound-on-film innovation that converted recorded sounds into visual representations that were printed on the film itself. Consequently, no separate machine was required because the visual and the audio components of the movie always matched.

Warner Bros. invested heavily in Vitaphone, whereas 20th Century Fox advocated Phonofilm. On October 6, 1927, Warner debuted Al Jolson's *The Jazz Singer* using the Vitaphone process.

Although not the first sound picture—there had been earlier experiments with recorded voices and music—*The Jazz Singer* was the first movie in which sound was used in a feature motion picture to tell a story (Weblink 12.9). The movie is forgettable except as a footnote in the history of sound presentations, although it included Jolson's famous ad-libbed line, "Wait a minute, wait a minute, you ain't heard nothin' yet." Nevertheless, it made $3.5 million ($42 million today) at the box office, and Warner's production head, Darryl F. Zanuck, received an Oscar during the first Academy Awards ceremony for the technical achievement.

More recent sound innovations include Ray Dolby's noise reduction technology introduced in the 1970s. Stanley Kubrick first used the process in the 1971 movie *A Clockwork Orange*. In 1990 Kodak introduced its Cinema Digital Sound for *Dick Tracy*. Dolby Digital was first heard in *Batman Returns* (1992), and in 1993 Digital Theater Systems (DTS) introduced its technology for *Jurassic Park*. Columbia used Sony Dynamic Digital Sound (SDDS) for *Last Action Hero*.

■ Color

Another technical innovation was the use of color. The tedious method of hand-tinting individual frames of a motion picture was used commercially as early as Porter's *The Great Train Robbery*. The first color film innovations were complicated, time-consuming, and expensive. The first full-length movie filmed and projected in color was *The World, the Flesh and the Devil* (1914). That British production used a short-lived, two-projector process called Kinemacolor. In 1915, the Technicolor Motion Picture Corporation announced its two-color process. A more advanced three-color Technicolor process was introduced in 1932. The next year the Walt Disney Studio won an Academy Award for its all-color animated classic *Flowers and Trees* (Weblink 12.10), and *Becky Sharp* (1935) was the first live action film shot with the three-color innovation (Weblink 12.11). Public acceptance of color began with the classic fantasy motion picture *The Wizard of Oz* (1939). Audiences reportedly burst into wild applause when Dorothy, played by Judy Garland, opened the door of her drab, sepia-toned Kansas home and entered the brightly hued world of Oz after her tornado trip.

■ Widescreen

Widescreen presentations were another attempt to lure viewers to the theater. Early in its history, the Academy of Motion Picture Arts and Sciences selected the 4:3 width-to-length aspect ratio as the industry standard for screen presentations in order to avoid costly differences in film stock, cameras, and theaters. The earlier, almost square proportions of the film image had to be widened in the 1930s for the Phonofilm process to allow for the sound track to run along the side of the film. Eventually, widescreen became the standard presentation format. In 1952, the first commercial widescreen format—Cinerama—was introduced. Although it was a complicated process that required a movie to be shot with three cameras and shown with four projectors (one reserved for the sound track), the widescreen, expansive look was a great success with the public. The next year Cinema-Scope (later called Panavision) provided directors with a widescreen process that needed only one camera and projector. Some early widescreen hits included

The Robe (1953), *How the West Was Won* (1962), and *It's a Mad, Mad, Mad, Mad World* (1963) (Weblink 12.12). The widescreen trend continues today with the IMAX and OMNIMAX presentation formats that require specially built auditoriums. IMAX theater screens are 40 × 28 yards.

With television enjoying its "Golden Age" in the 1950s and fewer leaving their couches for a movie theater's cushioned seat, another idea to bring in audiences were movies that took advantage of the fears sparked by the Cold War, the atomic bomb, and teenage alienation in the 1950s. Consequently, the studios produced low-budget "red menace" movies such as *I Married a Communist* (1949), several science fiction movies with subtle links to political issues such as *The Invasion of the Body Snatchers* (1956), movies with atom-bomb-created mutant creatures such as *Them!* (1954), and alienated teenager movies such as *The Wild One* (1954) and *Rebel Without a Cause* (1955) (Weblink 12.13).

■ Three-Dimensional Films

Three-dimensional (3-D), double feature, and drive-in movies were promoted to also try to compete with television. As early as 1915, Edwin Porter showed 3-D test films to audiences, but nothing became of his early attempt. In Los Angeles, the first 3-D movie shown to a paying audience was called *The Power of Love* in 1922. In the 1950s 3-D took off with *Bwana Devil* (1952), and the first feature-length 3-D motion picture presented in stereo sound was *The House of Wax* (1953), starring the great horror actor Vincent Price, who went on to star in three other 3-D movies. The great director Alfred Hitchcock even filmed

a 3-D version of his classic thriller *Dial M for Murder* in 1954. Audiences soon grew tired of the passing fad. However, the genre is enjoying a comeback with high quality 3-D effects as seen in Henry Selick's animated puppet movie *Coraline* (2009) and Disney's first computer-generated 3-D cartoon with Pixar, *Up* (2009) (Weblink 12.14). The 3-D technology company RealD supplies comfortable glasses for audience members and installs digital screens for theater operators such as AMC Entertainment, Cinemark USA, and Regal Entertainment Group. In James Cameron's *Avatar* (2010) the performance capture technology combined with 3-D movie making represent a quantum leap in motion pictures as important as sound, color, and widescreen.

■ Double Features and Drive-Ins

Double features began in the 1930s as a way to convince money-conscious viewers that they would get more for their money. With a newsreel, a cartoon, trailers, and two feature-length movies, moviegoers stayed in the theater for several hours while owners made money from drinks, popcorn, and candy sales. Double feature presentations survived until the 1970s and spawned a motion picture genre known as the "B" movie, a term that came from an ancient time when pop songs were produced on small, vinyl discs and played at 45 revolutions per minute. The "A side" was the popular tune of the time; the "B side," not so much. Cheaply produced, short B movies were needed to fill the bill with the main feature. One of the most notable movie directors of this era was Roger Corman, known as the "King of the B Movies." He produced almost 400 motion pictures and gave many in Hollywood their start in the industry, including James Cameron and

Ron Howard. During the 1950s, drive-in movies prospered throughout the country, with over 4,000 screens across America. Owners of cheap land away from city lights saw drive-ins as a way to put the unproductive real estate to better use. But television viewing competed with drive-ins too. Despite being a haven for lovers and parents with young children, drive-ins, with their colorfully painted front screens, are hard to find. Today, many are used as convenient open spaces for flea markets (Figure 12.19). Drive-in movies are making a bit of a comeback with large inflatable screens set up on swap meet locations, where the theaters used to be established. Home versions of the large screen can be purchased for as low as $200 for a back-yard viewing party.

■ *Multi-Screen Theaters*

Other casualties of the war with television were the large, often enchanting movie theaters that could hold up to 3,000 people. With architectural and sculptural curiosities, moody and mysterious lighting effects, and a huge screen behind a heavy maroon or blue curtain, these movie houses were truly magical places that matched the wonder of the motion pictures themselves. Today the trend is against large, single screens because owners can make more money with multi-screen theaters. Some cineplexes have as many as 27 separate theaters under one roof. Theater managers receive the films via mailed discs, satellite, or internet connections and project them digitally (Figure 12.20).

Multi- and megaplexes are here to stay with their stadium seating and convenient showing times. A fairly new trend are luxury theaters such as the ArcLight movie complex in Los Angeles, with reserved seating in plush leather chairs and premium food and drinks served to your seat. For about $30 a ticket with food and drinks extra, Gold Class Cinemas founded in Australia with theaters in California, Illinois, and Washington state offers "online seating reservations, free valet parking, [and] in-theater food and beverage service with a call button" that makes you feel like William Randolph Hearst watching a movie in his castle.

 *Technical Perspective*

As with the cartoon and photography media, movies primarily communicate in a visual format. By studying previous works and by being creative, directors have learned to exploit the visual considerations inherent in static or dynamic shots and film choices.

■ *The Shot*

The basic unit of a movie is the shot, defined as a continuous picture in which

Figure 12.19

Drive-in theaters have been nearly eliminated as places for showing movies, except in a few, mostly rural communities. In 2009 "The Spud" drive-in outside of Victor, Idaho, still serves up first-run movies such as Night at the Museum *and* Angels and Demons *during the summer season, along with their famous french fries.*

Courtesy of Paul Martin Lester

Figure 12.20

The movie complex at Universal Citywalk in Los Angeles includes 19 screens with one a giant IMAX theater all with stadium seating.

the camera doesn't stop. A shot can be as quick as 1/30th of a second—one frame— or can last the entire length of a picture. Graphic designer Saul Bass created the storyboards for one of the most memorable scenes in Hollywood history—the shower murder in *Psycho* (1960). Alfred Hitchcock, using storyboards from Bass, created an impressionistic murder with shocking intensity by using 67 separate editing cuts for the 90-second scene (Figure 12.21). On the opposite side of the quick cut, an incredible technical achievement was accomplished in 2002 when the Russian director Alexandr Sokurov used one continuous shot for his motion picture *Russian Ark*. The film traced over 300 years of Russian history by taking the viewer on a rhythmic, rambling stroll through 33 rooms of the State Hermitage Museum in St. Petersburg (Weblink 12.15).

■ Film Choices

Motion pictures can be shot in black and white, color, or a combination of the two. Movies also can be tinted or colorized. Black and white always has been associated with serious, documentary-style subjects, whereas, at first, color was thought to be a distracting attribute better used for fantasies. But black and white can be as colorful and sensational as color. Richard Brooks's haunting retelling of the story of two killers and their capture in the film *In Cold Blood* (1967) and Martin Scorsese's *Raging Bull* (1980), the story of boxer Jake LaMotta, were shot in black and white. The rich tones contribute to a documentary atmosphere in the telling of the brutal stories. Such directors as the indie favorite Jim Jarmusch in his *Stranger than Paradise* (1984), *Coffee and Cigarettes* (2003), and *Broken Flowers* (2005), and the Hollywood iconoclast Francis Ford Coppola in his personal story *Tetro* (2009), known for his colorful classics *The Godfather* (1972) and *Apocalypse Now* (1979), preferred to tell their stories in the less distracting format of black and white. Some directors combine

Figure 12.21

One of the most unforgettable moments in motion picture history is the shower murder scene with Janet Leigh and Anthony Perkins in Alfred Hitchcock's 1960 Psycho. *The terror of the scene is enhanced by the quick cuts, but after the Leigh character is killed, a slow transition between the shower drain and her eye is breathtaking.*

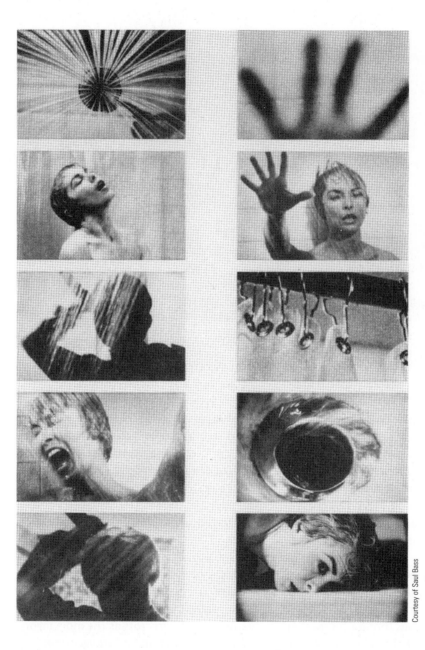

Courtesy of Saul Bass

black and white and color for dramatic contrast. Oliver Stone switched quickly back and forth between the two film formats in *Natural Born Killers* (1994). The same technique was employed by Guy Maddin in his wonderfully strange musical *The Saddest Music in the World* (2003) (Weblink 12.16).

 Ethical Perspective

Besides the issues associated with the other media discussed, there are three main ethical concerns for the movie industry: stereotypical portrayals, emphasis on violent themes, and the promotion of smoking. However, a fourth ethical consideration is taking hold within the industry due to the availability of motion pictures on the internet—copyright infringement.

■ Stereotypes

In 2001 the Oscars for best male and female actors went to two African Americans—Denzel Washington and Halle Berry for their work in *Training Day* and *Monster's Ball*, respectively, a first for the Awards. But since that time such films as *Soul Plane* (2004), *White Chicks* (2004), and *Norbit* (2007) were released (Weblink 12.17). Director Spike Lee said that *Plane* is "coonery and buffoonery," while another critic wrote that the film is "among the most offensive ever in terms of showing African Americans in a negative light." It seems that progress against stereotyping is always tempered by movies that are made to sell tickets and not to advance society.

African Americans aren't the only group to feel the sting of stereotyping in motion pictures. Native Americans, although seen in films frequently in the early westerns, almost always were portrayed as murderous savages. Lobbying from Arab groups, upset over the stereotypes in Disney's *Aladdin* (1992), convinced the studio to change offending lyrics in a song, although many other common Arab stereotypes remained. On the other hand, Sacha Baron Cohen's parody *Borat: Cultural Learnings of America for Make Benefit Glorious Nation of Kazakhstan* (2006) revealed in a comedic way the stereotypes and prejudices of middle-class Americans. His next film was produced for the same purpose and featured his character Bruno, a gay Austrian fashion writer, in *Bruno: Delicious Journeys Through America for the Purpose of Making Heterosexual Males Visibly Uncomfortable in the Presence of a Gay Foreigner in a*

Mesh T-Shirt (2009). The full title didn't fit on theater's marquees. Nevertheless, gay activists criticized the film for the character's stereotypical obsession with "anal sex, bondage wear and sex toys."

■ Violence

Offering the simplistic argument that the violence seen in motion pictures is responsible for all of the social problems in a society is always politically popular. Undeniably, action-adventure movies, always a popular genre, are filled with violent activities. Despite momentary sensitivity among U.S. film producers, violence will continue to be a staple of American films because violent films are enormously popular. One of the main reasons that the number of violent movies is increasing is the economic situation of the major studios. Studio executives need big blockbuster hits to maintain the economic health of their enterprises. And since about 80 percent of all movies shown in Europe are from the United States, executives have learned that action-adventure films are popular throughout the world because violence translates across cultures.

■ Smoking in the Movies

A five-year content analysis of U.S. motion pictures conducted by academic researchers and reported on the website "Smoke Free Movies" found that 80 percent of the "776 Hollywood and independent movies included tobacco use" (Weblink 12.18). About 90 percent of R-rated films, 80 percent of PG-13 movies, and 50 percent of G and PG motion pictures had at least one scene with an actor smoking. Furthermore, the major studios of "Time-Warner, Disney, and Sony accounted for more than half of all movies released with smoking." The number of scenes with characters smoking is higher today than it was during the 1950s, when the health issues related to smoking were not as well known. Because children are highly influenced by seeing stars smoke and the brands they choose, the advocacy group recommended that movies with characters who smoke should have an R rating and that cigarette brands not be visually identified in the films. In 2007 Disney announced it would no longer show characters smoking in its movies and discouraged directors of its Touchstone and Miramax adult labels from showing characters lighting up. In 2008 the six major movie studios announced that they would include anti-smoking public service announcements on DVD versions of any movies that depict smoking.

■ Copyright Infringement

An open letter presented on the website of the MPAA reads, "As with any business, the people and companies that create music, movies, and other copyrighted material rely on getting a fair reward for their creativity, time and hard work. That happens when people buy these works, but not when they steal them—including by copying or transmitting them without the permission of the copyright owners." Chairman and CEO Dan Glickman said in 2004 that the organization would combat piracy through three approaches: "improve [piracy deterring] technology, enforce the laws, and educate people." Computer network systems make the downloading of music, movies, and other materials easier than ever before in the history of the medium. Just as movie producers adapted to the competition from television, they will once again need to be

creative to overcome the trend toward an all-download future.

Cultural Perspective

Motion pictures, just like any art form, reflect the archetypes and myths that are popular within a particular culture at a particular time. All visual messages, movies included, help shape what we think of our society and ourselves. Hollywood stars give us ideals to strive for, and the mythic stories of good versus evil, social order versus anarchy, and group dependence versus independence strike deep, cultural chords. At least 12 genres, or types of stories created on film, reflect a society's cultural values—comedy, crime, documentary, epic, horror, musical, romance, science fiction, social impact, thriller, war, and western.

Comedy: *City Lights* (1931), *Some Like It Hot* (1959), and *Tropic Thunder* (2008)—from sophisticated situations and dialogue to a cynical production that parodies the war film genre and the motion picture industry (Figure 12.22).

Crime: *Scarface* (1932), *Bonnie and Clyde* (1967), and *The Dark Knight* (2008)—from stories with clear good and evil characters to sympathetic psychological profiles of dangerous criminals (Weblink 12.19). In his last performance, which won him an Oscar, Heath Ledger provided a brilliant and sympathetic look at a seriously disturbed criminal in *The Dark Knight*.

Documentary: *Nanook of the North* (1922), *Primary* (1960), and *Man on Wire* (2008)—balanced reporting, as with a journalistic report, is not as valued as advocating a point of view. *Man on Wire* was a sensitive and intimate portrait of a fascinating personality and is an example of the best the genre has to offer (Figure 12.23).

Epic: *Napoleon* (1926), *Lawrence of Arabia* (1962), and *Australia* (2008)—an important genre that is always underrepresented in filmmaking (Weblink 12.20). *Australia* is a sweeping, old-fashioned love story with beautiful people, scenery, and not much else.

Horror: *Frankenstein* (1931), *Night of the Living Dead* (1968), and *Saw VI* (2009)—from human-created to inhuman monsters (Weblink 12.21). With each sequel for *Saw*, audiences become harder to shock.

Musical: *The Wizard of Oz* (1939), *The Sound of Music* (1965), and *Footloose* (2010)—from unrealistic fantasies to serious character studies. The remake of the teen favorite *Footloose* indicates a lack of new ideas (Weblink 12.22).

Romance: *Gone with the Wind* (1939), *Casablanca* (1942), and *The Love Guru* (2008)—from love in the midst of civil and world war to a movie voted the worst of the year by the Golden Raspberry Award Foundation (Weblink 12.23).

Science fiction: *Metropolis* (1926), *2001: A Space Odyssey* (1968), and *Push* (2009)—from thoughtful commentaries about the future to a visually arresting feature with little interest in its characters and plot (Weblink 12.24).

Social impact: *The Grapes of Wrath* (1940), *Smoke Signals* (1998), and *An Inconvenient Truth* (2006)—always a strong film genre. *Truth* is essentially a lecture on the dangers of global warming to the planet by Academy Award, Grammy, and Nobel Prize winner Al Gore, which rivets your attention from start to finish (Weblink 12.25).

Thriller: *The Maltese Falcon* (1941), *Psycho* (1960), *The International* (2009)—from

United Artists / The Kobal Collection / The Picture Desk

The Everett Collection

Figure 12.22

Joe E. Brown (left) and Jack Lemmon in the famous final scene for Some Like It Hot. *After Lemmon removes his wig, he confesses, "I'm a man" to Brown, his groom-to-be. Brown responds, "Well, nobody's perfect." Back screen projection is often employed by directors to simulate an outdoor view. Here, the actors sat on a stationary boat in a studio while film of the ocean was displayed behind them.*

Figure 12.23

A good example of a "one sheet" promotional poster before the influence of the graphic designer Saul Bass is the one for Nanook of the North *(1922), considered the first true documentary dramatic film. Instead of one central graphic element, three textual descriptions and five illustrations attempt to intrigue a potential theater-goer to watch the black-and-white silent movie.*

well-written dramas with fine acting to a movie with fast-paced and intense action scenes that add dramatic effect to an otherwise ordinary plot (Weblink 12.26).

War: All Quiet on the Western Front (1930), *Apocalypse Now* (1979), and *Waltz with Bashir* (2008)—the best in this genre are critical examinations of why wars are sometimes necessary (Weblink 12.27). *Waltz with Bashir*, a critical examination of what happens to people on both sides of a gun's barrel, shows how moving and effective the animation medium can be (Weblink 12.28).

Western: Stagecoach (1939), *The Wild Bunch* (1969), and *Appaloosa* (2008)—as with the best films in this genre, the need for violent actions is questioned but sometimes cannot be avoided (Weblink 12.29).

Because motion pictures are visual media, they tell their mythic stories through visual symbolism. Myths are the stories of our culture, whereas symbols are the way those stories are communicated. Motion pictures are cultural artifacts. Movies affect us emotionally because the powerful visual messages, on a screen as large as a house and with sound quality that is better than being on a set, tell stories that we understand.

Critical Perspective

Movie attendance has been declining slowly since the 1950s because of the popularity of television, the computer, and the internet. The number of tickets sold annually in the United States immediately after World War II averaged about four billion. In 2008, the number of tickets sold dropped to about 1.37 billion. The movie industry is still profitable because ticket prices have risen, sales of refreshments have increased, and screens have been added to the 5,800 local theaters in the United States. With multiplex suburban theaters, first-run blockbuster movies with huge marketing budgets are sold out the first few weeks of their runs. But after attention wanes, you'll easily find a theater seat without anyone sitting in front of you. Nevertheless, total box-office sales for 2009 was $10.5 billion, a record year.

Today, many forms of entertainment are available to those who can afford them—restaurants, lectures, art museums, music concerts, comedy clubs, shopping malls, traditional theaters, athletic activities, and sporting events. But by far the biggest threat to the existence of motion pictures is in the home, with radio, broadcast television, cable and satellite television, videotapes, DVDs, board and video games, web presentations, reading, yard work, talking, dinner parties, and sex all keeping people occupied.

Moviemaking is a business. If anticipated blockbusters bomb embarrassingly at the box office, the studio executives responsible sometimes get the axe. This blockbuster mentality, in which most of the profits for a studio are made during the summer months, forces producers to make films that appeal to large audiences. More often than not, proven formulas from the past—remakes and sequels with sexual and violent themes—do well at the box office.

Moviemaking, it is sad to report, is still a man's business. During the summer blockbuster season of 2007, women directed none of the 30 top-grossing motion pictures. On average, only a paltry 6 percent of all the movies made during a year have women directors. Nevertheless, standout women directors include Kathryn Bigelow for *Point Break* (1991),

Strange Days (1995), and *The Hurt Locker* (2009), which was named the best drama of the year by the Los Angeles Film Critics Association and the American Film Institute, Gurinder Chadha for *Bend It Like Beckham* (2002) and *It's a Wonderful Afterlife* (2010), Jane Champion for *The Piano* (1993) and *Bright Star* (2009), Sanaa Hamri for *Sisterhood of the Traveling Pants 2* (2008) and *Acceptance* (2009), Catherine Hardwicke for *Twilight* (2008) and *Maximum Ride* (2010), Christine Jeffs for *Sunshine Cleaning* (2008), Phyllida Lloyd for *Mamma Mia!* (2008), Jennifer Lynch for *Boxing Helena* (1993) and *Surveillance* (2008), and Nia Vardalos for *I Hate Valentine's Day* (2009). In addition, women are being noted for their writing abilities, particularly Lorene Scafaria for her screenplay for *Nick & Norah's Infinite Playlist* (2008), Dana Fox for *What Happens in Vegas* (2008), and Diablo Cody who wrote *Jennifer's Body* (2009) and won an Oscar for her script for *Juno* (2007) (Weblink 12.30).

■ TRENDS TO WATCH FOR MOTION PICTURES

The most exciting trend for the motion picture medium involves technology and funding—admittedly not two of the most compelling topics. But high definition (hi-def) camcorders, called "Hollywood's filmless future" offer high-resolution, high-quality images and audio in a portable format using laptop editing software programs, combined with the steadicam, a stabilizing unit mounted to a camera that keeps the picture stable despite movements by the operator, allow independent directors to make movies with almost the same ease as multimedia presentations with sound.

With high quality but relatively inexpensive equipment, independent productions will continue to be vital to the movie industry. The 2009 Academy Award Best Picture and winner of seven other Oscars, the much-touted *Slumdog Millionaire*, for example, was a British production, co-financed by a French company, and starred an all-Indian cast. It debuted in only 10 theaters, but was marketed wisely by a small studio within media giant News Corp., Fox Searchlight. It also handled such surprise independent hits as *Juno* (2007), *Little Miss Sunshine* (2006), and *Sideways* (2004). Searchlight paid $2.5 million for distribution rights to *Slumdog*. As of this writing it has grossed more than $100 million.

With the six major studios—20th Century Fox, Disney, Paramount, Sony, Universal, and Warner Bros.—feeling the pinch from an economic downturn in 2009, independent movies ("indies") are having their way with the help of film festivals such as the Sundance Film Festival in Park City, Utah, and South by Southwest in Austin, Texas, television channels such as the Independent Film Channel, and the Spirit Awards that celebrate "independent, low-budget filmmaking." To attract attention to their work and also because they appreciate the aesthetic, some indie producers turn to 3-D technology. For his science fiction thriller *Duel* (2008), director Pavel Nikolajev made the $100,000 film in 3-D (Figure 12.24). Many indie directors are also bypassing traditional theater distribution and making their films available for internet downloading. For example, Robert Greenwald, director of *Rethinking Afghanistan* (2009), released the documentary in five parts from his website, and other independent producers make their work available through video-on-demand

(VOD) via cable providers or web services such as Amazon on Demand or YouTube Screening Room (Weblink 12.31).

A genre of indie film that is gaining in popularity is called "mumblecore." Concerning the first example, *Funny Ha Ha* (2005), David Denby notes that these "micro-budget independent movies . . . made by buddies, casual and serious lovers, and networks of friends . . . [are] a kind of lyrical documentary of American stasis and inarticulateness" (Weblink 12.32). Craig Brewer, director of *Hustle & Flow* (2005) and *Black Snake Moan* (2006), produced a mumblecore series in 2009 with his Memphis musician friends in "$5 Cover" for web and MTV (Weblink 12.33).

Film directors will continue to challenge themselves and sometimes their audiences by making movies based on traditional board games, turning video games into movies and movies into video games, and making commercials for television and the web. For example, Kevin Lima, director of *Enchanted* (2007), directed a movie based on the children's game Candy Land. The success of the 1996 video game "Tomb Raider" inspired directors Simon West and Jan de Bont to cast Angelina Jolie to play Lara Croft in the movie versions. Gore Verbinski, director of the *Pirates of the Caribbean* (2003–2007) movies, produced a first-shooter video game, "Bioshock," and Mike Newell of *Harry Potter and the Goblet of Fire* (2005) made "Prince of Persia: The Sands of Time." Famous directors are also enticed to produce television and web commercials. Joel and Ethan Coen (*Fargo*, 1996, and *No Country for Old Men*, 2007) made a humorous public service commercial for the "Reality Campaign" that criticized the concept of a clean coal facility (Weblink 12.34). Roman Polanski, the controversial director of the classic film noir *Chinatown* (1974), made an ad for a fake perfume brand, which was the concept of the Italian artist Francesco Vezzoli, in which actresses Natalie Portman and Michelle Williams fought over a bottle of "Greed," as a commentary on the state of the world in 2009 (Weblink 12.35).

With one-dollar rentals from Redbox vending machines located at many supermarkets, you can rent a DVD movie for a day and watch it wherever you want. But there are other, even more convenient ways to watch movies. The website Crackle.com, owned by Sony Pictures Entertainment Company, produces and presents original movies and series as well as previously released motion pictures.

Figure 12.24

Written and directed by Pavel Nikolajev, the indie 3-D film Duel (2008), in its storyline and visual style, attempts to emulate the Japanese anime style of movie-making. Except for the miscellaneous typeface family used for the title, the poster, on the other hand, does not reflect the anime style.

Courtesy of Nova Automatics

Netflix.com users can also download movies to their computers and watch them on their large, high-definition, widescreen monitors with digital sound connected to cable or satellite operators with seamless wireless access to the web that provides viewing of first-run movies before they are shown in local theaters. Perhaps taking a tip from Netflix, Warner Home Video announced in 2009 that it would make approximately 5,000 motion pictures in its DVD collection available per a customer's demand.

But in the short run, fads such as 3-D and 4-D (live action players on stage); guest lectures from movie producers, critics, and academics; concert performances in 3-D or live, simulcast operas; and seats installed with computer monitors for value-added information about the film won't get a mass audience off their couches. To remain a viable medium and to get people away from their home entertainment centers, movie producers will need to rely less on blockbuster movies to improve their bottom line and more on smaller, well-made, and compelling stories that are now mostly supplied by independent filmmakers. Theater owners must also think of new ways to enhance the viewing experience, including higher quality and healthier food offerings, Facebook-style friend group special screenings, and better soundproofing so that the explosions from the theater next door are silenced.

Will people continue to go to movie theaters? Of course they will. Humans are social animals and simply enjoy the company of one another too much to stay home for long.

■ KEY TERMS

- Archetypes
- Aspect ratio
- Black Power
- Camcorder
- CinemaScope
- Cinerama
- Contrast
- Golden Raspberry Award
- Indie
- Kinemacolor
- Kinetograph
- Kinetoscope
- Ku Klux Klan
- One-reel film
- Shooter video game
- Steadicam
- Technicolor
- Tracking shot
- Two-color process
- Vacuum tube
- Zoopraxiscope

 To locate active URLs for the weblinks mentioned in this chapter, please go to the companion site at http://communication.wadsworth.com/lester5 and select the proper chapter.

Chapter 13

Television

"The tribe has spoken."

If you don't own a TV or don't watch it, you will probably have trouble identifying that catchphrase. Host Jeff Probst always speaks the words toward the end of each episode of the consistent CBS hit, "Survivor." The implicit meanness of the phrase, which no contestant wants to hear because it means you are voted off the show, says a lot about the state of television programming and modern society as well. The phrase also signifies that reality or unscripted television has come a long way from "Smile, you're on Candid Camera," the innocent ending to a mild practical joke in the 1950s classic (Weblink 13.1).

Reality television includes an amazing number of unscripted programs. Besides the traditional offerings such as news, sports, and talk shows, included in the reality mix are programs based on documentaries, historical re-creations, dating, law enforcement and military subjects, makeovers, life changes, docu-soaps, hidden cameras, games, spoofs, talent searches, fantasies fulfilled, cooking, commercial sales, and situation comedies where actors ad-lib dialogue without a script (Figure 13.1).

Since 2000, the reality television genre has been a ratings powerhouse with reality shows such as "Who Wants to be a Millionaire?" in 2000, "Survivor: The Australian Outback" in 2001, and "American Idol" from 2005 to the present topping the charts over all other shows. One might think there is nothing but reality shows on television, but that is not the case, of course. Nevertheless, reality still dominates schedules and viewer preferences and is the hope for the relatively new broadcast network, The CW. Formed in 2006 after a merger with UPN, a Paramount/CBS network, and The WB, a joint venture of the Tribune Broadcasting and Warner Bros. Studios, The CW debuted with a two-hour season premiere of the quasi-talent show "America's Next Top Model." To attract the desired 18- to 34-year-old viewing audience, The CW plans to only air young prime-time soap operas and reality shows.

According to Nielsen Media Research for the 1994–1995 season, only two shows could be considered reality-based: "NFL Monday Night Football" and "60 Minutes." The ABC sitcom "Home Improvement" was the number one show. For the 2008–2009 season, six of the top ten rated programs were reality shows, with more than one quarter of the prime-time episodes as well as cable channels A&E, Bravo, Discovery, and the History Channel dedicated to the genre. "American Idol" topped the list and charges up to $1 million for a 30-second advertising spot. In a testament to the enduring popularity of "Idol," it was reported that home viewers cast almost 100 million votes during the final showdown of the 2009 season between favorite Adam Lambert and dark horse Kris Allen, with Kris winning the competition. Furthermore, the judge everyone loves to hate, the British music entrepreneur Simon Cowell, is also a judge for the Independent Television Network's (ITV) program "Britain's Got Talent," which received international interest after a 48-year-old Scottish church volunteer, Susan Boyle, stunned Cowell and the audience with her beautiful singing voice. A media blitz followed, resulting in over 100 million users watching her performances on YouTube. In a surprise finish, Boyle ended up taking second place, with a dance group taking first.

The founder of reality programming is Allen Funt (Weblink 13.2). During World

War II while serving in the Army Signal Corps, he experimented with portable radio equipment. He was a writer for "Sweetheart Soap," which was First Lady Eleanor Roosevelt's radio program; he came up with funny skits for the popular "Truth or Consequences" show; and he headed what he called "the stupidest show in radio," a program called "Funny Money Man," which was turned into a syndicated comic strip. His interest in gags that made fun of ordinary persons led to "Candid Microphone," which aired on the ABC Radio Network in 1946 (Weblink 13.3). The next year he took his show to television where it eventually became the smash hit "Candid Camera" in 1953. At one time or another it aired on all three major networks. The show originally consisted of good-humored practical jokes pulled on unsuspecting individuals who were unaware they were being filmed. When the joke had run its course, the catchphrase, "Smile, you're on Candid Camera" would be spoken amid laughter. But not everyone laughed. In an era in which security cameras were

Figure 13.1

In 2003 "The Joe Schmo Show" on the Spike TV cable channel parodied the reality game format by using actors to fool one contestant who thought the game was being played for real. Matt Kennedy Gould (center) never guessed that he was the star until he was told during the final episode. Receiving all the prizes and money offered during the show ameliorated some embarrassment he might have felt. But in a 2008 interview he confessed, "If I had to do it over again, I wouldn't do the show at all. Honestly, the show really made me feel dumb. And I never felt like that before. I did it because I needed the money." In 2004 the same producers debuted "Joe Schmo 2," which parodied the reality dating show genre.

not common, few appreciated the joke played on them. For every scenario that aired, about 20 were rejected because the person did not smile or sign a necessary release form for the show. Funt later produced a feature-length reality-based motion picture, What Do You Say to a Naked Lady? (1970).

The first documentary-style reality show seen in America, "An American Family," was broadcast on the Public Broadcasting Service (PBS) network in 1973. Directed by Alan and Susan Raymond, the 12-part series followed the highs and lows of an actual family—Bill and Patricia Loud of Santa Barbara, California, and their five children (Figure 13.2). The series became controversial as the family dealt with highly personal issues, including an impending divorce and their son Lance's homosexuality, using nonintrusive camera techniques similar to today's "Survivor." In 2002 TV Guide magazine listed the program as number 32 of the "50 Greatest TV Shows of All Time." The family reunited 30 years later for "A Death in An American Family," which documented Lance's addiction to crystal meth and his struggle with HIV/AIDS.

In March 1988, the Screen Actors Guild (SAG) and the Writers Guild of America (WGA), two important Hollywood unions that represented thousands of actors and writers, went on strike. The SAG strike was less than a month, but the WGA strike lasted five months and devastated the fall lineup of scripted shows. Since television producers did not have shows to air, many popular programs delayed their start until December. However, innovative executives realized, as some already knew, that there could be programs without the need for actors or writers.

Two hits begun in 1989 required little writing and acting—"Cops" and "America's Funniest Home Videos." "Cops" used actual footage from videographers riding along with police units. It was the brainchild of John Langley and Malcolm Barbour, who pitched the concept to Stephen Chao, a Fox television programming executive who liked the raw edge of the show, its inexpensive production costs, and its appeal to a young, male demographic valuable to advertisers (Weblink 13.4). Fox, the network that gave "The Simpsons" the green light, is known for being innovative when it comes to programming. "Cops" garnered four Emmy nominations and concerns from social critics about stereotyping African Americans and southern Anglos. "Funniest Home Videos" was produced by Vin Di Bona for the ABC network and was based on a popular Japanese show, "Fun TV." Each week the studio audience voted for a top video, with an end-of-the-season winner receiving a $100,000 prize. Originally hosted by comedian Bob Saget, Tom Bergeron is the present host (Weblink 13.5).

"Home Videos" put entertainment producers on notice that everyday persons with their video camcorders were potential contributors to their shows.

Figure 13.2

A family portrait of the Louds of Santa Barbara, California, doesn't reveal the hidden tensions that "An American Family" on the PBS network revealed. The show was the first documentary-style reality program on television.

Time Life Pictures / Getty Images

In 1991 this trend led directly to what is considered to be "the most famous home video of all time"—the beating of Rodney King by members of the police force, taken by amateur George Holliday. King was a recently released convict whose alcoholic father died at age 42. Holliday was an upper-middle-class son of an oil executive, who had been born in Canada but lived most of his life in Argentina. King was out of work and angry. Holliday was a manager of a plumbing company and contented. King was beaten severely by members of the Los Angeles Police Department (LAPD). Holliday was watching the beating through the viewfinder of his new $1,200 (about $2,000 today) Sony Handycam. King was African American, Holliday was Anglo. Excerpts were shown throughout the world, and when the police officers were initially found not guilty in April 1992, many blamed the video for causing unrest that led to the worst civil disturbance in the history of the United States (Weblink 13.6). The violence claimed over 50 lives, caused 2,300 injuries, resulted in hundreds of arrests, and cost more than $1 billion ($1.6 billion today) in property damage (Figure 13.3).

The year 1992 also introduced television producers and audience members to the strange world of voyeurism. "The Real World," the first reality-based series to appeal to an enormous television audience, premiered on MTV (Figure 13.4). Co-created by soap opera producer ("As the World Turns" and "Search for Tomorrow") Mary-Ellis Bunim and documentary filmmaker Jon Murray, "The Real World" featured a familiar scenario of several strangers living together in a beautifully furnished house in a major city while viewers watched how their relationships disintegrated or prospered. After a long battle with breast cancer, Bunim, 57, died in Burbank, Califor-

nia, in 2004. Nevertheless, Murray continues to produce reality-based programs. In 2009 MTV aired *Pedro*, a movie based on the "Real World: San Francisco" cast of 1994, which featured the sad but inspirational story of Cuban American HIV/AIDS victim Pedro Zamora (Weblink 13.7).

Figure 13.3

This high-contrast and blurry still image taken from a television monitor shows Los Angeles police officers Wind and Powell standing over the crouched form of Rodney King in front of his automobile.

Figure 13.4

In this publicity photograph of the fourth-season cast of "The Real World" (set in London), all act like the best of friends until they live together with intrusive microphones and cameras.

In 2009 the genre was criticized for seemingly exploiting willing, yet naïve participants by airing their public confessions and unusual behavior such that as shown on "The Bachelor" and "The Real Housewives of New Jersey," as well as the sensational breakup of Jon and Kate Gosselin in "Jon & Kate Plus 8" and the inner life and struggles of the single mother of 14 Nadya Suleman in "Octomom: The Incredible Unseen Footage." There was also concern among critics and television executives that some members of the general public might perform dangerous and unethical acts in order to get the attention of reality show producers. Richard Heene and his "balloon boy" hoax as well as Michaele and Tareq Salahi who crashed President Obama's first state dinner were all hoping to attract attention by their antics.

■ THE LIFE AND TIMES OF MARK BURNETT

Despite the criticisms of reality television, the title of "king of reality TV" has to go to a British citizen, Mark Burnett, 49, who almost single-handedly defined the reality genre. His list of hits is impressive: "Eco Challenge," "The Apprentice," "The Contender," "Are You Smarter than a 5th Grader?," and of course, the winner of them all, "Survivor."

His life sounds like a pitch for a new situation comedy show (Figure 13.5). Mark Burnett was born in England in 1960. At 18 years old he joined the British Army Parachute Regiment. He fought in Northern Ireland and in the Falkland Islands. After his discharge in 1982, he left for America. Since he had only $600 (about $1,500 today) in his pocket, he stayed with friends in Southern California. He hoped he might become a mercenary who helped train

Central American military forces in the ways of weapons, explosives, and tactics. But a talk with his mother convinced him to pursue a less romantic lifestyle—at least for the time being. Instead, he was hired as a babysitter for a Beverly Hills couple with a young son and then as a nanny for two boys in Malibu. His selling point to the parents was that he could do the dishes and be a bodyguard to his young charges. Not surprisingly, "Commando Nanny" was the name of a scripted pilot he sold to the WB network based on his early experiences living in Los Angeles.

From that toehold in America, he quickly advanced from selling himself to selling insurance, T-shirts, real estate, credit cards, and television programs. In fact, as a T-shirt salesman in Venice Beach, California, he realized that "the same strategies that applied to selling T-shirts apply to selling TV shows. I still use them today." His love for physical challenges and salesmanship came in handy when in 1992 he joined a team of fellow adventurers for the grueling "Raid Gauloises," in which four-person teams from around the world competed in a variety of athletic tests for five to seven days over four continents. Seeing the potential of "Raid" as a television program, Burnett sold the idea of his renamed "Eco-Challenge" to MTV executives with teams who biked, rafted, and climbed their way around Moab, Utah, in 1995. With the success of the show, Burnett was on his way to becoming a full-time television executive.

"Survivor" has its roots in Burnett's home country. In 1988 British television producer Charlie Parsons conceived of a show he called "Survive!" in which four contestants were shipwrecked on a desert island. The concept was inspired by William Golding's 1954 novel *Lord of the Flies*. Renamed "Castaway," the concept was pitched to the

CBS / Landov

Figure 13.5

As his towering pose and rugged, accessorized outfit suggest, Mark Burnett is a macho dude. He is a survivor not only of the British Army Parachute Regiment, but also of network television.

British Broadcasting Corporation (BBC) by Parsons for the Planet 24 television company, owned by the Irish political activist and rock star Bob Geldof. The BBC liked the idea so much they decided to produce their own version of the show, "Castaway 2000." Parsons and Geldof then sold the idea to a Swedish production company with the new name "Exhibition Robinson," in honor of the novels *Robinson Crusoe* by Daniel Defoe and *The Swiss Family Robinson* by Johann David Wyss. The Swedish program featured the setup now familiar to American audiences—16 contestants and a camera crew were left on an island for six weeks. Every week, one contestant was voted off until there was a winner. Controversy ensued after the first contestant voted off tragically killed himself. Nevertheless, by the fourth season the last episode was one of the highest rated shows in Swedish television history.

In 1996, Burnett talked with Parsons at a party and discussed buying the U.S. rights to the program. Burnett pitched the show to all the major networks without success. Finally CBS reconsidered and gave it a try. The first U.S. "Survivor" aired during the summer of 2000. It became more than a hit—it was a cultural phenomenon, watched by over 70 million viewers. It earned over $50 million for Viacom, the parent company of CBS. It gave its 16 contestants their 15 minutes of fame and then some. The star of the show and winner of $1 million was a "gay, overweight corporate trainer from Newport, Rhode Island," Richard Hatch. Later, Hatch was sentenced to four years in prison after he was convicted for not paying taxes on his winnings (Figure 13.6).

Since 2000, Mark Burnett has been the executive producer of more than 40 television programs, including "The Apprentice" for NBC, in which contestants or B-level celebrities vie to work for real estate tycoon Donald Trump and his comb-over; "The Casino" for Fox, which documented the efforts of owners, employees, and

CBS Broadcasting Inc., 2000

Figure 13.6
Although the infographic at the right of the website page indicates that viewers thought former Navy SEAL Rudy Boesch would win the $1 million, Richard Hatch came away with the cash. This website for the first "Survivor" contains familiar features—top four final words, profiles of the contestants, the logo and slogan "Outwit Outplay Outlast," and three promotional references for the next show, "Survivor: The Australian Outback."

gamblers during the reopening of the Las Vegas Golden Nugget Hotel and Casino; "The Contender" for NBC, produced with DreamWorks executive Jeffrey Katzenberg and actor Sylvester Stallone of *Rocky* (with boxers Sugar Ray Leonard and George Foreman conducting on-air interviews); and "Are You Smarter than a 5th Grader?" hosted by comedian Jeff Foxworthy for Fox. In 2009 Burnett ventured into the genre of documentaries when he produced a series for the History Channel, "Expedition Africa: Stanley & Livingstone," in which four adventurers retraced the 19th century journalist Henry Stanley's search for the explorer Dr. David Livingstone.

■ ANALYSIS OF "SURVIVOR"

Schadenfreude is a German word that literally translates to "harm's joy," but roughly means taking pleasure from

Figure 13.7
Jeff Probst shows off his Emmy award in 2009 after winning it for hosting "Survivor."

Robyn Beck / Afp / Getty Images

another's misfortune. This concept might explain why the personal shortcomings of celebrities are so popular in tabloid magazines and on television. It also explains why it is amusing to learn that "Survivor" host Jeff Probst "was stung by a jellyfish during Survivor 1, received an electric shock when he relieved himself on an electric fence in Survivor 2 and was stung by a scorpion in Survivor 3." Certainly the Emmy awards he won in 2008 and 2009 for his work as host of the show made him feel better (Figure 13.7).

Although there is little doubt that the popularity of the show is because it "is part escapism and part game show, a chance to watch attractive, scantily clad contestants battle physically and psychologically in beautiful, contrived settings, and guess who will be voted off the island each week," a chief factor in its success is also that each contestant is humiliated and humbled. With a wide range of ages, genders, races, ethnicities, and lifestyle choices among the participants, chances are a viewer somewhere will either identify with or wish ill of someone who happens to make it on one of the most popular television shows in America.

Toward that end, the application that everyone must fill out for the show is quite egalitarian. All are welcome to apply: You need only be at least 21 years old and willing to travel at your own expense for an initial interview, have a lot of time on your hands during the summer, be a U.S. citizen who is not running for a political office, be in excellent physical and mental health, and be able to produce a three-minute video about yourself. Those who are picked for the 16 spots are a familiar representation of people you might find standing alongside you in a post office or at a driver's license bureau. Mark Burnett makes that aspect of the show clear when he states, "My goal with 'Survivor' was to show how a small group of normal people would interact with one another when stranded under harsh conditions, while at [the same] time trying to win one million dollars."

"Survivor" works because we can all see ourselves as a survivor; but as most of us did not apply to be on the show, we take pleasure in passively watching our surrogate selves search for water, sleep in the rain, eat bugs, and survive the vote off the show. As Ghen Maynard, a CBS executive who was an early advocate of the show, admitted, "'Survivor' is very much about two things: The effect of deprivation and the fear of rejection. Both are social issues."

With humidity, rain, sand, and electrical power concerns, running, shooting, and editing the show is no easy matter. The 39-day shooting schedule requires a crew of 85 members. Ten teams of filmmakers—each consisting of one camera and one audio technician as well as several editors, art designers, construction personnel, island guides, a medical team, a makeup person, and various other technical members—are only part of the "Survivor" production team. Available light is used during daytime scenes, whereas the "Tribal Council" meeting scenes have stage lighting powered by portable generators and car batteries. Night scenes back at the camps are filmed with special low-light cameras.

One of the reasons Mark Burnett has been financially successful is that he has redefined the way advertising is shown; in fact, much of it is sold by Burnett himself. Because of its popularity, "Survivor" receives more than $400,000 per 30-second commercial. But Burnett also has been a leader in product and marketing "integration," in which he gets advertisers to pay extra for product placements. That

is why Jeff Probst, the host, often entices hungry and exhausted contestants with "a bag of Doritos and a can of Mountain Dew" as prizes for that week's competition. But those aren't the only sponsors. Contestants are also teased with products from Tylenol, Home Depot, Proctor & Gamble, and Chevrolet, among others. Mixing advertising and programming is unfortunately a fact of doing business in this age of TiVo, Video on Demand, and web television viewing options in an era in which viewers can control when and what they watch.

The most dramatic part of any episode, when members discuss each other and vote one of the group off the game, is a product of sophisticated editing techniques. The dénouement takes several hours of carefully worded questions from Probst with the scene edited down into a seven-minute segment. "At its purest level, there is really no such thing as reality TV," says Chris Cowen of the canceled show "Temptation Island." "As soon as you start condensing the minutes or hours of a day, it ceases to be reality and is now a manipulated form of reality." In addition, the producers do not always tell contestants all the information they need to know about living in the remote area. For example, in an episode of the "Survivor All-Stars," Sue Hawk caused other contestants to worry when she drank water right out of a well before it had been boiled to kill any parasites. But the water was safe to drink. The producers of the show didn't reveal that information to members of the tribe in order to heighten the drama.

The unscripted reality program format has inspired other producers to try a similar technique with their shows. Critically acclaimed but often audience-challenged shows such as HBO's "Curb

Your Enthusiasm," Comedy Central's "Reno 911!," and the cancelled Fox program "Arrested Development" all allowed the actors to ad-lib their lines after being given brief outlines with plot points. Such techniques may be the answer to any future writers' strike, since extensive writing is not required.

In many ways, "Survivor" and other game-oriented reality programs feature the best and worst elements about television and American society. The people chosen for the unscripted program, the situations and challenges they must overcome, and the dramatic camerawork and careful editing help sustain interest for 13 one-hour episodes. Each season epitomizes all the elements needed for a top television program when characters, situations, words, pictures, and audio come together within the confines of the screened medium and are combined with the comfort of watching the show at home (Weblink 13.8).

■ TELEVISION AND THE SIX PERSPECTIVES

Personal Perspective

Television is easy to criticize. Former Federal Communications Commission (FCC) chair Newton Minow in a 1961 speech called the medium "a vast wasteland." Philosopher Bertrand Russell growled that it is nothing more than "chewing gum for the eyes." In some cultures, it is hip to criticize "the boob tube." Mark Miller, in his book *Boxed In*, writes that "a great deal of the time when we are watching TV we know that it is stupid and enjoy the feeling of superiority." Mark Frost, co-creator with David Lynch of the short-lived and critically acclaimed "Twin Peaks"

television series, admits, "In this country, television is used primarily as a narcotic to prepare people for the commercial." David Chase, the creative force behind HBO's successful series "The Sopranos," also has a dim view of television. In a 2004 interview Chase said, "Television is at the base of a lot of our problems. It trivializes everything. So there's no more mystery, we've seen it all 50,000 times. And in order to make the boring interesting, everything is hyped." Tough words from someone who has been so successful with the medium.

Many viewers use a remote control device to flip from one program to another in the sometimes frustrating effort to find something interesting to watch. Called *channel grazing*, the curious habit of discovering a good program without the aid of a television guide evokes the wide-open plains of the Old West—the metaphor of a better life over the next hill or around the bend. That promise of a better program through the next push of a button is where television gets its power.

In the early history of the medium, viewers were content to be intrigued by the low-quality flickering pictures. With few stations and programs, people watched whatever was broadcast because they were easily fascinated. Today, viewers are more fickle, demanding constant entertainment. The reason is simple—television actually is radio with pictures, and radio has roots deep in vaudeville theater. Consequently, television always was meant to be more of an entertainment than an educational medium. The high ideals and educational hopes came later. If you learn something from "The Beverly Hillbillies" or "Masterpiece Theatre," it is only because entertainment has been made educational. Conversely, producers of more serious television fare hope that they make education entertaining.

Whether you don't watch television at all or watch it for several hours each day, one conclusion is clear: TV is a medium in which the viewer is charged with the task of making sense of it all. Jack Perkins said of the Arts & Entertainment cable network that it "shows the entire scope of television, which is, of course, the entire scope of life." Television is life because it reveals much about the lives of those inside and outside the screen. Whether conscious of television's effect or blissfully unaware, people eventually succumb to the enticing images that flicker across the glowing glass or plasma frame.

Probably the chief reason why television is so routinely criticized is the queasy feeling that comes from the thought that despite all the great moments presented—all the news, drama, comedy, and sports—television never has lived up to its potential. One source that helps to improve the medium's credibility is the Archive of American Television. It provides one of the best resources for the appreciation of television in a collection that contains more than 1,000 hours of interviews with producers, performers, and production personnel (Weblink 13.9). Regardless, there is always a feeling that television should be something more— something better. Stay tuned (Figure 13.8).

Historical Perspective

In the 1930s when Hollywood executives first learned about the new medium of television, they laughed at the idea of a radio with pictures. In the 1940s they were concerned enough to reduce ticket prices and offer double features. In the 1950s the war was over—television had

become the single most popular form of entertainment for Americans. The laughing stopped.

The birth of modern television began in 1922 after two scientists with Western Electric, the research arm of AT&T, started selling the cathode ray tube (CRT), a vacuum tube that accelerates a beam of electrons onto a florescent screen (Figure 13.9). That same year, an Idaho high school student, Philo (or Phil, as he preferred) Farnsworth, 14, inspired by the rows of upturned soil after plowing his family's field, invented a model for television (Weblink 13.10). Five years later, Farnsworth transmitted a vertical black line on a CRT that moved back and forth like his plow against a lit background. He

Figure 13.8

Old, small-screen television sets are a part of this historical display in the Amberley Working Museum, England.

Agri Press / Lifesize / Jupiter Images

Figure 13.9

This diagram for a black-and-white television receiver (color sets have three cathode ray tubes [CATs], one for each primary color) identifies its various parts. Within a vacuum tube, electron beams are focused on a fluorescent screen to make it glow with a picture. For the most part, plasma, liquid crystal, digital light processing (DLP), and organic light-emitting diodes (OLEDs) have replaced the CATs.

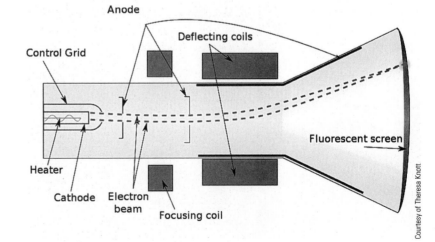

Courtesy of Theresa Knott

Figure 13.10

"Philo Farnsworth with a television set he invented," 1928. The profile of the woman on the small, round screen is most likely simulated for this publicity shot, because the quality of the TV image was never that good.

Figure 13.11

More than 44 million people attended the 1939 New York World's Fair held in Flushing Meadows, the author's birthplace. Part of the attraction was the NBC exhibition that featured television. President Franklin Roosevelt delivered an opening day speech that was televised by NBC for about 1,000 viewers watching on 200 sets in the New York area.

Courtesy of the San Francisco History Center, San Francisco Public Library

Bettmann / Corbis

called his device an "image dissector." In 1928, at 20 years old, he demonstrated his invention to investors at his San Francisco laboratory by showing them a transmission of, perhaps fittingly, a dollar sign. In 1929 his wife Elma, known as "Pem," posed for a live image with her eyes closed because of the bright light needed for the picture. Farnsworth later established research centers in Indiana and his birth state of Utah. He is credited with 300 U.S.

and international patents contributing to advances in radar, the electron microscope, and the astronomical telescope (Figure 13.10).

Because of the interest in television, GE, RCA, and Westinghouse scientists merged their research operations in 1930. Russian immigrant Vladimir Zworykin headed the television team. He visited Farnsworth and was impressed enough to have his engineers produce a copy. In their laboratory in New Jersey, the scientists improved on Farnsworth's invention with what they called the iconoscope electronic scanning tube for television with patents purchased from Kálmán Tihanyi. The Hungarian inventor introduced his Radioskop system in 1926. RCA's variation of television was more practical than Farnsworth's process because it required less light. Nevertheless, the first transmission was a crude, 60-line reproduction of a small cartoon drawing of the popular character Felix the Cat, the work of Australian cartoonist Pat Sullivan and American animator Otto Messmer. However, the first networked demonstration of television in the United States occurred on April 7, 1927, via the technology of AT&T Bell Telephone Laboratories. The live picture and voice of Secretary of Commerce Herbert Hoover was broadcast from a funeral home in Washington, D.C., to a receiver in an auditorium in New York City. "Today we have, in a sense, the transmission of sight for the first time in the world's history," Hoover said. "Human genius has now destroyed the impediment of distance in a new respect, and in a manner hitherto unknown." Later that same day another demonstration sent a televised image via a radio transmission.

However, with RCA's head start and financial advantage, the AT&T system couldn't compete. The iconoscope was soon improved with a 441-line picture scanner. The success of these experiments led David Sarnoff, president of RCA, to decide in 1932 to invest heavily in this new technology. It was Sarnoff who came up with the word *television*. The New York World's Fair in 1939 first introduced the American public to the new medium (Figure 13.11).

Concerned about competing technologies that would delay the spread of television, the Federal Communications Commission (FCC), a U.S. regulatory body overseeing radio and television, authorized sets to contain a 525-line electron scanner for black-and-white transmission in 1941. World War II temporarily halted the spread of television because of the need for the country to concentrate on the war effort. During the war years, only six stations were broadcasting to about 10,000 sets in the United States. Most of them were in bars, bowling alleys, appliance store windows, and the homes of wealthier families. Broadcasting was lim-

ited to a short time in the evening. Radio employees re-created their popular programs, announced some news, and narrated sporting events.

After the war, attention once again turned to television, and commercial television broadcasting began in earnest. NBC, CBS, and ABC dominated the market because of the expense of establishing a network and the limited number of stations operating in any one area. The popular vaudeville-style variety shows of Milton Berle and Ed Sullivan were typical broadcasts (Figure 13.12).

Many writers have dubbed the 1950s the "golden age" of television because of technological and programming innovations. One fact is clear: During the decade, television gained a tremendous number of viewers and became a true mass medium.

Fifteen million homes in the United States had television sets by 1956, and 500 broadcast stations in the United States were generating more than $1 billion

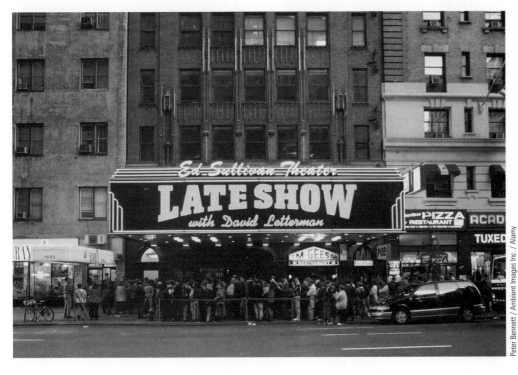

Figure 13.12

"The Ed Sullivan Show" was one of the most popular variety shows on television. Broadcast from 1948 to 1971, it was hosted by the genial yet awkward host Ed Sullivan. Elvis Presley and The Beatles are among the countless acts that were introduced to the American public on the show. Today the theater where the show originated is named after Sullivan, and it is where "The Late Show with David Letterman" is produced.

Peter Bennett / Ambient Images Inc. / Alamy

Figure 13.13

Host Jack Barry of the tainted television quiz show "Twenty-One" turns toward contestant Charles Van Doren as fellow contestant Vivienne Nearing looks on. Canceled in 1958 after a congressional investigation discovered that the show was rigged, the "Twenty-One" scandal had a lasting effect on all television game shows and their participants. Jack Barry was forced into exile and didn't work again on television until a decade later. Nearing, who at the time was a lawyer for Warner Bros. and beat champion Van Doren, was disbarred for six months after being convicted of lying to a grand jury about the show. Charles Van Doren resigned his position as an assistant professor at Columbia University, but he became an editor for the Encyclopædia Britannica, *author of several books, and is now an adjunct professor at the University of Connecticut, Torrington, for the English department, along with his wife, Gerry. Sponsor-controlled involvement in the playing of game shows was eliminated, and contestants were forbidden to have any personal conversations with a host.*

($8 billion today) in advertising sales. In addition to movie stars, theater actors were persuaded to perform on television in the mid-1950s. For example, the "I Love Lucy" show was a landmark production in 1951 for many reasons. Produced by Lucille Ball and Desi Arnaz through their Desilu production company in studios purchased from the failed movie studio RKO, the situation comedy was filmed with three cameras in front of a live audience and was enormously successful. Filmed productions meant that the shows could be shown again and again as reruns for additional profits.

Several attempts were made in the 1950s to censor content and individuals. In 1950, Senator Estes Kefauver led a movement to curtail violence portrayed on television programs. Kefauver's attempts at censorship coincided with another senator's effort to root out alleged Communists in the government and media. Joseph McCarthy of Wisconsin helped publish *Red Channels: The Report of Communist Influence in Radio and Television*. The report listed 151 suspects, whom the networks blacklisted because of fear of advertiser boycotts. In 1952, the FCC, concerned about the content of programs sent into homes, required that 10 percent (later increased to 35 percent) of a day's broadcasting be educational. This regulation marked the beginning of the FCC's shift from technical issues to content regulation. McCarthy was discredited and later censured by the Senate in 1954 after a news broadcast by Edward R. Murrow, the CBS journalist, who revealed McCarthy's unfair smear practices.

In 1958 a quiz show scandal rocked the television industry. A congressional investigation discovered that contestants had been coached with the correct answers in order to make the programs more dramatic. The networks canceled many quiz shows after Charles Van Doren testified that he had been given the answers for the show "Twenty-One" (Figure 13.13). Quiz shows soon returned to daytime

Library of Congress Prints and Photographs Division, LC-USZ62-126813

television, but under much stiffer regulations. The controversy was examined in the 1994 movie *Quiz Show*, directed by Robert Redford (Weblink 13.11).

Color, videotape, and cable were introduced in the 1950s. However, CBS and RCA proposed two different systems for camera and receiver color. The FCC tried to delay the switch to color, fearing that the transition would be too expensive. Nevertheless, the FCC approved RCA's color technology as the industry standard. The first color television set was introduced in 1954 at a cost of $1,000 (about $8,000 today). Because of the high cost of the sets and the time required for stations to convert to color, they were not immediately popular.

In the late 1950s, a southern California company, Ampex, who was more known for its sound equipment, began working on a videotape system. At the National Association of Broadcasters (NAB) annual convention in Chicago in 1956, Charles Ginsburg demonstrated the new method for recording programs. The convention was set up with closed-circuit television for those not able to get into the auditorium. Ginsburg tapped into the system, recorded a few minutes of the proceedings, and played the tape back for astonished attendees. Within days of the NAB convention, Ampex received about 50 orders for its $74,000 videotape system (about $600,000 today). CBS was one of the first customers and began rebroadcasting its nightly news program called "Douglas Edwards and the News" to its West Coast affiliates at a normal viewing time (Figure 13.14).

Another innovation of using videotape was that it allowed high-quality reproductions of programs, so that huge amounts of money could be made from showing reruns of previously aired shows. Desi

Arnaz no longer had a monopoly with his filmed reruns. In 1967 the public became aware of the potential for videotape technology to add to their viewing pleasure when instant replay was introduced during a Super Bowl football game. With the advent of instant replay technology for sports programs, ABC became a leading network. In addition, new sports leagues were formed to take advantage of the tremendous profits by selling commercials during televised sporting events.

Cable or pay television began as a way to bring television to communities in Pennsylvania that were nestled among mountains that prevented over-the-air reception. The cable company received television signals and then piped them into individual homes through coaxial cable links. Customers paid about $10 a month for the service (or about the price of cable today, $80). By 1960, more than 90 percent of the homes in the United States had at least one television set. Cable companies flourished, with more than 650,000 subscribers and 640 different cable firms. Besides better reception, viewers with cable could get many more channels and commercial-free sporting events and movies. In 1962, AT&T and

SSPL / The Image Works

Figure 13.14

Begun in 1944 by the Russian-born engineer Alexander M. Poniatoff, Ampex (his initials combined with "EX" for excellence) is an electronics company more known for its audio equipment. However, in 1956 the VR-1000A shown here was the first videotape recorder introduced by the company. One reel of tape cost $300 ($2,400 today), and the entire machine was priced at about $100,000 ($803,000 today).

NASA collaborated to develop and launch the first communications satellite, Telstar I. With other launches, live same-time programming across the United States became popular.

Action-adventure dramas produced outside of theater studios were the most popular shows. One of the most controversial was the Desilu production of "The Untouchables." With its Elliot Ness–inspired stories, car crashes, and flying bullets, the show, according to a Senate subcommittee, was "the most violent program on television." Concerned that Congress might seek censorship through legislation, network executives moved most of their production facilities to California, where Hollywood was responsible for mass appeal, inoffensive sitcoms such as "Mr. Ed," "Gilligan's Island," and "The Beverly Hillbillies."

Although most of these entertainment programs were criticized, news and sports during the politically troubled 1960s

were experiencing their own golden age. With satellite and videotape technology, news programs could cover many social and political events. The 1960 televised presidential debate between John Kennedy and Richard Nixon demonstrated to political managers the importance of a candidate's image on television for the first time (Figure 13.15). Vivid images of assassinations, civil rights marches, political speeches, and the Vietnam War had a tremendous impact on viewers who watched them on their home screens. The effect of bringing the outside world's problems into the home was that the social problems protested in the 1960s could not be ignored.

In the 1970s, the federal government became much more proactive in regulating television content. Congressional action banned cigarette commercials from television in 1972. (To avoid a similar fate, beer company advertisements never show a person actually drinking.) In that

Figure 13.15

During the 1960 presidential campaign, Senator John F. Kennedy and Vice President Richard M. Nixon agreed to have one of their debates televised for the first time ever. Broadcast from NBC studios in Washington, surveys conducted afterward indicated that those who heard the debate on the radio thought Nixon had won, whereas those who watched it on television thought Kennedy came out ahead. Consequently, the visual image of candidates became a serious consideration for politicians and their handlers even though the next televised presidential debate didn't occur until 1976, between Governor Jimmy Carter and President Gerald Ford.

Bettmann/Bettmann / Corbis

same year, cable became competitive with the broadcast networks when Home Box Office (HBO) started to air second-run movies. Also, spin-offs, or shows based on characters from previously broadcast programs, proliferated. For example, the popular sitcoms "All in the Family" and "The Mary Tyler Moore Show" resulted in 15 separate spin-offs and gave independent television production companies—Tandem for "Family" and MTM Productions for "Moore"—as much financial clout as the movie studios.

During this era, professional electronic news gathering (ENG) videotape trucks were equipped with all the switching and editing equipment found in a station's control room. Large ENG trucks became common sights outside sports stadiums when games were televised. When the technology became linked with satellites and the equipment grew smaller, local news stations could send news teams to cover events anywhere in a city or the world. To further increase the popularity of home video recording equipment, in the 1980s Sony introduced its Video 8 camera (the palmcorder). It was a small, lightweight camera that used high-quality 8-mm tape. Home users also desired the ability to record and watch feature-length movies. When videotaped movies became available for overnight rental in 1977 from a single store in Los Angeles, they were instantly enormously popular. That led Mel Brooks, the director of *Blazing Saddles* and *Young Frankenstein*, to remark that "pictures never die. They go to heaven. It's called video."

An economic downturn in the 1980s caused companies to merge to save money. Capital Cities Communication bought ABC, General Electric purchased NBC's parent company RCA, and Westinghouse bought CBS. Cost-cutting measures at all three networks resulted in fewer highly trained journalists in their news divisions. This move allowed Ted Turner's 24-hour news channel, the Cable News Network (CNN), to become the preeminent source for worldwide news. To further protect their investments, television networks, cable companies, and movie studios formed partnerships. In 1985, Australian tabloid mogul Rupert Murdoch bought half control of the movie studio 20th Century Fox. Two years later the Fox Broadcasting Company, a fourth broadcasting network, introduced one night per week of Fox-produced shows to its 105 independent stations. With the success of "The Simpsons" and "Cops," its programming, once dominated by reruns, expanded to include several original productions and news shows.

In 2009 a technological shift as fundamental as the move from black-and-white to color television sets took place: the transition from analog to digital broadcasting and receiving. Implementation of the switch to high definition, digital television (called HDTV or simply DTV) was delayed several times while regulators worked with manufacturers to make sure the technology was the best possible and the government worked with various agencies and public groups to make sure citizens were informed fully of what would be needed for the transition to digital. Despite all the publicity about the switch, anywhere from one to three million lower-income, elderly, disabled, young, and non-English-speaking U.S. households lost their television signal because they watched television via an antenna and failed to get a converter box for the DTV digital signal.

Equally transformational to the history of television is the way viewers can now watch their favorite programs. Seth

MacFarlane, the creator of the animated situation comedy "Family Guy" on the Fox network, said, "I think what we're seeing right now is a great cultural shift of how this country watches television." He was referring to the trend toward seeing shows on a computer. A Nielsen Media Research survey discovered that 25 percent of all internet users watch television episodes online. And with all those viewers, more programs are produced. For example, the successful team of Marshall Herskovitz and Edward Zwick ("My So-Called Life" and "thirtysomething") produced "quarterlife," a drama that was originally available to users of the MyspaceTV.com social networking site in 2007. The series also aired on NBC and Bravo (Weblink 13.12). Some critics have predicted that because of the switch to DTV, more viewers will forego watching programs on their actual television sets and use their computers and cell phones instead as higher-quality 4G (or Fourth Generation) wireless internet connections become the norm.

 Technical Perspective

Movie studio executives laughed when they first saw television because they never believed that the small, fuzzy black-and-white picture, with its poor audio component, would ever be a serious threat to their industry. What they did not imagine was how resourceful technicians would be in improving the medium. Over the years, cameras, transmission modes, and receivers have been refined continuously.

■ Cameras

A video camera's controls are similar to those of a still camera, and shot considerations are determined in the same way as those in motion pictures. A camera has a tube or microchip, called a *charge-coupled device* (CCD), that converts the image into an electrical equivalent. When a television operator focuses on a subject with the camera's lens, the picture strikes a layer of photosensitive material consisting of dots, which emit an electrical charge. A dot in a light part of a picture sends a higher charge than one in a darker part of the image. All the electrical charges from the dots strike a target and compose an electrical version of the image in the form of 525 lines (or 636 or 840 lines for non-U.S. systems). An electron gun in the back of the camera generates a steady stream of electrons that scan the target. In the U.S. system, the electron scanning starts with the odd-numbered lines and repeats the process with the even-numbered lines. The two scans take 1/30th of a second, or accomplishes the scanning at a rate of 30 frames a second.

The scanned electrical images are sent through a wire to monitors in the master control area of the station, where a director composes the program by switching from one camera's image to another. These images are recorded on videotape to be broadcast at a later time or are transmitted immediately.

■ Transmission Modes

Television signals can be sent to a home through the air and picked up from rooftop antennae and satellite dishes or by telephone lines and coaxial or fiber optic cable. Originally a home required a large roof-mounted antenna to pick up the audio and video signals sent by a broadcast television station. The sound signal was sent via an FM radio frequency. The pictures came from either VHF or UHF channels on the electromagnetic spectrum. Both VHF and UHF are known as line-of-sight carrier waves. The more powerful VHF stations can usually go around barriers such as buildings, mountains, or large weather systems, but UHF channels are susceptible to interference. The broadcasting of television programs by VHF and UHF stations first introduced television into people's homes. However, such methods are obsolete since the switch to DTV.

Since the 1970s, consumers have been able to buy large and expensive receiving dishes and point them in a southern direction to capture television images from a satellite in a geosynchronous orbit around the earth. People living in rural communities, where broadcast stations didn't reach and the distance

was too far for the local cable company to string wire to their houses, first used these dishes (Figure 13.16). But viewers in cities learned that they could receive hundreds of channels from all over the world and many premium cable networks (e.g., HBO, Showtime, the Playboy Channel, and others) without having to pay a monthly charge. Direct broadcast satellites (DBSs) are the new generation of reception technology that use digital transmission to send hundreds of channels to 18-inch-diameter, window-mounted dishes with high-quality images and sound. For example, Hughes Electronics Corporation, with its DirecTV service, has three high-powered satellites in space that enable home users to receive more than 185 television channels.

Figure 13.16

Many people living in rural communities are too far away to receive television broadcast signals and find that getting a cable connection is too expensive. Consequently, they are forced to buy satellite dishes. This photograph is a study in contrast. A woman outside Bloomington, Indiana, burns her own trash—an ancient chore—amid two satellite dishes; she explains, "I have two TVs."

Courtesy of Paul Martin Lester

However, most viewers of television don't use an antenna. The most common home connections for television are through cable. Coaxial cable comprises two wires that are separated by insulation; one cable transmits the sound, and the other transmits the picture. A cable company pays a fee to receive signals from program producers via a large satellite dish. The coaxial cable connects the operator's facility to a person's home. Depending on the services desired, a home can receive anywhere from 50 to 500 channels. The cable company supplies a converter box that connects to the television set and changes the cable signal so that the receiver can show the images. However, most new TV sets are "cable-ready," having a built-in signal converter.

■ *Receivers*

High-definition digital television (HDTV or DTV) presents pictures as sharp as high-quality photographs—ten times the picture resolution obtained by traditional analog television broadcasts. In addition, the sound is of DVD quality. In order to receive the digital signal, home users either are connected through their cable company or have a set-top box that converts the digital signal from an antenna to an analog version for a TV set. Many of the

Figure 13.17

Perhaps it's a bit much to ask of a big-screen TV set, but according to promotional material from Hitachi, the "Inspire the Next" slogan refers to the company's "being a new breath of air that will infuse the next generation and future societies, and expresses our attitude of applying the 'pioneering spirit' . . . to confront the challenges of that next generation."

estimated 15 million households who use antennas to receive a TV signal complained that the picture was poor and they lost some channels in the transmission.

With digital transmissions, television sets are interactive computers in which users can order shows when they want to view them, watch sporting events from specific cameras on the field, learn more information about a program's topic through the web, order products seen in shows, and so on (Figure 13.17). In 2009, plasma slim-screen DTV manufacturer Fujitsu offered a 50-inch monitor for $4,499. It was a bargain when compared with the 65-inch model, which was originally priced at $17,999. In addition, most plasma television sets require much more electrical power to operate, which adds, depending on the size, more than $100 to an annual bill. Panasonic makes a 103-inch plasma display that is too big for most home dens, but it can be seen in shopping areas and bars (Weblink 13.13). An alternative is a backlit LED (light-emitting diode) receiver such as Vizio Inc.'s 55-inch receiver, which is far less expensive and uses less energy as well. The granddaddy of big screens is the pair of HD monitors that hang over the playing field of the Dallas Cowboys football stadium. The largest in the world—60 yards wide and 20 yards tall—they use 36 million LEDs that show 25,000 square feet of football action. This Mitsubishi Electric Diamond Vision System cost $40 million. With such a huge, clear picture, will fans bother to watch the live action?

Receiver add-ons, such as amplified "surround sound" speaker systems and digital video players and recorders like those available from TiVo and other companies, are a necessity for many home viewers who want to duplicate a movie theater experience and/or watch a show

Figure 9.2

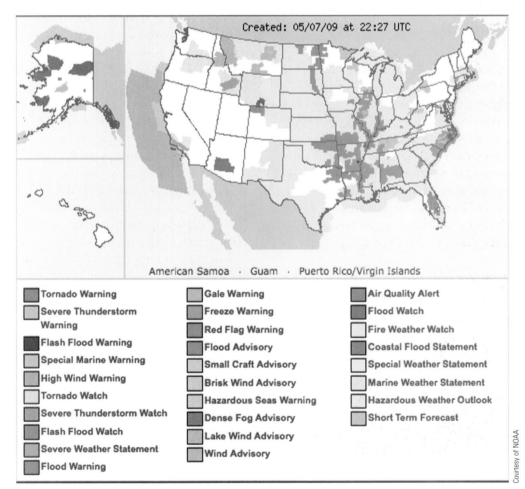

Created: 05/07/09 at 22:27 UTC

American Samoa · Guam · Puerto Rico/Virgin Islands

Tornado Warning	Gale Warning	Air Quality Alert
Severe Thunderstorm Warning	Freeze Warning	Flood Watch
Flash Flood Warning	Red Flag Warning	Fire Weather Watch
Special Marine Warning	Flood Advisory	Coastal Flood Statement
High Wind Warning	Small Craft Advisory	Special Weather Statement
Tornado Watch	Brisk Wind Advisory	Marine Weather Statement
Severe Thunderstorm Watch	Hazardous Seas Warning	Hazardous Weather Outlook
Flash Flood Watch	Dense Fog Advisory	Short Term Forecast
Severe Weather Statement	Lake Wind Advisory	
Flood Warning	Wind Advisory	

Figure 9.5

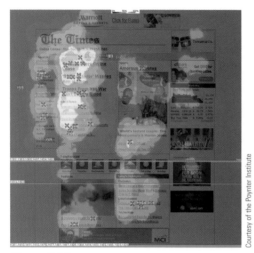

Figure 9.24

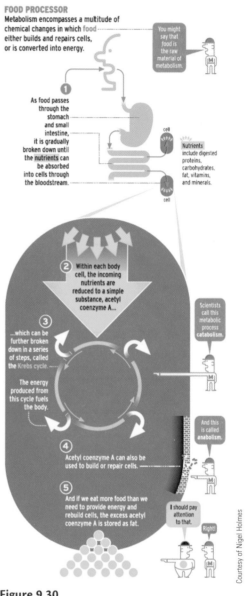

FOOD PROCESSOR

Metabolism encompasses a multitude of chemical changes in which food either builds and repairs cells, or is converted into energy.

You might say that food is the raw material of metabolism.

1 As food passes through the stomach and small intestine, it is gradually broken down until the nutrients can be absorbed into cells through the bloodstream.

cell

Nutrients include digested proteins, carbohydrates, fat, vitamins, and minerals.

cell

2 Within each body cell, the incoming nutrients are reduced to a simple substance, acetyl coenzyme A...

Scientists call this metabolic process catabolism.

3 ...which can be further broken down in a series of steps, called the Krebs cycle.

The energy produced from this cycle fuels the body.

And this is called anabolism.

4 Acetyl coenzyme A can also be used to build or repair cells.

5 And if we eat more food than we need to provide energy and rebuild cells, the excess acetyl coenzyme A is stored as fat.

I should pay attention to that.

Right!

Figure 9.30

Figure 10.1

Figure 10.22

Figure 10.30

Figure 11.22

Figure 11.39

Figure 11.42

at a later time. Similar to the technological war in the 1970s between videocassette tape formats Betamax and the Video Home System (VHS), the Japanese corporate giants Sony and Toshiba fought over the format of high-definition DVDs. Although named Blu-ray, Sony's discs actually use the violet-colored part of the electromagnetic spectrum and thus can hold much more video, audio, and text data than red-light CDs because of their faster wave frequency. Toshiba's HD DVD competing blue laser format was discontinued in 2008 after major movie studios and retailers went with the Blu-ray format.

Ethical Perspective

If you let water gush into a kitchen sink for hours, keep all the lights on during the day, or leave the doors and windows wide open at your home, chances are that eventually you will be criticized for such careless behavior. But a television set left on, even when no one is watching, is a cultural standard. Over a 20-year period, the average household will have a television set operating for almost six years. More disturbing, a 2004 study of 2,600 kids from birth to age seven found that for every hour preschool children watch television, their chances of acquiring a form of attention deficit disorder (ADD) go up to about 10 percent. Another study conducted by the Kaiser Family Foundation found that 36 percent of the 1,000 families surveyed had the TV on all day, and 43 percent of children between four and six years old had a TV in their bedrooms where they could watch programs unsupervised. Not surprisingly, it has been found that children who watch 10 or more hours of television a day have lower

reading scores than those who watch less TV. The American Academy of Pediatrics recommends that children under the age of two not watch any television.

It is no coincidence that a television set usually sits in the most comfortable room in a home. Although an impersonal appliance, it evokes the same emotional response as a favorite chair, a soft pillow, or an interesting friend. Television characters become comfortable personalities whom we invite into our lives. Talk-show hosts and nightly newscast announcers look right into the camera and talk directly to us. The television set must remain on—no one wants to offend a friend.

Television demands a price for its friendship. The cost is acceptance of the image of the moment as real and representative of society as a whole. Such a belief comes from the cultural notion that education and learning are bitter-tasting medicines that end once you are out of school. Acceptance of this notion comes from laziness and peer acceptance. The popular notion is that television is only a form of entertainment, meant to give a laugh or a thrill. Serious, sensitive social issues do not belong on television. Such programming is considered boring, high-minded, and elitist.

Entertainment and education have been merged into something called "edutainment." Programs and commercials all have the same interest level and visual style. Fiction and nonfiction in drama and news shows are jumbled together. Small, insignificant issues become important trends because the medium blows them out of proportion. Vital, important concerns get reduced to a small screen over dinner. Simpleminded stereotypes about people and generalizations about communities are reinforced.

As much as we love television, it is a medium that we love to hate—especially for its reliance on ratings, stereotyping, and sexual and violent themes.

■ *Ratings*

Lynn Gross, in her textbook *See/Hear: An Introduction to Broadcasting*, writes that an unnamed television executive once said, "There are only two rules in broadcasting: Keep the ratings as high as possible and don't get in any trouble." The only networks that sell entertainment in the tradition of Hollywood are the premium cable channels. All other networks, especially the "big four," rely on ratings. Shows need not only large audiences but also viewers who are younger, upscale, and likely to buy the advertised products. An emphasis on ratings relegates high-quality broadcasting to the low-rated Public Broadcasting Service (PBS), which depends on government support and viewer and corporate donations.

■ *Stereotypes*

Expecting television programs to be completely free from some kind of stereotyping of individuals is unreasonable. Someone, somewhere, is bound to object to a media characterization. But because of the enormous scope and influence of television, producers need to be especially sensitive to characterizations that have the potential to cause harm. The problem is that Anglo producers often are unaware of the concerns of those from other cultures. One way of ensuring sensitivity to cultural awareness is by hiring people from diverse cultures. The National Association for the Advancement of Colored People (NAACP) released a report in 2008 that chastised the industry for its Anglo-centric programs. But a surprising development of all the reality television shows is the diversity that can be seen on the programs. Asians, African Americans, and Latinos are often featured contestants in such shows as CBS's "The Amazing Race" and "Survivor," ABC's "Dancing with the Stars," and Fox's "Hell's Kitchen" and "American Idol." However, two exceptions are ABC's "The Bachelor" and "The Bachelorette." According to the *Los Angeles Times*, in 17 seasons, "neither show's main role has even been filled with a person of color" (Weblink 13.14).

■ *Sexual and Violent Themes*

A recent study of viewer behavior estimated that an American child who watches three hours of television a day will see 8,000 murders and some 100,000 other acts of violence by the time she is 12 years old. However, television critic Howard Rosenberg makes the point that, although the medium shows thousands of acts of violence, television also displays just as many acts of kindness. "Television violence," Rosenberg writes, "is too simple a solution for violence in the country. It's human nature to seek easy answers to complex questions. Rather than acknowledge the root causes of violence as being deep and complicated, there's a tendency on the part of many to automatically blame television." Sexual aggression and other violent acts committed by members of a culture are partly a result of societal factors—the easy availability of guns, few employment and educational opportunities, and family hardships—and not simply violent portrayals on the screen.

The best defense against gratuitous sex and violence, as well as stereotyping and an emphasis on ratings, is to make intelligent viewing choices. Parents should monitor the viewing habits of their children and explain scenes that disturb them. Offensive shows should not be watched, and uplifting shows should be supported. Because the content of television programs is a result of the collective will of at least part of the culture, each viewer has an ethical and moral responsibility to ensure that positive values are communicated through the media.

🌐 *Cultural Perspective*

Television actually is a mix of four preceding media: the theater, radio, motion pictures, and, perhaps more importantly, the comic book. From the theater came the familiar stage sets so common in sitcoms. The vaudeville theater also contributed the idea of variety acts to the medium. Radio brought its characters, personalities, and story-telling ideas—and the technology to broadcast programs to homes. From motion pictures, television producers learned how to tell their stories in a visual format with the use of multiple cameras and editing techniques. Finally, the comic book gave television its most important concept. Except for made-for-television movies, the basic unit of television isn't an individual program but a continuing series of episodes with the same characters in comfortable surroundings. From week to week and from episode to episode, viewers may live with television actors and their problems over a period of several years. Consequently, television is more a medium of personalities than stories. The screen is a poor place for dramatic action and spectacles. But subtle character development reinforced by close-up shots that fill the frame with the face of a friendly actor works well for television (Weblink 13.15).

In his book *TV Genres*, Brian Rose lists 18 different types of programs that have been shown on television since its inauguration: police, detective, western, medical melodramas, science fiction and fantasy, soap opera, made-for-television movies, docudramas, news, documentary reports, sports, game shows, variety shows, talk shows, children's programming, educational and cultural shows, religious programming, and commercials. Any classification scheme is bound to omit some types. For example, legal melodramas, adult programming, reality-based shows, instructional courses sponsored by local colleges, infomercials, home shopping programming, music videos, and web access and services also are important categories. The reason for the large number of categories for television, as compared with the number of categories for motion pictures, is that television is an intimate medium. Television images come right into the homes of viewers, whereas movies are a social experience separate from everyday home life. Consequently, television is able to explore many more commonly held cultural beliefs and values within a much more varied array of formats than motion pictures.

🔍 *Critical Perspective*

Television caused serious declines in all other mass communications media. But the media that survive are those that can adapt to the challenge offered by television. Many magazines in the 1960s and 1970s, such as *Colliers, Saturday Evening Post, Life,* and *Look,* ended publication because national advertisers preferred television. With advertisers tightening their belts during the 2009 economic downturn, present conditions are not much better. The Magazine Publishers of America reported that the industry suffered a 20 percent loss of revenue for the first three months of 2009 compared to the previous year. In response, newsmagazines such as *Time*, *Newsweek*, and others produce thoughtful, in-depth stories that try to take readers "beyond the headlines" of the 24/7 internet and cable television news channels. Newspapers also suffered severe declines because of television, with some offering web-only presentations and others quitting publication all together.

Polls show that 50 percent of those under 35 years of age prefer to learn about news events from television. But the news shows they are watching are more likely to be produced by MTV, "Entertainment Tonight," or Comedy Central. Many newspapers have folded, but others have hung on because of chain ownership, a more feature-oriented approach, zoned editions, colorful graphics, and engaging interactive web presentations. Radio quit airing dramatic serials and concentrated on obtaining specialized audiences for specific kinds of music and programs. Motion pictures made their screens larger, their pictures more vivid, the sound clearer, and the seats more comfortable. But more important, Hollywood swallowed its pride and accepted the power of television. It now works with TV producers instead of against them. Most sound stages on movie backlots are devoted to television production.

Commercial television emphasizes mainstream political, economic, and cultural values—and champions consumerism. It is no wonder that television can be both addicting and alienating. A research study released in 2009 found that the more time teenagers watch television, the more depressed they were as older adults. Wars and other personal tragedies

reduced to a small screen suddenly segue into a commercial. These curious transitions occur because the bottom line for television executives isn't to sell programs to audiences but to sell audiences to advertisers.

Until that system of funding changes, few innovations will occur in the types of shows the medium offers. But for the first time in its short history, television is getting serious competition from other media, which may fundamentally alter the way television is presented. More people than ever are spending less time watching network offerings, preferring cable programs, DVD movies, video games, and the web. The reason cable and alternative video sources are successful is that they rely on the diversity of audience interests—not advertisers' preferences.

As we gradually become a society that doesn't write letters and is dependent on visual signs and language, television can remind us, if we let it, that it is an important part of the making of history. More and more, we will be connected to the past by the images we have made. They become what we call our collective memory that will be passed to future generations. Television may be "a vast wasteland," but it allows a lot of space for the creation of memorable visual messages if a culture demands value from it. Viewers need to graze less and learn to settle for more.

■ TRENDS TO WATCH FOR TELEVISION

The old-fashioned idea of television as a one-way, anesthetizing viewing experience soon will be an anachronism. The days of videotape and DVD presentations may be numbered, as viewers become users able to download any program from web-based menu choices. Rental companies such as Blockbuster and West Coast Video long ago quit offering videotapes, making the switch to more durable and convenient DVD discs (Figure 13.18).

Television is being replaced by large, flat-screen, high-resolution digital computer monitors in which viewers can watch almost any program or movie made at any time, connect to the web to watch or learn more about a presentation, and talk to a friend over the telephone, all with the same device. Digital video players such as the Roku Netflix Player and the Apple TV connect a computer to a television monitor for easy viewing of movies and television programs. Websites such as Hulu.com, a joint venture of NBC Universal and News Corp., CBS Interactive's TV.com, Sony's Crackle.com, and Google's YouTube.com allow users to access videos of current and canceled television shows and movies, with many preceded by commercials just as with traditional TV. The Disney-ABC television group also includes its popular hit shows such as "Grey's Anatomy" and "Desperate Housewives" on Hulu (Weblink 13.16). The media giant felt that ABC and Disney needed a "broader distribution for is shows" than its dedicated websites. In 2009 Disney launched its Stage 9 website that featured original online series such as the 10-episode science fiction thriller "Trenches" and "Squeegees," a comedy about window washers (Weblink 13.17). Satellite TV for cars à la AT&T's Cruise-Cast, attachments to cell phones so you can project your favorite show on any surface available from Samsung, and large screen receivers that use less energy are becoming more common (Weblink 13.18). In addition, 3-D TV screens like those offered by Panasonic and Sony

Courtesy of Paul Martin Lester

Figure 13.18

A typical array of videotapes line a shelf at the author's home. Many people predict, however, that soon the format will be outdated as cable and wireless connections make them obsolete.

will gain in popularity as more 3-D programming is offered. As a test of viewer acceptance, in 2009 ESPN broadcast the first college football game, USC vs. Ohio State, in 3-D to audiences in venues in Los Angeles, Ohio, Connecticut, and Texas. In 2009 the Ubisoft video game company introduced "Avatar: The Game" based on James Cameron's motion picture with a version that plays on 3-D TV sets with users wearing special glasses.

As videotaped movies and programs for rent or sale are a quaint anachronism, so too will be DVD rentals. In 2009 Blockbuster teamed with TiVo to deliver movies on demand—users can collect and watch their favorite shows from the comfort of their homes on television, computers, game players such as Xbox, or on a cell phone screen.

How we access and watch television programs will change as well. South Korean subway riders were the first in the world to be able to watch TV from their cell phones in 2005. In 2009 the cable arm of media giant Time Warner announced "TV Everywhere," which allows subscribers to watch on-demand cable shows online—either through a home computer or a portable device such as a Black-Berry Storm, Pearl, or Curve, a Palm Inc. Pre, or an Apple iPhone, while Comcast Corp. started a wireless television service in Atlanta, Chicago, Philadelphia, and Portland, Oregon, using the high-speed WiMax network for laptop computer users only.

Since many people carry and use video and digital cameras as part of their cell phones, news organizations can now show dramatic video of tragic events shot by amateurs. Making video is made easier with the UltraHD camcorder from Flip video (Weblink 13.19). George Holliday's video of the Rodney King beating is a case in point, but "Seinfeld" actor Michael Richards also learned to be wary of the technology after shocked audience members recorded and uploaded to YouTube a racist rant he spewed at a comedy club in 2006 (Weblink 13.20). Reality-based television programs and electronic video monitoring systems are also common uses for the equipment. Security systems at homes and businesses record the actions of every passerby; police officers have digital cameras in their patrol cars to monitor the actions of those detained or arrested; and news teams hide cameras in their clothing to record illegal practices for the visually oriented nightly newscasts. Sometimes gruesome shootings during convenience store robberies captured by digital monitoring equipment are aired on newscasts. Made possible by the digital revolution, the spread of sensational news is a chief concern of many of television's social critics.

With the global economic downturn of 2009, many traditional television customers such as national car dealers have pulled their commercials off the air.

Consequently, TV executives who need the revenue are allowing once taboo products and services. Liquor ads are rarely seen on TV, but Absolut Vodka brought them back during the Grammy Awards show in 2009. The NBA reversed a long-time ban and allowed courtside liquor ads that can be seen by viewers at home. In addition, infomercials, once seen only in the middle of the night, can be seen during prime-time hours and hawk everything from "extramarital affairs and the intimate uses of K-Y Jelly" to Vince Offer's favorite product ShamWow! (Weblink 13.21).

The Emmy, one of the most prestigious awards given to television programs, and those who are responsible for them made history in 2008 with the 60th presentation as it was the first time a basic cable show—AMC channel's "Mad Men," about those who work for a 1960s-era advertising agency—won for best dramatic series (Weblink 13.22). The "Mad" feat was repeated the next year. Non-network programs won 59 of the 55 awards given out in 2009. HBO took 21 and AMC had 5. NBC led the networks with 16 Emmy statuettes. Consequently, there were more than a few nervous laughs from the audience after comedienne and former "Seinfeld" actress Julia Louis-Dreyfus remarked during the Emmy presentation that this is "the last official year of network television." Many broadcast executives don't find the joke funny.

NBC is a case in point. The Nielsen Company reported that during the 1952-1953 season, more than 30 percent of viewers watched NBC prime time programming. In 2010 that figure is down to about five percent. No wonder America's largest cable company, Comcast purchased NBC Universal from its parent company General Electric—but not because of the broadcasting network. The reason for the sale is to obtain the more lucrative cable channels—Bravo, CNBC, MSNBC, Syfy.

With cable as a model for future programming, television channels will necessarily become as content-specific as specialized magazines. NBC, CBS, ABC, and Fox can survive the competition from cable networks by sticking with a concept originated by the early motion picture studios—the star system. The big four can differentiate from all the other channels (as many as 1,500) by establishing a stable of well-known performers who are cast in familiar situations and dramas, always the most successful television strategy.

■ KEY TERMS

- 15 minutes of fame
- Ad-lib
- Analog
- Big Four
- Carrier wave
- Coaxial cable
- Digital
- Digital television (DTV)
- Electron scanner
- Federal Communications Commission (FCC)
- Green light
- HIV/AIDS
- Iconoscope

- On-demand
- Pilot
- Plasma television
- Prime time
- Screen Actors Guild (SAG)
- Situation comedy
- Soap operas
- Tabloid
- Time shifting
- Upper-middle class
- Vaudeville theater
- WiMax
- Writers Guild of America (WGA)

To locate active URLs for the weblinks mentioned in this chapter, please go to the companion site at http://communication.wadsworth.com/lester5 and select the proper chapter.

Chapter

14 Computers

Two memorable characters in motion picture history never complained about long working hours, costume problems, or the quality of the catered lunches. That's because they never spoke for themselves, were never paid, never wore clothes, and never ate anything. Many of the other actors never even saw them during filming—not until the movie was finished.

One was a gentle, compassionate, and positive living force; the other was a violent, insensitive, and cold-blooded killer. The smiling, rippling water snake, termed "water weenie" by the crew, that was featured in the motion picture *The Abyss* (1989) and the murderous T-1000 liquid-alloy robot in *Terminator 2: Judgment Day* (1991) introduced theater audiences not only to memorable visual messages but also to images totally fabricated through the use of the computer (Figures 14.1 and 14.2).

The success of those computer creatures, one critically and the other economically, was attributed to director James Cameron. And when he needed to show the last desperate moments of those who lost their lives on an ill-fated ocean liner, he didn't use only live stunt men and women. Cameron employed the knowledge he had learned from his previous motion pictures by creating computer-generated imagery (CGI) for his movie *Titanic*, which earned the Academy Award for Best Picture in 1998.

Born in 1954 in Kapuskasing, Ontario, Canada, about 700 miles north of Detroit, Cameron had an early fascination with science and movies. When his family moved to Fullerton, California, in 1971, he started making short films while attending school. After he saw *Star Wars* in 1977, Cameron was inspired to write a science fiction script, and he raised the funds

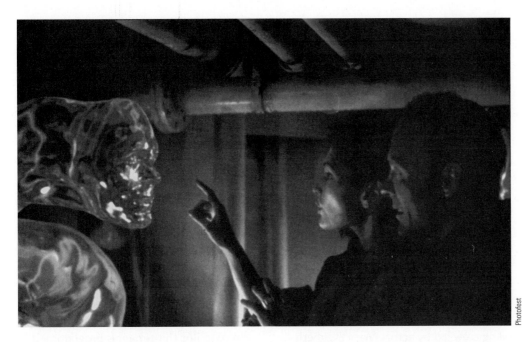

needed with two friends to make the little-seen science fiction thriller *Xenogenesis* (1978) (Weblink 14.1).

The care taken with the special effects piqued the curiosity of director and producer Roger Corman, who hired Cameron as a model maker. Two years later he was promoted to art director for Corman's big budget movie, *Battle Beyond the Stars*, which starred Richard Thomas, George Peppard, and Robert Vaughn (Weblink 14.2). And after the director hired for the horror film *Piranha II: The Spawning* (1981) quit unexpectedly, Cameron was asked to take over in his directorial, but forgettable, debut.

Although certainly not an auspicious beginning, Cameron's career moves following this start were the envy of Hollywood. In quick succession he was responsible for the low-budget *The Terminator* (1984) that earned more than $78 million; the sequel to Ridley Scott's *Alien* (1979), *Aliens* (1986), that was a critical and box office success; *The Abyss* (1989) that won an Academy Award for Best Visual Effects; *Terminator 2: Judgment Day* (1991) that smashed box office records around the world and won four Academy Awards; and then the motion picture that inspired his "King of the World" moment at the Academy Awards ceremony, *Titanic*

Figure 14.2

Two views of the T-1000 cyborg character in the movie Terminator 2. *Note how the use of light and shadow aids in creating the illusion of depth for the computer-generated images.*

(1997), that is estimated to have made more than $1.8 billion in global box office receipts and won a record-tying 11 Oscars including Best Picture and Best Director (Weblink 14.3).

The lessons learned in the making of *The Abyss* and *Terminator 2* taught Cameron that any situation with any type of character that could be imagined could be realized on the big screen. Furthermore, the success he experienced with his CGI-dependent motion pictures taught others—writers, directors, and producers—that with good stories and experienced actors, movies with a heavy dose of special effects could be great successes.

The 140-minute *Abyss* was a moderate box office success about an underwater oil rig crew led by actors Mary Elizabeth Mastrantonio and Ed Harris. The military recruits the aquanauts to retrieve a nuclear weapon from a damaged submarine. The plot twists when they discover an underwater civilization at the bottom of the ocean.

Computer-generated imaging technology took a breathtaking leap forward in the form of a creature that investigates the crew's vessel. Computer innovator Mark Dippé called the shimmering, water-filled pseudopod "one of the most significant pieces of computer animation done up until that time." The water entity is an astonishingly realistic water snake that playfully mimics the startled faces of Mastrantonio and Harris. When Mastrantonio pokes a finger into the being's "face," the computer-generated rippling effect adds to the realism of the moment. Dennis Muren of George Lucas's special effects company, Industrial Light and Magic (ILM), who worked on the effects for his *Star Wars* movie, created the "water weenie," which helped win him an Academy Award (Weblink 14.4).

In the first *Terminator*, a murderous cyborg played by Arnold ("I'll be back") Schwarzenegger is transported to the past from the future by advanced computers that have taken over control of the world from their human programmers. The robot's mission is to kill a woman who is to give birth to a son who will eventually lead a revolution against the machines. He's unsuccessful. In *T2* Linda Hamilton trains her son, portrayed by Edward Furlong, to take a leadership role in the upcoming rebellion. But images of a nuclear war eventually drive her insane, and she is committed to a mental hospital. Meanwhile, in the post-nuclear-war future, her now-grown son sends a reformatted Schwarzenegger robot back to the past. But this time it is programmed to protect the boy (himself) and his mother because the evil computers (are you following this?) have sent a new and improved model—the liquid metal, metamorphic cyborg, played in human form by Robert Patrick—to kill the family and anyone else who gets in its way. The T-1000 chrome robot in *Terminator 2* was one of 45 special CGI effects used in the blockbuster movie. Some of the most riveting scenes occur in the insane asylum in which the T-1000 character assumes the shape of a section of linoleum floor, makes his hands turn into deadly swords, has his "face" sliced in two by the force of Schwarzenegger's weapon (but it quickly reconstitutes itself), and changes back and forth between a uniformed police officer, a hospital security guard, and the chrome-colored, metal monster. The over-the-top visual effect, however, is when the cyborg oozes through the bars of a security gate to attack Hamilton, Furlong, and Schwarzenegger. Filming Patrick and the bars separately, and then matching a computer model of the actor's face with the live action film created the through-the-bars scene. The movie, unlike any other that used CGI, woke up Hollywood executives to the potential of computer graphics (Weblink 14.5).

After *Titanic*, Cameron received an honorary Doctorate of Fine Arts degree from California State University, Fullerton, the university where he studied physics and English until dropping out. In 2000 he created and wrote the television series "Dark Angel" for the Fox network, about a genetically enhanced young woman who works for a messenger service in Seattle after a magnetic bomb destroys every computer in the world. It was canceled after two seasons. In 2002 Cameron helped create a television documentary, "Expedition: Bismarck," detailing the demise of the famous battleship. The next year he produced an IMAX documentary titled *Volcanoes of the Deep Sea*, and directed *Ghosts of the Abyss*, a 3-D IMAX semi-documentary that takes a camera around and into the actual *Titanic* where they find, well, ghosts. Although he has personally terminated his fascination with the Terminator character, the franchise lives on with *Terminator 3: Rise of the Machines* (2003), *Terminator Salvation* (2009), and the Fox television series "Terminator: The Sarah Connor Chronicles." Continuing his fascination with the 3-D effect, Cameron's 2009 futuristic film *Avatar*, shown with a 3-D system he helped develop, was one of the most ambitious motion capture animated films ever produced and helped revolutionize and popularize the two technologies (Weblink 14.6). *Battle Angel*, another 3-D production based on a Japanese graphic novel shot in an *anime* style, is set for a 2011 release.

Although many directors have produced motion pictures with astounding special effects since James Cameron's *The Abyss*, the field of CGI would not be where it is today without his groundbreaking work.

■ ANALYSIS OF COMPUTER-GENERATED IMAGES

The history of computer-generated images for film goes back to 1961 when a student at the Massachusetts Institute of Technology (MIT), Ivan Sutherland, created a computer-drawing program called Sketchpad that allowed a user with a light pen to draw simple shapes on a computer screen and save them. Two years later Ed Zajac, a researcher for Bell Laboratories (now Lucent Technologies), produced the first computer-generated motion picture—a simulation of a trip around the Earth that a satellite might travel (Figure 14.3).

The first major motion picture that included any computer graphic effects was the 1968 Stanley Kubrick classic *2001: A Space Odyssey*. Simple lines and letters on monitors controlled by the HAL computer were the best computer graphics that could be achieved at that time (Weblink 14.7). Eight years later the robotic fantasy thriller *Futureworld* presented a brief line drawing of a human head on a computer

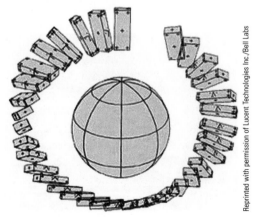

Figure 14.3

Although it's not the sexiest title one can imagine, Simulation of a Two-Giro Gravity Attitude Control System *is nevertheless considered to be the first computer-animated movie. Developed by Ed Zajac in 1963 on an IBM mainframe computer, the short motion picture shows how a satellite could be oriented as it orbits Earth.*

Reprinted with permission of Lucent Technologies Inc./Bell Labs

terminal, and in 1977 technology hadn't advanced much further when George Lucas directed *Star Wars*, summarized in the original trailer as "A story of a boy, a girl, and a universe." The movie presented simple computerized plans for the Death Star displayed on a large screen during a briefing about battle strategies to star fighters. All of the fight scenes seen in outer space in the original release were made with models (Weblink 14.8).

The first movie to feature the extensive use of computer graphics was the Disney box office disappointment *Tron* (1982). About 20 minutes of the film, much of it during the Light Cycle race, was produced with computers (Figure 14.4). *Newsweek*, *Time*, and *Rolling Stone* hailed computer graphics as an important advance in motion picture production. However, the technological benefits were delayed because the public wasn't interested in a story about a computer programmer who was trapped inside a computer (Weblink 14.9). Nevertheless, John Lasseter, who later went on to become CEO of Pixar Animation Studios, said, "Without *Tron*, there would be no *Toy Story*."

In 1984, *The Last Starfighter* was praised for its digital spacecraft dogfights. But again, as in *Tron*, the public wasn't interested in a teenage video game player who saves the universe. Two years later

the creative genius Jim Henson, best known for his Muppets, joined forces with George Lucas to create the visually stunning fantasy *Labyrinth* which featured computer-generated effects that helped propel the story line (Weblink 14.10).

If the stories sometimes suffered, at least the technology was improving. In 1990 Arnold Schwarzenegger starred in the science fiction action thriller *Total Recall*. It has the distinction of being the last major Hollywood movie in which most of the special effects were achieved through miniature models. An exception was an X-ray security view of Schwarzenegger's skeleton. The effect helped win a Special Achievement Academy Award for the film (Weblink 14.11). A year later in a Michael Jackson music video for his song "Black or White," the seamless and breathless transition from one diverse face to another using morphing software at the end of the six-minute-plus film was expertly maneuvered by director John Landis (Weblink 14.12).

Two years after the release of *Terminator 2*, a motion picture based on a novel by Michael Crichton and directed by Steven Spielberg astounded moviegoers with CGI dinosaurs on the screen so believable that many believed they had to actually live somewhere in this world. Stan Winston, the late great makeup and

Figure 14.4
With industrial designer Syd Mead as visual consultant for the motion picture Tron *(1982), the Light Cycle racers had a futuristic look. Mead also worked on another science fiction classic,* Blade Runner *(1982).*

effects artist, won an Academy Award for Best Visual Effects for *Jurassic Park* (1993) (Weblink 14.13).

Following Cameron's sinking of the *Titanic*, Pixar filmmaker John Lasseter was executive producer for the 2001 hit *Monsters, Inc.* The movie featured several innovations in computer animation technology, mostly related to how hair and clothing were rendered (Weblink 14.14). The fur of Sulley, an 800-pound monster, and the clothing of the human girl Boo were simulated to a level not previously achieved in cartoon animation. One of the reasons computer cartoons of the past had a plastic, unrealistic look, Lasseter explained, was because "the more organic something is, the harder it is to do." Despite advances in computer power, animators painstakingly re-created each hair of Sulley's fur coat—about three million of them—and took two years to write the software required for the clothing used in the film in order to achieve a natural and lifelike appearance. Lasseter wanted theatergoers to say, "Oh, we know it's not real, but it sure does look real."

Such realism comes at a high cost. The skills necessary to render believable CGI effects to an ever-increasingly sophisticated audience are enormously expensive to produce. The director Sam Raimi has the distinction of making one of the most expensive motion picture in the history of Hollywood, *Spider-Man 3* (2007) (Weblink 14.15). Largely because of the extensive use of CGI effects, the film cost a whopping $350 million. Nevertheless, audiences enjoy suspending their disbelief through the effects experience. Animated characters such as Dobby, the house elf in *Harry Potter and the Chamber of Secrets* (2002), and Gollum/Smeagol in Peter Jackson's *The Lord of the Rings* trilogy, who was portrayed by actor Andy Serkis, were created by vastly

different methods. Dobby was manufactured through traditional object animation techniques by George Lucas's Industrial Light and Magic using a rubber model and the stop-motion technique. Director Chris Columbus "wanted Dobby to be a character that felt very real and one that the audience would fall in love with." But Serkis interacted with his fellow cast members wearing a suit covered with tiny dots that were picked up with a digital camera, creating a more lifelike effect with the motion capture process (Weblink 14.16).

Determining whether any image—for print or screen media—is a picture of a live action actor or whether it is a completely computer-generated fabrication is almost at the point in which the difference is impossible to detect. Within the context of entertainment, viewers who want to be thrilled, writers and directors who want to turn their imaginations into screen reality, and producers who don't want to hire so many actors wait for the next generation of CGI with great anticipation. Agents, actors, stunt personnel, prop people, makeup artists, and even caterers are among those who will not be thrilled by such advances.

■ COMPUTERS AND THE SIX PERSPECTIVES

 Personal Perspective

Science fiction author and scientist Arthur C. Clarke once said, "Any significantly advanced technology is indistinguishable from magic." Computers, with the ability to create, access, and manipulate words, numbers, and images, certainly qualify as magical machines. The near future will be known for the way in which words and pictures are used together as equal partners in the communication process—a Convergent Era, in which all forms of communication are included through web access. Whatever the new era is called, computer technology clearly has grown to such an extent that imagining a world without them is difficult. From buying groceries to watching a movie, innovations brought about by the computer affect our lives for better or worse.

 Historical Perspective

The history of computers is rooted in complex ancient calculators. In 1901 under the waters off the Greek island of Antikythera, a mysterious object was found. It took almost 100 years for researchers to discover the secret of this barnacle-encrusted metal tool—it is the first mechanical calculator able to accurately predict various astronomical positions (Figure 14.5). Members of an ancient civilization created it over 2,100 years ago. One scientist said that the piece was "more valuable than the Mona Lisa."

Although Charles Babbage of London is credited with inventing the computer around 1822, in reality, he designed a steam-powered, program-controlled calculator he called a "difference engine." He claimed that his machine would mechanize the thought process itself. The huge, noisy contraption had pulleys and wheels that were used to make calculations. It weighed about 15 tons, but he never completed it. That's because he switched gears and started working on an improved design he named the "analytical engine." It was theoretically capable of storing 1,000 numbers of 50 decimal places each on punched cards, but once again it never got much beyond the lab bench stage. Nevertheless, his assistant, Ada Lovelace, daughter of the poet Lord Byron, is considered the first computer programmer. Lovelace wrote programs for Babbage's engine and also foresaw that the machine had capabilities beyond calculations. In 1991 a difference engine was constructed based on Babbage's design and successfully completed complex calculations beyond the capabilities of most pocket calculators. Babbage's machine and his brain are preserved at the Science Museum in London (Figure 14.6).

Herman Hollerith, an American, had more success with his device. He invented the first electric calculator, which was used for the enormous task of compiling the decennial U.S. Census. Hollerith invented an electromechanical system that could count and sort data from punched cards. Hollerith's device was first used for the 1890 Census (Figure 14.7). After favorable reviews, orders came from all over the world from governments, banks, insurance companies, and other institutions that required quick tabulations. In 1911, Hollerith had too much business to handle alone so he merged his company with three others to form the Computing-Tabulating-Recording Company (CTR).

Figure 14.5

A fragment of the 2,100-year-old Antikythera Mechanism, an astonishingly advanced device fabricated to calculate the position and movements of the sun, moon, and planets. With as many as 72 gears, the calculator was more complex than most intricate clocks.

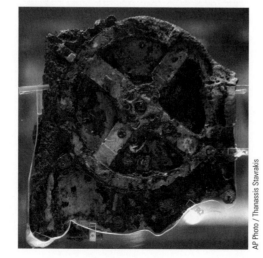

AP Photo / Thanassis Stavrakis

A salesperson for the National Cash Register Company, Thomas J. Watson needed a job and a good lawyer—he was found guilty as part of a conspiracy to run other cash register companies out of business. An appeals court ordered a new trial, but it never took place. Despite his conviction, a friend of Watson's gave him a job as general manager of CRT and when the president of CTR died, Watson was named to replace him (Figure 14.8).

In an effort to expand its business, in 1924 CTR changed its name to International Business Machines (IBM). The company grew tremendously during World War II and became the world's top producer of office equipment and data-processing machines for government and business applications. After Watson retired, his son, Thomas Watson, Jr., succeeded him.

IBM introduced its first personal computer in 1975. It was called the 5100 Portable Computer, weighed about 50 pounds, came in 12 models costing as much as $19,975 (more than $85,000 today). Not surprisingly, only about 15,000 were sold. Watson never thought computers for home users would be profitable. However, after Apple's success with its Apple II personal computer, released in 1977, IBM officials decided to try the personal computer market again. In 1981, it introduced the IBM PC, which was an instant hit. Through the company's worldwide distribution system, it sold more than 800,000 computers the first year. The letters "PC," standing for "personal computer," became synonymous with IBM desktop computing. IBM also allowed other companies to use its computer technological specifications to make their own products. The "clones" spread further the concept of the PC for home and office users. Nevertheless, in 2004 IBM sold its

Science & Society Picture Library / SSPL / Getty Images

personal computer business to a Chinese company, the Lenovo Group, essentially ending their interest in the consumer computer market.

Figure 14.6

Charles Babbage was never able to secure the funding to build his calculating machine during his lifetime. However, the Science Museum of London built a mechanism in 1991 based on the plans of his "Difference Engine No. 2" that could perform calculations with numbers up to 31 digits—more advanced than the average pocket calculator.

Figure 14.7

This 1890 issue of Scientific American *magazine introduced readers to Herman Hollerith's electrical tabulating machine. As noted by the illustrations with the article, information collected through interviews and other means was transferred to punch cards that were then input into Hollerith's device.*

Courtesy of International Business Machines, Inc.

Figure 14.8

Above: A middle-aged Thomas Watson, Sr., sits in his austere office and appears to be too absorbed in a document to notice the photographer. Below: A few years later, his portrait is radically different. Bound volumes of classical books—note the Holy Bible prominently displayed on the shelf to his right— within a wooden bookcase, a globe turned to Africa, a Foreign Affairs journal, a book entitled Chinese Art, the IBM company magazine Think (with the word repeated above), and direct eye contact with the camera combine to convey the image of a person of wealth, worldwide influence, and confidence.

Both courtesy of International Business Machines, Inc.

Before computers could be popular with the public, they had to have their own high-quality monitors, be small enough to conveniently fit on a desk, be relatively low in cost, and contain software programs that were useful and fun.

An important innovation for computers, which eventually led to visual displays, was the combination of computer and the cathode ray tube (CRT). At Manchester University in England, F. C. Williams and colleagues in 1948 used CRTs similar to those in television sets for their Manchester Mark I computer. The last room-sized computer of note that used vacuum tubes was the UNIVAC (for UNIVersal Automatic Computer). The SAGE (for Semi-Automatic Ground Environment) military project in 1955 expanded the computer monitor concept to include a handheld controller that later became known as a mouse. An operator seated in front of a large CRT monitor could aim a light pen at a specific point on the screen, and the computer would supply information about that plane and its location (Figure 14.9).

Early room-sized computers were hot and heavy because they operated through hundreds of integrated glass vacuum tubes that often burned out and had to be regularly replaced. One of the most important discoveries in the 20th century was announced to the public in 1948 with almost no coverage by the media. A team of scientists working for Bell Telephone Laboratories invented the transistor—a semiconductor with the same function as a vacuum tube but made of silicon, the chief component of sand. As opposed to tubes, silicon transistors didn't get hot, cost pennies to make, and could be as small as a pencil's eraser (Figure 14.10). In 1956 the Nobel Prize in physics was awarded to the three-person Bell team of William Shockley, Walter Braittain, and John Bardeen, who invented the transistor. One of its first applications was for hearing aid amplifiers in 1953. The next year transistor radios were introduced.

In 1958, Jack Kilby, who worked for Texas Instruments in Dallas, linked transistors on an integrated circuit board, allowing complex computer operations to occur in a vastly reduced space and at much faster speeds (Figure 14.11). In 1970 Kilby received the National Medal of Science in a ceremony at the White House for his important invention. Because of transistors linked on circuit boards, room-sized computers, commonly referred to as mainframes, were soon replaced with much smaller, faster, and cheaper machines (Figure 14.12).

At the time when computer companies such as IBM were concentrating on business computers, an underground amateur computer movement of interested hobbyists and entrepreneurs gathered in clubs to promote the technology. Many members of computer clubs wanted to build their own computers. To fill that need, a Florida dentist, Edward Roberts, sold computer kits to amateurs. A *Popular Electronics* cover story in 1971 about his Altair 8800 computer helped launch the personal computer industry (Figure 14.13). After the article was published, Roberts immediately received thousands of orders. However, the computer was a simple design that could be used only to play uncomplicated games. To become a more fully functional machine, it needed a built-in program that would allow the computer to understand commands from a user. When Harvard student Paul Allen saw the article about the computer at a newsstand, he was intrigued and showed it to his friend, fellow freshman William Henry "Bill" Gates. They called Roberts to offer their services in writing a basic program. Roberts hired Allen, and Gates dropped out of college to become a freelance computer software writer.

Both courtesy of International Business Machines, Inc.

Figure 14.9

The SAGE computer system was designed as an early warning defense system in the event of enemy attack. It was one of the first to use a monitor. Above: Military personnel study a large projection map generated by the computer system. Below: A technician obtains more information about a specific plane with a light pistol, a precursor of a computer mouse.

Allen and Gates eventually teamed up and formed the Microsoft Corporation, which became America's largest and most successful software company. Their first major client was IBM, who made one of the poorest business decisions in history when it gave the contract for writing its

All, courtesy of International Business Machines, Inc.

Figure 14.10

Advances in computer technology reduced machine cost and size and increased machine power and speed. The most important advances were from the vacuum tube (left) to the transistor (center) to the tiny silicon chip (the small square speck).

Figure 14.11

In 1958, Jack Kilby linked numerous transistors on a circuit board to give computers added speed and reliability.

Figure 14.12

Silicon chip circuit boards that could fit through the eye of a sewing needle further reduced size and cost without sacrificing speed or accuracy.

Courtesy of International Business Machines, Inc.

Courtesy of International Business Machines, Inc.

operating system to Microsoft instead of creating its own. Microsoft's Windows operating software and graphical interface, which many thought resembled Apple's user-friendly appearance, was popular mainly because at that time about 97 percent of all the desktop computers in the world were IBM or their clones. The two were paid a royalty for every PC that used the software, making them rich beyond their dreams.

Allen left Microsoft in 1983 to pursue other business interests. With his stock in Microsoft, Allen started Charter Communications Corp., the nation's third-largest cable operator, and bought the NBA's Portland Trailblazers and the NFL's Seattle Seahawks (Figure 14.14).

Gates stayed with Microsoft to become at one point the richest person in the world, personally worth an estimated $60 billion (Figure 14.15). However, in 2000 he started working part-time for Microsoft and devoted more of his efforts to the Bill & Melinda Gates Foundation, a charity organization founded with his wife. It is the fourth largest private foundation in the world. In 2008 at the age of 52, Gates retired from Microsoft to concentrate more on his charity work. It is estimated that the Foundation donates $1.5 billion annually for such causes as HIV/AIDS research, vaccines and immunizations, assistance to the poor, agricultural development, and educational programs worldwide.

One of the computer clubs inspired by Roberts's Altair homemade computer was the Homebrew Computer Club located in Silicon Valley (named for the many computer companies established south of San Francisco). Homebrew started with about 30 members who met for the first time in 1975 near Stanford University. Soon its membership was more than 500. Present at the first meeting was a young computer genius named Stephen Wozniak.

"Woz," as his friends know him, built a transistorized calculator when he was 13 years old. Although he attended colleges in Colorado and California, he dropped out because the courses didn't interest him. He got a job with the Hewlett-Packard (HP) Company, recognized as the first Silicon Valley computer company. Woz helped design mainframe computers for HP. In 1971, he met Steven Jobs, a 16-year-old, long-haired, and somewhat shy HP summer employee. Jobs left HP to attend college out of state, but soon dropped out and returned to California. He got a job as a technician for the video game company Atari. After a life-changing trip to India, Jobs met up again with Woz at a Homebrew meeting (Figure 14.16). In the meantime, Wozniak had made a simple computer that could be plugged into a television set to play video games. Jobs immediately searched for funding so the computer could be marketed to the public. He sold his Volkswagen bus, borrowed $5,000 from a friend and additional funds from multimillionaire A.C. "Mike" Markkula, and on that basis the two Steves formed the Apple Computer Company.

In 1975, the two introduced their Apple I computer, but only sold 175

AP Photo / Heinz Nixdorf Museumsforum

Figure 14.13

The Altair 8800 was a home-made computer, which started Bill Gates and Paul Allen on their road to found Microsoft Corporation.

Larry Busacca / WireImage / Getty Images

Figure 14.14

Paul Allen attends Time *magazine's "100 Most Influential People in the World" gala in 2008.*

Jeff J Mitchell / Getty Images

machines at $500 each (about $2,000 today) (Figure 14.17). While Wozniak worked on a more sophisticated model, Jobs cured his shyness and found additional financial backers. In 1977, the Apple II computer was introduced and became an enormous success. In the first year, sales of the $2,000 computer ($7,500 today) totaled $775,000. When Apple's stock went public in 1980, Wozniak was personally worth $88 million ($333 million today) and Jobs was $165 million ($625 million) richer by the end of the first day of over-the-counter trading. The next year annual sales had reached $335

Figure 14.15 (left)

Bill Gates speaks during the World Economic Forum in Davos, Switzerland in 2008.

Figure 14.16

Holding the first Apple I circuit board are the two Steves—Stephen Wozniak (left), the technical genius, and Steven Jobs, the innovative thinker and marketing wizard.

Figure 14.17

An inside view of the original Apple I computer, built by Stephen Wozniak in his garage. All that is missing is the monitor and keyboard. Wood-grain paneling regrettably never became a computer standard.

million, making Apple Computer one of the fastest-growing firms in American history.

But after almost losing his life in an airplane crash, Steve Wozniak stopped working at Apple in 1981. He enrolled in UC Berkeley and earned an undergraduate degree. He sponsored music festivals, developed the first universal remote control device for television sets, taught fifth grade students at a school near where he lived, and funded various charitable organizations. In 2009 Wozniak competed on the eighth season of the reality television show "Dancing with the Stars" with teammate Karina Smirnoff, a world champion

professional dancer. However, he was hampered in his effort after he injured his foot and had to wear a removable cast.

In 1983, Jobs brought in former Pepsi-Cola executive John Sculley to be Apple's CEO. In the middle of the Super Bowl telecast the next year, viewers watched what was called the greatest commercial of all time, produced by motion picture director Ridley Scott (*Blade Runner*, 1982). With an obvious link to George Orwell's novel *1984*, the advertisement presented a "Big Brother" (i.e., IBM) theme in which computer operators all looked alike and worked in drab surroundings. Suddenly a young, athletic woman wearing running clothes and carrying a sledgehammer runs toward the giant screen. When she throws the hammer at the picture of the leader, the screen crashes to reveal behind it the latest revolution in computing—the Macintosh. The commercial only ran once (Weblink 14.17). The Macintosh sold for less than $2,000 (about $4,000 today) and contained a graphic interface that made many of the functions of the computer intuitively simple for the average person. It was an immediate hit with visual communicators.

Desktop publishing was born with the Macintosh computer and the LaserWriter printer introduced in 1985 (Figure 14.18). However, Jobs left Apple in 1985 to start another computer company, NeXT, after a power struggle between Sculley and himself. The next year he purchased the computer graphics division of George Lucas's Lucasfilm, which became the Pixar Animation Studios. By 1996 Apple was struggling financially. After Sculley left the company, Jobs returned and guided Apple to several computer and portable gadget triumphs. In 2001 a slick, modern, and easy-to-use portable music player, the iPod, was introduced. Coupled with Apple's iTunes

Courtesy of Apple Computer, Inc.

Courtesy of Apple Computer, Inc.

Figure 14.18

Designed to compete with IBM's 5100 Portable Computer, Apple's Lisa 2 (left), introduced in 1978, included a graphic interface and a mouse. The computer's name is an acronym for Local Integrated Software Architecture; Jobs's first child, who was born the same year the computer was introduced, is also named Lisa. The computer proved to be a rare commercial failure for the company. Nevertheless, the Macintosh computer (right), introduced in 1984, was commercially successful with its intuitive visual screen functions, a mouse, and built-in sound. Many people discovered that the Macintosh was much easier to use than the IBM PC.

software for transferring music and videos, the device was an enormous success. Pixar was acquired by the Walt Disney Company in 2006, and is considered one of the most successful animation studios in Hollywood. The next year saw Apple's launch of the iPhone. The portable touch screen device plays music and videos like an iPod, links to the web, takes photographs, is able to play thousands of applications for educational and entertainment purposes, and, oh yes, acts like a telephone on occasion. It was another unqualified success for the company.

Jobs was diagnosed with a cancerous tumor on his pancreas in 2004. Appearing thin and weak at a conference two years later, speculation about his poor health flooded the media. In 2009 it was revealed that he received a liver transplant from the Memphis, Tennessee Methodist University Hospital Transplant Institute with an "excellent prognosis." He has since

returned to Apple working a few days a week at the company's headquarters and the rest of the week from home.

Technical Perspective

A computer has five basic components: memory, the central processing unit (CPU), a switching device, peripherals, and software (Figure 14.19).

■ Memory

This necessary part of a computer, also called storage, comes in two types: short-term memory that aids computer operations while you are using the machine and permanent memory that resides within the computer and on separate recording devices. As a general rule for visual communicators, computers should have as much short-term and permanent memory

Courtesy of Paul Martin Lester

Figure 14.19

A professional graphic designer and educator shows off her iMac computer with a Microsoft Word document presented on the screen. Note the external hard drive to the left for making backups in case of a computer crash, speakers in the back for multimedia audio productions, and a color printer for making proof pages.

as you can afford. You want to run more than one program at a time quickly and save all of your images, movies, and music. For processing high-resolution still and motion picture images, you need at least four to eight gigabytes (GB) of short-term memory (also called RAM, DRAM, and SDRAM), 320GB within a computer, a 500GB external hard drive, and at least a 1GB portable jump or flash drive. The large external hard drive is necessary in order to make regular backups of your work in case of a computer crash. Another alternative for data is to sign up for a storage company such as Google's GMail Drive, Putplace.com, or Mozy and keep your files on a remote site (Weblink 14.18).

■ CPU

For a CPU, the faster its chip or clock speed, the faster it can process information, and the more you will be able to accomplish. Fast, efficient chips also allow you to easily run more than one program at the same time. This capability is use-

ful when editing digital images for still or moving presentations. Introduced in 2006, one of the most popular computer chips is the Intel Core 2 brand that is used by Apple computers and others because of its fast speed and low power consumption. With Apple's MacBook Pro you can include a chip speed as high as 2.93 gigahertz, or 2.93 billion operations a second. However, many experts agree that RAM is more important in determining a computer's efficiency than its chip speed.

■ Switching Devices

These are simply cords that connect the CPU with all other functions of a computer. They can be telephone-type links or complex 64-pin devices called *small computer systems interface* (SCSI, pronounced "scuzzy") connectors. Program instructions and other information are sent through a switching device to the CPU and out to a monitor or printer depending on the need of the user. The Universal Serial Bus (USB), manufactured by Intel, and Firewire, an Apple product, are devices that have revolutionized peripheral connections by making them faster, more versatile, and easier to obtain. But computers without wire connections are the wave of the future. Apple's thin notebook computer, the Air, for example, does not contain a Firewire port but relies on a wireless connection.

■ Peripherals

The three types of peripherals are those that send data to the CPU (e.g., keyboard, mouse, tablet, voice, and scanner devices), those that deliver data from the CPU to a monitor and printer, and those that offer two-way communication between one computer user and another, such as through direct line, e-mail, and web applications.

■ *Software*

Without software, a computer, with all its storage, CPU, switching devices, and peripherals, is only good as a place to stick yellow Post-it notes. A visual communicator must be comfortable writing and editing words, creating and manipulating still and moving images, working with numerical output, and sorting and finding information on the web. You must also have a working knowledge of audio production and be able to put all the elements together in graphic designs for both print and screen presentations. Therefore, you should be familiar with at least nine programs: a word processing program such as *Word*, an illustrator program such as *Illustrator*, picture manipulation software such as *Photoshop*, spreadsheet software such as *Excel*, a page layout program such as *InDesign*, a presentation program such as *PowerPoint*, motion picture editing software such as *Final Cut Pro*, a motion graphics editor such as *Flash*, and a web editor such as *Dreamweaver*. Although you don't need to be proficient in all nine programs, you should be able to communicate with others who are.

Ethical Perspective

As with photography, motion pictures, and television, computer games have been accused of displaying scenarios that feature gratuitous sex, violence, and stereotypes. Many critics are concerned that children become obsessed with playing video games at home and thus are slow to learn how to interact socially with other people. As pressing as those issues are, there are also concerns about image manipulation.

■ *Violent Themes*

Video games began innocently with simple interactive graphics. The first interactive computer game is considered to be "Spacewar" by MIT student Steve Russel in 1962 (Weblink 14.19). The first arcade game in 1971, "Computer Space," helped launch Atari (Weblink 14.20). The next year a home system named Magnavox Odyssey was introduced, which plugged into your TV set so you could play a type of ping-pong game with a ball of light and two simulated paddles, along with 11 other educational and entertainment games (Weblink 14.21). The arcade version from Atari followed, and "Pong" could be found in many bars across the United States (Weblink 14.22).

Gradually, the games became more sophisticated in their story lines and their technology. As a result, realistic and often violent games were produced, such as "Street Fighter II" in 1991 and "Doom" in 1993, with near 3-D perspective (Weblink 14.23). With "Grand Theft Auto" in 1997, violent video games were established as a popular and lucrative staple of the industry (Weblink 14.24).

Using the fastest processing chips available, the newest game systems are much more lifelike than anything seen previously, but they don't mean much without the software. Increasingly, software involves interactive "shooter" games. Social critics raise important concerns about children who become obsessed with video game playing. Users often forsake homework, friends, family, and even meals as they move through the fantasy scenes alone or with others connected through online play. Most video games can be criticized because they reward a player for committing some kind of violent act. The object of most video games is to "kill" as many other video characters as possible with an often creative assortment of weapons and tactics. Critics point out that the games teach a child, as do violent examples in other media, that conflicts are easily resolved, not through compromise, but through direct, violent action. They believe that video game violence has a higher potential for contributing to adverse personality disorders among children than do motion pictures or television because a child is actually responsible for the actions in the game, rather than being a passive viewer.

After two young men killed 13 people and themselves at a Littleton, Colorado, high school in 1999, it was discovered they obsessively played two "first-person shooter" CD-ROM video games, *Doom* and *Quake* (Weblink 14.25). Consequently, Disney banished all violent video games from its theme parks and hotels. Another CD-ROM game that raised alarms of concern was *Mortal Kombat*,

which featured decapitations and spinal cord and heart removals (Figure 14.20). In 2009 Common Sense Media, a video game watchdog group, warned the public of "Grand Theft Auto IV," developed by Rockstar Games and published by Take-Two Interactive Software Inc. Common Sense spokesperson Marc Saltzman said that because of the game's heavy violence, it "should be kept away—far away from children." And yet, "Grand Theft Auto: Chinatown Wars" from Rockstar, filled with violence, mobsters, foul language, and drug references, was released for Nintendo's handheld model, the DS, a popular platform for children. Nevertheless, the U.S. 9th Circuit Court of Appeals upheld a lower court's ruling that such games cannot be banned from those younger than 18 because of First Amendment free speech protection. Although Midway Games, the maker of *Mortal Kombat*, filed for bankruptcy in 2009, expect more action titles after

Figure 14.20

This advertisement for the video game "Grand Theft Auto IV" for the Xbox 360 game system cannot disguise the violent nature of the game as the menacing character holds a handgun.

Jerry Bruckheimer, producer for such Hollywood hits as *Top Gun* (1986), *Con Air* (1997), and *Black Hawk Down* (2001), announced the formation of his own video game company, Jerry Bruckheimer Games Inc. In 2009 Ubisoft introduced "Avatar: The Game" based on James Cameron's blockbuster available for the Nintendo Wii and DS, PlayStation 3, Xbox 360, PC, and 3-D TV. Players who decide to be a human and take control of the planet Pandora, use weapons that mostly terrorize innocent animal life (Weblink 14.26).

■ Sexual Themes

Many interactive video and CD-ROM games feature soft pornography, as opposed to hard-core pornographic adult themes. Most of these CD-ROM games involve women characters that are willing to take their clothes off and perform sexual services in response to a mouse-generated command. Digitized video images and audio effects give the illusion of a one-on-one encounter. One of the first sex-oriented "games" was *MacPlaymate*, created by Mike Saenz. As the user clicked a mouse on various parts of the main character's cartoon clothing, Maxie would oblige by undressing. The program also contained a "panic button." If someone came into the room unexpectedly, the user could quickly switch the screen to a simulated spreadsheet program. Saenz also produced one of the most popular CD-ROM adult games, *Virtual Valerie 2*. The CD-ROM game was an enhanced animated version of the Maxie line drawing. Promotional material describes the CD as "the ultimate in cyberotica and the embodiment of every red-blooded technophile's deepest desires."

In the movie *The Lawnmower Man*, from a short story by Stephen King, the lead character has virtual reality (VR) sex with his girlfriend. The movie was forgettable, but the scene inspired many stories in the media (Weblink 14.27). Some writers have predicted that VR sex between partners thousands of miles from each other but linked through an online network may be the "killer app"—jargon among program developers for an application that everyone will want to have. A serious consequence of the increased realism of humans in computer games and presentations is the issue of where you draw the line between innovative presentations and child pornography. Responsible industry executives have established guidelines for adult themes. They state that no underage models, animals, sadistic and masochistic (S&M) practices, or violence toward women are to be featured in these programs. But they are only guidelines with which compliance is voluntary.

■ Image Manipulation

The manipulation of still digital photographs is a valuable tool for photographers who can easily and without chemicals perform all the functions that traditionally were reserved for darkrooms (Figure 14.21). However, critics are concerned that manipulations are going beyond simple cropping or color balance adjustments and altering the content of news editorial pictures. Computer technology allows taking parts from one film and combining them with another. For example, a Coca-Cola commercial featured living musician Elton John singing with several dead entertainers including Louis Armstrong, Humphrey Bogart, and James Cagney; Fred Astaire appeared to dance with a vacuum cleaner in a

Figure 14.21

A winery worker near San Luis Obispo, California, is easily added to a scene with the help of the Photoshop software program manufactured by Adobe Systems Incorporated. Or was the employee removed from the picture? That question points to the dilemma with computer manipulations—sometimes it is impossible to tell.

Courtesy of Paul Martin Lester

Dirt Devil commercial; and John Wayne popped up in a Coors Light ad.

Advertising manipulations are less of a concern than those for journalism presentations. Much of the apprehension over digital still and moving image manipulations is because the *original* often is altered. Once a picture is changed, it is changed forever. Photographic credibility—the idea that seeing is believing—may be a naive, old-fashioned concept. But *every* image in the mind's eye, every subject before a camera's lens, and every still and moving picture produced in the dark or light is manipulated. Because more people are learning how images are produced, fewer and fewer believe in the inherent truthfulness of a picture anymore.

When a picture's content no longer is credible, context and the words that accompany a photograph will become more crucial to deciding what should be believed. The credibility of a picture may rest more on a media outlet's reputation and the text used to explain an image than the picture itself in this computer manipulation age. Computer technology didn't start the decline in the credibility of pictures, but it has hastened it.

🌐 *Cultural Perspective*

Although many companies make desktop computers, Apple and IBM used to dominate the industry. Various publications carried stories that pitted the counterculture gurus with their long hair, beards, and sandals against the establishment executives with their white shirts, conservative ties, and blue suits. Steve Jobs parked his motorcycle next to several video game consoles and a grand piano in the lobby of Apple Computer. Uniformed security guards greet visitors to IBM sites. But never is the contrast between the two companies as clear as in their two logos.

The first Apple logo, probably one of the worst in logo history, was a black-and-white line drawing of Sir Isaac Newton sitting under a tree reading a book. Jobs and the third founding member of Apple, Ronald Wayne, drew the original logo (Figure 14.22). Above Newton's head is an apple that has just become detached from the branch and is on its way to inspire Newton to theorize about the law of gravity. Around the picture is the strangely cryptic quotation: "A mind forever voyaging through strange seas of thought—alone." The quote came from Book Three of William Wordsworth's *The Prelude* in which he describes viewing a marble statue of Newton.

Soon, however, the company changed the logo to a symbol that could be easily condensed into one simple, visual message. Rob Janoff, an experienced graphic artist, designed the rainbow-colored Apple with a bite taken out in 1976 (Figure 14.23). The logo had several possible interpretations that included a nod to Newton and the apple's role in his discovery of gravity, that knowledge was the pot of gold awaiting a user at the end of the Apple rainbow, or that the computer was the "forbidden fruit" and more fun than an IBM PC. It has also been said that the rainbow logo was a tribute to one of the founders of modern computing, the gay mathematician Alan Turing who died after eating an apple that contained cyanide. In 1998 the logo was changed to a solid color apple shape, perhaps reflecting the company's maturity in the business world. Regardless of its many interpretations, the logo perfectly summarized Apple Computer—bright, innovative, visual, and a bit anti-establishment.

However, the logo has not been without controversy. In 1978, Apple Corps, a company begun by the Beatles, sued Apple for trademark infringement. The computer company paid $80,000 and agreed to never get into the music business. But after iTunes was launched, Apple Corps took the company back to court. This time the settlement was pricier as Apple Computers paid $26.5 million in 1991 to settle the suit. In 2008 all was forgiven and Sir Paul McCartney agreed to make the Beatles song catalog available on iTunes. However, the two Apples have yet to agree on a price. It appears that it may be a long and winding road before users can hear Beatles songs on iTunes.

The IBM logo is a contrast in style (Figure 14.24). Designed by Paul Rand and architect Eliot Noyes in 1956, it originally comprised three black capital letters in a serious square serif typeface. Rand added the blue color and the distinctive horizontal stripes later because, as he wrote, "since

Courtesy of Apple Computer, Inc.

Figure 14.22

The original Apple Computer logo was a confusing array of text and graphics—not the kind of symbol that can be easily reduced and remembered by consumers. Nevertheless, the trademark introduced the world to the connection of the computer firm to Sir Isaac Newton and apples.

each letter is different, the parallel lines, which are the same, are the harmonious elements that link the letters together."

Courtesy of Apple Computer, Inc.

Figure 14.23

Apple Computer's previous trademark was a round, organic, colorful logo that emphasizes the computer's ease of use, enjoyment, and slightly irreverent company philosophy.

Courtesy of International Business Machines, Inc.

Figure 14.24

Paul Rand's IBM trademark presents bold, capital, square serif letters linked by horizontal white lines. The logo symbolizes the company's powerful position in the industry and its worldwide networking capabilities.

But for others, the stripes reminded them of a prison uniform. The logo is a no-nonsense, conservative design and, like the Apple logo, visually complements the underlying philosophy of the company. Interestingly, Rand, who was also responsible for the logos of such companies as ABC, Westinghouse, and UPS, posed for the grammatically challenged "Think Different" campaign from Apple Computers in 1998.

Despite the strict lines of the IBM logo, the stereotypical image of an individual (usually a male) with mussed hair, glasses held together at the bridge of the nose with tape, about ten pens and pencils carried in a shirt pocket protector, wrinkled clothing, and a laugh similar to a donkey's bray is identified in this culture as that of the "computer nerd." This stereotype emerged during the time when research scientists and technicians dominated the computer industry. The general public was all too eager to make fun of these learned yet socially awkward individuals because the technology scared most people. No culture ever generated a "printing press nerd" or a "typewriter nerd" because those machines never evoked the fears equal to that of computers.

During the 1950s, audiences were frightened by a computerized robot featured in *The Day the Earth Stood Still* (1951) that was so powerful it could halt the flow of electricity to every machine on the planet. Fear of nuclear armageddon, in which people would have no control over the powerful machines they had created to protect them, fueled such movies as *Failsafe* (1964) and *Dr. Strangelove or: How I Learned to Stop Worrying and Love the Bomb* (1964). In Arthur C. Clarke's *2001: A Space Odyssey* (1968), the benign, protective, and slightly condescending computer HAL (each letter in the name is one off

from the letters IBM) suddenly turned into a psychopathic killer. *The Matrix* trilogy (1999–2003) featured a world in which computers have so taken over their human creators that the human bodies are used as batteries for the machines while their minds are placated through an elaborate virtual world (Weblink 14.28). Even real-life serial killers are described in media reports as having the "calculating mind of a computer." With the vision of computers as so forceful that they control every aspect of a person's life, stereotyping the creators and operators of these mighty machines as impotent and unattractive isn't surprising.

The desktop publishing revolution helped end the nerd stereotype and the negative view of computers. The image of a sterile, serious, and a bit obsessed IBM executive has been replaced by the image of a passionate, relaxed, and a bit obsessed Apple user.

With easy-to-operate computers and software programs, anyone can learn how to operate the machine. Desktop publishing educated the average user about the difference between a software program and the task of computing. No longer does a computer user need to know how to write a program that makes a computer operate. Similar to the time when George Eastman invented roll film cameras so that anyone could enjoy photography, the diversity of tasks that can be performed relatively easily on a computer makes it a tremendously popular machine. The mystique of the computer is lessened further when elementary school children can write essays, process still and moving images, and make presentations for assignments. With computer chips now essential for the operation of such diverse machines as wristwatches, microwave ovens, and automobiles, computers and their users are admired by the culture that embraces such technology. A computer, especially in the home, is a status symbol—not nerdism. Its owners are considered to be forward thinking, progressive, and mentally sharp. The same terms were spoken about those in the 1950s who had a television set at home. Because today almost everyone has a TV set, the symbol of an upwardly mobile family is the computer.

Critical Perspective

Without question, computers represent a major technological breakthrough on a par with Gutenberg's printing press. All the media are becoming dependent on computers, and this convergence ensures that the world will never return to a pre-computer time. But computers simply are machines that reflect the culture that makes them. As with other means of expression, if a society accepts violence, sexism, and the perpetuation of cultural stereotypes, that type of content will pervade the digital medium. A society always gets the media images it deserves.

Computerphiles advance the simplistic notion that more computer technology can solve all the evils of the world. But capitalistic, free-market democracies have consistently demonstrated that almost any innovation divides people into those who can afford to use it and those who cannot. For example, some schools are better equipped to teach and some restaurants have higher-quality entrées because of the economic status of those who live nearby. Many experts look to interactive multimedia and network-connected machines on the web to help solve many of society's problems. As more people are educated through technol-

ogy, so the argument goes, the world will become a better and more tolerant place. At present, half of all the messages on worldwide electronic information networks are simple notes that could just as easily be sent by telephone or postcard. If computers turn out to be simply low-cost alternatives to telephone and postal services with unfair access, a potentially great societal benefit will be lost.

■ TRENDS TO WATCH FOR COMPUTERS

Speculating about the future of computers is always risky. Because of the delay between writing a manuscript, having it published, and your processing these words and images, this book already may be outdated in some respects. One trend is clear: Computers as they are presently known eventually will become as quaint and old-fashioned as manual typewriters and as ubiquitous as cell phones. American Alexander Bell could never have imagined that his invention of the telephone in 1876 would eventually lead to the most advanced achievement in technology. Handheld computers that provide voice, text, and imagery links to powerful worldwide networks are instigating a new revolution in communications technology and are also helping to eliminate an ancient human skill—writing by hand (Figure 14.25).

Despite an economic downturn in 2008, the U.S. stand-alone and online video game industry reached a record $22 billion in total annual sales, and $50 billion worldwide. Nintendo's Wii system sold more than 800,000 units in the month of December alone. The "Wii Fit" exercise game outsold the violent "Grand Theft Auto IV: The Lost and the Damned"

Courtesy of Paul Martin Lester

Figure 14.25

Two women text message on their handheld devices while sitting in a coffee shop. Let's hope they're not "talking" to each other.

which made $500 million during the first week of sales. Its DSi handheld model plays more than 800 DS games and includes a photo distortion function so you can make funny pictures of your friends. Equally high sales of Microsoft's Xbox 360 and Sony's PlayStation 3 were also reported for 2008. Xbox Live allows thousands of online players to compete against one another virtually in versions of television game shows such as "1 vs. 100," while a new technology named Project Natal from Microsoft for the game system lets users control the action with full-body movements in games such as "Ricochet," "Paint Party," and an as-yet-unnamed program in which users interact with a virtual character as if it were a real person. Still, video game sales are down 23 percent compared with the previous year.

Apple is a relatively new player in the video game genre. Although its iPhone and iPod Touch devices offer more than 25,000 apps that include educational, social networking, and travel uses, 75 percent of the apps that are sold are games. Their popularity is causing game producers to develop cheap, faster programs for the small screens. The multibillion-dollar

video game industry will prosper even more from independent producers. Major companies such as Microsoft and Sony Corp. are signing up amateur creators to produce games for their Xbox 360 and PlayStation 3. James Silva, 26, who once washed dishes to help pay for college, sold his game "The Dishwasher," about a ninja who fights his way out of a crowded kitchen, to Microsoft. Students from the DigiPen Institute of Technology located in Redmond, Washington, developed "Portal," in which a player must solve a series of puzzles in order to advance through the game. At the 2008 Game Developers Conference, "Portal" beat out such big-budget games as "Super Mario Galaxy," "Rock Band," "Bioshock," and "Call of Duty 4." With the success of "Portal," the sequels "Portal: Still Alive" and "Portal 2" were produced.

Educators are experimenting with computer–human interfaces in the form of online classes. Students, their professors, and guest speakers can be located anywhere in the world and connect through online virtual classroom software such as Blackboard and iLinc to have real-time discussions with text, audio, and video options.

One of the most promising platforms for teaching online is Second Life (SL), an avatar-based virtual social community launched in 2003 by Philip Rosedale of San Francisco's Linden Lab. Residents can walk, fly, drive a vehicle, and teleport to rural and urban simulated environments to engage in all kinds of activities. With a credit card, residents can accessorize their avatars with hair, skin, clothing, and a sexy walk. With a premiere account (SL is otherwise free to join), residents can buy land, build stores and homes, and sell their creations to other users of the program. Roughly inspired by Neal

Stephenson's 1992 science fiction classic *Snow Crash* about a user-dominated virtual reality, Second Life currently has more than 15 million registered users.

Although essentially an elaborate chatroom, SL combines the visual cues found in the real, analog world (color, form, depth, and movement) with an interactive communicative experience. In that sense it is possible to make the learning and teaching experience more real for online students than with the virtual classroom chat-based discussions provided by Blackboard. Presently there are over 150 educational institutions that have a presence on SL with many offering live, synchronous classroom instruction (Figure 14.26).

Businesses are also trying to save money by scheduling meetings on Second Life. The semiconductor manufacturer Sun Microsystems, Inc., owns seven islands on SL and conducts seminars on technical matters with employees located throughout the world. IBM first established a presence in the online virtual community in 2006 and uses it to "conduct meetings, train new employees and hold orientation sessions."

Computers and humans not only interact but are becoming one, as foretold by such artists as Kelly Dobson, a graduate of the renowned MIT Media Lab. Dobson created a video art presentation, *Blendie* (2004), in which she communicates through her voice with a 1950s Osterizer blender that responds in surprising ways (Weblink 14.29). In what seems like an episode of the 1970s kitschy television series "The Six Million Dollar Man" starring Lee Majors with "cybernetic parts," prosthetic limbs for those who need them employ computer chips that aid in more sophisticated movements, the simulation of touch, and the sensation of weight. With technological advances

Courtesy of Paul Martin Lester

Figure 14.26
Moments before a visual communication lecture class offered on Second Life, the students' avatars sit on rugs, comfortable couches, and "air chairs" while the professor in the foreground waits for the rest of the class to arrive.

precipitated from the high number of injuries to American soldiers during the wars in Afghanistan and Iraq, the U.S. Department of Defense in conjunction with outside vendors has made great strides in prosthetics. For example, the Scottish company Touch Bionics invented the "i-Limb," which has a computer chip that translates the wearer's electrical arm signals into hand movements. One Army soldier who lost his left arm after an explosive blast in Iraq said, "To have this movement, it's—it's amazing. My son tells me I'm half robot, half man."

And then there is Kevin Warwick of Reading University, England, who implanted a chip in his arm that linked his nervous system with a computer in a series of experiments called "Project Cyborg." With the implant he could "control doors, lights, heaters, and other computer-controlled devices." Another experiment involved his wife, who was also implanted with a computer chip that allowed the two of them to communicate through the internet and their nervous systems. Warwick's hope is that the technology might aid those with damaged spinal cords. An outspoken advocate for the field of robotics, he famously said, "There is no way I want to stay a mere human."

At the 2009 Technology, Entertainment, and Design (TED) conference held in Long Beach, California, Pattie Maes and Pranav Mistry of MIT's Fluid Interfaces Group demonstrated a $350 wearable computer that includes a webcam attached to a small portable projector with a wireless connection to a cell phone and web access; it can project images and other types of information on any surface. Called the "Sixth Sense," a user can use her hands in a framing gesture to take a picture, use a finger to make a circle on a wrist that turns into a projection of a watch, project numbers on fingers to make a phone call, and get product information by simply looking at an item on a store's shelf (Weblink 14.30). In the not-too-distant future these wearable computers may become what we call cell phones.

■ *KEY TERMS*

- Atari
- Chief executive officer
- Chip speed
- Convergent Era
- Crash
- DRAM
- Killer app
- Mainframe computer
- MIT Media Lab
- Mouse
- Operating system
- Over-the-counter stock
- Punch cards
- RAM
- SDRAM
- Silicon Valley
- Synchronous classroom
- Tablet
- Transistor
- Vacuum tube

To locate active URLs for the weblinks mentioned in this chapter, please go to the companion site at http://communication.wadsworth.com/lester5 and select the proper chapter.

Chapter 15

The Web

Have you ever heard a friend ask for a "Coke" to mean any flavor of carbonated sugar water, a "Kleenex" referring to any thin paper handkerchief substitute, or a "Band-Aid" for any sterile adhesive? A product is a huge success when its trademarked name becomes the generic term for all products of its type. (Other famous brands include Frisbee, Q-Tip, Taser, and Xerox.) But when the brand name also becomes a verb, there's a cultural phenomenon going on (Figure 15.1).

Soon after the simple amateur-friendly Kodak camera was introduced in the 19th century, "bring along the Kodak" meant to take a camera with you (Figure 15.2). In the 1913 version of *Webster's Revised Unabridged Dictionary*, *kodaking* was defined as "to photograph with a Kodak." Likewise, a decade after two hockey-playing brothers in Minneapolis adapted a pair of in-line roller skates to their specifications

in 1980, the world was introduced to two new terms based on their brand name—rollerblade, the noun form ("Let's go to the sporting goods store and buy a pair of rollerblades") and the verb form ("I'll rollerblade to the park and meet you").

All these products pale in comparison to another—one you can't even hold in your hand. It's a noun, it's a verb, and it's the search engine: Google (Figure 15.3).

Google is the name of one of the easiest, fastest, and most popular search engines available on the web. In 2009 there was an average of 31 billion searches made with it in a single month. A simple, uncluttered opening page with a cheery logo, an empty box to type in your keywords, a minimum number of buttons, and plenty of eye-pleasing white space, Google is a welcome change from most other overly busy and too-eager-to-please search portals (Weblink 15.1). Despite its humble

The web is the most important single outcome of the personal computer. It is the Gutenberg press that is democratizing information.

Bill Atkinson, b. 1951
SOFTWARE DESIGNER AND NATURE PHOTOGRAPHER

Courtesy of the U.S. Army

Figures 15.1 and 15.2

Nouns and verbs. The M26 Taser stun gun is the military and police version of the commercial weapon (left). Invented in 1974 by NASA scientist Jack Cover, the name is an acronym for Tom A. Swift's Electric Rifle—a weapon that appeared in a young adult adventure novel featuring Tom Swift that fired bolts of electricity, as described by author Victor Appleton in 1911. As a less-than-lethal weapon, the Taser is a noun, but if you are ever unfortunate enough to have it used on you as a verb, it is hoped you have a good lawyer. In this 1916 advertisement for a Kodak camera printed in a French magazine, the George Eastman invention is so popular worldwide that it is also thought of as a noun and a verb.

appearance, it operates at a blinding speed. Most searches on Google, no matter how complex, take less than a second to complete as it looks through its database collection of over 6 billion web pages.

Google is so popular that it has inspired games and parodies. "Googlewhacking" is a game in which you try to find a single website indexed on Google from two seemingly unrelated words such as "comparative unicyclist," "maladroit wheezer," and "blithering clops." "Weapons of Mass Destruction" and "French Military Victories" are examples of another game, "Google Bombing" in which knowledgeable tricksters manipulate the page-ranking program used by Google so that a specific website will be the first on the list (Weblink 15.2). "Google Fight" allows you to pit one name or concept against another (Weblink 15.3). Whichever has the most Google hits wins. For example, in a Google fight between Godzilla and King Kong, Godzilla wins with 7 million more results than the giant ape. One of the most popular games is to use Google as a verb and "Google someone" to see if you can discover any facts known about that person on the web. Singles and others have learned to Google potential dates or mates.

There are versions of Google in 90 languages, from Afrikaans to Zulu (Weblink 15.4). You can also select specialty languages or dialects that show many of the features Google has to offer, but printed in Latin, Pig Latin, or Elmer Fudd. In Klingon, "I'm feeling lucky" translates to "jlSuDrup." Plus, the folks at Google are constantly dreaming up new applications. Its website lists more than 40 search, programming, communications, and cell phone services available for free (Weblink 15.5).

Admittedly, Google owes much of its success to its catchy name. Some say it comes from "Googleplex Star Thinker," a computer character in *The Hitchhiker's Guide to the Galaxy* by Douglas Adams who could "calculate the trajectory of every single dust particle throughout a five-week Dangrabad Beta sand blizzard." Perhaps as a tribute to Adams, the home office for Google is called the Googleplex. However, Sergey Brin and Larry Page, the two visionary Stanford University students who created the search engine, say it comes from a mathematical term that refers to a number that is a 1 followed by 100 zeros, a "googol." That number is larger than all the atoms that make up the universe. So, googol became Google, a worthy name for a large-scale, worldwide search engine.

There have been many two-person teams in the history of computer innovations: Bill Hewlett and Dave Packard (HP), Paul Allen and Bill Gates (Microsoft), Stephen Wozniak and Steven Jobs (Apple), and David Filo and Jerry Yang (Yahoo!), to name a few. Perhaps that fact is an indication of the complicated nature of computer technology. Each one alone probably could never have achieved what the two accomplished together. And so it is with Sergey Brin and Larry Page. Both come from highly intelligent and motivated parents, showed early interest in computers, are under 40 years old, are Stanford University dropouts, drive Toyota Priuses, live in modest apartments with their wives, and are worth about $18.5 billion each (Figure 15.4).

Brin, a native of Moscow in the Soviet Union, moved at an early age with his family to College Park, Maryland, the home of the University of Maryland, where his father was a math professor and his mother was a scientist for NASA. Later, he received an undergraduate degree from the same university. In 2007 he married Anne Wojcicki, a biotech analyst who co-founded the personal genome service, where you can send in a sample of your DNA and get an analysis for $399 (Weblink 15.6). In 2008 *Time* magazine named it the "invention of the year." Through this process, Brin discovered that he has a chance of developing Parkinson's disease later in his life.

Larry Page is the son of Michigan State University computer science professor Dr. Carl Victor Page. When he was six years old he received his first computer. He earned a bachelor's of science degree in engineering at the University of Michigan and distinguished himself by building a programmable printer out of Lego toy blocks. In 2007 he married Lucinda Southworth who has a master's of science degree from Oxford University.

Brin and Page met in 1995 when Page was visiting the campus of Stanford University. Brin was one of a group of students assigned to show him around. The first Google database resided in Page's dorm room. The hard drive contained about 30 million web pages. When they moved their operation to a friend's garage in 1998, they dropped out of school and started to work for the company full-time.

One of the persons who encouraged them was David Filo, co-founder of Yahoo!.

By 2001 Brin and Page thought it was time to impose a grown-up structure to their company. They became co-presidents, with Brin concentrating on Google's worldwide growth and Page in charge of new product development. To run day-to-day operations, Eric Schmidt was named chair of the board and CEO. Schmidt had both master's and PhD degrees from the University of California, Berkeley, was on the research staff at the famous Xerox Palo Alto Research Center, and was an executive with Sun Microsystems and Novell.

Today, Google's offices, reminiscent of the early years at Apple Computers, are

Figure 15.3

While still in its testing (beta) phase in 1998, Sergey Brin created the Google logo on a computer. He added the exclamation mark to mimic the Yahoo! logo. The no-nonsense, yet playful appearance of the home page immediately appealed to search engine users because of its uncluttered appearance and its speed at finding information.

Figure 15.4

Larry Page (left) and Sergey Brin pose in front of a de stijl-inspired grid pattern. In 2007 PC World Magazine ranked Page and Brin as number one in the category of the "50 Most Important People on the Web."

located in Mountain View, California, in Silicon Valley, and are filled with perks to keep their employees happy and on the site working (Figure 15.5). They can eat in one of 11 cafeterias, enjoy one of two swimming pools, get a massage from a therapist, have their laundry cleaned for free, and can play pool, a baby grand piano, volleyball, or roller hockey. In 2007 solar panels were installed that generate 1.6 megawatts of electricity, the largest such installation in the United States.

Google makes money two ways: from advertisements that are above or to the side of the main result listings, and from selling search services to other companies. As a result, the company in 2008 had revenues of more than $5.37 billion. With its new browser, Google Chrome, the web can be searched even faster and easier while its Chrome OS (Operating System) is a direct competitor to Microsoft's OS, Azure. In 2009 the company announced that its popular video sharing website, YouTube, made deals with a number of companies including CBS, the BBC, Sony, MGM, and Lionsgate to provide programs

Figure 15.5

In the lobby of the Googleplex in Mountain View, California, participants of the Google Developers Day 2007 sit on beanbag chairs waiting for the next session.

Courtesy of AP Photo / Marcio Jose Sanchez

on its "YouTube Shows" section for the price of watching a brief opening commercial. Potentially, the search engine company may change the way we watch TV and movies. It's a Google world after all.

■ A BRIEF HISTORY OF SEARCHING

Bob Davis, former CEO of Lycos, an early web search engine, explains, "Search is the ultimate killer app. The internet without search is like a cruise missile without a guidance system." Why is searching so important? Imagine trying to find a book somewhere in a big city library without any clue to where it might be found. Searching and finding are critical to knowing.

James Burke, science historian and television producer, once remarked that before Gutenberg's printing press, palaces and monasteries employed scribes to make copies of all sorts of written materials, but those in charge weren't all that keen on organizing what was written. As a result, books, articles, edicts, census information, local news, sermons, and so on were often combined within a single leather-bound publication and stored on shelves in a haphazard way with hundreds of other books. To make matters worse for those who wanted to find a specific document, the title on the cover or spine of the volume might simply refer to the first work in the collection. The only way to know what else was in the book was to look through every page. Imagine trying to find a specific event recorded somewhere on an 8-hour cassette in a collection of hundreds of videotapes and you start to understand why many writings were lost to history.

Perhaps the monks of the Middle Ages should have taken a lesson from ancient

Indians. One of the first civilizations to start classifying ideas was that of India during the Vedic period (1500–326 BCE). These "Upanishads" or teachers divided knowledge into four categories: Dharma (law, religion, ethics, and sociology), Artha (history, politics, economics, and applied sciences), Kama (pure science, arts, and literature), and Moksha (spirituality and philosophy).

Taking a cue from the Vedic culture, the third president of the United States, Thomas Jefferson, had a library of about 6,700 volumes at his home in Monticello that he divided into three simple categories: memory (history), reason (philosophy and science), and imagination (fine arts). After the British destroyed the U.S. government's library during the burning of Washington, D.C., in 1812, Jefferson sold his library to Congress for $23,950 ($800,000 today) in 1815. His collection was the start of the Library of Congress (Figure 15.6).

Later, in 1876 Melvil Dewey from upstate New York at the age of 21 developed his categorizing system based on 10 classes of major subjects. His Dewey Decimal Classification system made him the founder of the modern library. It is used in 95 percent of all the city and public school libraries in the United States and in more than 135 countries worldwide. In 1897, Jefferson's simple classification method was replaced by the Library of Congress Classification (LCC) system that divided all works from his original 3 to 21 content categories. The letter–number scheme is still in wide use at many academic and research libraries.

In 1966 Gordon Foster, a retired professor of statistics at Trinity College in Dublin, Ireland, developed a nine-digit classification system for commercial booksellers to more easily organize their

Courtesy of the Library of Congress Prints and Photographs Division, LC-USZ62-387

Figure 15.6
With Benjamin Franklin smiling to the left, Thomas Jefferson sits beside a few of the books that he sold to the U.S. government in 1815, marking the inception of the Library of Congress. This portrait was painted by Gilbert Charles Stuart, an American painter who is best known for his portrait of President George Washington that appears on the one-dollar bill.

collections. One more number was added to his International Standard Book Number (ISBN) in 1970 and adopted as a worldwide system. In 2007 a 13-digit system was employed for newly published books. Bar codes on the back covers of books include the number with pricing information for use in bookstores.

Despite the popularity of the Library of Congress, Dewey, and ISBN systems, they are being replaced by online data searches that can hunt for works by author, title, and/or subject. With Google and other companies and academic institutions attempting to digitize all the books ever published, web users can easily find a book and read it off a screen or print it out. However, critics worry that the millions of books Google digitizes may be available only through a fee-based structure.

Although today it is common to use the web to find almost anything imaginable, the practice of searching online is relatively new. "Archie" was the name for the first computer-based networked data

Figure 15.7

Shown through Marc Andreessen's original Mosaic web browser, a typical Gopher page contained folder icons for its menu items. By the late 1990s Gopher was considered obsolete. However, search engine hobbyists still maintain about 125 servers throughout the world. By tradition, new Gopher servers are created only on April Fool's Day.

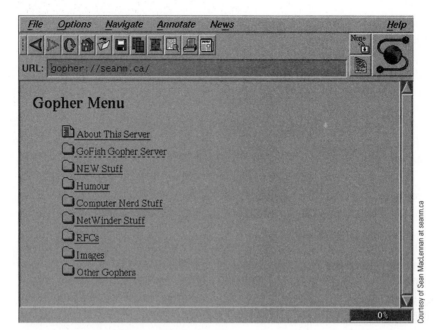

Courtesy of Sean MacLennan at seanm.ca

Figure 15.8

Yahoo! co-founders David Filo (left) and Jerry Yang in 1999.

Courtesy of Eric Sander / Getty images

organizer. Alan Emtage and Bill Heelan, students at McGill University in Montreal, created it in 1990. It was named either for its closeness to the word "archive" or after the teenager-inspired comic book *Archie*, which was first published in 1941, created by Bob Montana and drawn by Vic Bloom.

In 1991 a team of University of Minnesota students introduced "Gopher," named after the school's mascot (Figure 15.7). It was a menu-driven document retrieval program for the internet. Its search engine was called "Veronica," another character from the *Archie* comic book—thereby solidifying the link between computer users and cartoons.

Developers—from amateurs with their poorly designed home pages to professionals with their poorly designed online brochures—created millions of web pages. However, without knowing what specifically to look for, finding useful content was often a frustrating experience until the first successful organizer for much of the web was invented—Yahoo! (Weblink 15.7). The exclamation mark was added because several other companies had already trademarked the word Yahoo. In 1994 two Stanford University students, David Filo and Jerry Yang, created the popular data retrieval program (Figure 15.8). Initially a class project named "Jerry's Guide to the

World Wide Web," Yahoo! (aka "Yet Another Hierarchical Officious Oracle") was a collection of web pages that were divided into logical categories, as with the Library of Congress and Dewey systems. Initially, anyone with a website had to request that it be included into the Yahoo! database. Once it was accepted, the web pages were entered manually into the database. Yahoo! was enormously popular and respected as a great idea (Figure 15.9). After Yahoo!, data organizer programs such as Archie and Gopher became obsolete.

When Filo and Yang announced their public stock offering in 1996, they raised more than $30 million ($42 million today). With the money, Yahoo! was turned into a more commercial web portal, a type of webpage that offers news, entertainment, and e-mail, as well as search services. The company also was able to purchase other web entities such as GeoCites, other search engines Inktomi and AltaVista, the picture-sharing site Flickr, and the social bookmarking site del.icio.us.

Despite its aggressive marketing plan, Yahoo! made some missteps. In 2007, executives allegedly gave private e-mail registration information to the Chinese government about a dissident. He was

World Series · CLICK HERE TO VISIT THE STARS · YAHOO! LOS ANGELES · Weekly Picks

Search Options

Yellow Pages - People Search - City Maps -- Stock Quotes - Sports Scores

- **Arts and Humanities** - Architecture, Photography, Literature...

- **Business and Economy [Xtra!]** - Companies, Investments, Classifieds...

- **Computers and Internet [Xtra!]** - Internet, WWW, Software, Multimedia...

- **Education** - Universities, K-12, College Entrance...

- **Entertainment [Xtra!]** - Cool Links, Movies, Music, Humor...

- **Government** - Politics [Xtra!], Agencies, Law, Military...

- **Health [Xtra!]** - Medicine, Drugs, Diseases, Fitness...

- **News and Media [Xtra!]** - Current Events, Magazines, TV, Newspapers...

- **Recreation and Sports [Xtra!]** - Sports, Games, Travel, Autos, Outdoors...

- **Reference** - Libraries, Dictionaries, Phone Numbers...

- **Regional** - Countries, Regions, U.S. States...

- **Science** - CS, Biology, Astronomy, Engineering...

- **Social Science** - Anthropology, Sociology, Economics...

Figure 15.9

The Yahoo! hierarchical listing of categories in 1996 is preserved by the "Wayback Machine" (itself a tribute to a device made famous on the cartoon series "The Rocky and Bullwinkle Show") at archive.org.

later caught and sentenced to ten years in prison. Boycotts of all Yahoo! products and services were formed by a number of worldwide organizations. Sensing vulnerability and wanting to get more into the search engine market, the next year the giant Microsoft Corporation made a bid to buy Yahoo! for $44.6 billion, but the offer was turned down. Recently, the company had to lay off employees due to the economic downturn. However, in 2009 the two media giants agreed on a search engine partnership to compete with Google.

Since Yahoo!, search engines for the web have evolved from simple file finders created by innovative graduate students to sophisticated full-service portals maintained by major corporations such as Microsoft. Ask.com was started up in 1996 by two California entrepreneurs, Garrett Gruener and David Warthen, with a developer, Gary Chevsky, and a logo designed by Marcos Sorensen. It was originally named "Ask Jeeves," after the butler from stories by P. G. Wodehouse. In 2006 the butler was fired and replaced with a more modern logo after the media conglomerate InterActive Corp. (IAC), run by Barry Diller, purchased it. When he headed the Fox Broadcasting Company, Diller gave a green light to Matt Groening's series, "The Simpsons." "Jeeves" was unique in that you could simply type a question rather than worry about using an exact keyword. Microsoft introduced Live Search in 2007. Two years later it was replaced by Bing to further compete with Google. Bing is marketed not as a search engine necessarily, but a "decision engine" (Weblink 15.8).

Hunting and gathering is as old as history, but other more creative designers of search engines have expanded the definition of the web genre. While visit-

ing Hawaii in 1994, American computer developer Ward Cunningham was told to take a "wiki wiki," the name for the shuttle bus that travelled between terminals at the airport. Wiki is Hawaiian for fast. After he returned home, Cunningham named his online database the WikiWikiWeb, the first that allowed others to contribute information. Since then, user-supplemented databases or wikis have become common. The most successful wiki by far is Wikipedia, an online encyclopedia with more than 10 million topics that are constantly updated by about 75,000 contributors (Weblink 15.9). Begun in 2000 by Jimmy Wales and Larry Sanger of the online encyclopedia company Nupedia, Wikipedia is now an entity of the not-for-profit Wikipedia Foundation and used as a resource for learning about a vast array of subjects.

Called a "discovery search engine," Live Plasma was begun by the French developer Frédéric Vavrille in 2004. It generates a map of similarly evaluated songs and music groups from the one requested by a user (Weblink 15.10). For example, type in the 1980s alternative band The Pixies, and Live Plasma will generate pretty colored bubbles with related bands such as Sonic Youth, Frank Black, The Amps, and The Breeders. The size of each bubble denotes the number of web links associated with each band. Type "The Rolling Stones," and bubbles that stand for similar groups such as The Beatles, The Who, and Led Zeppelin appear.

Delocator began in 2005 after its creator, xtine burrough (she prefers her name lowercase), was frustrated that she couldn't find an independent coffee shop in Soho, New York City, amid the Starbucks stores on seemingly every corner. She collaborated with developer Jim Bursch, and the result of their efforts is a search engine in which you can type a zip code and a distance radius and receive a list of Starbucks and non-Starbucks coffee shops (Figure 15.10). Since the initial launch, a user can also find independent bookstores and movie theaters. A unique feature of the site is that users can add reviews, comments, and photographs for each entry (Weblink 15.11). This concept of adding user-generated content to build a sense of community is a key element in the so-called Web 2.0 (discussed later).

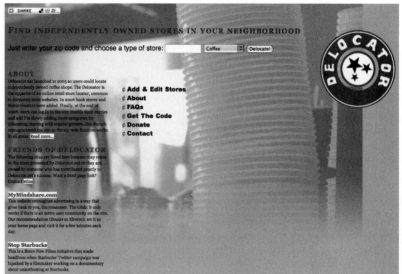

Figure 15.10

An alternative way of thinking about web search engines can be found with a website known as Delocator.net. Alternative coffee houses, with users adding pictures and brief descriptions, can be found by typing in your zip code. The coffee shop background image and dark green logo are perhaps meant to evoke a Starbucks alternative.

■ ANALYSIS OF GOOGLE

Google is used to search the web about 140,000 times every minute, or 200 million searches a day. That's 75 percent of all the daily searches that happen on the web. With income from advertising and search services, Sergey Brin and Larry Page are ranked as the 32nd and 33rd richest persons in the world and, if ranked by age, are the youngest billionaires in the world.

Based on an original idea from Sergey Brin, Ruth Kedar, an artist and designer, used the roman typeface Catull to design the original Google logo. The letters use the primary colors of red, green, and blue, with a yellow "o" to signify that the company doesn't follow the rules. A delightful aspect of the simple, uncluttered Google home page is the variations of its logo for special anniversaries or occasions. Dennis Hwang, a graphic artist born in Tennessee but raised in South Korea, started creating his own logos for the page in 2000 when Brin and Page wanted something a bit "more fun." Nicknamed "Google Doodles," Hwang definitely has fun. He claims to love each letter in "G-o-o-g-l-e" equally,

but he does favor the "O" (which has become a "Halloween pumpkin, a Nobel Prize medal, the Korean flag symbol and the planet Earth") and "L" (which has been used as a "flagpole, the Olympic flame cauldron or a snow ski"). For Piet Mondrian's birthday the logo mimicked one of his paintings using simple colored grids, whereas a tribute to Pablo Picasso used multiple faces in the "OOs" (Figure 15.11).

Critics have challenged the highly publicized corporate ethos of Google, "Don't be evil." Monopolistic tendencies, privacy, and other issues have been concerns with critics. As early as 1996, Brin and Page envisioned digitizing all of the library material in the world and using their search program to find any book online. After their company was formed, employees started working on the project in earnest. In 2004 Google struck a deal with major university libraries to digitize their collections and by 2010 book publishers and libraries throughout the world have joined the program. Nevertheless, a French court ordered Google to stop copying works from its country

Figure 15.11

The graphic designer for Google, Dennis Hwang, obviously enjoys playing with the logo to make "Google Doodles." From previous chapters of this textbook, it should be obvious that the grid-like Google at the top is a tribute to Piet Mondrian, while the multiview design is a nod to the painter Pablo Picasso. Other famous persons from Albert Einstein to Andy Warhol, as well as important dates such as Bastille, Veteran's, and Valentine's days have been Doodled.

Courtesy of Google

because of copyright concerns. Google has also been controversial at various times for mixing editorial and advertising content. Links that appear as a result of a user's search can be considered Google's editorial content, and commercial sites that pay Google to have their related links presented above and to the right are advertising. Sometimes the two get confused.

For example, when the first links presented after a search for the word "Jew" were to anti-Jewish websites, Google quickly added a disclaimer to explain why such results occur and pointed users to "informative and relevant" sites. But when lawyers representing the Church of Scientology asked Google to stop linking to what they considered to be an anti-Scientology site, the offending links were removed. The strict policy of not allowing "the advertisement of sites that promote hate, violence, racial intolerance, or *advocate against any individual, group, or organization* [emphasis added]" also disallows individuals and groups with political messages. In addition, after a request from the People's Republic of China, Google instituted keyword filters for its Chinese version to prevent users from obtaining information the government didn't want known.

Privacy issues are also a concern of many critics of Google, especially after the introduction of their e-mail service, Gmail, was launched April 1, 2004, as a beta release and made available to the public three years later. Started on April Fool's Day, many thought that giving those who sign up for Gmail 1GB of storage space was a joke, but the service is popular. With that much storage space, messages will never have to be deleted, and for an extra fee of $500 a year you can have up to 400GB of storage.

But Google is not simply offering this service out of the goodness of their hearts. Your e-mail messages are analyzed and advertising links are added pertaining to the content in your e-mails. For example, if you mention a motorcycle in a text message to a friend, a link to Harley-Davidson might appear to the side of your message. If you were writing about a friend who was involved in a motorcycle accident, you might not be in the mood to buy one. Google explained that it tries to refrain from placing ads next to sensitive e-mail topics. However, that seems to imply an actual person is reading and evaluating your e-mail messages.

Is Google and web searching too popular? In a recent poll, 71 percent of middle and high school students reported that they used the internet as their main source for research. Google leads all other search engines with 65 percent of all users and with products such as Google Earth with its Mars, Moon, Ocean, and Sky programs, Gmail, News, and the digitization of health records and books, almost 75 percent of all searches made in the world via the internet go through Google. Either because of convenience or laziness, many no longer visit libraries to check out books on a particular topic.

■ THE WEB AND THE SIX PERSPECTIVES

Personal Perspective

The web was originally developed by military officials who needed to find a way to communicate with one another in the event of a nuclear holocaust. However, since its inception, the web has come under attack for a wide variety of reasons. Social critics (mostly conservative) warn that the web is a plaything for those interested in corrupting young minds with a steady stream of easily accessible child pornography materials. Others assert that it is the subject of a relentless barrage of mass media hyperbole. Whether it is considered the future of mass media or a colossal waste of time and resources, the web has earned its place as a valuable resource for information, entertainment, and blatant commercialism—as all media eventually do.

The web is an important medium of communication because it is a convergence of all that has come before it. It gets its immediacy from radio and television, its totality of information from print, and its visual and audio qualities from motion pictures—and yet it is more than all those media. When the first automobile was introduced, no one predicted fast cars, the interstate road systems, highway deaths, mechanic garages, parts stores, the suburbs, pollution, reliance on foreign oil, global warming, and drive-through fast-food restaurants and liquor stores. One hundred years from now people will no doubt chuckle about how the web was used way back in the year 2010.

Historical Perspective

After World War II, the Cold War set in, a political "war" mainly between the United States and the Union of Soviet Socialist

Figure 15.12

An icon of the Cold War era is this aerial photograph taken by Major Richard Stephen Heyser during one of his five flights over Cuba in his U-2 spy photographic plane. It shows a Soviet truck convoy transporting nuclear missiles near San Cristobal, Cuba, on October 14, 1962. After a U.S. naval blockade of the island country and America's agreement to remove its missiles from Turkey along the Soviet border, the Soviet government removed the weapons. Called the "Cuban Missile Crisis," it was the closest the two superpowers have come to a nuclear war and inspired the U.S. military to create an alternative communications network that eventually became the internet. Heyser died at the age of 81 in 2008. It's not known whether he had an e-mail address.

Courtesy of U.S. Air Force

Republics. Its most terrifying moment was the Cuban missile crisis of 1962 when it was discovered that the Soviet Union was storing nuclear weapons on the island nation 90 miles from Key West, Florida (Figure 15.12). Concerned that there well might be a nuclear war in which major cities were destroyed, the U.S. military started to consider ways other than the telephone to communicate. With the help of the RAND Corporation, a governmental think tank, the Defense Department's Advanced Research Projects Agency (ARPA) started to develop a communications network via computers. The concept was that if communication was wiped out in some areas, the network could re-route messages around the blank spots. In 1969 the first e-mail message was sent between researchers at UCLA and the Stanford Research Institute using a computer network called the ARPAnet.

Coincidentally, others realized the need for networked communications. During the 1970s, powerful IBM and other mainframe computers were popular at government, business, and university research sites around the world. With all the activity generated by these machines, scientists soon realized that they needed communications links among these centers so that computer operators could transfer data and talk with each other electronically. Consequently, more and more computer users started using the ARPANET for work-related and personal messages (Figure 15.13). By 1983, the system had become so popular that it was divided into two—the original Arpanet for university use and Milnet for the military. When satellite links were added to the system, international communication became possible. Arpanet's name was changed to the International Network, or internet.

Gradually, users of the internet started to see commercial uses for this new communications technology. The first commercial use of networked computers was named *videotex* (called teletext or viewdata in Europe). Videotex was the name for communications systems that delivered information over a broadcast

Figure 15.13

Unlike telephone conversations that relied on a party-to-party single connection, the ARPANET (Advanced Research Projects Agency Network) divided communications into discrete packets that could be sent independent of each other through a variety of routes and reassembled so that routing of the message could still take place in case of a major catastrophe. This map shows the extent of the network in 1969, with the four original nodes (also called hosts or service providers) and their connections based at university institutions: UTAH (University of Utah), SRI (Stanford Research Institute), UCSB (UC Santa Barbara), and UCLA (UC Los Angeles). Based on the CIA World Factbook, in 2008 the United States topped the list of worldwide internet hosts with 316 million, while the rest of the world has an estimated 251 million providers. The majority of them are commercial sites.

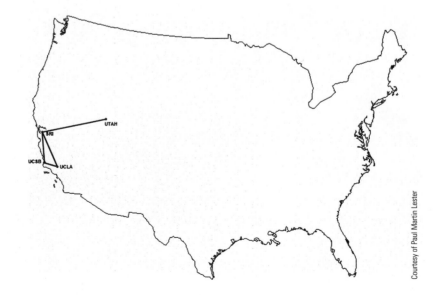

Courtesy of Paul Martin Lester

television signal to a person's home. With a small keypad and a television set-top box, a home user could control which frames were viewed. Viewers could access hundreds of televised "pages" that contained screens for news, shopping, and other kinds of information. In 1973, the British Broadcasting Corporation (BBC) began Ceefax, a one-way, text-only teletext system (Figure 15.14). British users received news and information scrolled along the bottom of their television screens.

In 1979, the British Post Office (known as British Telecom) began the first truly interactive system, Prestel. The Prestel system connected computer databases to the home through telephone lines. Users received about the same type of information as with Ceefax, but they could control what they wanted to read. Michael Aldrich invented and sold a computer he called a "teleputer" that could receive television programs using the Prestel system. However, Prestel proved unpopular as consumers had to buy a separate set-top box and pay extra telephone charges for the service.

One of the most successful communications systems in the world was the French government's Minitel system.

Begun in 1981 by the French Telecom telephone company, it provided low-cost computers to every telephone subscriber in France. The government saved millions of dollars by not having to print telephone directories because users obtained phone numbers through their home computers. Canada, Ireland, South Africa, and other countries experimented with versions of the Minitel system. However, the web made the system archaic. In 2009 the French Minitel service was discontinued.

In the United States, pay-for-use videotex services were never popular. A videotex system was tried in 1979 using terminals sold at Radio Shack stores and content provided by CompuServe, the first major online system in the United States. Two years later, the Knight-Ridder newspaper chain with content from the *Miami Herald* and technology from AT&T provided a videotex service called Viewtron to users in Coral Gables, Florida, an affluent suburb of Miami. In the initial experiment, users weren't asked to pay for the videotex terminals or the service. But beginning in 1983, home viewers had to pay $300 (almost $700 today) for a computer terminal and a monthly service

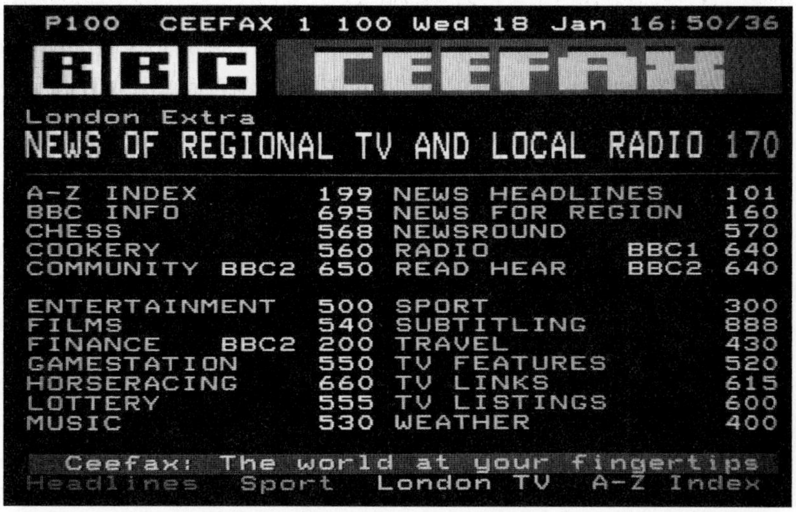

Figure 15.14
Users of the BBC's Ceefax teletext system are able to access news, games, and other information from their television sets.

Figure 15.15

More visually interesting than the Antiope system, the graphic look of the Viewtron Videotex Service was still simple by today's web standards. Nevertheless, the service made it easy for Miami-area users to shop online at a Burdines department store. They just didn't want to use this service in 1983.

Courtesy of Paul Martin Lester

Figure 15.16

The bulletin board service called Monochrome still has users who prefer the retro look of text-based displays.

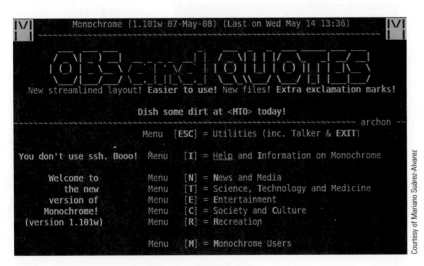

Courtesy of Mariano Suárez-Alvarez

charge of about $30 (about $70). After investing more than $50 million (more than $110 million today) in the electronic information experiment, Knight-Ridder abandoned the project (Figure 15.15).

Bulletin board systems (BBS) were initiated in 1978 by Chicago computer developers Ward Christensen and Randy Suess with information that could be accessed through telephone lines. At first, BBS were an added feature to users of home-made computers such as the Altair 8800. After IBM and Apple desktop computers became popular in the early 1980s, the use of these communication systems took off. At their height there were more than 100,000 boards worldwide (Figure 15.16). These BBS ranged from local text-only systems with a handful of users to worldwide networks that had millions of subscribers. They offered a wide range of services that included news, information, shopping, banking, software downloads, chatting, and airline reservations. Before the web, some of the most popular BBS were America Online, CompuServe, Delphi, Genie, Prodigy, the Source, the WELL, and ZiffNet. In the United Kingdom, the Monochrome BBS is still popular for "interactive chat, offline messaging and discussion files" (Weblink 15.12). Users also enjoy playing text-based role-playing multi-user dungeon (MUD) games such as "Banished Lands," "Discworld," and "Lands of Stone" (Weblink 15.13). Because a videotex system or bulletin board stored its data at a central location, users could only access what was made available to them. These systems, in other words, were similar to CD-ROM or DVD interactive programs—what was on a disc was all you could access. Much of the appeal of these systems was the interactive chats between other users.

Soon, however, a unique communications technology would change that limiting concept—the web.

In 1989, British computer scientist Timothy Berners-Lee, using a NeXT computer while working for the European Laboratory for Particle Physics (CERN) in Geneva, Switzerland, developed a computer language called Hypertext Transfer Protocol (HTTP), which created files that could be accessed from the internet. In 1991 HTTP was used for the first web browser that Berners-Lee called the WorldWideWeb. For his innovations in mass communications, *Time* magazine in 1999 listed him as one of the most influential persons of the 20th century, and in 2004 the Queen of England knighted him (Figure 15.17).

In 1993, interest in the internet expanded tremendously because of what was called its killer app—the Mosaic software program. Marc Andreessen developed it while a student at the University of Illinois. His web browser made accessing and downloading internet files that contained still and moving pictures with audio as simple as clicking a computer's mouse.

Web browsers turned the text-dominated internet into the colorful, content-filled surfing explosion that it is today. Apart from the program's graphic capa-

SEBASTIAN DERUNGS / AFP / Getty Images

bilities, much of the appeal of browsers comes from the fact that they allow a person to create and use a hypertext link to discover a seemingly inexhaustible amount of interrelated information and services. After administrators at the University of Illinois demanded that Andreessen give the browser to the school, he quit to form his own company he called Netscape (Figure 15.18). In 1995 he sold it to AOL, once owned by the media giant Time Warner. That same year Microsoft introduced its Internet Explorer (IE) web browser. By 2003 IE was the clear winner of the browser war because of its advantage in having its software residing on 95 percent of computers worldwide.

However, other web browsers are slowly eating away at IE's dominance. The Mozilla Corporation's Firefox, launched in 2004, and Apple's Safari, released in 2003, are strong competitors of Internet Explorer. Firefox and Safari each offer features not included with Internet Explorer. As of 2009, IE is used by 68 percent of web users, Firefox by 22 percent, Safari, 8 percent, and Netscape by only 1 percent.

Figure 15.17
Tim Berners-Lee poses with the first web server in 2009.

Figure 15.18

With its links to information, classified ads, and many more topics and services, the German version of the Netscape home page or portal resembles many other magazine, newspaper, radio, and televisions websites.

When this book's first edition was written in 1993, the internet had about 15 million users worldwide. More than 15 years later there are an estimated 1.5 *billion* users, or about 24 percent of the Earth's population. In the past ten years, those living in Africa and the Middle East have had the highest percentage of web use growth. Also, in 1993 the communications tool was called the all-capitalized "World Wide Web." Today, the web, as with the internet, are commonly spelled with lowercase initial letters like photography, movies, and television, and the "www" prefix for web addresses, called the Uniform Resource Locator (URL), is no longer necessary with most browsers. Rather than a demotion in status, the change indicates that the web is a democratizing, universal communications tool that has profoundly changed mass communications.

 *Technical Perspective*

Early in its history, those who envisioned the communication system known as the web realized that there needed to be a set of rules for those who create websites so that files could be viewed on any type of web browser and on any kind of computer. Tim Berners-Lee's simple software language HTML ensures that a web browser can request information from a web server so that you can see all the words and images on your own computer screen. For any website that has been downloaded to your computer, you can view the HTML source code and study how the site was created. A popular HTML editor from Adobe—*Dreamweaver*—makes the task of website creation much easier than writing software code from scratch.

Since the development of HTML, other valuable software tools have been created that enhance the efficiency and functionality of websites. These include Application Programming Interface (API), which helps in the creation of web-based software applications, and Cascading Style Sheets (CSS), in which specifications regarding colors, typefaces, fonts, and layout for a set of web pages can be housed within a separate file. In addition, the Extensible Markup Language (XML) Java, developed by James Gosling of Sun Microsystems in 1995, JavaScript, created by Brendan Eich of Netscape the same year, and its professional programming big brother, AJAX, allow developers to create applications that can more easily be shared between different computers and operating systems.

The technical information to create a website is beyond the scope of this book, but lessons can easily be found on the web and on bookstore shelves. However, you should be aware of how to analyze a website to make sure the information contained within it is credible. Researchers at the Stanford Web Credibility Project conducted a three-year project surveying more than 4,500 persons and came up with ten guidelines that improve a website's credibility (Weblink 15.14). The ten items are as follows:

1. Make it easy for the user to verify the accuracy of the information.

2. Identify the organization that sponsors the site.

3. Note any experts who provide information.

4. Detail the backgrounds of those involved with the site.

5. Make contact information readily available.

6. Make sure the use of typography, images, and graphic design elements looks professional.

7. Include navigational elements so that the site is easy to use.

8. Update the site often and report the last update.

9. Avoid advertisements.

10. Remove spelling, typographical, and linking errors.

One of the best examples of web design, technology, and credibility is the "Frontline" website, produced by PBS's affiliate WGBH in Boston. Since 1983, "Frontline" has been one of the best programs on television to view investigative documentaries (Weblink 15.15). Newsday calls the program "television's last fully serious bastion of journalism." The website is also an excellent example of the synergy among all of the media elements discussed in previous chapters.

■ Typography

The typographical presentations include headlines, text blocks, and captions printed in an easy-to-read sans serif typeface. Colored text, boldface, and backgrounds signal special areas and features so that a user can easily find them.

■ Graphic Design

The home page for the site is divided into discrete sections with each one clearly separated from another by colored backgrounds. Words and images are neatly displayed in a gridlike approach that denotes a serious attitude about the content of the site.

■ Photography

The mostly color still images, tightly cropped for added impact, and the images from main stories sliding automatically across the top of the page give a user a clear idea of what to expect after a mouse click.

■ Television

Using Adobe's Flash software player, investigative reports as seen on television can be watched on a user's computer screen at any time. Users also have the option to run the digital video in a small screen off to the side of a desktop or fill the monitor with the picture.

■ Computers

Unlike a motion picture or a television program, users can choose their own path through the website. Built-in interactive features allow users to search for specific information and programs and link to other websites and databases.

 Ethical Perspective

As can be imagined with a medium not two decades old, there are many ethical and legal issues that are worthy of serious discussion that have not yet been resolved. Every concern pointed out in the previous chapters' ethical perspective sections can certainly be applied to the web. For visual communicators, one of the most important issues is that of free speech versus governmental censorship. Social critics have sometimes described the web as a huge, unregulated book or video store in which a child can suddenly wander into a back room where all the pornographic magazines and lewd videos are shelved. But besides access to sexually explicit sites, there is also easy access to hate speech. With Google's SafeSearch Filtering feature set to the most adult setting of

"Do not filter my search results," the word "sex" resulted, as can be imagined, in over 62 million hits, with everything from links to free pornographic videos to a sex education website for teens sponsored by Rutgers University. The phrase "white power" produced more than a million websites that included pictures of swastikas and young men giving Nazi salutes. With Google's SafeSearch set to "strict filtering," a search for "sex" resulted in the Rutgers website, numerous links concerned with the television show "Sex and the City," and sexual predator criminal cases. Interestingly, switching to strict filtering didn't make much difference when "white power" was searched. The results were a similar array of Aryan supremacy websites and images, as if no filtering had been applied. The lesson might be that web culture is more concerned with sex than hate. Regardless, as with all media, parents need to be responsible for the materials their children watch. But in a public setting—as in a university or library—adults should be given the opportunity to view a wide variety of materials available on the web.

⊕ Cultural Perspective

Alexa Internet ranks the most popular websites among actual users by country worldwide. Currently the top ten worldwide sites in order of popularity are Google.com, Facebook.com, YouTube .com, Yahoo.com, Live.com, Wikipedia .org, Blogger.com, Baidu.com, MSN.com, and Yahoo.co.jp (Japan). All but one is a commercial site. Consistently, the web has moved far away from its research institution roots, but there are indications that the focus is changing back to educational uses. One of the places to find many non-commercial and alternative sites on the web is the annual Webby Awards (Weblink 15.16). Established in 1996 and presented by The International Academy of Digital Arts and Sciences, with judges such as internet inventor Vint Cerf, musicians Beck and David Bowie, and Matt Groening of "The Simpsons," the Webby awards honor those who create websites in almost 70 categories, from Activism to Weird.

Consequently, there has been a dramatic shift in the way the web works and is thought of by users and programs since its introduction in 1993. Mimicking release iterations of software products, the initial version of the medium is sometimes called Web 1.0. Non-users often criticized this form of the web because, for the most part, individuals and corporations simply displayed the equivalent of a flyer, brochure, and/or business card in simply designed home pages with bad typography and spinning animations. The most sophisticated element on a page might have been a visitor sign-in logbook.

Irish blogger Joe Drumgoole, CEO and founder of putplace.com, a website in which users can store their digital belongings, writes that Web 1.0 was about reading. It was often said that persons and companies created websites regardless of whether they were functional or viewed by anyone, so that they could *say* they had a website. The web, then, started as a static, page-driven family bulletin board or corporate tool with little user input or influence on the data.

A move in changing the way the web was regarded happened in 2004 when Tim O'Reilly of O'Reilly Media sponsored a Web 2.0 conference in San Francisco to spark development of what he thought should be the next generation. For Drumgoole, Web 2.0 is about writing and sharing. For many, user-generated content

sites such as Blogger, del.icio.us, Facebook, Flickr, YouTube, and Wikipedia epitomize this next generation of websites. With these websites you can easily share your ideas, bookmarks, personal stories, pictures, videos, and knowledge with others. With web feed formats, or Really Simple Syndication (RSS) utilities such as podcasts for audio or digital video file sharing and blog sites on any subject imaginable, good ideas get distributed at the speed of light.

Of the ten most used global websites mentioned previously, Google.com, YouTube.com, Facebook.com, Wikipedia .org, Blogger.com, and Baidu.com are Web 2.0 applications. Another popular example of this interactive web is the auction site eBay.com. Begun in 1995 by French-born Iranian computer developer Pierre Omidyar to sell used items online, eBay is one of the most successful auction sites with versions throughout the world. The company also owns PayPal for transactions, Skype for telephone calls, StubHub for tickets, and Kijiji for classified advertising, all with the .com suffix.

For many, Web 2.0 is also about creating social communities based on common interests. For others it is a way to take back the web from the large corporations. For visual communicators, the web is wide open. Just about anything conceptualized can be visualized. The one-way, force-feeding of tightly controlled words and images for mostly commercial purposes is being replaced by a two-way, more open user culture. Consequently, graphic designers and visual artists are teaming up with computer developers to create platforms for the web. Many of these collaborations are commonly called "mashups," so named because they combine two or more existing applications to create a distinct service. One of the first mashups was a combination of the popular craigslist.org classified advertising website and Google Maps called HousingMaps.com, in which users could find out about places to live pinpointed on a map of the area desired (Weblink 15.17). Digg.com is an enormously popular social network mashup of news and information websites with users in control of the stories that are displayed on the front page. Kevin Rose and Alex Albrecht host a video podcast, "diggNation," that features the top stories found on the Digg website. The two are also occasional guests on Jimmy Fallon's television show, "Late Night."

Michael Mandiberg, a senior fellow at New York City's Eyebeam, a center for the creation of experimental digital tools that "challenges convention, celebrates the hack, educates the next generation, encourages collaboration, freely offers its contributions to the community, and invites the public to share in a spirit of openness," is a strong advocate of mashups (Weblink 15.18). He is the creator of such websites as TheRealCosts.com, a Firefox plug-in that "adds CO_2 emissions information to airfare websites" and HowMuchItCosts.us that uses data from Google Maps and gasoline efficiency data from automobile manufacturers to calculate CO_2 costs for air or car travel. His assertion that "Platforms are the internet" has become a "meme," a cultural concept that has spread quickly throughout the internet because of user conversations through such social networking sites as Digg, Facebook, Twitter, and YouTube.

The internet, through the web, has certainly moved past its e-mail roots. Artist and educator xtine burrough who created Delocator.net and developer Michael Shafae produced a mashup, YourNeighborsBiz.com, a Facebook application that uses Google Maps (Weblink 15.19).

Users can locate friends who provide a service, such as cutting hair or giving yoga lessons, to sell or barter (Figure 15.19). Steve Lambert, CEO of AntiAdvertsingAgency .com, elicited developer friends to create a mashup of AdblockPlus.org and the Firefox web browser. His program replaces sometimes annoying website advertisements found on browsers with artwork from his site Add-Art.org. About his mashup, Lambert said, "It is very much a hack. It makes Firefox do what it wasn't designed to do." These innovative mashers combine an artist's eye with an anti-establishment, activist urgency.

Another outgrowth of the Web 2.0 philosophy that stresses user input and interactivity may be in how the concept influences the future of television. A growing body of original programming is being produced by seasoned motion picture and television veterans as well as independent newcomers and shown on such websites as Hulu.com, Live.com, Television.aol.com, YouTube.com, and the major network and cable websites, as well as sites named after the programs themselves, such as quarterlife.com. To make viewing easier, Intel and Yahoo! joined forces to provide the "Widget Channel." These "widgets" allow users to easily access web programming, photographs, and movies through their television sets and computers. Clicker.com helps users find television and web-based programs as well as motion pictures. An indication of the acceptance of the web as a medium for original programming is critical acclaim. In 2009 Joss Whedon, known for his television series "Buffy the Vampire Slayer" won a Primetime Emmy Award for his online-only creation, "Dr. Horrible's Sing-Along Blog" that starred Neil Patrick Harris as a lovesick supervillain. It can be purchased on iTunes (Weblink 15.20).

Figure 15.19

YourNeighborsBiz.com is a Web 2.0 interactive website in which users swap services and goods with their friends. As an alternative to classified websites such as craigslist in which strangers buy and sell to each other, Your Neighbor's Biz is a mashup that uses Google Maps and the social networking Facebook application so that you can buy and sell from friends or friends of friends.

The Showtime channel exemplifies the result of this TV/web (Tweb?) synergy. After the last episode of its six-season hit "The L Word" aired, fans had to access the cable channel's website to watch additional footage and learn how a main character died. Critical to almost all of these "webvision" sites and the reason they can be considered part of the Web 2.0 generation is that users have the opportunity to write comments on the Showtime site or on Facebook.com and critique and/or praise each episode. Such an interactive feature is not a part of the traditional television model.

A more serious use of the technology was in 2009 when President Obama gave the first online town hall meeting from the White House through streaming media. Prior to the webcast, more than 100,000 e-mail and video questions were sent to the president's website at whitehouse.gov. From this input, 3.6 million votes from users determined which questions the president would answer. You could watch the live broadcast on your computer. Although Obama's answers didn't make much news, the fact that the technology was used for the first time to connect persons with the government was featured on newspaper front pages and led many television news programs (Figure 15.20).

Critical Perspective

Science fiction writer William Gibson first used the word *cyberspace* to describe the ethereal world of the electronic highway

Figure 15.20

President Obama's Online Town Hall meeting was the first of its kind in the history of White House press conferences. Using Web 2.0 technology, anyone could ask questions in text or video formats, vote on their favorite questions, and then watch the President give responses live on the internet from a computer.

where unusual and unlimited communication links are available. He used the word in a short story called "Burning Chrome" in *Omni* magazine in 1982. Two years later his classic *Neuromancer* was published and introduced the word to popular culture. Space on the electronic highway comprises not asphalt or concrete, but electricity and light. Writer John Perry Barlow described cyberspace as having a lot in common with the 19th century West. "It is . . . vast, unmapped, culturally and legally ambiguous, verbally terse, hard to get around in, and up for grabs. . . . To enter it, one forsakes both body and place and becomes a thing of words alone. . . . It is, of course, a perfect breeding ground for outlaws and new ideas. . . ." Perhaps that critique was true at the beginning, but new media web designers are changing the face of the medium.

Nevertheless, the sheer popularity of the web is causing concerns. As more users download and upload movie clips, use social networking sites, and play online multiplayer games such as "World of Warcraft," internet traffic delays are clogging up the system for all. For example, the Irvine, California-based Blizzard Entertainment that produces "Warcraft" enjoys a fan-base of 11.5 million users with each playing the game about 20 to 30 hours a week. Three popular programs—Facebook, Skype, and YouTube—make the point.

The social networking website Facebook started as a program called Facemash by three Harvard computer science majors in 2003. It soon became popular with other Ivy League students at Columbia, Stanford, and Yale. In 2009 its *200 millionth user* was registered, with 70 percent of its members living outside the United States. Skype, a software program that allows users to make free telephone calls to each other using the internet, was begun in 2005 by entrepreneurs mostly based in Tallinn, Estonia. In 2009, on average more than 17 million users were online with Skype *at the same time.* Three friends who worked for the online payment company PayPal started YouTube.com in 2005. Now owned by

Google, it currently uses more bandwidth space than the *entire* internet in the year 2000. Estimates of the internet's growth are that for the foreseeable future, traffic on the global network will grow by 50 percent per year.

The web has brought human civilization to a great crossroads. Do we use the new tools of communication to perpetuate the same old themes of commercialism to feel better about ourselves and better than someone else; violence to resolve conflicts; sexual objectification to devalue relationships; and stereotypes to promote the dominant culture's way of life? Or do we use the technology to learn from one another in the hope of creating a world in which ideas are valued more than physical attributes?

Will you use the web to find the most titillating stories, pictures, and digital video found on websites such as Rotten (Weblink 15.21), which displays autopsy photographs, or Toxic Junction (Weblink 15.22), which offers gruesome car crash videos (Figure 15.21), or will you use the web to take one of hundreds of college courses offered online (Figure 15.22)? In either event, we live in an extremely exciting and challenging time in the history of communication—both in interpersonal relationships and the mass media.

■ TRENDS TO WATCH FOR THE WEB

Back in 1968, the future-thinking South Korean video artist Nam June Paik declared, "Paper is dead . . . except for toilet paper."

In 2009 the global economy was rocked by one of the worst economic downturns in recent history. In the United States,

bank failures, housing foreclosures, and unemployment numbers made many compare the situation with the Great Depression of the 1930s. Newspaper companies, already suffering from a steady decline in subscribers and advertising revenue and a steady rise in newsprint costs, are in crisis. Major chains and daily newspapers have filed for bankruptcy, including the Tribune Co., publisher of the *Chicago Tribune*, the *Los Angeles Times*, and the *Baltimore Sun*; the Journal Register Co. that owns 20 daily newspapers across the country, as well as newspapers such as the *Philadelphia Inquirer*, the Minneapolis *Star Tribune*; and the Sun-Times Media Group that publishes the *Chicago Sun-Times* and several suburban newspapers. The *Rocky Mountain News*, first published in 1859, quit publishing, a fate that also happened to the *Seattle Post-Intelligencer*. For years, many

Figure 15.21

There should be no mistake about the content within the pages of rotten.com. Users are warned of the site's content by the skeleton image, the red on white typography, and the text, "An archive of disturbing illustration." From autopsy and execution photographs to strange and eerie stories from around the world, rotten.com is not the place to spend a few pleasant, relaxing moments.

Figure 15.22

Every state in the United States sponsors some sort of long-distance educational opportunities via the web. The matter-of-fact graphics and typography indicate the serious nature of taking courses online—and lend a sense of credibility to that form of higher education, sometimes criticized for being impersonal.

advocates and critics of the newspaper industry have been saying that the web is the best hope for the newspaper industry.

The Knight-Ridder newspaper chain, the same company that was part of the videotex experiment in Florida in the 1980s, introduced one of the first online newspapers in the world, the *San Jose Mercury News'* Mercury Center (Figure 15.23). The newspaper was first introduced on the AOL bulletin board in 1993. In 1997, the newspaper chain introduced Real Cities network with 40 newspaper sites that contained news, information, and entertainment options from selected communities on the web. At the present time almost all of the 1,400 daily newspapers in the United States and most around the world have a version of their paper on the web. Given the trend toward a younger demographic of television and online news users, news printed on paper, a technology dating from the 16th century, may be on its way out. What we think of as "news," however, *will* survive as content

from news-providing entities, whether major corporations or enterprising individuals, will still be produced. Perhaps traditional publishing entities would be wise to learn from popular online tabloid entertainment gossip sites such as TMZ, owned by the media giant Time Warner. Short for "Thirty Mile Zone," a term used to describe a thirty-mile radius that includes where many Hollywood stars live and the motion picture and television production facilities where they work, TMZ is criticized for paying for tips from the general public, many received via Twitter, and financing still and video paparazzi. Nevertheless, the website scooped all other media in the world to be the first to announce the death of singer Michael Jackson in 2009 (Weblink 15.23).

It seems absurd during this present era of mass communications to think of television and newspapers as anything but separate. Television requires a complex machine that usually is the focus of the furniture within a room to comfortably

Figure 15.23

Like so many popular sites, the web version of the Los Angeles Times *is a portal, or entry, into news, services, and shopping.*

Richard B. Levine/News.com

watch the programs provided by a content provider. A newspaper, on the other hand, is a portable collection of paper sheets printed by inked presses, folded together, and physically delivered to homes, businesses, and pay-per-copy sidewalk boxes. When you are finished watching a television show you turn off the set. When you are done with a newspaper, you throw it in a recycle bin or leave it for someone else.

Web innovations have changed forever the perception of the two media as being separate. In fact, on the web there is little difference between portals, newspapers and magazines, and radio and television stations (Figure 15.24). All provide news, information, entertainment, and advertisements using still and moving images and audio with links to more. For the first time in mass communications history, the plural "media" have been transformed into the singular "medium" called the web. Those in the newspaper industry simply need to think of how to attract viewers and advertisers

who will be willing to pay for their product.

A "value-added" concept, similar to Apple's iTunes model in which users pay a few extra cents for engaging, interactive, and user-contributed presentations they choose to view about their neighbors and the world, is a model that will save the news and the journalism profession. News Corporation founder and Australian media mogul Rupert Murdoch exclaimed, "People reading news for free on the web, that's got to change." Publishers such as the Hearst Newspapers, *The New York Times*, Time Inc., and others have plans to charge users slight fees for stories. The Associated Press plans to charge websites, not readers, for the use of their stories. At Global Post, a news site with 65 reporters around the world, free major news items are supported by advertisements, but "passport" subscribers who pay $199 a year get access to "correspondents, conference calls and meetings with reporters, and breaking news e-mail messages from those journalists." Passport subscribers

Figure 15.24

The English language version of the Arab news television channel, Al Jazeera maintains an online website that is similar to other news portals.

Richard B. Levine/News.com

can also suggest story ideas. Perhaps still and moving outtakes as well as behind-the-scene tales of how a reporter covered a story would also be of interest to subscribers (Weblink 15.24).

Another trend to note is that computer manufacturers are selling affordable machines that help increase the number of web users. Clive Thompson of *Wired* magazine writes that most computer users don't need expensive computers with lots of memory. "It turns out that about 95 percent of what I do on a computer can now be accomplished through a browser," he writes. "I use it for updating Twitter and Facebook and for blogging. Meebo.com lets me log into several instant-messaging accounts simultaneously. Last.fm gives me tunes, and webmail does the email. I use Google Docs for word processing, and if I need to record video, I can do it directly from a webcam to YouTube." Rather than software-loaded laptops, much cheaper notebook computers connected wirelessly, referred as "cloud computing," are available from such manufacturers as Asustrk, Acer, Hewlett-Packard, OLPC, and Dell, which provide web computing for as low as $99.

Some web advocates and futurists are already planning for the next web generation. Web 3.0, sometimes referred to as the "semantic web," will be an example of human-computer interaction in which a user's specific needs are coupled with an advanced artificially intelligent computer agent that will not only deliver information that is salient for a specific user, but will anticipate that person's requirements and desires.

Imagine receiving an unexpected e-mail from an old friend inviting you to attend your high school reunion in your hometown 1,000 miles from where you presently live. Before you can reply to your friend, a pop-up screen appears on your desktop with information based on your schedule and bank account balance for flight, hotel, rental car, and dinner reservations that can be booked if you select the "OK" box. Or imagine that you're sitting in your political science class and your professor explains the five-page paper you have to write that is due in two weeks. The next time you open your computer, a list of topics and suggested sources are waiting for you. Sorry, you still have to write the paper yourself. Or imagine waking up each morning and your computer has an array of stories and/or images queued for you on the platform of your choice—portable player, radio, television, or computer—at home, in your car, or at the office. That is the promise of the Web 3.0. Your computer will have total access to your calendar, files, e-mails, web searches, bank accounts, medical records, shopping history, current circumstances including what you own or lease, personal habits and preferences, and on and on. With that information, your computer will be able to make a thousand choices for you.

Privacy issues are not a concern because with Web 3.0, the computer *is* you.

Information highways, with or without wires, are as valuable and necessary for communications as backwoods trails, shipping lanes, telegraph wires, railroad lines, roadways, and airline flight paths. The challenge for government agencies, corporate executives, creative producers, artists, educators, and concerned citizens is to ensure that everyone can ride the information highways as easily as those made of asphalt.

The author's great-grandmother lived to be 100 years old. She once admitted that she laughed when she first heard about automobiles. When asked why she found cars so funny, she replied simply, "How could everyone have their own train?" It's human nature to evaluate and anticipate technology based on previous experiences, but sometimes there are innovations in technologies and uses expressed by individuals who help us see the future. After all, in the 1870s the French artist and novelist Albert Robida and the British cartoonist George du Maurier envisioned a device that combined the telephone, television, and the web in which users watched 24-hour news and plays, had interactive communications, and took university courses all on a big screen in what was called the téléphonoscope (Figure 15.25).

The future of mass communication may have little to do with our understanding of the past or present. The best plan for anticipating the future is to keep learning with an open mind so that you will be prepared, to paraphrase Aldous Huxley, for the brave new (visual) world.

We can only hope that it is a world in which everyone is, can be, and wants to participate.

Punch Cartoons

Figure 15.25

Described as an "electric camera obscura," the téléphonoscope is illustrated in a parody of Thomas Edison and his inventions by George du Maurier in a 1978 issue of Punch *magazine.*

■ *KEY TERMS*

- Beta
- Blog
- Bookmark
- Browser
- CERN
- Chief executive officer (CEO)
- Cloud computing
- Cold War
- Computer agent
- Cyberspace
- Demographics
- Download
- Electronic highway
- Hack
- Hit
- Home page
- Hypertext
- Killer app
- Mainframe
- Meme
- Mouse
- Multi-User Dungeon (MUD)
- Operating system
- Platform
- Plug-in
- Podcast
- Portal
- Search engine
- Server
- Silicon Valley
- Streaming media
- Uniform Resource Locator (URL)
- Upload
- Widget
- Xerox Palo Alto Research Center (PARC)
- Yahoo!

 To locate active URLs for the weblinks mentioned in this chapter, please go to the companion site at http://communication.wadsworth.com/lester5 and select the proper chapter.

Chapter

16 The More You Know, The More You See

Google the title of Aldous Huxley's *The Art of Seeing* and in less than half a second you will be able to link to more than 100,000 hits. It will take you considerably more time, however, to visit all of the websites offered, but such a task would be a worthy assignment. That's because the phrase is associated with everything from philosophical uses to practical applications that cover the three types of visual messages—mental, direct, and mediated. In short, "the art of seeing" is one of the most important endeavors we should learn as humans, and it should not be surprising that its use is reported so often in a web search. No wonder then that the book by Huxley helped inspire this one (Figure 16.1). Huxley, like many others, realizes that true seeing is not exclusively a product of light, the eyes, and the brain. What is needed to turn sight into insight is an active, aware mind.

California photographer Pete Eckert understands more than most the art of seeing (Weblink 16.1). In a career that has spanned more than 20 years, Eckert has created a body of work that includes sensual portraits of friends and frenetic tributes to light that has been praised by museum curators, awards judges, magazine editors, and collectors. To other photographers who sometimes have difficulty finding images to focus upon he advises, "If you can't see, it's because your vision is getting in the way."

Eckert should know. His vision never gets in the way of his work. He's blind.

But before he realized he had trouble with his eyes, he graduated from the Art Institute of Boston in 1979 majoring in sculpture and ceramics and worked as a carpentry apprentice. Four years later, however, he was diagnosed with retinitis pigmentosa, or "tunnel vision," a condition that gradually narrows your field of view until you become blind. Nevertheless, he graduated from San Francisco State University in 1984 with two degrees—one in sculpture and the second in design and industry. As his eyesight dimmed, he thought it best to get a business degree and received an MBA from the University of Hartford in 1989. Wanting to challenge himself even more, he studied tae kwon do, received his first degree in that martial art in 1993, and developed techniques appropriate for blind persons.

After he became totally blind in 2000, he took up photography full-time. His main technique is to keep the shutter open for several seconds in a darkened room or outside at night and with a variety of light sources—flashlights, lasers, lighters, and candles—to create his images (Figure 16.2). As can be imagined, Eckert has much to teach the sighted about seeing. He explains, "The human brain is wired for optical input, for visualization. The optic nerve bundle is huge. Even with no input, or maybe especially with no input, the brain keeps creating images. I'm a very visual person, I just can't see."

Pete Eckert personifies Huxley's mantra, "The more you know, the more you see." The phrase is not simply a good idea—it is a simple fact of human nature. The eyes of a police officer on the lookout for criminal activity and the eyes of a youngster playing a video game are basically the same. Although there is no such thing as superhuman eyesight, a police officer knows how to find and catch a felon in the real world. A teenager, on the other hand, is better able to hunt down bad guys in a video game. If the situations were reversed, the officer and the youth would be lost in each other's unfamiliar environments.

Huxley understood that clear seeing is a combination of how much you

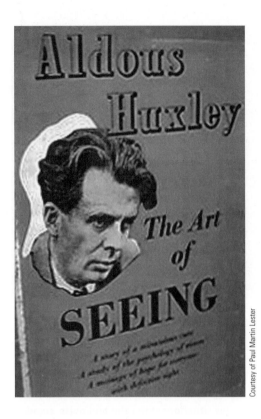

Courtesy of Paul Martin Lester

Figure 16.1

For the jacket of Aldous Huxley's 1942 book The Art of Seeing, *the graphic cutout behind his portrait makes him appear to be popping out of the cover. Despite the layout gimmick, his intense gaze dignifies the display and emphasizes the book's subject.*

know and how you feel at any particular moment. Your mental state is a vital link in the visual communication process. As he noted:

The most characteristic fact about the functioning of the total organism, or of any

Courtesy of Pete Eckert

Figure 16.2

With various non-traditional lighting techniques that include candles, flashlights, and lasers, San Francisco–based photographer Peter Eckert paints with light to create eerily ethereal human forms set within complex, urban scenes.

Courtesy of Steve Starr / CORBIS

Figure 16.3

The devastation of the Florida coastal city of Homestead after a 23-foot-high flood surge and several tornadoes generated by Hurricane Andrew in 1992 is clearly evident in this aerial photograph.

part of the organism, is that it is not constant, but highly variable. Sometimes we feel well, sometimes we feel poorly; sometimes our digestion is good, sometimes it is bad; sometimes we can face the most trying situations with calm and poise, sometimes the most trifling mishap will leave us irritable and nervous.

This non-uniformity of functionality is the price we pay for being living, self-conscious organisms, unremittingly involved in the process of adapting ourselves to changing conditions. Our organs of vision—the sensing eye, the transmitting nervous system, and the mind that selects and perceives—is no less variable than the functioning of the organism as a whole.

But this book, as strange as it may seem, isn't only concerned with seeing. Visual communication requires a two-way path between the producer and receiver of a message. Consequently, the focus of this work has more to do with *remembering* than seeing. If you learn to analyze a visual message in terms of its inventory, composition, visual cues, semiotic signs and codes, cognitive ele-

ments, purpose, and aesthetics, and to consider your personal reaction to the image, its historical context, how it was made, any ethical responsibilities of the producer and presenter, and its impact on society, you should be able to create and use memorable pictures because you will remember it.

More often than not, images that are remembered are the ones that combine aesthetically pleasing design elements with content that matters. The trouble is, works that combine both aesthetic beauty and meaning are enormously difficult to produce. Because emotional and intellectual attributes are culturally bound, the two seldom agree. Appreciating cultural similarities and differences are keys in effective mass communication.

Let's use our imaginations and think of archeologists 1,500 years from now uncovering the buried ruins of any major city in the world (Figure 16.3). They will no doubt find text on billboards, storefronts, traffic signs, and so on in the languages we know and use today throughout the world. These words, however, will probably not be understood by 36th century scientists because languages of today and the technologies that saved them will eventually become obsolete and forgotten.

Luckily, there may be an energetic and tenacious researcher with a well-used hand spade who will find along the viaducts and abandoned highways in the old cities evidence of writing that will be instantly recognized and easily read by those of his generation. For amid the buried rubble of civilizations long past will be elaborate and brightly colored signs and symbols created by graffiti artists that will last through the millennia (Figure 16.4).

This often scoffed and criminalized form of visual communication will in the future become the one, universally accepted language. In today's world, multi-colored spray-painted messages are labeled vandalism, graffiti, or tagging, depending on the speaker. These visual messages are actually a complex written form of communication. Graffiti messages may mean the mark of a territorial border, a plea for understanding and hope for the future, grief for a grief for a lost loved one, loved one, anger toward an enemy, a show of playfulness and humor, an act of criminal vandalism, or simply an individual expression that signals the writer's existence. As with any communicative system, if you do not know the language, you will have trouble deciphering the message.

The future of mass communications will not rely on the preservation of pencils, pens, paper, computers, or satellites. In the vast, inconceivable future our so-called advanced human representatives may understand ancient civilizations only because of paint in spray cans applied to walls. In the end, taggers with spray cans may be the ones to spread the message of our lost civilization.

That far-fetched, science fiction scenario is meant to help you ponder the importance of visual messages for the here and now. Is it any wonder why the human race created pictures on cave walls long before we formed them into words?

Before we are four years old, most of us have learned "The Alphabet Song." Sung to the same tune as "Twinkle Twinkle Little Star," it is unlike most other songs because no pictures come to mind when singing it. With "Twinkle," we can look up in the night's sky and imagine a little star out of the billions shining just for us. But a song about the letters of the alphabet does not carry any visual equivalents. Children soon match up, however,

Courtesy of Paul Martin Lester

Figure 16.4
Graffiti on a London, England, wall shows a combination of several different tags, the personal logos or signatures from writers, and a "throw-up," a quickly spray-painted two-color drawing. At least seven writers have tagged this small space, and yet they didn't draw over the graphic eye in the center.

concrete nouns with images for each letter in the song.

To learn to interpret the symbolic line drawing of a letter, children's books help to solve the mystery of the song with "A is for apple . . . ." Each letter of the alphabet becomes a picture that corresponds with an image. We no longer have to think of an actual red, juicy apple when we see the letter "A." But before anyone learns to read and write, they cannot tell the difference between a drawing and a letter.

When someone writes an "A" to someone who cannot read the letter, it is simply a picture, different than a face or a house, but still just another image drawn with a colored pen on paper. Soon we learn that combinations of these letter-pictures mean more complicated things. When the drawings

A   P   P   L   E

are combined, they form another picture, which we learn stands for the name of the fruit. Of course, other languages use different letter pictures for the same word:

When combined with other letter pictures they become word pictures that can spark other images in our minds. We further learn that these word pictures, when combined with other word pictures,

MOLLA	Albanian
ةحافت	Arabic
蘋 果	Chinese (Traditional)
苹 果	Chinese (Simplified)
JABUKA	Croatian
MANSANAS	Filipino
OMENA	Finnish
POMME	French
APFEL	German
ΜΉΛΟ	Greek
תפוח	Hebrew
MELA	Italian
リンゴ	Japanese
사 과	Korean
JABŁKO	Polish
ЯБЛОКО	Russian
MANZANA	Spanish
QUẢTÁO	Vietnamese

form sentence pictures, and so on. To a child, as with cave and graffiti artists, there is no difference between words and pictures—they are one and the same. The reason young Alice followed the scurrying rabbit down the hole that led to all kinds of wondrous adventures at the start of Lewis Carroll's *Alice in Wonderland* was because she was bored with the book her sister was reading that contained no illustrations. As she put it, "What is the use of a book without pictures?"

Soon, however, the mystery and magic of seeing the world visually is diminished. We are taught to make distinctions between words and pictures and to not think of them in the same way. We are taught that although we can gain meaning from each, reading words is

valued more than reading pictures. We are taught that pictures play a separate and subservient role to the words. And although we are taught how to *make* pictures with our colored pencils and our watercolor paints, we get much more instruction on how to form, with our large lead pencils, the lines and curves that make letters and words.

We are taught to read stories, but we are never taught how to read images.

In the Disney classic *Beauty and the Beast* (1991), the macho Gaston satirizes Belle's reading habits. "How can you read this?" he asks. "There are no pictures." She answers with a condescending, "Well, some people use their imagination." And yet, when the viewer of the animated movie is shown a close-up of a page in her book, she points to a picture of a castle.

There are strong indications that the status of images is improving. We live in a mediated blitz of images. They fill our newspapers, magazines, books, clothing, skin, billboards, theaters, television screens, and computer monitors as never before in the history of mass communications (Figure 16.5). Something is happening. We are becoming a visually mediated society. And that fact is changing us. For many, understanding of the world is accomplished not by reading words, but by reading images.

Critics blame everything from the rise in the crime rate to the deterioration of educational institutions on the concurrent rise in the number of mediated images that can be seen daily. Rebellious youth cling to visual symbols on walls, clothing, and stickers on laptop computers because words are associated with old ways of communicating and old ways of establishing social order. Many think that words are repressive while pictures are fascinating, easily understood within a particular culture, and can be made into personal forms of expression.

In 1955 a *Time* magazine story with the headline, "Why Johnny Can't Read," also the title of a best-selling book by Rudolf Flesch, alarmed many around the country. Parents, politicians, and educators worried about the poor thinking, reading, and writing capabilities of young adults. Their answer to Flesch's book was often simplistic: too many pictures and not enough words.

But there are other possible answers: Maybe there was little written that Johnny wanted to read. Maybe he felt there was no point in reading when there were no jobs that required reading. Maybe his parents didn't read and didn't support the habit in him. Or maybe Johnny *was* reading, but adults did not understand what he liked to read. Visual messages *are* being read, but this language means nothing to those who can only read words.

Although it is unclear what may be the economic, social, and educational effects this visual culture will have upon the world, strangely, the use of images may foster a return of the word's importance. Or rather, a communication medium in which words and pictures have equal status may be a result of the recent explosion in pictures.

Because images on television and the web cross all international borders, they become more easily understood by almost everyone. Words are easily forgotten, but pictures stay in our minds. We may not remember many of the facts that led to the brief student uprising in China's Tiananmen Square in 1989, but you can never forget the image of the lone protester standing defiantly in front of a line of menacing, green Chinese tanks (Weblink 16.2). If you have seen the still picture or video, you remember it not

Courtesy of British Museum / Art Resource, NY

only because it is a highly emotional image, but also because you have thought about the image in your mind with words. Words and pictures become one powerfully effective communicative medium inside your head. It shouldn't be a surprise that our minds are used as a model and metaphor for our communications technology. Computers, more than any other innovation, are responsible for the sudden increase in images.

Educational psychologist Jerome Bruner of New York University cites studies showing that people remember only 10 percent of what they hear, 30 percent of what they read, but about 80 percent of what they see and do. When all members of society, whether at home, in school, or on the job, use computers for word and picture processing, the switch is made from passive watching to active using. There will no longer be the barrier between the two symbolic structures.

Figure 16.5

Roshi Ensei, the heavily tattooed fictional hero of the popular Chinese story Shuihu zhuan (The Water Margin), *holds a wooden beam during a wrestling match in a woodblock print by the Japanese master Utagawa Kuniyoshi published in 1827. At an early age, the skin of Chinese wrestlers is tattooed with all-body designs that include flowers and lions. Born the son of a silk dyer in 1797, Kuniyoshi grew up with a keen appreciation of colors and fabrics from working with his father. As his reputation grew, he formed his own school (which bore his name) and taught many artists his woodblock printing techniques.*

Figure 16.6

The origination of the photography cliché "a picture is worth a thousand words" comes from this advertisement created by Fred Barnard, the National Advertising Manager for the Street Railways Advertising Company. Barnard's argument for using illustrations in ads is that words might fade from memory, but the picture of the boy's smiling and eager face will make a lasting impression on busy streetcar riders.

Words and pictures will become one powerful and memorable mode of communication just as in their beginning on cave walls.

Documentary photographer Lewis Hine, who often used words to accompany his photographs, once said, "If I could tell the story in words, I wouldn't need to lug a camera." It is beyond question that words and pictures are different symbolic structures. But each possess a language that some can interpret better than others. Photography philosopher John Berger admits "photographs supply information without having a language of their own. Photographs quote rather than translate from reality." Sol Worth, author of *Studying Visual Communication*, wrote of a compromise between the two points. "Pictures are not a language in the verbal sense. Pictures have no lexicon or syntax in a formal grammarian's sense. But they do have form, structure, convention and rules."

One of the most tired and ill-conceived clichés in photography is "a picture is worth a thousand words." Type the phrase in Google with quotation marks and you will get more than 175,000 hits. Go ahead. I'll wait. Back? Good. But the often-quoted phrase seen in many student essays is actually phony and not even comprised of the original words. Fred Barnard, an advertising executive in the 1920s for the Street Railways Advertising Company, was trying to convince advertisers in a *Printer's Ink* trade magazine ad that pictures get a busy streetcar rider's attention and should be included with text messages. To add some of Aristotle's pathos, Barnard added a picture of a boy with a big smile (Figure 16.6). For credibility, or ethos to his argument, a bit of phony ancient philosophy was added: "CHINESE PROVERB One picture is worth ten thousand words." Meaning that a picture of a boy's smile enjoying his mother's baked concoction is equal to 10,000 words explaining the benefits of baking powder. Over time, of course, it took 9,000 fewer words to describe a photograph. But whomever Barnard hired to create the Chinese translation got the proverb a bit wrong. Instead of stating that a picture is *worth* ten thousand words, the literal translation is, "A picture's meaning can express ten thousand words." Worth implies a crass, commercial connection, while the meaning of something is subjective and often personal. To say that an image is worth any number of words is a false equivalence. But meaning puts words and pictures on a respectful, equal footing. More eloquent writers than an advertising executive followed in that tradition.

The writer William Saroyan, who won a Pulitzer Prize for his play *The Time of Your Life* (1939), noted how the meaning of images comes from the mind when he remarked, "One picture is worth a thousand words. Yes, but only if you look at the picture and say or think the thousand words." Suzanne Langer, known for her book *Philosophy in a New Key: A Study in the Symbolism of Reason, Rite, and Art* (1942), wrote that because language names relationships rather than illustrating them, "one word can take care of a situation that would require a whole sheet of drawings to depict it." For her, one word can mean a thousand pictures.

Words and pictures are intricately linked for educational and persuasive contexts. Words printed with a photograph signal the importance of the subjects within the image. Words beside a picture in an advertisement explain a product and its attributes clearly to a potential customer. Words spoken by a professor give explanations and life to an otherwise dull PowerPoint slideshow projected from the ceiling. For the Tiananmen Square tank protestor mentioned earlier, the caption in the Western press to accompany the image mentioned the bravery of the man who risked his life to stop the column of tanks. The words from the Chinese government gave a different spin on the same visual message. Its caption for the picture remarked that it showed how much the military cared about its citizens by pausing their progress until the man left the scene. As with the "finding" and "looting" news photographs from New Orleans after Hurricane Katrina, discussed in Chapter 5, intent and perspective also infuse images with meaning through the words used to describe them—the pictures themselves are neutral.

As Wilson Hicks, an influential picture editor for *Life* magazine, wrote in his book *Words and Pictures* (1952), "It is not correct to say that either medium supplements the other. The right verb is 'complements.'"

Despite occasional problems in discerning the meaning of pictures and words in publications, the combination of the two symbolic systems is one of the most powerful communicative strategies known. Hicks wrote that when words and pictures are equally expressive, the two become one medium where "the meaning of the work can be achieved in one perceptual act." John Berger also celebrated the word and picture collaboration:

> In the relation between a photograph and words, the photograph begs for an interpretation, and the words usually supply it. The photograph, irrefutable as evidence but weak in meaning, is given meaning by the words. And the words, which by themselves remain at the level of generalization, are given specific authenticity by the irrefutability of the photograph. Together the two then become very powerful; an open question appears to have been fully answered.

Psychologists have found that concrete nouns are much more effectively remembered as an aid to recall than abstract ones. The concrete nouns of ball, book, bottle, baby, and so on are easier to visualize in the mind because of their link to real objects. Abstract concepts of freedom, peace, ethics, love, and so on are harder to link to a single image. But in 1836 for his book *Nature*, Ralph Waldo Emerson noted that the roots of all words—even abstract ones—are concrete in nature. "Every word which is used to express a moral or intellectual fact," he wrote, "if traced to its roots, is found to be borrowed from some material appearance." As the Greek poet Simonides wrote, "Words are the images of things," while

Aristotle wrote even more succinctly, "There can be no words without images."

When you carefully analyze a visual message, you consciously study each visual symbol within that picture's frame. The act of concentration is an important verbal exercise. Without thinking of the signs within an image, there is little chance of it being recalled in the future. The picture is lost from your memory because you have learned nothing from it. Images become real property of the mind and remembered only when language expresses them. Linguistic experts do not need to argue that images have no alphabet or syntax because such assertions are true. The alphabet and the syntax of images reside in the mind, not in the picture itself.

Ironically, societies with only a spoken language had better recall of objects and events because their mental symbol systems had to be highly developed. They passed on their knowledge to future generations in the form of songs and dances. Writing and the literacy that spread throughout the world decreased the need for memory because once an event is recorded on paper, it does not have to be remembered exactly as it originally happened. Consequently, the need for a complex system of visual signs within the mind decreased over time as words dominated communication. But as images become more prevalent, memory may once again reach the level of supposedly "primitive" cultures.

Early in her life, Dr. Temple Grandin was labeled as having a primitive mind. It wasn't until she was an adult that she was accurately diagnosed with Asperger's syndrome (AS), a form of autism in which individuals are nevertheless highly functional. Today she is a professor of animal science at Colorado State Univer-

sity and a leading advocate for the ethical treatment of animals and the author of several books. Grandin advised Dustin Hoffman for his role in the 1988 movie *Rain Man* while Claire Danes played her in the 2010 biopic *Temple Grandin* for HBO. Yet despite her extraordinary verbal skills, she does not think like most of us (Weblink 16.3).

Her mind is predominantly visual and pre-verbal, not dominated by thoughts that most of us consider "thinking." Her visual mind gives her an ability to empathize with animals that resulted in her revolutionary redesign of slaughterhouses to make them more humane. It also led to her writings that have helped autistic individuals and their caregivers.

Although Grandin is primarily a visual thinker, she is obviously a highly literate and verbal individual who would admit that although words are a second language, she would not be able to fully function in their absence. A world totally without language is one in which colors, forms, and movements can be recognized and compared, but meaning is largely lost. An image without a verbal accompaniment is similar to an amorphous, meaningless shape. Language gives meaning and substance to pictures.

Furthermore, signs have little meaning outside their context. Visual and verbal thoughts combine to create the context that links signs together to form symbols that can be remembered and recalled. Context is the glue that binds visual and verbal symbols together. Recognizing context is the chief function of a rational mind. The face of someone you know can be immediately recalled within your mind. But that face is not a literal, detailed, photographic image. The mind's picture is a combination of the perceptual elements—color, form, depth, and movement—that are needed to describe appearance combined with the verbal thoughts that define the person—lover, relative, friend, co-worker, stranger—and the context—home, work, vacation, chance meeting. Again, it is through analysis—a highly functional mental process—that context and meaning become one.

Memorable images, whether imagined, directly experienced, or seen through a mediated format, are those that you think about often. They are usually simple compositions with immediate impact. They are images that trigger the emotional *and* rational aspects of your mind. They are pictures you recall again and again long after the original object of perception has faded from your retinas.

In his classic works *The Gutenberg Galaxy: The Making of Typographic Man* (1962) and *Understanding Media* (1964), Canadian media critic and philosopher Marshall McLuhan wrote of the power of electronic communication to unite the world. Because this contact is practically instantaneous, it's as if we are all living in one, singular township—a global village (Weblink 16.4). McLuhan's metaphor is often employed to describe the power and the promise of the web to contradict the presumed economic imperialism of globalization. Globalization fails if it turns into cultural imperialism that is concerned only with spreading one country's cultural values—for better or worse—throughout the vast regions of the planet. Russia probably doesn't need more McDonald's cheeseburgers, and Tokyo has plenty of Starbucks coffees. Likewise, those living in poverty don't need to be further exploited and stigmatized through sweatshops that churn out clothing, shoes, electronic equipment, and cartoon animations. But McLuhan's

form of globalization, his global village, was not seen as a way to bring harmony to the world, but, as he said, to have "extreme concern with everybody else's business." And yet, harmony might be achieved through visual languages.

When words and images have equal status within all media of communication, the cultural cues that define a society will not only be more efficiently passed from one generation to the next, but within *this* generation, here and now, diverse cultures will be able to understand each other a little better. As with the de stijl artists with their peaceful, grid-like designs and Otto Neurath's Isotype written language that was based on the groundbreaking work by German philosopher Gottfried Leibniz in the 17th century toward a universal language, many throughout history have hoped to unite the planet through verbal and visual messages. In her book *In the Land of Invented Languages: Esperanto Rock Stars, Klingon Poets, Loglan Lovers, and the Mad Dreamers Who Tried to Build A Perfect Language* Arika Okrent details 500 manufactured languages that date from the year 1150. Some languages have been created for motion pictures. For example, the American linguist Marc Okrand developed the language for the fictitious Klingon alien race featured in several *Star Trek* movies while starting with a list of about three dozen words from director James Cameron, USC professor and linguistics expert Paul R. Frommer developed a language for the Na'vi tribe shown in the film *Avatar* (2009). In 1887 Ludwik Zamenhof, a Russian ophthalmologist or eye surgeon, published, under the pseudonym Doktoro Esperanto, his manual *Unua Libro* (*First Book*) that detailed his constructed language Esperanto in the hope that it would "foster peace and international

Figure 16.7

Aldous Huxley's famous phrase is the translation of this set of images from the Charles Bliss idiographic writing system, blissymbolics.

the more you know the more you see

Courtesy of Paul Martin Lester

understanding." Today the language is used for world travel and cultural exchanges. The Austrian semiotician Karl Blitz, who later changed his name to Charles Bliss, developed a visual language similar to Neurath's concept. After surviving the Dachau concentration camp during World War II, he invented his Blissymbolics pictograph system inspired from Chinese ideograms. In 1949 Bliss published the three-volume work *International Semantography: A Non-alphabetical Symbol Writing Readable in all Languages.* Although his 900-symbol visual language failed to bring about increased world understanding as he had hoped, in the 1960s it was found that children with severe cerebral palsy could be taught to communicate using Bliss's symbols (Figure 16.7).

Understanding and respecting each other's ways of communicating through words *and* pictures is a way for a positive form of globalization to occur. We *will* be concerned and care about everybody else's business because we will know each other a little better by the images we are able to view. As the noted photographic historian and collector Helmut Gernsheim wrote, "Photography is the only 'language' understood in all parts of the world, and bridging all nations and cultures."

Regardless of whether a presentation is meant for print or screen media, words and pictures have a better chance of being remembered if they are used together. That union is possible because of light. In fact, light links all the information presented in this book.

The visual cues of color, form, depth, and movement quickly sort light into helpful or harmful classifications. Gestalt,

constructivism, semiotics, and cognitive theories help explain why some light messages are remembered longer than others. Techniques used in advertising, public relations, and journalism help explain how light can so effectively attract, repel, and persuade. Light without reason or compassion produces pictorial stereotypes that mislead and harm.

Light forms the visual messages seen or discussed in all the chapters of this book (Figure 16.8).

From colorful iconic drawings of animals on cave walls came the symbolic marks of letterforms that Johannes Gutenberg used with his commercial printing press, and typographical designers of today strive to turn words into artistic expressions.

Saul Bass taught us that an entire motion picture's marketing image in print and its opening title sequence should be graphically linked. He and other designers use the art movements of art nouveau, dada, art deco, punk, new wave, pop art, hip-hop, de stijl, and bauhaus to make designs, regardless of the media, that respect word and picture combinations.

USA Today's weather map not only inspired renewed interest in weather and its reporting, it also helped spur the entire informational graphics profession. Innovative and technically savvy designers turn dull listings of numbers into displays that reveal significant details about the way the world works.

Evolving from short spots in a live-action comedy program, Matt Groening's enduring program *The Simpsons* is now the longest-running prime-time show in television history. It inspired the renaissance of animation we see today in print and on screens.

More than 100 years after the world's first photograph was taken (a fuzzy and

Figure 16.8

In this photograph taken by Jack Delano of the Farm Security Administration (FSA), light is a physical substance that has texture, weight, and can be touched (try it) as it streaks from windows of the waiting room of Union Station, Chicago, in 1943. Delano was born in Russia and moved to the United States with his family when he was nine years old. He became a noted photographer, musician, and filmmaker. As a member of the FSA, he worked on assignments throughout the United States. After completing a project in Puerto Rico, he moved there permanently in 1946 where he directed a 1953 documentary Los Peloteros (The Players) concerned with baseball and the poor children who love the game. He also composed classical works performed by the Puerto Rico Symphony Orchestra.

blurred view of buildings in France), the American photojournalist Dorothea Lange made a timeless portrait of a mother's concern for her future during the Great Depression. People of the 21st century now can try to duplicate her achievement with their cell phone cameras.

The motion picture medium started with a short film of a fake sneeze by an assistant to Thomas Edison and was transformed by Orson Welles's classic *Citizen Kane*. Movies can now be shown through 3-D projections onto multi-story screens, but the story still matters for the success of the show.

A vaudeville act converted to radio and transformed into an audio and visual experience became television. It started as a crude, hard-to-see means of entertainment for the wealthy and went on to become the most pervasive and powerful medium in the world.

Computers began as complex room-sized calculators, then progressed to become complex room-sized vacuum-filled programmable monoliths. They are now indispensible pocket-sized tools for everyday and sometimes extraordinary and magical uses.

Finally, the web was invented as a communication method in case of a nuclear holocaust and has become the one invention that has significantly altered and may replace most all other media.

Light in the form of typography, graphic design, informational graphics, cartoons, photography, motion pictures, television, computers, and the web makes us sad, angry, happy, tense, calm, smart, dumb, loving, cynical, or bored—but by all means, it always makes us *something*.

Light.

The light of day, the light of reason, and the light of compassion made us who we were, makes us who we are, will make us who we will become, and will determine how we will be remembered.

Huxley, however, probably wouldn't agree with too literal a reading of the phrase "the more you know, the more you see." Seeing certainly is a major component in visual communication, but it isn't the only way to know. That's because:

The more you know, the more you hear.
The more you know, the more you smell.
The more you know, the more you taste.
The more you know, the more you feel.
The more you know, the more you are you.

Your generation of communicators has the tools necessary to activate all the senses with words, pictures, and sounds. When you do, memorable messages—the only ones that challenge and enrich a person's life—will be the result.

■ *KEY TERMS*

- Globalization
- Hits
- Lexicon
- Optic nerve
- Syntax

 To locate active URLs for the weblinks mentioned in this chapter, please go to the companion site at http://communication.wadsworth.com/lester5 and select the proper chapter.

Glossary

15 minutes of fame: The phrase coined by pop artist Andy Warhol in 1968, "In the future everyone will be world-famous for 15 minutes," as a commentary is concerned with the rise of the entertainment industry and the discounting of celebrity status (13).

9/11: On the morning of Tuesday, September 11, 2001, 19 members of the terrorist group al Qaeda hijacked four airplanes that were used in attacks on American property and civilians. The twin towers of the World Trade Center in New York City were hit and destroyed as well as a significant portion of the Pentagon in Arlington, Virginia. A fourth airliner, bound for the Capitol or the White House, was overtaken by passengers and crashed in a field outside Shanksville, Pennsylvania. Nearly 3,000 victims were killed, and billions of dollars in damages resulted (1).

Abstract: A form of expression that may use the standard tools employed by artists of other forms of art but does not employ elements that are easily identified as being from the real world. The most obvious examples are paintings whose main subject matter are geometric forms (1).

Abu Ghraib: The name of a prison in Baghdad, Iraq, that became a symbol of American military misconduct after it was learned from a "60 Minutes II" television report and a Seymour Hersh *The New Yorker* magazine article in 2004 that systematic torture had been performed on numerous, mostly innocent prisoners. Much of the evidence of the torture came from snapshot photographs taken by American military guards (11).

Ad-lib: An abbreviation of the Latin *ad libitum* meaning "at one's pleasure," it refers to the dramatic technique in which actors are asked to improvise dialogue with their own, unscripted words and actions based on what they think their characters would say and do (13).

Adjusted for inflation: A comparison of the rise or fall of the price of goods and services for a time period based on the Consumer Price Index. The greater the difference in two dates, the more the comparison reflects the actual costs to citizens at the time (9).

Advertising campaign: A term used whenever an advertising agency develops a series of messages for a particular product or service within a set time frame (2).

Airbrush: An artistic technique that uses air to spray paint, ink, or dye on a substrate. It is also a pejorative term used to describe the manipulation of photographs by the removal of unwanted elements for political, economic, or aesthetic reasons (11).

Allegorical: Developed first by the Greeks with their mythic stories and later employed by interpreters of the New Testament, this analytical technique gives literal, sometimes ordinary events significant symbolic meaning (6).

Alloy: A solid solution of one or more elements combined to enhance the properties of both for a specific purpose.

Everything looked at closely

is full of wonder.

Jacob Grimm, 1785–1863
AUTHOR, LAWYER, AND PHILOLOGIST

For example, steel is made stronger by an alloy of iron and carbon (7).

American Civil Liberties Union (ACLU): Begun as an organization formed to protest America's involvement in World War I, the ACLU's mission statement is "to defend and preserve the individual rights and liberties guaranteed to every person in this country by the Constitution and laws of the United States." As such, it regularly offers legal advice and representation for liberal and conservative causes (11).

American Institute of Graphic Arts (AIGA): First organized in 1914, it is a professional and student organization composed of typographers, graphic designers, photographers, and other media artists. AIGA currently has more than 20,000 members in 65 worldwide chapters (7).

Analog: The term can apply to numerical information that is represented by measureable quantities, such as lengths or electrical signals, as well as real-world activities without the aid of a computer (7).

Anime: A term for Japanese-inspired animated cartoons (10).

Anorexia nervosa: A serious psychiatric eating disorder marked by extremely low body weight. About 90 percent of those affected are women (4).

Aperture: The opening or hole of a lens that allows light to travel through it. As the opening gets smaller, the image is more sharply focused (11).

Archetypal or archetypes: The Swiss psychologist Carl Jung and the American mythologist Joseph Campbell theorized the existence of universal stories through a "collective unconscious" that contain original models that inspire other things or ideas and teach about the commonalities of human nature (6).

Aspect ratio: The look or appearance of a screen or frame. Film and television screens originally used an aspect ratio of 4:3 in which the screen is four units across by three down. Movie theaters and digital television sets now use a ratio of 16:9 for a widescreen or letterbox view (12).

Assimilation: Sometimes termed "The Melting Pot," the blending of diverse cultural groups into the dominant society (5).

Atari: An arcade game company founded in 1972 that created the popular tennis-like game "Pong." Atari is a Japanese word meaning *to hit the target* (14).

Aztec culture: Refers to a group of ethnic peoples of central Mexico that dominated the region for about 300 years from the 14th century (5).

Banner: A form of advertisement or a title for a newspaper story that displays a message across an entire printed or web page (2).

Beehive hairdo: An elaborately high and teased head of hair invented in 1958. It was originally called a "B-52" after the shape of the front of an Air Force bomber of the same name (10).

Beta: A prototype version of a software product usually released to a select few for testing and comments before a general release to the public (15).

Big Four: Originally the "Big Three," referred to the American broadcast companies of ABC (American), CBS (Columbia), and NBC (National). The Fox Broadcasting Company was added to the list in 1986 (13).

Binocular vision: The act of using both eyes or two lenses at the same time (2).

Bitumen of Judea: Also known as asphalt, it is a sticky, molasses-like form of petroleum mainly used for paving roads. It was used in early photographic processes, most notably for heliography because it hardens from 10 minutes to several hours, depending on the amount of light it receives (11).

Black Power: A political and social movement begun in the 1960s in which African Americans communicated racial pride and economic advancement (12).

Blog: A contraction of the word weblog (web log), it was invented by the American computer programmer Jorn Barger to describe his activity of listing what he had read each day as "logging the web." Later, weblog was shortened to blog and now refers to any website that provides commentary in any form (text, audio, and/or video) with feedback possible from readers (3).

Blue-collar: A member of the working class who receives an hourly wage and engages in manual labor (10).

Bollywood: The Hindi-language film industry that originated in Mumbai, India, with most movies in the genre being melodramatic, love triangle, and daredevil musicals (10).

Bolshevik: A faction of the Marxist political party founded and led by Vladimir Lenin that took control of the Soviet Union during the 1917 Russian Revolution (6).

Bookmark: Originally a paper or leather insert to mark where you stopped reading a book, it can also mean a web address saved on a web browser so the user can easily return to the website without typing the entire address (15).

Briefs: As with an abstract for a research paper, it is a short synopsis of a story stressing its main points. They can be included in print and online editions as a list to update readers of public events or sent to editors by public relations personnel as a press release in the hope of getting coverage (3).

Broadsheet: Originally referring to one, large sheet of paper for the printing of news first used by a Dutch paper in 1618, it is the largest of the newspaper page formats that can be 22 inches or longer (3).

Bronze Age: An era of prehistoric times, estimated to be about a 2,000-year period from 3300 to 1200 BCE in which alloys, particularly the melting of copper and tin to create bronze, were used for art objects, weapons, and other items (7).

Browser: A software application intended for the purpose of retrieving information available from the web (15).

Bullet points: Named for the tip of a rifle's projectile, it is a graphic mark used to stress an item in a list (9).

Calligraphy: Greek for "beautiful writing," it is a style of handwritten letters originally used by Chinese scribes and can be found on the bones of animals and shells of tortoises dating from the 14th century BCE (7).

Camcorder: A portable **cam**era re**corder** for video and audio. One of the first was Sony's Betacam in 1982 with the recording tape holder built into the camera. Analog videotape camcorders are quickly being replaced by digital formats that can plug directly into computers for editing (12).

Caption: Informational text accompanying a picture (4).

Carrier wave: An electromagnetic frequency that can be used to transmit text, sounds, and images over long distances (13).

Cel: Short for celluloid, it is a clear sheet on which hand-drawn animated cartoons are created. Disney's *The Little Mermaid* (1989) was one of the studio's last films to use cels in its production (10).

CERN (European Organization for Nuclear Research): Established in 1954 in a suburb of Geneva, Switzerland, it provides particle accelerators and expertise for nuclear physics research for educators, scientists, and engineers. In 1991 the first website, developed by Tim Berners-Lee and Robert Calilliau, went online from the facility (15).

Chief executive officer (CEO): A high-ranking corporate employee who is responsible for the overall management of a company (14).

Chip speed: Sometimes called clock speed, it is a measurement of a computer processor's efficiency in calculating math, logic, and data functions (14).

Cholera: A highly infectious bacteria transmitted to humans through contaminated food and water. At the first sign of symptoms, a patient experiences a drop in blood pressure and can die within three hours without treatment (9).

Chroma key: Commonly used for background images during televised weather reports and special effects in motion pictures, it is a computer technique in which two images can be superimposed on one another. The process uses a large blue or green background screen, because skin is not one of those colors (9).

CinemaScope: A widescreen motion picture format that used special lenses to project the picture onto the screen. It was popular for 14 years from the release of *The Robe* (1953) (12).

Cinerama: A widescreen movie format that used three projectors with left, center, and right parts of the picture. Since the technique was enormously expensive and required specially designed movie theaters, it was soon replaced by single-projector Super Panavision 70 and then Ultra Panavision 70 formats (12).

Clip art: Inexpensive and usually simple illustrations used for personal and professional presentations, although many times their use is discouraged (10).

Closure: In graphics, it is the perception of elements within a layout when they are not a part of the design.

For example, a circle or line with gaps can be perceived as being whole. It is related to the gestalt law of continuation (3).

Cloud computing: A concept that can mean using an inexpensive computer and accessing software programs from an internet source whenever they are needed, or it can also mean the extent of a wireless reception area (15).

Coaxial cable: A transmission line comprising a wire (usually) surrounded by another wire that is insulated (13).

Cold War: The name of an era in which there was serious political tension between the United States and the Soviet Union from the end of World War II until the fall of the Soviet Union in 1991 (15).

Collodion: A substance produced when highly flammable nitrocellulose is dissolved in ether. It was used as a temporary dressing for wounded American Civil War soldiers and as a photographic emulsion to coat glass plates by photographers who might have taken pictures of those injured soldiers (11).

Composition: The arrangements of visual elements within a frame. In a 1957 interview, the photojournalist Henri Cartier-Bresson defined his concept of the "decisive moment" as the instant when "Your eye must see a composition or an expression that life itself offers you, and you must know with intuition when to click the camera." (2)

Computer agent: A software program that performs its tasks in the background, often with the user unaware of its operation (15).

Computer tomography (CT or CAT scan): A way of creating a three-dimensional image from a two-dimensional X-ray picture (2).

Consumerism: Any economic policy or habit that emphasizes consumption, usually with the assumption that such activity produces happiness (8).

Contrast: The relative extent of the difference between light and dark areas in a picture (11).

Convergent Era: A concept proposed by MIT professor Henry Jenkins in which the mass media are combining both technically and socially. As he puts it, "We are living in an age when changes in communications, storytelling, and information technologies are reshaping almost every aspect of contemporary life—including how we create, consume, learn, and interact with each other. A whole range of new technologies enable consumers to archive, annotate, appropriate, and re-circulate media content and in the process, these technologies have altered the ways that consumers interact with core institutions of government, education, and commerce." (14)

Copy: The words or text supplied by a writer for a print or screen media graphic design (4).

Cornea: Since this clear, outside layer of the eye does not have blood vessels—it gets nourishment directly from air—it was the first part of the body to be transplanted to another (2).

Cortex: See Visual cortex (2).

Crash: Whenever a software application or operating system stops working and freezes a computer. Oftentimes the only remedy is to restart the machine. However, if the hard drive has failed, data may be lost. It is always a good idea to regularly back up data onto an external hard drive (14).

Cropped: A picture with the edges removed (6).

Cultural relativism: The philosophy that states that a person's attitudes, beliefs, and activities should be understood within that person's own cultural understanding and values without input from ideas from other cultures (3).

Cut: The smallest portion of a film, the name is a holdover from when film was a physical object requiring the slicing of it for editing purposes. Several short cuts in a motion picture scene can add dramatic tension, whereas a long stretch of film without cuts can convey a calm, hypnotic rhythm (8).

Cyberspace: From the Greek word for "rudder," it refers to the various global communications technologies that make such tools as the internet and the web possible (8).

Dark Ages: A period of time in Western European history from the fall of the Roman Empire until the invention and widespread use of the commercial printing press, from about 476 to 1500 CE (7).

Darkroom: A specialized space with plumbing and controlled lighting to allow the processing of negatives and printing of photographs in the dark, or with non-photosensitive safelights (11).

Death penalty: A government's sanctioned murder of another person because of a major offense or capital crime (4).

Demographics: Data such as race, age, gender, economic status, and so on that is usually obtained through surveys and used in research about cultural trends and other purposes (15).

Depth of field: A term used in image making that describes the relative extent to which a scene is in focus. With a small aperture and longer shutter speed, the elements in the foreground to the background are more in focus than if a large aperture and a quick shutter speed were employed (6).

Digital: Within this book's context, it is any information or practice that must use a computer for its inception and presentation. Editing a document or a photograph is digital; holding a printout is analog (9).

Digital television (DTV): Part of a worldwide technological movement, it is the over-the-air reception of televised signals through computer rather than analog, broadcast transmissions. Several European countries made the switch to digital television starting in 2006. The United States switched on June 12, 2009. Japan and Canada will make the change in 2011, Great Britain in 2012, and China in 2015 (10).

Dioramas: Full- or small-scale models of usually a historically or environmentally significant event often seen in museum displays. They originated in France in 1822 by the co-inventor of the daguerreotype photographic process, Louis Jacques Mandé Daguerre. He created elaborate staged illusions in which audience members thought they were viewing reality. Modern examples can be found in the "Universe of Energy" pavilion at Epcot outside Orlando, Florida, "Pirates of the Caribbean" ride at Disney World and Disneyland, and in the movie *Night at the Museum: Battle of the Smithsonian* (2009) (11).

Discrimination: To act in a prejudiced or biased way toward people (usually) who have apparent, but not essential, differences (5).

DIY (do-it-yourself): A self, home, and world improvement philosophy that advocates creating and repairing things without resorting to paid experts. Activities that fall under the DIY umbrella can also include music recordings, website creation, and zine production (7).

Doctors Without Borders: A worldwide volunteer organization founded in France in 1971 composed of physicians, nurses, and journalists that provides aid to persons in need and publicizes their plight and recovery. As stated in the relief organization's website, it is "committed to bringing quality medical care to people caught in crisis regardless of race, religion, or political affiliation [and acts] independently of any political, military, or religious agendas." (10)

Double exposure: It traditionally refers to a negative image superimposed or overlaying another as a procedure within the camera or a darkroom, but can mean any multiple image effect regardless of how it is achieved (2).

Download: Refers to the act of transferring information—whether textual, audio, and/or visual—from one computer to another. To download means to receive, to upload means to send (15).

DRAM (dynamic random access memory): A form of computer memory that can contain a lot of information but is lost once the power supply is turned off (14).

Dust Bowl: An environmental catastrophe occurring in the United States for a decade starting in about 1930. Severe and continual drought conditions coupled with inefficient and ill-conceived farming methods (e.g., deep plowing, lack of crop rotation) affected more than 156,000 square miles of land, larger than the state of Montana, and was centered in the Oklahoma and Texas panhandle regions. Much of the topsoil of the region was blown away in powerful windstorms that blackened East Coast cities. The soil eventually was deposited into the Atlantic Ocean. More than half a million persons were left homeless, with more than 100,000 families arriving in California to find work (11).

eBay: Begun as an online auction website in 1995 named AuctionWeb, the name was changed to eBay two years later. Today it is the largest online auction and shopping website in the world (11).

Editorial picture: A photograph usually taken by a photojournalist for use within a news context (1).

Electromagnetic spectrum: Named by the Scottish physicist James Clerk Maxwell, who also invented the first color photography process, it is a range of wavelengths, some as long as the height of the tallest buildings in the world that support radio broadcasts and others as small as atomic nuclei known as gamma rays (2).

Electron scanner: A process in microphotography that uses beams of electrons instead of visible light, as with most microscopes, to provide extremely close-up pictures (13).

Electronic highway: An early metaphor to describe the internet. See cyberspace (15).

Emulsion: For analog photographic films, it is a layer that contains light-sensitive material within a medium of collodion, starch, or gelatin on a sheet of metal, glass, paper, or plastic (11).

Engraving: A technique used for printing illustrations that employs a steel tool called a burin to carve an image onto a metal plate. The plate is then used in the printing process (7).

Existentialist: A type of analysis that tries to find meaning by concentrating on actual human existence as an observer and participant of the world and espoused by such philosophers as Søren Kierkegaard, Friedrich Nietzsche, Jean-Paul Sartre, Simone de Beauvoir, and Albert Camus (6).

Family values: A political and cultural philosophy that has different meanings depending on your point of view. For conservatives, the most stable unit within society is a family with a married father and mother and their children that is pro-religion and against abortion. For liberals, it may mean that families are supported through childcare and maternity and paternity leaves (8).

Fascism: Perhaps best exemplified by Mussolini's pre–World War II Italian government, it is an authoritative ideology that is in constant conflict with its own citizens and other countries (3).

Federal Communications Commission (FCC): Established by the Communications Act of 1934 to regulate radio and television broadcasts and interstate wire, satellite, and cable, its five commissioners are selected by the president and confirmed by the U.S. Congress (13).

Feminist movement: Begun in the 19th century by women advocating the right to vote (that privilege was granted in 1920), it progressed in the 1960s to include protest against cultural restrictions placed on women including unfair pay structures compared with men; currently the movement attempts to celebrate the achievements of women in order to expand its political membership (2).

Field dressing: In hunting, a technique to preserve the meat of a killed animal by removing its organs from the carcass while in the wild (6).

Filmsetting: Also known as phototypesetting, it is a method of projecting pictures of typefaces at various sizes onto a photographic film that are then used in the printing process (7).

Flash: A technique used in photography in which artificial light is supplied by flash powder, bulbs, cubes, and/or electronic units (1).

Flash mob: Usually an event organized via e-mail in which mostly strangers gather at some public site and perform a group activity that either delights or annoys passersby (11).

Freelance: To sell work or services to clients without permanent employment status (9).

Freudian: Relating to an analytical technique inspired from the writings of the Austrian psychiatrist Sigmund Freud in which a person's subconscious mind is evoked in order to discover personal meaning for symbolic signs (6).

Frieze: An artistic expression usually found in classical architecture in which bas-relief, painted, or calligraphic figures are displayed between the roof and columns on exteriors and between the ceiling and moldings inside.

Functionalism: An analytical philosophy in which an object's role in society is valued more than its composition (8).

Gallup poll: Developed by the American educator and statistician George Gallup in 1935, it charts the public's opinion on a variety of political, social, and economic issues (5).

Gelatin: A by-product of the meat and leather industries, it is a clear protein substance derived from the bones and internal organs of cattle, pigs, and horses that is used for a variety of purposes including photographic film (11).

Geneva Conventions: A set of four international treaties first adopted in 1864 in Geneva, Switzerland, that details how prisoners and civilians should be treated during wars (11).

Genre: A particular type of written or visual work (2).

Geosynchronous orbit: Also known as "Clarke's orbit" after the science fiction writer Arthur C. Clarke's initial proposal, it is a procedure for stationing satellites in space with their speed the same as the Earth's rotation (2).

Gesture: A form of nonverbal body language that is used for communicative purposes, such as a finger to the mouth to indicate quiet or a wink when flirting (2).

GIF (graphics interchange format): Introduced by the bulletin board service CompuServe in 1987, it is a simple picture format often used for the web that also supports animation. GIF files are mostly used for company logos (11).

Globalization: A condition of cultural and/or economic development in which a local trend becomes accepted on a worldwide scale (16).

Golden Raspberry Award (The Razzie): Started as a parody of Hollywood award presentations by media critic John Wilson in 1980, it annually reports the worst motion picture performances and has become "the foremost authority on all things that suck on the big screen." (12)

Grain: A term that was originally a property of analog photographic film in which silver particles can be seen randomly dispersed throughout an emulsion. For digital materials, the condition is called "image noise." The amount of grain or noise that can be noticed by viewers is a creative option of photographers and directors (11).

Green light: As with a green traffic light that signifies "go," it refers to a company's approval after a creative pitch to start production of a television program or motion picture (13).

Hack: An activity by a hacker in which a computer program is changed from its original purpose either for a positive or a malicious reason (15).

Halftone: A printing technique for photographs in which the image is converted to tiny, differently sized dots through a screen, reproducing the tones on a printing press. First conceived by photographic inventor William Fox Talbot in the 1850s, the process was practically introduced by Stephen Horgan and later perfected by Frederic Ives, George Meisenbach, and Louis and Max Levy (2).

Handbills: A printed notice, usually related to advertising, and distributed by hand (7).

Hijab: Unlike a chadri or burqa in which a woman's entire body is covered, from the Arabic word meaning "to cover," a hijab is a head covering or scarf worn by Muslim women as a symbol of their religious and cultural heritage (5).

Hit: Usually refers to a successful web destination from using a search engine, but can also mean a request from a user to download a file (7).

HIV (Human Immunodeficiency Virus)/AIDS (Acquired Immunodeficiency Syndrome): AIDS is a chronic, life-threatening pandemic disease caused by HIV. First recognized in 1981, it is estimated that more than 2.1 million persons have died from the virus, about 300,000 of them children. Currently about 40 million persons worldwide have HIV/AIDS supported by expensive medications that slow its growth. There is no known cure (4).

Home page: Usually the first page that is presented on a website (15).

Hospice: A form of medical care available usually within special wings of hospitals reserved for terminally ill patients with a diagnosis of less than six months to live in which the physical needs, including pain management and emotional wants of the patient and friends and family, are supplied (4).

Hot spot: Refers to an area on a webpage, usually within a picture, that acts like a hypertext link. It also means an area where a Wi-Fi wireless connection is possible with a properly equipped computer (9).

Hypertext: One of the chief differences between print media and the web, it is text that is usually underlined to indicate a hyperlink where additional information is available from some other webpage or website (15).

Iconoscope: An early television camera tube developed by the Russian-born scientist Vladimir Zworykin for RCA that was used by German technicians to televise the 1936 Olympic Games and employed in American sets until it was replaced in 1946 by the highly light-sensitive image orthicon tube (13).

Ideograph: Unlike its cousin the pictograph that shows an actual object, it is an illustration of a concept or idea. Numbers, musical notations, emoticons, and the Blissymbolics from Charles Bliss are examples (7).

Impressionism: Inspired and influenced by the new invention of photography, Impressionist artists such as Claude Monet, Pierre-Auguste Renoir, and Edgar Degas broke many established "rules" of fine art with their choice of colors, brush strokes, and outdoor, natural settings (1).

Inca culture: First established around 1200 CE in the Cuzco region of southeastern Peru, the Inca empire eventually stretched from Colombia to southern Chile. The society was known to worship a sun god, were advanced architecturally as evidenced by the Machu Picchu site, used knotted strings in the accounting of inventories, and fabricated elaborate mountainside terraces for farming. With the 1533 invasion of the Spanish conquistadores, the Inca were practically wiped out (5).

Indie: An abbreviation of "independent," it is a term used mostly for music and filmmaking producers who sidestep major companies to create and distribute their art on their own. Indie also refers to a free, break-the-rules kind of attitude (12).

Industrial Revolution: Dated from improvements made by the Scottish inventor James Watt to the steam engine in 1775, the era lasted roughly until the end of the 19th century. It was marked by several applications of the engine—in train and boat travel, in mining, and in iron and textile production—as well as urban overcrowding, factories with their accompanying pollution, great differences in salaries and lifestyles between owners and workers, and the expansion of printing with advertisements to entice the new middle and upper classes (11).

Infomercials: Paid announcements in print or screen media masked as entertainment or educational presentations (9).

Islam: Based on the teachings of the Islamic prophet Muhammad who died in 632 CE, it is the second most prevalent religion in the world after Christianity. It is a monotheist religion with its religious history, principles, and social rules outlined in its holy book, the Qur'an. A person who practices Islam is called a Muslim (5).

Isobar: In meteorology, it is a line that indicates equal barometric pressure on a map (9).

Joe the Plumber: During the 2008 presidential campaign, it was the nickname given to Samuel Joseph Wurzelbacher after he questioned then-candidate Senator Barack Obama about his tax policies while videotaped by an ABCNews cameraperson. Although not a licensed plumber, he was supported by the Republican Party and candidate Senator John McCain for his outspoken opinions. By 2009, he had worn out his 15 minutes of fame (4).

JPG or JPEG (joint photographic experts group): A picture file format common to the web that compresses the file so it takes up less memory space on a computer (11).

Jungian: Inspired by the Swiss psychiatrist Carl Jung, it is an analytical method that attempts to understand symbolic images and concepts through the analysis of human archetypes and myths (6).

Killer app: A computer application that is such an innovative and desired program that it is an instant public success. Spreadsheet, banking, and communications software are popular examples (14).

Kinemacolor: A two-color (usually red and green) filter system for the taking and projecting of color motion pictures. It was the first color movie technology and was invented by British George Smith in 1906 (12).

Kinetograph and Kinetoscope: Although the American inventor Thomas Edison first thought of the technology, two of his employees, William Kennedy Laurie Dickson and William Heise, invented the movie camera and viewer. As a camera, the Kinetograph recorded images on long rolls of 35-mm-wide photographic film supplied by George Eastman's Kodak company, and mounted on perforated cylinders. Viewers watched the films through a peephole of a Kinetoscope (10).

Ku Klux Klan: A United States domestic terrorist organization founded in 1865 with veterans from the Confederate Army that was anti-Catholic, anti-Semitic, anti-Communism, and racist. By the 1870s the Klan was mostly suppressed due to the federal government's prosecution of members' crimes. However, with the popularity of and controversy surrounding D. W. Griffith's film *Birth of a Nation* that celebrated the Klan, membership increased so that by the 1920s it claimed more than six million members. Today the estimated membership is about 6,000 (3).

Large-format camera: Generally speaking, any analog camera that is 4 × 5 inches or larger, usually requiring a tripod and a black cloth over the head of the photographer for a clear look through the viewfinder (11).

Layout: The arrangement of all graphic elements for print or screen media (2).

Lexicon: Compared with the word "font" that refers to all the graphic variations of a typeface, it is all the words and expressions that make up a vocabulary (16).

Life **magazine**: A name for a publication with three major iterations—as a humor magazine from 1883 to 1936, a weekly news magazine from 1936 to 1972, a monthly from 1978 to 2000, and finally a weekly newspaper supplement from 2004 to 2007 when it quit publishing. During its second heyday, publisher Henry Luce helped make it one of the premiere places to see the best of photojournalism (4).

Literal: A term that refers to concepts and objects that are easily understood (1).

Lithography: A printing method that allows artwork and type to be printed at the same time (7).

Live-action: Works that are performed during the taping of television shows and the filming of motion pictures by human actors (10).

Logo: A distinctively identifying symbol for a company, publication, or screen presentation (2).

Long-term memory: In physiological terms, thoughts that stay in a person's mind from a few days to as long as a lifetime (1).

LP (long playing) record: A round vinyl phonograph album about 12 inches in diameter that played music stored in an analog format when amplified through a needle and spun on a turntable (4).

Magnetic resonance imaging (MRI): A medical technique that uses a powerful magnetic field to show highly detailed internal structures of the body (2).

Mainframe computer: Originally large, room-sized computers capable of complex and fast calculations for government and corporate purposes. Personal computer networks are gradually replacing them (14).

Manga: Graphic novels, often containing violent and sexual content, that are popular in Japan and other Asian countries (10).

Marxism: A political philosophy originating from the German economist Karl Marx and the German social scientist Friedrich Engels that presents a non-capitalist and non-religious view of how the world should work (6).

Maya: With its capital in the Yucatán Peninsula, the Maya civilization spanned from southern Mexico to western Honduras from about 2000 BCE until the arrival of the Spanish Conquistadores about 900 CE. At its height the society was one of the most complex cultures in the world with advances in art, architecture, writings, and political systems (7).

Meme: Invented by the British evolutionary biologist Richard Dawkins in his book *The Selfish Gene* (1976), used to describe the spread of musical, fashion, and religious ideas. It can be a familiar phrase or popular cultural concept such as the YouTube video of a piano-playing cat featured on the 2009 "MTV Movie Awards" show or "All your base are belong to us" from a poorly translated bit of dialogue from the Japanese Sega video game "Zero Wing." (8).

Memory card: A small electronic storage device used in digital cameras, audio devices, and as a stand-alone portable plug-in for the easy transfer of computer files (1).

Microelectrode: An electrode with an end so small it doesn't damage a cell's outer membrane that is used for monitoring electrical impulses (2).

MIT (Massachusetts Institute of Technology) Media Lab: A department of the School of Architecture and

Planning, its personnel have a reputation for innovations in communications including an initiative to develop a $100 laptop computer to improve educational opportunities for children around the world (14).

Moiré pattern: From a French word for a type of textile, it refers to visual interference that creates the illusion of internal vibration when an illustration with a set of parallel lines overlays another at a slight angle (2).

Montage: An artistic composition of several different parts (8).

Morphing: A computer-generated cross-fading special effect that seamlessly combines one image with another (10).

Mouse: Named by researchers at the Stanford Research Institute because of its small size and cord that looked like a tail, it is a sophisticated pointing device that allows a user to interact with software programs on a computer (8).

Mug shot: A head-and-shoulders portrait of a person usually looking into a camera's lens and displayed at a small size on a page whether for print or screen media (2).

Multi-User Dungeon (MUD): Online game playing with often-unknown partners on their computers anywhere in the world. An outgrowth of the board game "Dungeons and Dragons," the first MUD was named "Colossal Cave Adventure." Created by computer programmer and spelunker Will Crowther in 1975, the game's pathways are based on the Mammoth Cave system in Kentucky that he used to explore (15).

Muslims: See Islam (5).

Mythical: A form of analysis that evokes stories in words or pictures that persons in a culture understand because of their deeply held and common emotions (6).

News photograph: See editorial picture (1).

Newspaper chain: A family or corporate-owned business that owns more than one publication. Currently the largest chain in the United States is the Gannett Company that owns *USA Today* (9).

Noise: In visual communication, it can refer to the amount of grain that is noticed in a film or photograph as well as the number of elements within a frame or as part of a layout that distract from what should be the primary subject matter (9).

Olmec: A Mexican civilization occupying the south central part of the country for about 1500 years from 1200 BCE. Best known for their huge stone head artworks, they also performed ritualized body piercing and played ballgames in which the losing team was sometimes executed (7).

On-demand: Any number of user-controlled features that include watching video, working on a computer, using software, or printing whenever it is convenient (13).

One-reel film: In the early history of motion pictures, a single reel was 35 mm wide, based on the Thomas Edison standard, and 1,000 feet long, or about 11 minutes. Today's motion pictures comprise about five 2,000-foot reels, although most theaters have converted to digital material (12).

Operating system (OS): A software program that manages a computer's communication between an application and its hardware. Popular systems include Mac OS X, Windows Vista, Linux, and GNU, a free program created by the American developer and hacker Richard Stallman (14).

Optic nerve: Part of the central nervous system that connects visual information from the eyes to the brain (16).

Over-the-counter (OTC) stock: As opposed to exchange trading by large organizations such as the NASDAQ, New York, or London exchanges, it is the buying and selling of stocks directly from one party to another (14).

Pan or panning: A film technique in which the camera is moved horizontally (2).

Paparazzi: Usually freelance still photographers and/or videographers that take photographs and video of celebrities during public and sometimes private events (11).

Pater Noster House: With its slogan "Where Hope Comes Home," it is a 28-year-old licensed home located in Columbus, Ohio, that offers transitional housing for those with HIV/AIDS (4).

Petroglyphs: Images made by scratching or carving into rock surfaces (7).

Phenomenological: Espoused by the philosopher Edmund Husserl and his student Martin Heidegger, it is an analytical method similar to existentialism in which the phenomenon is used as a way of understanding all human knowledge (6).

Photocomposition: See filmsetting (7).

Photo-optic printing: Also known as photo or optical lithography, it is a technique used in the making of integrated circuits (7).

Photoshop: A software program usually reserved for editing still photographs created by the American software developer Thomas Knoll and introduced by Adobe in 1990 for Macintosh computers only. It has since been developed for almost all platforms and is the most popular program for photographic manipulation in the world (2).

Phototypesetting: A typesetting process in which different sized letters could be projected onto photographic paper, printed, and then set within a layout. Since the advent of personal desktop computers, it is now obsolete (7).

Pictographs: Also called pictograms, they are pictures that closely resemble a physical object they are meant to represent. In that way, they are similar to the semiotic iconic sign (7).

Pilot: A provisionary episode produced in the hope that a television series will be approved and financed (13).

Plasma television: A large flat-panel display in which two panels of glass confine a gas that when stimulated with an electrical impulse excites phosphorescent particles that creates a picture. The technology has been criticized for its excessive electrical expenditure (13).

Platen: Originally a wooden and later a metal weight pressed over a sheet of paper above an inked typeface surface during the printing process (7).

Plate: Made of paper, plastic, metal, stone, or other materials, an image on its surface is inked and transferred to paper directly, or in offset printing, transferred to a rubber surface that is then used to print the picture on paper (11).

Platform: It refers to all of the proprietary hardware and software components that allow a computer to work. The two major platforms are the PC, or IBM, computers and clones and Macintosh from Apple Computers (15).

Plug-in: Also known as an add-on or add-in, it is a software program that adds features to an application including ways to manipulate images and presentation formats for showing video (15).

Podcast: A digital media file that can contain still images, audio, and video that can be downloaded to a computer or portable player. A user can select a single program or subscribe to a producer's work so that presentations are automatically downloaded on a regular basis (3).

Polio: Short for poliomyelitis, it is a highly contagious viral disease that can cause severe symptoms, from stiffness of the neck to paralysis, but only in about 5 percent of those affected. Since the medical researcher Jonas Salk introduced a polio vaccine in 1955, the disease has been essentially eliminated. However, in countries such as India, Nigeria, and Pakistan, the incidence of infection is still about 1,500 a year (11).

Portal: Sometimes called a gateway, it is a major starting site for mainly commercial website users (15).

Poster child: A young person with a debilitating disease selected to have her picture included on posters in addition to making public appearances in order to generate sympathy and publicity to raise funds from the general public in order to provide for the treatment and research for the condition (5).

Prejudice: Bias for or against a person or idea without knowing all the facts (5).

Prime time: Regardless of the time zone, it is a three-hour fixed block of time from 8:00 until 11:00 p.m. when most viewers watch television and most surveys of audiences take place to establish ratings (13).

Proposition 8: A California voter-initiated ballot measure approved during a general election in 2008 that changed the state's constitution so that only marriages between a man and a woman would be considered valid. The section with the Prop 8 amendment begins, "All people are by nature free and independent and have inalienable rights. Among these are enjoying and defending life and liberty, acquiring, possessing, and protecting property, and pursuing and obtaining safety, happiness, and privacy." (5)

Public service announcement (PSA): Usually a radio, television, or web non-commercial message that raises awareness about a specific topic (2).

Ptolemy V: After his father died, he became Emperor of Egypt at the age of five in the year 204 BCE. Known for his cruelty in suppressing a rebellion and his skill at hunting, his main claim to fame comes from a scribe who wrote on the Rosetta Stone of a tax break he gave to a religious group (7).

Punch cards: Perforated stiff paper sheets with holes that defined quantitative data that could be input into early calculating machines and then computers. First used in 1725 in France for controlling the complex patterns of textile looms, their use could still be found by graduate students using university mainframe computers as late as 1985 (14).

Quantitative: Measurements such as time, distance, weight, public opinions, and demographics that can be defined by a specific unit and thus calculated, and conclusions made about any relationships between the measured elements (9).

Racial profiling: Discrimination usually conducted by law enforcement officials that is based on the assumption that some races are more suspicious or dangerous than others (5).

RAM (random access memory): A type of storage that is accessed quickly and is used to run software programs during a computer's operation; once the computer is turned off, the memory is erased (14).

Random dot stereogram: Two images composed of dots that when viewed by focusing behind them generate a 3-D image in the mind. First created by the Hungarian scientist Béla Julesz in 1959, his student Chris Tyler in 1979 used the principle to make the effect with a single image, called an autostereogram (2).

Realism: An artistic style in which actual scenes found in life were preferred over mythical or fantastical constructs. The Italian Michelangelo Merisi da Caravaggio in the 16th century as well as trompe l'oeil artists were advocates of the art genre (1).

Reductionism: A means of analysis in which complex ideas or images are reduced to their simplest element. It dates from the Greek philosopher Democritus' theory of atomism and much later by the French philosopher René Descartes who thought of life like a complex clock with identifiable and explainable parts (8).

Renaissance: An era of intense cultural growth for about 300 years dating from the 14th century that began in Italy and then spread to the rest of the Western world largely because of the advent of Johannes Gutenberg's commercial printing press (2).

Retinas: A lining of tissue within the back of each eye that contains the photosensitive cells known as rods, sensitive to low-light situations and movement, and cones, used for sharp focus and color perception (2).

Reuben award: An honor given to the "Cartoonist of the Year" by the National Cartoonist Society. Named after Rube Goldberg, a Pulitzer Prize–winning political cartoonist, best known for his humorous comic strip in which he devised overly intricate and complex devices in order to complete an ordinarily simple task. The first recipient was given in 1946 to Milton Caniff for his strip "Terry and the Pirates." (10)

Rhetorical: An analytical methodology often used in persuasion scenarios in which often intriguing questions are asked and concepts pondered without the expectation of receiving an answer (6).

Rituals: A wide variety of acts made by a single individual or a group usually performed on certain dates or for some known cultural reason such as birthday parties, weddings, and funerals (3).

Roman Empire: During its heyday in 117 CE, the Italian-based realm ruled north to England, south to Egypt, east to Mesopotamia, and west to northern Africa. Starting with ancient Rome in the 10th century BCE and continuing through the Roman Republic that dated from about 510 BCE and had a monarchy that could be influenced by its citizens until it was overthrown through civil wars, the Roman Empire had a single emperor that ruled dictatorially. The Empire had enormous influence over architecture, language, and political thought until its demise in 1453 when the Ottoman Turks captured Constantinople (7).

Rule: A thin, usually horizontal line used in layouts to graphically separate different sections (8).

Sarcophagus: Any stone coffin, but usually Egyptian (7).

Screen Actors Guild (SAG): A union affiliated with the AFL-CIO begun in 1933 that represents about 120,000 actors in "motion pictures, television, commercials, industrials, video games, Internet and all new media formats." (13)

Scribe: A person employed as a copyist of manuscripts (7).

SDRAM (synchronous dynamic random access memory): A quick, powerful, and stable technology for delivering data for computer operations (14).

Search engine: A software application that allows a user to find information on the web through keyword input (15).

Secularism: A manifestation of the concept of the separation between church and state, it is the idea that government agencies and their decisions should not be guided by religious beliefs (7).

Serial: A continuing plot for radio, television, and web stories that reveal more plot twists as a season unfolds (10).

Serif: Seen in all the typeface families except sans serif, a continuation of a letter's stroke that comes from the cursive writing style in which handwritten letters were joined (7).

Server: A broad term that can mean a software program that is a part of a dedicated computer that accepts data requests from users' web browsers (15).

Shooter video game: A type of video game that can be "first-person" (e.g., "Bioshock" and "Doom 3" for Xbox 360), in which the player controls the firearms supplied by the game, or "third-person" (e.g., "Quantum" for PlayStation 3 and "Damnation" for Xbox 360) in which the player follows along with the action (12).

Short: In the early history of Hollywood, it was typically a two-reel film less than 25 minutes long. Today these "short subjects" are less than 45 minutes. The "Festival des Très Court" is an annual film festival founded in Paris highlighting films of three minutes or less (10).

Short-term memory: Lasting only a few seconds, it is the ability of humans to store brief bits of verbal and visual data such as phone numbers and visual arrays that sometimes are used in the making of long-term memories (3).

Shot: A single photographic image or continuous take in motion pictures (2).

Shrine: Usually a religiously sacred place worshipped by those who believe in its historical significance, although it can refer to any setting where heroes and idols are remembered with wonder and admiration (3).

Shutter speed: A camera's setting that determines the length of time an aperture allows light to strike the recording medium, either analog or digital. Settings of 125th of a second and longer are considered long or slow, whereas those that are over are considered short or fast (6).

Sidebar: Similar to a fact box infographic, it can be a text-related story, pictures, or a collection of hyperlinks, usually graphically separated from the main article for print and online publications (3).

Silicon Valley: Originally used in a trade magazine in 1971 to describe the burgeoning semiconductor industry centered south of San Francisco near San Jose, California, the Silicon Valley is home of some of the world's leading high technology companies including Adobe Systems, Apple, Inc., eBay, Google, Hewlett-Packard, Intel, and Yahoo! (14).

Silver bromide and nitrate: Crystalline halides (others are silver with chloride, iodide, and fluoride) used in black and white photographic film and paper because they turn dark when exposed to light (11).

Situation comedy (sitcom): A television episodic genre for animated or live-action actors in which continuing characters are presented with different and hopefully humorous conditions from week to week (8).

Slander: Unlike its print and broadcast counterpart libel, it is defamation of a person's character that is made orally and in public (7).

Small press books: A concept related to the indie film movement, these are publishers that typically produce fewer than 10 titles per year. Many times they feature superior, handmade papers, bindings, and graphic designs (7).

Soap operas: A television genre that features long-running, continual story lines, usually shown during the daytime hours (13).

Social symbols: Verbal and nonverbal signs that have meaning to individuals in public settings that aid in human communication. Examples might be a greeting, handshake, kiss, or a brand name on a T-shirt (3).

Steadicam: A trademarked product of the Tiffen Manufacturing Corporation, it is an aid to shooting motion picture film that produces a steady, jiggle-free shot regardless of how much the operator moves. It was invented in 1976 by the American cinematographer Garrett Brown, who won an Academy Award of Merit in 1978 for his technology (12).

Stereotype plate: A technology of early hot press printing that is a cost-saving procedure in which a mold of papier-mâché or plastic is cast for an entire block of type that can be reused without setting individual letters by hand (7).

Storyboard: A cartoon version of a film used as a way to organize individual frames of a motion picture originally developed by the Walt Disney Studio in the 1930s. Directors such as James Cameron and Joel and Ethan Coen use storyboards almost exclusively in the preparation for shooting (8).

Streaming media: In order to speed the delivery of multimedia programming through an internet network, an end-user can enjoy the material from the beginning instead of waiting until the entire piece is downloaded (15).

Structural: A form of analysis in which elements are studied based on their relationships with each other rather than their history (6).

Stylus: A device for writing first used by cuneiform scribes with the tips of reeds and bones pressed into soft clay. Later, inked quills from the wings of birds and pencils, crayons, fountain and roller ball pens, and computer touch screen markers were employed (7).

Substrate: The first layer in which all others are included (7).

Surrealism: A form of art that surprises the viewer through grotesque or fantastic elements (3).

Symbolic: A form of analysis that stresses any aural, verbal, or visual element that represents some other, non-literal meaning for the viewer (1).

Synchronous classroom: A type of online instruction in which the instructor and students use a "virtual classroom" chat room to have same-time discussions and meetings just as with a face-to-face class (14).

Syndication: A term that applies to print, broadcast, and web media in which a story, column, comic strip, television show, or presentation is made available to a larger network for a fee (10).

Syntax: All of the rules and conditions that describe how sentences should be constructed (3).

Tablet: Any flat pad or panel used for the production of a presentation (14).

Tabloid: Originally a pharmaceutical term to describe a pill that contains compressed medicine, it is a newspaper and television format usually known for its exploitation of sensational news and entertainment stories. However, it can also refer to smaller sized newspapers that are traditional in content (3).

Teasers: These are eye-catching photographs and/or text blocks that hint at a story on an inside page that might be of interest to a reader (3).

Technicolor: A proprietary color process named for MIT, where one of the inventors, Herbert Kalmus, received his undergraduate degree. It was widely used for motion pictures from 1922 until 1952, first as a two-color system and then as a full-color process by Walt Disney Studios for its animated cartoons and for *The Wizard of Oz* (1939) (12).

Terrorists: Those who espouse a philosophy of terrorism that usually involves committing violent acts against innocent citizens for the purpose of disrupting social and economic activities (5).

TIF or TIFF (tagged image format): Invented by the Aldus desktop publishing company, now Adobe Systems, it is a high-quality image file preferred by publishers for printed work (11).

Time shifting: A user-controlled feature of television technology in which programs are recorded for viewing at a later, more convenient time (13).

Tracking shot: Also known as a dolly shot, it is a technique used in filmmaking, often through the use of a Steadicam, in which action is followed by a camera operator for an extended length of time without a cut. Famously long tracking shots in motion pictures include Alfred Hitchcock's *Rope* (1948), Orson Welles's *Touch of Evil* (1958), Michelangelo Antonioni's *The Passenger* (1975), Robert Altman's *The Player* (1992), and Aleksandr Sokurov's *Russian Ark* (2002) (12).

Transistor: A semiconductor device used for the sending and amplification of an electrical signal (14).

Two-color process: A motion picture and photographic technology with examples such as Kinemacolor, an additive process for movies, and the Eastman Kodak subtractive slide film Kodachrome introduced in 1935, one of the finest quality color films, popularized by *National Geographic* photographers (12).

Type mold: Similar to casting, it is a hollow block of metal for making typefaces that contains the shape of a letter that is created after a liquid alloy is poured into it and cooled (7).

Uniform resource locator (URL): The address for a website (15).

Upload: See download (15).

Upper-middle class: A designation of a social group in which its members are signified by higher income levels and educational achievement and more prestigious occupations than the middle class (10).

Uruk, Iraq: An ancient city of Mesopotamia in which about 80,000 residents lived around the year 2900 BCE and located about 150 miles southeast of Baghdad. Home of King Gilgamesh and thought to be the inspiration of the Garden of Eden as told in the Bible, the city was abandoned around 100 CE. Baghdad's National Museum of Iraq was looted of priceless artifacts from the region during the beginning of the Iraq War in 2003 (7).

Vacuum tube: A sealed glass or metal tube once commonly used in electronic devices (12).

Vaudeville: Any stage show that consists of a variety of entertainment genres—songs, animal acts, and comedy sketches (5).

Vellum: French for *calfskin*, a tough and lasting substrate mainly reserved for printed materials made from the flesh of mammals, particularly cattle. Copies of Johannes Guttenberg's Bible printed on vellum have outlasted those he made with paper (7).

Victorian era: A period in history when Queen Victoria ruled England from 1837 until 1901 and marked by significant advances in art, literature, the middle class, and technology (8).

Viral videos: Similar to a meme, a video clip that becomes wildly popular through e-mail and instant message sharing. Examples include a digital short titled "Dick in a Box" first shown on "Saturday Night Live;" the Scottish church singer Susan Boyle's surprising debut on "Britain's Got Talent;" and the "Star Wars Kid," 14-year-old French Canadian Ghyslain Raza's personal video that he made while pretending to fight with a light saber (10).

Virtual reality: A term used to describe a technology that simulates an actual, living experience for the user (8).

Visual array: The elements you can see with both eyes open under normal lighting conditions. For an adult, the angle of view is approximately equivalent to a 24-mm wide-angle lens (2).

Visual cortex: An area in the back of the brain where sight-related nerve cells are located (2).

Visual journalist: A professional in the mass communication field who works with words, images, and graphic designs for print and/or screen media (9).

Visual perception: Understanding in a literal and symbolic sense what it is your mind is focused upon within a visual array (3).

Wavelength: The distance between two crests of a waveform with a trough between them. A wave that is more energetic or has a higher frequency has a shorter wavelength than one with a lower frequency and longer wavelength. The distance for a wavelength of the color violet is about 400 nanometers (or 0.000016 of an inch), whereas red is longer at about 700 nm (0.000028 of an inch) (2).

Web perfecting press: The name for the extremely fast and efficient rotary printing press invented by the American Richard Hoe in 1843 in which words and images are placed on a curved cylinder (7).

Western culture: Sometimes known as Western civilization, it is a culmination of art, custom, religion, and technology commencing from Western Europe and including immigrants to other parts of the globe, most specifically in the Americas and Australia (1).

Widget: Tools, games, and other presentations that can be accessed from a computer or cell phone that are easily installed and quickly accessed, such as calendar, clock, and weather applications (15).

WiMax (Worldwide Interoperability for Microwave Access): Established by the WiMax Forum, a non-profit organization formed in 2001, it is a communications technology that offers a greater range and faster access speeds than common Wi-Fi wireless networks (13).

Wirephoto: A method for sending photographs via telegraph or telephone lines introduced by Western Union in 1921 and used by the Associated Press (AP) news agency to quickly send images to member newspapers until 2004 when the web made the technology obsolete (9).

Working class: See blue-collar worker (10).

World Press Photo: A non-profit organization founded in 1955 and based in Amsterdam that promotes the best of photojournalism through its annual contest (4).

Writers Guild of America (WGA): A United States–based labor organization with its eastern branch representing television and motion picture writers who live in the New York City area and the western branch for the same in southern California. Begun in 1921, it has about 8,000 members (13).

Xerox Palo Alto Research Center (PARC): Founded in 1970 in California's Silicon Valley as an experimental lab supporting innovations in computing, scientists at the Center developed the laser printer, the local area network known as the Ethernet, and the graphical user interface (GUI) that inspired Apple Computer engineers to include it in their Macintosh—one of the most important features in its computers. Much later, Xerox sued Apple for copyright violation, but the suit was dismissed due to the expiration of the statute of limitations (15).

Yahoo!: Although fully explained in Chapter 15, the term was included in this glossary so that every letter of the alphabet would be represented.

Zapf Dingbats: ✢□❊✿▼✳✳ ❂❙ ▼✳✳ ✧✳□○❂■ ▼❙□✳❂✿✳✳ ✳✳▲✣✳■✳□ ★✳□○○❂■■ ✳❂□✳✨ ❱✣□ ❂❂▲□ ✳■✣✿✳■▼✳✳ ▼✳✳ □□□◆❂❂□ □□○❂■ ✳✳○✳❂❙ ▼❙□✳❂✳✳ □✳ ☆❂❂❂▼✳■□ ❂■✳ ▼✳✳ ▲❂■▲ ▲✳□✳✳ ★□▼✳○❂✨ ✳▼ ✳▲ ❂ ○✳▲✳✳❂❂❂❂■✳□◆▲ ▲✳▼ □✳ ✳□❂□✳✳✳ ▲❙○□❂▲ ▲✳❂■□○ ◆▲✳✳ ❂❙ ✳□❂□✳✳✳ ✳✳▲✳✳■✳□▲✎ (7).

Zapotec: A pre-Columbian (before the arrival of Christopher Columbus) civilization centered in south central Mexico dating from about 500 BCE. Known for their elaborate tombs and jewelry, they also developed a written form of communication with symbols representing the syllables of their language that influenced the later cultures of the Maya and Aztec (7).

Zoom: A film technique in which a camera is connected to a special lens so that its focal length can change from a wide to a close-up view (2).

Zoopraxiscope: One of the first devices for showing animated images invented by Eadweard Muybridge in 1879 (12).

Index